The Poems of George Meredith

Volume 1

Photograph of George Meredith by Frederick Hillyer, 1887.

The Poems of George Meredith

EDITED BY

Phyllis B. Bartlett

VOLUME 1

New Haven and London, Yale University Press

1978

Designed by Helen Buzyna and John O. C. McCrillis
and set in Times New Roman type.
Printed in the United States of America by
The Murray Printing Co., Westford, Massachusetts.

Published in Great Britain, Europe, Africa, and
Asia (except Japan) by Yale University Press, Ltd., London.
Distributed in Latin America by Kaiman & Polon,
Inc., New York City; in Australia and New Zealand
by Book & Film Services, Artarmon, N.S.W., Australia;
and in Japan by Harper & Row, Publishers,
Tokyo Office.

The decorative device used on the binding
is from the title page of George Meredith,
Poems (London: Constable and Company Ltd., 1910).

Contents

VOLUME 1

PART I

POEMS COLLECTED BY MEREDITH

Poems (1851)

Modern Love
and
Poems of the English Roadside,
with Poems and Ballads (1862)

Poems and Ballads

Poems and Lyrics
of the Joy of Earth (1883)

Ballads and Poems
of Tragic Life (1887)

A Reading of Life
with Other Poems (1901)

VOLUME 2

PART II

Poems Published but Not Collected by Meredith

PART III

Posthumously Published Poems and Trivia

PART IV

UNPUBLISHED POEMS AND FRAGMENTS

Publisher's Note

When Phyllis Bartlett died in 1973, the first galley proofs for these volumes had just begun to arrive from the printer. Thus the final check for accuracy in the texts and annotation had to be carried out by the Press. The publishers are particularly grateful to Mrs. Gillian Beer, Mrs. Margaret Harris, and Miss Marjorie Wynne for their advice and help in correcting the proofs. Errors no doubt remain and the publishers will be glad to receive corrections which will be incorporated in any subsequent edition.

Introduction

This edition of Meredith's poems is divided into four parts. The first section contains those poems Meredith included in collected volumes of his poetry. In the second section, arranged in chronological order of their publication, appear those poems published during Meredith's lifetime but not included by him in any collection of his verse. The third section comprises posthumously published poems and trivia, and the fourth section previously unpublished poems and fragments.

There is no evidence that the heretofore unpublished poems were sent out for publication. Meredith himself rejected them—and rightly—often because they were downright sentimental or silly. Frequently he jotted down a few lines and abandoned them. But however fragmentary or trivial, all of this verse is here included and makes up something like a fifth or sixth of the bulk of Meredith's poetic work. The number of trivia will not surprise those readers already acquainted with him as the jovial companion revealed in his letters and the memoirs of friends. Indeed, he approved of "light literature," recommending it to his older son Arthur as a help to "freshness of style and elegance in graver writings."

More extensive are the early drafts of published poems. All such extant drafts are to be found here in the apparatus criticus, so that the close student of Meredith's poetry can discover for himself the ways in which the poet worked his poems into final shape.

Once Meredith had chosen the poems for a volume, he was careful of their arrangement, as letters to his publishers show, but whether the arrangement was based on a principle or was arbitrary is not revealed. Study of the volumes indicates only that songs or lyrics were usually interspersed between poems of heavier matter. In his earliest volume six light poems appear between the poems on classical subjects, *Antigone* and *The Shipwreck of Idomeneus*, and in

his last volume the exquisite *Song in the Songless* separates the
difficult *Hueless Love* from *Union in Disseverance.*

Early Notebooks and Problems of Handwriting

Much of the hitherto unpublished material included here is taken
from two notebooks now in the Beinecke Library at Yale. They
appear to have been custom-made for young Meredith. The leaves
of both measure $7\frac{3}{4} \times 10\frac{7}{16}$ inches, but the bindings and paper
differ.

The one most used in this edition is here referred to as NB A–B.
The paper in this notebook is a bluish gray, and most of the leaves
have been torn out. Notebook A starts at the end now facing the
Yale University Library bookplate, B at the other end and upside
down. The extant text of A begins, after a number of stubs from
leaves torn out, with a doodled list of titles of poems characteristic of
Meredith early in his career (see Appendix II). NB B starts with a
translation of Schiller's "Evening, after a Picture."

The other, less mutilated, notebook at Yale is made up of a brighter
blue paper. It is referred to here as WW, because its chief interest is
the long, relatively fair passage for Meredith's most ambitious
unpublished early poem, "Wandering Willie." A scheme for this
poem and a specimen title page face the Yale University Library
bookplate. The other end of the notebook begins with financial
forms, such as a bill of exchange signed "Anthony Chuzzlewit" and
accepted by "Dick Swiveller" and a promissory note signed "Charles
Dickens." These are followed by the fragment of a tale, "The Land
of Flowers," and a long essay on the Austrian dramatist Grillparzer.

Since the first two of the financial forms bear the dates "10 May
1849" and "1 June 1849," it was apparently in the spring of that
year that Meredith had both notebooks made up and started to use
them. He worked prodigiously in 1849 and 1850, drafting poems in
his notebooks, polishing some of them as anonymous contributions
to Dickens's new magazine *Household Words,* and preparing for his
first volume.

Unfortunately, the order of the poems and fragments in these
notebooks is no help in the dating of them. In NB A–B Meredith not
only wrote from both ends but also filled the space left in corners or

margins at a later time than the original drafts. Moreover, he had two scripts, a cursive and a copybook. While the cursive was used for letters and for rough drafts of poems, the bold copybook hand, which appears in both diminutive and larger forms, at its best could find place in any manual of calligraphy. Because the two hands were used at different times and with different points, the handwriting can take on the appearance of as many as five different scripts on a single page. The dating of material from the notebooks must therefore be highly conjectural.

The vigorous half-lettering of Meredith's middle years is a fusion of the two early hands. Blue aniline ink appeared on the London market for the first time in 1858, and from 1859 on to the end of his life, except for letters written on mourning paper after the death of his second wife, he used it constantly. As he grew older, his writing got larger, but, although it is sometimes rough, the ataxia from which he suffered does not show itself positively until 1896. From then on the shakiness of his writing increases till the end. The change of ink and the development and ultimate degeneration of Meredith's handwriting have helped the editor arrange the unpublished material in an approximately chronological order.

Meredith's Career as a Published Poet

"The Monthly Observer"

The earliest known poems by Meredith are found in a manuscript literary magazine issued monthly by an informal group of young Londoners to display and criticize each other's writing. Five numbers of "The Monthly Observer"—beginning with Number 11 of January 1849 and including the March, April, June, and July numbers—were preserved by Dr. Richard Stephen Charnock, the young solicitor to whom the twenty-year-old Meredith was at that time articled for training in the legal profession. Now in the Widener Collection at Harvard, these numbers were first described by Meredith's bibliographer Maurice Buxton Forman,[1] who later published them.[2]

1. In *George Meredith and the "Monthly Observer"* (London: privately printed, 1911).
2. *The Contributions of George Meredith to the "Monthly Observer," January–July 1849* (Edinburgh: printed for private circulation, 1928).

Poems (1851)

The chief contemporary influence on Meredith's verse from 1848 through 1852 was Richard Henry (or Hengist) Horne (1803–84) who, after an exciting military life in Mexico, had taken up poetry as a temporary career and had made some name for himself in 1843 with his epic *Orion*, sensationally sold at a farthing as a symbol of the low esteem in which poetry was held at the time. When Meredith, knowing that Horne encouraged young writers, approached him with a copy of his own classical poem "Daphne" and a tribute in verse,[3] Horne responded favorably. He introduced his young admirer to *Household Words*, helping him with three poems for that magazine and giving advice on the contents of his first volume. In partial return for these favors, Meredith quoted a passage from Horne's *Orion* on the title page of *Poems* (1851).[4] On the title page of the copy inscribed to Horne[5] he wrote: "To R. H. Horne, Esqʳ: by whose generous appreciation & trusty criticism these 'Poems' were chiefly fostered."

The poems collected in 1851 would perhaps have been more to Horne's taste than to that of Thomas Love Peacock, to whom the volume is dedicated with "profound admiration and affectionate respect." Although as the years went by it became increasingly apparent that Meredith and his father-in-law had much in common—wit, talent for song writing, antisentimentalism—the young poet's first volume displayed none of his future characteristics except lyrical power.

The volume was published, at the poet's expense, by John W. Parker and Son, West Strand, London, in May 1851, in an issue of 500 copies of which only 100 were bound.[6] On December 12, 1850, Meredith sent Parker the basic material for this volume, and on December 17 he wrote again, comparing his modest poetic start with that of Tennyson. He anticipated a financial loss, a sum that late in life he remembered as fifty or sixty pounds,[7] but believed that he would eventually win his laurels. Meredith deferentially sought

3. See p. 817.
4. (London: J. Miller, 1843), bk. 3, canto 1, p. 102.
5. The Widener Collection at Harvard.
6. MBF, p. 8. For abbreviations here and throughout see Sigla, p. xlvii.
7. Ibid.

Parker's advice and was willing to understand if he would rather not publish the poems because of his own reputation. After Horne wrote to Parker's printer, James Vizetelly, on behalf of the volume, the publishing arrangements were completed.

Although *Poems* was a financial failure, as anticipated, it received welcome tributes. Edmund Ollier and Tennyson, the new Poet Laureate, wrote letters to Meredith in praise of the volume, while Charles Kingsley and William Michael Rossetti reviewed it favorably in the press.[8]

In a flurry of optimism about *Poems*, Meredith had one copy interleaved with his bluish gray stationery and specially bound. In it he wrote poems he hoped to include in a later edition. This fascinating document is in the Berg Collection of the New York Public Library and is identified in this edition as Berg (see Sigla). The book contains forty-one poems or fragments, only nine of which were subsequently published, three of the nine meriting inclusion in the *Modern Love* volume of 1862. It bears an unidentified penciled description on the flyleaf: "The Gift of the Author. Copsham Cottage. Esher."[9] Meredith left Copsham Cottage in the autumn of 1864 when he married Marie Vulliamy, the latest possible date at which he might have given away this interleaved copy, but there is no evidence that any of the poems in this curious copybook were written later than the winter of 1853.

Ten years later he was already calling *Poems* his "boy's book,"[10] and in later years he wished that it could be destroyed, but, realizing that no such miracle would happen, he consented to revise the text for the Edition de Luxe, *Poems* 3 (1898).

In the summer of 1855, when patriotism over the Crimean War was high, Meredith approached his first publisher, John W. Parker, with a volume of "British Poems,"[11] for which he insisted that he be paid, but was rebuffed. The many nationalistic poems completed or

8. Their reviews are quoted in J. A. Hammerton, *George Meredith, His Life and Art in Anecdote and Criticism* (Edinburgh: John Grant, 1911), p. 8.

9. See Phyllis Bartlett, "George Meredith: Early Poems in the Berg Collection," *Bulletin of the New York Public Library* 61 (August 1957): 396–415. The Sale Catalogue of Messrs. Sotheby, Wilkinson and Hodge, 17–21 March 1902, adds the assurance that the inscription was written by "the father of the owner of this volume, and the father and Mr. Meredith were most intimate in their youth," MBF, p. 10.

10. WMM, p. 45.

11. Cline, Letter 30.

suggested in NB A–B and the Berg interleaved *Poems* (1851) were doubtless included in this effort to pick up some money.

During the next several years Meredith was chiefly engaged in writing the prose fantasies, *The Shaving of Shagpat* (1855) and *Farina* (1857), and his first novel, *The Ordeal of Richard Feverel* (1859), but he did contribute several poems to the magazine *Once a Week*.

Modern Love and Poems of the English Roadside, with Poems and Ballads (1862)

In contrast to the austere title of Meredith's first book of *Poems*, which imitated Coleridge, Tennyson, and others, the title *Modern Love* had descriptive value. The volume was published on April 28, 1862 by Chapman & Hall, the firm for which Meredith had become a regularly employed reader in 1860, a job that he retained for thirty-five years. *Modern Love* was "Affectionately Inscribed to Captain Maxse, R.N." A naval hero of the Crimean War, Frederick Augustus Maxse had been so revolted by the mismanagement of the war that he became a zealous pamphleteering radical. Meredith later modeled Nevil Beauchamp in his novel *Beauchamp's Career* (1875) after him. They were devoted lifetime friends.

Twentieth-century critics have generally considered the title poem, *Modern Love*, Meredith's poetic masterpiece. Meredith, in later years the advocate of the comic spirit and of common sense, probably would not have accepted the high verdict of latter-day critics about his tragic poem; yet he reprinted it in 1892. The death of his first wife, Mary Ellen Peacock Nicolls, in October of 1861, opened his way to an imaginative transcendence of the tragedy of their marriage in a poem that is as much fictional as it is autobiographical. (Mary did not commit suicide, and there is no evidence that Meredith took a mistress.) The headnote to the poem (p. 115) reconstructs the history of its composition.

The first, rough draft of the poem I surmise to have been among the many pages torn from NB A–B. Interestingly, in the summer of 1965 a manuscript of thirty-six sonnets for *Modern Love* emerged, unheralded.[12] It is a fair copy revised, and one of the thirty-six

---

12. See Phyllis Bartlett, "A Manuscript of Meredith's 'Modern Love,'" *The Yale University Library Gazette* 40 (April 1966): 185–87.

sonnets was not used in the published sequence of fifty. Through the courtesy of the late Mr. Bertram Rota and the generosity of Mr. Frank Altschul and of Yale, this manuscript now reposes in Yale's Beinecke Library.

Contemporary reviewers condemned the poem for its unorthodox presentation of married love and sex. The most vitriolic of these reviews, in the influential *Spectator*, May 24, 1862, was answered by Algernon Charles Swinburne, a relatively new friend of Meredith's, in a glowing letter to the editor òf the *Spectator* (printed in the issue of June 7, 1862), which praised the poem enthusiastically. The aggregate of the reviews, however, rescued Meredith from the misconception that his poems would earn him money. For this reason he turned chiefly to fiction, publishing seven novels during the twenty-one years that lapsed before the next publication of a volume of poems. Occasionally, however, he returned to poetry, placing poems in such excellent magazines as the *Cornhill*, the *Fortnightly Review*, and *Macmillan's*.

Poems and Lyrics of the Joy of Earth (*1883*)

Meredith's third volume of poetry, *Poems and Lyrics of the Joy of Earth*, was brought out by Macmillan on June 7, 1883. Again he had to pay the costs, but there were so many misprints in the volume that, as he wrote Maxse on July 20, Frederick Macmillan reprinted it at his own expense. It contained several poems previously printed in periodicals but even more hitherto unpublished. Meredith's letters for the two years preceding the publication of this volume repeatedly record that he was experiencing an upsurge of verse, and we may assume that most of the poems were written during these years.

The volume was "Inscribed to James Cotter Morison. *Antistans mihi milibus trecentis.*"[13] Meredith must have met Morison (1832–1888) at about the same time that he met John Morley (see p. xxxvii), probably in 1861. Morison's knowledge of French language, literature, and history, and his athletic abilities would naturally have made him attractive to Meredith, but he also had a vivacious and pleasing personality. Philosophically, Morison believed in positivism. He is best known for his learned *Life of St. Bernard*, published in 1863.

13. 'Standing ahead of me by three hundred thousand.'

The volume begins with *The Woods of Westermain*, probably the best known today of Meredith's philosophical poems. It is an allegory in which Self, an inflated belief in the importance of one's own personality, is the Dragon in the woods of life that must be tamed by an evolutionary process into becoming a useful servant of society. Several of Meredith's most sustained and elegant poems—including his own favorites, *The Day of the Daughter of Hades* and *Earth and Man*—appeared in *Poems and Lyrics of the Joy of Earth* together with all of his best disparate sonnets. Because in substance, if not in essence, the version of *Love in the Valley* reprinted here from *Macmillan's Magazine*, October 1878, was a new poem, not merely a tinkering with the early version that appeared in *Poems* (1851) (see p. 62 and note), both versions appear complete in the present edition.

Poems and Lyrics of the Joy of Earth was not favorably reviewed. After summarizing the widely divergent range of critical opinion, Meredith's biographer Lionel Stevenson explains: "Sure that his genius was primarily poetical, Meredith regarded his first book of verse in twenty years as an event of literary moment. The qualified and impercipient praise that it received seemed to him no better than an insult, and he became convinced that no critic was willing to recognize the merits of his poetry. From this time onward the surest way to gain his good graces was to declare his poems superior to his novels."[14]

Ballads and Poems of Tragic Life (1887)

Macmillan also published *Ballads and Poems of Tragic Life* on May 10, 1887. There seems to be no record of who paid for it— probably Meredith—and it carries no dedication. Although six of the poems had appeared in periodicals before the publication of *Poems and Lyrics of the Joy of Earth* (1883), their subjects precluded their inclusion under the title of that volume. Within this collection *The Nuptials of Attila*, dating from the *New Quarterly Magazine* of January 1879, was long a favorite with its author; and *France, December 1870*, written during the siege of Paris and published in the *Fortnightly Review* of January 1, 1871, spoke ardently the belief

14. LS, p. 250.

that France would make an "aureole" of her "calamity" and regain her leadership among nations. From it sprang the later, elaborate *Odes in Contribution to the Song of French History* (1898) in which *France, December 1870*, was reprinted as the third ode.

Ballads and Poems of Tragic Life received scant praise from the press, thus confirming Meredith's conviction that his poetry was unappreciated. In this volume, on the verso of the leaf preceding the half title, Macmillan advertised as "forthcoming" the next collection.

A Reading of Earth (1888)

On December 20, 1888, Macmillan published the collection, *A Reading of Earth*. On February 16, 1887, Meredith had written to his Scottish friend, George Stevenson, that the volume following *Ballads and Poems of Tragic Life* would be "of more spiritual flavour," and indeed it was. *A Reading of Earth* contains the profoundly soul-searching poems written during the painful, lingering, and fatal struggle with cancer of his second wife, Marie Vulliamy. During the last months of her life Meredith had tried to equal her courage, and the effort is revealed in such poems as *The Thrush in February* and *A Faith on Trial*. The experience had indeed been a test of the rhetorical question that he had asked himself about a quarter of a century earlier before he had met Marie Vulliamy:

> Into the breast that gives the rose,
> Shall I with shuddering fall?[15]

After *A Reading of Earth* was published, Meredith wrote Mrs. George Stevenson on January 4, 1889: "You will not be troubled by notices of it in the press. I no longer give out volumes of verse for review." Nevertheless, the volume was voluntarily and favorably reviewed by a few admirers.

Modern Love, A Reprint, to which is added
The Sage Enamoured and the Honest Lady (1892)

Meredith wrote to an admirer, the journalist Clement K. Shorter, on October 20, 1891, that the reprint of *Modern Love* was in the printer's hands, "But the book will not be sent out for review.

---

15. *Ode to the Spirit of Earth in Autumn*, 161–62.

Critics have enough of me as a novelist." Thus he followed the policy begun with *A Reading of Earth*. The volume was published by Macmillan on January 26, 1892, and Meredith rededicated it: "To Admiral Maxse in Constant Friendship"[16] (see p. 115).

Poems: The Empty Purse, with Odes to the Comic Spirit, To Youth in Memory, and Verses (1892)

At the end of *A Reading of Earth* (1888) Macmillan had advertised, "Forthcoming Volume. The Empty Purse: A Sermon to our Later Prodigal Son," but the volume was not published until October 1892. It is not known whether the delay was caused by complications in the elaborate revision of *The Empty Purse* or by the decision to complete and polish the other new poems that accompanied it.

Complimentary copies of *The Empty Purse* went out to a number of important people. Chiefly on account of his novels, Meredith was by then a celebrity, recently honored with the LL.D. from the University of St. Andrews. Lionel Stevenson reports that "In spite of austere title and forbidding style, the book sold better than its predecessors. Shortly after publication, when Meredith wanted to give a copy to a friend, he found that the supply of the first issue was already exhausted."[17]

Selected Poems (1897)

Guaranteed on p. [viii] to have been made "under the supervision of the Author," *Selected Poems* was curiously long in the making. On November 30, 1891, Meredith had written Frederick Greenwood, editor of the *Anti-Jacobin*, that he had "a volume of Selections . . . ready," and there seems to be no other identification for this volume than the *Selected Poems* of 1897. It was not until February 1894, however, that this volume took shape, because in the Meredith Collection at Yale there is a collection of bound leaves stamped "R. & R. Clark, Printers. Brandon St. Edinburgh," and dated February 1894. These leaves were torn from the volumes from which the poems were selected and a number are marked by Meredith with the instruction: "Revise." Many, but not all, of these instructions were followed in the 1897 edition. Why the selection set up in 1894

16. Maxse had retired from the Navy in 1867 as a Rear-Admiral.
17. LS, p. 304.

was abandoned is not known. R. and R. Clark printed for Macmillan, however, and Meredith left that firm for Archibald Constable & Co. after his son by his second marriage, William Maxse Meredith, took a position with Constable in about 1895.[18] In 1897, *Selected Poems* was published by Constable; all the verbal corrections made by Meredith have been noted in the present edition.

Odes in Contribution to the Song of French History (1898)

The volume *Odes*, which, on October 21, 1898, was also published by Constable, was dedicated to John Morley, statesman, biographer, and abiding friend of Meredith.[19] In asking Morley on July 6, 1898, whether he would accept a dedication, Meredith assured him that his acceptance would not imply sponsorship: "But you may have objections to the parade in a dedication, however plainly worded. I have no taste for the like. At the same time, your knowledge of French History, sympathy with France, and our old friendship, form a sort of plea, with the reminder that I must soon be going."

Of the four *Odes in Contribution to the Song of French History*, the three composed in the 1890s (*The Revolution, Napoléon,* and *Alsace-Lorraine*) are elaborately interlocked in diction and metaphor. The ode *France, December 1870*, which was written during the siege of Paris in 1870, is fitted into them chronologically but not stylistically.

In his book on Meredith, a French admirer, Constantin Photiadès, quoted a letter that Meredith wrote to him on September 19, 1908. "It is true that at all times my heart has beaten for France; and it is not less true that, even up to this day, I have not acknowledged by an adequate testimony the debt that mankind owes to her. My *Odes in Contribution to the Song of French History* are an effort in this direction. If I were younger, I should do still better work. . . ."[20]

A Reading of Life (1901)

Published by Constable in May 1901, *A Reading of Life* was the last collection of verse for which Meredith himself was responsible. Previously, all except three short poems had been printed in periodicals.

18. LS, p. 316.
19. See *Lines to a Friend Visiting America* and *To J. M.*
20. *George Meredith, His Life, Genius & Teaching*, trans. Arthur Price (London: Constable, 1913), pp. 245–46.

Posthumous Collections

Two collections of Meredith's poems were rushed to press after his death in 1909. One was a privately printed book limited to twenty-five copies called *Twenty Poems*, containing heretofore unattributed publications in *Household Words*, December 28, 1850, to November 1, 1856. In 1911 B. W. Matz, editor of *Twenty Poems*, disclosed that he had found the titles of these poems and the sums paid to Meredith for them in the account book of *Household Words* while preparing the "National" edition of Dickens's works.[21] William Maxse Meredith was reluctant to acknowledge most of these poems as his father's, but on the basis of evidence in the early notebooks and the account books I have included all of them in Part II. The second posthumous collection of 1909 was *Last Poems*, edited by William Maxse Meredith and published by Constable in October of that year. This helter-skelter collection of poems published in periodicals from 1893 until after Meredith's death is not ordered chronologically. It ends with a tombstone epitaph of 1884. Meredith's son was an unreliable editor, as his father's letters to him often reveal, and I have not hesitated to disassemble this volume in order to present the poems chronologically in Part II of this edition.

Collected Editions

The most important collection of Meredith's works is the Edition de Luxe, published by Constable in thirty-six volumes from 1896 to 1911. The edition was edited by William Maxse Meredith, who was supervised by his father through volume 32 (essays). The poems are contained in volumes 29–31 (1898) and 33 (1910), also numbered 1–4, and there seems to be no rationale in their ordering. Volume 1 begins with the reprint of *Modern Love* (1892), including *The Sage Enamoured and the Honest Lady*, which had first been published with this reprint, then reverts to *Poems and Lyrics of the Joy of Earth* (1883). Volume 2 consists of *Ballads and Poems of Tragic Life* (1887) and *A Reading of Earth* (1888). Volume 3 continues chronologically with *The Empty Purse*, "Etc." (1892), but arbitrarily adds three poems from *Modern Love* (1862) and one from *Ballads and Poems of*

---

21. MBF, p. 145. This account book is now in the Library of Princeton University.

Tragic Life. It then reverts to "Poems Written in Early Youth: 1851" (*Poems*, 1851) and "Poems from 'Modern Love': 1862," both categories set in very small type, as are the "Scattered Poems," twelve poems printed in periodicals from August 1851 to November 1890, that conclude the volume. The posthumous volume 4 picks up the two volumes *Odes in Contribution to the Song of French History* (1898) and *A Reading of Life* (1901). Then follow *Last Poems* (1909) and four addenda to "Poems Written in Youth," large type this time. "Errata in the Poems" appears in volume 36 (1911), *Bibliography and Various Readings*.

The three volumes of *Poems* in the Memorial Edition (1910), also edited by Meredith's son, improve the arrangement of the Edition de Luxe in that they proceed chronologically, although not adhering strictly to the table of contents of each original volume. Thus, there is no title for the *Poems* of 1851, and *The Doe*, which came at the end of the *Modern Love* volume of 1862, now precedes the 1851 poems, as do two poems published in journals before the collection of 1851. The "Scattered Poems" are rescattered throughout the collected works, placed wherever their original publication in journals apparently suggested.

The most important posthumous edition of Meredith's poetry was *Poetical Works*, edited by the subsequently famous historian George Macaulay Trevelyan and published by Constable in October 1912. The text follows that of the Memorial Edition, but Trevelyan notes in his preface that he made "two or three substantial emendations, in making which I had the concurrence of the Editor of the text of the Memorial Edition." I include these substantive changes which, in fact, number six: the addition of two passages of poetry from the fantasy *The Shaving of Shagpat* (1855), the full text of *By the Rosanna*, as printed in *Once a Week* (October 19, 1861) and in *Modern Love* (1862), two passages of poetry from the novel *Vittoria* (1867), and the long passage from *In the Woods*, published in the *Fortnightly Review* (August 1870) and never republished by Meredith.

The organization of Trevelyan's edition of *Poetical Works* is eccentric. With many exceptions, he arranged the poems in the chronological order of their appearance in periodicals, if they had appeared in periodicals before Meredith collected them into volumes.

He gave some of the titles of the volumes, but not all. For instance, after the contents of *Modern Love and Poems of the English Roadside, with Poems and Ballads* (1862)—a long and important title which does not appear in the table of contents—is a poem published in a periodical in 1865, then a poem unaccountably separated from the contents of the unnamed *Modern Love* volume of 1862 and, without a break, most of the contents of *Poems and Lyrics of the Joy of Earth* (1883). Following the sonnets from this volume is the title of the volume *Poems and Lyrics of the Joy of Earth*. Apart from the chronological organization, the Trevelyan edition contains two subject categories— "Poems on National Affairs" (1867–1908) and "Epitaphs," the latter composed of the seven "Epitaphs" with which Meredith had concluded *A Reading of Earth* (1888) and six that had been published elsewhere. Despite its unorthodox organization, Trevelyan's edition has served readers well. Although some of his explanatory notes seem superfluous to readers trained in the rigors of twentieth-century poetry, many are still useful to the understanding of Meredith's poems, and I have borrowed a few of them with acknowledgment.

Practices in Composition

A study of Meredith's manuscripts shows chiefly that he was a liberal reviser of his poems and that this carefulness increased as he grew older. Unlike Wordsworth, he had no objection to copying his own writing. The clearest evidence of his willingness to write and to rewrite is found in the multiple drafts of a late poem, *The Empty Purse*. Although their survival is accidental, it is fair to conjecture that this diligence was characteristic. As his reputation grew, so did his thoughtful labor. The apparatus criticus of the present edition, light for the early years, grows increasingly ponderous. His most conspicuous technical and artistic concerns are sketched in the following paragraphs.

The improvement of meter, especially classical meters, was Meredith's chief concern in his drafts and subsequent revisions. He was first stung into carefulness by Charles Kingsley who, in a review of his first volume, *Poems* (1851), criticized *Pastorals VII* as "careless as hexameters. . . ." When late in life he reluctantly consented to include these "Poems Written in Youth" in the Edition de Luxe, he revised this pastoral more thoroughly than any other poem in his first volume, adding and dropping syllables to even the meter.

Almost forty years after *Pastorals VII* he attempted hexameters more deliberately when translating fragments of the *Iliad*. Some of these fragments were published in the *Illustrated London News* (1891) and letters to the editor of that journal evidence his continuing concern for metrics—he advises the editor that he needs a revise to amend "a spondee or two" (March 28, 1891), and that he wants to omit the accents he marked because he has "falsified" one (April 1, 1891).

His most ambitious effort in classical metrics was his experiment with the Galliambic measure in *Phäethon* (*Fortnightly Review*, 1867). When reprinting the poem in *Ballads and Poems of Tragic Life* (1887), he added a note from Hermann's *Elementa Doctrinae Metricae* to explain Galliambics, commenting that "A perfect conquest of the measure is not possible in our tongue." He also omitted four lines from the poem and added or dropped a syllable in six others to improve the meter.

Meredith was not much concerned with the fine points of grammar when composing a first draft but resolved the distinction between "that" and "which," "she" and "her," "like" and "as" in reworking and polishing the poem. By far the most frequent discrimination he made was that between "towards" and "toward." The apparatus criticus records eight corrections of "towards" to "toward" in the republication of poems written between 1851 and 1871.

He liked hard-sounding words. "Corusant," "immarcessible," and "expugnant" were second thoughts, and he delighted in his invention of "therminous" to rhyme with "*nous.*" In *The Empty Purse* he advises the young man not to join "the ranks of the thermonous," then emends this to an admonishment not to fight "With the tigerly zeal of the therminous," and finally—harder still—

> Not as Cybele's beast will thy head lash tail
> So praeter-determinedly thermonous.

Although Meredith had a tendency to add lines and stanzas while polishing a poem, when he prepared his poems for the Edition de Luxe he ruthlessly discarded whole completed sections. His most drastic cut from the *Modern Love* volume of 1862 was in *By the Rosanna* from 178 to 20 lines, leaving only a short description of the river in the Tyrol. The excised section was some sort of private message for "rallying" his friend Frederick Maxse; it had confused uninitiated readers at the time and is no more illuminating today. Similarly, by discarding the second part of *The Orchard and the Heath* when taking it from *Macmillan's Magazine* (1868) for inclusion in *Poems and Lyrics of the Joy of Earth* (1883), he omitted the message, a public one this time, in which the "light of Heaven" preached that

> Never till men rejoice in being one
> Shall any of them hold a perfect heart,

and that only by a life of service can enlightened men unite the affluent children of the orchard and the poor children of the heath. The poem was thus left as a simple descriptive episode with no weight of didactic comment.

Artistic judgment intervened between the three fair copies of *Night of Frost in May*, titled in manuscript "The Poet's Night," and the first publication of the poem in *The Empty Purse* volume of 1892. The published poem consists of eighty-two lines describing one of Meredith's favorite scenes. In manuscript this description had been the first part of a two-part poem, the second part fulfilling the original title by inviting a number of English poets to delight in the scene. The allusions to Chaucer, Shakespeare, Milton, Coleridge, Keats, Wordsworth, Shelley, and Tennyson are banal; the catalogue is a facile dither, wisely discarded.

Another poem cut drastically between the earliest extant manuscript and its first publication was *Foresight and Patience*, which appeared in the *National Review* (1894). About 150 lines were amputated from this rather tedious didactic poem, although many of them were emended in the *National Review* version, which was only slightly retouched for its final form of 282 lines in the Edition de Luxe. As Meredith said of his tortuous *Empty Purse* this "is not poetry. The muse shuns that paedagogue." *The Empty Purse*, which had grown considerably through its ten or more versions, would have profited by the judgment Meredith applied to *Foresight and Patience*.

Some of Meredith's poetic concerns can be seen at work in *The South-Wester*, first published in *A Reading of Earth* (1888). For this poem, which attempts to describe his favorite kind of day—one when a strong southwest wind was blowing—we have as evidence of composition a working draft, five fragments, and a fair copy.

Meredith seldom had trouble beginning a poem, and the opening lines of *The South-Wester* come through intact from the working draft:

> Day of the clouds in fleets! O day
> Of wedded white and blue, that sail
> Immingled, with a footing ray
> In shadow-sandals down our vale!—

This naval metaphor, which appears in the unpublished "Wandering Willie" written nearly forty years earlier (see p. 893), is illustrative of his ability to recall and put to use favorite figures of speech long after composing them. Several notes in the present edition call attention to lines that hark back to his early notebooks.

The South-Wester grew characteristically by the addition of a few lines here and there from 109 in a working draft to 133 in the published version. Three of the five fragments were variants that led on to the fair copy. The octosyllabics that he often used offered no difficulty, but the accent over the noun "ímmortal," which he had supplied in his fair copy, was omitted in the printing; this distressed him, as he wrote to a friend on February 25, 1889, because "The word is an anti-Bacchic. . . . On this I take my stand." He was careful to make the distinction between "like" and "as," as witnessed by the correction of "like" to "as" in line 9 of the working draft. He did not use hard-sounding words, but twice made comparable revisions by steering away from obvious allusions. The "high . . . volumed blot" of line 90 is impossible to visualize, but the working draft indicates that one should see it as heavy and bumpy, for in the margin there are the undeleted variants: "knotted" or "volumed Python Club." Later in the poem we are invited to "a glimpse of Python slain," so it is possible that he did not want two disparate references to the serpent Python. An allusion that might escape the non-classicist, the "Dream-messenger" of line 107, is easily explained by "Iris," explicitly named, although deleted, in the early draft. The obscurity of Meredith's images, so often castigated by his contemporaries, is often seen from a reading of the manuscripts to be deliberate.

The ease with which he opened *The South-Wester* contrasts with the difficulty he found in closing the poem. A much-labored fragment shows that he wished city children could be brought out to the country on this "freër, cheerer" day when the southwester was blowing. Four times he tried to use these adjectives, then gave up his benevolent fresh-air project altogether.

Editorial Procedures

The text of the poems in this edition is based on the last version that Meredith himself saw through the press, or corrected. Thus, the text of *Poems* (1851), *Modern Love* (1862), *Poems and Lyrics of the Joy of Earth* (1883), *Ballads and Poems of Tragic Life* (1887), *A Reading of Earth* (1888), *Modern Love* (1892), and *The Empty Purse* (1892) is taken from the Edition de Luxe. The text of *Odes* (1898) and *A Reading of Life* (1901) is based on the original volumes published by Constable, not on the posthumous volume 4 of *Poems* in the Edition de Luxe.

In this edition, poems untitled by Meredith are referred to by their first lines and in text carry an ornament in place of a title.*

Unfortunately, when superintending the printing of his poems, Meredith did not catch everything that he would have wanted to change, because he was a bad proofreader; he wrote to John Morley on April 4, 1877, "I am the worst of correctors of my own writing." Nor was his son William Maxse, who was responsible for seeing the Edition de Luxe through the press and for the fourth, posthumous volume (1910), much better. The corrections on the proof sheets at Yale show that Meredith desired to change the following contractions:

& to *and*
'd to *ed*
tho' to *though*
thro' to *through*

---

* Some untitled poems were apparently given titles by Phyllis Bartlett; these titles appear in brackets.—Press Ed.

Whether or not Meredith made these corrections, I have adhered to the copy-text. Whereas in early life he had inconsistently used "Oh" and "O," he finally settled on "O"; and whereas he had inconsistently used "gray" and "grey," he finally settled on "grey." He reduced his early capitalized "Heaven" and "Heavens" to lower case, and he strove for consistency in capitalizing the first letter in the names of the seasons and the points of the compass. In revising his punctuation, he shed many illogical commas and exclamation marks when they interrupted the syntax of a sentence. He had an increasing taste for using hyphens in compound words.

Both previous editors of the poems, W. M. Meredith and Trevelyan, clearly improved the meaning of many sentences by the addition or omission of punctuation marks, but in the interest of fidelity to the copy-text the present edition retains Meredith's often careless punctuation. Clarity, however, has been allowed to dictate the regularization of quotation marks in the poems from manuscript. Deviant spellings have been retained throughout: as in the early "ancle" and "chesnut." In about 1886 Meredith decided that when a verb ends with *e* the *e* should be retained before a suffix. For example, "unconsumable" in *France, December 1870* (IV. 2), thus spelled when the poem was published in the *Fortnightly Review*, 1871, became "unconsum*e*able" in the volume of 1887. (Neither W. M. Meredith nor Trevelyan followed the later spelling.) In the same passage, however, the 1871 "plunging" (IV. 22) survived in the 1887 volume but was corrected to "plung*e*ing" in the Edition de Luxe. Meredith did not attempt to introduce this medial *e* into the text of poems published before 1887 and was inconsistent in his use of it thereafter. Evidently the habit was hard to develop.

Since this is a critical edition, not a description of manuscripts, illegible deletions have been ignored when they are replaced by legible words except when necessary to fill out the meter, in which case they are indicated by [?]. At the Huntington Library it was determined that neither infrared nor ultraviolet ray rendered legible the heavy cancellations made in the process of composition. By and large, it is easier to read deletions made later. Where Meredith left two or more readings, the last one written has been chosen for the main text because, as proved by the textual variants to the published poems, he usually preferred his last alternative.

A word on annotation is perhaps in order. The aim has been to provide in headnotes sufficient information to explain the context of the particular poem in Meredith's life and work, with more detailed elucidation reserved for the Explanatory Notes. Textual variants are noted at the foot of the relevant page, and there is in addition a group of Supplementary Textual Notes, which mainly comprises variants too lengthy or complicated to be conveniently accommodated as footnotes, in particular sections of poems which Meredith rejected at some stage from the finally accepted version.

The form of the textual notes has been made as clear as possible. The abbreviation "*del.*" is not to be taken literally; in this edition it simply denotes a change: sometimes the addition or superscription of a letter, a word or words, sometimes a transposition.

In Meredith's early handwriting the capital *E* and small *e* are indistinguishable, and I may not always have interpreted his intention correctly.

Every fragment that can reasonably be associated with a printed text has been so recorded.

Standard reference books, biographies, and histories from which informatory notes have been eclectically derived are not named unless directly quoted. All quotations from Meredith's letters, unless noted "WMM," come from C. L. Cline's recent edition; I have followed Cline's practice of enclosing in brackets dates for undated letters or letters dated with the day of the week only; conjectural dates are preceded by a question mark. Whenever an obscure allusion remains unannotated, it is to be assumed that it has eluded the search of several helpers and myself, as well as those who like to answer published enquiries.

Apart from allusions, the basic reasons for the obscurity in Meredith's later poetry were analyzed by M. R. Ridley.[22] Part of the pleasure that the obscure poems give is the intellectual exercise that they afford, and I decided at the outset of this edition that in such matters as idiosyncrasy of grammar and syntax I would not intervene between the poet and the reader.

22. "Meredith's Poetry," *Second Thoughts* (London: Dent, 1965), pp. 146–71.

Sigla

1851 *Poems*
1862 *Modern Love and Poems of the English Roadside, with Poems and Ballads*
1883 *Poems and Lyrics of the Joy of Earth*
1887 *Ballads and Poems of Tragic Life*
1888 *A Reading of Earth*
1892 *Modern Love, A Reprint, to which is added The Sage Enamoured and the Honest Lady*
1892 *Poems: The Empty Purse, with Odes to the Comic Spirit, To Youth in Memory, and Verses*
1894 Second Edition of *Modern Love, A Reprint*
1897 *Selected Poems*
1898 *Odes in Contribution to the Song of French History*
1901 *A Reading of Life*

Edition de Luxe, 1–4   *Poems* in *The Works of George Meredith*, ed. William Maxse Meredith (London: Constable, 1898–1911). Volumes 29–31 (also numbered 1–3) published in 1898 under GM's supervision. Volume 33 (also numbered 4) published posthumously in 1910.

Edition de Luxe, 1911   "Errata in the Poems," *Bibliography and Various Readings*, Volume 36 (1911) of *The Works of George Meredith*, ed. William Maxse Meredith.

GMT   *The Poetical Works of George Meredith*, with some notes by G. M. Trevelyan (London: Constable, 1912).

LP   George Meredith, *Last Poems*, ed. W. M. Meredith (London: Constable, 1909).

Mem. Ed.   Memorial Edition, *The Works of George Meredith*, 29 vols. (New York: Scribner, 1909–12).

TP   George Meredith, *Twenty Poems* (from *Household Words*), ed. B. W. Matz (London: privately printed, 1909).

Altschul   *A Catalogue of the Altschul Collection of George Meredith in the Yale University Library*, comp. Bertha Coolidge (privately printed, 1931).

Berg   Interleaved Copy 7 of *Poems* (1851), in the Henry W. and Albert A. Berg Collection of the New York Public Library.

Butcher   Lady Butcher (Alice Brandreth Gordon), *Memories of George Meredith, O.M.* (New York: Scribner, 1919).

Century   *The Century Illustrated Monthly Magazine.*

Cline   *The Letters of George Meredith*, ed. C. L. Cline, 3 vols. (Oxford: Clarendon, 1970).

Clodd   Edward Clodd, *Memories* (New York: Putnam, 1916).

Cornhill   *The Cornhill Magazine.*

Ellis   S. M. Ellis, *George Meredith: His Life and Friends in Relation to His Work* (London: Grant Richards, 1919).

English   *The English Illustrated Magazine.*
  Illustrated

Fortnightly   *The Fortnightly Review.*

Fraser's   *Fraser's Magazine.*

Galland   René Galland, *George Meredith: Les Cinquante Premières Années, 1828–1878* (Paris: Les Presses Françaises, 1923).

Hardman   *The Hardman Papers: A Further Selection (1865–1868) from the Letters and Memoirs of Sir William Hardman*, ed. S. M. Ellis (London: Constable, 1930).

Houghton   The Houghton Library, Harvard University.

Huntington   The Huntington Library, San Marino, California.

LS   Lionel Stevenson, *The Ordeal of George Meredith: A Biography* (New York: Scribner, 1953).

Macmillan's   *Macmillan's Magazine.*

MBF	Maurice Buxton Forman, *A Bibliography of the Writing in Prose and Verse of George Meredith* (Edinburgh: The Bibliographical Society, 1922).
MLQ	*The Modern Language Quarterly.*
"Monthly Observer"	MS periodical, Widener Collection, Harvard University.
Morley	Viscount John Morley, *Recollections*, 2 vols. (New York: Macmillan, 1917).
MVP	*A Mid-Victorian Pepys: The Letters and Memoirs of Sir William Hardman*, ed. S. M. Ellis (New York: George H. Doran, [1923]).
NB A	Early notebook in the Beinecke Library, Yale University, beginning after end paper with bookplate.
NB B	Opposite end of NB A.
NB WW	Early notebook in the Beinecke Library, Yale University, used primarily for fair copies of passages of "Wandering Willie."
New Quarterly	*The New Quarterly Magazine.*
OED	*Oxford English Dictionary.*
Ross	Janet Duff Gordon Ross, *The Fourth Generation* (New York: Scribner, 1912).
Scribner's	*Scribner's Magazine.*
Sencourt	Robert Esmonde Sencourt, *The Life of George Meredith* (New York: Scribner, 1929).
Texas	The University of Texas Library, Austin, Texas.
TLS-I	Edward Clodd, "Meredith's Conversations with Clodd—I," *Times Literary Supplement*, 8 May 1953.
TLS-II	Edward Clodd, "Meredith's Conversations with Clodd—II," *Times Literary Supplement*, 15 May 1953.
WMM	*Letters of George Meredith*, ed. his son (William Maxse Meredith), 2 vols. (New York: Scribner, 1912).
Yale	Yale University Library.

Part I
Poems Collected by Meredith

POEMS
(1851)

The Olive Branch

According to the July 1, 1851–June 30, 1852 edition of *Lloyd's Register of British and Foreign Shipping*, four ships named *Olive Branch* were afloat, two of them fishing smacks and thus not appropriate to GM's poem. He would, therefore, have had in mind either the 114-ton schooner, mastered by J. Dunnet, built in 1845, or the 320-ton barque, mastered by R. Hudson, built in 1837. The larger of the two seems the more likely choice as a vessel of an international good will.

A dove flew with an Olive Branch;
It crossed the sea and reached the shore,
And on a ship about to launch,
Dropped down the happy sign it bore.

'An omen' rang the glad acclaim!
The Captain stooped and picked it up,
'Be then the Olive Branch her name,'
Cried she who flung the christening cup.

The vessel took the laughing tides;
It was a joyous revelry   10
To see her dashing from her sides
The rough, salt kisses of the sea.

And forth into the bursting foam
She spread her sail and sped away,
The rolling surge her restless home,
Her incense wreaths the showering spray.

MS: NB A, [*p. 15*], *lines 29–40, 71–73, 79–86, forming a continuous fragment. Variants are from this MS.*

Far out, and where the riot waves
Run mingling in tumultuous throngs,
She danced above a thousand graves,
And heard a thousand briny songs.   20

Her mission with her manly crew,
Her flag unfurl'd, her title told,
She took the Old World to the New,
And brought the New World to the Old.

Secure of friendliest welcomings,
She swam the havens sheening fair;
Secure upon her glad white wings,
She fluttered on the ocean air.

To her no more the bastioned fort
Shot out its swarthy tongue of fire;   30
From bay to bay, from port to port,
Her coming was the world's desire.

And tho' the tempest lashed her oft,
And tho' the rocks had hungry teeth,
And lightnings split the masts aloft,
And thunders shook the planks beneath,

And tho' the storm, self-willed and blind,
Made tatters of her dauntless sail,
And all the wildness of the wind
Was loosed on her, she did not fail;   40

But gallantly she ploughed the main,
And gloriously her welcome pealed,
And grandly shone to sky and plain
The goodly bales her decks revealed;

30 fire] flame *del.*
32 the] a
35 split] lick'd
38 dauntless] milky

Brought from the fruitful eastern glebes
Where blow the gusts of balm and spice,
Or where the black blockaded ribs
Are jammed 'mongst ghostly fleets of ice,

Or where upon the curling hills
Glow clusters of the bright-eyed grape,   50
Or where the hand of labour drills
The stubbornness of earth to shape.

Rich harvestings and wealthy germs,
And handicrafts and shapely wares,
And spinnings of the hermit worms,
And fruits that bloom by lions' lairs.

Come, read the meaning of the deep!
The use of winds and waters learn!
'Tis not to make the mother weep
For sons that never will return;   60

'Tis not to make the nations show
Contempt for all whom seas divide;
'Tis not to pamper war and woe,
Nor feed traditionary pride;

'Tis not to make the floating bulk
Mask death upon its slippery deck,
Itself in turn a shattered hulk,
A ghastly raft, a bleeding wreck.

It is to knit with loving lip
The interests of land to land;   70
To join in far-seen fellowship
The tropic and the polar strand.

61 nations] sailor
62 whom] the
69 loving] heart &
71 join] bid *del.*   far-seen] hearty *del.* mutual

It is to make that foaming Strength
Whose rebel forces wrestle still
Thro' all his boundaried breadth and length,
Become a vassal to our will.

It is to make the various skies,
And all the various fruits they vaunt,
And all the dowers of earth we prize,
Subservient to our household want.   80

And more, for knowledge crowns the gain
Of intercourse with other souls,
And Wisdom travels not in vain
The plunging spaces of the poles.

The wild Atlantic's weltering gloom,
Earth-clasping seas of North and South,
The Baltic with its amber spume,
The Caspian with its frozen mouth;

The broad Pacific, basking bright,
And girdling lands of lustrous growth,   90
Vast continents and isles of light,
Dumb tracts of undiscovered sloth.

She visits these, traversing each;
They ripen to the common sun;
Thro' diverse forms and different speech,
The world's humanity is one.

O may her voice have power to say
How soon the wrecking discords cease,
When every wandering wave is gay
With golden argosies of peace!   100

77 skies] fruits *or* skies
Between 77 and 78 del.: Subservient to the household
82 souls] homes
84 The vastness of the ocean foams

Now when the ark of human fate,
Long baffled by the wayward wind,
Is drifting with its peopled freight,
Safe haven on the heights to find;

Safe haven from the drowning slime
Of evil deeds and Deluge wrath;—
To plant again the foot of Time
Upon a purer, firmer path;

'Tis now the hour to probe the ground,
To watch the Heavens, to speak the word,   110
The fathoms of the deep to sound,
And send abroad the missioned bird.

On strengthened wing for evermore,
Let Science, swiftly as she can,
Fly seaward on from shore to shore,
And bind the links of man to man;

And like that fair propitious Dove,
Bless future fleets about to launch;
Make every freight a freight of love,
And every ship an Olive Branch.   120

Song

Love within the lover's breast
Burns like Hesper in the west,
O'er the ashes of the sun,
Till the day and night are done;
Then when dawn drives up her car—
Lo! it is the morning star.

Love! thy love pours down on mine
As the sunlight on the vine,
As the snow-rill on the vale,
As the salt breeze in the sail;   10
As the song unto the bird,
On my lips thy name is heard.

As a dewdrop on the rose
In thy heart my passion glows,
As a skylark to the sky,
Up into thy breast I fly;
As a sea-shell of the sea
Ever shall I sing of thee.

The Wild Rose and the Snowdrop

The Snowdrop is the prophet of the flowers;
It lives and dies upon its bed of snows;
And like a thought of spring it comes and goes,
Hanging its head beside our leafless bowers.
The sun's betrothing kiss it never knows,
Nor all the glowing joy of golden showers;
But ever in a placid, pure repose,
More like a spirit with its look serene,
Droops its pale cheek veined thro' with infant green.

Queen of her sisters is the sweet Wild Rose,   10
Sprung from the earnest sun and ripe young June;
The year's own darling and the Summer's Queen!
Lustrous as the new-throned crescent moon.
Much of that early prophet look she shows,
Mixed with her fair espoused blush which glows,
As if the ethereal fairy blood were seen;
Like a soft evening over sunset snows,
Half twilight violet shade, half crimson sheen.

Twin-born are both in beauteousness, most fair
In all that glads the eye and charms the air;   20
In all that wakes emotions in the mind
And sows sweet sympathies for human kind.
Twin-born, albeit their seasons are apart,
They bloom together in the thoughtful heart;
Fair symbols of the marvels of our state,
Mute speakers of the oracles of fate!

For each fulfilling nature's law, fulfils
Itself and its own aspirations pure;
Living and dying; letting faith ensure
New life when deathless Spring shall touch the hills.   30
Each perfect in its place; and each content
With that perfection which its being meant:
Divided not by months that intervene,
But linked by all the flowers that bud between.
Forever smiling thro' its season brief,
The one in glory and the one in grief:
Forever painting to our museful sight,
How lowlihead and loveliness unite.

Born from the first blind yearning of the earth
To be a mother and give happy birth,   40
Ere yet the northern sun such rapture brings,
Lo, from her virgin breast the Snowdrop springs;
And ere the snows have melted from the grass,
And not a strip of greensward doth appear,
Save the faint prophecy its cheeks declare,
Alone, unkissed, unloved, behold it pass!
While in the ripe enthronement of the year,
Whispering the breeze, and wedding the rich air
With her so sweet, delicious bridal breath,—
Odorous and exquisite beyond compare,   50
And starr'd with dews upon her forehead clear,
Fresh-hearted as a Maiden Queen should be
Who takes the land's devotion as her fee,—
The Wild Rose blooms, all summer for her dower,
Nature's most beautiful and perfect flower.

The Death of Winter

When April with her wild blue eye
    Comes dancing over the grass,
And all the crimson birds so shy
    Peep out to see her pass;

As lightly she loosens her showery locks
   And flutters her rainy wings;
      Laughingly stoops
         To the glass of the stream,
      And loosens and loops
         Her hair by the gleam,   10
While all the young villagers blithe as the flocks
   Go frolicking round in rings;—
Then Winter, he who tamed the fly,
Turns on his back and prepares to die,
For he cannot live longer under the sky.

Down the valleys glittering green,
Down from the hills in snowy rills,
He melts between the border sheen
   And leaps the flowery verges!
He cannot choose, but brighten their hues,   20
And tho' he would creep, he fain must leap,
   For the quick Spring spirit urges.
Down the vale and down the dale,
He leaps and lights, till his moments fail,
Buried in blossoms, red and pale,
   While the sweet birds sing his dirges!

O Winter! I'd live that life of thine,
With a frosty brow and an icicle tongue,
And never a song my whole life long,—
Were such delicious burial mine!   30
To die and be buried, and so remain
A wandering brook in April's train,
Fixing my dying eyes for aye
On the dawning brows of maiden May.

Song

The moon is alone in the sky
   As thou in my soul;
The sea takes her image to lie
   Where the white ripples roll

All night in a dream,
With the light of her beam,
Hushedly, mournfully, mistily up to the shore.
The pebbles speak low
In the ebb and the flow,
As I when thy voice came at intervals, tuned to adore: 10
Nought other is stirr'd
Save my heart all unheard
Beating to bliss that is past evermore.

John Lackland

A wicked man is bad enough on earth;
But O the baleful lustre of a chief
Once pledged in tyranny!   O star of dearth
Darkly illumining a nation's grief!
How many men have worn thee on their brows!
Alas for them and us!   God's precious gift
Of gracious dispensation got by theft—
The damning form of false unholy vows!
The thief of God and man must have his fee:
And thou John Lackland, despicable prince—   10
Basest of England's banes before or since!
Thrice traitor, coward, thief!   O thou shalt be
The historic warning, trampled and abhorr'd
Who dared to steal and stain the symbols of the Lord!

The Sleeping City

A princess in the eastern tale
Paced thro' a marble city pale,
And saw on ghastly shapes of stone,
The sculptured life she breathed alone;

SONG: THE MOON IS ALONE IN THE SKY

11 is] *om. de L; corr. GM Berg Copy 1*   stirr'd] heard *1851; corr. GM Berg Copy 1*
12 all unheard] like a bird *1851*; all unheard *corr. GM Berg Copy 1*
13 evermore, evermore *1851*; *2nd* evermore *del. GM in proof for de L*

THE SLEEPING CITY

3 on] *1851, de L*; in *Mem. Ed., GMT*

Saw, where'er her eye might range,
Herself the only child of change;
And heard her echoed footfall chime
Between Oblivion and Time;

And in the squares where fountains played,
And up the spiral balustrade,   10
Along the drowsy corridors,
Even to the inmost sleeping floors,

Surveyed in wonder chilled with dread,
The seemingness of Death, not dead;
Life's semblance but without its storm,
And silence frosting every form;

Crowned figures, cold and grouping slaves,
Like suddenly arrested waves
About to sink, about to rise,—
Strange meaning in their stricken eyes.   20

And cloths and couches live with flame
Of leopards fierce and lions tame,
And hunters in the jungle reed,
Thrown out by sombre glowing brede;

Dumb chambers hushed with fold on fold,
And cumbrous gorgeousness of gold;
White casements o'er embroidered seats,
Looking on solitudes of streets,—

On palaces and column'd towers,
Unconscious of the stony hours;   30
Harsh gateways startled at a sound,
With burning lamps all burnish'd round;—

Surveyed in awe this wealth and state,
Touched by the finger of a Fate,
And drew with slow-awakening fear,
The sternness of the atmosphere;—

And gradually with stealthier foot,
Became herself a thing as mute,
And listened,—while with swift alarm
Her alien heart shrank from the charm;   40

Yet as her thoughts dilating rose,
Took glory in the great repose,
And over every postured form
Spread lava-like and brooded warm,—

And fixed on every frozen face,
Beheld the record of its race,
And in each chiselled feature knew
The stormy life that once blushed thro';—

The ever-present of the past
There written; all that lightened last,   50
Love, anguish, hope, disease, despair,
Beauty and rage, all written there;—

Enchanted Passions! whose pale doom
Is never flushed by blight or bloom,
But sentinelled by silent orbs,
Whose light the pallid scene absorbs.—

Like such a one I pace along
This City with its sleeping throng;
Like her with dread and awe, that turns
To rapture, and sublimely yearns;—   60

For now the quiet stars look down
On lights as quiet as their own;
The streets that groaned with traffic, show
As if with silence paved below;

The latest revellers are at peace,
The signs of in-door tumult cease,
From gay saloon and low resort,
Comes not one murmur or report:

The clattering chariot rolls not by,
The windows show no waking eye,   70
The houses smoke not, and the air
Is clear, and all the midnight fair.

The centre of the striving world,
Round which the human fate is curled,
To which the future crieth wild,—
Is pillowed like a cradled child.

The palace roof that guards a crown,
The mansion swathed in dreamy down,
Hovel, court, and alley-shed,
Sleep in the calmness of the dead.   80

Now while the many-motived heart
Lies hushed—fireside and busy mart,
And mortal pulses beat the tune,
That charms the calm cold ear o' the moon

Whose yellowing crescent down the West
Leans listening, now when every breast
Its basest or its purest heaves,
The soul that joys, the soul that grieves;—

While Fame is crowning happy brows
That day will blindly scorn, while vows   90
Of anguished love long hidden, speak
From faltering tongue and flushing cheek;

The language only known to dreams,
Rich eloquence of rosy themes!
While on the Beauty's folded mouth,
Disdain just wrinkles baby youth;

While Poverty dispenses alms
To outcasts, bread, and healing balms;
While old Mammon knows himself
The greater beggar for his pelf;   100

100 greater] *1851*; greatest *de L*; *corr. errata, de L 1911*

While noble things in darkness grope,
The Statesman's aim, the Poet's hope;
The Patriot's impulse gathers fire,
And germs of future fruits aspire;—

Now while dumb nature owns its links,
And from one common fountain drinks,
Methinks in all around I see
This Picture in Eternity;—

A marbled City planted there
With all its pageants and despair;   110
A peopled hush, a Death not dead,
But stricken with Medusa's head;—

And in the Gorgon's glance for aye
The lifeless immortality
Reveals in sculptured calmness all
Its latest life beyond recall.

The Poetry of Chaucer

Grey with all honours of age! but fresh-featured and ruddy
As dawn when the drowsy farm-yard has thrice heard
    Chaunticlere.
Tender to tearfulness—childlike, and manly, and motherly;
Here beats true English blood richest joyance on sweet English
    ground.

The Poetry of Spenser

Lakes where the sunsheen is mystic with splendour and
    softness;
Vales where sweet life is all Summer with golden romance;
Forests that glimmer with twilight round revel-bright palaces;
Here in our May-blood we wander, careering 'mongst ladies and
    knights.

The Poetry of Shakespeare

Picture some Isle smiling green 'mid the white-foaming
     ocean;—
Full of old woods, leafy wisdoms, and frolicsome fays;
Passions and pageants; sweet love singing bird-like above it;
Life in all shapes, aims, and fates, is there warm'd by one great
     human heart.

The Poetry of Milton

Like to some deep-chested organ whose grand inspiration,
Serenely majestic in utterance, lofty and calm,
Interprets to mortals with melody great as its burthen,
The mystical harmonies chiming for ever throughout the bright
     spheres.

The Poetry of Southey

Keen as an eagle whose flight towards the dim empyréan
Fearless of toil or fatigue ever royally wends!
Vast in the cloud-coloured robes of the balm-breathing Orient
Lo! the grand Epic advances, unfolding the humanest truth.

The Poetry of Coleridge

A brook glancing under green leaves, self-delighting, exulting,
And full of a gurgling melody ever renewed—
Renewed thro' all changes of Heaven, unceasing in sunlight,
Unceasing in moonlight, but hushed in the beams of the holier orb.

The Poetry of Shelley

See'est thou a Skylark whose glistening winglets ascending
Quiver like pulses beneath the melodious dawn?
Deep in the heart-yearning distance of heaven it flutters—
Wisdom and beauty and love are the treasures it brings down at eve.

The Poetry of Wordsworth

A breath of the mountains, fresh born in the regions majestic,
That look with their eye-daring summits deep into the sky.
The voice of great Nature; sublime with her lofty conceptions,
Yet earnest and simple as any sweet child of the green lowly vale.

The Poetry of Keats

The song of a nightingale sent thro' a slumbrous valley,
Low-lidded with twilight, and tranced with the dolorous sound,
Tranced with a tender enchantment; the yearning of passion
That wins immortality even while panting delirious with death.

Violets

Violets, shy violets!
    How many hearts with you compare!
      Who hide themselves in thickest green,
        And thence unseen,
    Ravish the enraptured air
    With sweetness, dewy fresh and rare!

Violets, shy violets!
    Human hearts to me shall be
      Viewless violets in the grass,
        And as I pass,   10
    Odours and sweet imagery
    Will wait on mine and gladden me!

Angelic Love

Angelic love that stoops with heavenly lips
    To meet its earthly mate;
Heroic love that to its sphere's eclipse,
    Can dare to join its fate

VIOLETS

2 you] ye *1851*

With one beloved devoted human heart,
And share with it the passion and the smart,
  The undying bliss
  Of its most fleeting kiss;
  The fading grace
  Of its most sweet embrace:—   10
 Angelic love, heroic love!
 Whose birth can only be above,
 Whose wandering must be on earth,
 Whose haven where it first had birth!
Love that can part with all but its own worth,
  And joy in every sacrifice
  That beautifies its Paradise!
And gently like a golden-fruited vine,
With earnest tenderness itself consign,
And creeping up deliriously entwine   20
  Its dear delicious arms
   Round the beloved being!
  With fair unfolded charms,
   All-trusting, and all-seeing,—
Grape-laden with full bunches of young wine!
While to the panting heart's dry yearning drouth
  Buds the rich dewy mouth—
   Tenderly uplifted,
   Like two rose-leaves drifted
Down in a long warm sigh of the sweet South! 30
  Such love, such love is thine,
  Such heart is mine
O thou of mortal visions most divine!

Twilight Music

 Know you the low pervading breeze
  That softly sings
 In the trembling leaves of twilight trees,
As if the wind were dreaming on its wings?

And have you marked their still degrees
Of ebbing melody, like the strings
Of a silver harp swept by a spirit's hand
 In some strange glimmering land,
   'Mid gushing springs,
   And glistenings   10
Of waters and of planets, wild and grand!
 And have you marked in that still time,
 The chariots of those shining cars
 Brighten upon the hushing dark,
   And bent to hark
That Voice, amid the poplar and the lime,
 Pause in the dilating lustre
   Of the spheral cluster;
 Pause but to renew its sweetness, deep
As dreams of heaven to souls that sleep!   20
 And felt, despite earth's jarring wars,
   When day is done
   And dead the sun,
 Still a voice divine can sing,
 Still is there sympathy can bring
   A whisper from the stars!
Ah, with this sentience quickly will you know,
How like a tree I tremble to the tones
   Of your sweet voice!
   How keenly I rejoice   30
 When in me with sweet motions slow
The spiritual music ebbs and moans—
Lives in the lustre of those heavenly eyes,
Dies in the light of its own paradise,—
Dies, and relives eternal from its death,
Immortal melodies in each deep breath;
Sweeps thro' my being, bearing up to thee
Myself, the weight of its eternity;
Till nerved to life from its ordeal fire,
It marries music with the human lyre,   40
Blending divine delight with loveliest desire.

Requiem

The subject of this poem may be Julia Hay Hobhouse, daughter of John Cam Hobhouse (best known as Byron's friend), later Lord Broughton. Julia contracted cholera in Guernsey and died at the family home, Erle Stoke in West Wiltshire on September 5, 1849 (Lord Broughton, *Recollections of a Long Life* [London: Murray, 1911], 6:246). Hobhouse was a friend of Thomas Love Peacock, GM's father-in-law, who wrote a poem on the occasion of Julia's death, *Lines on the Death of Julia, Lord Broughton's Eldest Daughter, 1849* (in *Works*, Halliford ed. [London: Constable, 1923–34], 7:253).

Where faces are hueless, where eyelids are dewless,
    Where passion is silent and hearts never crave;
Where thought hath no theme, and where sleep hath no dream,
    In patience and peace thou art gone—to thy grave!
Gone where no warning can wake thee to morning,
    Dead tho' a thousand hands stretch'd out to save.

Thou cam'st to us sighing, and singing and dying,
    How could it be otherwise, fair as thou wert?
Placidly fading, and sinking and shading,
    At last to that shadow, the latest desert;   10
Wasting and waning, but still, still remaining,
    Alas for the hand that could deal the death-hurt!

The Summer that brightens, the Winter that whitens,
    The world and its voices, the sea and the sky,
The bloom of creation, the tie of relation,
    All—all is a blank to thine ear and thine eye;
The ear may not listen, the eye may not glisten,
    Nevermore waked by a smile or a sigh.

The tree that is rootless must ever be fruitless;
    And thou art alone in thy death and thy birth;   20
No last loving token of wedded love broken,
    No sign of thy singleness, sweetness and worth;
Lost as the flower that is drowned in the shower,
    Fall'n like a snowflake to melt in the earth.

The Flower of the Ruins

Take thy lute and sing
By the ruined castle walls,
Where the torrent-foam falls,
And long weeds wave:
Take thy lute and sing,
O'er the grey ancestral grave!
Daughter of a King,
Tune thy string.

Sing of happy hours,
In the roar of rushing time;   10
Till all the echoes chime
To the days gone by;
Sing of passing hours
To the ever-present sky;—
Weep—and let the showers
Wake thy flowers.

Sing of glories gone:—
No more the blazoned fold
From the banner is unrolled;
The gold sun is set.   20
Sing his glory gone,
For thy voice may charm him yet;
Daughter of the dawn,
He is gone!

Pour forth all thy grief!
Passionately sweep the chords,
Wed them quivering to thy words;
Wild words of wail!
Shed thy withered grief—
But hold not Autumn to thy bale   30
The eddy of the leaf
Must be brief!

Sing up to the night:
Hard it is for streaming tears
To read the calmness of the spheres,
Coldly they shine;
Sing up to their light;
They have views thou may'st divine—
Gain prophetic sight
From their light!   40

On the windy hills
Lo, the little harebell leans
On the spire-grass that it queens,
With bonnet blue;
Trusting love instils
Love and subject reverence true,
Learn what love instils
On the hills!

By the bare wayside
Placid snowdrops hang their cheeks,   50
Softly touch'd with pale green streaks,
Soon, soon, to die;
On the clothed hedgeside
Bands of rosy beauties vie,
In their prophecied
Summer pride.

From the snowdrop learn;
Not in her pale life lives she,
But in her blushing prophecy.
Thus be thy hopes,   60
Living but to yearn
Upwards to the hidden copes;—
Even within the urn
Let them burn!

Heroes of thy race—
Warriors with golden crowns,
Ghostly shapes with marbled frowns
Stare thee to stone;

Matrons of thy race
Pass before thee making moan;   70
Full of solemn grace
Is their pace.

Piteous their despair!
Piteous their looks forlorn!
Terrible their ghostly scorn!
Still hold thou fast;—
Heed not their despair!—
Thou art thy future, not thy past;
Let them glance and glare
Thro' the air.   80

Thou the ruin's bud,
Be not that moist rich-smelling weed
With its arras-sembled brede,
And ruin-haunting stalk;
Thou the ruin's bud,
Be still the rose that lights the walk,
Mix thy fragrant blood
With the flood!

The Rape of Aurora

Never, O never,
Since dewy sweet Flora,
Was ravished by Zephyr,
Was such a thing heard
In the valleys so hollow!
Till rosy Aurora,
Uprising as ever,
Bright Phosphor to follow,
Pale Phoebe to sever,
Was caught like a bird   10
To the breast of Apollo!

Wildly she flutters,
    And flushes all over
With passionate mutters
    Of shame to the hush
        Of his amorous whispers:
    But, O such a lover
Must win when he utters
    Thro' rosy red lispers,
The pains that discover   20
    The wishes that gush
        From the torches of Hesperus.

One finger just touching
    The Orient chamber,
Unflooded the gushing
    Of light that illumed
        All her lustrous unveiling.
    On clouds of glow amber,
Her limbs richly blushing,
    She lay sweetly wailing,   30
In odours that gloomed
    On the God as he bloomed
        O'er her loveliness paling.

Great Pan in his covert
    Beheld the rare glistening,
The cry of the love-hurt,
    The sigh and the kiss
        Of the latest close mingling:
    But love, thought he, listening,
Will not do a dove hurt   40
    I know,—and a tingling,
Latent with bliss,
    Prickt thro' him, I wis,
        For the Nymph he was singling.

South-West Wind in the Woodland

GM sent this poem, with *The Olive Branch* and *Will o' the Wisp*, to the printer, James Vizetelly, after the main bulk of *Poems*, probably in February 1851. On receiving an appreciative letter from Edmund Ollier, son of the publisher of Shelley and Keats, and himself a versifier (Cline, Letter 23, n.1) after the publication of *Poems*, GM defended the versification of this poem as follows: "What you say of my blank octo-syllabic may be true, and is quite just; but the 'S. W. Wind in the Woodland'—in which I used it—is a subject which, in my opinion, would have been marred by rhyme—Nor could I find any other (better) mode of giving my impression of the reckless rushing rapidity, and sweeping sound of the great wind among the foliage which I felt impelled to do in such manner that the ear should only be conscious of swiftness, and no sweetness; and that there should be no direct pause throughout."

For an earlier treatment of this theme, see "Wandering Willie" (canto 2, pp. 907–933); for a later one, see *The South-Wester* (pp. 405–408). In *The Egoist* "the South-west driving the clouds, gallantly firm in commotion," is flatteringly used for the appearance of the heroine, Clara Middleton, and the wind itself is eulogized by GM (Mem. Ed., 13:201, 14:20).

> The silence of preluded song—
> Æolian silence charms the woods;
> Each tree a harp, whose foliaged strings
> Are waiting for the master's touch
> To sweep them into storms of joy,
> Stands mute and whispers not; the birds
> Brood dumb in their foreboding nests,
> Save here and there a chirp or tweet,
> That utters fear or anxious love,
> Or when the ouzel sends a swift   10
> Half warble, shrinking back again
> His golden bill, or when aloud
> The storm-cock warns the dusking hills
> And villages and valleys round:
> For lo, beneath those ragged clouds
> That skirt the opening west, a stream
> Of yellow light and windy flame
> Spreads lengthening southward, and the sky
> Begins to gloom, and o'er the ground

MS: NB WW, *fragment, white scrap of paper pasted into MS, verso of* "Thou tremblest," *see p. 972, lines 86–91 + 13 lines. Variants are from this fragment.*

A moan of coming blasts creeps low   20
And rustles in the crisping grass;
Till suddenly with mighty arms
Outspread, that reach the horizon round,
The great South-West drive o'er the earth,
And loosens all his roaring robes
Behind him, over heath and moor.
He comes upon the neck of night,
Like one that leaps a fiery steed
Whose keen black haunches quivering shine
With eagerness and haste, that needs   30
No spur to make the dark leagues fly!
Whose eyes are meteors of speed;
Whose name is as a flashing foam;
Whose hoofs are travelling thunder-shocks;—
He comes, and while his growing gusts,
Wild couriers of his reckless course
Are whistling from the daggered gorse,
And hurrying over fern and broom,
Midway, far off, he feigns to halt
And gather in his streaming train.   40

Now, whirring like an eagle's wing
Preparing for a wide blue flight;
Now, flapping like a sail that tacks
And chides the wet bewildered mast;
Now, screaming like an anguish'd thing
Chased close by some down-breathing beak;
Now, wailing like a breaking heart,
That will not wholly break, but hopes
With hope that knows itself in vain;
Now, threatening like a storm-charged cloud;   50
Now, cooing like a woodland dove;
Now, up again in roar and wrath
High soaring and wide sweeping; now
With sudden fury dashing down
Full-force on the awaiting woods.

Long waited there, for aspens frail
That tinkle with a silver bell,
To warn the Zephyr of their love,
When danger is at hand, and wake
The neighbouring boughs, surrendering all   60
Their prophet harmony of leaves,
Had caught his earliest windward thought,
And told it trembling; naked birk
Down showering her dishevelled hair,
And like a beauty yielding up
Her fate to all the elements,
Had swayed in answer; hazels close,
Thick brambles and dark brushwood tufts,
And briared brakes that line the dells
With shaggy beetling brows, had sung   70
Shrill music, while the tattered flaws
Tore over them, and now the whole
Tumultuous concords, seized at once
With savage inspiration,—pine,
And larch, and beech, and fir, and thorn,
And ash, and oak, and oakling, rave
And shriek, and shout, and whirl, and toss,
And stretch their arms, and split, and crack,
And bend their stems, and bow their heads,
And grind, and groan, and lion-like   80
Roar to the echo-peopled hills
And ravenous wilds, and crake-like cry
With harsh delight, and cave-like call
With hollow mouth, and harp-like thrill
With mighty melodies, sublime,
From clumps of column'd pines that wave
A lofty anthem to the sky,
Fit music for a prophet's soul—
And like an ocean gathering power,
And murmuring deep, while down below,   90

90 down] reigns

Reigns calm profound;—not trembling now
The aspens, but like freshening waves
That fall upon a shingly beach;—
And round the oak a solemn roll
Of organ harmony ascends,
And in the upper foliage sounds
A symphony of distant seas.

The voice of nature is abroad
This night; she fills the air with balm;
Her mystery is o'er the land;   100
And who that hears her now and yields
His being to her yearning tones,
And seats his soul upon her wings,
And broadens o'er the wind-swept world
With her, will gather in the flight
More knowledge of her secret, more
Delight in her beneficence,
Than hours of musing, or the lore
That lives with men could ever give!
Nor will it pass away when morn   110
Shall look upon the lulling leaves,
And woodland sunshine, Eden-sweet,
Dreams o'er the paths of peaceful shade;—
For every elemental power
Is kindred to our hearts, and once
Acknowledge, wedded, once embraced,

91 Among the ferns profoundest calm—
After 91:

> Still sweeping from the quivering chords
> A leafy lamentation loud,
> A multitudinous murmuring plaint,
> A dirge of showering griefs that rise
> To one wild shouting jubilee
> And ebb again in dirgelike falls
> As of a distant torrent foam—
> A ringing change of joy and woe
> Like bells in cadence, heard at eve,
> When tempest threatens and the spire
> Points upward to the lightning cloud.

Margin: The wilderness of greenery

Once taken to the unfettered sense,
Once claspt into the naked life,
The union is eternal.

Will o' the Wisp

The will-o'-the-wisp is akin to Lantern Jack (lines 49 ff.), the Jack-o'-lantern, a phosphorescent light, also known as *ignis fatuus*, that leads night wanderers into dangerous places.

Follow me, follow me,
Over brake and under tree,
Thro' the bosky tanglery,
        Brushwood and bramble!
Follow me, follow me,
        Laugh and leap and scramble!
Follow, follow,
Hill and hollow,
Fosse and burrow,
Fen and furrow,   10
Down into the bulrush beds,
'Midst the reeds and osier heads,
In the rushy soaking damps,
Where the vapours pitch their camps,
        Follow me, follow me,
                For a midnight ramble!
O! what a mighty fog,
What a merry night O ho!
Follow, follow, nigher, nigher—
Over bank, and pond, and briar,   20
Down into the croaking ditches,
        Rotten log,
        Spotted frog,
        Beetle bright
        With crawling light,
                What a joy O ho!
Deep into the purple bog—
                What a joy O ho!

Where like hosts of puckered witches,
All the shivering agues sit   30
Warming hands and chafing feet,
By the blue marsh-hovering oils:
O the fools for all their moans!
Not a forest mad with fire
Could still their teeth, or warm their bones,
Or loose them from their chilly coils.
     What a clatter,
     How they chatter!
     Shrink and huddle,
     All a muddle,   40
       What a joy O ho!
Down we go, down we go,
       What a joy O ho!
Soon shall I be down below,
Plunging with a grey fat friar,
Hither, thither, to and fro,
Breathing mists and whisking lamps,
Plashing in the slimy swamps;
While my cousin Lantern Jack,
With cock ears and cunning eyes,   50
Turns him round upon his back,
Daubs him oozy green and black,
Sits upon his rolling size,
Where he lies, where he lies,
Groaning full of sack—
Staring with his great round eyes!
       What a joy O ho!
Sits upon him in the swamps
Breathing mists and whisking lamps!
       What a joy O ho!   60
Such a lad is Lantern Jack,
When he rides the black nightmare

Between 46 and 47: What a joy O ho! *1851*
Between 48 and 49: What a joy O ho! *1851*
48 slimy] *1851*; shiny *de L*; *corr. errata, de L 1911*

Through the fens, and puts a glare
In the friar's track.
Such a frolic lad, good lack!
To turn a friar on his back,
Trip him, clip him, whip him, nip him.
Lay him sprawling, smack!
Such a lad is Lantern Jack!
Such a tricksy lad, good lack!   70
    What a joy O ho!
  Follow me, follow me,
Where he sits, and you shall see!

Song

Fair and false!   No dawn will greet
    Thy waking beauty as of old;
The little flower beneath thy feet
    Is alien to thy smile so cold;
The merry bird flown up to meet
Young morning from his nest i' the wheat,
    Scatters his joy to wood and wold,
    But scorns the arrogance of gold.

False and fair!   I scarce know why,
    But standing in the lonely air,   10
And underneath the blessed sky,
    I plead for thee in my despair;—
For thee cut off, both heart and eye
From living truth; thy spring quite dry;
    For thee, that heaven my thought may share,
    Forget—how false! and think—how fair!

Song

Two wedded lovers watched the rising moon,
    That with her strange mysterious beauty glowing,
    Over misty hills and waters flowing,

Crowned the long twilight loveliness of June:
  And thus in me, and thus in me, they spake,
The solemn secret of first love did wake.

Above the hills the blushing orb arose;
  Her shape encircled by a radiant bower,
  In which the nightingale with charméd power,
Poured forth enchantment o'er the dark repose: 10
  And thus in me, and thus in me they said,
  Earth's mists did the sweet new spirit wed.

Far up the sky with ever purer beam,
  Upon the throne of night the moon was seated,
  And down the valley glens the shades retreated,
And silver light was on the open stream.
  And thus in me, and thus in me, they sighed,
  Aspiring Love has hallowed Passion's tide.

Song

I cannot lose thee for a day,
  But like a bird with restless wing,
My heart will find thee far away,
  And on thy bosom fall and sing,
    My nest is here, my rest is here;—
  And in the lull of wind and rain,
  Fresh voices make a sweet refrain,
    'His rest is there, his nest is there.'

With thee the wind and sky are fair,
  But parted, both are strange and dark;   10
And treacherous the quiet air
  That holds me singing like a lark,
    O shield my love, strong arm above!
  Till in the rush of wind and rain,
  Fresh voices make a rich refrain,
    'The arm above, will shield thy love.'

SONG: I CANNOT LOSE THEE FOR A DAY

5 rest is] rest in *misp. GMT*
14 rush] hush *misp. all eds., corr. GM Berg*

Daphne

Musing on the fate of Daphne,
Many feelings urged my breast,
For the God so keen desiring,
And the Nymph so deep distrest.

Never flashed thro' sylvan valley,
Visions so divinely fair!
He with early ardour glowing,
She with rosy anguish rare.

Only still more sweet and lovely
For those terrors on her brows,   10
Those swift glances wild and brilliant,
Those delicious panting vows.

Timidly the timid shoulders
Shrinking from the fervid hand!
Dark the tide of hair back-flowing
From the blue-veined temples bland!

Lovely, too, divine Apollo
In the speed of his pursuit;
With his eye an azure lustre,
And his voice a summer lute!   20

Looking like some burnished eagle
Hovering o'er a fluttered bird;
Not unseen of silver Naiad,
And of wistful Dryad heard!

Many a morn the naked beauty
Saw her bright reflection drown
In the flowing smooth-faced river,
While the god came sheening down.

Down from Pindus bright Peneus
Tells its muse-melodious source;   30
Sacred is its fountained birthplace,
And the Orient floods its course.

Many a morn the sunny darling
Saw the rising chariot-rays,
From the winding river-reaches,
Mellowing in amber haze.

Thro' the flaming mountain gorges
Lo, the River leaps the plain;
Like a wild god-stridden courser,
Tossing high its foamy mane.   40

Then he swims thro' laurelled sunlight,
Full of all sensations sweet,
Misty with his morning incense,
To the mirrored maiden's feet!

Wet and bright the dinting pebbles
Shine where oft she paused and stood;
All her dreamy warmth revolving,
While the chilly waters wooed.

Like to rosy-born Aurora,
Glowing freshly into view,   50
When her doubtful foot she ventures
On the first cold morning blue.

White as that Thessalian lily,
Fairest Tempe's fairest flower,
Lo, the tall Peneïan virgin,
Stands beneath her bathing bower.

29 *1851*: Peneus from the heights of Pindus; *corr. GM, Berg, and on errata leaf of presentation copy to R. H. Horne, Widener Collection, Harvard*: Penëus from lofty Pindus
30 Tells] Takes *1851*

Between 40 and 41 1851:

Soon the sweetness of the scenery,
And the balm of flower and herb,
Soothe his senses, check his swiftness,
Smoothe him with a gentle curb!

41 Then] And *1851*

There the laurell'd wreaths o'erarching
Crown'd the dainty shuddering maid;
There the dark prophetic laurel
Kiss'd her with its sister shade.   60

There the young green glistening leaflets
Hush'd with love their breezy peal;
There the little opening flowerets
Blush'd beneath her vermeil hccl!

There among the conscious arbours,
Sounds of soft tumultuous wail,
Mysteries of love, melodious,
Came upon the lyric gale!

Breathings of a deep enchantment,
Effluence of immortal grace,   70
Flitted round her faltering footstep,
Spread a balm about her face!

Witless of the enamour'd presence,
Like a dreamy lotus bud
From its drowsy stem down-drooping,
Gazed she in the glowing flood.

Softly sweet with fluttering presage,
Felt she that ethereal sense,
Drinking charms of love delirious,
Reaping bliss of love intense!   80

All the air was thrill'd with sunrise,
Birds made music of her name,
And the god-impregnate water
Claspt her image ere she came.

Richer for that glance unconscious!
Dearer for that soft dismay!
And the sudden self-possession!
And the smile as bright as day!

Plunging 'mid her scattered tresses,
With her blue invoking eyes;   90
See her like a star descending!
Like a rosebud see her rise!

Like a rosebud in the morning
Dashing off its jewell'd dews,
Ere unfolding all its fragrance
It is gathered by the muse!

Beauteous in the foamy laughter,
Bubbling round her shrinking waist,
Lo! from locks and lips and eyelids
Rain the glittering pearl-drops chaste!   100

And about the maiden rapture
Still the ruddy ripples play'd,
Ebbing round in startled circlets
When her arms began to wade.

Flowing in like tides attracted,
To the glowing crescent shine!
Clasping her ambrosial whiteness
Like an Autumn-tinted vine!

Sinking low with love's emotion!
Levying with look and tone   110
All love's rosy arts to mimic
Cytherea's magic zone!

Trembling up with adoration
To the crimson daisy tip,
Budding from the snowy bosom—
Fainter than the rose-red lip!

Rising in a storm of wavelets,
That for shelter, feigning fright,
Prest to those twin-heaving havens,
Harbour'd there beneath her light.   120

Gleaming in a whirl of eddies
Round her lucid throat and neck;
Eddying in a gleam of dimples
Up against her bloomy cheek.

Bribing all the breezy water
With rich warmth, the nymph to keep
In a self-imprison'd pleasance,
Tempting her from deep to deep.

Till at last delirious passion
Thrill'd the god to wild excess,   130
And the fervour of a moment
Made divinity confess;

And he stood in all his glory!
But so radiant, being near,
That her eyes were frozen on him
In a fascinated fear!

All with orient splendour shining,—
All with roseate birth aglow,
Gleam'd the golden god before her,
With his golden crescent bow.   140

Soon the dazzled light subsided,
And he seem'd a beauteous youth,
Form'd to gain the maiden's murmurs,
And to pledge the vows of truth.

Ah! that thus he had continued!
O, that such for her had been!
Graceful with all godlike beauty,
But so humanly serene!

Cheeks, and mouth, and mellow ringlets,
Bounteous as the mid-day beam;   150
Pleading looks and wistful tremour,
Tender as a maiden's dream!

127 pleasance] *errata leaf 1851*; plaisance *1851, de L*

Palms that like a bird's throbb'd bosom
Palpitate with eagerness,
Lips, the bridals of the roses,
Dewy sweet from the caress!

Lips and limbs, and eyes and ringlets,
Swaying, praying to one prayer,
Like a lyre, swept by a spirit,
In the still, enraptur'd air.   160

Like a lyre in some far valley,
Uttering ravishments divine!
All its strings to viewless fingers
Yearning, modulations fine!

Yearning with melodious fervour!
Like a beauteous maiden flower,
When the young beloved, three paces
Hovers from the bridal bower.

Throbbing thro' the dawning stillness
As a heart within a breast,   170
When the young beloved is stepping
Radiant to the nuptial nest.

O for Daphne! gentle Daphne!
Ever warmer by degrees
Whispers full of hopes and visions,
Throng her ears like honey bees!

Never yet was lonely blossom
Woo'd with such delicious voice!
Never since hath mortal maiden
Dwelt on such celestial choice!   180

Love-suffused she quivers, falters—
Falters, sighs, but never speaks,
All her rosy blood up-gushing,
Overflows her ripe young cheeks.

Blushing, sweet with virgin blushes,
All her loveliness a-flame,
Stands she in the orient waters,
Stricken o'er with speechless shame!

Ah! but lovelier, ever lovelier,
As more deep the colour glows,   190
And the honey-laden lily
Changes to the fragrant rose.

While the god with meek embraces,
Whispering all his sacred charms,
Softly folds her, gently holds her,
In his white encircling arms!

But, O Dian! veil not wholly
Thy pale crescent from the morn!
Vanish not, O virgin goddess,
With that look of pallid scorn!   200

Still thy pure protecting influence
Shed from those fair watchful eyes!—
Lo! her angry orb has vanished,
And the bright sun thrones the skies!

Voicelessly the forest Virgin
Vanished! but one look she gave—
Keen as Niobean arrow
Thro' the maiden's heart it drave.

Thus toward that throning bosom
Where all earth is warmed,—each spot   210
Nourished with autumnal blessings—
Icy chill was Daphne caught.

Icy chill! but swift revulsion
All her gentler self renewed,
Even as icy Winter quickens
With bud-opening warmth imbued.

209 toward] towards *1851*

Even as a torpid brooklet
That to the night-gleaming moon
Flashed in turn the frozen glances,—
Melts upon the breast of noon.   220

But no more—O never, never,
Turns she to that bosom bright,
Swiftly all her senses counsel—
All her nerves are strung to flight.

O'er the brows of radiant Pindus
Rolls a shadow dark and cold,
And a sound of lamentation
Issues from its mournful fold.

Voice of the far-sighted Muses!
Cry of keen foreboding song!   230
Every cleft of startled Tempe
Tingles with it sharp and long.

Over bourn and bosk and dingle,
Over rivers, over rills,
Runs the sad subservient Echo
Toward the dim blue distant hills!

And another and another!
'Tis a cry more wild than all;
And the hills with muffled voices
Answer 'Daphne!' to the call.   240

And another and another!
'Tis a cry so wildly sweet,
That her charmed heart turns rebel
To the instinct of her feet;

236 Toward] Towards *1851*

Between 236 and 237 1851:

          And another and another!
          And a cry more keen and strong,
          Sends the babbling nymph to follow
          That first message of wild song.

And she pauses for an instant;
But his arms have scarcely slid
Round her waist in cestian girdles,
And his low voluptuous lid

Lifted pleading, and the honey
Of his mouth for her's athirst,   250
Ruby glistening, raised for moisture—
Like a bud that waits to burst

In the sweet espousing showers—
And his tongue has scarce begun
With its inarticulate burthen—
And the clouds scarce show the sun

As it pierces thro' a crevice
Of the mass that closed it o'er,
When again the horror flashes—
And she turns to flight once more!   260

And again o'er radiant Pindus
Rolls the shadow dark and cold,
And the sound of lamentation
Issues from its sable fold!

And again the light winds chide her
As she darts from his embrace—
And again the far-voiced echoes
Speak their tidings of the chase.

Loudly now as swiftly, swiftly,
O'er the glimmering sands she speeds;   270
Wildly now as in the furzes
From the piercing spikes she bleeds.

Deeply and with direful anguish
As above each crimson drop,
Passion checks the god Apollo,
And love bids him weep and stop.—

He above each drop of crimson
Shadowing—like the laurel leaf
That above himself will shadow,—
Sheds a fadeless look of grief.   280

Then with love's remorseful discord,
With its own desire at war,
Sighing turns, while dimly fleeting
Daphne flies the chase afar.

But all nature is against her!
Pan with all his sylvan troop,
Thro' the vista'd woodland valleys
Blocks her course with cry and whoop!

In the twilights of the thickets
Trees bend down their gnarled boughs,   290
Wild green leaves and low curved branches,
Hold her hair and beat her brows.

Many a brake of brushwood covert
Where cold darkness slumbers mute,
Slips a shrub to thwart her passage,
Slides a hand to clutch her foot.

Glens and glades of lushest verdure
Toil her in their tawny mesh,
Wilder-woofed ways and alleys
Lock her struggling limbs in leash.   300

Feathery grasses, flowery mosses,
Knot themselves to make her trip;
Sprays and stubborn sprigs outstretching,
Put a bridle on her lip;—

Many a winding lane betrays her,
Many a sudden bosky shoot,
And her knee makes many a stumble
O'er some hidden damp old root,

Whose quaint face peers green and dusky
'Mongst the matted growth of plants,   310
While she rises wild and weltering,
Speeding on with many pants.

Tangles of the wild red strawberry
Spread their freckled trammels frail;
In the pathway creeping brambles
Catch her in their thorny trail.

All the widely sweeping greensward
Shifts and swims from knoll to knoll;
Grey rough-fingered oak and elm wood
Push her by from bole to bole.   320

Groves of lemon, groves of citron,
Tall high-foliaged plane and palm,
Bloomy myrtle, light-blue olive,
Wave her back with gusts of balm.

Languid jasmine, scrambling briony,
Walls of close-festooning braid,
Fling themselves about her, mingling
With her wafted locks, waylaid.

Twisting bindweed, honey'd woodbine,
Cling to her, while, red and blue,   330
On her rounded form, ripe berries
Dash and die in gory dew.

Running ivies dark and lingering,
Round her light limbs drag and twine;
Round her waist with languorous tendrils
Reels and wreathes the juicy vine;—

Reining in the flying creature
With its arms about her mouth;
Bursting all its mellowing bunches
To seduce her husky drouth.   340

Crowning her with amorous clusters;
Pouring down her sloping back
Fresh-born wines in glittering rillets,
Following her in crimson track.

Buried, drenched in dewy foliage,
Thus she glimmers from the dawn,
Watched by every forest creature,
Fleet-foot Oread, frolic Faun,

Silver-sandalled Arethusa
Not more swiftly fled the sands,   350
Fled the plains and fled the sunlights,
Fled the murmuring ocean strands.

O, that now the earth would open!
O, that now the shades would hide!
O, that now the gods would shelter!
Caverns lead and seas divide!

Not more faint soft-lowing Io
Panted in those starry eyes,
When the sleepless midnight meadows
Piteously implored the skies!   360

Still her breathless flight she urges
By the sanctuary stream,
And the god with golden swiftness
Follows like an eastern beam.

Her the close bewildering greenery
Darkens with its duskiest green,—
Him each little leaflet welcomes,
Flushing with an orient sheen.

Thus he nears, and now all Tempe
Rings with his melodious cry,   370
Avenues and blue expanses
Beam in his large lustrous eye!

All the branches start to music!
As if from a secret spring
Thousands of sweet bills are bubbling
In the nest and on the wing.

Gleams and shines the glassy river
And rich valleys every one;
But of all the throbbing beauty
Brightest! singled by the Sun!　　　　　　　　　　　380

Ivy round her glimmering ancle,
Vine about her glowing brow,
Never sure was bride so beauteous,
Daphne, chosen nymph as thou!

Thus he nears! and now she feels him
Breathing hot on every limb;
And he hears her own quick pantings—
Ah! that they might be for him.

O, that like the flower he tramples,
Bending from his golden tread,　　　　　　　　　　　390
Full of fair celestial ardours,
She would bow her bridal head.

O, that likc the flower she presses,
Nodding from her lily touch,
Light as in the harmless breezes,
She would know the god for such!

See! the golden arms are round her—
To the air she grasps and clings!
See! his glowing arms have wound her—
To the sky she shrieks and springs!　　　　　　　　　400

See! the flushing chase of Tempe
Trembles with Olympian air—
See! green sprigs and buds are shooting
From those white raised arms of prayer!

396 for] as *1851*

In the earth her feet are rooting!—
Breasts and limbs and lifted eyes,
Hair and lips and stretching fingers,
Fade away—and fadeless rise.

And the god whose fervent rapture
Clasps her, finds his close embrace   410
Full of palpitating branches,
And new leaves that bud apace,

Round his wonder-stricken forehead;—
While in ebbing measures slow,
Sounds of softly dying pulses,
Pause and quiver, pause and go.

Go, and come again, and flutter
On the verge of life,—then flee!
All the white ambrosial beauty
Is a lustrous Laurel Tree!   420

Still with the great panting love-chase
All its running sap is warmed;—
But from head to foot the virgin
Is transfigured and transformed.

Changed!—yet the green Dryad nature
Is instinct with human ties,
And above its anguish'd lover
Breathes pathetic sympathies.

Sympathies of love and sorrow;—
Joy in her divine escape!   430
Breathing through her bursting foliage
Comfort to his bending shape.

Vainly now the floating Naiads
Seek to pierce the laurel maze,
Nought but laurel meets their glances,
Laurel glistens as they gaze.

Nought but bright prophetic laurel!
Laurel over eyes and brows,
Over limbs and over bosom,
Laurel leaves and laurel boughs!   440

And in vain the listening Dryad
Shells her hand against her ear!—
All is silence—save the echo
Travelling in the distance drear.

Song

Should thy love die;
O bury it not under ice-blue eyes!
And lips that deny,
With a scornful surprise,
The life it once lived in thy breast when it wore no disguise.

Should thy love die;
O bury it where the sweet wild-flowers blow!
And breezes go by,
With no whisper of woe;
And strange feet cannot guess of the anguish that slumbers
below.   10

Should thy love die;
O wander once more to the haunt of the bee!
Where the foliaged sky,
Is most sacred to see,
And thy being first felt its wild birk like a wind-wakened
tree.

Should thy love die;
O dissemble it! smile! let the rose hide the thorn!
While the lark sings on high,
And no thing looks forlorn,
Bury it, bury it, bury it where it was born.   20

SONG: SHOULD THY LOVE DIE

5 when] where *1851*

London by Lamplight

In sending this poem to James Vizetelly, on February 20, 1851, GM wrote: "London by the lamplight I have quite cut to pieces. You will see I have transformed 'Midnight' into the 'Sleeping City' and 'Night' about half its original length stands now under the title of 'London by Lamplight.' 'Dusk of Eve' will not be published."

> There stands a singer in the street,
> He has an audience motley and meet;
> Above him lowers the London night,
> And around the lamps are flaring bright.
>
> His minstrelsy may be unchaste—
> 'Tis much unto that motley taste,
> And loud the laughter he provokes
> From those sad slaves of obscene jokes.
>
> But woe is many a passer by
> Who as he goes turns half an eye,   10
> To see the human form divine
> Thus Circe-wise changed into swine!
>
> Make up the sum of either sex
> That all our human hopes perplex,
> With those unhappy shapes that know
> The silent streets and pale cock-crow.
>
> And can I trace in such dull eyes
> Of fireside peace or country skies?
> And could those haggard cheeks presume
> To memories of a May-tide bloom?   20
>
> Those violated forms have been
> The pride of many a flowering green;
> And still the virgin bosom heaves
> With daisy meads and dewy leaves.
>
> But stygian darkness reigns within,
> The river of death from the founts of sin;
> And one prophetic water rolls
> Its gas-lit surface for their souls.

I will not hide the tragic sight—
Those drown'd black locks, those dead lips white,   30
Will rise from out the slimy flood,
And cry before God's throne for blood!

Those stiffened limbs, that swollen face,—
Pollution's last and best embrace,
Will call as such a picture can,
For retribution upon man.

Hark! how their feeble laughter rings,
While still the ballad-monger sings,
And flatters their unhappy breasts
With poisonous words and pungent jests.   40

O how would every daisy blush
To see them 'mid that earthy crush!
O dumb would be the evening thrush,
And hoary look the hawthorn bush!

The meadows of their infancy
Would shrink from them, and every tree,
And every little laughing spot,
Would hush itself and know them not.

Precursor to what black despairs
Was that child's face which once was theirs!   50
And O to what a world of guile
Was herald that young angel smile!

That face which to a father's eye
Was balm for all anxiety;
That smile which to a mother's heart
Went swifter than the swallow's dart!

O happy homes! that still they know
At intervals, with what a woe
Would ye look on them, dim and strange,
Suffering worse than winter change!   60

41 how] *corr. errata, de L 1911*; now, *1851, de L*

And yet could I transplant them there,
To breathe again the innocent air
Of youth, and once more reconcile
Their outcast looks with nature's smile;

Could I but give them one clear day
Of this delicious loving May,
Release their souls from anguish dark,
And stand them underneath the lark;—

I think that Nature would have power
To graft again her blighted flower   70
Upon the broken stem, renew
Some portion of its early hue:—

The heavy flood of tears unlock,
More precious than the Scriptured rock;
At least instil a happier mood,
And bring them back to womanhood.

Alas! how many lost ones claim
This refuge from despair and shame!
How many, longing for the light,
Sink deeper in the abyss this night!   80

O, crying sin!   O, blushing thought!
Not only unto those that wrought
The misery and deadly blight;
But those that outcast them this night!

O, agony of grief! for who
Less dainty than his race, will do
Such battle for their human right,
As shall awake this startled night?

Proclaim this evil human page,
Will ever blot the Golden Age,   90
That poets dream and saints invite,
If it be unredeemed this night!

This night of deep solemnity,
And verdurous serenity,
While over every fleecy field,
The dews descend and odours yield.

This night of gleaming floods and falls,
Of forest glooms and sylvan calls,
Of starlight on the pebbly rills,
And twilight on the circling hills.   100

This night! when from the paths of men
Grey error steams as from a fen;
As o'er this flaring City wreathes
The black cloud-vapour that it breathes!

This night from which a morn will spring
Blooming on its orient wing;
A morn to roll with many more
Its ghostly foam on the twilight shore.

Morn! when the fate of all mankind
Hangs poised in doubt, and man is blind.   110
His duties of the day will seem
The fact of life, and mine the dream.

The destinies that bards have sung,
Regeneration to the young;
Reverberation of the truth,
And virtuous culture unto youth!

Youth! in whose season let abound
All flowers and fruits that strew the ground,
Voluptuous joy where love consents,
And health and pleasure pitch their tents: 120

All rapture and all pure delight;
A garden all unknown to blight,
But never the unnatural sight
That throngs the shameless song this night!

123 sight] *1851*; night *misp. de L*; *corr. errata, de L 1911*

Song

In a letter, September 20, 1877, to W. Davenport Adams, editor of *Latter-Day Lyrics, Being Poems of Sentiment and Reflection by Living Writers* (1878), GM wrote that he would rather not see this poem included in the collection because it "has a tone of *niaiserie pastorale*, not perfectly pleasant to me." He approved the inclusion of *Violets* and *Song: Love within the lover's breast* (Cline, Letter 602, n.1).

Under boughs of breathing May,
In the mild spring-time I lay,
Lonely, for I had no love;
  And the sweet birds all sang for pity,
  Cuckoo, lark, and dove.

Tell me, cuckoo, then I cried,
Dare I woo and wed a bride?
I, like thee, have no home-nest;
  And the twin notes thus tuned their ditty,—
  'Love can answer best.'   10

Nor, warm dove with tender coo,
Have I thy soft voice to woo,
Even were a damsel by;
  And the deep woodland crooned its ditty,—
  'Love her first and try.'

Nor have I, wild lark, thy wing,
That from bluest heaven can bring
Bliss, whatever fate befall;
  And the sky-lyrist trilled this ditty,—
  'Love will give thee all.'   20

So it chanced while June was young,
Wooing well with fervent song,
I had won a damsel coy;
  And the sweet birds that sang for pity,
  Jubileed for joy.

Pastorals

[I]

How sweet on sunny afternoons,
For those who journey light and well,
To loiter up a hilly rise
Which hides the prospect far beyond,
And fancy all the landscape lying
     Beautiful and still.

Beneath a sky of summer blue,
Whose rounded cloudlets, folded soft,
Gaze on the scene which we await
And picture from their peacefulness;   10
So calmly to the earth inclining
     Float those loving shapes!

Like airy brides, each singling out
A spot to love and bless with love,
Their creamy bosoms glowing warm,
Till distance weds them to the hills,
And with its latest gleam the river
     Sinks in their embrace.

And silverly the river runs,
And many a graceful wind he makes,   20
By fields where feed the happy flocks,
And hedge-rows hushing pleasant lanes,
The charms of English home reflected
     In his shining eye.

Ancestral oak, broad-foliaged elm,
Rich meadows sunned and starred with flowers,
The cottage breathing tender smoke
Against the brooding golden air,
With glimpses of a stately mansion
     On a woodland sward.   30

And circling round as with a ring,
The distance spreading amber haze,
Enclosing hills and pastures sweet;
A depth of soft and mellow light
Which fills the heart with sudden yearning
      Aimless and serene!

No disenchantment follows here,
For nature's inspiration moves
The dream which she herself fulfils;
And he whose heart like valley warmth,   40
Steams up with joy at scenes like this
      Shall never be forlorn.

And O for any human soul
The rapture of a wide survey—
A valley sweeping to the West
With all its wealth of loveliness,
Is more than recompense for days
      That taught us to endure.

[II]

Yon upland slope which hides the sun
Ascending from his eastern deeps,
And now against the hues of dawn,
One level line of tillage rears;
The furrowed brow of toil and time;
To many it is but a sweep of land!

To others 'tis an Autumn trust,
But unto me a mystery;—
An influence strange and swift as dreams;
A whispering of old romance;   10
A temple naked to the clouds;
Or one of nature's bosoms fresh revealed,

Heaving with adoration! there
The work of husbandry is done,
And daily bread is daily earned;

Nor seems there ought to indicate
The springs which move in me such thoughts,
But from my soul a spirit calls them up.

All day into the open sky,
All night to the eternal stars,   20
For ever both at morn and eve
When mellow distances draw near,
And shadows lengthen in the dusk,
Athwart the heavens it rolls its glimmering line!

When twilight from the dream-hued West
Sighs hush! and all the land is still;
When from the lush empurpling East,
The twilight of the crowing cock,
Dawns on the drowsy village roofs,
Athwart the heavens that glimmering line is seen.   30

And now beneath the rising sun,
Whose shining chariot overpeers,
The irradiate ridge, while fetlock deep
In the rich soil his coursers plunge—
How grand in robes of light it looks!
How glorious with rare suggestive grace!

The ploughman mounting up the height
Becomes a glowing shape, as though
'Twere young Triptolemus, plough in hand,
While Ceres in her amber scarf,   40
With gentle love directs him how
To wed the willing earth and hope for fruits!

The furrows running up, are fraught
With meanings; there the goddess walks,
While Proserpine is young, and there—
'Mid the late autumn sheaves, her voice
Sobbing and choked with dumb despair—
The nights will hear her wailing for her child!

29 Dawns] *errata 1851*; Peers *all eds.*

Whatever dim tradition tells,
Whatever history may reveal,   50
Or fancy, from her starry brows,
Of light or dreamful lustre shed,
Could not at this sweet time increase
The quiet consecration of the spot.

Blest with the sweat of labour, blest
With the young sun's first vigorous beams,
Village hope and harvest prayer,—
The heart that throbs beneath it, holds
A bliss so perfect in itself
Men's thoughts must borrow rather than bestow.   60

III

Now standing on this hedgeside path,
Up which the evening winds are blowing
Wildly from the lingering lines
   Of sunset o'er the hills;
Unaided by one motive thought,
My spirit with a strange impulsion
Rises, like a fledgling,
Whose wings are not mature, but still
Supported by its strong desire,
Beats up its native air and leaves   10
   The tender mother's nest.

Great music under heaven is made,
And in the track of rushing darkness
Comes the solemn shape of night,
   And broods above the earth.
A thing of Nature am I now,
Abroad, without a sense or feeling
Born not of her bosom;
Content with all her truths and fates;
Ev'n as yon strip of grass that bows   20
Above the new-born violet bloom,
   And sings with wood and field.

IV

Lo, as a tree, whose wintry twigs
Drink in the sun with fibrous joy,
And down into its dampest roots
Thrills quickened with the draught of life,
I wake unto the dawn, and leave my griefs to drowse.

I rise and drink the fresh sweet air:
Each draught a future bud of Spring;
Each glance of blue a birth of green;
I will not mimic yonder oak
That dallies with dead leaves ev'n while the primrose peeps.   10

But full of these warm-whispering beams,
Like Memnon in his mother's eye,—
Aurora! when the statue stone
Moaned soft to her pathetic touch,—
My soul shall own its parent in the founts of day!

And ever in the recurring light,
True to the primal joy of dawn,
Forget its barren griefs; and aye
Like aspens in the faintest breeze,
Turn all its silver sides and tremble into song.   20

V

Now from the meadow floods the wild duck clamours,
Now the wood pigeon wings a rapid flight,
Now the homeward rookery follows up its vanguard,
And the valley mists are curling up the hills.

Three short songs gives the clear-voiced throstle,
Sweetening the twilight ere he fills the nest;
While the little bird upon the leafless branches
Tweets to its mate a tiny loving note.

Deeper the stillness hangs on every motion;
Calmer the silence follows every call;   10
Now all is quiet save the roosting pheasant,
The bell-wether tinkle and the watch-dog's bark.

Softly shine the lights from the silent kindling homestead,
Stars on the hearth to the shepherd in the fold;
Springs of desire to the traveller on the roadway;
Ever breathing incense to the ever-blessing sky!

VI

How barren would this valley be,
Without the golden orb that gazes
On it, broadening to hues
Of rose, and spreading wings of amber;
Blessing it before it falls asleep.

How barren would this valley be,
Without the human lives now beating
In it, or the throbbing hearts
Far distant, who their flower of childhood
Cherish here, and water it with tears!   10

How barren should I be, were I
Without above that loving splendour,
Shedding light and warmth! without
Some kindred natures of my kind
To joy in me, or yearn towards me now!

VII

In February 1851 GM sent to the publisher of *Poems* a poem in "Hexameters" to be placed among the "Pastorals." This is the Pastoral to which Charles Kingsley alluded in his review of the volume in *Fraser's Magazine*, December 1851. After quoting lines 38–48, he wrote: "Careless as hexameters; but honest landscape-painting; and only he who begins honestly ends greatly." GM, evidently stung by the charge of careless versification, wrote in the copy presented to his friend Tom Taylor (Berg, Copy 1): "Lines, not Hexameters" [top of p. 94]. Even so, the meter of the poem was surely intended to be classic hexameters, and GM revised it more thoroughly than any other poem when preparing the text of this first volume for inclusion in the Edition de Luxe.

Summer glows warm on the meadows, and speedwell, and
    gold-cups, and daisies,
Darken 'mid deepening masses of sorrel, and shadowy grasses
Show the ripe hue to the farmer, and summon the scythe and the
    hay-makers

Down from the village; and now, even now, the air smells of the
    mowing,
And the sharp song of the scythe whistles daily; from dawn, till the
    gloaming
Wears its cool star; sweet and welcome to all flaming faces afield
    now;
Heavily weighs the hot season, and drowses the darkening foliage,
Drooping with languor; the white cloud floats, but sails not, for
    windless
Heaven's blue tents it; no lark singing up in its fleecy white valleys;

Up in its fairy white valleys, once feathered with minstrels;
    melodious   10
With the invisible joy that wakes dawn o'er the green fields of
    England.
Summer glows warm on the meadows; then come, let us roam thro'
    them gaily,
Heedless of heat, and the hot-kissing sun, and the fear of dark
    freckles.
Never one kiss will he give on a neck, or a lily-white forehead,
Chin, hand, or bosom uncovered, all panting, to take the chance
    coolness,—
But full sure the fiery pressure leaves seal of espousal.
Heed him not; come, tho' he kiss till the soft little upper-lip loses
Half its pure whiteness; just speck'd where the curve of the rosy
    mouth reddens.

Come, let him kiss, let him kiss, and his kisses shall make thee the
    sweeter.
Thou art no nun, veiled and vowed; doomed to nourish a withering
    pallor!   20
City exotics beside thee would show like bleached linen at mid-day,

Between 6 and 7 1851: Besprinkled with labour, and with the pure brew of the malt right
cheery!
9 Heaven's blue] The blue heaven *1851*
14 Never] For never *1851*
15 bosom] fair bosom *1851*
16 *1851:* But surely the hot fiery pressure shall leave its brown seal of espousal.
17 Heed] Still heed *1851*

Hung upon hedges of eglantine!   Thou in the freedom of nature,
Full of her beauty and wisdom, gentleness, joyance, and kindness!
Come, and like bees will we gather the rich golden honey of
    noontide;
Deep in the sweet summer meadows, border'd by hillside and river;
Lined with long trenches half-hidden, where, smell of white
    meadow-sweet, sweetest
Blissfully hovers—O sweetest! but pluck it not! even in the
    tenderest
Grasp it will lose breath and wither; like many, not made for a
    posy.

See, the sun slopes down to the meadows, where all the flowers are
    falling!
Falling unhymned; for the nightingale scarce ever charms the long
    twilight: 30
Mute with the cares of the nest; only known by a 'chuck, chuck,'
    and dovelike
Call of content, but the finch and the linnet and blackcap pipe
    loudly.
Round on the western hill-side warbles the rich-billed ouzel;
And the shrill throstle is filling the tangled thickening copses;
Singing o'er hyacinths hid, and most honey'd of flowers, white
    field-rose.
Joy thus to revel all day in the grass of our own beloved country;
Revel all day, till the lark mounts at eve with his sweet 'tirra-lirra':
Trilling delightfully. See, on the river the slow-rippled surface
Shining; the slow ripple broadens in circles; the bright surface
    smoothens;
Now it is flat as the leaves of the yet unseen water-lily.   40
There dart the lives of a day, ever-varying tactics fantastic.

23 kindness] kindliness *1851*
26 smell of white meadow-sweet, sweetest] sweetest, the smell of white meadow-sweet
1851
32 Call] Low call *1851*
33 Round on] From elms round *1851*
34 tangled] dusky *1851*
36 Joy] O Joy *1851*

There, by the wet-mirrored osiers, the emerald wing of the
    kingfisher
Flashes, the fish in his beak! there the dab-chick dived, and the
    motion
Lazily undulates all thro' the tall standing army of rushes.

Joy thus to revel all day, till the twilight turns us homeward!
Till all the lingering deep-blooming splendour of sunset is over,
And the one star shines mildly in mellowing hues, like a spirit
Sent to assure us that light never dieth, tho' day is now buried.
Saying: to-morrow, to-morrow, few hours intervening, that interval
Tuned by the woodlark in heaven, to-morrow my semblance, far
    eastward,   50
Heralds the day 'tis my mission eternal to seal and to prophecy.

Come then, and homeward; passing down the close path of the
    meadows.
Home like the bees stored with sweetness; each with a lark in the
    bosom,
Trilling for ever, and oh! will you lark ever cease to sing up there?

Song

SPRING

When buds of palm do burst and spread
    Their downy feathers in the lane,
And orchard blossoms, white and red,
    Breathe Spring delight for Autumn gain;
    And the skylark shakes his wings in the rain;

O then is the season to look for a bride!
    Choose her warily, woo her unseen;
For the choicest maids are those that hide
    Like dewy violets under the green.

PASTORALS VII

45 Joy] O joy *1851*
53 Home like] *1851*; Home-like *de L; corr. errata, de L 1911*

SONG: SPRING
4 for] and *1851*

Song

AUTUMN

When nuts behind the hazel-leaf
    Are brown as the squirrel that hunts them free,
And the fields are rich with the sun-burnt sheaf,
        'Mid the blue cornflower and the yellowing tree;
        And the farmer glows and beams in his glee;

O then is the season to wed thee a bride!
    Ere the garners are filled and the ale-cups foam;
For a smiling hostess is the pride
    And flower of every Harvest Home.

Love in the Valley

Correcting only the punctuation and capitalization, GM allowed the
1851 version of *Love in the Valley* to stand among the "Poems Written in
Early Youth" in Edition de Luxe 3. For the final, rewritten, and greatly
expanded version of the poem, see page 250.

The meter, as has often been pointed out, was probably suggested by
George Darley's *Serenade of a Loyal Martyr*, first published in the
Athenaeum, 23 January 1836.

Muirhead's guide to *England*, second edition (1924), states that "Juniper
Bottom" on the north slope of Box Hill is the scene of GM's "Happy
Valley," an allusion, it would seem, to *Love in the Valley*.

Title: possibly taken from Tennyson's idyl in *The Princess* (1847),
"Come down, O maid, from yonder mountain height":

> And come, for Love is of the valley, come,
> For Love is of the valley, come thou down
> And find him;
>
> (7–9)

Under yonder beech-tree standing on the green-sward,
    Couched with her arms behind her little head,
Her knees folded up, and her tresses on her bosom,
    Lies my young love sleeping in the shade.

SONG: AUTUMN

5 in his] with *1851*

Had I the heart to slide one arm beneath her,
    Press her dreaming lips as her waist I folded slow,
Waking on the instant she could not but embrace me—
    Ah! would she hold me, and never let me go?

Shy as the squirrel, and wayward as the swallow;
    Swift as the swallow when athwart the western flood   10
Circleting the surface he meets his mirrored winglets,—
    Is that dear one in her maiden bud.
Shy as the squirrel whose nest is in the pine-tops;
    Gentle—ah! that she were jealous as the dove!
Full of all the wildness of the woodland creatures,
    Happy in herself is the maiden that I love!

What can have taught her distrust of all I tell her?
    Can she truly doubt me when looking on my brows?
Nature never teaches distrust of tender love-tales,
    What can have taught her distrust of all my vows?   20
No, she does not doubt me! on a dewy eve-tide
    Whispering together beneath the listening moon,
I pray'd till her cheek flush'd, implored till she faltered—
    Fluttered to my bosom—ah! to fly away so soon!

The first drafts of stanza 1, a part of stanza 3, and stanzas 4, 5 and 8 are written in minuscule script across the copybook handwriting of the beginning of a poem called "The Soul" (see frontispiece of vol. 2 and p. 887). On the verso of this leaf are the first drafts of stanzas 6 and 10; these were reproduced in facsimile, *Poems* 2, Mem. Ed., facing p. 80. Abandoned fragments on these two pages are given in the Supplementary Textual Notes.

MS: NB A, [*pp. 7–8*], *spaced as quatrains. Variants are from this MS.*

1 Underneath the beech tree standing in the forest *or* from its fellows
2 behind] underneath
3 With her long brown tresses heaving[?] down her bosom
4 Lies my young love] My young loves lies
5 Had I now the courage to slip one hand beneath her
6 Hold her waist encircled & kiss *or* press her dreaming lips *or* Press her dreaming lips as her waist I circled slow
9–16 *not in MS*
17–19
                  What has taught her distrust of lovers vows
                  And honest brows—nature has not taught her
                  This then why pretend to doubt?

When her mother tends her before the laughing mirror,
    Tying up her laces, looping up her hair,
Often she thinks—were this wild thing wedded,
    I should have more love, and much less care.
When her mother tends her before the bashful mirror,
    Loosening her laces, combing down her curls,   30
Often she thinks—were this wild thing wedded,
    I should lose but one for so many boys and girls.

Clambering roses peep into her chamber,
    Jasmine and woodbine breathe sweet, sweet,
White-necked swallows twittering of summer,
    Fill her with balm and nested peace from head to feet.
Ah! will the rose-bough see her lying lonely,
    When the petals fall and fierce bloom is on the leaves?
Will the Autumn garners see her still ungathered,
    When the fickle swallows forsake the weeping eaves?   40

Comes a sudden question—should a strange hand pluck her!
    Oh! what an anguish smites me at the thought.
Should some idle lordling bribe her mind with jewels!—
    Can such beauty ever thus be bought?
Sometimes the huntsmen prancing down the valley
    Eye the village lasses, full of sprightly mirth;
They see as I see, mine is the fairest!
    Would she were older and could read my worth!

Are there not sweet maidens if she still deny me?
    Show the bridal heavens but one bright star?   50
Wherefore thus then do I chase a shadow,
    Clattering one note like a brown eve-jar?

25 tends] helps *del.*   laughing] rosy *del.*   27–32 *and* 33–40 *reverse order*
29 tends] helps   bashful] rosy   32 lose but] but lose
33 peep] breathe *del.* gaze
37 Soon will she know how sweet things wither *or* Ah may her white bed see her not
more lonely
38 fierce bloom is on the] the roses shrink their
39 Ah! may the [?] moon fold me close beside her
40 When the fickle] Ere the flying   41 question] thought *or* question
42 smites] bites   43 Should a lovely lordling win her with his riches,
44 Can such beauty] No lord [?] such loveliness *del.*
45 down] thro'   valley] village *del.*   49–56 *not in MS*

So I rhyme and reason till she darts before me—
    Thro' the milky meadows from flower to flower she flies,
Sunning her sweet palms to shade her dazzled eyelids
    From the golden love that looks too eager in her eyes.

When at dawn she wakens, and her fair face gazes
    Out on the weather thro' the window-panes,
Beauteous she looks! like a white water-lily
    Bursting out of bud on the rippled river plains.   60
When from bed she rises clothed from neck to ankle
    In her long nightgown, sweet as boughs of May,
Beauteous she looks! like a tall garden lily
    Pure from the night and perfect for the day!

Happy, happy time, when the grey star twinkles
    Over the fields all fresh with bloomy dew;
When the cold-cheeked dawn grows ruddy up the twilight,
    And the gold sun wakes, and weds her in the blue.
Then when my darling tempts the early breezes,
    She the only star that dies not with the dark!   70
Powerless to speak all the ardour of my passion
    I catch her little hand as we listen to the lark.

57 fair] sweet *del.*
60 rippled] smooth *or* rippled
61 from bed] at dawn *or* from bed   neck] head *del.*
62 sweet as boughs of May] new white as any cloud *or* morning ray
65–70 *not in MS*
Facing stanzas 8 and 9, lines 58–72, Berg, between pp. 104–05:

    Rains that at night time in the winter weather,
        Beat against her windows, borne on wailing wind;
    When the doors and floors with sobs and shrieks are shaken,
        And the house is crazed, and all the earth is blind;—
    Rains that at night time beat against her windows,
        Weep like the tears from her true love's eye!
    Full of drowning passion, full of death and anguish;
        Teach her to pity or to fear me lest I die.
    Rains that at night time in the turning Season,
        Drop from the cloud that is like a mother's breast;
    When the earth is sweet and awake in balmy freshness,
        And light is on the valley, and love is in the nest;—
    Rains that at night time feed the baby Season,
        Fall to the flower that is dying pale and dumb,
    Sink to the seed that is striving in the darkness—
        Teach it to dream of the days that are to come.

Shall the birds in vain then valentine their sweethearts?
    Season after season tell a fruitless tale;
Will not the virgin listen to their voices?
    Take the honeyed meaning, wear the bridal veil.
Fears she frosts of winter, fears she the bare branches?
    Waits she the garlands of spring for her dower?
Is she a nightingale that will not be nested
    Till the April woodland has built her bridal bower?   80

Then come merry April with all thy birds and beauties!
    With thy crescent brows and thy flowery, showery glee;
With thy budding leafage and fresh green pastures;
    And may thy lustrous crescent grow a honeymoon for me!
Come merry month of the cuckoo and the violet!
    Come weeping Loveliness in all thy blue delight!
Lo! the nest is ready, let me not languish longer!
    Bring her to my arms on the first May night.

Beauty Rohtraut

(FROM MÖRICKE)

Eduard Mörike (1804–75), who caught the essence of the *Volkslied*, is considered by many as the greatest of the Swabian lyric poets. *Schön-Rohtraut* (1838) is one of his best-known ballads.

    What is the name of King Ringang's daughter?
    Rohtraut, Beauty Rohtraut!
    And what does she do the livelong day,

LOVE IN THE VALLEY

75 tell a fruitless tale] in [thro' *del.*] unhappy vale *or* year after year *del.* tell a fruitless tale
Between 75 and 76 del.: Ah! tho' the branches are bare
78 Waits] Wants *or* Waits
80 Till April has built her dewy woodland bower?
81–88 *not in MS*
See Supplementary Textual Notes.

BEAUTY ROHTRAUT

Previously printed in the Leader *1 (14 September 1850), title* The Ballad of Beauty Rohtraut.

Since she dare not knit and spin alway?
O hunting and fishing is ever her play!
And, heigh! that her huntsman I might be!
I'd hunt and fish right merrily!
       Be silent, heart!

And it chanced that, after this some time,
      Rohtraut, Beauty Rohtraut,   10
The boy in the Castle has gained access,
And a horse he has got and a huntsman's dress,
To hunt and to fish with the merry Princess;
And, O! that a king's son I might be!
Beauty Rohtraut I love so tenderly.
       Hush! hush! my heart.

Under a grey old oak they sat,
      Beauty, Beauty Rohtraut!
She laughs: 'Why look you so slyly at me?
If you have heart enough, come, kiss me.'   20
Cried the breathless boy, 'kiss thee?'
But he thinks, kind fortune has favoured my youth;
And thrice he has kissed Beauty Rohtraut's mouth.
       Down! down! mad heart.

Then slowly and silently they rode home,—
Rohtraut, Beauty Rohtraut!
The boy was lost in his delight:
'And, wert thou Empress this very night,
I would not heed or feel the blight;
Ye thousand leaves of the wild wood wist   30
How Beauty Rohtraut's mouth I kiss'd.
       Hush! hush! wild heart.'

17 Under a grey old oak] Beneath an old oak-tree once *L*

To a Skylark

This poem obviously echoes the main theme of Shelley's *To a Skylark* (1820). As a mature poet, GM wrote the philosophic poem *The Lark Ascending*; see page 238.

O skylark! I see thee and call thee joy!
Thy wings bear thee up to the breast of the dawn;
I see thee no more, but thy song is still
The tongue of the heavens to me!

Thus are the days when I was a boy;
Sweet while I lived in them, dear now they're gone:
I feel them no longer, but still, O still
They tell of the heavens to me.

Sorrows and Joys

Bury thy sorrows, and they shall rise
As souls to the immortal skies,
And there look down like mothers' eyes.

But let thy joys be fresh as flowers,
That suck the honey of the showers,
And bloom alike on huts and towers.

So shall thy days be sweet and bright;
Solemn and sweet thy starry night,
Conscious of love each change of light.

The stars will watch the flowers asleep,   10
The flowers will feel the soft stars weep,
And both will mix sensations deep.

With these below, with those above,
Sits evermore the brooding dove,
Uniting both in bonds of love.

SORROWS AND JOYS

Previously printed in Household Words *1 (24 August 1850). Variants are from* HW.

3 there] then
14 dove] Dove

For both by nature are akin;
Sorrow, the ashen fruit of sin,
And joy, the juice of life within.

Children of earth are these; and those
The spirits of divine repose—   20
Death radiant o'er all human woes.

O, think what then had been thy doom,
If homeless and without a tomb,
They had been left to haunt the gloom!

O, think again what now they are—
Motherly love, tho' dim and far,
Imaged in every lustrous star.

For they, in their salvation, know
No vestige of their former woe,
While thro' them all the heavens do flow.   30

Thus art thou wedded to the skies,
And watched by ever-loving eyes,
And warned by yearning sympathies.

Song

The Flower unfolds its dawning cup,
And the young sun drinks the star-dews up,
At eve it droops with the bliss of day,
And dreams in the midnight far away.

SORROWS AND JOYS
19–21 *come before* 16–18   19 earth] Earth
20 divine] intense
Between 21 and 22:

> O, make thy sorrows holy—wise—
> So shall their buried memories rise,
> Celestial, e'en in mortal skies.

22 thy] their   23 homeless and] all unshriven—
25–27 *not in HW, instead:*

> O, think again what they will be
> Beneath God's bright serenity,
> When thou art in eternity!

30 heavens] Heavens

So am I in thy sole, sweet glance,
Pressed with a weight of utterance;
Lovingly all my leaves unfold,
And gleam to the beams of thirsty gold.

At eve I droop, for then the swell
Of feeling falters forth farewell;—   10
At midnight I am dreaming deep,
Of what has been, in blissful sleep.

When—ah! when will love's own light
Wed me alike thro' day and night,
When will the stars with their linking charms
Wake us in each other's arms?

Song

Thou to me art such a spring,
As the Arab seeks at eve,
Thirsty from the shining sands;
There to bathe his face and hands,
While the sun is taking leave,
And dewy sleep is a delicious thing.

Thou to me art such a dream,
As he dreams upon the grass,
While the bubbling coolness near,
Makes sweet music in his ear;   10
And the stars that slowly pass,
In solitary grandeur o'er him gleam.

Thou to me art such a dawn,
As the dawn, whose ruddy kiss
Wakes him to his darling steed;
And again the desert speed,
And again the desert bliss,
Lightens thro' his veins, and he is gone!

Antigone

The speaker in this poem is the shade of Antigone's brother Polynices.

The buried voice bespake Antigone.

'O Sister! couldst thou know as thou wilt know,
The bliss above, the reverence below,
Enkindled by thy sacrifice for me;
Thou wouldst at once with holy ecstasy,
Give thy warm limbs into the yearning earth.
Sleep, Sister! for Elysium's dawning birth,—
And faith will fill thee with what is to be!
Sleep, for the Gods are watching over thee!
Thy dream will steer thee to perform their will,   10
As silently their influence they instil.
O Sister! in the sweetness of thy prime,
Thy hand has plucked the bitter flower of death;
But this will dower thee with Elysian breath,
That fade into a never-fading clime,
Dear to the Gods are those that do like thee
A solemn duty! for the tyranny
Of kings is feeble to the soul that dares
Defy them to fulfil its sacred cares:
And weak against a mighty will are men.   20
O, Torch between two brothers! in whose gleam
Our slaughtered House doth shine as one again,
Tho' severed by the sword; now may thy dream
Kindle desire in thee for us, and thou,
Forgetting not thy lover and his vow,
Leaving no human memory forgot,
Shalt cross, not unattended, the dark stream
Which runs by thee in sleep and ripples not.
The large stars glitter thro' the anxious night,
And the deep sky broods low to look at thee: 30
The air is hush'd and dark o'er land and sea,
And all is waiting for the morrow light:
So do thy kindred spirits wait for thee.

O Sister! soft as on the downward rill,
Will those first daybeams from the distant hill
Fall on the smoothness of thy placid brow,
Like this calm sweetness breathing thro' me now:
And when the fated sounds shall wake thine eyes,
Wilt thou, confiding in the supreme will,
In all thy maiden steadfastness arise,   40
Firm to obey and earnest to fulfil;
Remembering the night thou didst not sleep,
And this same brooding sky beheld thee creep,
Defiant of unnatural decree,
To where I lay upon the outcast land;
Before the iron gates upon the plain;
A wretched, graveless ghost, whose wailing chill,
Came to thy darkened door imploring thee;
Yearning for burial like my brother slain;—
And all was dared for love and piety!   50
This thought will nerve again thy virgin hand
To serve its purpose and its destiny.'

She woke, they led her forth, and all was still.

Swathed round in mist and crown'd with cloud,
O Mountain! hid from peak to base—
Caught up into the heavens and clasped
In white ethereal arms that make
Thy mystery of size sublime!
What eye or thought can measure now
Thy grand dilating loftiness!
What giant crest dispute with thee
Supremacy of air and sky!
What fabled height with thee compare!   10
Not those vine-terraced hills that seethe
The lava in their fiery cusps;
Nor that high-climbing robe of snow,

Whose summits touch the morning star,
And breathe the thinnest air of life;
Nor crocus-couching Ida, warm
With Juno's latest nuptial lure;
Nor Tenedos whose dreamy eye
Still looks upon beleaguered Troy;
Nor yet Olympus crown'd with gods,   20
Can boast a majesty like thine,
O Mountain! hid from pcak to base,
And image of the awful power
With which the secret of all things
That stoops from heaven to garment earth,
Can speak to any human soul,
When once the earthly limits lose
Their pointed heights and sharpened lines,
And measureless immensity
Is palpable to sense and sight.   30

Song

No, no, the falling blossom is no sign
    Of loveliness destroy'd and sorrow mute;
The blossom sheds its loveliness divine;—
    Its mission is to prophecy the fruit.

Nor is the day of love for ever dead,
    When young enchantment and romance are gone;
The veil is drawn, but all the future dread
    Is lightened by the finger of the dawn.

Love moves with life along a darker way,
    They cast a shadow and they call it death: 10
But rich is the fulfilment of their day;
    The purer passion and the firmer faith.

The Two Blackbirds

The subject of this poem is taken from one that Mary Nicolls, soon to become Mrs. George Meredith, had given to the "Monthly Observer." Mrs. Nicolls's poem is dated June 1, 1849:

THE BLACKBIRD

Being the true history of a Blackbird known to me.

Rains of sorrow, fruitful showers,
Calling forth the leaves and flowers
Of holy charity,
That unwept from ductless eyes,
In the spirit do surprise
Germs of mystery;

Not alone in human bosoms
Flourish the immortal blossoms
Of divinity,
But in earth's most careless creature
Dwells a link, or blooms a feature,
Of immortality.

They shot the happy Blackbird's mate,
Long rose the heart cry, desolate,
From his golden bill;
Dimly an angel voice is heard
In the bosom of the bird,—
"There are sadder still,

"Of love, and liberty, that be
"Chief blessings unto thine and thee,
"One leaveth thee,
"Look down, where, hung by yonder cot,
"A cagéd brother knoweth not,
"What either be,

"To him the pulse of love doth seem
"The vision of a hopeless dream
"And mockery,
"That sea of air where others sport
"To him a mist where shadows float,
"No verity."

Previously printed in Household Words *2 (9 November 1850). Variants are from* HW.

Whisper of the viewless Angel,
Uttered he in clear evangel
From his quivering throat,
And ever round the cagéd bird
His legendary song is heard
On the breeze to float,

And to the loveless prisoner
Choice blackbird dainties, quaint, and rare,
He with care doth bring;
Sorrow from his heart departeth
At each solace he imparteth
In his communing.

(Mrs. Nicolls confusingly closed every line of the evangelical voice with
quotation marks, here omitted.)

A Blackbird in a wicker cage,
    That hung and swung 'mid fruits and flowers,
Had learnt the song-charm, to assuage
    The drearness of its wingless hours.

And ever when the song was heard,
    From trees that shade the grassy plot
Warbled another glossy bird,
    Whose mate not long ago was shot.

Strange anguish in that creature's breast,
    Unwept like human grief, unsaid,   10
Has quickened in its lonely nest
    A living impulse from the dead.

Not to console its own wild smart,—
    But with a kindling instinct strong,
The novel feeling of its heart
    Beats for the captive bird of song.

And when those mellow notes are still,
    It hops from off its choral perch,
O'er path and sward, with busy bill,
    All grateful gifts to peck and search.   20

6 that shade] around
7 Warbled] Frisk'd
9–12 *not in* HW

Store of ouzel dainties choice
    To those white swinging bars it brings;
And with a low consoling voice,
    It talks between its fluttering wings.

Deeply in their bitter grief
    Those sufferers reciprocate,
The one sings for its woodland life,
    The other for its murdered mate.

But deeper doth the secret prove,
    Uniting those sad creatures so;   30
Humanity's great link of love,
    The common sympathy of woe.

Well divined from day to day,
    Is the swift speech between them twain;
For when the bird is scared away,
    The captive bursts to song again.

Yet daily with its flattering voice,
    Talking amid its fluttering wings,
Store of ouzel dainties choice,
    With busy bill the poor bird brings.   40

And shall I say, till weak with age,
    Down from its drowsy branch it drops,
It will not leave that captive cage,
    Nor cease those busy searching hops?

Ah, no! the moral will not strain;
    Another sense will make it range,
Another mate will soothe its pain,
    Another season work a change.

But thro' the live-long summer, tried,
    A pure devotion we may see;   50
The ebb and flow of Nature's tide;
    A self-forgetful sympathy.

27 woodland] wingéd
52 self-forgetful] pitying, loving

July

I

Blue July, bright July,
    Month of storms and gorgeous blue;
 Violet lightnings o'er thy sky,
    Heavy falls of drenching dew;
Summer crown! o'er glen and glade
Shrinking hyacinths in their shade;
I welcome thee with all thy pride,
I love thee like an Eastern bride.
    Though all the singing days are done
    As in those climes that clasp the sun;   10
    Though the cuckoo in his throat,
    Leaves to the dove his last twin note;
Come to me with thy lustrous eye,
Golden-dawning oriently,
Come with all thy shining blooms,
Thy rich red rose and rolling glooms.
    Though the cuckoo doth but sing 'cuk, cuk,'
        And the dove alone doth coo;
    Though the cushat spins her coo-r-roo, r-r-roo—
        To the cuckoo's halting 'cuk.'   20

II

Sweet July, warm July!
    Month when mosses near the stream,
Soft green mosses thick and shy,
    Are a rapture and a dream.
Summer Queen! whose foot the fern
Fades beneath while chesnuts burn;
I welcome thee with thy fierce love,
Gloom below and gleam above.
    Though all the forest trees hang dumb,
    With dense leafiness o'ercome;   10
    Though the nightingale and thrush,
    Pipe not from the bough or bush;

Come to me with thy lustrous eye,
Azure-melting westerly,
The raptures of thy face unfold,
And welcome in thy robes of gold!
Though the nightingale broods—
'sweet-chuck-sweet'—
And the ouzel flutes so chill,
Tho' the throstle gives but one shrilly trill
To the nightingale's 'sweet-sweet.'   20

Song

I would I were the drop of rain
That falls into the dancing rill,
For I should seek the river then,
And roll below the wooded hill,
Until I reached the sea.

And O, to be the river swift
That wrestles with the wilful tide,
And fling the briny weeds aside
That o'er the foamy billows drift,
Until I came to thee!   10

I would that after weary strife,
And storm beneath the piping wind,
The current of my true fresh life,
Might come unmingled, unimbrined,
To where thou floatest free.

Might find thee in some amber clime,
Where sunlight charms the languid sail,
And dreaming of our plighted vale,
Might seal the dream, and bless the time,
With maiden kisses three.   20

SONG: I WOULD I WERE THE DROP OF RAIN

17 charms the languid] dazzles on the *all eds., corr. GM, Berg*

Song

Come to me in any shape!
　　As a victor crown'd with vine,
In thy curls the clustering grape,—
　　　　Or a vanquished slave:
'Tis thy coming that I crave,
　　And thy folding serpent twine,
　　　　　　Close and dumb;
Ne'er from that would I escape;
Come to me in any shape!
　　　　　　Only come!   10

Only come, and in my breast
　　Hide thy shame or show thy pride;
In my bosom be caressed,
　　　　Never more to part;
Come into my yearning heart;
　　I, the serpent, golden -eyed,
　　　　　　Twine round thee;
Twine thee with no venomed test,
Absence makes the venomed nest;
　　　　　　Come to me!   20

Come to me, my lover, come!
　　Violets on the tender stem
Die and wither in their bloom,
　　　　Under dewy grass;
Come, my lover, or, alas!
　　I shall die, shall die like them,
　　　　　　Frail and lone;
Come to me, my lover, come!
Let thy bosom be my tomb:
　　　　　　Come, my own!   30

The Shipwreck of Idomeneus

This poem is based on a post-Homeric account of the return of
Idomeneus from the siege of Troy to Crete. The myth that GM elaborates
was first given literary currency by Servius (fourth century A.D.) in his
note to Virgil's *Aeneid* 3.121.

Swept from his fleet upon that fatal night
When great Poseidon's sudden-veering wrath
Scattered the happy homeward-floating Greeks
Like foam-flakes off the waves, the King of Crete
Held lofty commune with the dark Sea-god.
His brows were crowned with victory, his cheeks
Were flushed with triumph, but the mighty joy
Of Troy's destruction and his own great deeds
Passed, for the thoughts of home were dearer now,
And sweet the memory of wife and child,   10
And weary now the ten long, foreign years,
And terrible the doubt of short delay—
More terrible, O Gods! he cried, but stopped;
Then raised his voice upon the storm and prayed.
O thou, if injured, injured not by me,
Poseidon! whom sea-deities obey
And mortals worship, hear me! for indeed
It was our oath to aid the cause of Greece,
Not unespoused by gods, and most of all
By thee, if gentle currents, havens calm,   20
Fair winds and prosperous voyage, and the Shape
Impersonate in many a perilous hour,
Both in the stately councils of the Kings,
And when the husky battle murmured thick,
May testify of services performed!
But now the seas are haggard with thy wrath,
Thy breath is tempest! never at the shores
Of hostile Ilium did thy stormful brows
Betray such fierce magnificence! not even
On that wild day when mad with torch and glare,   30
The frantic crowds with eyes like starving wolves,

Burst from their ports impregnable, a stream
Of headlong fury toward the hissing deep;
Where then full-armed I stood in guard, compact
Beside thee, and alone, with brand and spear,
We held at bay the swarming brood, and poured
Blood of choice warriors on the foot-ploughed sands!
Thou, meantime, dark with conflict, as a cloud
That thickens in the bosom of the West
Over quenched sunset, circled round with flame.   40
Huge as a billow running from the winds
Long distances, till with black shipwreck swoln,
It flings its angry mane about the sky.
And like that billow heaving ere it burst;
And like that cloud urged by impulsive storm
With charge of thunder, lightning, and the drench
Of torrents, thou in all thy majesty
Of mightiness didst fall upon the war!
Remember that great moment! Nor forget
The aid I gave thee; how my ready spear   50
Flew swiftly seconding thy mortal stroke,
Where'er the press was hottest; never slacked
My arm its duty, nor mine eye its aim,
Though terribly they compassed us, and stood
Thick as an Autumn forest, whose brown hair,
Lustrous with sunlight, by the still increase
Of heat to glowing heat conceives like zeal
Of radiance, till at the pitch of noon
'Tis seized with conflagration and distends
Horridly over leagues of doom'd domain.   60
Mingling the screams of birds, the cries of brutes,
The wail of creatures in the covert pent,
Howls, yells, and shrieks of agony, the hiss
Of seething sap, and crash of falling boughs
Together in its dull voracious roar.
　　So closely and so fearfully they throng'd,
Savage with phantasies of victory,

33 toward] towards *1851*

A sea of dusky shapes; for day had passed
And night fell on their darkened faces, red
With fight and torchflare; shrill the resonant air   70
With eager shouts, and hoarse with angry groans;
While over all the dense and sullen boom,
The din and murmur of the myriads,
Rolled with its awful intervals, as though
The battle breathed, or as against the shore
Waves gather back to heave themselves anew.
That night sleep dropped not from the dreary skies,
Nor could the prowess of our chiefs oppose
That sea of raging men. But what were they?
Or what is man opposed to thee? His hopes   80
Are wrecks, himself the drowning, drifting weed
That wanders on thy waters; such as I
Who see the scattered remnants of my fleet,
Remembering the day when first we sailed,
Each glad ship shining like the morning star
With promise for the world. Oh! such as I
Thus darkly drifting on the drowning waves.
O God of waters! 'tis a dreadful thing
To suffer for an evil unrevealed;
Dreadful it is to hear the perishing cry   90
Of those we love; the silence that succeeds
How dreadful! Still my trust is fixed on thee
For those that still remain and for myself.
And if I hear thy swift foam-snorting steeds
Drawing thy dusky chariot, as in
The pauses of the wind I seem to hear,
Deaf thou art not to my entreating prayer!
Haste then to give us help, for closely now
Crete whispers in my ears, and all my blood
Runs keen and warm for home, and I have yearning,   100
Such yearning as I never felt before,
To see again my wife, my little son,
My Queen, my pretty nursling of five years,

84 we] *1851*; he *misp. de L; corr. errata, de L 1911*

The darling of my hopes, our dearest pledge
Of marriage, and our brightest prize of love,
Whose parting cry rings clearest in my heart.
O lay this horror, much-offended God!
And making all as fair and firm as when
We trusted to thy mighty depths of old,—
I vow to sacrifice the first whom Zeus   110
Shall prompt to hail us from the white seashore
And welcome our return to royal Crete,
An offering, Poseidon, unto thee!

Amid the din of elemental strife,
No voice may pierce but Deity supreme:
And Deity supreme alone can hear,
Above the hurricane's discordant shrieks,
The cry of agonized humanity.

Not unappeased was He who smites the waves,
When to his stormy ears the warrior's vow   120
Entered, and from his foamy pinnacle
Tumultuous, he beheld the prostrate form,
And knew the mighty heart. Awhile he gazed,
As doubtful of his purpose, and the storm,
Conscious of that divine debate, withheld
Its fierce emotion, in the luminous gloom
Of those so dark irradiating eyes!
Beneath whose wavering lustre shone revealed
The tumult of the purpling deeps, and all
The throbbing of the tempest, as it paused,   130
Slowly subsiding, seeming to await
The sudden signal, as a faithful hound
Pants with the forepaws stretched before its nose,
Athwart the greensward, after an eager chase;
Its hot tongue thrust to cool, its foamy jaws
Open to let the swift breath come and go,
Its quick interrogating eyes fixed keen

133 the] its *1851*

Upon the huntsman's countenance, and ever
Lashing its sharp impatient tail with haste:
Prompt at the slightest sign to scour away,   140
And hang itself afresh by the bleeding fangs,
Upon the neck of some death-singled stag,
Whose royal antlers, eyes, and stumbling knees,
Will supplicate the gods in mute despair.
This time not mute, nor yet in vain this time!
For still the burden of the earnest voice
And all the vivid glories it revoked,
Sank in the god, with that absorbed suspense
Felt only by the Olympians, whose minds
Unbounded like our mortal brain, perceive   150
All things complete, the end, the aim of all;
To whom the crown and consequence of deeds
Are ever present with the deed itself.

And now the pouring surges, vast and smooth,
Grew weary of restraint, and heaved themselves
Headlong beneath him, breaking at his feet
With wild importunate cries and angry wail;
Like crowds that shout for bread and hunger more.
And now the surface of their rolling backs
Was ridged with foam-topt furrows, rising high   160
And dashing wildly, like to fiery steeds,
Fresh from the Thracian or Thessalian plains,
High-blooded mares just tempering to the bit,
Whose manes at full-speed stream upon the winds,
And in whose delicate nostrils when the gust
Breathes of their native plains, they ramp and rear,
Frothing the curb, and bounding from the earth,
As though the Sun-god's chariot alone
Were fit to follow in their flashing track.
Anon with gathering stature to the height   170
Of those colossal giants, doomed long since
To torturous grief and penance, that assailed
The sky-throned courts of Zeus, and climbing, dared

For once in a world the Olympic wrath, and braved
The electric spirit which from his clenching hand
Pierces the dark-veined earth, and with a touch
Is death to mortals, fearfully they grew!
And with like purpose of audacity,
Threatened Titanic fury to the god.
Such was the agitation of the sea   180
Beneath Poseidon's thought-revolving brows,
Storming for signal. But no signal came.
And as when men who congregate to hear
Some proclamation from the regal fount
With eager questioning and anxious phrase,
Betray the expectation of their hearts,
Till after many hours of fretful sloth,
Weary with much delay, they hold discourse
In sullen groups and cloudy masses, stirred
With rage irresolute and whispering plot,   190
Known more by indication than by word,
And understood alone by those whose minds
Participate;—even so the restless waves
Began to lose all sense of servitude,
And worked with rebel passions, bursting, now
To right, and now to left, but evermore
Subdued with influence, and controlled with dread
Of that inviolate Authority.

Then, swiftly as he mused, the impetuous God
Seized on the pausing reins, his coursers plunged,   200
His brows resumed the grandeur of their ire;
Throughout his vast divinity the deeps
Concurrent thrilled with action, and away,
As sweeps a thunder-cloud across the sky
In harvest-time, preluded by dull blasts;
Or some black-visaged whirlwind, whose wide folds
Rush, wrestling on with all 'twixt heaven and earth,
Darkling he hurried, and his distant voice,

207 wrestling on] wrestling *1851*

Not softened by delay, was heard in tones
Distinctly terrible, still following up   210
Its rapid utterance of tremendous wrath
With hoarse reverberations; like the roar
Of lions when they hunger, and awake
The sullen echoes from their forest sleep,
To speed the ravenous noise from hill to hill
And startle victims; but more awful, He,
Scudding across the hills that rise and sink,
With foam, and splash, and cataracts of spray,
Clothed in majestic splendour; girt about
With sea-gods and swift creatures of the sea;   220
Their briny eyes blind with the showering drops;
Their stormy locks, salt tongues, and scaly backs,
Quivering in harmony with the tempest, fierce
And eager with tempestuous delight;—
He like a moving rock above them all
Solemnly towering while fitful gleams
Brake from his dense black forehead, which display'd
The enduring chiefs as their distracted fleets,
Tossed, toiling with the waters, climbing high,
And plunging downward with determined beaks,   230
In lurid anguish; but the Cretan king
And all his crew were 'ware of under-tides,
That for the groaning vessel made a path,
On which the impending and precipitious waves
Fell not, nor suck'd to their abysmal gorge.

O, happy they to feel the mighty God,
Without his whelming presence near: to feel
Safety and sweet relief from such despair,
And gushing of their weary hopes once more
Within their fond warm hearts, tired limbs, and eyes   240
Heavy with much fatigue and want of sleep!
Prayers did not lack; like mountain springs they came,
After the earth has drunk the drenching rains,
And throws her fresh-born jets into the sun

With joyous sparkles;—for there needed not
Evidence more serene of instant grace,
Immortal mercy! and the sense which follows
Divine interposition, when the shock
Of danger hath been thwarted by the Gods,
Visibly, and through supplication deep,—   250
Rose in them, chiefly in the royal mind
Of him whose interceding vow had saved.
Tears from that great heroic soul sprang up;
Not painful as in grief, nor smarting keen
With shame of weeping; but calm, fresh, and sweet;
Such as in lofty spirits rise, and wed
The nature of the woman to the man;
A sight most lovely to the Gods! They fell
Like showers of starlight from his stedfast eyes,
As ever towards the prow he gazed, nor moved   260
One muscle, with firm lips and level lids,
Motionless; while the winds sang in his ears,
And took the length of his brown hair in streams
Behind him. Thus the hours passed, and the oars
Plied without pause, and nothing but the sound
Of the dull rowlocks and still watery sough,
Far off, the carnage of the storm, was heard.
For nothing spake the mariners in their toil,
And all the captains of the war were dumb;
Too much oppressed with wonder, too much thrilled   270
By their great chieftain's silence, to disturb
Such meditation with poor human speech.
Meantime the moon through slips of driving cloud
Came forth, and glanced athwart the seas a path
Of dusky splendour, like the Hadean brows,
When with Elysian passion they behold
Persephone's complacent hueless cheeks.

260 towards] *GM failed to make his usual correction to* toward
262 sang] sung *1851*
277 Persephone's] *errata 1851:* "for *Persephonias'* read *Persephonia's.*"
complacent hueless] fresh complacent *1851*

Soon gathering strength and lustre, as a ship
That swims into some blue and open bay
With bright full-bosomed sails, the radiant car   280
Of Artemis advanced, and on the waves
Sparkled like arrows from her silver bow,
The keenness of her pure and tender gaze.

Then, slowly, one by one the chiefs sought rest;
The watches being set, and men to relieve
The rowers at midseason. Fair it was
To see them as they lay! Some up the prow,
Some round the helm, in open-handed sleep;
With casques unloosed, and bucklers put aside;
The ten years' tale of war upon their cheeks,   290
Where clung the salt wet locks, and on their breasts
Beards, the thick growth of many a proud campaign;
And on their brows the bright invisible crown
Victory sheds from her own radiant form,
As o'er her favourites' heads she sings and soars.
But dreams came not so calmly, as around
Turbulent shores wild waves and swamping surf
Prevail, while seaward, on the tranquil deeps,
Reign placid surfaces and solemn peace,
So from the troubled strands of memory, they   300
Launched and were tossed, long ere they found the tides
That lead to the gentle bosoms of pure rest.
And like to one who from a ghostly watch
In a lone house where murder hath been done,
And secret violations, pale with stealth
Emerges, staggering on the first chill gust
Wherewith the morning greets him, feeling not
Its balmy freshness on his bloodless cheek,—
But swift to hide his midnight face afar,
'Mongst the old woods and timid-glancing flowers   310
Hastens, till on the fresh reviving breasts
Of tender Dryads folded, he forgets

The pallid witness of those nameless things,
In renovated senses lapt, and joins
The full, keen joyance of the day, so they
From sights and sounds of battle smeared with blood,
And shrieking souls on Acheron's bleak tides,
And wail of execrating kindred, slid
Into oblivious slumber and a sense
Of satiate deliciousness complete.   320

Leave them, O Muse, in that so happy sleep!
Leave them to reap the harvest of their toil,
While fast in moonlight the glad vessel glides,
As if instinctive to its forest home.
O Muse, that in all sorrows and all joys,
Rapturous bliss and suffering divine,
Dwellest with equal fervour, in the calm
Of thy serene philosophy, albeit
Thy gentle nature is of joy alone,
And loves the pipings of the happy fields,   330
Better than all the great parade and pomp,
Which forms the train of heroes and of kings,
And sows, too frequently, the tragic seeds
That choke with sobs thy singing,—turn away
Thy lustrous eyes back to the oath-bound man!
For as a shepherd stands above his flock,
The lofty figure of the king is seen,
Standing above his warriors as they sleep:
And still as from a rock grey waters gush,
While still the rock is passionless and dark,   340
Nor moves one feature of its giant face,
The tears fall from his eyes, and he stirs not.

And O, bright Muse! forget not thou to fold
In thy prophetic sympathy, the thought
Of him whose destiny has heard its doom:
The Sacrifice thro' whom the ship is saved.

Haply that Sacrifice is sleeping now,
And dreams of glad to-morrows. Haply now,
His hopes are keenest, and his fervent blood
Richest with youth, and love, and fond regard!   350
Round him the circle of affections blooms,
And in some happy nest of home he lives,
One name oft uttering in delighted ears,
Mother! at which the hearts of men are kin
With reverence and yearning. Haply, too,
That other name, twin holy, twin revered,
He whispers often to the passing winds
That blow toward the Asiatic coasts;
For Crete has sent her bravest to the war,
And multitudes pressed forward to that rank,   360
Men with sad weeping wives and little ones.
That other name—O Father! who art thou,
Thus doomed to lose the star of thy last days?
It may be the sole flower of thy life,
And that of all who now look up to thee!
Oh! Father, Father! unto thee even now
Fate cries; the future with imploring voice,
Cries 'Save me,' 'Save me,' though thou hearest not,
And Oh! thou Sacrifice, foredoomed by Zeus.
Even now the dark inexorable deed   370
Is dealing its relentless stroke, and vain
Are prayers, and tears, and struggles, and despair!
The mother's tears, the nation's stormful grief,
The people's indignation and revenge!
Vain the last childlike pleading voice for life,
The quick resolve, the young heroic brow,
So like, so like, and vainly beautiful!
Oh! whosoe'er ye are the Muse says not,
And sees not, but the gods look down on both.

351 blooms] bloom *1851*
354 hearts] *1851*; heart *misp. de L, GMT*
358 toward] towards *1851*

The Longest Day

On yonder hills soft twilight dwells
    And Hesper burns where sunset dies,
Moist and chill the woodland smells
    From the fern-covered hollows uprise;
    Darkness drops not from the skies,
But shadows of darkness are flung o'er the vale
    From the boughs of the chesnut, the oak, and the elm,
While night in yon lines of eastern pines
    Preserves alone her inviolate realm
        Against the twilight pale.   10

Say, then say, what is this day,
    That it lingers thus with half-closed eyes,
When the sunset is quenched and the orient ray
    Of the roseate moon doth rise,
    Like a midnight sun o'er the skies!
'Tis the longest, the longest of all the glad year,
    The longest in life and the fairest in hue,
When day and night, in bridal light,
    Mingle their beings beneath the sweet blue,
        And bless the balmy air!   20

MS: Yale, *a completed poem of two stanzas, fair copy corrected. Variants are from this MS.*

1 yonder] western   soft] clear
2 And Hesper] The *del.* A white star   sunset] colour
3 Moist and chill the woodland] Rich & cool the sand-earth
4 uprise] arise
6 But cowering shadows are over [the *del.*] our vale
7 Round branches of chestnut & maple & elm;
8 yon] those   eastern] high ranked
9 [Furls *del.*] Holds the black banner of her old realm
Stanza 2:

      Grave light, that seemest by angels borne,
      A corse held pure of dark decay;
      Or spirit [watching *del.*] watchful for the morn,
        To leap in the orient ray;
        Deathless through night is thy day.
      And high on thy throne of the midsummer now,
      Spirit or corse, thou wearest thy dream
      With rapturous grace, as though off the face   [*Cf.·lines 28–29*]
      Of [the *del.*] an unveiled Infinity one far beam
        Had fall'n on thy sighting brow.

Upward to this starry height
 The culminating seasons rolled;
On one slope green with spring delight,
 The other with harvest gold,
 And treasures of Autumn untold:
And on this highest throne of the midsummer now
 The waning but deathless day doth dream,
With a rapturous grace, as tho' from the face
 Of the unveiled infinity, lo, a far beam
  Had fall'n on her dim-flushed brow!   30

Prolong, prolong that tide of song
 O leafy nightingale and thrush!
Still earnest-throated blackcap throng
 The woods with that emulous gush
 Of notes in tumultuous rush.
Ye summer souls raise up one voice!
 A charm is afloat all over the land;
The ripe year doth fall to the Spirit of all,
 Who blesses it with outstretched hand,
  Ye summer souls rejoice!   40

To Robin Redbreast

Merrily 'mid the faded leaves,
 O Robin of the bright red breast!
Cheerily over the Autumn eaves,
 Thy note is heard, bonny bird;
Sent to cheer us, and kindly endear us
 To what would be a sorrowful time

TO ROBIN REDBREAST

MS: NB B, [*p. 8*], *working draft, faint pencil. Variants are from this MS.*

1 'mid] 'mongst
2 red breast] *corr. errata, de L 1911*; redbreast *1851, de L*
4 bonny] thou bonny

Without thee in the weltering clime:
Merry art thou in the boughs of the lime,
    While thy fadeless waistcoat glows on thy breast,
    In Autumn's reddest livery drest.   10

A merry song, a cheery song!
    In the boughs above, on the sward below,
Chirping and singing the live day long,
    While the maple in grief sheds its fiery leaf,
And all the trees waning, with bitter complaining,
    Chesnut, and elm, and sycamore,
    Catch the wild gust in their arms, and roar
Like the sea on a stormy shore,
       Till wailfully they let it go,
       And weep themselves naked and weary with woe.   20

Merrily, cheerily, joyously still
    Pours out the crimson-crested tide.
The set of the season burns bright on the hill,
    Where the foliage dead falls yellow and red,
Picturing vainly, but foretelling plainly
    The wealth of cottage warmth that comes
    When the frost gleams and the blood numbs,
And then, bonny Robin, I'll spread thee out crumbs
       In my garden porch for thy redbreast pride,
       The song and the ensign of dear fireside.   30

---

9 fadeless waistcoat glows] warm red waistcoat burns
10 In Autumns [fine? *del.*] warm red livery drest Robin of the downy breast *del.* In Autumn livery drest *del.*
12 *blank*
18 sea on a stormy] flakes [?] on a windy
22 crested] breasted
23 set] sunset *del.*
25 Picturing] Mimicking *del.*
26 cottage] winter
27 frost gleams] dews freeze
29 redbreast pride] breasted *or* redbreast tide

Song

The daisy now is out upon the green;
    And in the grassy lanes
    The child of April rains,
The sweet fresh-hearted violet is smelt and loved unseen.

Along the brooks and meads, the daffodil
    Its yellow richness spreads,
    And by the fountain-heads
Of rivers, cowslips cluster round, and over every hill.

The crocus and the primrose may have gone,
    The snowdrop may be low,   10
    But soon the purple glow
 Of hyacinths will fill the copse, and lilies watch the dawn.

And in the sweetness of the budding year,
    The cuckoo's woodland call,
    The skylark over all,
And then at eve, the nightingale, is doubly sweet and dear.

My soul is singing with the happy birds,
    And all my human powers
    Are blooming with the flowers,
My foot is on the fields and downs, among the flocks and herds.   20

Deep in the forest where the foliage droops,
    I wander, fill'd with joy.
    Again as when a boy,
The sunny vistas tempt me on with dim delicious hopes.

The sunny vistas, dim with hanging shade,
    And old romantic haze:—
    Again as in past days,
The spirit of immortal Spring doth every sense pervade.

Oh! do not say that this will ever cease;—
    This joy of woods and fields,   30
    This youth that nature yields,
Will never speak to me in vain, tho' soundly rapt in peace.

25 hanging] *corr. errata, de L 1911*; hurying *1851*; hurrying *de L*

Sunrise

The clouds are withdrawn
And their thin-rippled mist,
That stream'd o'er the lawn
To the drowsy-eyed west.
Cold and grey
They slept in the way,
And shrank from the ray
Of the chariot East:
But now they are gone
And the bounding light   10
Leaps thro' the bars
Of doubtful dawn;
Blinding the stars,
And blessing the sight;
Shedding delight
On all below;
Glimmering fields,
And wakening wealds,
And rising lark,
And meadows dark,   20
And idle rills,
And labouring mills,
And far-distant hills
Of the fawn and the doe.
The sun is cheered
And his path is cleared,
As he steps to the air
From his emerald cave,
His heel in the wave,
Most bright and bare;   30
In the tide of the sky
His radiant hair;
From his temples fair,
Blown back on high;

17 Glimmering] Green glimmering *1851*

As forward he bends,
And upward ascends,
Timely and true,
To the breast of the blue;
His warm red lips
Kissing the dew,   40
Which sweetened drips
On his flower cupholders;
Every hue
From his gleaming shoulders
Shining anew
With colour sky-born,
As it washes and dips
In the pride of the morn.
Robes of azure,
Fringed with amber,   50
Fold upon fold
Of purple and gold,
Vine-leaf bloom,
And the grape's ripe gloom,
When season deep
In noontide leisure,
With clustering heap
The tendrils clamber,
Full in the face
Of his hot embrace,   60
Fill'd with the gleams
Of his firmest beams.
Autumn flushes,
Roseate blushes,
Vermeil tinges,
Violet fringes,
Every hue
Of his flower cupholders,
O'er the clear ether
Mingled together,   70
Shining anew

From his gleaming shoulders!
Circling about
In a coronal rout,
And floating behind,
The way of the wind,
As forward he bends,
And upwards ascends,
Timely and true,
To the breast of the blue.   80
His bright neck curved,
His clear limbs nerved,
Diamond keen
On his front serene,
While each white arm strains
To the racing reins,
As plunging, eyes flashing,
Dripping, and dashing,
His steeds triple grown,
Rear up to his throne,   90
Ruffling the rest
Of the sea's blue breast,
From his flooding, flaming crimson crest!

Pictures of the Rhine

The *Pictures* were written in reminiscence of GM's wedding trip with
Mary Ellen Peacock Nicolls in the late summer of 1849 (see also *Rhine-
Land*, p. 761). In sending a selection of his poems to John W. Parker, the
publisher, GM wrote on December 12, 1850, that he had more of these
Pictures of the Rhine but that he thought six were enough.

I refer to the *Pictures* as "sonnets" because they reflect GM's early
experimentation with varying the two conventional sonnet patterns. Later
he experimented more boldly in the 16-line "sonnets" of *Modern Love*.
Perhaps he was jolted into these experiments by Keats's experimental
sonnet on the sonnet, "If by dull rhymes our English must be chain'd,"
first published in 1848.

I

The spirit of Romance dies not to those
Who hold a kindred spirit in their souls:
Even as the odorous life within the rose

Lives in the scattered leaflets and controls
Mysterious adoration, so there glows
Above dead things a thing that cannot die;
Faint as the glimmer of a tearful eye,
Ere the orb fills and all the sorrow flows.
Beauty renews itself in many ways;
The flower is fading while the new bud blows;   10
And this dear land as true a symbol shows,
While o'er it like a mellow sunset strays
The legendary splendour of old days,
Invisible, inviolate repose.

II

About a mile behind the viny banks,
How sweet it was, upon a sloping green,
Sunspread, and shaded with a branching screen,
To lie in peace half-murmuring words of thanks!
To see the mountains on each other climb,
With spaces for rich meadows flowering bright;
The winding river freshening the sight
At intervals, the trees in leafy prime;
The distant village-roofs of blue and white,
With intersections of quaint-fashioned beams   10
All slanting crosswise, and the feudal gleams
Of ruined turrets, barren in the light;—
To watch the changing clouds, like clime in clime,
Oh! sweet to lie and bless the luxury of time.

III

Fresh blows the early breeze, our sail is full;
A merry morning and a mighty tide.
Cheerily O! and past St. Goar we glide,
Half hide in misty dawn and mountain cool.
The river is our own! and now the sun
In saffron clothes the warming atmosphere;
The sky lifts up her white veil like a nun,
And looks upon the landscape blue and clear;—

The lark is up; the hills, the vines in sight;
The river broadens with his waking bliss   10
And throws up islands to behold the light;
Voices begin to rise, all hues to kiss;—
Was ever such a happy morn as this!
Birds sing, we shout, flowers breathe, trees shine with one delight!

IV

Between the two white breasts of her we love,
A dewy blushing rose will sometimes spring;
Thus Nonnenwerth like an enchanted thing
Rises mid-stream the crystal depths above.
On either side the waters heave and swell,
But all is calm within the little Isle;
Content it is to give its holy smile,
And bless with peace the lives that in it dwell.
Most dear on the dark grass beneath its bower
Of kindred trees embracing branch and bough,   10
To dream of fairy foot and sudden flower;
Or haply with a twilight on the brow,
To muse upon the legendary hour,
And Roland's lonely love and Hildegard's sad vow.

V

Hark! how the bitter winter breezes blow
Round the sharp rocks and o'er the half-lifted wave,
While all the rocky woodland branches rave
Shrill with the piercing cold, and every cave,
Along the icy water-margin low,
Rings bubbling with the whirling overflow;
And sharp the echoes answer distant cries
Of dawning daylight and the dim sunrise,
And the gloom-coloured clouds that stain the skies
With pictures of a warmth, and frozen glow   10
Spread over endless fields of sheeted snow;
And white untrodden mountains shining cold,
And muffled footpaths winding thro' the wold,
O'er which those wintry gusts cease not to howl and blow.

VI

Rare is the loveliness of slow decay!
With youth and beauty all must be desired,
But 'tis the charm of things long past away,
They leave, alone, the light they have inspired:
The calmness of a picture; Memory now
Is the sole life among the ruins grey,
And like a phantom in fantastic play,
She wanders with rank weeds stuck on her brow,
Over grass-hidden caves and turret-tops,
Herself almost as tottering as they;   10
While, to the steps of Time, her latest props
Fall stone by stone, and in the Sun's hot ray
All that remains stands up in rugged pride,
And bridal vines drink in his juices on each side.

To a Nightingale

O nightingale! how hast thou learnt
    The note of the nested dove?
While under thy bower the fern hangs burnt
    And no cloud hovers above!
Rich July has many a sky
With splendour dim, that thou mightst hymn,
And make rejoice with thy wondrous voice,
    And the thrill of thy wild pervading tone!
But instead of to woo, thou hast learnt to coo:
Thy song is mute at the mellowing fruit,   10
And the dirge of the flowers is sung by the hours
    In silence and twilight alone.

O nightingale! 'tis this, 'tis this
    That makes thee mock the dove!
That thou hast past thy marriage bliss,
    To know a parent's love.

The waves of fern may fade and burn,
The grasses may fall, the flowers and all,
And the pine-smells o'er the oak dells
    Float on their drowsy and odorous wings,   20
But thou wilt do nothing but coo,
Brimming the nest with thy brooding breast,
'Midst that young throng of future song,
    Round whom the Future sings!

MODERN LOVE
AND
POEMS OF THE ENGLISH ROADSIDE,
WITH
POEMS AND BALLADS
(1862)

Grandfather Bridgeman

According to the journal of William Hardman, GM was working on this poem in September 1861. On the Hardmans' return from a morning walk, GM read to Hardman "the result of his morning's work—portion of a very pretty idyll called *Grandfather Bridgeman*" (*MVP*, p. 56). GM described the poem in a long letter to Mrs. Janet Ross, November 19, 1861, as "an idyll: true to English life, and containing a war episode, approved by friends who have heard it." Since Samuel Lucas, editor of *Once a Week*, did not care for the poem, GM withheld it from that publication (letter of January 5, 1862).

I

'Heigh, boys!' cried Grandfather Bridgeman, 'it's time before
    dinner to-day.'
He lifted the crumpled letter, and thumped a surprising 'Hurrah!'
Up jumped all the echoing young ones, but John, with the starch
    in his throat,
Said, 'Father, before we make noises, let's see the contents of the
    note.'

MODERN LOVE (1862)

The presentation copies of Modern Love and Poems of the English Roadside, with Poems and Ballads *cited in the notes are situated as follows: Mrs. Shirley Brooks, wife of the novelist* (Berg, Copy 1), *Robert Browning* (Yale), *Dante Gabriel Rossetti* (BM Ashley 1135), *A. C. Swinburne* (the private library of Arthur A. Houghton, Jr.), *A. Trollope* (Widener Collection, Harvard), *W. C. Bonaparte Wyse* (The Pierpont Morgan Library).

The old man glared at him harshly, and, twinkling made answer:
    'Too bad!
John Bridgeman, I'm always the whisky, and you are the water,
    my lad!'

II

But soon it was known thro' the house, and the house ran over for
    joy,
That news, good news, great marvels, had come from the soldier
    boy;
Young Tom, the luckless scapegrace, offshoot of Methodist John;
His grandfather's evening tale, whom the old man hailed as his son.
And the old man's shout of pride was a shout of his victory, too;
For he called his affection a method: the neighbours' opinions he
    knew.

III

Meantime, from the morning table, removing the stout breakfast
    cheer,
The drink of the three generations, the milk, the tea, and the beer
(Alone in its generous reading of pints stood the Grandfather's jug),
The women for sight of the missive came pressing to coax and to
    hug.
He scattered them quick, with a buss and a smack; thereupon he
    began
Diversions with John's little Sarah: on Sunday, the naughty old
    man!

IV

Then messengers sped to the maltster, the auctioneer, miller, and all
The seven sons of the farmer who housed in the range of his call.
Likewise the married daughters, three plentiful ladies, prime cooks,
Who bowed to him while they condemned, in meek hope to stand
    high in his books.

II.3 offshoot] the offshoot *1862*

'John's wife is a fool at a pudding,' they said, and the light carts up
    hill
Went merrily, flouting the Sabbath: for puddings well made mend a
    will.

V

The day was a van-bird of summer: the robin still piped, but the
    blue,
As a warm and dreamy palace with voices of larks ringing thro',
Looked down as if wistfully eyeing the blossoms that fell from its
    lap:
A day to sweeten the juices: a day to quicken the sap.
All round the shadowy orchard sloped meadows in gold, and the
    dear
Shy violets breathed their hearts out: the maiden breath of the year!

VI

Full time there was before dinner to bring fifteen of his blood,
To sit at the old man's table: they found that the dinner was good.
But who was she by the lilacs and pouring laburnums concealed,
When under the blossoming apple the chair of the Grandfather
    wheeled?
She heard one little child crying, 'Dear brave Cousin Tom!' as it
    leapt;
Then murmured she: 'Let me spare them!' and passed round the
    walnuts, and wept.

VII

Yet not from sight had she slipped ere feminine eyes could detect
The figure of Mary Charlworth. 'It's just what we all might expect,'
Was uttered: and: 'Didn't I tell you?' Of Mary the rumour
    resounds,
That she is now her own mistress, and mistress of five thousand
    pounds.
'Twas she, they say, who cruelly sent young Tom to the war.
Miss Mary, we thank you now! If you knew what we're thanking
    you for!

V.2 As a] A *1862*   dreamy] *1851*; dreary *de L*; *corr. errata, de L 1911*
VII.1 had] has *1862*   ere feminine] ere sharp feminine *1862*

VIII

But, 'Have her in: let her hear it,' called Grandfather Bridgeman,
    elate,
While Mary's black-gloved fingers hung trembling with flight on the
    gate.
Despite the women's remonstrance, two little ones, lighter than deer,
Were loosed, and Mary imprisoned, her whole face white as a tear,
Came forward with culprit footsteps. Her punishment was to
    commence:
The pity in her pale visage they read in a different sense.

IX

'You perhaps may remember a fellow, Miss Charlworth, a sort of
    black sheep,'
The old man tuned his tongue to ironical utterance deep:
'He came of a Methodist dad, so it wasn't his fault if he kicked.
He earned a sad reputation, but Methodists are mortal strict.
His name was Tom, and, dash me! but Bridgeman I think you might
    add:
Whatever he was, bear in mind that he came of a Methodist dad.'

X

This prelude dismally lengthened, till Mary, starting, exclaimed,
'A letter, Sir, from your grandson?' 'Tom Bridgeman that rascal is
    named,
The old man answered, and further, the words that sent Tom to the
    ranks,
Repeated as words of a person to whom they all owed mighty
    thanks.
But Mary never blushed: with her eyes on the letter, she sate,
And twice interrupting him faltered, 'The date, may I ask, Sir, the
    date?

XI

'Why, that's what I never look at in a letter,' the farmer replied:
'Facts first! and now I'll be parson.' The Bridgeman women
    descried

IX.2 tuned] turned *misp. all eds., corr. GM in presentation copy to Robert Browning*
IX.4 are] *are ital. 1862*

A quiver on Mary's eyebrows. One turned, and while shifting her
    comb,
Said low to a sister: 'I'm certain she knows more than we about
    Tom.
She wants him now he's a hero!' The same, resuming her place,
Begged Mary to check them the moment she found it a tedious case.

XII

Then as a mastiff swallows the snarling noises of cats,
The voice of the farmer opened. '"Three cheers, and off with your
    hats!"'
—That's Tom. "We've beaten them, Daddy, and tough work it was,
    to be sure!
A regular stand-up combat: eight hours smelling powder and gore.
I entered it Serjeant-Major,"—and now he commands a salute,
And carries the flag of old England! Heigh! see him lift foes on his
    foot!

XIII

'—An officer! ay, Miss Charlworth, he is, or he is so to be;
You'll own war isn't such humbug: and Glory means something,
    you see.
"But don't say a word," he continues, "against the brave French
    any more."
—That stopt me: we'll now march together. I couldn't read further
    before.
That "brave French" I couldn't stomach. He can't see their
    cunning to get
Us Britons to fight their battles, while best half the-winnings they
    net!'

XIV

The old man sneered, and read forward. It was of that desperate
    fight;—
The Muscovite stole thro' the mist-wreaths that wrapped the chill
    Inkermann height,

Where stood our silent outposts: old England was in them that day!
O sharp worked his ruddy wrinkles, as if to the breath of the fray
They moved! He sat bareheaded: his long hair over him slow,
Swung white as the silky bog-flowers in purple heath-hollows that
    grow.

XV

And louder at Tom's first person: acute and in thunder the 'I'
Invaded the ear with a whinny of triumph, that seem'd to defy
The hosts of the world. All heated, what wonder he little could
    brook
To catch the sight of Mary's demure puritanical look?
And still as he led the onslaught, his treacherous side-shots he sent
At her who was fighting a battle as fierce, and who sat there unbent.

XVI

'"We stood in line, and like hedgehogs the Russians rolled under us
    thick.
They frightened me there."—He's no coward; for when, Miss, they
    came at the quick,
The sight, he swears, was a breakfast.—"My stomach felt tight: in
    a glimpse
I saw you snoring at home with the dear cuddled-up little imps.
And then like the winter brickfields at midnight, hot fire lengthened
    out.
Our fellows were just leashed bloodhounds: no heart of the lot
    faced about.

XVII

'"And only that grumbler, Bob Harris, remarked that we stood one
    to ten:
'Ye fool,' says Mick Grady, 'just tell 'em they know how to
    compliment men!'
And I sang out your old words: 'If the opposite side isn't God's,
Heigh! after you've counted a dozen, the pluckiest lads have the
    odds.'

XVII.2 how] *om. misp. 1862, added in presentation copies to Mrs. Brooks, Browning,
Swinburne, and Trollope; om. de L*

Ping-ping flew the enemies' pepper: the Colonel roared, Forward,
    and we
Went at them. 'Twas first like a blanket: and then a long plunge in
    the sea.

XVIII

'"Well, now about me and the Frenchman: it happened I can't
    tell you how:
And, Grandfather, hear, if you love me, and put aside prejudice
    now":
He never says "Grandfather"—Tom don't—save it's a serious
    thing.
"Well, there were some pits for the rifles, just dug on our French-
    leaning wing:
And backwards, and forwards, and backwards we went, and at last
    I was vexed,
And swore I would never surrender a foot when the Russians
    charged next.

XIX

'"I know that life's worth keeping."—Ay, so it is, lad; so it is!—
"But my life belongs to a woman."—Does that mean Her Majesty,
    Miss?—
"These Russians came lumping and grinning: they're fierce at it,
    though they are blocks.
Our fellows were pretty well pumped, and looked sharp for the little
    French cocks.
Lord, didn't we pray for their crowing! when over us, on the
    hill-top,
Behold the first line of them skipping, like kangaroos seen on the
    hop.

XX

'"That sent me into a passion, to think of them spying our flight!"
Heigh, Tom! you've Bridgeman blood, boy! And, "'Face them!'
    I shouted: 'All right;
Sure, Serjeant, we'll take their shot dacent, like gentlemen,' Grady
    replied.

XVIII.3 save] unless *1862*

A ball in his mouth, and the noble old Irishman dropped by my
    side.
Then there was just an instant to save myself, when a short wheeze
Of bloody lungs under the smoke, and a red-coat crawled up on his
    knees.

XXI

'"'Twas Ensign Baynes of our parish."—Ah, ah, Miss Charlworth,
    the one
Our Tom fought for a young lady? Come, now we've got into the
    fun!—
"I shouldered him: he primed his pistol, and I trailed my musket,
    prepared."
Why, that's a fine pick-a-back for ye, to make twenty Russians look
    scared!
"They came—never mind how many: we couldn't have run very
    well,
We fought back to back: 'face to face, our last time!' he said,
    smiling, and fell.

XXII

'"Then I strove wild for his body: the beggars saw glittering rings,
Which I vowed to send to his mother. I got some hard knocks and
    sharp stings,
But felt them no more than an angel, or devil, except in the wind.
I know that I swore at a Russian for showing his teeth, and he
    grinned
The harder: quick, as from heaven, a man on a horse rode
    between,
And fired, and swung his bright sabre: I can't write you more of
    the scene.

XXIII

'"But half in his arms, and half at his stirrup, he bore me right
    forth,
And pitched me among my old comrades: before I could tell south
    from north,

XXII.3 an angel] angel *misp. all eds., corr. GM in presentation copies to Browning,
Rossetti, Swinburne, and Trollope*

He caught my hand up, and kissed it! Don't ever let any man speak
A word against Frenchmen, I near him! I can't find his name, tho'
    I seek.
But French, and a General, surely he was, and God bless him!
    thro' him
I've learnt to love a whole nation,"' The ancient man paused,
    winking dim.

XXIV

A curious look, half woeful, was seen on his face as he turned
His eyes upon each of his children, like one who but faintly
    discerned
His old self in an old mirror. Then gathering sense in his fist,
He sounded it hard on his knee-cap. 'Your hand, Tom, the French
    fellow kissed!
He kissed my boy's old pounder! I say he's a gentleman!' Straight
The letter he tossed to one daughter; bade her the remainder relate.

XXV

Tom properly stated his praises in facts, but the lady preferred
To deck the narration with brackets, and drop her additional word.
What nobler Christian natures these women could boast, who 'twas
    known,
Once spat at the name of their nephew, and now made his praises
    their own!
The letter at last was finished, the hearers breathed freely, and sign
Was given, 'Tom's health!'—Quoth the farmer: 'Eh, Miss? are
    you weak in the spine?'

XXVI

For Mary had swayed, and her body was shaking, as if in a fit.
Tom's letter she held, and her thumb-nail the month when the letter
    was writ
Fast-dinted, while she hung sobbing: 'O, see, Sir, the letter is old!
O, do not be too happy!'—'If I understand you, I'm bowled!'

XXVI.1 swayed] sunk *all eds., corr. GM copy of* Modern Love *for de L, Yale*

Said Grandfather Bridgeman, 'and down go my wickets!—not
    happy! when here
Here's Tom like to marry his General's daughter—or widow—I'll
    swear!

XXVII

'I wager he knows how to strut, too! It's all on the cards that the
    Queen
Will ask him to Buckingham Palace, to say what he's done and
    he's seen.
Victoria's fond of her soldiers: and she's got a nose for a fight.
If Tom tells a cleverish story—there is such a thing as a knight!
And don't he look roguish and handsome!—To see a girl snivelling
    there—
By George, Miss, it's clear that you're jealous!'—'I love him!'
    she answered his stare.

XXVIII

'Yes! now!' breathed the voice of a woman.—'Ah! now!' quiver'd
    low the reply.
'And "now"'s just a bit too late, so it's no use your piping your
    eye.'
The farmer added bluffly: 'Old Lawyer Charlworth was rich;
You followed his instructions in kicking Tom into the ditch.
If you're such a dutiful daughter, that doesn't prove Tom is a fool.
Forgive and forget's my motto! and here's my grog growing cool!'

XXIX

'But, Sir,' Mary faintly repeated: 'for four long weeks I have failed
To come and cast on you my burden; such grief for you always
    prevailed!
My heart has so bled for you!' The old man burst on her speech:
'You've chosen a likely time, Miss! a pretty occasion to preach!'
And was it not outrageous, that now, of all times, one should come
With incomprehensible pity! Far better had Mary been dumb.

XXX

But when again she stammered in this bewildering way,
The farmer no longer could bear it, and begged her to go, or to stay,
But not to be whimpering nonsense at such a time. Pricked by a
    goad,
''Twas you who sent him to glory:—you've come here to reap what
    you sowed.
Is that it?' he asked; and the silence the elders preserved, plainly
    said,
On Mary's heaving bosom this begging-petition was read.

XXXI

And that it was scarcely a bargain that she who had driven him wild,
Should share now the fruits of his valour, the women expressed, as
    they smiled.
The family pride of the Bridgemans was comforted; still, with
    contempt,
They looked on a monied damsel of modesty quite so exempt.
'O give me force to tell them!' cried Mary, and even as she spoke,
A shout and a hush of the children: a vision on all of them broke.

XXXII

Wheeled, pale, in a chair, and shattered, the wreck of their hero
    was seen;
The ghost of Tom drawn slow o'er the orchard's shadowy green.
Could this be the martial darling they joyed in a moment ago?
'He knows it?' to Mary Tom murmured, and closed his weak lids
    at her 'No.'
'Beloved!' she said, falling by him, 'I have been a coward: I thought
You lay in the foreign country, and some strange good might be
    wrought.

XXXIII

'Each day I have come to tell him, and failed, with my hand on
    the gate.
I bore the dreadful knowledge, and crushed my heart with its
    weight.

The letter brought by your comrade—he has but just read it aloud!
It only reached him this morning!' Her head on his shoulder she
    bowed.
Then Tom with pity's tenderest lordliness patted her arm,
And eyed the old white-head fondly, with something of doubt and
    alarm.

XXXIV

O, take to your fancy a sculptor whose fresh marble offspring
    appears
Before him, shiningly perfect, the laurel-crown'd issue of years:
Is heaven offended? for lightning behold from its bosom escape,
And those are mocking fragments that made the harmonious shape!
He cannot love the ruins, till feeling that ruins alone
Are left, he loves them threefold. So passed the old grandfather's
    moan.

XXXV

John's text for a sermon on Slaughter, he heard, and he did not
    protest.
All rigid as April snowdrifts, he stood, hard and feeble; his chest
Just showing the swell of the fire as it melted him. Smiting a rib,
'Heigh! what have we been about, Tom! Was this all a terrible fib?'
He cried, and the letter forth-trembled. Tom told what the cannon
    had done.
Few present but ached to see falling those aged tears on his heart's
    son!

XXXVI

Up lanes of the quiet village, and where the mill-waters rush red
Thro' browning summer meadows to catch the sun's crimsoning
    head,
You meet an old man and a maiden who has the soft ways of a wife
With one whom they wheel, alternate; whose delicate flush of new
    life
Is prized like the early primrose. Then shake his right hand, in the
    chair—
The old man fails never to tell you: 'You've got the French
    General's there!'

The Meeting

GM sent this poem [? August 1860], along with others, to Samuel Lucas, hoping that "[John Everett] Millais might catch a sentiment from one or two of the enclosed. I would rather not have my name to them, as they are productions of my coxcombical and too imitative youth. Initials, if you like." The poem was published in *Once a Week* on September 1, signed "G.M." and illustrated by Millais. Probable date of composition: 1849–51.

GM must have thought better of the poem when he saw it in print with Millais's illustration since he included it in the *Modern Love* volume (1862).

The old coach-road through a common of furze,
With knolls of pine ran white;
Berries of autumn, with thistles, and burrs,
And spider-threads, droop'd in the light.

The light in a thin blue veil peered sick;
The sheep grazed close and still;
The smoke of a farm by a yellow rick
Curled lazily under a hill.

No fly shook the round of the silver net;
No insect the swift bird chased;   10
Only two travellers moved and met
Across that hazy waste.

One was a girl with a babe that throve,
Her ruin and her bliss;
One was a youth with a lawless love,
Who clasped it the more for this.

The girl for her babe hummed prayerful speech;
The youth for his love did pray;
Each cast a wistful look on each,
And either went their way.   20

Previously printed in Once A Week *3 (1 September 1860).*

2 pine] pines *OaW, 1862*
17 hummed] made *OaW*

The Promise in Disturbance

This sonnet does not appear in the volume of 1862. It was written to preface *Modern Love, A Reprint,* 1892.

> How low when angels fall their black descent,
> Our primal thunder tells: known is the pain
> Of music, that nigh throning wisdom went,
> And one false note cast wailful to the insane.
> Now seems the language heard of Love as rain
> To make a mire where fruitfulness was meant.
> The golden harp gives out a jangled strain,
> Too like revolt from heaven's Omnipotent.
> But listen in the thought; so may there come
> Conception of a newly-added chord,   10
> Commanding space beyond where ear has home.
> In labour of the trouble at its fount,
> Leads Life to an intelligible Lord
> The rebel discords up the sacred mount.

Modern Love

In a long letter of November 19, 1861, to Mrs. Janet Ross, GM speaks of "A Love-Match" as one of his later pieces; then goes on to say that when the six poems he mentions "are out," by which he would mean in *Once a Week*, he will set himself "seriously to work on a long poem. For if I have the power to do it, why should I not?"

In a postscript to a letter to Frederick A. Maxse, probably written in early December 1861, he wrote: "I have done a great deal of the 'Love-Match.' Rossetti says it's my best. I contrast it mentally with yours, which is so very much better!" GM must have worked diligently on his poem that December, for by January 5, 1862, he wrote Maxse that he wanted to send him "the proofs of 'A Tragedy of Modern Love', for inspection. . . . The poem goes into the volume to be dedicated to you, and which I am now preparing to publish." A few days later he sent Maxse "a portion of proofs of the 'Tragedy of Modern Love'," saying that, "There are wanting to complete it, 13 more sonnets. Please read, and let me have the honest judgment. When done with, return. This poem will come in the middle of the book."

MODERN LOVE

MS: Yale, *fair copy corrected, sonnets 1–9, unpublished sonnet 10, sonnets 11–36, no sonnet numbered 18, sonnets 18–36 numbered 19–37.*

I have argued elsewhere that I think these proofs for Maxse were made from the manuscript now in the possession of Yale ("A Manuscript of Meredith's 'Modern Love'," *Yale University Library Gazette* 40 [April 1966]: 185–87). In this manuscript there is no sonnet 18, and it is more likely to have been extracted than to have been left out inadvertently. With number 18 in place, the manuscript would have run to the length of the thirty-seven sonnets GM sent Maxse, lacking the "13 more sonnets" needed to round out the fifty that GM planned.

GM wrote of the poem to Augustus Jessopp, a schoolmaster, on September 20, 1862: "'Modern Love' as a dissection of the sentimental passion of these days, could only be apprehended by the few who would read it many times. I have not looked for it to succeed. Why did I write it?—Who can account for pressure?"

On June 16, 1891, he wrote George Stevenson, "I rather meditate a new issue of *Modern Love*." Whereupon he made a number of revisions in the poem. By October 20, 1891, he was able to inform Clement K. Shorter, "My reprint of *Modern Love* is in the printer's hands."

The following epigraph attached to *Modern Love* in the first edition, was omitted in the reprint.

> This is not meat
> For little people or for fools.
> *Book of the Sages*

Stevenson must have questioned GM about the extent of the wife's infidelity, because GM wrote him on February 5, 1892, "As to the Lady in 'Modern Love,' her husband never accurately knew; therefore we ought not to inquire; but flesh totters on the decline when irritated by anything."

I

By this he knew she wept with waking eyes:
That, at his hand's light quiver by her head,
The strange low sobs that shook their common bed,
Were called into her with a sharp surprise,
And strangled mute, like little gaping snakes,
Dreadfully venomous to him. She lay
Stone-still, and the long darkness flowed away
With muffled pulses. Then, as midnight makes
Her giant heart of Memory and Tears
Drink the pale drug of silence, and so beat   10
Sleep's heavy measure, they from head to feet
Were moveless, looking through their dead black years,

I.4 surprise] surprize *MS*

By vain regret scrawled over the blank wall.
Like sculptured effigies they might be seen
Upon their marriage-tomb, the sword between;
Each wishing for the sword that severs all.

II

It ended, and the morrow brought the task.
Her eyes were guilty gates, that let him in
By shutting all too zealous for their sin:
Each sucked a secret, and each wore a mask.
But, oh, the bitter taste her beauty had!
He sickened as at breath of poison-flowers:
A languid humour stole among the hours,
And if their smiles encountered, he went mad
And raged deep inward, till the light was brown
Before his vision, and the world forgot,   10
Looked wicked as some old dull murder-spot.
A star with lurid beams, she seemed to crown
The pit of infamy: and then again
He fainted on his vengefulness, and strove
To ape the magnanimity of love,
And smote himself, a shuddering heap of pain.

III

This was the woman; what now of the man?
But pass him. If he comes beneath a heel,
He shall be crushed until he cannot feel,
Or, being callous, haply till he can.
But he is nothing:—nothing? Only mark
The rich light striking out from her on him!
Ha! what a sense it is when her eyes swim
Across the man she singles, leaving dark
All else! Lord God, who mad'st the thing so fair,

II.4 sucked a] hid the *del. MS*
III.1 what now of the] where [?] the *del. MS*
III.2 a] our *MS, 1862*
III.6 out from her on him!] from her unto him: *MS, 1862*
III.9 the thing so] her very *del. MS*

See that I am drawn to her even now!   10
It cannot be such harm on her cool brow
To put a kiss? Yet if I meet him there!
But she is mine! Ah, no! I know too well
I claim a star whose light is overcast:
I claim a phantom-woman in the Past.
The hour has struck, though I heard not the bell!

                              IV

All other joys of life he strove to warm,
And magnify, and catch them to his lip:
But they had suffered shipwreck with the ship,
And gazed upon him sallow from the storm.
Of if Delusion came, 'twas but to show
The coming minute mock the one that went.
Cold as a mountain in its star-pitched tent,
Stood high Philosophy, less friend than foe:
Whom self-caged Passion, from its prison-bars,
Is always watching with a wondering hate.   10
Not till the fire is dying in the grate,
Look we for any kinship with the stars.
Oh, wisdom never comes when it is gold,
And the great price we pay for it full worth:
We have it only when we are half-earth.
Little avails that coinage to the old!

                              V

A message from her set his brain aflame.
A world of household matters filled her mind,
Wherein he saw hypocrisy designed:
She treated him as something that is tame,
And but at other provocation bites.

III.16 The hour] Something *del. MS*
IV.1 joys] *MS, 1862, corr. errata, de L 1911;* joy *1892, 1894, de L*
IV.7 *MS del.:* Cold in the whiteness of its own cold Laws,
IV.12 *MS del.:* See we our kinship with the quenchless stars!
IV.14 *MS del.:* And that great wealth we squandered for it, worth
IV.15 have] know *del. MS*
V.3 hypocrisy] hypocriscy *MS*

Familiar was her shoulder in the glass,
Through that dark rain: yet it may come to pass
That a changed eye finds such familiar sights
More keenly tempting than new loveliness.
The 'What has been' a moment seemed his own: 10
The splendours, mysteries, dearer because known,
Nor less divine: Love's inmost sacredness,
Called to him, 'Come!'—In his restraining start,
Eyes nurtured to be looked at, scarce could see
A wave of the great waves of Destiny
Convulsed at a checked impulse of the heart.

VI

It chanced his lips did meet her forehead cool.
She had no blush, but slanted down her eye.
Shamed nature, then, confesses love can die:
And most she punishes the tender fool
Who will believe what honours her the most!
Dead! is it dead? She has a pulse, and flow
Of tears, the price of blood-drops, as I know,
For whom the midnight sobs around Love's ghost,
Since then I heard her, and so will sob on.
The love is here; it has but changed its aim.   10
O bitter barren woman! what's the name?
The name, the name, the new name thou hast won?
Behold me striking the world's coward stroke!
That will I not do, though the sting is dire.
—Beneath the surface this, while by the fire
They sat, she laughing at a quiet joke.

VII

She issues radiant from her dressing-room,
Like one prepared to scale an upper sphere:
—By stirring up a lower, much I fear!

V.13 his] that *MS, 1862*
VI.3 love] Love *MS; cf. line 8*
VI.10 aim] name *del. MS*
VI.16 They sat] We sit *del. MS*

How deftly that oiled barber lays his bloom!
That long-shanked dapper Cupid with frisked curls,
Can make known women torturingly fair;
The gold-eyed serpent dwelling in rich hair,
Awakes beneath his magic whisks and twirls.
His art can take the eyes from out my head,
Until I see with eyes of other men;   10
While deeper knowledge crouches in its den,
And sends a spark up:—is it true we are wed?
Yea! filthiness of body is most vile,
But faithlessness of heart I do hold worse.
The former, it were not so great a curse
To read on the steel-mirror of her smile.

VIII

Yet it was plain she struggled, and that salt
Of righteous feeling made her pitiful.
Poor twisting worm, so queenly beautiful!
Where came the cleft between us? whose the fault?
My tears are on thee, that have rarely dropped
As balm for any bitter wound of mine:
My breast will open for thee at a sign!
But, no: we are two reed-pipes, coarsely stopped:
The God once filled them with his mellow breath;
And they were music till he flung them down,   10
Used! used! Hear now the discord-loving clown
Puff his gross spirit in them, worse than death!
I do not know myself without thee more:
In this unholy battle I grow base:
If the same soul be under the same face,
Speak, and a taste of that old time restore!

VII.7 The gold-eyed] And all the *del. MS*   rich] deep[?] *del. MS*
VII.11 its] the[?] *del. MS*
VII.12 up:—is it] is't *del. MS*   we are] we're *MS, 1862*
VIII.3 Poor twisting] O abject *MS, 1862*
VIII.10 And they were music] Ah! sweet the music *del. MS*
VIII.11 Hear] And *del. MS*
VIII.12 Puff] Puffs *del. MS*

IX

He felt the wild beast in him betweenwhiles
So masterfully rude, that he would grieve
To see the helpless delicate thing receive
His guardianship through certain dark defiles.
Had he not teeth to rend, and hunger too?
But still he spared her. Once: 'Have you no fear?'
He said: 'twas dusk; she in his grasp; none near.
She laughed: 'No, surely; am I not with you?'
And uttering that soft starry 'you,' she leaned
Her gentle body near him, looking up;   10
And from her eyes, as from a poison-cup,
He drank until the flittering eyelids screened.
Devilish malignant witch! and oh, young beam
Of heaven's circle-glory! Here thy shape
To squeeze like an intoxicating grape—
I might, and yet thou goest safe, supreme.

X

But where began the change; and what's my crime?
The wretch condemned, who has not been arraigned,
Chafes at his sentence. Shall I, unsustained,

IX.3 helpless] tender *del. MS*
IX.9 soft starry] sweet[?] star-like *del. MS*

Sonnet X not in MS, instead:

Contest not, we learn much from misery.
I knew not women till I suffer'd thus:
[All that *del.*] The things they are, and may be, unto us.
She gives the key with her inconstancy.
They must see Love to feel him, & no less
He dies if his pursuing [eyes *del.*] gaze they miss:
[As *del.*] Lo, if you break the habit of a kiss,
And it comes strange, so comes their bashfulness!
Narrow'd in that hot centre of their life
Where instincts rule, they bind you to its laws,
These shifting sandbanks [that *del.*] which the ebb-tide draws!—
You have a one-month's bride, & then a wife
Who weens that time deposes her; rebels:
While you are living upward to the air,
Those passions that are spawn of low despair,
She clasps, & gets the comfort that is Hell's.
Del.: for hungry comfort, even Hell's!

Drag on Love's nerveless body thro' all time?
I must have slept, since now I wake. Prepare,
You lovers, to know Love a thing of moods:
Not like hard life, of laws. In Love's deep woods,
I dreamt of loyal Life:—the offence is there!
Love's jealous woods about the sun are curled;
At least, the sun far brighter there did beam.—   10
My crime is, that the puppet of a dream,
I plotted to be worthy of the world.
Oh, had I with my darling helped to mince
The facts of life, you still had seen me go
With hindward feather and with forward toe,
Her much-adored delightful Fairy Prince!

                         XI

Out in the yellow meadows, where the bee
Hums by us with the honey of the Spring,
And showers of sweet notes from the larks on wing,
Are dropping like a noon-dew, wander we.
Or is it now? or was it then? for now,
As then, the larks from running rings pour showers:
The golden foot of May is on the flowers,
And friendly shadows dance upon her brow.
What's this, when Nature swears there is no change
To challenge eyesight? Now, as then, the grace   10
Of heaven seems holding earth in its embrace.
Nor eyes, nor heart, has she to feel it strange?
Look, woman, in the West. There wilt thou see

XI.2 Hums] Hummed *del. MS*
XI.4 *MS del.*: Were dropping like a dewy noon, wander'd we.
XI.5 is] was *del. MS*
XI.6 pour] shed *MS;* send *1862, 1892*
XI.7 is] was *del. MS*
XI.8 dance] danc'd *del. MS*
XI.9 change] change? *MS*
XI.10 To challenge eyesight?] Which is the liar? *MS*   grace] race *del. MS*
XI.12 *MS:* Discerneth she the difference, sad & strange?

An amber cradle near the sun's decline:
Within it, featured even in death divine,
Is lying a dead infant, slain by thee.

XII

Not solely that the Future she destroys,
And the fair life which in the distance lies
For all men, beckoning out from dim rich skies:
Nor that the passing hour's supporting joys
Have lost the keen-edged flavour, which begat
Distinction in old times, and still should breed
Sweet Memory, and Hope,—earth's modest seed,
And heaven's high-prompting: not that the world is
    flat
Since that soft-luring creature I embraced,
Among the children of Illusion went: 10
Methinks with all this loss I were content,
If the mad Past, on which my foot is based,
Were firm, or might be blotted: but the whole
Of life is mixed: the mocking Past will stay:
And if I drink oblivion of a day,
So shorten I the stature of my soul.

XIII

'I play for Seasons; not Eternities!'
Says Nature, laughing on her way. 'So must
All those whose stake is nothing more than dust!'
And lo, she wins, and of her harmonies
She is full sure! Upon her dying rose,
She drops a look of fondness, and goes by,
Scarce any retrospection in her eye;
For she the laws of growth most deeply knows,
Whose hands bear, here, a seed-bag—there, an urn.

XI.14 amber] golden *del. MS*   cradle [hanging *del.*] near *MS*
XII.2 the fair] that fair *del. MS*   which] that *del. MS*
XII.6 times] time *MS, 1862*
XII.12 the] that *del. MS*
XII.14 will] must *MS, 1862*

Pledged she herself to aught, 'twould mark her end!   10
This lesson of our only visible friend,
Can we not teach our foolish hearts to learn?
Yes! yes!—but, oh, our human rose is fair
Surpassingly! Lose calmly Love's great bliss,
When the renewed for ever of a kiss
Whirls life within the shower of loosened hair!

XIV

What soul would bargain for a cure that brings
Contempt the nobler agony to kill?
Rather let me bear on the bitter ill,
And strike this rusty bosom with new stings!
It seems there is another veering fit,
Since on a gold-haired lady's eyeballs pure,
I looked with little prospect of a cure,
The while her mouth's red bow loosed shafts of wit.
Just heaven! can it be true that jealousy
Has decked the woman thus? and does her head   10
Swim somewhat for possessions forfeited?
Madam, you teach me many things that be.
I open an old book, and there I find,
That 'Women still may love whom they deceive.'
Such love I prize not, madam: by your leave,
The game you play at is not to my mind.

XV

I think she sleeps: it must be sleep, when low
Hangs that abandoned arm toward the floor;
The face turned with it. Now make fast the door.
Sleep on: it is your husband, not your foe.

XIII.13 fair] sweet[?] *del. MS*
XIII.14 Love's] that *del. MS*
XIII.15 for ever] forever *MS, 1862*
XIII.16 *MS, 1862:* Sounds thro' the listless hurricane of hair!
XIV.1 *MS:* Not such a cure, not such a cure, which brings
XIV.2 kill?] kill! *MS*
XIV.6 on a] in that *del. MS*   eyeballs] eyeballs *del.* eyelids [?] *MS*
XIV.11 *MS, 1862:* Whirl giddily for what she forfeited?
XIV.14 whom] tho[?] *del. MS*
XV.2 toward] towards *MS, 1862*
XV.3 face] head *MS, 1862*

The Poet's black stage-lion of wronged love,
Frights not our modern dames:—well if he did!
Now will I pour new light upon that lid,
Full-sloping like the breasts beneath. 'Sweet dove,
Your sleep is pure. Nay, pardon: I disturb.
I do not? good!' Her waking infant-stare   10
Grows woman to the burden my hands bear:
Her own handwriting to me when no curb
Was left on Passion's tongue. She trembles through;
A woman's tremble—the whole instrument:—
I show another letter lately sent.
The words are very like: the name is new.

XVI

In our old shipwrecked days there was an hour,
When in the firelight steadily aglow,
Joined slackly, we beheld the red chasm grow
Among the clicking coals. Our library-bower
That eve was left to us: and hushed we sat
As lovers to whom Time is whispering.
From sudden-opened doors we heard them sing:
The nodding elders mixed good wine with chat.
Well knew we that Life's greatest treasure lay
With us, and of it was our talk. 'Ah, yes!   10
Love dies!' I said: I never thought it less.
She yearned to me that sentence to unsay.
Then when the fire domed blackening, I found
Her cheek was salt against my kiss, and swift
Up the sharp scale of sobs her breast did lift:—
Now am I haunted by that taste! that sound!

XV.7 lid] open *del.* lid *MS*
XV.8 *MS del.:* That slopes as slopes the bosom. "Gentle dove!
XV.9 Your sleep is pure] Awake! 'tis I! *del. MS*
XV.10 good] well *MS, 1862*
XV.11 Grows woman to] Slowly discerns *del. MS*   my] his *del. MS*
XV.16 words are very] wondrous[?] *del.* tone is very *del. MS*
XVI.3 red chasm] chasm *MS, 1862*
XVI.11 thought] felt *MS*
XVI.13 domed] was[?] *del. MS*
XVI.15 sobs] tears *del. MS*

XVII

At dinner, she is hostess, I am host.
Went the feast ever cheerfuller? She keeps
The Topic over intellectual deeps
In buoyancy afloat. They see no ghost.
With sparkling surface-eyes we ply the ball:
It is in truth a most contagious game:
HIDING THE SKELETON, shall be its name.
Such play as this, the devils might appal!
But here's the greater wonder; in that we
Enamoured of an acting nought can tire,   10
Each other, like true hypocrites, admire;
Warm-lighted looks, Love's ephemerioe,
Shoot gaily o'er the dishes and the wine.
We waken envy of our happy lot.
Fast, sweet, and golden, shows the marriage-knot.
Dear guests, you now have seen Love's corpse-light
    shine.

XVIII

Here Jack and Tom are paired with Moll and Meg.
Curved open to the river-reach is seen
A country merry-making on the green.
Fair space for signal shakings of the leg.

XVII.2 Went the feast ever] Did ever feast run *del. MS*
XVII.10–11 *MS del.:*
                    Enamour'd of each other's acting, feel
                    An admiration we cannot conceal.
      MS, 1862:
                    Enamour'd of our acting and our wits,
                    Admire each other like true hypocrites.
XVII.12 Warm-lighted looks] The glances that are *del. MS;* Warm-lighted glances *MS,*
1862   ephemerioe] Ephemeræ *MS, 1862;* ephemeridæ *Mem. Ed.*
XVII.14–15 *MS del.:*
                    And we are envied?—Why not? for so complete
                    A union few behold & fewer meet.
XVII.14 We waken] There is much *del. MS*
XVII.15 the] our *MS, 1862*
XVII.16 Dear guests] Fair friends *del. MS*

Sonnet XVIII, sonnet 19 MS
XVIII.1 Here] Here's *MS*   are] well *MS*

That little screwy fiddler from his booth,
Whence flows one nut-brown stream, commands the
    joints
Of all who caper here at various points.
I have known rustic revels in my youth:
The May-fly pleasures of a mind at ease.
An early goddess was a country lass: 10
A charmed Amphion-oak she tripped the grass.
What life was that I lived? The life of these?
Heaven keep them happy! Nature they seem near.
They must, I think, be wiser than I am;
They have the secret of the bull and lamb.
'Tis true that when we trace its source, 'tis beer.

XIX

No state is enviable. To the luck alone
Of some few favoured men I would put claim.
I bleed, but her who wounds I will not blame.
Have I not felt her heart as 'twere my own
Beat thro' me? could I hurt her? heaven and hell!
But I could hurt her cruelly! Can I let
My Love's old time-piece to another set,
Swear it can't stop, and must for ever swell?
Sure, that's one way Love drifts into the mart
Where goat-legged buyers throng. I see not plain:—   10
My meaning is, it must not be again.
Great God! the maddest gambler throws his heart.

XVIII.6 nut-brown stream] one stream of beer *del. MS*
XVIII.10 An early] [?] my first *del.* My earliest *del. MS*   country] *MS, 1862, corr.*
errata, de L 1911; county *1892, 1894, de L*
XVIII.13 Heaven] God *MS, 1862*   seem] are *MS, 1862*
XVIII.15 *MS del.*: There roars a human bull: here frisks a lamb.
XVIII.16 *MS del.*: But half of this *or* 'Tis true the whole may find its source in beer
trace its] ask the *del.* seek its *MS*

Sonnet XIX, sonnet 20 MS

XIX.3 her] she *MS, 1862*
XIX.9 Love] they *del. MS*
XIX.10 see] am *del.*
XIX.12 throws] stakes *del. MS*

If any state be enviable on earth,
'Tis yon born idiot's, who, as days go by,
Still rubs his hands before him, like a fly,
In a queer sort of meditative mirth.

XX

I am not of those miserable males
Who sniff at vice and, daring not to snap,
Do therefore hope for heaven. I take the hap
Of all my deeds. The wind that fills my sails,
Propels; but I am helmsman. Am I wrecked,
I know the devil has sufficient weight
To bear: I lay it not on him, or fate.
Besides, he's damned. That man I do suspect
A coward, who would burden the poor deuce
With what ensues from his own slipperiness.   10
I have just found a wanton-scented tress
In an old desk, dusty for lack of use.
Of days and nights it is demonstrative,
That, like some aged star, gleam luridly.
If for those times I must ask charity,
Have I not any charity to give?

XXI

We three are on the cedar-shadowed lawn;
My friend being third. He who at love once laughed,
Is in the weak rib by a fatal shaft
Struck through, and tells his passion's bashful dawn

XIX.14 'Tis yon born] Yon village *del. MS*
XIX.15 Still] Yet[?] *del. MS*
XIX.16 queer] strange *del. MS*   mirth] glee *del. MS*

Sonnet XX, sonnet 21 MS

XX.10 what ensues from] that which comes of *del. MS*
XX.12 desk, dusty] drawer put by *del. MS*
XX.14 some aged] a blasted *del. MS*
XX.15 those times] that time *MS, 1862*

Sonnet XXI, sonnet 22 MS

XXI.1 on the cedar-shadowed] sitting on the Summer *del. MS*

And radiant culmination, glorious crown,
When 'this' she said: went 'thus': most wondrous she.
Our eyes grow white, encountering: that we are three,
Forgetful; then together we look down.
But he demands our blessing; is convinced
That words of wedded lovers must bring good.   10
We question; if we dare! or if we should!
And pat him, with light laugh. We have not winced.
Next, she has fallen. Fainting points the sign
To happy things in wedlock. When she wakes,
She looks the star that thro' the cedar shakes:
Her lost moist hand clings mortally to mine.

XXII

What may the woman labour to confess?
There is about her mouth a nervous twitch.
'Tis something to be told, or hidden:—which?
I get a glimpse of hell in this mild guess.
She has desires of touch, as if to feel
That all the household things are things she knew.
She stops before the glass. What sight in view?
A face that seems the latest to reveal!
For she turns from it hastily, and tossed
Irresolute, steals shadow-like to where   10
I stand; and wavering pale before me there,
Her tears fall still as oak-leaves after frost.
She will not speak. I will not ask. We are
League-sundered by the silent gulf between.
You burly lovers on the village green,
Yours is a lower, and a happier star!

XXI.12 *MS del.:* We laugh [?] & pat him. Neither winced
XXI.14 wedlock] marriage *del. MS*
XXI.16 lost] round [?] *del. MS*
Sonnet XXII, sonnet 23 MS
XXII.1 the] this *MS, 1862*
XXII.7 sight in] does she *MS, 1862*
XXII.9 tossed] steals *del.* tost *MS*
XXII.10 steals shadow-like] comes [?] up *del. MS*
XXII.13 will] must *del. MS*
XXII.16 and] but *MS, 1862*

XXIII

'Tis Christmas weather, and a country house
Receives us: rooms are full: we can but get
An attic-crib. Such lovers will not fret
At that, it is half-said. The great carouse
Knocks hard upon the midnight's hollow door,
But when I knock at hers, I see the pit.
Why did I come here in that dullard fit?
I enter, and lie couched upon the floor.
Passing, I caught the coverlet's quick beat:—
Come, Shame, burn to my soul! and Pride, and
    Pain—   10
Foul demons that have tortured me, enchain!
Out in the freezing darkness the lambs bleat.
The small bird stiffens in the low starlight.
I know not how, but shuddering as I slept,
I dreamed a banished angel to me crept:
My feet were nourished on her breasts all night.

XXIV

The misery is greater, as I live!
To know her flesh so pure, so keen her sense,
That she does penance now for no offence,
Save against Love. The less can I forgive!
The less can I forgive, though I adore
That cruel lovely pallor which surrounds
Her footsteps; and the low vibrating sounds
That come on me, as from a magic shore.
Low are they, but most subtle to find out
The shrinking soul. Madam, 'tis understood   10
When women play upon their womanhood;

Sonnet XXIII, sonnet 24 MS

XXIII.9 caught] saw *del. MS*   coverlet's] coverlid's *MS, 1862*
XXIII.11 enchain] sustain *MS, 1862*
XXIII.13 bird] birds *del. MS*   low] great *del. MS*

Sonnet XXIV, sonnet 25 MS

XXIV.8 a] the *MS*
XXIV.10 The shrinking soul. Madam,] The loathing soul *del.* The soul that still would loathe *del. MS*

It means, a Season gone. And yet I doubt
But I am duped. That nun-like look waylays
My fancy. Oh! I do but wait a sign!
Pluck out the eyes of pride! thy mouth to mine!
Never! though I die thirsting. Go thy ways!

XXV

You like not that French novel? Tell me why.
You think it quite unnatural. Let us see.
The actors are, it seems, the usual three:
Husband, and wife, and lover. She—but fie!
In England we'll not hear of it. Edmond,
The lover, her devout chagrin doth share;
Blanc-mange and absinthe are his penitent fare,
Till his pale aspect makes her over-fond:
So, to preclude fresh sin, he tries rosbif.
Meantime the husband is no more abused: 10
Auguste forgives her ere the tear is used.
Then hangeth all on one tremendous IF:—
If she will choose between them. She does choose;
And takes her husband, like a proper wife.
Unnatural? My dear, these things are life:
And life, some think, is worthy of the Muse.

XXVI

Love ere he bleeds, an eagle in high skies,
Has earth beneath his wings: from reddened eve
He views the rosy dawn. In vain they weave
The fatal web below while far he flies.

Sonnet XXV, sonnet 26 MS

XXV.2 quite] most *MS, 1862*
XXV.3 it seems] methinks *del. MS*
XXV.6 her devout chagrin doth share] is most surely[?] penitent *del. MS*
XXV.7 penitent fare] nourishment *del. MS*
XXV.11 the] one *MS*
XXV.12 Then hangeth all] Now doth all hang *del. MS*
XXV.14 proper] worthy *del. MS*
XXV.16 some think] they say *MS, 1862*

Sonnet XXVI, sonnet 27 MS

But when the arrow strikes him, there's a change.
He moves but in the track of his spent pain,
Whose red drops are the links of a harsh chain,
Binding him to the ground, with narrow range.
A subtle serpent then has Love become.
I had the eagle in my bosom erst: 10
Henceforward with the serpent I am cursed.
I can interpret where the mouth is dumb.
Speak, and I see the side-lie of a truth.
Perchance my heart may pardon you this deed:
But be no coward:—you that made Love bleed,
You must bear all the venom of his tooth!

XXVII

Distraction is the panacea, Sir!
I hear my oracle of Medicine say.
Doctor! that same specific yesterday
I tried, and the result will not deter
A second trial. Is the devil's line
Of golden hair, or raven black, composed?
And does a cheek, like any sea-shell rosed,
Or clear as widowed sky, seem most divine?
No matter, so I taste forgetfulness.
And if the devil snare me, body and mind,   10
Here gratefully I score:—he seemëd kind,
When not a soul would comfort my distress!
O sweet new world, in which I rise new made!
O Lady, once I gave love: now I take!
Lady, I must be flattered. Shouldst thou wake
The passion of a demon, be not afraid.

XXVI.6 pain] blood *del. MS*
XXVI.16 *MS del.:* Yea, in a kiss take venom from his tooth!

Sonnet XXVII, sonnet 28 MS

XXVII.8 clear] fair *MS, 1862*   widowed sky] twilight Heavens *del.* widow'd Heaven
MS   sky] Heaven *1862*
XXVII.12 comfort] solace *del. MS*

XXVIII

I must be flattered. The imperious
Desire speaks out. Lady, I am content
To play with you the game of Sentiment,
And with you enter on paths perilous;
But if across your beauty I throw light,
To make it threefold, it must be all mine.
First secret; then avowed. For I must shine
Envied,—I, lessened in my proper sight!
Be watchful of your beauty, Lady dear!
How much hangs on that lamp you cannot tell.   10
Most earnestly I pray you, tend it well:
And men shall see me as a burning sphere;
And men shall mark you eyeing me, and groan
To be the God of such a grand sunflower!
I feel the promptings of Satanic power,
While you do homage unto me alone.

XXIX

Am I failing? For no longer can I cast
A glory round about this head of gold.
Glory she wears, but springing from the mould;
Not like the consecration of the Past!
Is my soul beggared? Something more than earth
I cry for still: I cannot be at peace
In having Love upon a mortal lease.
I cannot take the woman at her worth!
Where is the ancient wealth wherewith I clothed
Our human nakedness, and could endow   10
With spiritual splendour a white brow
That else had grinned at me the fact I loathed?

Sonnet XXVIII, sonnet 29 MS

XXVIII.4 with you enter] enter with you *del. MS*
XXVIII.12 as a] like the *MS, 1862*
XXVIII.13 groan] long[?] *del. MS*
XXVIII.15 promptings] surgings[?] *del. MS*

Sonnet XXIX, sonnet 30 MS

A kiss is but a kiss now! and no wave
Of a great flood that whirls me to the sea.
But, as you will! we'll sit contentedly,
And eat our pot of honey on the grave.

XXX

What are we first? First, animals; and next
Intelligences at a leap; on whom
Pale lies the distant shadow of the tomb,
And all that draweth on the tomb for text.
Into which state comes Love, the crowning sun:
Beneath whose light the shadow loses form.
We are the lords of life, and life is warm.
Intelligence and instinct now are one.
But Nature says: 'My children most they seem
When they least know me: therefore I decree   10
That they shall suffer.' Swift doth young Love flee,
And we stand wakened, shivering from our dream.
Then if we study Nature we are wise.
Thus do the few who live but with the day:
The scientific animals are they.—
Lady, this is my sonnet to your eyes.

XXXI

This golden head has wit in it. I live
Again, and a far higher life, near her.
Some women like a young philosopher;
Perchance because he is diminutive.
For woman's manly god must not exceed
Proportions of the natural nursing size.

Sonnet XXX, sonnet 31 MS

XXX.3 Pale] There *del. MS*   distant] heavy *del. MS*
XXX.5 which] this *MS, 1862*
XXX.9 Nature] *MS, 1862; cf. line 13;* nature *1892, 1894, de L*
XXX.10 they least] least they *MS*
XXX.11 Swift] Then *del. MS*
XXX.16 sonnet] love-chant *MS*

Sonnet XXXI, sonnet 32 MS

XXXI.3 Some women like] She rather likes *del. MS*

Great poets and great sages draw no prize
With women: but the little lap-dog breed,
Who can be hugged, or on a mantel-piece
Perched up for adoration, these obtain   10
Her homage. And of this we men are vain?
Of this! 'Tis ordered for the world's increase!
Small flattery! Yet she has that rare gift
To beauty, Common Sense. I am approved.
It is not half so nice as being loved,
And yet I do prefer it. What's my drift?

XXXII

Full faith I have she holds that rarest gift
To beauty, Common Sense. To see her lie
With her fair visage an inverted sky
Bloom-covered, while the underlids uplift,
Would almost wreck the faith; but when her mouth
(Can it kiss sweetly? sweetly!) would address
The inner me that thirsts for her no less,
And has so long been languishing in drouth,
·I feel that I am matched; that I am man!
One restless corner of my heart or head,   10
That holds a dying something never dead,
Still frets, though Nature giveth all she can.
It means, that woman is not, I opine,
Her sex's antidote. Who seeks the asp
For serpents' bites? 'Twould calm me could I clasp
Shrieking Bacchantes with their souls of wine!

XXXI.10 obtain] are they *MS*
XXXI.11 *MS*: Who win her homage. Know I what I say?
XXXI.12 Of this! 'Tis ordered] Yes, certainly, 'Tis *MS*
XXXI.14 beauty] women *del. MS*

Sonnet XXXII, sonnet 33 MS

XXXII.4 Bloom-covered] Beneath me *MS*   underlids] blue *del.* underlids *MS*
XXXII.8 And] That *del. MS*
XXXII.12 frets] fumes *del. MS*
XXXII.13 It means, that woman is not] Woman is not her own cure *del. MS*
XXXII.14 Her sex's] Its[?] *del. MS*
XXXII.15 serpents'] *MS, 1862, corr. errata, de L 1911;* serpent's *1892, 1894, de L*
could I] still[?] to *del. MS*

XXXIII

'In Paris, at the Louvre, there have I seen
The sumptuously-feathered angel pierce
Prone Lucifer, descending. Looked he fierce,
Showing the fight a fair one? Too serene!
The young Pharsalians did not disarray
Less willingly their locks of floating silk:
That suckling mouth of his, upon the milk
Of heaven might still be feasting through the fray.
Oh, Raphael! when men the Fiend do fight,
They conquer not upon such easy terms.   10
Half serpent in the struggle grow these worms.
And does he grow half human, all is right.'
This to my Lady in a distant spot,
Upon the theme: *While mind is mastering clay,*
Gross clay invades it. If the spy you play,
My wife, read this! Strange love talk, is it not?

XXXIV

Madam would speak with me. So, now it comes:
The Deluge or else Fire! She's well; she thanks
My husbandship. Our chain on silence clanks.
Time leers between, above his twiddling thumbs.
Am I quite well? Most excellent in health!
The journals, too, I diligently peruse.
Vesuvius is expected to give news:
Niagara is no noisier. By stealth

Sonnet XXXIII, sonnet 34 MS

XXXIII.1 there have I] I have *del. MS*
XXXIII.8 heaven] stars *MS, 1862*
XXXIII.9 do fight] engage *del. MS*
XXXIII.10 conquer not upon] do not conquer on *del. MS*
XXXIII.12 *MS del.:* Let's hope he grows half human, from his rage.
XXXIII.16 read this] my spy *del. MS*

Sonnet XXXIV, sonnet 35 MS

XXXIV.3 on] through *MS, 1862*
XXXIV.4 above his twiddling] us, twiddling his *MS, 1862*
XXXIV.8 Niagara is no noisier] From earth's hot centre. Than our eyes *del. MS*

Our eyes dart scrutinizing snakes. She's glad
I'm happy, says her quivering under-lip.   10
'And are not you?' 'How can I be?' 'Take ship!
For happiness is somewhere to be had.'
'Nowhere for me!' Her voice is barely heard.
I am not melted, and make no pretence.
With commonplace I freeze her, tongue and sense.
Niagara or Vesuvius is deferred.

XXXV

It is no vulgar nature I have wived.
Secretive, sensitive, she takes a wound
Deep to her soul, as if the sense had swooned,
And not a thought of vengeance had survived.
No confidences has she: but relief
Must come to one whose suffering is acute.
O have a care of natures that are mute!
They punish you in acts: their steps are brief.
What is she doing? What does she demand
From Providence or me? She is not one   10
Long to endure this torpidly, and shun
The drugs that crowd about a woman's hand.
At Forfeits during snow we played, and I
Must kiss her. 'Well performed!' I said: then she:
''Tis hardly worth the money, you agree?'
Save her? What for? To act this wedded lie!

XXXVI

My Lady unto Madam makes her bow.
The charm of women is, that even while
You're probed by them for tears, you yet may smile,
Nay, laugh outright, as I have done just now.
The interview was gracious: they anoint

XXXIV.9 Our eyes dart] Dart out the *del. MS*
XXXIV.15 commonplace] truisms *MS, 1862*
Sonnet XXXV, sonnet 36 MS
XXXV.13 during snow] that[?] night *del. MS*
XXXV.16 wedded] two-scorn'd *MS*
Sonnet XXXVI, sonnet 37 MS

(To me aside) each other with fine praise:
Discriminating compliments they raise,
That hit with wondrous aim on the weak point:
My Lady's nose of Nature might complain.
It is not fashioned aptly to express   10
Her character of large-browed steadfastness.
But Madam says: Thereof she may be vain!
Now, Madam's faulty feature is a glazed
And inaccessible eye, that has soft fires,
Wide gates, at love-time only. This admires
My Lady. At the two I stand amazed.

XXXVII

Along the garden terrace, under which
A purple valley (lighted at its edge
By smoky torch-flame on the long cloud-ledge
Whereunder dropped the chariot), glimmers rich,
A quiet company we pace, and wait
The dinner-bell in prae-digestive calm.
So sweet up violet banks the Southern balm
Breathes round, we care not if the bell be late:
Though here and there grey seniors question Time
In irritable coughings. With slow foot   10
The low rosed moon, the face of Music mute,
Begins among her silent bars to climb.
As in and out, in silvery dusk, we thread,
I hear the laugh of Madam, and discern
My Lady's heel before me at each turn.
Our tragedy, is it alive or dead?

XXXVIII

Give to imagination some pure light
In human form to fix it, or you shame
The devils with that hideous human game:—
Imagination urging appetite!

XXXVI.6 (To me aside) each other] Each other subsequently *del. MS*
XXXVI.11 steadfastness] stedfastness *MS, 1862*
XXXVI.15 Wide gates, at love-time only] And open gates at love-time *del. MS*
End of MS

Thus fallen have earth's greatest Gogmagogs,
Who dazzle us, whom we can not revere:
Imagination is the charioteer
That, in default of better, drives the hogs.
So, therefore, my dear Lady, let me love!
My soul is arrowy to the light in you.   10
You know me that I never can renew
The bond that woman broke: what would you have?
'Tis Love, or Vileness! not a choice between,
Save petrifaction! What does Pity here?
She killed a thing, and now it's dead, 'tis dear.
Oh, when you counsel me, think what you mean!

XXXIX

She yields: my Lady in her noblest mood
Has yielded: she, my golden-crownëd rose!
The bride of every sense! more sweet than those
Who breathe the violet breath of maidenhood.
O visage of still music in the sky!
Soft moon! I feel thy song, my fairest friend!
True harmony within can apprehend
Dumb harmony without. And hark! 'tis nigh!
Belief has struck the note of sound: a gleam
Of living silver shows me where she shook   10
Her long white fingers down the shadowy brook,
That sings her song, half-waking, half in dream.
What two come here to mar this heavenly tune?
A man is one: the woman bears my name,
And honour. Their hands touch! Am I still tame?
God, what a dancing spectre seems the moon!

XL

I bade my Lady think what she might mean.
Know I my meaning, I? Can I love one,
And yet be jealous of another? None
Commits such folly. Terrible Love, I ween,

XXXVIII.10 arrowy] arrow'd *1862*
XL.4 Commits] Commit *1862*

Has might, even dead, half sighing to upheave
The lightless seas of selfishness amain:
Seas that in a man's heart have no rain
To fall and still them. Peace can I achieve,
By turning to this fountain-source of woe,
This woman, who's to Love as fire to wood?   10
She breathed the violet breath of maidenhood
Against my kisses once! but I say, No!
The thing is mocked at! Helplessly afloat,
I know not what I do, whereto I strive,
The dread that my old love may be alive,
Has seized my nursling new love by the throat.

XLI

How many a thing which we cast to the ground,
When others pick it up becomes a gem!
We grasp at all the wealth it is to them;
And by reflected light its worth is found.
Yet for us still 'tis nothing! and that zeal
Of false appreciation quickly fades.
This truth is little known to human shades,
How rare from their own instinct 'tis to feel!
They waste the soul with spurious desire,
That is not the ripe flame upon the bough.   10
We two have taken up a lifeless vow
To rob a living passion: dust for fire!
Madam is grave, and eyes the clock that tells
Approaching midnight. We have struck despair
Into two hearts. O, look we like a pair
Who for fresh nuptials joyfully yield all else?

XLII

I am to follow her. There is much grace
In women when thus bent on martyrdom.
They think that dignity of soul may come,
Perchance, with dignity of body. Base!

XLII.2 women] *1862, corr. errata, de L 1911;* woman *1892, 1894, de L*

But I was taken by that air of cold
And statuesque sedateness, when she said
'I'm going'; lit a taper, bowed her head,
And went, as with the stride of Pallas bold.
Fleshly indifference horrible! The hands
Of Time now signal: O, she's safe from me!   10
Within those secret walls what do I see?
Where first she set the taper down she stands:
Not Pallas: Hebe shamed! Thoughts black as death,
Like a stirred pool in sunshine break. Her wrists
I catch: she faltering, as she half resists,
'You love . . .? love . . .? love . . .?' all on an indrawn
    breath.

XLIII

Mark where the pressing wind shoots javelin-like,
Its skeleton shadow on the broad-backed wave!
Here is a fitting spot to dig Love's grave;
Here where the ponderous breakers plunge and strike,
And dart their hissing tongues high up the sand:
In hearing of the ocean, and in sight
Of those ribbed wind-streaks running into white.
If I the death of Love had deeply planned,
I never could have made is half so sure,
As by the unblest kisses which upbraid   10
The full-waked sense; or failing that, degrade!
'Tis morning: but no morning can restore
What we have forfeited. I see no sin:
The wrong is mixed. In tragic life, God wot,
No villain need be! Passions spin the plot:
We are betrayed by what is false within.

XLIV

They say, that Pity in Love's service dwells,
A porter at the rosy temple's gate.
I missed him going: but it is my fate
To come upon him now beside his wells;

XLII.7 a] the *1862*   XLII.16 on] in *1862, 1892, 1894*

Whereby I know that I Love's temple leave,
And that the purple doors have closed behind.
Poor soul! if in those early days unkind,
Thy power to sting had been but power to grieve,
We now might with an equal spirit meet,
And not be matched like innocence and vice.   10
She for the Temple's worship has paid price,
And takes the coin of Pity as a cheat.
She sees through simulation to the bone:
What's best in her impels her to the worst:
Never, she cries, shall Pity soothe Love's thirst,
Or foul hypocrisy for truth atone!

XLV

It is the season of the sweet wild rose,
My Lady's emblem in the heart of me!
So golden-crownëd shines she gloriously,
And with that softest dream of blood she glows:
Mild as an evening heaven round Hesper bright!
I pluck the flower, and smell it, and revive
The time when in her eyes I stood alive.
I seem to look upon it out of Night.
Here's Madam, stepping hastily. Her whims
Bid her demand the flower, which I let drop.   10
As I proceed, I feel her sharply stop,
And crush it under heel with trembling limbs.
She joins me in a cat-like way, and talks
Of company, and even condescends
To utter laughing scandal of old friends.
These are the summer days, and these our walks.

XLVI

At last we parley: we so strangely dumb
In such a close communion! It befell
About the sounding of the Matin-bell,
And lo! her place was vacant, and the hum

Of loneliness was round me. Then I rose,
And my disordered brain did guide my foot
To that old wood where our first love-salute
Was interchanged: the source of many throes!
There did I see her, not alone. I moved
Toward her, and made proffer of my arm.   10
She took it simply, with no rude alarm;
And that disturbing shadow passed reproved.
I felt the pained speech coming, and declared
My firm belief in her, ere she could speak.
A ghastly morning came into her cheek,
While with a widening soul on me she stared.

XLVII

We saw the swallows gathering in the sky,
And in the osier-isle we heard them noise.
We had not to look back on summer joys,
Or forward to a summer of bright dye:
But in the largeness of the evening earth
Our spirits grew as we went side by side.
The hour became her husband and my bride.
Love that had robbed us so, thus blessed our dearth!
The pilgrims of the year waxed very loud
In multitudinous chatterings, as the flood   10
Full brown came from the West, and like pale blood
Expanded to the upper crimson cloud.
Love that had robbed us of immortal things,
This little moment mercifully gave,
Where I have seen across the twilight wave
The swan sail with her young beneath her wings.

XLVIII

Their sense is with their senses all mixed in,
Destroyed by subtleties these women are!
More brain, O Lord, more brain! or we shall mar
Utterly this fair garden we might win.

XLVI.10 Toward] Towards *1862*
XLVII.2 them] their *1862, 1892, 1894*
XLVII.15 Where I have seen] And still I see *1862*

Behold! I looked for peace, and thought it near.
Our inmost hearts had opened, each to each.
We drank the pure daylight of honest speech.
Alas! that was the fatal draught, I fear.
For when of my lost Lady came the word,
This woman, O this agony of flesh!   10
Jealous devotion bade her break the mesh,
That I might seek that other like a bird.
I do adore the nobleness! despise
The act! She has gone forth, I know not where.
Will the hard world my sentience of her share?
I feel the truth; so let the world surmise.

XLIX

He found her by the ocean's moaning verge,
Nor any wicked change in her discerned;
And she believed his old love had returned,
Which was her exultation, and her scourge.
She took his hand, and walked with him, and seemed
The wife he sought, though shadow-like and dry.
She had one terror, lest her heart should sigh,
And tell her loudly she no longer dreamed.
She dared not say, 'This is my breast: look in.'
But there's a strength to help the desperate weak.   10
That night he learned how silence best can speak
The awful things when Pity pleads for Sin.
About the middle of the night her call
Was heard, and he came wondering to the bed.
'Now kiss me, dear! it may be, now!' she said.
Lethe had passed those lips, and he knew all.

L

Thus piteously Love closed what he begat:
The union of this ever-diverse pair!
These two were rapid falcons in a snare,
Condemned to do the flitting of the bat.

Lovers beneath the singing sky of May,
They wandered once; clear as the dew on flowers:
But they fed not on the advancing hours:
Their hearts held cravings for the buried day.
Then each applied to each that fatal knife,
Deep questioning, which probes to endless dole.   10
Ah, what a dusty answer gets the soul
When hot for certainties in this our life!—
In tragic hints here see what evermore
Moves dark as yonder midnight ocean's force,
Thundering like ramping hosts of warrior horse,
To throw that faint thin line upon the shore!

Roadside Philosophers

Juggling Jerry

GM wrote to Samuel Lucas [July 7, 1859] asking him to send proofs of this poem, and he added: "Don't be too rigorous about our friend's rhythm. I'll do what I can, but I do not wish to destroy the emphasis of his phrases."

When he prepared his poems for the Edition de Luxe, he removed this poem from the group entitled *Poems from " Modern Love": 1862* and placed it, together with *The Old Chartist* and *Martin's Puzzle*, under the heading *Verses* (Edition de Luxe 3).

I

Pitch here the tent, while the old horse grazes:
    By the old hedge-side we'll halt a stage.
It's nigh my last above the daisies:
    My next leaf'll be man's blank page.

JUGGLING JERRY

Previously printed in Once a Week *1 (3 September 1859), title:* The Last Words of Juggling Jerry. *Variants are from* OaW.

Yes, my old girl! and it's no use crying:
    Juggler, constable, king, must bow.
One that outjuggles all's been spying
    Long to have me, and he has me now.

II

We've travelled times to this old common:
    Often we've hung our pots in the gorse.
We've had a stirring life, old woman!
    You, and I, and the old grey horse.
Races, and fairs, and royal occasions,
    Found us coming to their call:
Now they'll miss us at our stations:
    There's a Juggler outjuggles all!

III

Up goes the lark, as if all were jolly!
    Over the duck-pond the willow shakes.
Easy to think that grieving's folly,
    When the hand's firm as driven stakes!
Ay, when we're strong, and braced, and manful,
    Life's a sweet fiddle: but we're a batch
Born to become the Great Juggler's han'ful:
    Balls he shies up, and is safe to catch.

IV

Here's where the lads of the village cricket:
    I was a lad not wide from here:
Couldn't I whip off the bail from the wicket?
    Like an old world those days appear!
Donkey, sheep, geese, and thatched ale-house—I
    know them!
    They are old friends of my halts, and seem,
Somehow, as if kind thanks I owe them:
    Juggling don't hinder the heart's esteem.

I.8 he has] has
III.3 Easy] It's easy
IV.3 whip off the bail from] juggle the bale [*sic*] off
IV.5 them] 'em
IV.6 They are] They're
IV.7 them] 'em

V

Juggling's no sin, for we must have victual:
    Nature allows us to bait for the fool.
Holding one's own makes us juggle no little;
    But, to increase it, hard juggling's the rule.
You that are sneering at my profession,
    Haven't you juggled a vast amount?
There's the Prime Minister, in one Session,
    Juggles more games than my sins'll count.

VI

I've murdered insects with mock thunder:
    Conscience, for that, in men don't quail.
I've made bread from the bump of wonder:
    That's my business, and there's my tale.
Fashion and rank all praised the professor:
    Ay! and I've had my smile from the Queen:
Bravo, Jerry! she meant: God bless her!
    Ain't this a sermon on that scene?

VII

I've studied men from my topsy-turvy
    Close, and, I reckon, rather true.
Some are fine fellows: some, right scurvy:
    Most, a dash between the two.
But it's a woman, old girl, that makes me
    Think more kindly of the race:
And it's a woman, old girl, that shakes me
    When the Great Juggler I must face.

VIII

We two were married, due and legal:
    Honest we've lived since we've been one.
Lord! I could then jump like an eagle:
    You danced bright as a bit o' the sun.

Birds in a May-bush we were! right merry!
    All night we kiss'd, we juggled all day.
Joy was the heart of Juggling Jerry!
    Now from his old girl he's juggled away.

IX

It's past parsons to console us:
    No, nor no doctor fetch for me:
I can die without my bolus;
    Two of a trade, lass, never agree!
Parson and Doctor!—don't they love rarely,
    Fighting the devil in other men's fields!
Stand up yourself and match him fairly:
    Then see how the rascal yields!

X

I, lass, have lived no gipsy, flaunting
    Finery while his poor helpmate grubs:
Coin I've stored, and you won't be wanting:
    You sha'n't beg from the troughs and tubs.
Nobly you've stuck to me, though in his kitchen
    Many a Marquis would hail you Cook!
Palaces you could have ruled and grown rich in,
    But your old Jerry you never forsook.

XI

Hand up the chirper! ripe ale winks in it;
    Let's have comfort and be at peace.
Once a stout draught made me light as a linnet.
    Cheer up! the Lord must have his lease.
May be—for none see in that black hollow—
    It's just a place where we're held in pawn,
And, when the Great Juggler makes as to swallow,
    It's just the sword-trick—I ain't quite gone!

X.6 Marquis would hail] Duke might kneel to call
X.8 But your old] But old
XI.7 as] us

XII

Yonder came smells of the gorse, so nutty,
    Gold-like and warm: it's the prime of May.
Better than mortar, brick and putty,
    Is God's house on a blowing day.
Lean me more up the mound; now I feel it:
    All the old heath-smells! Ain't it strange?
There's the world laughing, as if to conceal it,
    But He's by us, juggling the change.

XIII

I mind it well, by the sea-beach lying,
    Once—it's long gone—when two gulls we beheld,
Which, as the moon got up, were flying
    Down a big wave that sparked and swelled.
Crack, went a gun: one fell: the second
    Wheeled round him twice, and was off for new
        luck:
There in the dark her white wing beckon'd:—
    Drop me a kiss—I'm the bird dead-struck!

The Old Chartist

This poem was one of three that GM offered to Samuel Lucas for *Once a Week* [before June 12, 1861], if he would "*pay the Muse better.*" GM wrote that this poem would be the best that Lucas had had and suggested Charles Keane as the illustrator for it. The illustration, in fact, was made by the artist Frederick Sandys.

On November 13, 1861, GM wrote Augustus Jessopp, "Note the 'Old Chartist,' and the 'Patriot Engineer,' that will also appear in *Once a Week*. They may not please you; but I think you will admit they have a truth condensed in them. They are flints perhaps, and not flowers."

In the Edition de Luxe this poem was moved from the *Modern Love* poems and placed under the heading *Verses* (Edition de Luxe 3).

JUGGLING JERRY

XII.8 He's] He is
XIII.8 Drop] Give

THE OLD CHARTIST

Previously printed in Once a Week *6 (8 February 1862); reprinted on the same day by the* Ipswich Journal, *and* Suffolk, Norfolk, Essex and Cambridgeshire Advertiser.

I

Whate'er I be, old England is my dam!
    So there's my answer to the judges, clear.
I'm nothing of a fox, nor of a lamb;
        I don't know how to bleat nor how to leer:
            I'm for the nation!
        That's why you see me by the wayside here,
            Returning home from transportation.

II

It's Summer in her bath this morn, I think.
    I'm fresh as dew, and chirpy as the birds:
And just for joy to see old England wink
        Thro' leaves again, I could harangue the herds:
            Isn't it something
        To speak out like a man when you've got words,
            And prove you're not a stupid dumb thing?

III

They shipp'd me off for it; I'm here again.
    Old England is my dam, whate'er I be!
Says I, I'll tramp it home, and see the grain:
    If you see well, you're king of what you see:
            Eyesight is having,
        If you're not given, I said, to gluttony.
            Such talk to ignorance sounds as raving.

IV

You dear old brook, that from his Grace's park
    Come bounding! on you run near my old town:
My lord can't lock the water; nor the lark,
        Unless he kills him, can my lord keep down.
            Up, is the song-note!
        I've tried it, too:—for comfort and renown,
            I rather pitch'd upon the wrong note.

V

I'm not ashamed: Not beaten's still my boast:
   Again I'll rouse the people up to strike.
But home's where different politics jar most.
   Respectability the women like.
      This form, or that form,—
   The Government may be hungry pike,
     But don't you mount a Chartist platform!

VI

Well, well! Not beaten—spite of them, I shout;
   And my estate is suffering for the Cause.—
Now, what is yon brown water-rat about,
   Who washes his old poll with busy paws?
      What does he mean by 't?
   It's like defying all our natural laws,
     For him to hope that he'll get clean by 't.

VII

His seat is on a mud-bank, and his trade
   Is dirt:—he's quite contemptible; and yet
The fellow's all as anxious as a maid
   To show a decent dress, and dry the wet.
      Now it's his whisker,
   And now his nose, and ear: he seems to get
     Each moment at the motion brisker!

VIII

To see him squat like little chaps at school,
   I could let fly a laugh with all my might.
He peers, hangs both his fore-paws:—bless that fool,
   He's bobbing at his frill now!—what a sight!
      Licking the dish up,
   As if he thought to pass from black to white,
     Like parson into lawny bishop.

VI.3 Now] No *misp. 1897*
VIII.2 I could let fly a laugh] I can't help laughing out *OaW, 1862*

IX

The elms and yellow reed-flags in the sun,
    Look on quite grave:—the sunlight flecks his side;
And links of bindweed-flowers round him run,
    And shine up doubled with him in the tide.
        I'm nearly splitting,
    But nature seems like seconding his pride,
        And thinks that his behaviour's fitting.

X

That isle o' mud looks baking dry with gold,
    His needle-muzzle still works out and in.
It really is a wonder to behold,
    And makes me feel the bristles of my chin,
        Judged by appearance,
    I fancy of the two I'm nearer Sin,
        And might as well commence a clearance.

XI

And that's what my fine daughter said:—she meant:
    Pray, hold your tongue, and wear a Sunday face.
Her husband, the young linendraper, spent
    Much argument thereon:—I'm their disgrace.
        Bother the couple!
    I feel superior to a chap whose place
        Commands him to be neat and supple.

XII

But if I go and say to my old hen:
    I'll mend the gentry's boots, and keep discreet,
Until they grow *too* violent,—why, then,
    A warmer welcome I might chance to meet:
        Warmer and better.
    And if she fancies her old cock is beat,
        And drops upon her knees—so let her!

XIII

She suffered for me:—women, you'll observe,
   Don't suffer for a Cause, but for a man.
When I was in the dock she show'd her nerve:
      I saw beneath her shawl my old tea-can
         Trembling . . . she brought it
      To screw me for my work: she loath'd my plan,
         And therefore doubly kind I thought it.

XIV

I've never lost the taste of that same tea:
   That liquor on my logic floats like oil,
When I state facts, and fellows disagree.
      For human creatures all are in a coil;
         All may want pardon.
      I see a day when every pot will boil
         Harmonious in one great Tea-garden!

XV

We wait the setting of the Dandy's day,
   Before that time!—he's furbishing his dress,—
He *will* be ready for it!—and I say,
      That yon old dandy rat amid the cress,—
         Thanks to hard labour!—
      If cleanliness is next to godliness,
         The old fat fellow's heaven's neighbour!

XVI

You teach me a fine lesson, my old boy!
   I've looked on my superiors far too long,
And small has been my profit as my joy.
      You've done the right while I've denounced the
         wrong.
         Prosper me later!
      Like you I will despise the sniggering throng,
         And please myself and my Creator.

XVII

I'll bring the linendraper and his wife
    Some day to see you; taking off my hat.
Should they ask why, I'll answer: in my life
    I never found so true a democrat.
        Base occupation
    Can't rob you of your own esteem, old rat!
    I'll preach you to the British nation.

The Beggar's Soliloquy

I

Now, this, to my notion, is pleasant cheer,
    To lie all alone on a ragged heath,
Where your nose isn't sniffing for bones or beer,
    But a peat-fire smells like a garden beneath.
The cottagers bustle about the door,
    And the girl at the window ties her strings.
She's a dish for a man who's a mind to be poor;
    Lord! women are such expensive things.

II

We don't marry beggars, says she: why, no:
    It seems that to make 'em is what you do;
And as I can cook, and scour, and sew,
    I needn't pay half my victuals for you.
A man for himself should be able to scratch,
    But tickling's a luxury:—love, indeed!
Love burns as long as the lucifer match,
    Wedlock's the candle! Now, that's my creed.

III

The church-bells sound water-like over the wheat;
    And up the long path troop pair after pair.
The man's well-brushed, and the woman looks neat:
    It's man and woman everywhere!

THE BEGGAR'S SOLILOQUY

Previously printed in Once a Week *4 (30 March 1861). Variants are from* OaW.

Unless, like me, you lie here flat,
    With a donkey for friend, you must have a wife:
She pulls out your hair, but she brushes your hat.
    Appearances make the best half of life.

IV

You nice little madam! you know you're nice.
    I remember hearing a parson say
You're a plateful of vanity pepper'd with vice;
    Yon chap at the gate thinks t'other way.
On his waistcoat you read both his head and his heart:
    There's a whole week's wages there figured in gold!
Yes! when you turn round you may well give a start:
    It's fun to a fellow who's getting old.

V

Now, that's a good craft weaving waistcoats and flowers,
    And selling of ribbons, and scenting of lard:
It gives you a house to get in from the showers,
    And food when your appetite jockeys you hard.
You live a respectable man; but I ask
    If it's worth the trouble? You use your tools,
And spend your time, and what's your task?
    Why, to make a slide for a couple of fools.

VI

You can't match the colour o' these heath mounds,
    Nor better that peat-fire's agreeable smell.
I'm clothed-like with natural sights and sounds;
    To myself I'm in tune: I hope you're as well.
You jolly old cot! though you don't own coal:
    It's a generous pot that's boiled with peat.
Let the Lord Mayor o' London roast oxen whole:
    His smoke, at least, don't smell so sweet.

VII

I'm not a low Radical, hating the laws,
    Who'd the aristocracy rebuke.
I talk o' the Lord Mayor o' London because
    I once was on intimate terms with his cook.
I served him a turn, and got pensioned on scraps,
    And, Lord, Sir! didn't I envy his place,
Till Death knock'd him down with the softest of taps,
    And I knew what was meant by a tallowy face!

VIII

On the contrary, I'm Conservative quite;
    There's beggars in Scripture 'mongst Gentiles and Jews:
It's nonsense, trying to set things right,
    For if people will give, why, who'll refuse?
That stopping old custom wakes my spleen:
    The poor and the rich in giving agree:
Your tight-fisted shopman's the Radical mean:
    There's nothing in common 'twixt him and me.

IX

He says I'm no use! but I won't reply.
    You're lucky not being of use to him!
On week-days he's playing at Spider and Fly,
    And on Sundays he sings about Cherubim!
Nailing shillings to counters is his chief work:
    He nods now and then at the name on his door:
But judge of us two, at a bow and a smirk,
    I think I'm his match: and I'm honest—that's more.

X

No use! well, I mayn't be. You ring a pig's snout,
    And then call the animal glutton! Now, he,
Mr. Shopman, he's nought but a pipe and a spout
    Who won't let the goods o' this world pass free.

VII.4 on intimate terms] acquainted
VII.7 taps] raps

This blazing blue weather all round the brown crop,
    He can't enjoy! all but cash he hates.
He's only a snail that crawls under his shop;
    Though he has got the ear o' the magistrates.

XI

Now, giving and taking's a proper exchange,
    Like question and answer: you're both content.
But buying and selling seems always strange;
    You're hostile, and that's the thing that's meant.
It's man against man—you're almost brutes;
    There's here no thanks, and there's there no pride.
If Charity's Christian, don't blame my pursuits,
    I carry a touchstone by which you're tried.

XII

—'Take it,' says she, 'it's all I've got':
    I remember a girl in London streets:
She stood by a coffee-stall, nice and hot,
    My belly was like a lamb that bleats.
Says I to myself, as her shilling I seized,
    You haven't a character here, my dear!
But for making a rascal like me so pleased,
    I'll give you one, in a better sphere!

XIII

And that's where it is—she made me feel
    I was a rascal: but people who scorn,
And tell a poor patch-breech he isn't genteel,
    Why, they make him kick up—and he treads on a corn.
It isn't liking, it's curst ill-luck,
    Drives half of us into the begging-trade:
If for taking to water you praise a duck,
    For taking to beer why a man upbraid?

XI.6 there's there] there's here *misp. de L;* there's there *corr. errata, de L 1911*

XIV

The sermon's over: they're out of the porch,
    And it's time for me to move a leg;
But in general people who come from church,
    And have themselves sinners, hate chaps to beg.
I'll wager they'll all of 'em dine to-day!
    I was easy half a minute ago.
If that isn't pig that's baking away,
    May I perish!—we're never contented—heigho!

The Patriot Engineer

In a letter written about June 26, 1861, GM remarked that he had just
polished this poem.
    He did not allow it admission into the Edition de Luxe, but the editors
brought it back after his death at the end of the fourth volume (Edition
de Luxe 4).
    If the poem is a personal reminiscence, it must refer to GM's wedding
trip in 1849; see explanatory note to lines 49–60.

        'Sirs! may I shake your hands?
            My countrymen, I see!
        I've lived in foreign lands
            Till England's Heaven to me.
        A hearty shake will do me good,
        And freshen up my sluggish blood.'

        Into his hard right hand we struck,
        Gave the shake, and wish'd him luck.

        '—From Austria I come,
            An English wife to win,   10
        And find an English home,
            And live and die therein.
        Great Lord! how many a year I've pined
        To drink old ale and speak my mind!'

THE PATRIOT ENGINEER

Previously printed in Once a Week *5 (14 December 1861); reprinted on the same day by the*
Ipswich Journal, and Suffolk, Norfolk, Essex and Cambridgeshire Advertiser.

Loud rang our laughter, and the shout
Hills round the Meuse-boat echoed about.

'—Ay, no offence: laugh on,
　　Young gentlemen: I'll join.
Had you to exile gone,
　　Where free speech is base coin,   20
You'd sigh to see the jolly nose
Where Freedom's native liquor flows!'

He this time the laughter led,
Dabbing his oily bullet head.

'—Give me, to suit my moods,
　　An ale-house on a heath,
I'll hand the crags and woods
　　To B'elzebub beneath.
A fig for scenery! what scene
Can beat a Jackass on a green?'   30

Gravely he seem'd with gaze intense,
Putting the question to common sense.

'—Why, there's the ale-house bench:
　　The furze-flower shining round:
And there's my waiting-wench,
　　As lissome as a hound.
With "hail Britannia!" ere I drink,
I'll kiss her with an artful wink.'

Fair flash'd the foreign landscape while
Breath'd we thus our native Isle.   40

24 Dabbing] Dabbling *misp. de L*; *corr. errata, de L 1911*
40 Breath'd we thus] *1862*; We breath'd again *OaW, de L 1910. The posthumous vol. 4
of* Poems *took its text from OaW, not from the revised text of 1862.*

'—The geese may swim hard-by;
  They gabble, and you talk:
 You're sure there's not a spy
  To mark your name with chalk.
My heart's an oak, and it won't grow
In flower-pots, foreigners must know.'

Pensive he stood: then shook his head
Sadly; held out his fist, and said:

'—You've heard that Hungary's floor'd?
  They've got her on the ground.   50
 A traitor broke her sword:
  Two despots hold her bound.
I've seen her gasping her last hope:
I've seen her sons strung up b' the rope.

'Nine gallant gentlemen
  In Arad they strung up!
 I work'd in peace till then:—
  That poison'd all my cup.
A smell of corpses haunted me:
My nostril sniff'd like life for sea.   60

'Take money for my hire
  From butchers?—not the man!
 I've got some natural fire,
  And don't flash in the pan;—
A few ideas I reveal'd:—
'Twas well old England stood my shield!

'Said I, "The Lord of Hosts
  Have mercy on your land!
 I see those dangling ghosts,—
  And you may keep command,   70
And hang, and shoot, and have your day:
They hold your bill, and you must pay.

52 hold] held *misp. de L*; *corr. errata, de L 1911*

'"You've sent them where they're strong,
        You carrion Double-Head!
I hear them sound a gong
        In Heaven above!"—I said.
"My God, what feathers won't you moult
For this!" says I: and then I bolt.

'The Bird's a beastly Bird,
        And what is more, a fool.   80
I shake hands with the herd
        That flock beneath his rule.
They're kindly; and their land is fine.
I thought it rarer once than mine.

'And rare would be its lot,
        But that he baulks its powers:
It's just an earthen pot
        For hearts of oak like ours.
Think! Think!—four days from those frontiers,
And I'm a-head full fifty years.   90

'It tingles to your scalps,
        To think of it, my boys!
Confusion on their Alps,
        And all their baby toys!
The mountains Britain boasts are men:
And scale you them, my brethren!'

Cluck, went his tongue; his fingers, snap.
Britons were proved all heights to cap.

And we who worshipp'd crags,
        Where purple splendours burn'd,   100
Our idol saw in rags,
        And right about were turn'd.
Horizons rich with trembling spires
On violet twilights lost their fires.

And heights where morning wakes
    With one cheek over snow;—
And iron-wallèd lakes
    Where sits the white moon low;—
For us on youthful travel bent,
The robing picturesque was rent.   110

Wherever Beauty show'd
    The wonders of her face,
This man his Jackass rode,
    Despotic in the place.
Fair dreams of our enchanted life,
Fled fast from his shrill island fife.

And yet we liked him well;
    We laugh'd with honest hearts:—
He shock'd some inner spell,
    And rous'd discordant parts.   120
We echoed what we half abjured:
And hating, smilingly endured.

Moreover, could we be
    To our deal land disloyal?
And were not also we
    Of History's blood-Royal?
We glow'd to think how donkeys graze
In England, thrilling at their brays.

For there a man may view
    An aspect more sublime   130
Than Alps against the blue:—
    The morning eyes of Time!
The very Ass participates
The glory Freedom radiates!

114 Despotic in] High despot of *OaW, de L 1910. The posthumous vol. 4 of* Poems *took its text from OaW, not from the revised text of 1862.*

Poems and Ballads

Cassandra

GM had originally intended to finish this poem in time for inclusion in *Poems* (1851), describing it in a letter to his publisher, John W. Parker, December 12, 1850, as his "best work." But it was not until a letter written about June 26, 1861, that we hear of his having polished the poem to his satisfaction. On October 19, [1861], he wrote a friend that he intended to publish the poem in *Once a Week* with an illustration by Dante Gabriel Rossetti. He later, [? January, 1862], decided "not to trouble Rossetti about 'Cassandra' and then it will be decidedly better to withdraw it from *Once a Week* for which I've always thought it unsuitable."

Rossetti did, in fact, make a drawing of Cassandra. For the date of the drawing and its relation to GM's poem, see Carl A. Peterson, "*The Iliad*, George Meredith's 'Cassandra,' and D. G. Rossetti's 'Cassandra' Drawing," *Texas Studies in Literature and Language* 7 (1966): 329–37. On page 334 Mr. Peterson writes that "A reading of Meredith's poem shows that Rossetti got his initial idea for a picture of Cassandra prophesying from the battlements from the following lines (stanza III, repeated verbatim as stanza IX). . . ."

I

Captive on a foreign shore,
Far from Ilion's hoary wave,
Agamemnon's bridal slave
Speaks Futurity no more:
Death is busy with her grave.

II

Thick as water, bursts remote
Round her ears the alien din,
While her little sullen chin
Fills the hollows of her throat:
Silent lie her slaughter'd kin.

MS: NB B, [*p. 10*], *stanza 1 as printed, followed by stanza not in 1862:*

Captive, and a thing of scorn,
Under that cold alien sky,
To the death that she must die
Pale *or* Young Cassandra walks forlorn:
——Shrouded is the golden eye.

III

Once to many a pealing shriek,
Lo, from Ilion's topmost tower,
Ilion's fierce prophetic flower
Cried the coming of the Greek!
Black in Hades sits the hour.

IV

Eyeing phantoms of the Past,
Folded like a prophet's scroll,
In the deep's long shoreward roll
Here she sees the anchor cast:
Backward moves her sunless soul.

V

Chieftains, brethren of her joy,
Shades, the white light in their eyes
Slanting to her lips, arise,
Crowding quick the plains of Troy:
Now they tell her not she lies.

VI

O the bliss upon the plains
Where the joining heroes clashed
Shield and spear, and, unabashed,
Challenged with hot chariot-reins
Gods!—they glimmer ocean-washed.

VII

Alien voices round the ships,
Thick as water, shouting Home.
Argives, pale as midnight foam,
Wax before her awful lips:
White as stars that front the gloom.

VIII

Like a torch-flame that by day
Up the daylight twists, and, pale,
Catches air in leaps that fail,
Crushed by the inveterate ray,
Through her shines the Ten-Years' Tale.

IX

Once to many a pealing shriek,
Lo, from Ilion's topmost tower,
Ilion's fierce prophetic flower,
Cried the coming of the Greek!
Black in Hades sits the hour.

X

Still upon her sunless soul,
Gleams the narrow hidden space
Forward, where her fiery race
Falters on its ashen goal:
Still the Future strikes her face.

XI

See, toward the conqueror's car
Step the purple Queen whose hate
Wraps red-armed her royal mate
With his Asian tempest-star:
Now Cassandra views her Fate.

XII

King of men! the blinded host
Shout:—she lifts her brooding chin:
Glad along the joyous din
Smiles the grand majestic ghost:
Clytemnestra leads him in.

XI.1 toward] towards *1862*

XIII

Lo, their smoky limbs aloof,
Shadowing heaven and the seas,
Fates and Furies, tangling Threes,
Tear and mix above the roof:
Fates and fierce Eumenides.

XIV

Is the prophetess with rods
Beaten, that she writhes in air?
With the Gods who never spare,
Wrestling with the unsparing Gods,
Lone, her body struggles there.

XV

Like the snaky torch-flame white,
Levelled as aloft it twists,
She, her soaring arms, and wrists
Drooping, struggles with the light,
Helios, bright above all mists!

XVI

In his orb she sees the tower,
Dusk against its flaming rims,
Where of old her wretched limbs
Twisted with the stolen power:
Ilion all the lustre dims!

XVII

O the bliss upon the plains,
Where the joining heroes clashed
Shield and spear, and, unabashed,
Challenged with hot chariot-reins
Gods!—they glimmer ocean-washed.

XV.3 her] with *1862*
XVI.5 Ilion] *inexplicably corr. GM to* Ilium *proof for de L; corr. errata, de L 1911, to conform with spelling throughout poem*

XVIII

Thrice the Sun-god's name she calls;
Shrieks the deed that shames the sky;
Like a fountain leaping high,
Falling as a fountain falls:
Lo, the blazing wheels go by!

XIX

Captive on a foreign shore,
Far from Ilion's hoary wave,
Agamemnon's bridal slave
Speaks Futurity no more:
Death is busy with her grave.

The Young Usurper

On my darling's bosom
Has dropped a living rosy-bud,
　　Fair as brilliant Hesper
　　Against the brimming flood.
　　　　She handles him,
　　　　She dandles him,
　　She fondles him and eyes him:
And if upon a tear he wakes,
　　With many a kiss she dries him:
She covets every move he makes,   10
　　And never enough can prize him.
　　　　Ah, the young Usurper!
　　　　I yield my golden throne:
　　Such angel bands attend his hands
　　To claim it for his own.

Margaret's Bridal-Eve

I

The old grey mother she thrummed on her knee:
　　There is a rose that's ready;
And which of the handsome young men shall it be?
　　There's a rose that's ready for clipping.

My daughter, come hither, come hither to me:
There is a rose that's ready;
Come, point me your finger on him that you see:
There's a rose that's ready for clipping.

O mother, my mother, it never can be:
There is a rose that's ready;
For I shall bring shame on the man marries me:
There's a rose that's ready for clipping.

10

Now let your tongue be deep as the sea:
There is a rose that's ready;
And the man'll jump for you, right briskly will he:
There's a rose that's ready for clipping.

Tall Margaret wept bitterly;
There is a rose that's ready;
And as her parent bade did she;
There's a rose that's ready for clipping.

20

O the handsome young man dropped down on his knee;
There is a rose that's ready;
Pale Margaret gave him her hand, woe's me!
There's a rose that's ready for clipping.

II

O mother, my mother, this thing I must say,
There is a rose in the garden;
Ere he lies on the breast where that other lay:
And the bird sings over the roses.

Now, folly, my daughter, for men are men:
There is a rose in the garden;
You marry them blindfold, I tell you again:
And the bird sings over the roses.

O mother, but when he kisses me!
  There is a rose in the garden;   10
My child, 'tis which shall sweetest be!
  And the bird sings over the roses.

O mother, but when I awake in the morn!
  There is a rose in the garden;
My child, you are his, and the ring is worn;
  And the bird sings over the roses.

Tall Margaret sighed and loosened a tress;
  There is a rose in the garden;
Poor comfort she had of her comeliness;
  And the bird sings over the roses.   20

My mother will sink if this thing be said:
  There is a rose in the garden;
That my first betrothed came thrice to my bed;
  And the bird sings over the roses.

He died on my shoulder the third cold night;
  There is a rose in the garden;
I dragged his body all through the moonlight;
  And the bird sings over the roses.

But when I came by my father's door;
  There is a rose in the garden;   30
I fell in a lump on the stiff dead floor;
  And the bird sings over the roses.

O neither to heaven, nor yet to hell;
  There is a rose in the garden;
Could I follow the lover I loved so well!
  And the bird sings over the roses.

II.9 My mother, but when I am kiss'd! *GM's autograph variant in presentation copy to Swinburne.*
II.11 'tis which shall sweetest be!] no mouth then knows what's missed. *GM's autograph variant in presentation copy to Swinburne.*

III

The bridesmaids slept in their chambers apart;
    There is a rose that's ready;
Tall Margaret walked with her thumping heart;
    There's a rose that's ready for clipping.

The frill of her nightgown below the left breast,
    There is a rose that's ready;
Had fall'n like a cloud of the moonlighted West;
    There's a rose that's ready for clipping.

But where the West-cloud breaks to a star;
    There is a rose that's ready;   10
Pale Margaret's breast showed a winding scar;
    There's a rose that's ready for clipping.

O few are the brides with such a sign!
    There is a rose that's ready;
Though I went mad the fault was mine;
    There's a rose that's ready for clipping.

I must speak to him under this roof to-night;
    There is a rose that's ready;
I shall burn to death if I speak in the light;
    There's a rose that's ready for clipping.   20

O my breast! I must strike you a bloodier wound;
    There is a rose that's ready;
Than when I scored you red and swooned,
    There's a rose that's ready for clipping.

I will stab my honour under his eye;
    There is a rose that's ready;
Though I bleed to the death, I shall let out the lie;
    There's a rose that's ready for clipping.

O happy my bridesmaids! white sleep is with you!
    There is a rose that's ready;   30
Had he chosen among you he might sleep too!
    There's a rose that's ready for clipping.

O happy my bridesmaids! your breasts are clean;
   There is a rose that's ready;
You carry no mark of what has been!
   There's a rose that's ready for clipping.

     IV

An hour before the chilly beam,
   Red rose and white in the garden;
The bridegroom started out of a dream,
   And the bird sings over the roses.

He went to the door, and there espied
   Red rose and white in the garden;
The figure of his silent bride,
   And the bird sings over the roses.

He went to the door, and let her in;
   Red rose and white in the garden;   10
Whiter looked she than a child of sin;
   And the bird sings over the roses.

She looked so white, she looked so sweet;
   Red rose and white in the garden;
She looked so pure he fell at her feet;
   And the bird sings over the roses.

He fell at her feet with love and awe;
   Red rose and white in the garden;
A stainless body of light he saw;
   And the bird sings over the roses.   20

O Margaret, say you are not of the dead!
   Red rose and white in the garden;
My bride! by the angels at night are you led?
   And the bird sings over the roses.

I am not led by the angels about;
    Red rose and white in the garden;
But I have a devil within to let out;
    And the bird sings over the roses.

O Margaret! my bride and saint!
    Red rose and white in the garden;   30
There is on you no earthly taint:
    And the bird sings over the roses.

I am no saint, and no bride can I be,
    Red rose and white in the garden;
Until I have opened my bosom to thee;
    And the bird sings over the roses.

To catch at her heart she laid one hand;
    Red rose and white in the garden;
She told the tale where she did stand;
    And the bird sings over the roses.   40

She stood before him pale and tall;
    Red rose and white in the garden;
Her eyes between his, she told him all;
    And the bird sings over the roses.

She saw how her body grew freckled and foul;
    Red rose and white in the garden;
She heard from the woods the hooting owl;
    And the bird sings over the roses.

With never a quiver her mouth did speak;
    Red rose and white in the garden;   50
O when she had done she stood so meek!
    And the bird sings over the roses.

The bridegroom stamped and called her vile;
    Red rose and white in the garden;
He did but waken a little smile;
    And the bird sings over the roses.

The bridegroom raged and called her foul;
   Red rose and white in the garden;
She heard from the woods the hooting owl;
   And the bird sings over the roses.   60

He muttered a name full bitter and sore;
   Red rose and white in the garden;
She fell in a lump on the still dead floor;
   And the bird sings over the roses.

O great was the wonder, and loud the wail,
   Red rose and white in the garden;
When through the household flew the tale;
   And the bird sings over the roses.

The old grey mother she dressed the bier;
   Red rose and white in the garden;   70
With a shivering chin and never a tear;
   And the bird sings over the roses.

O had you but done as I bade you, my child!
   Red rose and white in the garden;
You would not have died and been reviled;
   And the bird sings over the roses.

The bridegroom he hung at midnight by the bier;
   Red rose and white in the garden;
He eyed the white girl thro' a dazzling tear;
   And the bird sings over the roses.   80

O had you been false as the women who stray;
   Red rose and white in the garden;
You would not be now with the Angels of Day!
   And the bird sings over the roses.

IV.63 still] stiff *1862; cf. II.31*
IV.65 loud the] loud was the *1862*

Marian

This poem is generally accepted as a depiction of GM's first wife, the former Mary Peacock Nicolls. Revising his manuscript at a later time than the first fair draft, GM was, however, careful to avoid the identification and changed the wife into a maiden. Mary, who had deserted him, died shortly before the publication of *Modern Love*. In titling his poem *Marian*, GM may have wished the reader to associate the poem, as René Galland suggested, with his father-in-law's (Peacock's) Maid Marian who was "gentle as a ring-dove, yet high-soaring as a falcon" (Galland, p. 52). Thomas Love Peacock's novel was *Maid Marian* (1822).

I

She can be as wise as we,
        And wiser when she wishes;
She can knit with cunning wit,
        And dress the homely dishes.
She can flourish staff or pen,
        And deal a wound that lingers;
She can talk the talk of men,
        And touch with thrilling fingers.

II

Match her ye across the sea,
        Natures fond and fiery;
Ye who zest the turtle's nest
        With the eagle's eyrie.
Soft and loving is her soul,
        Swift and lofty soaring;
Mixing with its dove-like dole
        Passionate adoring.

MS: Berg, *between pp.* [16] *and 17, title:* "*Song.*" *Variants are from this MS.*

I.4 the homely] her husband's *del.*   I.5 staff] sword *del.*

Between stanzas I and II:

                Such a she who'll match with me   [*III.1*]
                        Throughout the little island:
                When in green she walks between
                        The barley & the rye land?
                Match her for her woman's worth,
                        And its blushing leaven:
                Match her as a thing of Earth,
                        And a Saint of Heaven.

II.6 Swift] High *or* Swift   II.7 its] her *or* its

III

Such a she who'll match with me?
In flying or pursuing,
Subtle wiles arc in her smiles
To set the world a-wooing.
She is steadfast as a star,
And yet the maddest maiden:
She can wage a gallant war,
And give the peace of Eden.

The Head of Bran the Blest

On October 3, 1859, GM wrote the editor of *Once a Week*: "What are you going to do with 'The Head of Bran.' It is the best thing you have yet had of mine; but it is enough for me that you have to consider the multitude."

When the poem appeared in the issue of February 4, 1860, it bore the following foreword:

> For an account of this British worthy, see "The Mabinogion," Lady Charlotte Guest's translation [*The Mabinogion, from the Llyfr Coch o Hergest, and other ancient Welsh manuscripts, with an English Translation and Notes*, 3 vols. (London: Longman, 1849), 3:130–32]. He was the son of Llyr, king of Britain, and said to be the first convert to Christianity in these islands. Hence his title, "Bendigeid, the Blessed." Taliesin, the bard, the "radiant brow," was one of the seven princes to whom it was committed to carry the Head to its resting-place.
>
> The Head was buried, looking towards France, in the Gwnvryn, or White Mount, site of the Tower of London. And this was called "the third goodly concealment of the isles of Britain;" for that no invasion from across sea came to this island while the Head was in that concealment. Arthur, "the blameless king," had it disinterred, refusing, in his pride, to trust to the charm. And this the Triads term the third ill-fated disclosure of the isles of Britain, invasion and general disaster following it.

MARIAN
Stanza III, stanza [4] MS
III.1 Wild and free and [full of *del.*] fresh with glee
III.2 And tender to *or* laughing with her true love:
III.3 Let her veer, but never fear
III.4 Her old love is her new love.   III.6 And yet the maddest] Wayward as a

THE HEAD OF BRAN THE BLEST
Previously printed in Once a Week 2 *(4 February 1860), title:* The Head of Bran. *MS: first 4 stanzas,* NB B, *[p. 47], title: "The Head of Bran"; facsimile Mem. Ed.,* Poems 1, *facing p. 142.*

I

When the Head of Bran
    Was firm on British shoulders,
God made a man!
    Cried all beholders.

Steel could not resist
    The weight his arm would rattle;
He, with naked fist,
    Has brain'd a knight in battle.

He marched on the foe,
    And never counted numbers;   10
Foreign widows know
    The hosts he sent to slumbers.

As a street you scan,
    That's towered by the steeple,
So the Head of Bran
    Rose o'er his people.

II

'Death's my neighbour,'
    Quoth Bran the Blest;
'Christian labour
    Brings Christian rest.

From the trunk sever
    The Head of Bran,
That which never
    Has bent to man!

I.5–8 *MS*:

    He with naked fist
        Could brain a knight in battle:
    Steel could not resist
        The weight his [blows *del.*] sword *or* arm would rattle.

I.12 sent to] fell'd[?] with *MS*
I.16 Rose o'er] Shone above *or* o'er *MS*

'That which never
            To men has bowed,   10
Shall live ever
            To shame the shroud:
Shall live ever
            To face the foe;
Sever it, sever,
            And with one blow.

'Be it written,
            That all I wrought
Was for Britain,
            In deed and thought: 20
Be it written,
            That while I die,
Glory to Britain!
            Is my last cry.

'Glory to Britain!
            Death echoes me round.
Glory to Britain!
            The world shall resound.
Glory to Britain!
            In ruin and fall,   30
Glory to Britain!
            Is heard over all.'

III

Burn, Sun, down the sea!
Bran lies low with thee.

Burst, Morn, from the main!
Bran so shall rise again.

Blow, Wind, from the field!
Bran's Head is the Briton's shield.

Beam, Star, in the West!
Bright burns the Head of Bran the Blest.

IV

Crimson-footed, like the stork,
    From great ruts of slaughter,
Warriors of the Golden Torque,
    Cross the lifting water.
Princes seven, enchaining hands,
    Bear the live Head homeward.
Lo! it speaks, and still commands:
    Gazing far out foamward.

Fiery words of lightning sense,
    Down the hollows thunder;   10
Forest hostels know not whence
    Comes the speech, and wonder.
City-Castles, on the steep,
    Where the faithful Seven
House at midnight, hear, in sleep,
    Laughter under heaven.

Lilies, swimming on the mere,
    In the castle shadow,
Under draw their heads, and Fear
    Walks the misty meadow.   20
Tremble not! it is not Death
    Pledging dark espousal:
'Tis the Head of endless breath,
    Challenging carousal!

Brim the horn! a health is drunk,
    Now, that shall keep going:
Life is but the pebble sunk;
    Deeds, the circle growing!

IV.6 Head] head *misp. 1862, de L*
IV.8 far out] *1862;* out far *de L, corr. errata, de L 1911*

Fill, and pledge the Head of Bran!
    While his lead they follow,   30
Long shall heads in Britain plan
    Speech Death cannot swallow!

By Morning Twilight

Night, like a dying mother,
Eyes her young offspring, Day.
The birds are dreamily piping.
And O, my love, my darling!
    The night is life ebb'd away:
    Away beyond our reach!
A sea that has cast us pale on the beach;
    Weeds with the weeds and the pebbles
That hear the lone tamarisk rooted in sand,
          Sway   10
With the song of the sea to the land.

BY MORNING TWILIGHT

1862 part:

II.

Night has eyes of Heaven:
    Eyes of Earth has Day.
How darkly over the pillow
    The locks from your forehead stray!
How like yon tangled darkness
    From the arch of pearly gray!
And now the blush steals on it, like the stream
Of rose across the crocus-bed
    In the pearly eastern arch.
I'm half in love with morning,   10
    Morning fresh on her march,
To see you: but O for the shadowy gleam
    Of our dark-jewell'd mistress,
    Bearing the baby-dream
    On the infinite vales of her bosom!
    My love! I must up and away.

Autumn Even-Song

S. M. Ellis (p. 112) claims that this poem was written in the autumn of 1859 at Copsham, but I date the manuscript several years earlier. The combination of "lake" (a broadening of the Thames) and river sounds like the scene at Weybridge and Lower Halliford where the Merediths spent most of their time from 1850 through 1854. Meredith probably revised his poem in 1859 for publication in *Once a Week*, in which case the "old hall" referred to in the added third stanza may well have been Claremont Park, near his new abode at Esher.

> The long cloud edged with streaming grey,
> > Soars from the West;
> The red leaf mounts with it away,
> > Showing the nest
> A blot among the branches bare:
> There is a cry of outcasts in the air.

> Swift little breezes, darting chill,
> > Pant down the lake;
> A crow flies from the yellow hill,
> > And in its wake   10
> A baffled line of labouring rooks:
> Steel-surfaced to the light the river looks.

> Pale on the panes of the old hall
> > Gleams the lone space
> Between the sunset and the squall;
> > And on its face
> Mournfully glimmers to the last:
> Great oaks grow mighty minstrels in the blast.

Previously printed in Once a Week *1 (3 December 1859); MS: Berg, between pp. [48] and [49], stanzas 1–2, 4.*

1 long] dark *MS*
6 *MS del.*: Wild music shudders up the air.
7–9 *MS*:
> > The timid breeze pants blue and chill
> > > Athwart the lake:
> > One crow flaps from the western hill;

11 baffled] windy *MS*
12 *MS del.*: In the wind's pauses sing the brooks. *OaW*: A purple bow the shadowless river looks.

Pale the rain-rutted roadways shine
    In the green light   20
Behind the cedar and the pine:
    Come, thundering night!
Blacken broad earth with hoards of storm:
For me yon valley-cottage beckons warm.

Unknown Fair Faces

    The subject of this sonnet may have been suggested by Keats's sonnet
that begins, "Time's sea hath been five years at its slow ebb," formally
titled by Douglas Bush as *To a Lady Seen for a Few Moments at
Vauxhall.*

Though I am faithful to my loves lived through,
And place them among Memory's great stars,
Where burns a face like Hesper: one like Mars:
Of visages I get a moment's view,
Sweet eyes that in the heaven of me, too,
Ascend, tho' virgin to my life they passed.
Lo, these within my destiny seem glassed
At times so bright, I wish that Hope were new.
A gracious freckled lady, tall and grave,
Went in a shawl voluminous and white,   10
Last sunset by; and going sow'd a glance.
Earth is too poor to hold a second chance;
I will not ask for more than Fortune gave:
My heart she goes from—never from my sight!

AUTUMN EVEN-SONG

22–24 *MS*:

        But coming night
    Blackens all with its hoard of storm:
    Del.: The birds are shelter'd close and warm.
    Nestle to me, my love, and keep thee warm.

Phantasy

Carl H. Ketcham in "Meredith and the Wilis," *Victorian Poetry*, November 1963, convincingly argues that the source of this dream poem was the "popular ballet *Giselle ou les Wilis,* first produced in Paris in 1841." The Wilis in Slavonic legend are "betrothed maidens, over-fond of dancing, who had died before marriage and cannot rest in their graves." They are snow-white and dance in their bridal dresses by moonlight, luring men to destruction. The ballet was often performed in London as well as in Paris. Ketcham adds that "in addition to the ballet itself, Meredith may have seen Ernest-Augustin Gendron's interpretation of the legend in his popular masterpiece *Les Willis* [*sic*], which was painted in the mid-forties, or the lithograph of it by Michele Fanoli."

The poem was written before GM's walking trip with his son Arthur and his friend William Charles Bonaparte Wyse in the summer of 1861. It probably was one of the three that GM offered Samuel Lucas some time before June 12, 1861, if he would "*pay the Muse better*." About June 26, 1861, he reported that the poem "is remoulded and made presentable." Lucas evidently raised objections to the poem because GM wrote him [October 1861]: "'Phantasy,' if you read it attentively, will really stand as it is very well. I leave it to you, of course (to strike out—: not to alter), but I do think that the effect would be spoilt by the scissors."

Compare the early manuscript poem, "Time," page 978, lines 1–4.

I

Within a Temple of the Toes,
    Where twirled the passionate Wili,
I saw full many a market rose,
    And sighed for my village lily.

II

With cynical Adrian then I took flight
    To that old dead city whose carol
Bursts out like a reveller's loud in the night,
    As he sits astride his barrel.

III

We two were bound the Alps to scale,
    Up the rock-reflecting river;
Old times blew thro' me like a gale,
    And kept my thoughts in a quiver.

Previously printed in Once a Week 5 *(23 November 1861).*

IV

Hawking ruin, wood-slope, and vine,
    Reeled silver-laced under my vision,
And into me passed, with the green-eyed wine
    Knocking hard at my head for admission.

V

I held the village lily cheap,
    And the dream around her idle:
Lo, quietly as I lay to sleep,
    The bells led me off to a bridal.

VI

My bride wore the hood of a Béguine,
    And mine was the foot to falter;
Three cowled monks, rat-eyed, were seen;
    The Cross was of bones o'er the altar.

VII

The Cross was of bones; the priest that read,
    A spectacled necromancer:
But at the fourth word, the bride I led,
    Changed to an Opera dancer.

VIII

A young ballet-beauty, who perked in her place,
    A darling of pink and spangles;
One fair foot level with her face,
    And the hearts of men at her ankles.

IX

She whirled, she twirled, the mock-priest grinned,
    And quickly his mask unriddled;
'Twas Adrian! loud his old laughter dinned;
    Then he seized a fiddle, and fiddled.

X

He fiddled, he glowed with the bottomless fire,
    Like Sathanas in feature:
All through me he fiddled a wolfish desire
    To dance with that bright creature.

VI.1 Béguine] Benguine *misp. de L*; *corr. errata, de L 1911*

XI

And gathering courage I said to my soul,
    Throttle the thing that hinders!
When the three cowled monks, from black as coal,
    Waxed hot as furnace-cinders.

XII

They caught her up, twirling: they leapt between-whiles:
    The fiddler flickered with laughter:
Profanely they flew down the awful aisles,
    Where I went sliding after.

XIII

Down the awful aisles, by the fretted walls,
    Beneath the Gothic arches:—
King Skull in the black confessionals
    Sat rub-a-dub-dubbing his marches.

XIV

Then the silent cold stone warriors frowned,
    The pictured saints strode forward:
A whirlwind swept them from holy ground;
    A tempest puffed them nor'ward.

XV

They shot through the great cathedral door;
    Like mallards they traversed ocean:
And gazing below, on its boiling floor,
    I marked a horrid commotion.

XVI

Down a forest's long alleys they spun like tops:
    It seemed that for ages and ages,
Thro' the Book of Life bereft of stops,
    They waltzed continuous pages.

XVII

And ages after, scarce awake,
    And my blood with the fever fretting,
I stood alone by a forest-lake,
    Whose shadows the moon were netting.

XVIII

Lilies, golden and white, by the curls
  Of their broad flat leaves hung swaying.
A wreath of languid twining girls
  Streamed upward, long locks disarraying.

XIX

Their cheeks had the satin frost-glow of the moon;
  Their eyes the fire of Sirius.
They circled, and droned a monotonous tune,
  Abandoned to love delirious.

XX

Like lengths of convolvulus torn from the hedge,
  And trailing the highway over,
The dreamy-eyed mistresses circled the sedge,
  And called for a lover, a lover!

XXI

I sank, I rose through seas of eyes,
  In odorous swathes delicious:
They fannd me with impetuous sighs,
  They bit me with kisses vicious.

XXII

My ears were spelled, my neck was coiled,
  And I with their fury was glowing,
When the marbly waters bubbled and boiled
  At a watery noise of crowing.

XXIII

They dragged me low and low to the lake:
  Their kisses more stormily showered;
On the emerald brink, in the white moon's wake,
  An earthly damsel cowered.

XXIV

Fresh heart-sobs shook her knitted hands
  Beneath a tiny suckling,
As one by one of the doleful bands
  Dived like a fairy duckling.

XXV

And now my turn had come—O me!
  What wisdom was mine that second!
I dropped on the adorer's knee;
  To that sweet figure I beckoned.

XXVI

Save me! save me! for now I know
  The powers that Nature gave me,
And the value of honest love I know:—
  My village lily! save me!

XXVII

Come 'twixt me and the sisterhood,
  While the passion-born phantoms are fleeing!
Oh, he that is true to flesh and blood,
  Is true to his own being!

XXVIII

And he that is false to flesh and blood,
  Is false to the star within him:
And the mad and hungry sisterhood
  All under the tides shall win him!

XXIX

My village lily! save me! save!
  For strength is with the holy:—
Already I shuddered to feel the wave,
  As I kept sinking slowly:—

XXX

I felt the cold wave and the under-tug
  Of the Brides, when—starting and shrinking—
Lo, Adrian tilts the water-jug!
  And Bruges with morn is blinking.

XXXI

Merrily sparkles sunny prime
On gabled peak and arbour:
Merrily rattles belfry-chime
The song of Sevilla's Barber.

Shemselnihar

Shemselnihar was the beautiful and favored concubine of the caliph Haroun Alrashid in the story "Commencing with the hundred and fifty-third night, and ending with the hundred and sixty-ninth" in the *Arabian Nights*. Her lover was Ali the Son of Becar. When word came to the caliph of her infidelity he refused to believe it and treasured her faithfully. Both lovers died of their frustrated passion. The poem was probably inspired by the rereading of the *Arabian Nights* that fathered *The Shaving of Shagpat* (1855).

O my lover! the night like a broad smooth wave
Bears us onward, and morn, a black rock, shines wet.
How I shuddered—I knew not that I was a slave,
Till I looked on thy face:—then I writhed in the net.
Then I felt like a thing caught by fire, that her star
Glowed dark on the bosom of Shemselnihar.

SHEMSELNIHAR

MSS: Berg, *10 stanzas that include the 7 of the published version, between pp. 6 and 7;* NB B, [*p. 22*], *has a draft of an opening stanza, also in* Berg *MS.*

NB B

Let us die, O my lover! in this long kiss.
   [Of love we can never know *del*.] Let us die stretcht together
      close close in the night.
Let me die & be dust when they break [my *del*.] our bliss,
   And cut thee away from my breast & my sight.
Let us die & be dust as the pale flowers are,
For thou art the life-blood of Shemselnihar.

Variants B:

2 stretch'd *or* lockt
4 And] When they
5 us] me   flowers] lilies

1 B:

O love, O my lover, thy love like a wave
   Overwhelm'd me, it drown'd me in one deep desire:
I shudder'd; I knew not that I was a slave
   Till I look'd on thy face: how the world spun with fire!
I look'd and remember'd what anguish would mar
The first and sole passion of Shemselnihar.

And he came, whose I am: O my lover! he came:
    And his slave, still so envied of women, was I:
And I turned as a hissing leaf spits from the flame,
    Yes, I shrivelled to dust from him, haggard and dry.   10
O forgive her:—she was but as dead lilies are:
The life of her heart fled from Shemselnihar.

Yet with thee like a full throbbing rose how I bloom!
    Like a rose by the fountain whose showering we hear,
As we lie, O my lover! in this rich gloom,
    Smelling faint the cool breath of the lemon-groves near.
As we lie gazing out on that glowing great star—
Ah! dark on the bosom of Shemselnihar.

Yet with thee am I not as an arm of the vine,
    Firm to bind thee, to cherish thee, feed thee sweet?   20
Swear an oath on my lip to let none disentwine
    The life that here fawns to give warmth to thy feet.
I on thine, thus! no more shall that jewelled Head jar
The music thou breathest on Shemselnihar.

9 hissing leaf spits] wither'd leaf turns *B*
10–12 *B*:
> And I shrunk into Death in his arms, dark and dry.
> Take me close! clasp me now! hide me quite! may no bar
> Burn again 'twixt thy bosom and Shemselnihar.

13 full] hot *B*
16 Smelling faint the cool] And smell the faint *B*
18 Ah! dark on the bosom of] Which shows thee so darkly to *B*
19 an arm of the] a strong-climbing *B*
20–22 *B*:
> Firm to bind, full to cherish: deliriously sweet?
> Death alone, O my lover! shall e'er disentwine
> The life that rills over thee, neck, waist and feet.

22 The life] The fair life *1862*
23 I on thine, thus! no more] No! never again *B*
24 The] With the *B*
Between 24 and 25, B:
> Yet with thee, am I not as a fair sailing ship
> That dares the wild tempest—that trusts the strange sea?
> Hanging thus over thee, full on thy lip;
> Hoping and trusting *or* living in nothing but thee:
> My lover! in thee! and if wreckt shall each spar
> Show thee how truthful was Shemselnihar.

Far away, far away, where the wandering scents
    Of all flowers are sweetest, white mountains among,
There my kindred abide in their green and blue tents:
    Bear me to them, my lover! they lost me so young.
Let us slip down the stream and leap steed till afar
None question thy claim upon Shemselnihar.   30

O that long note the bulbul gave out—meaning love!
    O my lover, hark to him and think it my voice!
The blue night like a great bell-flower from above
    Drooping low and gold-eyed: O, but hear him rejoice!
Can it be? 'twas a flash! that accurst scimitàr
In thought even cuts thee from Shemselnihar.

Yes, I would that, less generous, he would oppress,
    He would chain me, upbraid me, burn deep brands for hate,
Than with this mask of freedom and gorgeousness,
    Bespangle my slavery, mock my strange fate.   40
Would, would, would, O my lover, he knew—dared debar
Thy coming, and earn curse of Shemselnihar!

25 Far away] Away *B*
27 There my] My *B*
29 Let us slip] Slip, slip *B*   leap] mount *B*
Between 31 and 32, B:

        Away, far away from this radiance that swoons
           Sick in my vision without thee! away
        Far, from the splendour *or* O my lover of these hush'd saloons,
           Far!—How the bulbul sings from the dark *or* black spray,
        Scattering to [joy *del.*] bliss his long wail with a bar
        Of sweetness like thine over Shemselnihar.

31–36 *B:*

        He pants pants with love: only love, only love,
           Only love, O my lover! yearns up in his voice.
        The night like a great flower bends from Above,
           Odorous, breathing in sighs that are joys:
        Joys even as ours where the *or* tho' his keen scimetar
        So jealously watches *or* hovers o'er Shemselnihar.

37 Yes, I would] Would *B*
38 *B:* Bind me, upbraid me, brand [give *del.*] deep ground for hate,
39 mask of freedom] tyrannous *B*
40 Bespangle] Dress up *or* Spangle *B*; Spangle over *1862*
41 *B:* Would, O my lover! he knew to [did but *del.*] debar
42 curse] hate *del. B*

A Roar through the Tall Twin Elm-Trees

A roar thro' the tall twin elm-trees
 The mustering storm betrayed:
The South-wind seized the willow
 That over the water swayed.

Then fell the steady deluge
 In which I strove to doze,
Hearing all night at my window
 The knock of the winter rose.

The rainy rose of winter!
 An outcast it must pine.   10
And from thy bosom outcast
 Am I, dear lady mine.

When I would image

When I would image her features,
 Comes up a shrouded head:
I touch the outlines, shrinking;
 She seems of the wandering dead.

A ROAR THROUGH THE TALL TWIN ELM-TREES

MS: NB B, [*p. 45*]. *Variants are from this MS.*

1 through] in tall twin] double
2 mustering] burst of the
3 South-wind seized] cassia &
4 That over the water] By strenuous gusts were
5–8:
   The [anger *del.*] wasting of the tempest
    Awoke me to my woes: *or* Swept chords of shrouded woes
   And all night long at my window
    Knock'd the winter rose.

10 it] of *misp. 1862, de L; corr. GM in presentation copies to Browning, Rossetti, Swin-burne, and Trollope, corr. errata, de L 1911*
11 And outcast from thy bosom,
12 dear] O

But when love asks for nothing,
    And lies on his bed of snow,
The face slips under my eyelids,
    All in its living glow.

Like a dark cathedral city,
    Whose spires, and domes, and towers   10
Quiver in violet lightnings,
    My soul basks on for hours.

I chafe at darkness

I chafe at darkness in the night,
    But when 'tis light,
Hope shuts her eyes; the clouds are pale;
The fields stretch cold into a distance hard:
I wish again to draw the veil
    Thousand-starred.

Am I of them whose blooms are shed,
    Whose fruits are spent,
Who from dead eyes see Life half dead;—
Because desire is feeble discontent?   10
    Ah, no! desire and hope should die,
    Thus were I.

But in me something clipped of wing,
    Within its ring
Frets; for I have lost what made
The dawn-breeze magic, and the twilight beam
A hand with tidings o'er the glade
    Waving seem.

By the Rosanna

TO F. M.

STANZER THAL. TYROL.

"F. M." is Frederick A. Maxse (see Introduction, p. xlii). Stanzer Thal is the low Alpine valley where GM, with his young son Arthur and with Bonaparte Wyse, paused on a walking tour in the summer of 1861, a vacation taken on doctor's orders. The mountain with a glacier that dominates the valley (lines 1–4) is the Riffler. In the pocket notebook that GM carried on this trip (Yale, numbered 3) he noted: "Stanzer-Thal. The sea-green Rosanna flowing through it to the Inn, with noise & foam, under the mountain pines in one long defile." He added the epigram: "Rosanna born from a kiss of the mountains & the cloud."

In a letter to Maxse from Merano, July 28, 1861, GM wrote: "The Rosanna, by the way, put me in mind of you—nay, sang of you with a mountain voice, somehow, I don't know how. Perhaps because it is both hearty and gallant, subtle, and *sea-green*. You never saw so lovely a brawling torrent. Clear, ice-cold, foaming. You shall have the verses it *inspired*." In October GM asked Samuel Lucas for proofs of "the lines." "I insist upon it that they are good of their kind. If you don't think so, let me hear. Return them and reproachfully shall they face you in alien pages!" Lucas, however, published them on October 19, 1861.

Shortly thereafter GM received a letter from Augustus Jessopp, who was to become a close friend and teacher of his son Arthur. The letter GM felt to be "generous" in praise of his poems, but Jessopp had evidently objected to *By the Rosanna*, for GM, in replying on November 13, 1861, felt called upon to justify the poem. "Apropos of the 'Rosanna,' it was written from the Tyrol, to a friend . . . and the short passage of description was a literal transcript of the scene. Moreover, though the style is open to blame, there is an idea running through the verses, which, while I was rallying my friend, I conceived to have some point for a larger audience." In the same month he made much the same explanation to Lucas and said that he was sorry for Lucas's "sake that it confuses people." On March 24, [1862], he explained to Jessopp: "A council of friends say that the Rosanna poem must be published, as embodying something of *me*!" So the poem was included in the *Modern Love* volume.

> The old grey Alp has caught the cloud,
> And the torrent river sings aloud;
> The glacier-green Rosanna sings
> An organ song of its upper springs.

Previously printed in Once a Week 5 (*19 October 1861*). *MS:* Yale, *pocket notebook numbered 3, lines 9–12.*

Foaming under the tiers of pine,
I see it dash down the dark ravine,
And it tumbles the rocks in boisterous play,
With an earnest will to find its way.
Sharp it throws out an emerald shoulder,
    And, thundering ever of the mountain,   10
Slaps in sport some giant boulder,
    And tops it in a silver fountain.
A chain of foam from end to end,
And a solitude so deep, my friend,
You may forget that man abides
Beyond the great mute mountain-sides.
Yet to me, in this high-walled solitude
Of river and rock and forest rude,
The roaring voice through the long white chain,
Is the voice of the world of bubble and brain.   20

Ode to the Spirit of Earth in Autumn

GM hoped that this ode would please Frederick A. Maxse. (Cline, [ca. April 1, 1862]; June 9, 1862; June 23, 1862. See also headnote to *By the Rosanna*, p. 192).

As was true of the second version of *Love in the Valley* a few years later (see p. 250), the *Ode* was inspired by GM's rereading of his own early verses: namely, Canto 2 of "Wandering Willie," "The Inspiration of the Great West Wind," lines 80–588 (see pp. 911–933). The personae of "Wandering Willie" are dropped, but there are many echoes in the *Ode* from the "Inspiration" of the poet and of Willie. The "holloa'd" of line 22 was suggested by the "hallooing" of "W.W.," line 231; the martial imagery of lines 52–55 echoes that of "W.W.," 106–14; the catalogue of trees, 55–67, is adapted from "W.W.," 86–97; the "wines of heaven," 84–88, and the important concept of Earth as a "Bacchante Mother," 157–62, are adapted from "W.W.," 341–54. Thus a passage (157–62) in

BY THE ROSANNA

9 *MS*: Here it leans an ice-green shoulder
12 tops] leaps *MS*

See Supplementary Textual Notes.

ODE TO THE SPIRIT OF EARTH IN AUTUMN

MS: NB B, [*p. 49*], *lines 191–204, a passage from "Wandering Willie."*

the *Ode*, often quoted in explanation of GM's philosophy of nature, is
very early in origin. The closest verbal correspondence, however, is the
concluding passage of the *Ode* on the "western war-chief," 190–208; see
textual notes to the *Ode to the Spirit of Earth in Autumn*.

Fair Mother Earth lay on her back last night,
To gaze her fill on Autumn's sunset skies,
When at a waving of the fallen light,
Sprang realms of rosy fruitage o'er her eyes.
A lustrous heavenly orchard hung the West,
Wherein the blood of Eden bloomed again:
Red were the myriad cherub-mouths that pressed,
Among the clusters, rich with song, full fain,
But dumb, because that overmastering spell
Of rapture held them dumb: then, here and there,   10
A golden harp lost strings; a crimson shell
Burnt grey; and sheaves of lustre fell to air.
The illimitable eagerness of hue
Bronzed, and the beamy winged bloom that flew
'Mid those bunched fruits and thronging figures failed.
A green-edged lake of saffron touched the blue,
With isles of fireless purple lying through:
And Fancy on that lake to seek lost treasures sailed.

Not long the silence followed:
The voice that issues from the breast,   20
O glorious South-west,
Along the gloom-horizon holloa'd;
Warning the valleys with a mellow roar
Through flapping wings; then sharp the woodland bore
A shudder and a noise of hands:
A thousand horns from some far vale
In ambush sounding on the gale.
Forth from the cloven sky came bands
Of revel-gathering spirits; trooping down,
Some rode the tree-tops; some on torn cloud-strips,   30
Burst screaming thro' the lighted town:
And scudding seaward, some fell on big ships:

Or mounting the sea-horses blew
Bright foam-flakes on the black review
Of heaving hulls and burying beaks.

Still on the farthest line, with outpuffed cheeks,
'Twixt dark and utter dark, the great wind drew
From heaven that disenchanted harmony
To join earth's laughter in the midnight blind:
Booming a distant chorus to the shrieks   40
                         Preluding him: then he,
His mantle streaming thunderingly behind,
Across the yellow realm of stiffened Day,
Shot thro' the woodland alleys signals three;
    And with the pressure of a sea,
Plunged broad upon the vale that under lay.

Night on the rolling foliage fell:
But I, who love old hymning night,
And know the Dryad voices well,
Discerned them as their leaves took flight,   50
Like souls to wander after death:
Great armies in imperial dyes,
And mad to tread the air and rise,
The savage freedom of the skies
To taste before they rot. And here,
Like frail white-bodied girls in fear,
The birches swung from shrieks to sighs;
The aspens, laughers at a breath,
In showering spray-falls mixed their cries,
Or raked a savage ocean-strand   60
With one incessant drowning screech.
Here stood a solitary beech,
That gave its gold with open hand,
And all its branches, toning chill,
Did seem to shut their teeth right fast,
To shriek more mercilessly shrill,
And match the fierceness of the blast.

But heard I a low swell that noised
Of far-off ocean, I was 'ware
Of pines upon their wide roots poised,   70
Whom never madness in the air
Can draw to more than loftier stress
Of mournfulness, not mournfulness
For melancholy, but Joy's excess,
That singing, on the lap of sorrow faints:
And Peace, as in the hearts of saints
Who chant unto the Lord their God;
Deep Peace below upon the muffled sod,
The stillness of the sea's unswaying floor.
Could I be sole there not to see   80
The life within the life awake;
The spirit bursting from the tree,
And rising from the troubled lake?
Pour, let the wines of Heaven pour!
The Golden Harp is struck once more,
And all its music is for me!
Pour, let the wines of Heaven pour!
And, ho, for a night of Pagan glee!

There is a curtain o'er us.
For once, good souls, we'll not pretend   90
To be aught better than she who bore us,
And is our only visible friend.
Hark to her laughter! who laughs like this,
Can she be dead, or rooted in pain?
She has been slain by the narrow brain,
But for us who love her she lives again.
Can she die? O, take her kiss!

The crimson-footed nymph is panting up the glade,
With the wine-jar at her arm-pit, and the drunken
    ivy-braid

70 wide] old *1862*
74 For melancholy] Not mournfulness *1862*
91 she] her *all eds., corr. GM in presentation copies to Mrs. Brooks, Swinburne, Trollope, and Wyse*

Round her forehead, breasts, and thighs: starts a
    Satyr, and they speed: 100
Hear the crushing of the leaves: hear the cracking of
    the bough!
And the whistling of the bramble, the piping of the
    weed!

    But the bull-voiced oak is battling now:
    The storm has seized him half-asleep,
    And round him the wild woodland throngs
    To hear the fury of his songs,
    The uproar of an outraged deep.
    He wakes to find a wrestling giant
    Trunk to trunk and limb to limb,
    And on his rooted force reliant,   110
    He laughs and grasps the broadened giant,
    And twist and roll the Anakim;
And multitudes acclaiming to the cloud,
    Cry which is breaking, which is bowed.

    Away, for the cymbals clash aloft
    In the circles of pine, on the moss-floor soft.
    The nymphs of the woodland are gathering there.
They huddle the leaves, and trample, and toss;
They swing in the branches, they roll in the moss,
    They blow the seed on the air.   120
Back to back they stand and blow
The winged seed on the cradling air,
A fountain of leaves over bosom and back.
The pipe of the Faun comes on their track,
And the weltering alleys overflow
With musical shrieks and wind-wedded hair.
The riotous companies melt to a pair.
    Bless them, mother of kindness!

116 circles] circle *1862*

A star has nodded through
The depths of the flying blue.   130
Time only to plant the light
Of a memory in the blindness.
But time to show me the sight
Of my life thro' the curtain of night;
Shining a moment, and mixed
With the onward-hurrying stream,
Whose pressure is darkness to me;
Behind the curtain, fixed,
Beams with endless beam
That star on the changing sea.   140

Great Mother Nature! teach me, like thee,
To kiss the season and shun regrets.
And am I more than the mother who bore,
Mock me not with thy harmony!
    Teach me to blot regrets,
    Great Mother! me inspire
    With faith that forward sets
    But feeds the living fire.
    Faith that never frets
    For vagueness in the form.   150
    In life, O keep me warm!
    For, what is human grief?
    And what do men desire?
Teach me to feel myself the tree,
    And not the withered leaf.
Fixed am I and await the dark to-be!

    And O, green bounteous Earth!
Bacchante Mother! stern to those
Who live not in thy heart of mirth;
Death shall I shrink from, loving thee?   160
Into the breast that gives the rose,
    Shall I with shuddering fall?

141 Great] Oh *1862*

Earth, the mother of all
Moves on her stedfast way,
Gathering, flinging, sowing.
Mortals, we live in her day,
She in her children is growing.

She can lead us, only she,
Unto Good's footstool, whither she reaches:
Loved, enjoyed, her gifts must be,   170
Reverenced the truths she teaches,
Ere a man may hope that he
Ever can attain the glee
Of things without a destiny!

She knows not loss:
She feels but her need,
Who the winged seed
With the leaf doth toss.

And may not men to this attain?
That the joy of motion, the rapture of being,   180
Shall throw strong light when our season is fleeing,
Nor quicken aged blood in vain,
At the gates of the vault, on the verge of the plain?
Life thoroughly lived is a fact in the brain,
While eyes are left for seeing.

Behold, in yon stripped Autumn, shivering grey,
Earth knows no desolation.
She smells regeneration
In the moist breath of decay.

Prophetic of the coming joy and strife,   190
Like the wild western war-chief sinking
Calm to the end he eyes unblinking,
Her voice is jubilant in ebbing life.

Between 174 and 175 see Supplementary Textual Notes.

181 our] their *1862*
191 *MS del.*: Then like the noble savage
192 *MS*: Down to the death he views unblinking,—
193 *MS*: Her dirge [becomes *del.*] swells to a jubilee!

He for his happy hunting-fields,
Forgets the droning chant, and yields
His numbered breaths to exultation
In the proud anticipation:
Shouting the glories of his nation,
Shouting the grandeur of his race,
Shouting his own great deeds of daring: 200
And when at last death grasps his face,
And stiffened on the ground in peace
He lies with all his painted terrors glaring;
Hushed are the tribe to hear a threading cry:
Not from the dead man;
Not from the standers-by:
The spirit of the red man
Is welcomed by his fathers up on high.

The Doe: A Fragment

(FROM 'WANDERING WILLIE')

For the story of "Wandering Willie" and the manuscript text, see pages 893–971. The chase is described in fragment 3, lines 161–280, pages 950–954.

And—'Yonder look! yoho! yoho!
Nancy is off!' the farmer cried,
Advancing by the river side,
Red-kerchieft and brown-coated;—'So,
My girl, who else could leap like that?
So neatly! like a lady! 'Zounds!
Look at her how she leads the hounds!'
And waving his dusty beaver hat,

ODE TO THE SPIRIT OF EARTH IN AUTUMN
195 droning chant] muttered chaunt *MS*
196 numbered breaths] ebbing life *MS*
201 grasps] sets *del. MS*
202 stiffened on the ground] on the grass he lies *MS*
203 He lies with all] With all *MS*
204 *MS*:

His tribes know [he has left *del.*] well he leaves the place,
[And *del.*] To [*paper torn*] father's in the chase.

He cheered across the chase-filled water,
And clapt his arm about his daughter,   10
And gave to Joan a courteous hug,
And kiss that, like a stubborn plug
From generous vats in vastness rounded,
The inner wealth and spirit sounded;
Eagerly pointing South, where, lo,
The daintiest, fleetest-footed doe
Led o'er the fields and thro' the furzc
Beyond: her lively delicate ears
Prickt up erect, and in her track
A dappled lengthy-striding pack.   20

Scarce had they cast eyes upon her,
When every heart was wagered on her,
And half in dread, and half delight,
They watched her lovely bounding flight;
As now across the flashing green,
And now beneath the stately trees,
And now far distant in the dene,
She headed on with graceful ease:
Hanging aloft with doubled knees,
At times athwart some hedge or gate;   30
And slackening pace by slow degrees,
As for the foremost foe to wait.
Renewing her outstripping rate
Whene'er the hot pursuers neared,
By garden wall and paled estate,
Where clambering gazers whooped and cheered.
Here winding under elm and oak,
And slanting up the sunny hill:
Splashing the water here like smoke
Among the mill-holms round the mill.   40

And—'Let her go; she shows her game,
My Nancy girl, my pet and treasure!'
The farmer sighed: his eyes with pleasure
Brimming: ''Tis my daughter's name,

My second daughter lying yonder.'
And Willie's eye in search did wander,
And caught at once, with moist regard,
The white gleams of a grey churchyard.
'Three weeks before my girl had gone,
And while upon her pillows propped,   50
She lay at eve; the weakling fawn—
For still it seems a fawn just dropt
A se'nnight—to my Nancy's bed
I brought to make my girl a gift:
The mothers of them both were dead:
And both to bless it was my drift,
By giving each a friend; not thinking
How rapidly my girl was sinking.
And I remember how, to pat
Its neck, she stretched her hand so weak,   60
And its cold nose against her cheek
Pressed fondly: and I fetched the mat
To make it up a couch just by her,
Where in the lone dark hours to lie:
For neither dear old nurse nor I
Would any single wish deny her.
And there unto the last it lay;
And in the pastures cared to play
Little or nothing: there its meals
And milk I brought: and even now   70
The creature such affection feels
For that old room that, when and how,
'Tis strange to mark, it slinks and steals
To get there, and all day conceals.
And once when nurse who, since that time,
Keeps house for me, was very sick,
Waking upon the midnight chime,
And listening to the stair-clock's click,
I heard a rustling, half uncertain,
Close against the dark bed-curtain: 80

48 gleams] gleam *1862*

And while I thrust my leg to kick,
And feel the phantom with my feet,
A loving tongue began to lick
My left hand lying on the sheet;
And warm sweet breath upon me blew,
And that 'twas Nancy then I knew.
So, for her love, I had good cause
To have the creature "Nancy" christened.'

He paused, and in the moment's pause,
His eyes and Willie's strangely glistened.   90
Nearer came Joan, and Bessy hung
With face averted, near enough
To hear, and sob unheard; the young
And careless ones had scampered off
Meantime, and sought the loftiest place
To beacon the approaching chase.

'Daily upon the meads to browse,
Goes Nancy with those dairy cows
You see behind the clematis:
And such a favourite she is,   100
That when fatigued, and helter skelter,
Among them from her foes to shelter,
She dashes when the chase is over,
They'll close her in and give her cover,
And bend their horns against the hounds,
And low, and keep them out of bounds!
From the house dogs she dreads no harm,
And is good friends with all the farm,
Man, and bird, and beast, howbeit
Their natures seem so opposite.   110
And she is known for many a mile,
And noted for her splendid style,
For her clear leap and quick slight hoof;
Welcome she is in many a roof.
And if I say, I love her, man!
I say but little: her fine eyes full

Of memories of my girl, at Yule
And May-time, make her dearer than
Dumb brute to men has been, I think.
So dear I do not find her dumb.   120
I know her ways, her slightest wink,
So well; and to my hand she'll come,
Sideling, for food or a caress,
Just like a loving human thing.
Nor can I help, I do confess,
Some touch of human sorrowing
To think there may be such a doubt
That from the next world she'll be shut out,
And parted from me! And well I mind
How, when my girl's last moments came,   130
Her soft eyes very soft and kind,
She joined her hands and prayed the same,
That she "might meet her father, mother,
Sister Bess, and each dear brother,
And with them, if it might be, one
Who was her last companion."
Meaning the fawn—the doe you mark—
For my bay mare was then a foal,
And time has passed since then:—but hark!'

For like the shrieking of a soul   140
Shut in a tomb, a darkened cry
Of inward-wailing agony
Surprised them, and all eyes on each
Fixed in the mute-appealing speech
Of self-reproachful apprehension:
Knowing not what to think or do:
But Joan, recovering first, broke through
The instantaneous suspension,
And knelt upon the ground, and guessed
The bitterness at a glance, and pressed   150

123 Sideling] Sidelong *misp. de L*; *corr. errata, de L 1911*
141 Shut] Stifled *1862*

Into the comfort of her breast,
The deep-throed quaking shape that drooped
In misery's wilful aggravation,
Before the farmer as he stooped,
Touched with accusing consternation:
Soothing her as she sobbed aloud:—
'Not me! not me! Oh, no, no, no!
Not me! God will not take me in!
Nothing can wipe away my sin!
I shall not see her: you will go;   160
You and all that she loves so:
Not me! not me! Oh, no, no, no!'
Colourless, her long black hair,
Like seaweed in a tempest tossed
Tangling astray, to Joan's care
She yielded like a creature lost:
Yielded, drooping toward the ground,
As doth a shape one half-hour drowned,
And heaved from sea with mast and spar,
All dark of its immortal star.   170
And on that tender heart, inured
To flatter basest grief, and fight
Despair upon the brink of night,
She suffered herself to sink, assured
Of refuge; and her ear inclined
To comfort; and her thoughts resigned
To counsel; her wild hair let brush
From off her weeping brows; and shook
With many little sobs that took
Deeper-drawn breaths, till into sighs   180
Long sighs they sank; and to the 'hush!'
Of Joan's gentle chide, she sought
Childlike to check them as she ought,
Looking up at her infantwise.

167 toward] towards *1862*
169 from] from the old *1862*
177 her wild] and her *1862*
181 sank] sunk *1862*

And Willie, gazing on them both,
Shivered with bliss through blood and brain,
To see the darling of his troth
Like a maternal angel strain
The sinful and the sinless child
At once on either breast, and there   190
In peace and promise reconciled
Unite them: nor could Nature's care
With subtler sweet beneficence
Have fed the springs of penitence,
Still keeping true, though harshly tried,
The vital prop of human pride.

193 subtler sweet] subtler *1862*

POEMS AND LYRICS
OF THE JOY OF EARTH
(1883)

The Woods of Westermain

The woods in Norbury Park were "the quickening inspiration" of *The Woods of Westermain* (Clodd, p. 138). This park lies by the village of Mickleham, the home of GM's second wife, Marie Vulliamy.

I

Enter these enchanted woods,
 You who dare.
Nothing harms beneath the leaves
More than waves a swimmer cleaves.
Toss your heart up with the lark,
Foot at peace with mouse and worm,
 Fair you fare.
Only at a dread of dark
Quaver, and they quit their form:
Thousand eyeballs under hoods   10
 Have you by the hair.
Enter these enchanted woods,
 You who dare.

II

Here the snake across your path
Stretches in his golden bath:
Mossy-footed squirrels leap
Soft as winnowing plumes of Sleep:

Yaffles on a chuckle skim
Low to laugh from branches dim:
Up the pine, where sits the star,
Rattles deep the moth-winged jar.
Each has business of his own;
But should you distrust a tone,   10
    Then beware.
Shudder all the haunted roods,
All the eyeballs under hoods
    Shroud you in their glare.
Enter these enchanted woods,
    You who dare.

III

Open hither, open hence,
Scarce a bramble weaves a fence,
Where the strawberry runs red,
With white star-flower overhead;
Cumbered by dry twig and cone,
Shredded husks of seedlings flown,
Mine of mole and spotted flint:
Of dire wizardry no hint,
Save mayhap the print that shows
Hasty outward-tripping toes,   10
Heels to terror, on the mould.
These, the woods of Westermain,
Are as others to behold,
Rich of wreathing sun and rain;
Foliage lustreful around
Shadowed leagues of slumbering sound.
Wavy tree-tops, yellow whins,
Shelter eager minikins,
Myriads, free to peck and pipe:
Would you better? would you worse?   20
You with them may gather ripe
Pleasures flowing not from purse.
Quick and far as Colour flies
Taking the delighted eyes,

You of any well that springs
May unfold the heaven of things;
Have it homely and within,
And thereof its likeness win,
Will you so in soul's desire:
This do sages grant t' the lyre.   30
This is being bird and more,
More than glad musician this;
Granaries you will have a store
Past the world of woe and bliss;
Sharing still its bliss and woe;
Harnessed to its hungers, no.
On the throne Success usurps,
You shall seat the joy you feel
Where a race of water chirps,
Twisting hues of flourished steel: 40
Or where light is caught in hoop
Up a clearing's leafy rise,
Where the crossing deerherds troop
Classic splendours, knightly dyes.
Or, where old-eyed oxen chew
Speculation with the cud,
Read their pool of vision through,
Back to hours when mind was mud;
Nigh the knot, which did untwine
Timelessly to drowsy suns;   50
Seeing Earth a slimy spine,
Heaven a space for winging tons.
Farther, deeper, may you read,
Have you sight for things afield,
Where peeps she, the Nurse of seed,
Cloaked, but in the peep revealed;
Showing a kind face and sweet:
Look you with the soul you see't.
Glory narrowing to grace,
Grace to glory magnified,   60
Following that will you embrace

Close in arms or aëry wide.
Banished is the white Foam-born
Not from here, nor under ban
Phebus lyrist, Phoebe's horn,
Pipings of the reedy Pan.
Loved of Earth of old they were,
Loving did interpret her;
And the sterner worship bars
None whom Song has made her stars.   70
You have seen the huntress moon
Radiantly facing dawn,
Dusky meads between them strewn
Glimmering like downy awn:
Argent Westward glows the hunt,
East the blush about to climb;
One another fair they front,
Transient, yet outshine the time;
Even as dewlight off the rose
In the mind a jewel sows.   80
Thus opposing grandeurs live
Here if Beauty be their dower:
Doth she of her spirit give,
Fleetingness will spare her flower.
This is in the tune we play,
Which no spring of strength would quell;
In subduing does not slay;
Guides the channel, guards the well:
Tempered holds the young blood-heat,
Yet through measured grave accord,   90
Hears the heart of wildness beat
Like a centaur's hoof on sward.
Drink the sense the notes infuse,
You a larger self will find:
Sweetest fellowship ensues
With the creatures of your kind.
Ay, and Love, if Love it be
Flaming over *I* and *ME*,

Love meet they who do not shove
Cravings in the van of Love.   100
Courtly dames are here to woo,
Knowing love if it be true.
Reverence the blossom-shoot
Fervently, they are the fruit.
Mark them stepping, hear them talk,
Goddess, is no myth inane,
You will say of those who walk
In the woods of Westermain.
Waters that from throat and thigh
Dart the sun his arrows back;   110
Leaves that on a woodland sigh
Chat of secret things no lack;
Shadowy branch-leaves, waters clear,
Bare or veiled they move sincere;
Not by slavish terrors tripped;
Being anew in nature dipped,
Growths of what they step on, these;
With the roots the grace of trees.
Casket-breasts they give, nor hide,
For a tyrant's flattered pride,   120
Mind, which nourished not by light,
Lurks the shuffling trickster sprite:
Whereof are strange tales to tell;
Some in blood writ, tombed in hell.
Here the ancient battle ends,
Joining two astonished friends,
Who the kiss can give and take
With more warmth than in that world
Where the tiger claws the snake,
Snake her tiger clasps infurled,   130
And the issue of their fight
Peoples lands in snarling plight.
Here her splendid beast she leads
Silken-leashed and decked with weeds

III.124 hell] bell *1883, de L; corr. errata, de L 1911*

Wild as he, but breathing faint
Sweetness of unfelt constraint.
Love, the great volcano, flings
Fires of lower Earth to sky;
Love, the sole permitted, sings
Sovereignly of *ME* and *I*.   140
Bowers he has of sacred shade,
Spaces of superb parade,
Voiceful . . . But bring you a note
Wrangling, howsoe'er remote,
Discords out of discord spin
Round and round derisive din:
Sudden will a pallor pant
Chill at screeches miscreant;
Owls or spectres, thick they flee;
Nightmare upon horror broods;   150
Hooded laughter, monkish glee,
       Gaps the vital air.
Enter these enchanted woods
       You who dare.

                    IV

You must love the light so well
That no darkness will seem fell.
Love it so you could accost
Fellowly a livid ghost.
Whish! the phantom wisps away,
Owns him smoke to cocks of day.
In your breast the light must burn
Fed of you, like corn in quern
Ever plumping while the wheel
Speeds the mill and drains the meal.   10
Light to light sees little strange,
Only features heavenly new;
Then you touch the nerve of Change,
Then of Earth you have the clue;

Then her two-sexed meanings melt
Through you, wed the thought and felt.
Sameness locks no scurfy pond
Here for Custom, crazy-fond:
Change is on the wing to bud
Rose in brain from rose in blood.   20
Wisdom throbbing shall you see
Central in complexity;
From her pasture 'mid the beasts
Rise to her ethereal feasts,
Not, though lightnings track your wit
Starward, scorning them you quit:
For be sure the bravest wing
Preens it in our common spring,
Thence along the vault to soar,
You with others, gathering more,   30
Glad of more, till you reject
Your proud title of elect,
Perilous even here while few
Roam the arched greenwood with you.
      Heed that snare.
Muffled by his cavern-cowl
Squats the scaly Dragon-fowl,
Who was lord ere light you drank,
And lest blood of knightly rank
Stream, let not your fair princess   40
Stray: he holds the leagues in stress,
      Watches keenly there.
Oft has he been riven; slain
Is no force in Westermain.
Wait, and we shall forge him curbs,
Put his fangs to uses, tame,
Teach him, quick as cunning herbs,
How to cure him sick and lame.
Much restricted, much enringed,
Much he frets, the hooked and winged,   50
      Never known to spare.

'Tis enough: the name of Sage
Hits no thing in nature, nought;
Man the least, save when grave Age
From yon Dragon guards his thought.
Eye him when you hearken dumb
To what words from Wisdom come.
When she says how few are by
Listening to her, eye his eye.
      Self, his name declare.   60
Him shall Change, transforming late,
Wonderously renovate.
Hug himself the creature may:
What he hugs is loathed decay.
Crying, slip thy scales, and slough!
Change will strip his armour off;
Make of him who was all maw,
Inly only thrilling-shrewd,
Such a servant as none saw
Through his days of dragonhood.   70
 Days when growling o'er his bone,
Sharpened he for mine and thine;
Sensitive within alone;
Scaly as in clefts of pine.
Change, the strongest son of Life,
Has the Spirit here to wife.
Lo, their young of vivid breed,
Bear the lights that onward speed,
Threading thickets, mounting glades,
Up the verdurous colonnades,   80
Round the fluttered curves, and down,
Out of sight of Earth's blue crown,
Whither, in her central space,
Spouts the Fount and Lure o' the chase.
Fount unresting, Lure divine!
There meet all: too late look most.
Fire in water hued as wine,
Springs amid a shadowy host;

IV.60 *added in* Selected Poems, *1897*

Circled: one close-headed mob,
Breathless, scanning divers heaps   90
Where a Heart begins to throb,
Where it ceases, slow, with leaps.
And 'tis very strange, 'tis said,
How you spy in each of them
Semblance of that Dragon red,
As the oak in bracken-stem.
And, 'tis said, how each and each:
Which commences, which subsides:
First my Dragon! doth beseech
Here who food for all provides.   100
And she answers with no sign;
Utters neither yea nor nay;
Fires the water hued as wine;
Kneads another spark in clay.
Terror is about her hid;
Silence of the thunders locked;
Lightnings lining the shut lid;
Fixity on quaking rocked.
Lo, you look at Flow and Drought
Interflashed and interwrought: 110
Ended is begun, begun
Ended, quick as torrents run.
Young Impulsion spouts to sink;
Luridness and lustre link;
'Tis your come and go of breath;
Mirrored pants the Life, the Death;
Each of either reaped and sown:
Rosiest rosy wanes to crone.
See you so? your senses drift;
'Tis a shuttle weaving swift.   120
Look with spirit past the sense,
Spirit shines in permanence.
That is She, the view of whom
Is the dust within the tomb,
Is the inner blush above,
Look to loathe, or look to love;

Think her Lump, or know her Flame;
Dread her scourge, or read her aim;
Shoot your hungers from their nerve;
Or, in her example, serve.   130
Some have found her sitting grave;
Laughing, some; or, browed with sweat,
Hurling dust of fool and knave
In a hissing smithy's jet.
More it were not well to speak;
Burn to see, you need but seek.
Once beheld she gives the key
Airing every doorway, she.
Little can you stop or steer
Ere of her you are the seër.   140
On the surface she will witch,
Rendering Beauty yours, but gaze
Under, and the soul is rich
Past computing, past amaze.
Then is courage that endures
Even her awful tremble yours.
Then, the reflex of that Fount
Spied below, will Reason mount
Lordly and a quenchless force,
Lighting Pain to its mad source,   150
Scaring Fear till Fear escapes,
Shot through all its phantom shapes.
Then your spirit will perceive
Fleshly seed of fleshly sins;
Where the passions interweave,
How the serpent tangle spins
Of the sense of Earth misprised,
Brainlessly unrecognized;
She being Spirit in her clods,
Footway to the God of Gods.   160
Then for you are pleasures pure,
Sureties as the stars are sure:

Not the wanton beckoning flags
Which, of flattery and delight,
Wax to the grim Habit-Hags
Riding souls of men to night:
Pleasures that through blood run sane,
Quickening spirit from the brain.
Each of each in sequent birth,
Blood and brain and spirit, three   170
(Say the deepest gnomes of Earth),
Join for true felicity.
Are they parted, then expect
Some one sailing will be wrecked:
Separate hunting are they sped,
Scan the morsel coveted.
Earth that Triad is: she hides
Joy from him who that divides;
Showers it when the three are one
Glassing her in union.   180
Earth your haven, Earth your helm,
You command a double realm;
Labouring here to pay your debt,
Till your little sun shall set;
Leaving her the future task:
Loving her too well to ask.
Eglantine that climbs the yew,
She her darkest wreathes for those
Knowing her the Ever-new,
And themselves the kin o' the rose.   190
Life, the chisel, axe and sword,
Wield who have her depths explored:
Life, the dream, shall be their robe,
Large as air about the globe;
Life, the question, hear its cry
Echoed with concordant Why;
Life, the small self-dragon ramped,
Thrill for service to be stamped.

Ay, and over every height
Life for them shall wave a wand: 200
That, the last, where sits affright,
Homely shows the stream beyond.
Love the light and be its lynx,
You will track her and attain;
Read her as no cruel Sphinx
In the woods of Westermain.
Daily fresh the woods are ranged;
Glooms which otherwhere appal,
Sounded: here, their worths exchanged,
Urban joins with pastoral: 210
Little lost, save what may drop
Husk-like, and the mind preserves.
Natural overgrowths they lop,
Yet from nature neither swerves,
Trained or savage: for this cause:
Of our Earth they ply the laws,
Have in Earth their feeding root,
Mind of man and bent of brute.
Hear that song; both wild and ruled.
Hear it: is it wail or mirth?   220
Ordered, bubbled, quite unschooled?
None, and all: it springs of Earth.
O but hear it! 'tis the mind;
Mind that with deep Earth unites,
Round the solid trunk to wind
Rings of clasping parasites.
Music have you there to feed
Simplest and most soaring need.
Free to wind, and in desire
Winding, they to her attached   230
Feel the trunk a spring of fire,
And ascend to heights unmatched,
Whence the tidal world is viewed
As a sea of windy wheat,
Momently black, barren, rude;
Golden-brown, for harvest meet;

Dragon-reaped from folly-sown;
Bride-like to the sickle-blade:
Quick it varies, while the moan,
Moan of a sad creature strayed,   240
Chiefly is its voice. So flesh
Conjures tempest-flails to thresh
Good from worthless. Some clear lamps
Light it; more of dead marsh-damps.
Monster is it still, and blind,
Fit but to be led by Pain.
Glance we at the paths behind,
Fruitful sight has Westermain.
There we laboured, and in turn
Forward our blown lamps discern,   250
As you see on the dark deep
Far the loftier billows leap,
    Foam for beacon bear.
Hither, hither, if you will,
Drink instruction, or instil,
Run the woods like vernal sap,
Crying, hail to luminousness!
    But have care.
In yourself may lurk the trap:
On conditions they caress.   260
Here you meet the light invoked:
Here is never secret cloaked.
Doubt you with the monster's fry
All his orbit may exclude;
Are you of the stiff, the dry,
Cursing the not understood;
Grasp you with the monster's claws;
Govern with his truncheon-saws;
Hate, the shadow of a grain;
You are lost in Westermain: 270
Earthward swoops a vulture sun,
Nighted upon carrion:
Straightway venom winecups shout
Toasts to One whose eyes are out:

Flowers along the reeling floor
Drip henbane and hellebore:
Beauty, of her tresses shorn,
Shrieks as nature's maniac:
Hideousness on hoof and horn
Tumbles, yapping in her track: 280
Haggard Wisdom, stately once,
Leers fantastical and trips:
Allegory drums the sconce,
Impiousness nibblenips.
Imp that dances, imp that flits,
Imp o' the demon-growing girl,
Maddest! whirl with imp o' the pits
Round you, and with them you whirl
Fast where pours the fountain-rout
Out of Him whose eyes are out: 290
Multitudes on multitudes,
Drenched in wallowing devilry:
And you ask where you may be,
      In what reek of a lair
Given to bones and ogre-broods:
      And they yell you Where.
Enter these enchanted woods,
      You who dare.

A Ballad of Past Meridian

I

Last night returning from my twilight walk
I met the grey mist Death, whose eyeless brow
Was bent on me, and from his hand of chalk
He reached me flowers as from a withered bough:
O Death, what bitter nosegays givest thou!

A BALLAD OF PAST MERIDIAN

Previously printed in the Fortnightly *25 (1 June 1876).*

I.1 Last] One *F*

II

Death said, I gather, and pursued his way.
Another stood by me, a shape in stone,
Sword-hacked and iron-stained, with breasts of clay,
And metal veins that sometimes fiery shone:
O Life, how naked and how hard when known!

III

Life said, As thou hast carved me, such am I.
Then memory, like the nightjar on the pine,
And sightless hope, a woodlark in night sky,
Joined notes of Death and Life till night's decline:
Of Death, of Life, those inwound notes are mine.

The Day of the Daughter of Hades

GM evidently read this poem to Frederick Sandys, early in March 1881, for on March 3 he had invited Sandys to come to see him and on March 11 wrote: "'Skiageneia' 'Born of a Shade' is the title of the poem, and I am glad you like it."
The myth is GM's invention.
For "Skiageneia" compare GM's "skiamachy" in *The Amazing Marriage* (1895). Woodseer had been trying to describe Carinthia to Lord Fleetwood: "Perhaps he was not clear; it was a piece of skiamachy [presumably, the device of a shade], difficult to render clear to the defeated" (Mem. Ed., 19:81).

I

He who has looked upon Earth
Deeper than flower and fruit,
Losing some hue of his mirth,
As the tree striking rock at the root,
Unto him shall the marvellous tale
Of Callistes more humanly come
With the touch on his breast than a hail
From the markets that hum.

II

Now the youth footed swift to the dawn.
'Twas the season when wintertide,
In the higher rock-hollows updrawn,
Leaves meadows to bud, and he spied,
By light throwing shallow shade,
Between the beam and the gloom,
Sicilian Enna, whose Maid
Such aspect wears in her bloom
Underneath since the Charioteer
Of Darkness whirled her away,   10
On a reaped afternoon of the year,
Nigh the poppy-droop of Day.
O and naked of her, all dust,
The majestic Mother and Nurse,
Ringing cries to the God, the Just,
Curled the land with the blight of her curse:
Recollected of this glad isle
Still quaking. But now more fair,
And momently fraying the while
The veil of the shadows there,   20
Soft Enna that prostrate grief
Sang through, and revealed round the vines,
Bronze-orange, the crisp young leaf,
The wheat-blades tripping in lines,
A hue unillumined by sun
Of the flowers flooding grass as from founts:
All the penetrable dun
    Of the morn ere she mounts.

III

Nor had saffron and sapphire and red
Waved aloft to their sisters below,
When gaped by the rock-channel head
Of the lake, black, a cave at one blow,

Reverberant over the plain:
A sound oft fearfully swung
For the coming of wrathful rain:
And forth, like the dragon-tongue
Of a fire beaten flat by the gale,
But more as the smoke to behold,   10
A chariot burst. Then a wail
Quivered high of the love that would fold
Bliss immeasurable, bigger than heart,
Though a God's: and the wheels were stayed,
And the team of the chariot swart
Reared in marble, the six, dismayed,
Like hoofs that by night plashing sea
Curve and ramp from the vast swan-wave:
For, lo, the Great Mother, She!
And Callistes gazed, he gave   20
His eyeballs up to the sight:
The embrace of the Twain, of whom
To men are their day, their night,
Mellow fruits and the shearing tomb:
Our Lady of the Sheaves
And the Lily of Hades, the Sweet
Of Enna: he saw through leaves
The Mother and Daughter meet.
They stood by the chariot-wheel,
Embraced, very tall, most like   30
Fellow poplars, wind-taken, that reel
Down their shivering columns and strike
Head to head, crossing throats: and apart,
For the feast of the look, they drew,
Which Darkness no longer could thwart;
And they broke together anew,
Exulting to tears, flower and bud.
But the mate of the Rayless was grave:
She smiled like Sleep on its flood,
That washes of all we crave: 40

Like the trance of eyes awake
And the spirit enshrouded, she cast
The wan underworld on the lake.
        They were so, and they passed.

IV

He tells it, who knew the law
Upon mortals: he stood alive
Declaring that this he saw:
        He could see, and survive.

V

Now the youth was not ware of the beams
With the grasses intertwined,
For each thing seen, as in dreams,
Came stepping to rear through his mind,
Till it struck his remembered prayer
To be witness of this which had flown
Like a smoke melted thinner than air,
That the vacancy doth disown.
And viewing a maiden, he thought
It might now be morn, and afar   10
Within him the memory wrought
Of a something that slipped from the car
When those, the august, moved by:
Perchance a scarf, and perchance
This maiden. She did not fly,
Nor started at his advance:
She looked, as when infinite thirst
Pants pausing to bless the springs,
Refreshed, unsated. Then first
He trembled with awe of the things   20
He had seen; and he did transfer,
Divining and doubting in turn,
His reverence unto her;
Nor asked what he crouched to learn:

The whence of her, whither, and why
Her presence there, and her name,
Her parentage: under which sky
Her birth, and how hither she came,
So young, a virgin, alone,
Unfriended, having no fear,   30
As Oreads have; no moan,
Like the lost upon earth; no tear;
Not a sign of the torch in the blood,
Though her stature had reached the height
When mantles a tender rud
In maids that of youths have sight,
If maids of our seed they be:
For he said: A glad vision art thou!
And she answered him: Thou to me!
    As men utter a vow.   40

VI

Then said she, quick as the cries
Of the rainy cranes: Light! light!
And Helios rose in her eyes,
That were full as the dew-balls bright,
Relucent to him as dews
Unshaded. Breathing, she sent
Her voice to the God of the Muse,
And along the vale it went,
Strange to hear: not thin, not shrill:
Sweet, but no young maid's throat: 10
The echo beyond the hill
Ran falling on half the note:
And under the shaken ground
Where the Hundred-headed groans
By the roots of great Ætna bound,
As of him were hollow tones
Of wondering roared: a tale
Repeated to sunless halls.
But now off the face of the vale
Shadows fled in a breath, and the walls   20

Of the lake's rock-head were gold,
And the breast of the lake, that swell
Of the crestless long wave rolled
To shore-bubble, pebble and shell.
A morning of radiant lids
O'er the dance of the earth opened wide:
The bees chose their flowers, the snub kids
Upon hindlegs went sportive, or plied,
Nosing, hard at the dugs to be filled:
There was milk, honey, music to make: 30
Up their branches the little birds billed:
Chirrup, drone, bleat and buzz ringed the lake.
O shining in sunlight, chief
After water and water's caress,
Was the young bronze-orange leaf,
That clung to the tree as a tress,
Shooting lucid tendrils to wed
With the vine-hook tree or pole,
Like Arachne launched out on her thread.
Then the maiden her dusky stole   40
In the span of the black-starred zone,
Gathered up for her footing fleet.
As one that had toil of her own
She followed the lines of wheat
Tripping straight through the field, green blades,
To the groves of olive grey,
Downy-grey, golden-tinged: and to glades
Where the pear-blossom thickens the spray
In a night, like the snow-packed storm:
Pear, apple, almond, plum: 50
Not wintry now: pushing, warm!
And she touched them with finger and thumb,
As the vine-hook closes: she smiled,
Recounting again and again,
Corn, wine, fruit, oil! like a child,
With the meaning known to men.
For hours in the track of the plough

And the pruning-knife she stepped,
And of how the seed works, and of how
Yields the soil, she seemed adept.   60
Then she murmured that name of the dearth,
The Beneficent, Hers, who bade
Our husbandmen sow for the birth
Of the grain making earth full glad.
She murmured that Other's: the dirge
Of life-light: for whose dark lap
Our locks are clipped on the verge
Of the realm where runs no sap.
She said: We have looked on both!
And her eyes had a wavering beam   70
Of various lights, like the froth
Of the storm-swollen ravine stream
In flame of the bolt. What links
Were these which had made him her friend?
He eyed her, as one who drinks,
    And would drink to the end.

VII

Now the meadows with crocus besprent,
And the asphodel woodsides she left,
And the lake-slopes, the ravishing scent
Of narcissus, dark-sweet, for the cleft
That tutors the torrent-brook,
Delaying its forceful spleen
With many a wind and crook
Through rock to the broad ravine.
By the hyacinth-bells in the brakes,
And the shade-loved white windflower, half hid,   10
And the sun-loving lizards and snakes
On the cleft's barren ledges, that slid
Out of sight, smooth as waterdrops, all,
At a snap of twig or bark
In the track of the foreign foot-fall,
She climbed to the pineforest dark,

Overbrowing an emerald chine
Of the glass-billows. Thence, as a wreath,
Running poplar and cypress to pine,
The lake-banks are seen, and beneath,   20
Vineyard, village, groves, rivers, towers, farms,
The citadel watching the bay,
The bay with the town in its arms,
The town shining white as the spray
Of the sapphire sea-wave on the rock,
Where the rock stars the girdle of sea,
White-ringed, as the midday flock,
Clipped by heat, rings the round of the tree.
That hour of the piercing shaft
Transfixes bough-shadows, confused   30
In veins of fire, and she laughed,
With her quiet mouth amused,
To see the whole flock, adroop,
Asleep, hug the tree-stem as one,
Imperceptibly filling the loop
Of its shade at a slant of sun.
The pipes under pent of the crag,
Where the goatherds in piping recline,
Have whimsical stops, burst and flag
Uncorrected as outstretched swine: 40
For the fingers are slack and unsure,
And the wind issues querulous:—thorns
And snakes!—but she listened demure,
Comparing day's music with morn's.
Of the gentle spirit that slips
From the bark of the tree she discoursed,
And of her of the wells, whose lips
Are coolness enchanting, rock-sourced.
And much of the sacred loon,
The frolic, the Goatfoot God,   50
For stories of indolent noon
In the pineforest's odorous nod,
She questioned, not knowing: he can

Be waspish, irascible, rude,
He is oftener friendly to man,
And ever to beasts and their brood.
For the which did she love him well,
She said, and his pipes of the reed,
His twitched lips puffing to tell
In music his tears and his need,   60
Against the sharp catch of his hurt.
Not as shepherds of Pan did she speak,
Nor spake as the schools, to divert,
But fondly, perceiving him weak
Before Gods, and to shepherds a fear,
A holiness, horn and heel.
All this she had learnt in her ear
From Callistes, and taught him to feel.
Yea, the solemn divinity flushed
Through the shaggy brown skin of the beast,   70
And the steeps where the cataract rushed,
And the wilds where the forest is priest,
Were his temple to clothe him in awe,
While she spake: 'twas a wonder: she read
The haunts of the beak and the claw
As plain as the land of bread,
But cities and martial States,
Whither soon the youth veered his theme,
Were impervious barrier-gates
To her: and that ship, a trireme,   80
Nearing harbour, scarce wakened her glance,
Though he dwelt on the message it bore
Of sceptre and sword and lance
To the bee-swarms black on the shore,
Which were audible almost,
So black they were. It befell
That he called up the warrior host
Of the Song pouring hydromel
In thunder, the wide-winged Song.
And he named with his boyish pride   90

The heroes, the noble throng
Past Acheron now, foul tide!
With his joy of the godlike band
And the verse divine, he named
The chiefs pressing hot on the strand,
Seen of Gods, of Gods aided, and maimed.
The fleetfoot and ireful; the King;
Him, the prompter in stratagem,
Many-shifted and masterful: Sing,
O Muse! But she cried: Not of them!   100
She breathed as if breath had failed,
And her eyes, while she bade him desist,
Held the lost-to-light ghosts grey-mailed,
As you see the grey river-mist
Hold shapes on the yonder bank.
A moment her body waned,
The light of her sprang and sank:
Then she looked at the sun, she regained
Clear feature, and she breathed deep.
She wore the wan smile he had seen,   110
As the flow of the river of Sleep,
On the mouth of the Shadow-Queen.
In sunlight she craved to bask,
Saying: Life! And who was she? who?
Of what issue? He dared not ask,
    For that partly he knew.

VIII

A noise of the hollow ground
Turned the eye to the ear in debate:
Not the soft overflowing of sound
Of the pines, ranked, lofty, straight,
Barely swayed to some whispers remote,
Some swarming whispers above:
Not the pines with the faint airs afloat,
Hush-hushing the nested dove:

It was not the pines, or the rout
Oft heard from mid-forest in chase,   10
But the long muffled roar of a shout
Subterranean. Sharp grew her face.
She rose, yet not moved by affright;
'Twas rather good haste to use
Her holiday of delight
In the beams of the God of the Muse.
And the steeps of the forest she crossed,
On its dry red sheddings and cones
Up the paths by roots green-mossed,
Spotted amber, and old mossed stones.   20
Then out where the brook-torrent starts
To her leap, and from bend to curve
A hurrying elbow darts
For the instant-glancing swerve,
Decisive, with violent will
In the action formed, like hers,
The maiden's, ascending; and still
Ascending, the bud of the furze,
The broom, and all blue-berried shoots
Of stubborn and prickly kind,   30
The juniper flat on its roots,
The dwarf rhododaphne, behind
She left, and the mountain sheep
Far behind, goat, herbage and flower.
The island was hers, and the deep,
All heaven, a golden hour.
Then with wonderful voice that rang
Through air as the swan's nigh death,
Of the glory of Light she sang,
She sang of the rapture of Breath.   40
Nor ever, says he who heard,
Heard Earth in her boundaries broad,
From bosom of singer or bird
A sweetness thus rich of the God
Whose harmonies always are sane.

She sang of furrow and seed,
The burial, birth of the grain,
The growth, and the showers that feed,
And the green blades waxing mature
For the husbandman's armful brown.   50
O, the song in its burden ran pure,
And burden to song was a crown.
Callistes, a singer, skilled
In the gift he could measure and praise,
By a rival's art was thrilled,
Though she sang but a Song of Days,
Where the husbandman's toil and strife
Little varies to strife and toil:
But the milky kernel of life,
With her numbered: corn, wine, fruit, oil!   60
The song did give him to eat:
Gave the first rapt vision of Good,
And the fresh young sense of Sweet:
The grace of the battle for food,
With the issue Earth cannot refuse
When men to their labour are sworn.
'Twas a song of the God of the Muse
        To the forehead of Morn.

                        IX

Him loved she. Lo, now was he veiled:
Over sea stood a swelled cloud-rack:
The fishing-boat havenward sailed,
Bent abeam with a whitened track,
Surprised, fast hauling the net,
As it flew: sea dashed, earth shook.
She said: Is it night? O not yet!
With a travail of thoughts in her look.
The mountain heaved up to its peak:
Sea darkened: earth gathered her fowl: 10
Of bird or of branch rose the shriek.

Night? but never so fell a scowl
Wore night, nor the sky since then
When ocean ran swallowing shore,
And the Gods looked down for men.
Broke tempest with that stern roar
Never yet, save when black on the whirl
Rode wrath of a sovereign Power.
Then the youth and the shuddering girl,
Dim as shades in the angry shower,   20
Joined hands and descended a maze
Of the paths that were racing alive
Round boulder and bush, cleaving ways,
Incessant, with sound of a hive.
The height was a fountain-urn
Pouring streams, and the whole solid height
Leaped, chasing at every turn
The pair in one spirit of flight
To the folding pineforest. Yet here,
Like the pause to things hunted, in doubt,   30
The stillness bred spectral fear
Of the awfulness ranging without,
And imminent. Downward they fled,
From under the haunted roof,
To the valley aquake with the tread
Of an iron-resounding hoof,
As of legions of thunderful horse
Broken loose and in line tramping hard.
For the rage of a hungry force
Roamed blind of its mark over sward: 40
They saw it rush dense in the cloak
Of its travelling swathe of steam,
All the vale through a thin thread-smoke
Was thrown back to distance extreme:
And dull the full breast of it blinked,
Like a buckler of steel breathed o'er,
Diminished, in strangeness distinct,
Glowing cold, unearthly, hoar:

An Enna of fields beyond sun,
Out of light, in a lurid web,   50
And the traversing fury spun
Up and down with a wave's flow and ebb;
As the wave breaks to grasp and to spurn,
Retire, and in ravenous greed,
Inveterate, swell its return.
Up and down, as if wringing from speed
Sights that made the unsighted appear,
Delude and dissolve, on it scoured.
Lo, a sea upon land held career
Through the plain of the vale half-devoured.   60
Callistes of home and escape
Muttered swiftly, unwitting of speech.
She gazed at the Void of shape,
She put her white hand to his reach,
Saying: Now have we looked on the Three.
And divided from day, from night,
From air that is breath, stood she,
        Like the vale, out of light.

                            X

Then again in disorderly words
He muttered of home, and was mute,
With the heart of the cowering birds
Ere they burst off the fowler's foot.
He gave her some redness that streamed
Through her limbs in a flitting glow.
The sigh of our life she seemed,
The bliss of it clothing in woe.
Frailer than flower when the round
Of the sickle encircles it: strong   10
To tell of the things profound,
Our inmost uttering song,
Unspoken. So stood she awhile
In the gloom of the terror afield,
And the silence about her smile
Said more than of tongue is revealed.

I have breathed: I have gazed: I have been:
It said: and not joylessly shone
The remembrance of light through the screen
Of a face that seemed shadow and stone.   20
She led the youth trembling, appalled,
To the lake-banks he saw sink and rise
Like a panic-struck breast. Then she called,
And the hurricane blackness had eyes.
It launched like the Thunderer's bolt.
Pale she drooped, and the youth by her side
Would have clasped her and dared a revolt
Sacrilegious as ever defied
High Olympus, but vainly for strength
His compassionate heart shook a frame   30
Stricken rigid to ice all its length.
On amain the black traveller came.
Lo, a chariot, cleaving the storm,
Clove the fountaining lake with a plough,
And the lord of the steeds was in form
He, the God of implacable brow,
Darkness: he: he in person: he raged
Through the wave like a boar of the wilds
From the hunters and hounds disengaged,
And a name shouted hoarsely: his child's.   40
Horror melted in anguish to hear.
Lo, the wave hissed apart for the path
Of the terrible Charioteer,
With the foam and torn features of wrath,
Hurled aloft on each arm in a sheet;
And the steeds clove it, rushing at land
Like the teeth of the famished at meat.
    Then he swept out his hand.

XI

This, no more, doth Callistes recall:
He saw, ere he dropped in swoon,
On the maiden the chariot fall,
As a thundercloud swings on the moon.

Forth, free of the deluge, one cry
From the vanishing gallop rose clear:
And: Skiágeneia! the sky
Rang: Skiágeneia! the sphere.
And she left him therewith, to rejoice,
Repine, yearn, and know not his aim,   10
The life of their day in her voice,
    Left her life in her name.

XII

Now the valley in ruin of fields
And fair meadowland, showing at eve
Like the spear-pitted warrior's shields
After battle, bade men believe
That no other than wrathfullest God
Had been loose on her beautiful breast,
Where the flowery grass was clod,
Wheat and vine as a trailing nest.
The valley, discreet in grief,
Disclosed but the open truth,   10
And Enna had hope of the sheaf:
There was none for the desolate youth
Devoted to mourn and to crave.
Of the secret he had divined
Of his friend of a day would he rave:
How for light of our earth she pined:
For the olive, the vine and the wheat,
Burning through with inherited fire:
And when Mother went Mother to meet,
She was prompted by simple desire   20
In the day-destined car to have place
At the skirts of the Goddess, unseen,
And be drawn to the dear earth's face.
She was fire for the blue and the green
Of our earth, dark fire; athirst
As a seed of her bosom for dawn,
White air that had robed and nursed

Her mother. Now was she gone
With the Silent, the God without tear,
Like a bud peeping out of its sheath   30
To be sundered and stamped with the sere.
And Callistes to her beneath,
As she to our beams, extinct,
Strained arms: he was shade of her shade.
In division so were they linked.
But the song which had betrayed
Her flight to the cavernous ear
For its own keenly wakeful: that song
Of the sowing and reaping, and cheer
Of the husbandman's heart made strong   40
Through droughts and deluging rains
With his faith in the Great Mother's love:
O the joy of the breath she sustains,
And the lyre of the light above,
And the first rapt vision of Good,
And the fresh young sense of Sweet:
That song the youth ever pursued
In the track of her footing fleet.
For men to be profited much
By her day upon earth did he sing: 50
Of her voice, and her steps, and her touch
On the blossoms of tender Spring,
Immortal: and how in her soul
She is with them, and tearless abides,
Folding grain of a love for one goal
In patience, past flowing of tides.
And if unto him she was tears,
He wept not: he wasted within:
Seeming sane in the song, to his peers,
Only crazed where the cravings begin.   60
Our Lady of Gifts prized he less
Than her issue in darkness: the dim
Lost Skiágeneia's caress
Of our earth made it richest for him.

And for that was a curse on him raised,
And he withered rathe, dry to his prime,
Though the bounteous Giver he praised
Through the island with rites of old time
Exceedingly fervent, and reaped
Veneration for teachings devout,   70
Pious hymns when the corn-sheaves are heaped,
And the wine-presses ruddily spout,
And the olive and apple are juice
At a touch light as hers lost below.
Whatsoever to men is of use
Sprang his worship of them who bestow,
In a measure of songs unexcelled:
But that soul loving earth and the sun
From her home of the shadows he held
For his beacon where beam there is none: 80
And to join her, or have her brought back,
In his frenzy the singer would call,
Till he followed where never was track,
      On the path trod of all.

The Lark Ascending

He rises and begins to round,
He drops the silver chain of sound,
Of many links without a break,
In chirrup, whistle, slur and shake,
All intervolved and spreading wide,
Like water-dimples down a tide
Where ripple ripple overcurls
And eddy into eddy whirls;
A press of hurried notes that run

THE DAY OF THE DAUGHTER OF HADES

XII.67 he] be *1883, de L; corr. errata, de L 1911*

THE LARK ASCENDING

Previously printed in the Fortnightly *35 (1 May 1881). Variant from* F.

So fleet they scarce are more than one,   10
Yet changeingly the trills repeat
And linger ringing while they fleet,
Sweet to the quick o' the ear, and dear
To her beyond the handmaid ear,
Who sits beside our inner springs,
Too often dry for this he brings,
Which seems the very jet of earth
At sight of sun, her music's mirth,
As up he wings the spiral stair,
A song of light, and pierces air   20
With fountain ardour, fountain play,
To reach the shining tops of day,
And drink in everything discerned
An ecstasy to music turned,
Impelled by what his happy bill
Disperses; drinking, showering still,
Unthinking save that he may give
His voice the outlet, there to live
Renewed in endless notes of glee,
So thirsty of his voice is he,   30
For all to hear and all to know
That he is joy, awake, aglow,
The tumult of the heart to hear
Through pureness filtered crystal-clear,
And know the pleasure sprinkled bright
By simple singing of delight,
Shrill, irreflective, unrestrained,
Rapt, ringing, on the jet sustained
Without a break, without a fall,
Sweet-silvery, sheer lyrical,   40
Perennial, quavering up the chord
Like myriad dews of sunny sward
That trembling into fulness shine,
And sparkle dropping argentine;
Such wooing as the ear receives
From zephyr caught in choric leaves

Of aspens when their chattering net
Is flushed to white with shivers wet;
And such the water-spirit's chime
On mountain heights in morning's prime,   50
Too freshly sweet to seem excess,
Too animate to need a stress;
But wider over many heads
The starry voice ascending spreads,
Awakening, as it waxes thin,
The best in us to him akin;
And every face to watch him raised,
Puts on the light of children praised,
So rich our human pleasure ripes
When sweetness on sincereness pipes,   60
Though nought be promised from the seas,
But only a soft-ruffling breeze
Sweep glittering on a still content,
Serenity in ravishment.

For singing till his heaven fills,
'Tis love of earth that he instils,
And ever winging up and up,
Our valley is his golden cup,
And he the wine which overflows
To lift us with him as he goes: 70
The woods and brooks, the sheep and kine,
He is, the hills, the human line,
The meadows green, the fallows brown,
The dreams of labour in the town;
He sings the sap, the quickened veins;
The wedding song of sun and rains
He is, the dance of children, thanks
Of sowers, shouts of primrose-banks,
And eye of violets while they breathe;
All these the circling song will wreathe,   80

Between 70 and 71:

> But not from earth is he divorced,
> He joyfully to fly enforced;

And you shall hear the herb and tree,
The better heart of men shall see,
Shall feel celestially, as long
As you crave nothing save the song.

Was never voice of ours could say
Our inmost in the sweetest way,
Like yonder voice aloft, and link
All hearers in the song they drink.
Our wisdom speaks from failing blood,
Our passion is too full in flood,   90
We want the key of his wild note
Of truthful in a tuneful throat,
The song seraphically free
Of taint of personality,
So pure that it salutes the suns
The voice of one for millions,
In whom the millions rejoice
For giving their one spirit voice.

Yet men have we, whom we revere,
Now names, and men still housing here,   100
Whose lives, by many a battle-dint
Defaced, and grinding wheels on flint,
Yield substance, though they sing not, sweet
For song our highest heaven to greet:
Whom heavenly singing gives us new,
Enspheres them brilliant in our blue,
From firmest base to farthest leap,
Because their love of Earth is deep,
And they are warriors in accord
With life to serve, and pass reward,   110
So touching purest and so heard
In the brain's reflex of yon bird:
Wherefore their soul in me, or mine,
Through self-forgetfulness divine,
In them, that song aloft maintains,
To fill the sky and thrill the plains

With showerings drawn from human stores,
As he to silence nearer soars,
Extends the world at wings and dome,
More spacious making more our home,   120
Till lost on his aërial rings
In light, and then the fancy sings.

Phoebus with Admetus

Phoebus, exiled from heaven for having killed the Cyclops, hired himself
to Admetus, king of Thessaly, as a shepherd and abided with him for nine
years before "the mandate was revoked" (I. 1–2).

At the end of *Poems and Lyrics of the Joy of Earth* (1883) there is the
following note: "PHOEBUS WITH ADMETUS. The measure runs:

$$\_\,u\,\_\,u\,\_\,\_\,u\,\_\,u\,\_\,u\,\_$$
$$\_\,u\,\_\,u\,\_\,\_\,u\,\_'\,\_'\,\_'\,$$ "

I

When by Zeus relenting the mandate was revoked,
    Sentencing to exile the bright Sun-God,
Mindful were the ploughmen of who the steer had yoked,
    Who: and what a track showed the upturned sod!
Mindful were the shepherds as now the noon severe
    Bent a burning eyebrow to brown evetide,
How the rustic flute drew the silver to the sphere,
    Sister of his own, till her rays fell wide.
        God! of whom music
        And song and blood are pure,   10
        The day is never darkened
        That had thee here obscure.

II

Chirping none the scarlet cicalas crouched in ranks:
    Slack the thistle-head piled its down-silk grey:
Scarce the stony lizard sucked hollows in his flanks:
    Thick on spots of umbrage our drowsed flocks lay.

PHOEBUS WITH ADMETUS

Previously printed in Macmillan's *43 (December 1880).*

Sudden bowed the chestnuts beneath a wind unheard,
   Lengthened ran the grasses, the sky grew slate:
Then amid a swift flight of winged seed white as curd,
   Clear of limb a Youth smote the master's gate.
            God! of whom music
            And song and blood are pure,   10
            The day is never darkened
            That had thee here obscure.

III

Water, first of singers, o'er rocky mount and mead,
   First of earthly singers, the sun-loved rill,
Sang of him, and flooded the ripples on the reed,
   Seeking whom to waken and what ear fill.
Water, sweetest soother to kiss a wound and cool,
   Sweetest and divinest, the sky-born brook,
Chuckled, with a whimper, and made a mirror-pool
      Round the guest we welcomed, the strange hand
         shook.
            God! of whom music
            And song and blood are pure,   10
            The day is never darkened
            That had thee here obscure.

IV

Many swarms of wild bees descended on our fields:
   Stately stood the wheatstalk with head bent high:
Big of heart we laboured at storing mighty yields,
   Wool and corn, and clusters to make men cry!
Hand-like rushed the vintage; we strung the bellied skins
   Plump, and at the sealing the Youth's voice rose:
Maidens clung in circle, on little fists their chins;
   Gentle beasties through pushed a cold long nose.
            God! of whom music
            And song and blood are pure,   10
            The day is never darkened
            That had thee here obscure.

V

Foot to fire in snowtime we trimmed the slender shaft:
    Often down the pit spied the lean wolf's teeth
Grin against his will, trapped by masterstrokes of craft;
    Helpless in his froth-wrath as green logs seethe!
Safe the tender lambs tugged the teats, and winter sped
    Whirled before the crocus, the year's new gold.
Hung the hooky beak up aloft the arrowhead
    Reddened through his feathers for our dear fold.
        God! of whom music
        And song and blood are pure,   10
        The day is never darkened
        That had thee here obscure.

VI

Tales we drank of giants at war with Gods above:
    Rocks were they to look on, and earth climbed air!
Tales of search for simples, and those who sought of love
    Ease because the creature was all too fair.
Pleasant ran our thinking that while our work was good,
    Sure as fruits for sweat would the praise come fast.
He that wrestled stoutest and tamed the billow-brood
    Danced in rings with girls, like a sail-flapped mast.
        God! of whom music
        And song and blood are pure,   10
        The day is never darkened
        That had thee here obscure.

VII

Lo, the herb of healing, when once the herb is known,
    Shines in shady woods bright as new-sprung flame.
Ere the string was tightened we heard the mellow tone,
    After he had taught how the sweet sounds came.
Stretched about his feet, labour done, 'twas as you see
    Red pomegranates tumble and burst hard rind.
So began contention to give delight and be
    Excellent in things aimed to make life kind.

God! of whom music
And song and blood are pure,   10
The day is never darkened
That had thee here obscure.

VIII

You with shelly horns, rams! and, promontory goats,
 You whose browsing beards dip in coldest dew!
Bulls, that walk the pastures in kingly-flashing coats!
 Laurel, ivy, vine, wreathed for feasts not few!
You that build the shade-roof, and you that court the
   rays,
 You that leap besprinkling the rock stream-rent:
He has been our fellow, the morning of our days;
 Us he chose for housemates, and this way went.
   God! of whom music
   And song and blood are pure,   10
   The day is never darkened
   That had thee here obscure.

Melampus

At the end of *Poems and Lyrics of the Joy of Earth* GM gave the
"measure" of *Melampus*:

   u — u — uu — u — uu —
    u — u — uu — uu — u —

I

With love exceeding a simple love of the things
 That glide in grasses and rubble of woody wreck;
Or change their perch on a beat of quivering wings
 From branch to branch, only restful to pipe and
   peck;
Or, bristled, curl at a touch their snouts in a ball;
 Or cast their web between bramble and thorny hook;
The good physician Melampus, loving them all,
 Among them walked, as a scholar who reads a book.

II

For him the woods were a home and gave him the key
    Of knowledge, thirst for their treasures in herbs and
        flowers.
The secrets held by the creatures nearer than we
    To earth he sought, and the link of their life with
        ours:
And where alike we are, unlike where, and the veined
    Division, veined parallel, of a blood that flows
In them, in us, from the source by man unattained
    Save marks he well what the mystical woods disclose.

III

And this he deemed might be boon of love to a breast
    Embracing tenderly each little motive shape,
The prone, the flitting, who seek their food whither best
    Their wits direct, whither best from their foes escape:
For closer drawn to our mother's natural milk,
    As babes they learn where her motherly help is great:
They know the juice for the honey, juice for the silk,
    And need they medical antidotes find them straight.

IV

Of earth and sun they are wise, they nourish their broods,
    Weave, build, hive, burrow and battle, take joy and
        pain
Like swimmers varying billows: never in woods
    Runs white insanity fleeing itself: all sane
The woods revolve: as the tree its shadowing limns
    To some resemblance in motion, the rooted life
Restrains disorder: you hear the primitive hymns
    Of earth in woods issue wild of the web of strife.

V

Now sleeping once on a day of marvellous fire,
    A brood of snakes he had cherished in grave regret
That death his people had dealt their dam and their sire,
    Through savage dread of them, crept to his neck,
        and set

Their tongues to lick him: the swift affectionate tongue
    Of each ran licking the slumberer: then his ears
A forked red tongue tickled shrewdly: sudden upsprung,
    He heard a voice piping: Ay, for he has no fears!

VI

A bird said that, in the notes of birds, and the speech
    Of men, it seemed: and another renewed: He moves
To learn and not to pursue, he gathers to teach;
    He feeds his young as do we, and as we love loves.
No fears have I of a man who goes with his head
    To earth, chance looking aloft at us, kind of hand:
I feel to him as to earth of whom we are fed;
    I pipe him much for his good could he understand.

VII

Melampus touched at his ears, laid finger on wrist:
    He was not dreaming, he sensibly felt and heard.
Above, through leaves, where the tree-twigs thick
        intertwist,
    He spied the birds and the bill of the speaking bird.
His cushion mosses in shades of various green,
    The lumped, the antlered, he pressed, while the sunny
        snake
Slipped under: draughts he had drunk of clear
        Hippocrene,
    It seemed, and sat with a gift of the Gods awake.

VIII

Divinely thrilled was the man, exultingly full,
    As quick well-waters that come of the heart of earth,
Ere yet they dart in a brook are one bubble-pool
    To light and sound, wedding both at the leap of
        birth.
The soul of light vivid shone, a stream within stream;
    The soul of sound from a musical shell outflew;
Where others hear but a hum and see but a beam,
    The tongue and eve of the fountain of life he knew.

IX

He knew the Hours: they were round him, laden with
        seed
Of hours bestrewn upon vapour, and one by one
They winged as ripened in fruit the burden decreed
    For each to scatter; they flushed like the buds in sun,
Bequeathing seed to successive similar rings,
        Their sisters, bearers to men of what men have
            earned:
He knew them, talked with the yet unreddened; the stings,
    The sweets, they warmed at their bosoms divined,
        discerned.

X

Not unsolicited, sought by diligent feet,
    By riddling fingers expanded, oft watched in growth
With brooding deep as the noon-ray's quickening wheat,
        Ere touch'd, the pendulous flower of the plants of
            sloth,
The plants of rigidness, answered question and squeeze,
    Revealing wherefore it bloomed uninviting, bent,
Yet making harmony breathe of life and disease,
    The deeper chord of a wonderful instrument.

XI

So passed he luminous-eyed for earth and the fates
    We arm to bruise or caress us: his ears were
        charged
With tones of love in a whirl of voluble hates,
    With music wrought of distraction his heart enlarged.
Celestial-shining, though mortal, singer, though mute,
    He drew the Master of harmonies, voiced or stilled,
To seek him; heard at the silent medicine-root
    A song, beheld in fulfilment the unfulfilled.

XII

Him Phoebus, lending to darkness colour and form
    Of light's excess, many lessons and counsels gave;
Showed Wisdom lord of the human intricate swarm,
     And whence prophetic it looks on the hives that
        rave,
And how acquired, of the zeal of love to acquire,
     And where it stands, in the centre of life a sphere;
And Measure, mood of the lyre, the rapturous lyre,
     He said was Wisdom, and struck him the notes to
        hear.

XIII

Sweet, sweet: 'twas glory of vision, honey, the breeze
    In heat, the run of the river on root and stone,
All senses joined, as the sister Pierides
    Are one, uplifting their chorus, the Nine, his own.
In stately order, evolved of sound into sight,
    From sight to sound intershifting, the man descried
The growths of earth, his adored, like day out of night,
    Ascend in song, seeing nature and song allied.

XIV

And there vitality, there, there solely in song,
    Resides, where earth and her uses to men, their needs,
Their forceful cravings, the theme are: there is it strong,
    The Master said: and the studious eye that reads,
(Yea, even as earth to the crown of Gods on the mount),
    In links divine with the lyrical tongue is bound.
Pursue thy craft: it is music drawn of a fount
    To spring perennial; well-spring is common ground.

XV

Melampus dwelt among men: physician and sage,
    He served them, loving them, healing them; sick or
        maimed
Or them that frenzied in some delirious rage
    Outran the measure, his juice of the woods reclaimed.

He played on men, as his master, Phoebus, on strings
   Melodious: as the God did he drive and check,
Through love exceeding a simple love of the things
   That glide in grasses and rubble of woody wreck.

Love in the Valley

See page 62 for the early version of this poem. Both versions are given
in this edition because this later one is a genuine re-creation rather than
a revision.

At the end of *Poems and Lyrics of the Joy of Earth* there is the following
note: "LOVE IN THE VALLEY: Trochaic, variable in short syllables
according to stress of the accent. A sketch of this poem appeared in a
volume published many years back, now extinct." GM's "extinct" was
obviously wishful thinking. The memorable meter of this poem was
probably derived from George Darley's *Serenade of a Loyal Martyr*.

Under yonder beech-tree single on the green-sward,
   Couched with her arms behind her golden head,
Knees and tresses folded to slip and ripple idly,
   Lies my young love sleeping in the shade.
Had I the heart to slide an arm beneath her,
   Press her parting lips as her waist I gather slow,
Waking in amazement she could not but embrace me:
   Then would she hold me and never let me go?

Shy as the squirrel and wayward as the swallow,
   Swift as the swallow along the river's light   10
Circleting the surface to meet his mirrored winglets,
   Fleeter she seems in her stay than in her flight.
Shy as the squirrel that leaps among the pine-tops,
   Wayward as the swallow overhead at set of sun,
She whom I love is hard to catch and conquer,
   Hard, but O the glory of the winning were she won!

LOVE IN THE VALLEY

Previously printed in Macmillan's *38* (*October 1878*).

When her mother tends her before the laughing mirror,
    Tying up her laces, looping up her hair,
Often she thinks, were this wild thing wedded,
    More love should I have, and much less care.   20
When her mother tends her before the lighted mirror,
    Loosening her laces, combing down her curls,
Often she thinks, were this wild thing wedded,
    I should miss but one for many boys and girls.

Heartless she is as the shadow in the meadows
    Flying to the hills on a blue and breezy noon.
No, she is athirst and drinking up her wonder:
    Earth to her is young as the slip of the new moon.
Deals she an unkindness, 'tis but her rapid measure,
    Even as in a dance; and her smile can heal no less: 30
Like the swinging May-cloud that pelts the flowers with
      hailstones
Off a sunny border, she was made to bruise and bless.

Lovely are the curves of the white owl sweeping
    Wavy in the dusk lit by one large star.
Lone on the fir-branch, his rattle-note unvaried,
    Brooding o'er the gloom, spins the brown evejar.
Darker grows the valley, more and more forgetting:
    So were it with me if forgetting could be willed.
Tell the grassy hollow that holds the bubbling wellspring;
    Tell it to forget the source that keeps it filled.   40

Stepping down the hill with her fair companions,
    Arm in arm, all against the raying West,
Boldly she sings, to the merry tune she marches,
    Brave is her shape, and sweeter unpossessed.
Sweeter, for she in what my heart first awaking
    Whispered the world was; morning light is she.
Love that so desires would fain keep her changeless;
    Fain would fling the net, and fain have her free.

24 for many] for the many *1897*
45 in] is *misp. de L; corr. errata, de L 1911*

Happy happy time, when the white star hovers
    Low over dim fields fresh with bloomy dew,   50
Near the face of dawn, that draws athwart the darkness,
    Threading it with colour, as yewberries the yew.
Thicker crowd the shades as the grave East deepens
    Glowing, and with crimson a long cloud swells.
Maiden still the morn is; and strange she is, and secret;
    Strange her eyes; her cheeks are cold as cold
        seashells.

Sunrays, leaning on our southern hills and lighting
    Wild cloud-mountains that drag the hills along,
Oft ends the day of your shifting brilliant laughter
    Chill as a dull face frowning on a song.   60
Ay, but shows the South-West a ripple-feathered bosom
    Blown to silver while the clouds are shaken and
        ascend
Scaling the mid-heavens as they stream, there comes a
        sunset
    Rich, deep like love in beauty without end.

When at dawn she sighs, and like an infant to the
        window
    Turns grave eyes craving light, released from dreams,
Beautiful she looks, like a white water-lily
    Bursting out of bud in havens of the streams.
When from bed she rises clothed from neck to ankle
    In her long nightgown sweet as boughs of May,   70
Beautiful she looks, like a tall garden lily
    Pure from the night, and splendid for the day.

Mother of the dews, dark eye-lashed twilight,
    Low-lidded twilight, o'er the valley's brim,
Rounding on thy breast sings the dew-delighted skylark,
    Clear as though the dewdrops had their voice in him.

52 as] like *M and all eds., although the correction to* as *appears on the errata slip, 1883*

Hidden where the rose-flush drinks the rayless planet,
    Fountain-full he pours the spraying fountain-
        showers.
Let me hear her laughter, I would have her ever
    Cool as dew in twilight, the lark above the flowers.   80

All the girls are out with their baskets for the primrose;
    Up lanes, woods through, they troop in joyful bands.
My sweet leads: she knows not why, but now she loiters,
    Eyes the bent anemones, and hangs her hands.
Such a look will tell that the violets are peeping,
    Coming the rose: and unaware a cry
Springs in her bosom for odours and for colour,
Covert and the nightingale; she knows not why.

Kerchiefed head and chin she darts between her tulips,
    Streaming like a willow grey in arrowy rain: 90
Some bend beaten cheek to gravel, and their angel
    She will be; she lifts them, and on she speeds again.
Black the driving raincloud breasts the iron gateway:
    She is forth to cheer a neighbour lacking mirth.
So when sky and grass met rolling dumb for thunder
    Saw I once a white dove, sole light of earth.

Prim little scholars are the flowers of her garden,
    Trained to stand in rows, and asking if they please.
I might love them well but for loving more the wild ones:
    O my wild ones! they tell me more than these.   100
You, my wild one, you tell of honied field-rose,
    Violet, blushing eglantine in life; and even as they,
They by the wayside are earnest of your goodness,
    You are of life's, on the banks that line the way.

Peering at her chamber the white crowns the red rose,
    Jasmine winds the porch with stars two and three.
Parted is the window; she sleeps; the starry jasmine
    Breathes a falling breath that carries thoughts of me.

77 where the rose-flush] where rose-flush *M*

Sweeter unpossessed, have I said of her my sweetest?
   Not while she sleeps: while she sleeps the jasmine
      breathes,   110
Luring her to love; she sleeps; the starry jasmine
   Bears me to her pillow under white rose-wreaths.

Yellow with birdfoot-trefoil are the grass-glades;
   Yellow with cinquefoil of the dew-grey leaf;
Yellow with stonecrop; the moss-mounds are yellow;
   Blue-necked the wheat sways, yellowing to the sheaf.
Green-yellow bursts from the copse the laughing yaffle;
   Sharp as a sickle is the edge of shade and shine:
Earth in her heart laughs looking at the heavens,
   Thinking of the harvest: I look and think of mine.   120

This I may know: her dressing and undressing
   Such a change of light shows as when the skies in sport
Shift from cloud to moonlight; or edging over thunder
   Slips a ray of sun; or sweeping into port
White sails furl; or on the ocean borders
   White sails lean along the waves leaping green.
Visions of her shower before me, but from eyesight
   Guarded she would be like the sun were she seen.

Front door and back of the mossed old farmhouse
   Open with the morn, and in a breezy link   130
Freshly sparkles garden to stripe-shadowed orchard,
   Green across a rill where on sand the minnows wink.
Busy in the grass the early sun of summer
   Swarms, and the blackbird's mellow fluting notes
Call my darling up with round and roguish challenge:
   Quaintest, richest carol of all the singing throats!

Cool was the woodside; cool as her white dairy
   Keeping sweet the cream-pan; and there the boys
      from school,
Cricketing below, rushed brown and red with sunshine;
   O the dark translucence of the deep-eyed cool!   140

Spying from the farm, herself she fetched a pitcher
 Full of milk, and tilted for each in turn the beak.
Then a little fellow, mouth up and on tiptoe,
 Said, 'I will kiss you': she laughed and leaned her
  cheek.

Doves of the fir-wood walling high our red roof
 Through the long noon coo, crooning through the
  coo.
Loose droop the leaves, and down the sleepy roadway
 Sometimes pipes a chaffinch; loose droops the blue.
Cows flap a slow tail knee-deep in the river,
 Breathless, given up to sun and gnat and fly.   150
Nowhere is she seen; and if I see her nowhere,
 Lightning may come, straight rains and tiger sky.

O the golden sheaf, the rustling treasure-armful!
 O the nutbrown tresses nodding interlaced!
O the treasure-tresses one another over
 Nodding! O the girdle slack about the waist!
Slain are the poppies that shot their random scarlet
 Quick amid the wheatears: wound about the waist,
Gathered, see these brides of Earth one blush of ripeness!
 O the nutbrown tresses nodding interlaced!   160

Large and smoky red the sun's cold disk drops,
 Clipped by naked hills, on violet shaded snow:
Eastward large and still lights up a bower of moonrise,
 Whence at her leisure steps the moon aglow.
Nightlong on black print-branches our beech-tree
 Gazes in this whiteness: nightlong could I.
Here may life on death or death on life be painted.
 Let me clasp her soul to know she cannot die!

Gossips count her faults; they scour a narrow chamber
 Where there is no window, read not heaven or her. 170
'When she was a tiny,' one aged woman quavers,
 Plucks at my heart and leads me by the ear.

Faults she had once as she learnt to run and tumbled:
    Faults of feature some see, beauty not complete.
Yet, good gossips, beauty that makes holy
    Earth and air, may have faults from head to feet.

Hither she comes; she comes to me; she lingers,
    Deepen her brown eyebrows, while in new surprise
High rise the lashes in wonder of a stranger;
    Yet am I the light and living of her eyes.   180
Something friends have told her fills her heart to
        brimming,
    Nets her in her blushes, and wounds her, and
        tames.—
Sure of her haven, O like a dove alighting,
    Arms up, she dropped: our souls were in our names.

Soon will she lie like a white-frost sunrise.
    Yellow oats and brown wheat, barley pale as rye,
Long since your sheaves have yielded to the thresher,
    Felt the girdle loosened, seen the tresses fly.
Soon will she lie like a blood-red sunset.
    Swift with the to-morrow, green-winged Spring!   190
Sing from the South-West, bring her back the truants,
    Nightingale and swallow, song and dipping wing.

Soft new beech-leaves, up to beamy April
    Spreading bough on bough a primrose mountain, you
Lucid in the moon, raise lilies to the skyfields,
    Youngest green transfused in silver shining through:
Fairer than the lily, than the wild white cherry:
    Fair as in image my seraph love appears
Borne to me by dreams when dawn is at my eyelids:
    Fair as in the flesh she swims to me on tears.   200

Could I find a place to be alone with heaven,
    I would speak my heart out: heaven is my need.
Every woodland tree is flushing like the dogwood,
    Flashing like the whitebeam, swaying like the reed.

Flushing like the dogwood crimson in October;
   Streaming like the flag-reed South-West blown;
Flashing as in gusts the sudden-lighted whitebeam:
   All seem to know what is for heaven alone.

The Three Singers to Young Blood

Carols nature, counsel men.
Different notes as rook from wren,
Hear we when our steps begin,
And the choice is cast within,
Where a robber raven's tale
Urges passion's nightingale.

Hark to the three, Chimed they in one,
Life were music of the sun.
Liquid first, and then the caw,
Then the cry that knows not law.   10

I

As the birds do, so do we,
Bill our mate, and choose our tree.
Swift to building work addressed,
Any straw will help a nest.
Mates are warm, and this is truth,
Glad the young that come of youth.
They have bloom i' the blood and sap
Chilling at no thunder-clap.
Man and woman on the thorn,
Trust not Earth, and have her scorn.   10
They who in her lead confide,
Wither me if they spread not wide!
Look for aid to little things,
You will get them quick as wings,
Thick as feathers; would you feed,
Take the leap that springs the need.

II

Contemplate the rutted road:
Life is both a lure and goad.
Each to hold in measure just,
Trample appetite to dust.
Mark the fool and wanton spin:
Keep to harness as a skin.
Ere you follow nature's lead,
Of her powers in you have heed;
Else a shiverer you will find
You have challenged humankind.   10
Mates are chosen marketwise:
Coolest bargainer best buys.
Leap not, nor let leap the heart:
Trot your track, and drag your cart.
So your end may be in wool,
Honoured, and with manger full.

III

O the rosy light! it fleets,
Dearer dying that all sweets.
That is life: it waves and goes;
Solely in that cherished Rose
Palpitates, or else 'tis death.
Call it love with all thy breath.
Love! it lingers: Love! it nears:
Love! O Love! the Rose appears,
Blushful, magic, reddening air.
Now the choice is on thee: dare!   10
Mortal seems the touch, but makes
Immortal the hand that takes.
Feel what sea within thee shames
Of its force all other claims,
Drowns them. Clasp! the world will be
Heavenly Rose to swelling sea.

The Orchard and the Heath

I chanced upon an early walk to spy
A troop of children through an orchard gate:
    The boughs hung low, the grass was high;
    They had but to lift hands or wait
For fruits to fill them; fruits were all their sky.

They shouted, running on from tree to tree,
And played the game the wind plays, on and round.
    'Twas visible invisible glee
    Pursuing; and a fountain's sound
Of laughter spouted, pattering fresh on me.   10

I could have watched them till the daylight fled,
Their pretty bower made such a light of day.
    A small one tumbling sang, 'Oh! head!'
    The rest to comfort her straightway
Seized on a branch and thumped down apples red.

The tiny creature flashing through green grass,
And laughing with her feet and eyes among
    Fresh apples, while a little lass
    Over as o'er breeze-ripples hung:
That sight I saw, and passed as aliens pass.   20

My footpath left the pleasant farms and lanes,
Soft cottage-smoke, straight cocks a-crow, gay flowers;
    Beyond the wheel-ruts of the wains,
    Across a heath I walked for hours,
And met its rival tenants, rays and rains.

Previously printed in Macmillan's *17 (February 1868). Variants are from* M.
20 That] This
25 rays] sun

Still in my view mile-distant firs appeared,
When, under a patched channel-bank enriched
    With foxglove whose late bells drooped seared,
    Behold, a family had pitched
Their camp, and labouring the low tent upreared.   30

Here, too, were many children, quick to scan
A new thing coming; swarthy cheeks, white teeth:
    In many-colored rags they ran,
    Like iron runlets of the heath.
Dispersed lay broth-pot, sticks, and drinking-can.

Three girls, with shoulders like a boat at sea
Tipped sideways by the wave (their clothing slid
    From either ridge unequally),
    Lean, swift and voluble, bestrid
A starting-point, unfrocked to the bent knee.   40

They raced; their brothers yelled them on, and broke
In act to follow, but as one they snuffed
    Wood-fumes, and by the fire that spoke
    Of provender, its pale flame puffed,
And rolled athwart dwarf furzes grey-blue smoke.

Soon on the dark edge of a ruddier gleam,
The mother-pot perusing, all, stretched flat,
    Paused for its bubbling-up supreme:
    A dog upright in circle sat,
And oft his nose went with the flying steam.   50

I turned and looked on heaven awhile, where now
The moor-faced sunset broaden'd with red light;
    Threw high aloft a golden bough,
    And seemed the desert of the night
Far down with mellow orchards to endow.

28 drooped] dropped *misp. GMT*
51 on] in
See Supplementary Textual Notes.

Martin's Puzzle

Although George Smith of the *Cornhill Magazine* personally admired this poem, he rejected it for publication, thinking that it would "'offend many of his readers'" (Cline, [November 21, 1864]).

In preparing his poems for the Edition de Luxe GM removed *Martin's Puzzle* from *Poems and Lyrics of the Joy of Earth* and placed it, together with *Juggling Jerry* and *The Old Chartist*, under the heading *Verses* (Edition de Luxe 3).

I

There she goes up the street with her book in her hand,
    And her Good morning, Martin! Ay, lass, how d'ye
      do?
Very well, thank you, Martin!—I can't understand!
    I might just as well never have cobbled a shoe!
I can't understand it. She talks like a song;
    Her voice takes your ear like the ring of a glass;
She seems to give gladness while limping along,
    Yet sinner ne'er suffer'd like that little lass.

II

First, a fool of a boy ran her down with a cart.
    Then, her fool of a father—a blacksmith by trade—
Why the deuce does he tell us it half broke his heart?
    His heart!—where's the leg of the poor little maid!

Previously printed in the Fortnightly *1 (1 June 1865). MS:* Fitzwilliam Museum, *fair copy.*

I.8 sinner ne'er] no sinner has *or* sinner ne'er MS

Between stanzas I and II, stanza 2, MS and F:

        Now, I'm a rough fellow—what's happen'd to me?
           Since last I left Falmouth I've not had a fight
        With a miner come down for a dip in the sea;
           I cobble contented from morning to night.
        The Lord gives me all that a man should require;
           Protects me, and "cuddles me up", as it were.
        But what have I done to be saved from the fire?
           And why does His punishment fall upon her?

Well, that's not enough; they must push her downstairs,
    To make her go crooked: but why count the list?
If it's right to suppose that our human affairs
    Are all order'd by heaven—there, bang goes my fist!

III

For if angels can look on such sights—never mind!
    When you're next to blaspheming, it's best to be
        mum.
The parson declares that her woes weren't designed;
    But, then, with the parson it's all kingdom-come.
Lose a leg, save a soul—a convenient text;
    I call it Tea doctrine, not savouring of God.
When poor little Molly wants 'chastening,' why, next
    The Archangel Michael might taste of the rod.

IV

But, to see the poor darling go limping for miles
    To read books to sick people!—and just of an age
When girls learn the meaning of ribands and smiles!
    Makes me feel like a squirrel that turns in a cage.
The more I push thinking the more I revolve:
    I never get farther:—and as to her face,
It starts up when near on my puzzle I solve,
    And says, 'This crush'd body seems such a sad case.'

V

Not that she's for complaining: she reads to earn pence;
    And from those who can't pay, simple thanks are
        enough.
Does she leave lamentation for chaps without sense?
    Howsoever, she's made up of wonderful stuff.

III.7 poor] our poor *MS*
IV.3 ribands] ribbons *MS*, *F*

Ay, the soul in her body must be a stout cord;
    She sings little hymns at the close of the day,
Though she has but three fingers to lift to the Lord,
    And only one leg to kneel down with to pray.

VI

What I ask is, Why persecute such a poor dear,
    If there's Law above all? Answer that if you can!
Irreligious I'm not; but I look on this sphere
    As a place where a man should just think like a man.
It isn't fair dealing! But, contrariwise,
    Do bullets in battle the wicked select?
Why, then it's all chance-work! And yet, in her eyes,
    She holds a fixed something by which I am checked.

VII

Yonder riband of sunshine aslope on the wall,
    If you eye it a minute'll have the same look:
So kind! and so merciful! God of us all!
    It's the very same lesson we get from the Book.
Then, is Life but a trial? Is that what is meant?
    Some must toil, and some perish, for others below:
The injustice to each spreads a common content;
    Ay! I've lost it again, for it can't be quite so.

VIII

She's the victim of fools: that seems nearer the mark.
    On earth there are engines and numerous fools.
Why the Lord can permit them, we're still in the dark;
    He does, and in some sort of way they're His tools.

VII.1 riband] ribbon *MS, F*
VII.2 you] you'll *MS*
VII.4 the very same lesson] the *del.* a lesson—the lesson *or* the very same lesson *MS*
the Book] Thy Book *MS, F*
VII.8 Ay] Hey *MS*

It's a roundabout way, with respect let me add,
    If Molly goes crippled that we may be taught:
But, perhaps, it's the only way, though it's so bad;
    In that case we'll bow down our heads,—as we ought.

IX

But the worst of *me* is, that when I bow my head,
    I perceive a thought wriggling away in the dust,
And I follow its tracks, quite forgetful, instead
    Of humble acceptance: for, question, I must!
Here's a creature made carefully—carefully made!
        Put together with craft, and then stamped on, and
        why?
The answer seems nowhere: it's discord that's played.
    The sky's a blue dish!—an implacable sky!

X

Stop a moment: I seize an idea from the pit.
        They tell us that discord, though discord, alone,
Can be harmony when the notes properly fit:
        Am I judging all things from a single false tone?
Is the Universe one immense Organ, that rolls
        From devils to angels? I'm blind with the sight.
It pours such a splendour on heaps of poor souls!
        I might try at kneeling with Molly to-night.

Earth and Man

On October 15, 1906, GM wrote to Mrs. M. Sturge Henderson on the
subject of her book, *George Meredith, Novelist, Poet, Reformer* (New
York: Scribner, 1907), to which Basil de Selincourt had contributed four

MARTIN'S PUZZLE
VIII.6 goes] is *MS*
X.2 though] is *MS*
X.3 Can be] But is *MS*
X.8 I might try at] I think I'll try *MS*; Suppose I try *F*

chapters on GM's poetry. "Express, I beg, my obligation to Mr. de Selincourt for his exposition of 'Nature and Man'—a poem hitherto unnoticed, except by one pronouncing it obscure." "Nature and Man" is a slip for *Earth and Man*, and, since GM expressly approved of Basil de Selincourt's exposition of the poem, it is here quoted.

The true function of the senses is to put you in touch with a world outside yourself, a world which you share with mankind. But if, mis-understanding their intention, you value not the object revealed by them, but the feeling which accompanies the revelation, you are identifying yourself with something which belongs to yourself alone, and the spiritual life, the life of fellowship, is shut out. You are a prisoner, and your own senses have imprisoned you. Narrowness, confinement, is the essence of the sensual life, and to this Meredith traces it, as well in its most obvious, as in its most subtle forms, including all in the one idea of "selfishness." [Here de Selincourt quoted stanzas 34–36.] ... Only when this distempered devil [of selfishness] is cast out of him, can he burst from the chrysalis and be free. The natural function of the senses, then, is to be roads by which the mind may travel towards the attainment of truth. The danger is that they may get converted into mere conduits of pleasure. Thus converted they fly in the face of Nature, and Nature's retribution follows in due course. You have asked Pleasure of an instrument not, in the main, planned to give it to you: you get, what you least wanted, Pain. At least, that is how it works out in the long run. For the individual who aims at securing private satisfaction is aiming at something which it is no interest of Nature's that he should have. Her whip descends upon him, causing in him much horror at Nature's cruelty, much pity for himself; and at times he will fly for refuge to the defences of the cynic or the sentimentalist. Only, let wisdom lie but a little deeper in him than the skin, and the recurring stroke points him at last to the fundamental error, and teaches him to change his aim. [Pp. 216–17]

De Selincourt summarizes "this great ode" (pp. 188–92), without naming it till page 192. The gist of his summary is that when man has shed the veil of Self he will learn, as Earth has learned, "to live, not for himself, but for his kind, for the generations yet to be" (p. 193).

I

On her great venture, Man,
Earth gazes while her fingers dint the breast
Which is his well of strength, his home of rest,
And fair to scan.

II

More aid than that embrace,
That nourishment, she cannot give: his heart
Involves his fate; and she who urged the start
Abides the race.

III

For he is in the lists
Contentious with the elements, whose dower
First sprang him; for swift vultures to devour
If he desists.

IV

His breath of instant thirst
Is warning of a creature matched with strife,
To meet it as a bride, or let fall life
On life's accursed.

V

No longer forth he bounds
The lusty animal, afield to roam,
But peering in Earth's entrails, where the gnome
Strange themes propounds.

VI

By hunger sharply sped
To grasp at weapons ere he learns their use,
In each new ring he bears a giant's thews,
An infant's head.

VII

And ever that old task
Of reading what he is and whence he came,
Whither to go, finds wilder letters flame
Across her mask.

VIII

She hears his wailful prayer,
When now to the Invisible he raves
To rend him from her, now of his mother craves
Her calm, her care.

IX

The thing that shudders most
Within him is the burden of his cry.
Seen of his dread, she is to his blank eye
The eyeless Ghost.

X

Or sometimes she will seem
Heavenly, but her blush, soon wearing white,
Veils like a gorsebush in a web of blight,
With gold-buds dim.

XI

Once worshipped Prime of Powers,
She still was the Implacable: as a beast,
She struck him down and dragged him from the feast
She crowned with flowers.

XII

Her pomp of glorious hues,
Her revelries of ripeness, her kind smile,
Her songs, her peeping faces, lure awhile
With symbol-clues.

XIII

The mystery she holds
For him, inveterately he strains to see,
And sight of his obtuseness is the key
Among those folds.

VIII.3 now of] *corr. errata, de L 1911*; now, *1883, de L*; now—*errata 1883*

XIV

He may entreat, aspire,
He may despair, and she has never heed
She drinking his warm sweat will soothe his need,
Not his desire.

XV

She prompts him to rejoice,
Yet scares him on the threshold with the shroud.
He deems her cherishing of her best-endowed
A wanton's choice.

XVI

Albeit thereof he has found
Firm roadway between lustfulness and pain;
Has half transferred the battle to his brain,
From bloody ground;

XVII

He will not read her good,
Or wise, but with the passion Self obscures;
Through that old devil of the thousand lures,
Through that dense hood:

XVIII

Through terror, through distrust;
The greed to touch, to view, to have, to live:
Through all that makes of him a sensitive
Abhorring dust.

XIX

Behold his wormy home!
And he the wind-whipped, anywhither wave
Crazily tumbled on a shingle-grave
To waste in foam.

XX

Therefore the wretch inclines
Afresh to the Invisible, who, he saith,
Can raise him high: with vows of living faith
For little signs.

XXI

Some signs he must demand,
Some proofs of slaughtered nature; some prized few,
To satisfy the senses it is true,
And in his hand,

XXII

This miracle which saves
Himself, himself doth from extinction clutch,
By virtue of his worth, contrasting much
With brutes and knaves.

XXIII

From dust, of him abhorred,
He would be snatched by Grace discovering worth.
'Sever me from the hollowness of Earth!
Me take, dear Lord!'

XXIV

She hears him. Him she owes
For half her loveliness a love well won
By work that lights the shapeless and the dun,
Their common foes.

XXV

He builds the soaring spires,
That sing his soul in stone: of her he draws,
Though blind to her, by spelling at her laws,
Her purest fires.

XXVI

Through him hath she exchanged,
For the gold harvest-robes, the mural crown,
Her haggard quarry-features and thick frown
Where monsters ranged.

XXVII

And order, high discourse,
And decency, than which is life less dear,
She has of him: the lyre of language clear,
Love's tongue and source.

XXVIII

She hears him, and can hear
With glory in his gains by work achieved:
With grief for grief that is the unperceived
In her so near.

XXIX

If he aloft for aid
Imploring storms, her essence is the spur.
His cry to heaven is a cry to her
He would evade.

XXX

Not elsewhere can he tend.
Those are her rules which bid him wash foul sins;
Those her revulsions from the skull that grins
To ape his end.

XXXI

And her desires are those
For happiness, for lastingness, for light.
'Tis she who kindles in his haunting night
The hoped dawn-rose.

XXXII

Fair fountains of the dark
Daily she waves him, that his inner dream
May clasp amid the glooms a springing beam,
A quivering lark:

XXXIII

This life and her to know
For Spirit: with awakenedness of glee
To feel stern joy her origin: not he
The child of woe.

XXXIV

But that the senses still
Usurp the station of their issue mind,
He would have burst the chrysalis of the blind:
As yet he will;

XXXV

As yet he will, she prays,
Yet will when his distempered devil of Self;—
The glutton for her fruits, the wily elf
In shifting rays;—

XXXVI

That captain of the scorned;
The coveter of life in soul and shell,
The fratricide, the thief, the infidel,
The hoofed and horned;—

XXXVII

He singularly doomed
To what he execrates and writhes to shun;—
When fire has passed him vapour to the sun,
And sun relumed,

XXXVIII

Then shall the horrid pall
Be lifted, and a spirit nigh divine,
'Live in thy offspring as I live in mine,'
Will hear her call.

XXXIX

Whence looks he on a land
Whereon his labour is a carven page;
And forth from heritage to heritage
Nought writ on sand.

XL

His fables of the Above,
And his gapped readings of the crown and sword,
The hell detested and the heaven adored,
The hate, the love,

XLI

The bright wing, the black hoof,
He shall peruse, from Reason not disjoined,
And never unfaith clamouring to be coined
To faith by proof.

XLII

She her just Lord may view,
Not he, her creature, till his soul has yearned
With all her gifts to reach the light discerned
Her spirit through.

XLIII

Then in him time shall run
As in the hour that to young sunlight crows;
And—'If thou hast good faith it can repose,'
She tells her son.

XLIV

Meanwhile on him, her chief
Expression, her great word of life, looks she;
Twi-minded of him, as the waxing tree,
Or dated leaf.

A Ballad of Fair Ladies in Revolt

GM wrote to a poet and feminist, Miss Louisa Shore, on August 11, 1876, the month that this poem was published in the *Fortnightly Review*, "Will you say, that I have not assumed the present situation in 'Fair Ladies,' but one which it is to be understood that the beautiful, *i.e.* the most thoughtless of the sex hitherto, turn the chief weapon of the sex to the benefit of their sisters—having learnt to say 'we' for 'I': and thus, partly by beauty, partly by earnest argument, win one champion, and make their antagonist melancholy. Be certain that in such a combat the senses will not be excluded. Proud women may struggle against the assertion, but all experience is with that view."

On August 15 he wrote John Morley, editor of the *Fortnightly*: "You were wonderfully good in allowing my ballad to run to that length: I was ashamed, and yet I had to exercise restraint to keep back more verses."

Thirty-one years later, November 14, 1907, he wrote to Mrs. Florence J. Greenwood who had inquired about the *Ballad*: "There were no public circumstances to call it forth. It came of my study of the position and the aims of women, not much mentioned by them then, though strong in their hearts—the feeling and thinking portion of them; and I read them from sympathy. The poem was not noticed at the time. I wish you success, but fear that the combatant Suffragists are doing injury to a good cause. I would gladly see all the avenues of the Professions open to women. That would be a larger education for them."

Morley, who had first published this long ballad, wrote in his *Recollections* (see headnote, p. 296) that in 1869 he had handed GM John Stuart Mill's new *Subjection of Women*. "Meredith eagerly seized the book, fell to devouring it in settled silence, and could not be torn from it all day. He had more experience than Mill of some types of women and the particular arts, 'feline chiefly,' to which some have recourse to make their way in the world. It was a memorable day when he found the case set out, with a breadth, strength, and grasp, that raised the question brought up in France by Condorcet at the end of the eighteenth century, to a new

A BALLAD OF FAIR LADIES IN REVOLT

Previously printed in the Fortnightly 26 (*1 August 1876*).

and active position in English-speaking countries in the nineteenth"
(Morley, 1:47).

I

See the sweet women, friend, that lean beneath
The ever-falling fountain of green leaves
Round the white bending stem, and like a wreath
Of our most blushful flower shine trembling through,
To teach philosophers the thirst of thieves:
    Is one for me? is one for you?

II

—Fair sirs, we give you welcome, yield you place,
And you shall choose among us which you will,
Without the idle pastime of the chase,
If to this treaty you can well agree:
To wed our cause, and its high task fulfil.
    He who's for us, for him are we!

III

—Most gracious ladies, nigh when light has birth,
A troop of maids, brown as burnt heather-bells,
And rich with life as moss-roots breathe of earth
In the first plucking of them, past us flew
To labour, singing rustic ritornells:
    Had they a cause? are they of you?

IV

—Sirs, they are as unthinking armies are
To thoughtful leaders, and our cause is theirs.
When they know men they know the state of war:
But now they dream like sunlight on a sea,
And deem you hold the half of happy pairs.
    He who's for us, for him are we!

V

—Ladies, I listened to a ring of dames;
  Judicial in thc robe and wig; secure
  As venerated portraits in their frames;
  And they denounced some insurrection new
  Against sound laws which keep you good and pure.
      Are you of them? are they of you?

VI

—Sirs, they are of us, as their dress denotes,
  And by as much: let them together chime:
  It is an ancient bell within their throats,
  Pulled by an aged ringer; with what glee
  Befits the yellow yesterdays of time.
      He who's for us, for him are we!

VII

—Sweet ladies, you with beauty, you with wit;
  Dowered of all favours and all blessed things
  Whereat the ruddy torch of Love is lit;
  Wherefore this vain and outworn strife renew,
  Which stays the tide no more than eddy-rings?
      Who is for love must be for you.

VIII

—The manners of the market, honest sirs,
  'Tis hard to quit when you behold the wares.
  You flatter us, or perchance our milliners
  You flatter; so this vain and outworn She
  May still be the charmed snake to your soft airs!
      A higher lord than Love claim we.

IX

—One day, dear lady, missing the broad track,
  I came on a wood's border, by a mead,
  Where golden May ran up to moted black:

And there I saw Queen Beauty hold review,
With Love before her throne in act to plead.
    Take him for me, take her for you.

                           X

—Ingenious gentleman, the tale is known.
    Love pleaded sweetly: Beauty would not melt:
    She would not melt: he turned in wrath: her throne
    The shadow of his back froze witheringly,
    And sobbing at his feet Queen Beauty knelt.
        O not such slaves of Love are we!

                           XI

—Love, lady, like the star above that lance
    Of radiance flung by sunset on ridged cloud,
    Sad as the last line of a brave romance!—
    Young Love hung dim, yet quivering round him
            threw
    Beams of fresh fire while Beauty waned and bowed.
        Scorn Love, and dread the doom for you.

                           XII

—Called she not for her mirror, sir? Forth ran
    Her women: I am lost, she cried, when lo,
    Love in the form of an admiring man
    Once more in adoration bent the knee
    And brought the faded Pagan to full blow:
        For which her throne she gave: not we!

                          XIII

—My version, madam, runs not to that end.
    A certain madness of an hour half past,
    Caught her like fever: her just lord no friend
    She fancied; aimed beyond beauty, and thence grew
    The prim acerbity, sweet Love's outcast.
        Great heaven ward off that stroke from you!

XIV

—Your prayer to heaven, good sir, is generous:
 How generous likewise that you do not name
 Offended nature! She from all of us
 Couched idle underneath our showering tree,
 May quite withhold her most destructive flame;
     And then what woeful women we!

XV

—Quite, could not be, fair lady; yet your youth
 May run to drought in visionary schemes:
 And a late waking to perceive the truth,
 When day falls shrouding her supreme adieu,
 Shows darker wastes than unaccomplished dreams:
     And that may be in store for you.

XVI

—O sir, the truth, the truth! is't in the skies,
 Or in the grass, or in this heart of ours?
 But O the truth, the truth! the many eyes
 That look on it! the diverse things they see,
 According to their thirst for fruit or flowers!
     Pass on: it is the truth seek we.

XVII

—Lady, there is a truth of settled laws
 That down the past burns like a great watch-fire.
 Let youth hail changeful mornings; but your cause,
 Whetting its edge to cut the race in two,
 Is felony: you forfeit the bright lyre,
     Much honour and much glory you!

XVIII

—Sir, was it glory, was it honour, pride,
 And not as cat and serpent and poor slave,
 Wherewith we walked in union by your side?

Spare to false womanliness her delicacy,
Or bid true manliness give ear, we crave:
   In our defence thus chained are we.

XIX

—Yours, madam, were the privileges of life
Proper to man's ideal; you were the mark
Of action, and the banner in the strife:
Yea, of your very weakness once you drew
The strength that sounds the wells, outflies the lark:
   Wrapped in a robe of flame were you!

XX

—Your friend looks thoughtful. Sir, when we were chill,
You clothed us warmly; all in honour! when
We starved you fed us; all in honour still:
Oh, all in honour, ultra-honourably!
Deep is the gratitude we owe to men,
   For privileged indeed were we!

XXI

—You cite exceptions, madam, that are sad,
But come in the red struggle of our growth.
Alas, that I should have to say it! bad
Is two-sexed upon earth: this which you do,
Shows animal impatience, mental sloth:
   Man monstrous, pining seraphs you!

XXII

—I fain would ask your friend ... but I will ask
You, sir, how if in place of numbers vague,
Your sad exceptions were to break that mask

XXII.5 *present*] tainting *F*

They wear for your cool mind historically,
And blaze like black lists of a *present* plague?
    But in that light behold them we.

XXIII

—Your spirit breathes a mist upon our world,
  Lady, and like a rain to pierce the roof
And drench the bed where toil-tossed man lies curled
  In his hard-earned oblivion! You are few,
Scattered, ill-counselled, blinded: for a proof,
    I have lived, and have known none like you.

XXIV

—We may be blind to men, sir: we embrace
  A future now beyond the fowler's nets.
Though few, we hold a promise for the race
  That was not at our rising: you are free
To win brave mates; you lose but marionnettes.
    He who's for us, for him are we.

XXV

—Ah! madam, were they puppets who withstood
  Youth's cravings for adventure to preserve
The dedicated ways of womanhood?
  The light which leads us from the paths of rue,
That light above us, never seen to swerve,
    Should be the home-lamp trimmed by you.

XXVI

—Ah! sir, our worshipped posture we perchance
  Shall not abandon, though we see not how,
Being to that lamp-post fixed, we may advance
  Beside our lords in any real degree,
Unless we move: and to advance is now
    A sovereign need, think more than we.

XXVII

—So push you out of harbour in small craft,
  With little seamanship; and comes a gale,
  The world will laugh, the world has often laughed,
  Lady, to see how bold when skies are blue,
  When black winds churn the deeps how panic-pale,
      How swift to the old nest fly you!

XXVIII

—What thinks your friend, kind sir? We have escaped
  But partly that old half-tamed wild beast's paw
  Whereunder woman, the weak thing, was shaped:
  Men too have known the cramping enemy
  In grim brute force, whom force of brain shall awe:
      Him our deliverer, await we!

XXIX

—Delusions are with eloquence endowed,
  And yours might pluck an angel from the spheres
  To play in this revolt whereto you are vowed,
  Deliverer, lady! but like summer dew
  O'er fields that crack for rain your friends drop tears,
      Who see the awakening for you.

XXX

—Is he our friend, there silent? he weeps not.
  O sir, delusion mounting like a sun
  On a mind blank as the white wife of Lot,
  Giving it warmth and movement! if this be
  Delusion, think of what thereby was won
      For men, and dream of what win we.

XXXI

—Lady, the destiny of minor powers,
  Who would recast us, is but to convulse:
  You enter on a strife that frets and sours;

You can but win sick disappointment's hue;
And simply an accelerated pulse,
    Some tonic you have drunk moves you.

XXXII

—Thinks your friend so? Good sir, your wit is bright;
But wit that strives to speak the popular voice,
Puts on its nightcap and puts out its light;
Curfew, would seem your conqueror's decree
To women likewise: and we have no choice
    Save darkness or rebellion, we!

XXXIII

—A plain safe intermediate way is cleft
By reason foiling passion: you that rave
Of mad alternatives to right and left
Echo the tempter, madam: and 'tis due
Unto your sex to shun it as the grave,
    This later apple offered you.

XXXIV

—This apple is not ripe, it is not sweet;
Nor rosy, sir, nor golden: eye and mouth
Are little wooed by it; yet we would eat.
We are somewhat tired of Eden, is our plea.
We have thirsted long; this apple suits our drouth:
    'Tis good for men to halve, think we.

XXXV

—But say, what seek you, madam? 'Tis enough
That you should have dominion o'er the springs
Domestic and man's heart: those ways, how rough,
How vile, outside the stately avenue
Where you walk sheltered by your angel's wings,
    Are happily unknown to you.

XXXVI

—We hear women's shrieks on them. We like your
  phrase,
 Dominion domestic! And that roar,
 'What seek you?' is of tyrants in all days.
 Sir, get you something of our purity,
 And we will of your strength: we ask no more.
  That is the sum of what seek we.

XXXVII

—O for an image, madam, in one word,
 To show you as the lightning night reveals,
 Your error and your perils: you have erred
 In mind only, and the perils that ensue
 Swift heels may soften; wherefore to swift heels
  Address your hopes of safety you!

XXXVIII

—To err in mind, sir . . . your friend smiles: he may!
 To err in mind, if err in mind we can,
 Is grievous error you do well to stay.
 But O how different from reality
 Men's fiction is! how like you in the plan,
  Is woman, knew you her as we!

XXXIX

—Look, lady, where yon river winds its line
 Toward sunset, and receives on breast and face
 The splendour of fair life: to be divine,
 'Tis nature bids you be to nature true,
 Flowing with beauty, lending earth your grace,
  Reflecting heaven in clearness you.

XL

—Sir, you speak well: your friend no word vouchsafes.
To flow with beauty, breeding fools and worse,
Cowards and worse: at such fair life she chafes
Who is not wholly of the nursery,
Nor of your schools: we share the primal curse;
    Together shake it off, say we!

XLI

—Hear, then, my friend, madam! Tongue-restrained he
    stands
Till words are thoughts, and thoughts, like swords
    enriched
With traceries of the artificer's hands,
Are fire-proved steel to cut, fair flowers to view.—
Do I hear him? Oh, he is bewitched, bewitched!
    Heed him not! Traitress beauties you!

XLII

—We have won a champion, sisters, and a sage!
—Ladies, you win a guest to a good feast!
—Sir spokesman, sneers are weakness veiling rage.
—Of weakness, and wise men, you have the key.
—Then are there fresher mornings mounting East
    Than ever yet have dawned, sing we!

XLIII

—False ends as false began, madam, be sure!
—What lure there is the pure cause purifies!
—Who purifies the victim of the lure?
—That soul which bids us our high light pursue.
—Some heights are measured down: the wary wise
    Shun Reason in the masque with you!

XLI.1 Hear] *1883*; Here *de L; corr. errata, de L 1911*

XLIV

—Sir, for the friend you bring us, take our thanks.
Yes, Beauty was of old this barren goal;
A thing with claws; and brute-like in her pranks!
But could she give more loyal guarantee
Than wooing wisdom, that in her a soul
     Has risen? Adieu: content are we!

XLV

Those ladies led their captive to the flood's
Green edge. He floating with them seemed the most
Fool-flushed old noddy ever crowned with buds.
Happier than I! Then, why not wiser too?
For he that lives with Beauty, he may boast
     His comrade over me and you.

XLVI

Have women nursed some dream since Helen sailed
Over the sea of blood the blushing star,
That beauty, whom frail man as Goddess hailed,
When not possessing her (for such is he!),
Might in a wondering season seen afar,
     Be tamed to say not 'I,' but 'we'?

XLVII

And shall they make of Beauty their estate,
The fortress and the weapon of their sex?
Shall she in her frost-brilliancy dictate,
More queenly than of old, how we must woo,
Ere she will melt? The halter's on our necks,
     Kick as it likes us, I and you.

XLVIII

Certain it is, if Beauty has disdained
Her ancient conquests, with an aim thus high:
If this, if that, if more, the fight is gained.

But can she keep her followers without fee?
Yet ah! to hear anew those ladies cry,
 He who's for us, for him are we!

Sonnets

Lucifer in Starlight

Lucifer, the light-bringer and daystar, has been interpreted as a surrogate name for Satan in Isa. 14:12–15.

Paradise Lost is, naturally, echoed in this sonnet. Milton had described Satan's face as "intrencht" with "Deep scars of Thunder" (1. 601), and explained that "awe from above had quell'd / His Heart, not else dismay'd" (4. 860–61).

On a starred night Prince Lucifer uprose.
Tired of his dark dominion swung the fiend
Above the rolling ball in cloud part screened,
Where sinners hugged their spectre of repose.
Poor prey to his hot fit of pride were those.
And now upon his western wing he leaned,
Now his huge bulk o'er Afric's sands careened,
Now the black planet shadowed Arctic snows.
Soaring through wider zones that pricked his scars
With memory of the old revolt from Awe,   10
He reached a middle height, and at the stars,
Which are the brain of heaven, he looked, and sank.
Around the ancient track marched, rank on rank,
The army of unalterable law.

LUCIFER IN STARLIGHT

7 Afric's sands] Africa *1883*

The Star Sirius

Bright Sirius! that when Orion pales
To dotlings under moonlight still art keen
With cheerful fervour of a warrior's mien
Who holds in his great heart the battle-scales:
Unquenched of flame though swift the flood assails,
Reducing many lustrous to the lean:
Be thou my star, and thou in me be seen
To show what source divine is, and prevails.
Long watches through, at one with godly night,
I mark thee planting joy in constant fire;   10
And thy quick beams, whose jets of life inspire
Life to the spirit, passion for the light,
Dark Earth since first she lost her lord from sight
Has viewed and felt them sweep her as a lyre.

Sense and Spirit

The senses loving Earth or well or ill,
Ravel yet more the riddle of our lot.
The mind is in their trammels, and lights not
By trimming fear-bred tales; nor does the will
To find in nature things which less may chill
An ardour that desires, unknowing what.
Till we conceive her living we go distraught,
At best but circle-windsails of a mill.
Seeing she lives, and of her joy of life
Creatively has given us blood and breath   10
For endless war and never wound unhealed,
The gloomy Wherefore of our battle-field
Solves in the Spirit, wrought of her through strife
To read her own and trust her down to death.

Earth's Secret

Not solitarily in fields we find
Earth's secret open, though one page is there;
Her plainest, such as children spell, and share
With bird and beast; raised letters for the blind.
Not where the troubled passions toss the mind,
In turbid cities, can the key be bare.
It hangs for those who hither thither fare,
Close interthreading nature with our kind.
They, hearing History speak, of what men were,
And have become, are wise. The gain is great   10
In vision and solidity; it lives.
Yet at a thought of life apart from her,
Solidity and vision lose their state,
For Earth, that gives the milk, the spirit gives.

The Spirit of Shakespeare

GM sent the next two sonnets to Norman MacColl of the *Athenaeum* on February 1, 1883, with the following comment: "Enclosed are two sonnets, to be printed in company, if they are suitable to your columns. They come out of a body of sonnets, forming a portion of a volume I have in hand, called *Poems and Lyrics of the Joy of Earth*: but whether these two, as they stand by themselves, carry sufficient animation of the anti-Pessimism of the bulk, to have meaning enough for your readers, I cannot judge— therefore excuse you for a negative decision."

Thy greatest knew thee, Mother Earth; unsoured
He knew thy sons. He probed from hell to hell
Of human passions, but of love deflowered
His wisdom was not, for he knew thee well.
Thence came the honeyed corner at his lips,

THE SPIRIT OF SHAKESPEARE and THE SPIRIT OF SHAKESPEARE: CONTINUED

Previously printed in the Athenaeum *81 (10 February 1883).*
5 the] that *Ath.*

The conquering smile wherein his spirit sails
Calm as the God who the white sea-wave whips,
Yet full of speech and intershifting tales,
Close mirrors of us: thence had he the laugh
We feel is thine: broad as ten thousand beeves   10
At pasture! thence thy songs, that winnow chaff
From grain, bid sick Philosophy's last leaves
Whirl, if they have no response—they enforced
To fatten Earth when from her soul divorced.

The Spirit of Shakespeare: Continued

How smiles he at a generation ranked
In gloomy noddings over life! They pass.
Not he to feed upon a breast unthanked,
Or eye a beauteous face in a cracked glass.
But he can spy that little twist of brain
Which moved some weighty leader of the blind,
Unwitting 'twas the goad of personal pain,
To view in curst eclipse our Mother's mind,
And show us of some rigid harridan
The wretched bondmen till the end of time.   10
O lived the Master now to paint us Man,
That little twist of brain would ring a chime
Of whence it came and what it caused, to start
Thunders of laughter, clearing air and heart.

Internal Harmony

Assured of worthiness we do not dread
Competitors; we rather give them hail
And greeting in the lists where we may fail:
Must, if we bear an aim beyond the head!

My betters are my masters: purely fed
By their sustainment I likewise shall scale
Some rocky steps between the mount and vale;
Meanwhile the mark I have and I will wed.
So that I draw the breath of finer air,
Station is nought, nor footways laurel-strewn,   10
Nor rivals tightly belted for the race.
Good speed to them! My place is here or there;
My pride is that among them I have place:
And thus I keep this instrument in tune.

Grace and Love

Two flower-enfolding crystal vases she
I love fills daily, mindful but of one:
And close behind pale morn she, like the sun
Priming our world with light, pours, sweet to see,
Clear water in the cup, and into me
The image of herself: and that being done,
Choice of what blooms round her fair garden run
In climbers or in creepers or the tree,
She ranges with unerring fingers fine,
To harmony so vivid that through sight   10
I hear, I have her heavenliness to fold
Beyond the senses, where such love as mine,
Such grace as hers, should the strange Fates withhold
Their starry more from her and me, unite.

Appreciation

Earth was not Earth before her sons appeared,
Nor Beauty Beauty ere young Love was born:
And thou when I lay hidden wast as morn

APPRECIATION

3 wast] wert *1883*

At city-windows, touching eyelids bleared;
To none by her fresh wingedness endeared;
Unwelcome unto revellers outworn.
I the last echoes of Diana's horn
In woodland heard, and saw thee come, and cheered.
No longer wast thou then mere light, fair soul!
And more than simple duty moved thy feet.   10
New colours rose in thee, from fear, from shame,
From hope, effused: though not less pure a scroll
May men read on the heart I taught to beat:
That change in thee, if not thyself, I claim.

The Discipline of Wisdom

Rich labour is the struggle to be wise,
While we make sure the struggle cannot cease.
Else better were it in some bower of peace
Slothful to swing, contending with the flies.
You point at Wisdom fixed on lofty skies,
As mid barbarian hordes a sculptured Greece:
She falls. To live and shine, she grows her fleece,
Is shorn, and rubs with follies and with lies.
So following her, your hewing may attain
The right to speak unto the mute, and shun   10
That sly temptation of the illumined brain,
Deliveries oracular, self-spun.
Who sweats not with the flock will seek in vain
To shed the words which are ripe fruit of sun.

The State of Age

Rub thou thy battered lamp: nor claim nor beg
Honours from aught about thee. Light the young.
Thy frame is as a dusty mantle hung,

APPRECIATION
9 wast] wert *1883*

O grey one! pendant on a loosened peg.
Thou art for this our life an ancient egg,
Or a tough bird: thou hast a rudderless tongue,
Turning dead trifles, like the cock of dung;
Which runs, Time's contrast to thy halting leg.
Nature, it is most sure, not thee admires.
But hast thou in thy season set her fires   10
To burn from Self to Spirit through the lash,
Honoured the sons of Earth shall hold thee high:
Yea, to spread light when thy proud letter I
Drops prone and void as any thoughtless dash.

Progress

Compare GM's early sonnet "Progression," p. 1041.

In Progress you have little faith, say you:
Men will maintain dear interests, wreak base hates,
By force, and gentle women choose their mates
Most amorously from the gilded fighting crew:
The human heart Bellona's mad halloo
Will ever fire to dicing with the Fates.
'Now at this time,' says History, 'those two States
'Stood ready their past wrestling to renew.
'They sharpened arms and showed them, like the brutes
'Whose haunches quiver. But a yellow blight   10
'Fell on their waxing harvests. They deferred
'The bloody settlement of their disputes
'Till God should bless them better.' They did right.
And naming Progress, both shall have the word.

The World's Advance

Judge mildly the tasked world; and disincline
To brand it, for it bears a heavy pack.
You have perchance observed the inebriate's track

At night when he has quitted the inn-sign:
He plays diversions on the homeward line,
Still that way bent albeit his legs are slack:
A hedge may take him, but he turns not back,
Nor turns this burdened world, of curving spine.
'Spiral,' the memorable Lady terms
Our mind's ascent: our world's advance presents   10
That figure on a flat; the way of worms.
Cherish the promise of its good intents,
And warn it, not one instinct to efface
Ere Reason ripens for the vacant place.

A Certain People

As Puritans they prominently wax,
And none more kindly gives and takes hard knocks.
Strong psalmic chanting, like to nasal cocks,
They join to thunderings of their hearty thwacks
But naughtiness, with hoggery, not lacks
When Peace another door in them unlocks,
Where conscience shows the eyeing of an ox
Grown dully apprehensive of an Axe.
Graceless they are when gone to frivolousness,
Fearing the God they flout, the God they glut.   10
They need their pious exercises less
Than schooling in the Pleasures: fair belief
That these are devilish only to their thief,
Charged with an Axe nigh on the occiput.

The Garden of Epicurus

That Garden of sedate Philosophy
Once flourished, fenced from passion and mishap,
A shining spot upon a shaggy map;

Where mind and body, in fair junction free,
Luted their joyful concord; like the tree
From root to flowering twigs a flowing sap.
Clear Wisdom found in tended Nature's lap,
Of gentlemen the happy nursery.
That Garden would on light supremest verge,
Were the long drawing of an equal breath   10
Healthful for Wisdom's head, her heart, her aims.
Our world which for its Babels wants a scourge,
And for its wilds a husbandman, acclaims
The crucifix that came of Nazareth.

A Later Alexandrian

The poet here described is probably Dante Gabriel Rossetti, who had
died in 1882, the year before the appearance of the sonnet in *Poems and
Lyrics of the Joy of Earth*.

An inspiration caught from dubious hues,
Filled him, and mystic wrynesses he chased;
For they lead farther than the single-faced,
Wave subtler promise when desire pursues.
The moon of cloud discoloured was his Muse,
His pipe the reed of the old moaning waste.
Love was to him with anguish fast enlaced,
And Beauty where she walked blood-shot the dews.
Men railed at such a singer; women thrilled
Responsively: he sang not Nature's own   10
Divinest, but his lyric had a tone,
As 'twere a forest-echo of her voice:
What barrenly they yearn for seemed distilled
From what they dread, who do through tears rejoice.

An Orson of the Muse

Trevelyan added a subtitle: "[Walt Whitman]" in GMT. Probably
GM had identified the subject of the sonnet for him. Rossetti had also

used the name "Orson" for Whitman (Galland, p. 217 n.).

In 1877 GM, in his "Essay on the Idea of Comedy and of The Uses of the Comic Spirit" had used the term "Orson" for German controversialists. Orson was the twin in the French medieval tale of *Valentine and Orson*, who was suckled by a bear and grew up with rough manners.

> Her son, albeit the Muse's livery
> And measured courtly paces rouse his taunts,
> Naked and hairy in his savage haunts,
> To Nature only will he bend the knee;
> Spouting the founts of her distillery
> Like rough rock-sources; and his woes and wants,
> Being Nature's, civil limitation daunts
> His utterance never; the nymphs blush, not he.
> Him, when he blows of Earth, and Man, and Fate,
> The Muse will hearken to with graver ear   10
> Than many of her train can waken: him
> Would fain have taught what fruitful things and dear
> Must sink beneath the tidewaves, of their weight,
> If in no vessel built for sea they swim.

The Point of Taste

> Unhappy poets of a sunken prime!
> You to reviewers are as ball to bat.
> They shadow you with Homer, knock you flat
> With Shakespeare: bludgeons brainingly sublime
> On you the excommunicates of Rhyme,
> Because you sing not in the living Fat.
> The wiry whizz of an intrusive gnat
> Is verse that shuns their self-producing time.
> Sound them their clocks, with loud alarum trump,
> Or watches ticking temporal at their fobs,   10
> You win their pleased attention. But, bright God
> O' the lyre, what bully-drawlers they applaud!
> Rather for us a tavern-catch, and bump
> Chorus where Lumpkin with his Giles hobnobs.

Camelus Saltat

What say you, critic, now you have become
An author and maternal?—in this trap
(To quote you) of poor hollow folk who rap
On instruments as like as drum to drum.
You snarled tut-tut for welcome to tum-tum,
So like the nose fly-teased in its noon's nap.
You scratched an insect-slaughtering thunder-clap
With that between the fingers and the thumb.
It seemeth mad to quit the Olympian couch,
Which bade our public gobble or reject.   10
O spectacle of Peter, shrewdly pecked,
Piper, by his own pepper from his pouch!
What of the sneer, the jeer, the voice austere,
You dealt?—the voice austere, the jeer, the sneer.

Camelus Saltat: Continued

Oracle of the market! thence you drew
The taste which stamped you guide of the inept.—
A North-sea pilot, Hildebrand yclept,
A sturdy and a briny, once men knew.
He loved small beer, and for that copious brew,
To roll ingurgitation till he slept,
Rations exchanged with flavour for the adept:
And merrily plied him captain, mate and crew.
At last this dancer to the Polar star
Sank, washed out within, and overboard was pitched,   10
To drink the sea and pilot him to land.
O captain-critic! printed, neatly stitched,
Know, while the pillory-eggs fly fast, they are
Not eggs, but the drowned soul of Hildebrand.

To J. M.

GM wrote this sonnet to his friend John Morley in 1867 just after Morley had been appointed editor of the *Fortnightly*, a position that he held for fifteen years. In the first half of his tenure he built the *Fortnightly* into an important liberal journal; later it developed into the most important radical journal. His policy of signed articles was an innovation. Many years later John, who had become Viscount Morley, quoted this "sonnet of exhortation" when writing about GM's "animating counsels to a junior in whose future usefulness he had faith" (Morley, 1:38).

See also *Lines to a Friend Visiting America*, page 621.

> Let Fate or Insufficiency provide
> Mean ends for men who what they are would be:
> Penned in their narrow day no change they see
> Save one which strikes the blow to brutes and pride.
> Our faith is ours and comes not on a tide:
> And whether Earth's great offspring, by decree,
> Must rot if they abjure rapacity,
> Not argument but effort shall decide.
> They number many heads in that hard flock:
> Trim swordsmen they push forth: yet try thy steel.   10
> Thou, fighting for poor humankind, wilt feel
> The strength of Roland in thy wrist to hew
> A chasm sheer into the barrier rock,
> And bring the army of the faithful through.

To a Friend Lost

(TOM TAYLOR)

Tom Taylor, editor of *Punch* from 1874 until his death on July 12, 1880, was eleven years GM's senior and had been a dear friend since 1849 or

TO J. M.: LET FATE

Previously printed in the Fortnightly 7 *(1 June 1867), title*: Sonnet, To ——; *and in* English Sonnets by Living Writers, *ed. Samuel Waddington (London: Bell & S, 1880)*.

TO A FRIEND LOST (TOM TAYLOR)

Previously printed in the Cornhill 42 *(October 1880), title:* To a Friend recently Lost. T. T.; *1883, and the Edition de Luxe:* To a Friend Lost, (T. T.); *corrected in errata, de L 1911:* To a Friend Lost (Tom Taylor).

1850. Tom Taylor was many things: a barrister who did not practice, a
free-lance journalist, an art critic, and a prolific dramatist.

When I remember, friend, whom lost I call,
Because a man beloved is taken hence,
The tender humour and the fire of sense
In your good eyes; how full of heart for all,
And chiefly for the weaker by the wall,
You bore that lamp of sane benevolence;
Then see I round you Death his shadows dense
Divide, and at your feet his emblems fall.
For surely are you one with the white host,
Spirits, whose memory is our vital air   10
Through the great love of Earth they had: lo, these,
Like beams that throw the path on tossing seas,
Can bid us feel we keep them in the ghost,
Partakers of a strife they joyed to share.

My Theme

Of me and of my theme think what thou wilt:
The song of gladness one straight bolt can check.
But I have never stood at Fortune's beck:
Were she and her light crew to run atilt
At my poor holding little would be spilt;
Small were the praise for singing o'er that wreck.
Who courts her dooms to strife his bended neck;
He grasps a blade, not always by the hilt.
Nathless she strikes at random, can be fell
With other than those votaries she deals   10
The black or brilliant from her thunder-rift.
I say but that this love of Earth reveals
A soul beside our own to quicken, quell,
Irradiate, and through ruinous floods uplift.

TO A FRIEND LOST
6 lamp] light C
10 is] in 1883, de L; corr. errata, de L 1911

My Theme: Continued

'Tis true the wisdom that my mind exacts
Through contemplation from a heart unbent
By many tempests may be stained and rent:
The summer flies it mightily attracts.
Yet they seem choicer than your sons of facts,
Which scarce give breathing of the sty's content
For their diurnal carnal nourishment:
Which treat with Nature in official pacts.
The deader body Nature could proclaim.
Much life have neither. Let the heavens of wrath   10
Rattle, then both scud scattering to froth.
But during calms the flies of idle aim
Less put the spirit out, less baffle thirst
For light than swinish grunters, blest or curst.

Time and Sentiment

I see a fair young couple in a wood,
And as they go, one bends to take a flower,
That so may be embalmed their happy hour,
And in another day, a kindred mood,
Haply together, or in solitude,
Recovered what the teeth of Time devour
The joy, the bloom, and the illusive power,
Wherewith by their young blood they are endued
To move all enviable, framed in May,
And of an aspect sisterly with Truth: 10
Yet seek they with Time's laughing things to wed:
Who will be prompted on some pallid day
To lift the hueless flower and show that dead,
Even such, and by this token, is their youth.

TIME AND SENTIMENT

Previously printed in the Fortnightly *13 (1 April 1870), title:* Sonnet. A Mark in Time.

BALLADS AND POEMS

OF

TRAGIC LIFE

(1887)

The Two Masks

The composition of this poem can be dated from the drafts in the
Huntington Library, San Marino, California, since a fragment for the
opening of the poem *To Colonel Charles* appears on the same piece of
paper as a draft of the second part of *The Two Masks*. The same pen and
ink were used for the drafts of both poems. *To Colonel Charles* appeared
in the *Pall Mall Gazette*, February 16, 1887 and was dated "February
1887" when collected into *Poems: The Empty Purse*, etc. (1892).

I

Melpomene among her livid people,
Ere stroke of lyre, upon Thaleia looks,
Warned by old contests that one museful ripple
Along those lips of rose with tendril hooks,

MSS: Huntington HM6762. *MS 1, rough draft of two stanzas; MS 2, fair copy of stanza
II, no title. Variants are from these MSS.*

MS 1:
I.2 stroke of] striking

299

Forebodes disturbance in the springs of pathos,
Perchance may change of masks midway demand,
Albeit the man rise mountainous as Athos,
The woman wild as Cape Leucadia stand.

II

For this the Comic Muse exacts of creatures
Appealing to the fount of tears: that they
Strive never to outleap our human features,
And do Right Reason's ordinance obey,
In peril of the hum to laughter nighest.
But prove they under stress of action's fire
Nobleness, to that test of Reason highest,
She bows: she waves them for the loftier lyre.

I.5 disturbance] convulsions
I.6 *Del.*: A change of masks will ruthlessly demand,   midway] may oft *del.*
I.7 mountainous] mountain-high
I.8 woman wild as Cape Leucadia] woman on the rock Leucadian *or* [woman]'s form on
Cape Leucadia
I.6–8

> Perchance a change of masks forebodes midway
> Albeit the man stand
> The woman's form on Cape Leucadia sway.

II

> To her likewise the Sister Muse delivers
> A many who with laughter's opening note *or* chorus led,
> *Del.*: Away from perfect reason,
> Until the deeper instrument with shivers
> Caught them on tears
> But haps it that together for a season
> For this the Comic Muse exacts of either,
> That they [shall have *del.*] right Reason's ordinance obey;
> Else with *or* on an arm the Goddesses together
> Pull, & the creature soon is Laughter's prey,
> Though big, though woeful *or* tearful, tearful *or* harrowing, all in season,
> But does it in the fire of action wave
> Nobleness, to that highest tool of reason
> The laughing eyes are with the sorrowing

10

MS 2: 9 lines instead of 8:
II.5 hum] sounds
II.6–8

> But have they in the fire of action wrought
> Nobleness, to that test of Reason highest,
> The laughing eyes are with the grave in thought
> She bows; she waves them to the loftier lyre.

Archduchess Anne

This dramatic narrative is fictitious.

I

I

In middle age an evil thing
    Befell Archduchess Anne:
She looked outside her wedding-ring
    Upon a princely man.

II

Count Louis was for horse and arms;
    And if its beacon waved,
For love; but ladies had not charms
    To match a danger braved.

III

On battlefields he was the bow
    Bestrung to fly the shaft:
In idle hours his heart would flow
    As winds on currents waft.

IV

His blood was of those warrior tribes
    That streamed from morning's fire,
Whom now with traps and now with bribes
    The wily Council wire.

MSS: Huntington HM6763. *Fair copy; later fragment, part III.11–28. Title and I.1.2*
Anne; *thereafter* Ann

I.III.1 battlefields] battlefield *MS*
I.III.4 on] the *del. MS*

V

Archduchess Anne the Council ruled,
    Count Louis his great dame;
And woe to both when one had cooled!
    Little was she to blame.

VI

Among her chiefs who spun their plots,
    Old Kraken stood the sword:
As sharp his wits for cutting knots
    Of babble he abhorred.

VII

He reverenced her name and line,
    Nor other merit had
Save soldierwise to wait her sign,
    And do the deed she bade.

VIII

He saw her hand jump at her side
    Ere royally she smiled
On Louis and his fair young bride
    Where courtly ranks defiled.

IX

That was a moment when a shock
    Through the procession ran,
And thrilled the plumes, and stayed the clock,
    Yet smiled Archduchess Anne.

I.VI.3 wits] mind *MS*
I.VII.3 soldierwise] soldierly *del. MS*

X

No touch gave she to hound in leash,
    No wink to sword in sheath:
She seemed a woman scarce of flesh;
    Above it, or beneath.

XI

Old Kraken spied with kennelled snarl,
    His Lady deemed disgraced.
He footed as on burning marl,
    When out of Hall he paced.

XII

'Twas seen he hammered striding legs,
    And stopped, and strode again.
Now Vengeance has a brood of eggs,
    But Patience must be hen.

XIII

Too slow are they for wrath to hatch,
    Too hot for time to rear.
Old Kraken kept unwinking watch;
    He marked his day appear.

XIV

He neighed a laugh, though moods were rough
    With standards in revolt:
His nostrils took the news for snuff,
    His smacking lips for salt.

I.XI.2 Lady] mistress *MS*
I.XIII.3 kept] held *MS*

XV

Count Louis' wavy cock's plumes led
　　His troops of black-haired manes,
A rebel; and old Kraken sped
　　To front him on the plains.

XVI

Then camp opposed to camp did they
　　Fret earth with panther claws
For signal of a bloody day,
　　Each reading from the Laws.

XVII

'Forefend it, heaven!' Count Louis cried,
　　'And let the righteous plead:
My country is a willing bride,
　　Was never slave decreed.

XVIII

'Not we for thirst of blood appeal
　　To sword and slaughter curst;
We have God's blessing on our steel,
　　Do we our pleading first.'

XIX

Count Louis, soul of chivalry,
　　Put trust in plighted word;
By starlight on the broad brown lea,
　　To bar the strife he spurred.

I.XIX.3 brown] black[?] *del. MS*

XX

Across his breast a crimson spot,
　　That in a quiver glowed,
The ruddy crested camp-fires shot,
　　As he to darkness rode.

XXI

He rode while omens called, beware
　　Old Kraken's pledge of faith!
A smile and waving hand in air,
　　And outward flew the wraith.

XXII

Before pale morn had mixed with gold,
　　His army roared, and chilled,
As men who have a woe foretold,
　　And see it red fulfilled.

XXIII

Away and to his young wife speed,
　　And say that Honour's dead!
Another word she will not need
　　To bow a widow's head.

XXIV

Old Kraken roped his white moustache
　　Right, left, for savage glee:
—To swing him in his soldier's sash,
　　Were kind for such as he!

I.XXII.2 roared] stamped *MS*

XXV

Old Kraken's look hard Winter wears
    When sweeps the wild snow-blast:
He had the hug of Arctic bears
    For captives he held fast.

II

I

Archduchess Anne sat carved in frost,
    Shut off from priest and spouse.
Her lips were locked, her arms were crossed,
    Her eyes were in her brows.

II

One hand enclosed a paper scroll,
    Held as a strangled asp.
So may we see the woman's soul
    In her dire tempter's grasp.

III

Along that scroll Count Louis' doom
    Throbbed till the letters flamed.
She saw him in his scornful bloom,
    She saw him chained and shamed.

IV

Around that scroll Count Louis' fate
    Was acted to her stare,
And hate in love and love in hate
    Fought fell to smite or spare.

II.I.3 lips were] mouth was *MS*
II.IV.3 *MS*: And ancient love in present hate

V

Between the day that struck her old,
    And this black star of days,
Her heart swung like a storm-bell tolled
    Above a town ablaze.

VI

His beauty pressed to intercede,
    His beauty served him ill.
—Not Vengeance, 'tis his rebel's deed,
    'Tis Justice, not our will!

VII

Yet who had sprung to life's full force
    A breast that loveless dried?
But who had sapped it at the source,
    With scarlet to her pride!

VIII

He brought her waning heart as 'twere
    New message from the skies.
And he betrayed, and left on her
    The burden of their sighs.

IX

In floods her tender memories poured;
    They foamed with waves of spite:
She crushed them, high her heart outsoared,
    To keep her mind alight.

II.VI.4 Justice] duty *del. MS*
II.VIII.1 waning heart] withered wane *MS*; human wane *1887*
II.VIII.2 New] A *MS*
II.IX.3 crushed them, high] kept them down, *MS*
II.IX.4 keep] hold *MS*

X

—The crawling creature, called in scorn
        A woman!—with this pen
We sign a paper that may warn
        His crowing fellowmen.

XI

—We read them lesson of a power
        They slight who do us wrong.
That bitter hour this bitter hour
        Provokes; by turns the strong!

XII

—That we were woman once is known:
        That we are Justice now,
Above our sex, above the throne,
        Men quaking shall avow.

XIII

Archduchess Anne ascending flew,
        Her heart outsoared, but felt
The demon of her sex pursue,
        Incensing or to melt.

XIV

Those counterfloods below at leap,
        Still in her breast blew storm,
And farther up the heavenly steep,
        Wrestled in angels' form.

II.XIV.2 Still in] Within *del. MS*   blew] was[?] *del. MS*
II.XIV.3 farther] higher *MS*

XV

To disentangle one clear wish
    Not of her sex, she sought;
And womanish to womanish,
    Discerned in lighted thought.

XVI

With Louis' chance it went not well
    When at herself she raged;
A woman, of whom men might tell
    She doted, crazed and aged.

XVII

Or else enamoured of a sweet
    Withdrawn, a vengeful crone!
And say, what figure at her feet
    Is this that utters moan?

XVIII

The Countess Louis from her head
    Drew veil: 'Great Lady, hear!
My husband deems you Justice dread,
    I know you Mercy dear.

XIX

'His error upon him may fall;
    He will not breathe a nay.
I am his helpless mate in all,
    Except for grace to pray.

II.XV.4 lighted] highest *MS*
II.XVIII.2 Drew] Raised *MS*   Great] Dear *MS*

XX

'Perchance on me his choice inclined,
        To give his House an heir:
I had not marriage with his mind,
        His counsel could not share.

XXI

'I brought no portion for his weal
        But this one instinct true,
Which bids me in my weakness kneel,
        Archduchess Anne, to you.'

XXII

The frowning Lady uttered, 'Forth!'
        Her look forbade delay:
'It is not mine to weigh your worth;
        Your husband's others weigh.

XXIII

'Hence with the woman in your speech,
        For nothing it avails
In woman's fashion to beseech
        Where Justice holds the scales.'

XXIV

Then bent and went the lady wan,
        Whose girlishness made grey
The thoughts that through Archduchess Anne
        Shattered like stormy spray.

II.XX.1 on] to del. MS
II.XXII.2 look] eyes MS

XXV

Long sat she there, as flame that strives
  To hold on beating wind:
—His wife must be the fool of wives,
  Or cunningly designed!

XXVI

She sat until the tempest-pitch
  In her torn bosom fell;
—His wife must be a subtle witch
  Or else God loves her well!

III

I

Old Kraken read a missive penned
  By his great Lady's hand.
Her condescension called him friend,
  To raise the crest she fanned.

II

Swiftly to where he lay encamped
  It flew, yet breathed aloof
From woman's feeling, and he stamped
  A heel more like a hoof.

III

She wrote of Mercy: 'She was loth
  Too hard to goad a foe.'
He stamped, as when men drive an oath
  Devils transcribe below.

II.XXVI.2 torn] stung[?] *del.* worn *del. MS*

IV

She wrote: 'We have him half by theft.'
    His wrinkles glistened keen:
And see the Winter storm-cloud cleft
    To lurid skies between!

V

When read old Kraken: 'Christ our Guide,'
    His eyes were spikes of spar:
And see the white snow-storm divide
    About an icy star!

VI

'She trusted him to understand,'
    She wrote, and further prayed
That policy might rule the land.
    Old Kraken's laughter neighed.

VII

Her words he took; her nods and winks
    Treated as woman's fog.
The man-dog for his mistress thinks,
    Not less her faithful dog.

VIII

She hugged a cloak old Kraken ripped;
    Disguise to him he loathed.
—Your mercy, madam, shows you stripped,
    While mine will keep you clothed.

III.VII.1 took] read *del. MS*
III.VII.4 her] a *del. MS*

IX

A rough ill-soldered scar in haste
    He rubbed on his cheek-bone.
—Our policy the man shall taste;
    Our mercy shall be shown.

X

'Count Louis, honour to your race
    Decrees the Council-hall:
You 'scape the rope by special grace,
    And like a soldier fall.'

XI

—I am a man of many sins,
    Who for one virtue die,
Count Louis said.—They play at shins,
    Who kick, was the reply.

XII

Uprose the day of crimson sight,
    The day without a God.
At morn the hero said Good-night:
    See there that stain on sod!

XIII

At morn the Countess Louis heard
    Young light sing in the lark.
Ere eve it was that other bird,
    Which brings the starless dark.

III.XII.1 sight] light *del. MS*
III.XII.4 *MS*: They stretched him on red sod.
III.XIII.1 the] his *frag.*
III.XIII.3 that other] the blanker *frag.*

XIV

To heaven she vowed herself, and yearned
      Beside her lord to lie.
Archduchess Anne on Kraken turned,
      All white as a dead eye.

XV

If I could kill thee! shrieked her look:
      If lightning sprang from Will!
An oaken head old Kraken shook,
      And she might thank or kill.

XVI

The pride that fenced her heart in mail,
      By mortal pain was torn.
Forth from her bosom leaped a wail,
      As of a babe new-born.

XVII

She clad herself in courtly use,
      And one who heard them prate,
Had said they differed upon views
      Where statecraft raised debate.

XVIII

The wretch detested must she trust,
      The servant master own:
Confide to godless cause so just,
      And for God's blessing moan.

III.XIV.4 dead] corpse- *MS*
III.XV.1 shrieked] said *MS*
III.XVI.1 fenced] ringed *MS*
III.XVI.3 Forth from her bosom leaped] Out from her breast there leapt *MS*
III.XVII.2 heard them prate] witness bore *MS*
III.XVII.4 *MS*: Of statecraft, & no more.
III.XVIII *stanza xxii in MS*

XIX

Austerely she her heart kept down,
 Her woman's tongue was mute
When voice of People, voice of Crown,
 In cannon held dispute.

XX

The Crown on seas of blood, like swine,
 Swam forefoot at the throat:
It drank of its dear veins for wine,
 Enough if it might float!

XXI

It sank with piteous yelp, resurged
 Electrical with fear.
O had she on old Kraken urged
 Her word of mercy clear!

XXII

O had they with Count Louis been
 Accordant in his plea!
Cursed are the women vowed to screen
 A heart that all can see!

III.XIX *not in MS, instead:*

xviii

Like her, the gasping empire swims
 Where round the vortex boils:
To keep the form of head & limbs,
 It conjures python-coils:

III.XX *MS:*

xix

On seas of blood it swims like swine,
 The fore-hoofs at the throat:
It drinks of its dear veins for wine;
 It paddles, drifts to float.

III.XX.2 forefoot] fore-hoof *frag.*

XXIII

The godless drove unto a goal
    Was worse than vile defeat.
Did vengeance prick Count Louis' soul
    They dressed him luscious meat.

XXIV

Worms will the faithless find their lies
    In the close treasure-chest.
Without a God no day can rise,
    Though it should slay our best.

XXV

The Crown it furled a draggled flag,
    It sheathed a broken blade.
Behold its triumph in the hag
    That lives with looks decayed!

XXVI

And lo, the man of oaken head,
    Of soldier's honour bare,
He fled his land, but most he fled
    His Lady's frigid stare.

III.XXIII.1 unto] it to *MS*
III.XXIV *xxvii in MS*
III.XXIV.2 the] their *MS, frag.*
III. *before xxv MS:*

xxiv

Enough: you know: from wreck to debt
    With usury enslaved,
The empire triumphed; seeming set,
    The land Count Louis saved.

III.XXV.1 Crown it] empire *MS*
III.XXV.2 It] And *MS*
III.XXV.3 *MS:* What further, read: our tongues we wag
III.XXV.4 *MS:* On times of dust long laid.
    That] Which *frag.*

XXVII

Judged by the issue we discern
        God's blessing, and the bane.
Count Louis' dust would fill an urn,
        His deeds are waving grain.

XXVIII

And she that helped to slay, yet bade
        To spare the fated man,
Great were her errors, but she had
        Great heart, Archduchess Anne.

III.XXVI–XXVIII *not in MS, instead:*

xxvi

But he was first to make the stand,
        And try, with power for blows,
The means of peace; wherefore his land
        To him God's blessing owes.

xxvii *text XXIV*

xxviii

Count Louis now, Count Louis then,
        He towers a princely man,
And worthier when he braved than when
        He pleased Archduchess Ann.

III.XXVII.2 and] from *del. frag.*   the] his *frag.*
III.XXVII.3 would] might *frag.*
III.XXVIII.1 that] who *frag.*
III.XXVIII.2 fated] princely *frag.*

The Song of Theodolinda

In *Cornhill*, September 1872, and in *Ballads and Poems of Tragic Life* (1887), the following note was appended to this poem: "The legend of the Iron Crown of Lombardy, formed of a nail of the true Cross by order of the devout Queen Theodolinda, is well known. In the above dramatic song she is seen passing through one of the higher temptations of the believing Christian."

In a letter to Hilda de Longueuil, June 8, 1887, GM wrote in reference to an unfavorable review of his volume: "Poor Theodolinda is 'enigmatical.' . . . Theodolinda is in a white heat. Having (as I invent) branded her breast with the fiery Nail, she conceives herself elect, almost the Bride of the Crucified, and again, in a flash, corrects her presumption by the extreme of Christian prostration etc., etc. The recurrence is like an interchange of alternate black and bright."

I

Queen Theodolind has built
In the earth a furnace-bed:
There the Traitor Nail that spilt
Blood of the anointed Head,
Red of heat, resolves in shame:
White of heat, awakes to flame.
    Beat, beat! white of heat,
    Red of heat, beat, beat!

II

Mark the skeleton of fire
Lightening from its thunder-roof:
So comes this that saw expire
Him we love, for our behoof!
Red of heat, O white of heat,
This from off the Cross we greet.

Previously printed in the Cornhill 26 *(September 1872). MS: Texas, title: "The Song of the Blessed Nail."*
I.1 Theodolind] Theodolind' *MS*
After II.6 MS, C:
                    Beat, beat! white of heat,
                    Red of heat, beat, beat!

III

Brown-cowled hammermen around
Nerve their naked arms to strike
Death with Resurrection crowned,
Each upon that cruel spike.
Red of heat the furnace leaps,
White of heat transfigured sleeps.

IV

Hard against the furnace core
Holds the Queen her streaming eyes:
Lo! that thing of piteous gore
In the lap of radiance lies,
Red of heat, as when He takes,
White of heat, whom earth forsakes.

V

Forth with it, and crushing ring
Iron hymns, for men to hear
Echoes of the deeds that sting
Earth into its graves, and fear!
Red of heat, He maketh thus,
White of heat, a crown of us.

III.1 *MS*: Monkish hammermen are those
III.2 Nerve their] Nerving *MS*
III.3 *MS*: Dumb, the Passion's cleansing blows
After III.6 MS, C: refrain repeated, as in stanza I, after each stanza. MS: after stanzas
III, IV, VI [MS, stanza 7], VII [MS, stanza 10] GM originally inverted the "white" and
"Red" of the refrain but corrected his slips.
IV.2 Holds] Keeps *MS*
V.1 crushing ring] ring thro' earth *MS*; ring amain *C*
V.2 for men to hear] that men may know *MS*
V.3–6 *MS:*

> Pain & Joy, His death & birth,
> Pulses of their life below!
> Red of heat, O white of heat,
> Ring it to the Judgment seat.

V.3 sting] stain *C*

VI

This that killed Thee, kissed Thee, Lord!
Touched Thee, and we touch it: dear,
Dark it is; adored, abhorred:
Vilest, yet most sainted here.
Red of heat, O white of heat,
In it hell and heaven meet.

VII

I behold our morning day
When they chased Him out with rods
Up to where this traitor lay
Thirsting; and the blood was God's!
Red of heat, it shall be pressed,
White of heat, once on my breast!

Between stanzas V and VI, MS:

6

Of this Nail we make a Crown:
In this bondage we are free:
From this anguish we look down
Star-like on [the *del.*] our savage sea:
Red of heat, the mortal rose,
White of heat, immortal glows.
        Beat, beat! [red *del.*] white of heat,
        [White *del.*] Red of heat, beat, beat!

VI.4 sainted] blissful *del. MS, stanza 7*

Between stanzas VI and VII, MS:

8

This shall bind the brows of kings,
This shall tame the vice of kings,
This shall seal the vows of kings,
This the pride suffice of kings.
Red of heat, His precious blood:
White of heat, His Passion's flood.
        Beat, beat! &c

9

As this Nail, once lowly priced,
Priceless is, for none to buy,
So the basest, touching Christ,
Shall be lifted sovereign high.
Red of heat, O white of heat,
Blest who touch his hands & feet.
        Beat, beat! [red *del.*] white of heat,
        [White *del.*] Red of heat, beat, beat!

VIII

Quick! the reptile in me shrieks,
Not the soul. Again; the Cross
Burn there. Oh! this pain it wreaks
Rapture is: pain is not loss.
Red of heat, the tooth of Death,
White of heat, has caught my breath.

IX

Brand me, bite me, bitter thing!
Thus He felt, and thus I am
One with Him in suffering,
One with Him in bliss, the Lamb.
Red of heat, O white of heat,
Thus is bitterness made sweet.

X

Now am I, who bear that stamp
Scorched in me, the living sign
Sole on earth—the lighted lamp
Of the dreadful day divine.
White of heat, beat on it fast!
Red of heat, its shape has passed.

XI

Out in angry sparks they fly,
They that sentenced Him to bleed:
Pontius and his troop: they die,
Damned for ever for the deed!
White of heat in vain they soar:
Red of heat they strew the floor.

Stanza VIII not in MS
X.5 beat on] strike, strike *MS, stanza 12*
XI.3 *MS, stanza 13*: Strike them out, & see them die

XII

Fury on it! have its debt!
Thunder on the Hill accurst,
Golgotha, be ye! and sweat
Blood, and thirst the Passion's thirst.
Red of heat and white of heat,
Champ it like fierce teeth that eat.

XIII

Strike it as the ages crush
Towers! for while a shape is seen
I am rivalled. Quench its blush,
Devil! But it crowns me Queen,
Red of heat, as none before,
White of heat, the circlet wore.

XIV

Lowly I will be, and quail,
Crawling, with a beggar's hand:
On my breast the branded Nail,
On my head the iron band.
Red of heat, are none so base!
White of heat, none know such grace!

XV

In their heaven the sainted hosts,
Robed in violet unflecked,
Gaze on humankind as ghosts:
I draw down a ray direct.
Red of heat, across my brow,
White of heat, I touch Him now.

Stanza XII not in MS

XIII.2 a] the *del. MS, stanza 14*
XIV.1 I will] let me *del. MS, stanza 15*

XVI

Robed in violet, robed in gold,
Robed in pearl, they make our dawn.
What am I to them? Behold
What ye are to me, and fawn.
Red of heat, be humble, ye!
White of heat, O teach it me!

XVII

Martyrs! hungry peaks in air,
Rent with lightnings, clad with snow,
Crowned with stars! you strip me bare,
Pierce me, shame me, stretch me low,
Red of heat, but it may be,
White of heat, some envy me!

XVIII

O poor enviers! God's own gifts
Have a devil for the weak.
Yea, the very force that lifts
Finds the vessel's secret lcak.
Red of heat, I rise o'er all:
White of heat, I faint, I fall.

XVI.6 0] & *del. MS, stanza 17*
Between stanzas XVI and XVII, MS:

18

Red of heat is man's desire,
Burning in his pits of pride:
White of heat is Heaven's fire,
Wherein we stand purified.
Red of heat to white of heat,
Saints, blow on me, I entreat!
Beat, beat! &c

XVII.1 *MS, stanza 19*: Martyrs, that are mountain heights,
XVII.3 you strip me bare] the holy nights *MS, stanza 19*
XVII.4 *MS, stanza 19*: Lift you, for that ye were low!
XVII.5 but it may be] the flesh contends *MS, stanza 19*
XVII.6 some envy me] the soul ascends *MS, stanza 19*

XIX

Those old Martyrs sloughed their pride,
Taking humbleness like mirth.
I am to His Glory tied,
I that witness Him on earth!
Red of heat, my pride of dust,
White of heat, feeds fire in trust.

XX

Kindle me to constant fire,
Lest the nail be but a nail!
Give me wings of great desire,
Lest I look within, and fail!
Red of heat, the furnace light,
White of heat, fix on my sight.

Stanzas XVIII–XXI not in MS, instead:

20

Martyrs, to the lilied skies
Climbing, never climbed by flower!
On the furnace fix my eyes;
Stir in me the throes of Power,
Red of heat, that I may tread,
White of heat, its demons dead.
    Beat, beat! white of heat,
    Red of heat, beat, beat!

21

Queen Theodolind' has sung.
Silent are the hammers laid.
Wide the iron hymn has rung.
Of the Nail a Crown is made.
Red of heat the firebrands die.
White of heat the ashes lie.
    Beat, beat! white of heat,
    Red of heat, beat, beat!

XIX.6 in] of *C*
C, 1887:

xxii

Red of heat the firebrands die.
White of heat the ashes lie.

XXI

Never for the Chosen peace!
Know, by me tormented know,
Never shall the wrestling cease
Till with our outlasting Foe,
Red of heat to white of heat,
Roll we to the Godhead's feet!
  Beat, beat! white of heat,
  Red of heat, beat, beat!

A Preaching from a Spanish Ballad

The popular ballad is to be found in J. G. Lockhart's translation of *The Spanish Ballads* (New York: Scribner, Wedford and Armstrong, n.d. [1873?]) with the title, *The Ill-Married Lady*. Lockhart's version runs to eight quatrains as against GM's twenty-three, so that most of the preaching is GM's.

I

Ladies who in chains of wedlock
Chafe at an unequal yoke,
Not to nightingales give hearing;
Better this, the raven's croak.

II

Down the Prado strolled my seigneur,
Arm at lordly bow on hip,
Fingers trimming his moustachios,
Eyes for pirate fellowship.

A PREACHING FROM A SPANISH BALLAD

Previously printed in the Fortnightly *46 (August 1886). MS:* Huntington HM6764, *fair copy corrected, title: "A Spanish Ballad."*
I.2 at an unequal] at a solitary *del. MS*
II.2 Arm at lordly bow] Laughing loosely, hand *del. MS*
II.3 Fingers trimming] Hand at trim of *del. MS*
II.4 *MS:* Eyes on foot & waist & lip *or* pirate fellowship.

III

Home sat she that owned him master;
Like the flower bent to ground
Rain-surcharged and sun-forsaken;
Heedless of her hair unbound.

IV

Sudden at her feet a lover
Palpitating knelt and wooed;
Seemed a very gift from heaven
To the starved of common food.

V

Love me? she his vows repeated:
Fiery vows oft sung and thrummed:
Wondered, as on earth a stranger;
Thirsted, trusted, and succumbed.

VI

O beloved youth! my lover!
Mine! my lover! take my life
Wholly: thine in soul and body,
By this oath of more than wife!

VII

Know me for no helpless woman;
Nay, nor coward, though I sink
Awed beside thee, like an infant
Learning shame ere it can think.

IV.3 a very] he half a *del. MS*
IV.4 To the starved of common] Brought her mouth forgotten *or* To the starved of common *MS*
VII.1 Know me for] Mine! I am *or* Know me for *MS*
VII.2 nor] no *F*
VII.3 like] as *MS*

VIII

Swing me hence to do thee service,
Be thy succour, prove thy shield;
Heaven will hear!—in house thy handmaid,
Squire upon the battlefield.

IX

At my breasts I cool thy footsoles;
Wine I pour, I dress thy meats;
Humbly, when my lord it pleaseth,
Lie with him on perfumed sheets:

X

Pray for him, my blood's dear fountain,
While he sleeps, and watch his yawn
In that wakening babelike moment,
Sweeter to my thought than dawn!—

XI

Thundered then her lord of thunders;
Burst the door, and flashing sword,
Loud disgorged the woman's title:
Condemnation in one word.

XII

Grand by righteous wrath transfigured,
Towers the husband who provides
In his person judge and witness,
Death's black doorkeeper besides!

VIII.4 upon] across *del. MS*
IX.1 At] On *del. MS*
X.1 dear] own *MS*
X.2 his] him *del. MS*
X.4 thought] soul *MS*
XI.3 Loud disgorged] Bellowed forth *MS*

XIII

Round his head the ancient terrors,
Conjured of the stronger's law,
Circle, to abash the creature
Daring twist beneath his paw.

XIV

How though he hath squandered Honour
High of Honour let him scold:
Gilding of the man's possession,
'Tis the woman's coin of gold.

XV

She inheriting from many
Bleeding mothers bleeding sense,
Feels 'twixt her and sharp-fanged nature
Honour first did plant the fence.

XVI

Nature, that so shrieks for justice;
Honour's thirst, that blood will slake;
These are women's riddles, roughly
Mixed to write them saint or snake.

XVII

Never nature cherished woman:
She throughout the sexes' war
Serves as temptress and betrayer,
Favouring man, the muscular.

XIII.1 the] the *del.* those *MS*
XIII.3 abash] confound *MS*
XIII.4 twist] move[?] *del. MS*
XIV.2 High] Loud *MS*
XVI.4 write] make *del. MS*
XVII.1 woman] women *MS*
XVII.2 sexes'] sex's *MS*

XVIII

Lureful is she, bent for folly;
Doating on the child which crows:
Yours to teach him grace in fealty,
What the bloom is, what the rose.

XIX

Hard the task: your prison-chamber
Widens not for lifted latch
Till the giant thews and sinews
Meet their Godlike overmatch.

XX

Read that riddle, scorning pity's
Tears, of cockatrices shed:
When the heart is vowed for freedom,
Captaincy it yields to head.

XXI

Meanwhile you, freaked nature's martyrs,
Honour's army, flower and weed,
Gentle ladies, wedded ladies,
See for you this fair one bleed.

XXII

Sole stood her offence, she faltered;
Prayed her lord the youth to spare;
Prayed that in the orange garden
She might lie, and ceased her prayer.

XVIII.1 Lureful] Naked *MS*
XVIII.3 in] & *MS*
XIX.3 thews and sinews] thew & sinew *MS*
XIX.4 Meet] Find *MS*
XX.2 Tears] Tear *MS*
XXI.1 freaked] stern *del. MS*
XXI.4 fair one] victim *MS*
XXII.1 stood] was *MS*
XXII.4 ceased] closed *MS*

XXIII

Then commending to all women
Chastity, her breasts she laid
Bare unto the self-avenger.
Man in metal was the blade.

The Young Princess

A BALLAD OF OLD LAWS OF LOVE

I

I

When the South sang like a nightingale
    Above a bower in May,
The training of Love's vine of flame
Was writ in laws, for lord and dame
    To say their yea and nay.

II

When the South sang like a nightingale
    Across the flowering night,
And lord and dame held gentle sport,
There came a young princess to Court,
    A frost of beauty white.

III

The South sang like a nightingale
    To thaw her glittering dream:
No vine of Love her bosom gave,
She drank no wine of Love, but grave
    She held them to Love's theme.

A PREACHING FROM A SPANISH BALLAD

XXIII.3 unto] before *MS*

THE YOUNG PRINCESS, A BALLAD OF OLD LAWS OF LOVE

Previously printed in the English Illustrated *4 (December 1886).*

IV

The South grew all a nightingale
    Beneath a moon unmoved:
Like the banner of war she led them on;
She left them to lie, like the light that has gone
    From wine-cups overproved.

V

When the South was a fervid nightingale,
    And she a chilling moon,
'Twas pity to see on the garden swards,
Against Love's laws, those rival lords
    As willow-wands lie strewn.

VI

The South had throat of a nightingale
    For her, the young princess:
She gave no vine of Love to rear,
Love's wine drank not, yet bent her ear
    To themes of Love no less.

II

I

The lords of the Court they sighed heart-sick,
    Heart-free Lord Dusiote laughed:
I prize her no more than a fling o' the dice,
But, or shame to my manhood, a lady of ice,
    We master her by craft!

II

Heart-sick the lords of joyance yawned,
    Lord Dusiote laughed heart-free:
I count her as much as a crack o' my thumb,
But, or shame of my manhood, to me she shall come
    Like the bird to roost in the tree!

III

At dead of night when the palace-guard
    Had passed the measured rounds,
The young princess awoke to feel
A shudder of blood at the crackle of steel
    Within the garden-bounds.

IV

It ceased, and she thought of whom was need,
    The friar or the leech;
When lo, stood her tirewoman breathless by:
Lord Dusiote, madam, to death is nigh,
    Of you he would have speech.

V

He prays you of your gentleness,
    To light him to his dark end.
The princess rose, and forth she went,
For charity was her intent,
    Devoutly to befriend.

VI

Lord Dusiote hung on his good squire's arm,
    The priest beside him knelt:
A weeping handkerchief was pressed
To stay the red flood at his breast,
    And bid cold ladies melt.

VII

O lady, though you are ice to men,
    All pure to heaven as light
Within the dew within the flower,
Of you 'tis whispered that love has power
    When secret is the night.

VIII

I have silenced the slanderers, peace to their souls!
    Save one was too cunning for me.
I die, whose love is late avowed,
He lives, who boasts the lily has bowed
    To the oath of a bended knee.

IX

Lord Dusiote drew breath with pain,
    And she with pain drew breath:
On him she looked, on his like above;
She flew in the folds of a marvel of love,
    Revealed to pass to death.

X

You are dying, O great-hearted lord,
    You are dying for me, she cried;
O take my hand, O take my kiss,
And take of your right for love like this,
    The vow that plights me bride.

XI

She bade the priest recite his words
    While hand in hand were they,
Lord Dusiote's soul to waft to bliss;
He had her hand, her vow, her kiss,
    And his body was borne away.

III

I

Lord Dusiote sprang from priest and squire;
    He gazed at her lighted room:
The laughter in his heart grew slack;
He knew not the force that pushed him back
    From her and the morn in bloom.

II

Like a drowned man's length on the strong flood-tide,
        Like the shade of a bird in the sun,
He fled from his lady whom he might claim
As ghost, and who made the daybeams flame
        To scare what he had done.

III

There was grief at Court for one so gay,
        Though he was a lord less keen
For training the vine than at vintage-press;
But in her soul the young princess
        Believed that love had been.

IV

Lord Dusiote fled the Court and land,
        He crossed the woeful seas,
Till his traitorous doing seemed clearer to burn,
And the lady beloved drew his heart for return,
        Like the banner of war in the breeze.

V

He neared the palace, he spied the Court,
        And music he heard, and they told
Of foreign lords arrived to bring
The nuptial gifts of a bridegroom king
        To the princess grave and cold.

VI

The masque and the dance were cloud on wave,
        And down the masque and the dance
Lord Dusiote stepped from dame to dame,
And to the young princess he came,
        With a bow and a burning glance.

VII

Do you take a new husband to-morrow, lady?
    She shrank as at prick of steel.
Must the first yield place to the second, he sighed.
Her eyes were like the grave that is wide
    For the corpse from head to heel.

VIII

My lady, my love, that little hand
    Has mine ringed fast in plight:
I bear for your lips a lawful thirst,
And as justly the second should follow the first,
    I come to your door this night.

IX

If a ghost should come a ghost will go:
    No more the lady said,
Save that ever when he in wrath began
To swear by the faith of a living man,
    She answered him, You are dead.

IV

I

The soft night-wind went laden to death
    With smell of the orange in flower;
The light leaves prattled to neighbour ears;
The bird of the passion sang over his tears;
    The night named hour by hour.

II

Sang loud, sang low the rapturous bird
    Till the yellow hour was nigh,
Behind the folds of a darker cloud:
He chuckled, he sobbed, alow, aloud;
    The voice between earth and sky.

III

O will you, will you, women are weak;
　　The proudest are yielding mates
For a forward foot and a tongue of fire:
So thought Lord Dusiote's trusty squire,
　　At watch by the palace-gates.

IV

The song of the bird was wine in his blood,
　　And woman the odorous bloom:
His master's great adventure stirred
Within him to mingle the bloom and bird,
　　And morn ere its coming illume.

V

Beside him strangely a piece of the dark
　　Had moved, and the undertones
Of a priest in prayer, like a cavernous wave,
He heard, as were there a soul to save
　　For urgency now in the groans.

VI

No priest was hired for the play this night:
　　And the squire tossed head like a deer
At sniff of the tainted wind; he gazed
Where cresset-lamps in a door were raised,
　　Belike on a passing bier.

VII

All cloaked and masked, with naked blades,
　　That flashed of a judgement done,
The lords of the Court, from the palace-door,
Came issuing silently, bearers four,
　　And flat on their shoulders one.

VIII

They marched the body to squire and priest,
    They lowered it sad to earth:
The priest they gave the burial dole,
Bade wrestle hourly for his soul,
    Who was a lord of worth.

IX

One said, farewell to a gallant knight!
    And one, but a restless ghost!
'Tis a year and a day since in this place
He died, sped high by a lady of grace,
    To join the blissful host.

X

Not vainly on us she charged her cause,
    The lady whom we revere
For faith in the mask of a love untrue
To the Love we honour, the Love her due,
    The Love we have vowed to rear.

XI

A trap for the sweet tooth, lures for the light,
    For the fortress defiant a mine:
Right well! But not in the South, princess,
Shall the lady snared of her nobleness
    Ever shamed or a captive pine.

XII

When the South had voice of a nightingale
    Above a Maying bower,
On the heights of Love walked radiant peers;
The bird of the passion sang over his tears
    To the breeze and the orange-flower.

King Harald's Trance

I

Sword in length a reaping-hook amain
Harald sheared his field, blood up to shank:
    'Mid the swathes of slain,
    First at moonrise drank.

II

Thereof hunger, as for meats the knife,
Pricked his ribs, in one sharp spur to reach
    Home and his young wife,
    Nigh the sea-ford beach.

MS: Huntington HM6765, *fair copy heavily corrected, title: "The Trance of Harald Hammerskull." Variants are from this MS.*

I.1 amain] he cropped *dr. 1*; he lopped *dr. 3*
I.2 *dr. 1*: Richly at one sweep, blood over shank: field] foe *dr. 2*   up to] over *dr. 2*
dr. 3: Limbs *or* Arms, heads, right, left, thick; blood over shank:
I.3 *dr. 1*: Marked the sliced & lopped; *or* Mid his dozens lopped   *dr. 3*: Mid his dozens cropped,
I.4 at] nigh *or* at *dr. 1*

Between stanzas I and II:

ii

Shouldering from foes flung *or* hewn swathe on swathe—,
Home to his young wife, his last plucked flower,
    [Fast *del.*] Swift up forest-path
    Rode the man of power.

Stanza II, (iii in MS) drs. verso of leaf 1, not incorporated into this dr.:

Therewith hunger pricked his ribs for home,
Sharp as spear-points,

Therewith hunger sharp as spear-points pricked

Therewith sharp as spear-points

Thereof hunger, as for meats the knife,
Pricked his ribs, to gain ere [end of night *del.*] break of day
    Home & his young wife,
    Nigh the sea-ford grey.

Where the stonework stood
Under a low moon

III

After battle keen to feed was he:
Smoking flesh the thresher washed down fast,
    Like an angry sea
    Ships from keel to mast.

IV

Name us glory, singer, name us pride
Matching Harald's in his deeds of strength;
    Chiefs, wife, sword by side,
    Foemen stretched their length!

V

Half a winter night the toasts hurrahed,
Crowned him, clothed him, trumpeted him high,
    Till awink he bade
    Wife to chamber fly.

VI

Twice the sun had mounted, twice had sunk,
Ere his ears took sound; he lay for dead;
    Mountain on his trunk,
    Ocean on his head.

VII

Clamped to couch, his fiery hearing sucked
Whispers that at heart made iron-clang:
    Here fool-woman clucked,
    There men held harangue.

III.2 flesh] meats *or* flesh   thresher] shearer *del.*
Stanzas IV and V reverse order
IV.1 Name us] Know you *del.*   name us] know you *del.*
V.3 Till awink] Then *or* Till his wife *or* Then awink
V.4 Wife] Straight *or* Wife
VI.1 Twice] Thrice   twice] thrice

VIII

Burial to fit their lord of war,
They decreed him: hailed the kingling: ha!
    Hateful! but this Thor
    Failed a weak lamb's baa.

IX

King they hailed a branchlet, shaped to fare,
Weighted so, like quaking shingle spume,
    When his blood's own heir
    Ripened in the womb!

X

Still he heard, and doglike, hoglike, ran
Nose of hearing till his blind sight saw:
    Woman stood with man
    Mouthing low, at paw.

XI

Woman, man, they mouthed; they spake a thing
Armed to split a mountain, sunder seas:
    Still the frozen king
    Lay and felt him freeze.

XII

Doglike, hoglike, horselike now he raced,
Riderless, in ghost across a ground
    Flint of breast, blank-faced,
    Past the fleshly bound.

VIII.2 hailed] named   kingling] tonist *del.*
IX.1 branchlet] branching *del.*
XI.1 spake] spoke[?]
XII.2 a ground] an earth
XII.4 Rimmed in devil's girth.

XIII

Smell of brine his nostrils filled with might:
Nostrils quickened eyelids, eyelids hand:
    Hand for sword at right
    Groped, the great haft spanned.

XIV

Wonder struck to ice his people's eyes:
Him they saw, the prone upon the bier,
    Sheer from backbone rise,
    Sword uplifting peer.

XV

Sitting did he breathe against the blade,
Standing kiss it for that proof of life:
    Strode, as netters wade,
    Straightway to his wife.

XVI

Her he eyed: his judgement was one word,
Foulbed! and she fell: the blow clove two.
    Fearful for the third,
    All their breath indrew.

XVII

Morning danced along the waves to beach;
Dumb his chiefs fetched breath for what might hap:
    Glassily on each
    Stared the iron cap.

XIV.2 prone] length
XV.3 Strode] Stalked
XVI.3 Fearful for] Feared to be
XVII.2 *Del.*: Dumb for fetch of breath his chiefs hung round.

XVIII

Sudden, as it were a monster oak
Split to yield a limb by stress of heat,
    Strained he, staggered, broke
    Doubled at their feet.

Whimper of Sympathy

Compare *The Ordeal of Richard Feverel* (1859) where GM declares
against protective parents: "I think yonder old thrush on the lawn who
has just kicked the last of her lank offspring out of the nest to go shift for
itself, much the kinder of the two, though sentimental people do shrug
their shoulders at these unsentimental acts of the creatures who never
wander from nature" (Mem. Ed., 2: 287–88).
    This poem may have been intended as an answer to Tennyson's *In
Memoriam* (1850), lyric 55, in which the poet bemoans Nature's careless-
ness "of the single life." In Tennyson's poem the poet falters and falls,
thus exhibiting, in GM's words (line 8), "The feelings of the totter-knee'd."

Hawk or shrike has done this deed
Of downy feathers: rueful sight!
Sweet sentimentalist, invite
Your bosom's Power to intercede.

So hard it seems that one must bleed
Because another needs will bite!
All round we find cold Nature slight
The feelings of the totter-knee'd.

KING HARALD'S TRANCE

XVIII.1 it were] were it
XVIII.2 Seized by winds unfelt at Summer heat,

WHIMPER OF SYMPATHY

Previously printed in the Fortnightly *14 (1 August 1870), as stanza vi of* In the Woods.
MS: Yale, revision of F.
2 rueful] a cruel *F*
3 invite] intercede *F*
4 *F:* With Providence: it is not right!
5–8 *F:*
                Complain, revolt [of it *MS*]; say heaven is wrong,
                Say nature is [Call nature *MS*] vile, that can allow
                The [These *MS*] innocent to be torn, the strong
                To tower and govern—witness how!

O it were pleasant, with you
To fly from this tussle of foes,
The shambles, the charnel, the wrinkle!
To dwell in yon dribble of dew
On the cheek of your sovereign rose,
And live the young life of a twinkle.

10

Young Reynard

I

Gracefullest leaper, the dappled fox-cub
Curves over brambles with berries and buds,
Light as a bubble that flies from the tub,
Whisked by the laundry-wife out of her suds.
Wavy he comes, woolly, all at his ease,
Elegant, fashioned to foot with the deuce;
Nature's own prince of the dance: then he sees
Me, and retires as if making excuse.

II

Never closed minuet courtlier! Soon
Cub-hunting troops were abroad, and a yelp
Told of sure scent: ere the stroke upon noon
Reynard the younger lay far beyond help.
Wild, my poor friend, has the fate to be chased;
Civil will conquer: were 't other 'twere worse,
Fair, by the flushed early morning embraced,
Haply you live a day longer in verse.

WHIMPER OF SYMPATHY

10 tussle] struggle *F*
12 *F*: To be housed in the drop of dew *MS*: To house in the droplet of dew
13 *F*: That hangs on the cheek of the rose,
14 young life] life *F*

Manfred

A blast against Byron's "projection" of the guilty, lonely, romantic character Manfred, in his play *Manfred* (1817), written in the mood of *Childe Harold* 3 (1816). Compare the following poem, *Hernani*.

I

Projected from the bilious Childe,
This clatterjaw his foot could set
On Alps, without a breast beguiled
To glow in shedding rascal sweat.
Somewhere about his grinder teeth,
He mouthed of thoughts that grilled beneath,
And summoned Nature to her feud
With bile and buskin Attitude.

II

Considerably was the world
Of spinsterdom and clergy racked
While he his hinted horrors hurled,
And she pictorially attacked.
A duel hugeous. Tragic? Ho!
The cities, not the mountains, blow
Such bladders; in their shapes confessed
An after-dinner's indigest.

Hernani

While a mountaineer exile, Hernani, hero of Victor Hugo's play *Hernani* (1830), had given the horn that he used to rouse his followers to Don Leo, the elderly kinsman and betrothed of his beloved Zanthe. Don Leo, as a point of honor, had saved Hernani's life from his ancestral enemy, the king of Spain, and Hernani in giving Leo his horn had sworn that if Leo ever sounded it Leo could claim Hernani's life. At the end of the tragedy

MANFRED

I.8 and] & *de L; corr. errata, de L 1911*

HERNANI

MS: by kind permission of the Lawrence family, transcribed by C. L. Cline.

Leo claims this "obstructive debt" by sounding the horn after the wedding festivities of Zanthe and Hernani, the latter now legitimately reestablished as Duke of Arragaon. Zanthe and Hernani take poison and die; Leo, regarding them, also expires. Compare GM's attitude toward another romantic tragedy in the previous poem, *Manfred*.

GM's Cistercian monks do not appear in Hugo's drama. The poet imagines them as astute onlookers.

This poem can probably be dated late 1885 or early 1886 when GM sent the draft, from which the textual notes are taken, to his friends the Misses Mary and Louisa Lawrence, sisters of Sir Trevor Lawrence, Member of Parliament for the Surrey constituency with which GM voted.

Cistercians might crack their sides
With laughter, and exemption get,
At sight of heroes clasping brides,
And hearing—O the horn! the horn!
The horn of their obstructive debt!

But quit the stage, that note applies
For sermons cosmopolitan,
Hernani. Have we filched our prize,
Forgetting . . . ? O the horn! the horn!
The horn of the Old Gentleman!   10

The Nuptials of Attila

GM wrote to Frederick A. Maxse on August 15, 1874, four and a half years before the publication of this poem in the *New Quarterly Magazine*, "I am finishing a Poem, 'The Nuptials of Attila'—about forty pages." He must have put the poem aside, because he wrote Bonaparte Wyse on October 6, 1876, "I have been writing quantities of verse and in verse of late. I should like you to read them. I think 'The Nuptials of Attila'

HERNANI

6 that] thy *MS*
7 sermons] preachings *MS*

THE NUPTIALS OF ATTILA

Previously printed in the New *Quarterly, n.s. 22 (January 1879). MS: fragment, Berg, stanza XIX, lines 11–17. Proof for* NQ *corrected by printer:* Huntington 19162.

might give you a thrill." GM continued to like this poem and recommended
it to Wilfrid Scawen Blunt in 1894 (*My Diaries*, 2 vols. [New York:
Knopf, 1921] 2:143).

The source of the poem was almost undoubtedly Edward Gibbon's
Decline and Fall of the Roman Empire, chapters 34 and 35. The scene is
Attila's famous wooden palace beyond the Danube; the year is 453. Attila
had had many wives before Ildico. As GM told Edward Clodd in 1905, the
subject of the poem is not a love-story but "the fall of an empire" (Clodd,
p. 146).

I

Flat as to an eagle's eye,
      Earth hung under Attila.
Sign for carnage gave he none.
In the peace of his disdain,
Sun and rain, and rain and sun,
Cherished men to wax again,
Crawl, and in their manner die.
On his people stood a frost.
Like the charger cut in stone,
Rearing stiff, the warrior host,   10
Which had life from him alone,
Craved the trumpet's eager note,
As the bridled earth the Spring.
Rusty was the trumpet's throat.
He let chief and prophet rave;
Venturous earth around him string
Threads of grass and slender rye,
Wave them, and untrampled wave.
O for the time when God did cry,
      Eye and have, my Attila!   20

II

Scorn of conquest filled like sleep
Him that drank of havoc deep
When the Green Cat pawed the globe:
When the horsemen from his bow

I.19 *proof*: Flat as to an eagle's eye,
I.20 *proof*: Earth hung under Attila.

Shot in sheaves and made the foe
Crimson fringes of a robe,
Trailed o'er towns and fields in woe;
When they streaked the rivers red,
When the saddle was the bed.
    Attila, my Attila!   10

III

He breathed peace and pulled a flower.
    Eye and have, my Attila!
This was the damsel Ildico,
Rich in bloom until that hour:
Shyer than the forest doe
Twinkling slim through branches green.
Yet the shyest shall be seen.
    Make the bed for Attila!

IV

Seen of Attila, desired,
She was led to him straightway:
Radiantly was she attired;
Rifled lands were her array,
Jewels bled from weeping crowns,
Gold of woeful fields and towns.
She stood pallid in the light.
How she walked, how withered white,
From the blessing to the board,
She who should have proudly blushed   10

Between parts II and III proof:

II

War, the fire shut in his breast,
War, the torchfire he flung west.
Waned upon his people's face:
Waned like rocks of Danube's crest,
Wearing grey in flames that fly,
Leaving there a livid trace.
O for the time when God did cry,
    Eye and have, my Attila!

IV.10 should] would *1897*

Women whispered, asking why,
Hitting of a youth, and hushed.
Was it terror of her lord?
Was she childish? was she sly?
Was it the bright mantle's dye
Drained her blood to hues of grief
Like the ash that shoots the spark?
See the green tree all in leaf:
See the green tree stripped of bark!—
    Make the bed for Attila!   20

V

Round the banquet-table's load
Scores of iron horsemen rode;
Chosen warriors, keen and hard;
Grain of threshing battle-dints;
Attila's fierce body-guard,
Smelling war like fire in flints.
Grant them peace be fugitive!
Iron-capped and iron-heeled,
Each against his fellow's shield
Smote the spear-head, shouting, Live,   10
    Attila! my Attila!
Eagle, eagle of our breed,
Eagle, beak the lamb, and feed!
Have her, and unleash us! Live,
    Attila! my Attila!

VI

He was of the blood to shine
Bronze in joy, like shies that scorch.
Beaming with the goblet wine
In the wavering of the torch,
Looked he backward on his bride.
    Eye and have, my Attila!

V.14 Live] live *all eds., but cf. line 10*
VI.5 Looked he backward] Attila looked *NQ*

Fair in her wide robe was she:
Where the robe and vest divide,
Fair she seemed surpassingly:
Soft, yet vivid as the stream   10
Danube rolls in the moonbeam
Through rock-barriers: but she smiled
Never, she sat cold as salt:
Open-mouthed as a young child
Wondering with a mind at fault.
    Make the bed for Attila!

VII

Under the thin hoop of gold
Whence in waves her hair outrolled,
'Twixt her brows the women saw
Shadows of a vulture's claw
Gript in flight: strange knots that sped
Closing and dissolving aye:
Such as wicked dreams betray
When pale dawn creeps o'er the bed.
They might show the common pang
Known to virgins, in whom dread   10
Hunts their bliss like famished hounds;
While the chiefs with roaring rounds
Tossed her to her lord, and sang
Praise of him whose hand was large,
Cheers for beauty brought to yield,
Chirrups of the trot afield,
Hurrahs of the battle-charge.

VIII

Those rock-faces hung with weed
Reddened: their great days of speed,
Slaughter, triumph, flood and flame,
Like a jealous frenzy wrought,
Scoffed at them and did them shame,

VII *after 17, NQ*: Make the bed for Attila!

Quaffing idle, conquering naught.
O for the time when God decreed
        Earth the prey of Attila!
God called on thee in his wrath,
Trample it to mire! 'Twas done.   10
Swift as Danube clove our path
Down from East to Western sun.
Huns! behold your pasture, gaze,
Take, our king said: heel to flank
(Whisper it, the warhorse neighs!)
Forth we drove, and blood we drank
Fresh as dawn-dew: earth was ours:
Men were flocks we lashed and spurned:
Fast as windy flame devours,
Flame along the wind, we burned.   20
Arrow, javelin, spear, and sword!
Here the snows and there the plains;
On! our signal: onward poured
Torrents of the tightened reins,
Foaming over vine and corn
Hot against the city-wall.
Whisper it, you sound a horn
To the grey beast in the stall!
Yea, he whinnies at a nod.
O for sound of the trumpet-notes!   30
O for the time when thunder-shod,
He that scarce can munch his oats,
Hung on the peaks, brooded aloof,
Champed the grain of the wrath of God,
Pressed a cloud on the cowering roof,
Snorted out of the blackness fire!
Scarlet broke the sky, and down,
Hammering West with print of his hoof,
He burst out of the bosom of ire
Sharp as eyelight under thy frown,   40
        Attila, my Attila!

VIII.38 West with print] the west with the print *NQ*

IX

Ravaged cities rolling smoke
Thick on cornfields dry and black,
Wave his banners, bear his yoke.
Track the lightning, and you track
Attila. They moan: 'tis he!
Bleed: 'tis he! Beneath his foot
Leagues are deserts charred and mute;
Where he passed, there passed a sea.
　　　Attila, my Attila!

X

—Who breathed on the king cold breath?
Said a voice amid the host,
He is Death that weds a ghost,
Else a ghost that weds with Death?
Ildico's chill little hand
Shuddering he beheld: austere
Stared, as one who would command
Sight of what has filled his ear:
Plucked his thin beard, laughed disdain.
Feast, ye Huns! His arm he raised,   10
Like the warrior, battle-dazed,
Joining to the fight amain.
　　　Make the bed for Attila!

XI

Silent Ildico stood up.
King and chief to pledge her well,
Shocked sword sword and cup on cup,
Clamouring like a brazen bell.
Silent stepped the queenly slave.
Fair, by heaven! she was to meet
On a midnight, near a grave,
Flapping wide the winding-sheet.

X.6 beheld] let fall *NQ*
XI *after 8*, *NQ:* Make the bed for Attila!

XII

Death and she walked through the crowd,
Out beyond the flush of light.
Ceremonious women bowed
Following her: 'twas middle night.
Then the warriors each on each
Spied, nor overloudly laughed;
Like the victims of the leech,
Who have drunk of a strange draught.

XIII

Attila remained. Even so
Frowned he when he struck the blow,
Brained his horse that stumbled twice,
On a bloody day in Gaul,
Bellowing, Perish omens! All
Marvelled at the sacrifice,
But the battle, swinging dim,
Rang off that axe-blow for him.
        Attila, my Attila!

XIV

Brightening over Danube wheeled
Star by star; and she, most fair,
Sweet as victory half-revealed,
Seized to make him glad and young;
She, O sweet as the dark sign
Given him oft in battles gone,
When the voice within said, Dare!
And the trumpet-notes were sprung
Rapturous for the charge in line:
She lay waiting: fair as dawn   10
Wrapped in folds of night she lay;
Secret, lustrous; flaglike there,

XII *after 8, NQ:* Make the bed for Attila!

Waiting him to stream and ray,
With one loosening blush outflung,
Colours of his hordes of horse
Ranked for combat: still he hung
Like the fever-dreading air,
Cursed of heat; and as a corse
Gathers vultures, in his brain
Images of her eyes and kiss   20
Plucked at the limbs that could remain
Loitering nigh the doors of bliss.
     Make the bed for Attila!

XV

Passion on one hand, on one,
Destiny led forth the Hun.
Heard ye outcries of affright,
Voices that through many a fray,
In the press of flag and spear,
Warned the king of peril near?
Men were dumb, they gave him way,
Eager heads to left and right,
Like the bearded standard, thrust,
As in battle, for a nod   10
From their lord of battle-dust.
     Attila, my Attila!
Slow between the lines he trod.
Saw ye not the sun drop slow
On this nuptial day, ere eve
Pierced him on the couch aglow?
     Attila, my Attila?
Here and there his heart would cleave
Clotted memory for a space:
Some stout chief's familiar face,   20

XIV.17 fever-dreading] fever dreading *de L; corr. errata, de L 1911*

Choicest of his fighting brood,
Touched him, as 'twere one to know
Ere he met his bride's embrace.
    Attila, my Attila!
Twisting fingers in a beard
Scant as winter underwood,
With a narrowed eye he peered;
Like the sunset's graver red
Up old pine-stems. Grave he stood
Eyeing them on whom was shed   30
Burning light from him alone.
    Attila, my Attila!
Red were they whose mouths recalled
Where the slaughter mounted high,
High on it, o'er earth appalled,
He; heaven's finger in their sight
Raising him on waves of dead:
Up to heaven his trumpets blown.
O for the time when God's delight
    Crowned the head of Attila!   40
Hungry river of the crag
Stretching hands for earth he came:
Force and Speed astride his name
Pointed back to spear and flag.
He came out of miracle cloud,
Lightning-swift and spectre-lean.
Now those days are in a shroud:
Have him to his ghostly queen.
    Make the bed for Attila!

XVI

One, with winecups overstrung,
Cried him farewell in Rome's tongue.
Who? for the great king turned as though
•   Wrath to the shaft's head strained the bow.
Nay, not wrath the king possessed,
But a radiance of the breast.

XVI.1 with] in *NQ*

In that sound he had the key
Of his cunning malady.
Lo, where gleamed the sapphire lake,
Leo, with his Rome at stake,   10
Drew blank air to hues and forms;
Whereof Two that shone distinct,
Linked as orbed stars are linked,
Clear among the myriad swarms,
In a constellation, dashed
Full on horse and rider's eyes
Sunless light, but light it was—
Light that blinded and abashed,
Froze his members, bade him pause,
Caught him mid-gallop, blazed him home.   20
  Attila, my Attila!
What are streams that cease to flow?
What was Attila, rolled thence,
Cheated by a juggler's show?
Like that lake of blue intense,
Under tempest lashed to foam,
Lurid radiance, as he passed,
Filled him, and around was glassed,
When deep-voiced he uttered, Rome!

XVII

Rome! the word was: and like meat
Flung to dogs the word was torn.
Soon Rome's magic priests shall bleat
Round their magic Pope forlorn!
Loud they swore the king had sworn
Vengeance on the Roman cheat,
Ere he passed as, grave and still,
Danube through the shouting hill:
Sworn it by his naked life!
Eagle, snakes these women are: 10
Take them on the wing! but war,
Smoking war's the warrior's wife!

XVI *after 29, NQ:* Make the bed for Attila!

Then for plunder! then for brides
Won without a winking priest!—
Danube whirled his train of tides
Black toward the yellow East.
    Make the bed for Attila!

XVIII

Chirrups of the trot afield,
Hurrahs of the battle-charge,
How they answered, how they pealed,
When the morning rose and drew
Bow and javelin, lance and targe,
In the nuptial casement's view!
    Attila, my Attila!
Down the hillspurs, out of tents
Glimmering in mid-forest, through
Mists of the cool morning scents,   10
Forth from city-alley, court,
Arch, the bounding horsemen flew,
Joined along the plains of dew,
Raced and gave the rein to sport,
Closed and streamed like curtain-rents
Fluttered by a wind, and flowed
Into squadrons: trumpets blew,
Chargers neighed, and trappings glowed
Brave as the bright Orient's.
Look on the seas that run to greet   20
Sunrise: look on the leagues of wheat:
Look on the lines and squares that fret
Leaping to level the lance blood-wet.
Tens of thousands, man and steed,
Tossing like field-flowers in Spring;
Ready to be hurled at need

XVIII *between 23 and 24, NQ:* Attila, my Attila!

Whither their great lord may sling.
Finger Romeward, Romeward, King!
    Attila, my Attila!
Still the woman holds him fast   30
As a night-flag round the mast.

XIX

Nigh upon the fiery noon,
Out of ranks a roaring burst.
'Ware white women like the moon!
They are poison: they have thirst
First for love, and next for rule.
Jealous of the army, she?
Ho, the little wanton fool!
We were his before she squealed
Blind for mother's milk, and heeled
Kicking on her mother's knee.   10
His in life and death are we:
She but one flower of a field.
We have given him bliss tenfold
In an hour to match her night:
    Attila, my Attila!
Still her arms the master hold,
As on wounds the scarf winds tight.

XX

Over Danube day no more,
Like the warrior's planted spear,
Stood to hail the King: in fear
Western day knocked at his door.
    Attila, my Attila!

XVIII *after 31, NQ:* Make the bed for Attila!
XIX.11 in] for *frag.*
XIX.12 of] in *frag.*
XIX.17 on] round *frag.*
XIX *after 17, frag., proof:* Make the bed for Attila!

Sudden in the army's eyes
Rolled a blast of lights and cries:
Flashing through them: Dead are ye!
Dead, ye Huns, and torn piecemeal!
See the ordered army reel   10
Stricken through the ribs: and see,
Wild for speed to cheat despair,
Horsemen, clutching knee to chin,
Crouch and dart they know not where.
    Attila, my Attila!
Faces covered, faces bare,
Light the palace-front like jets
Of a dreadful fire within.
Beating hands and driving hair
Start on roof and parapets.   20
Dust rolls up; the slaughter din.
—Death to them who call him dead!
Death to them who doubt the tale!
Choking in his dusty veil,
Sank the sun on his death-bed.
    Make the bed for Attila!

XXI

'Tis the room where thunder sleeps.
Frenzy, as a wave to shore
Surging, burst the silent door,
And drew back to awful deeps,
Breath beaten out, foam-white. Anew
Howled and pressed the ghastly crew,
Like storm-waters over rocks.
    Attila, my Attila!
One long shaft of sunset red
Laid a finger on the bed.   10
Horror, with the snaky locks,
Shocked the surge to stiffened heaps,
Hoary as the glacier's head

Faced to the moon. Insane they look.
God it is in heaven who weeps
Fallen from his hand the Scourge he shook.
        Make the bed for Attila!

XXII

Square along the couch, and stark,
Like the sea-rejected thing
Sea-sucked white, behold their King.
        Attila, my Attila!
Beams that panted black and bright,
Scornful lightnings danced their sight:
Him they see an oak in bud,
Him an oaklog stripped of bark:
Him, their lord of day and night,
White, and lifting up his blood   10
Dumb for vengeance. Name us that,
Huddled in the corner dark,
Humped and grinning like a cat,
Teeth for lips!—'tis she! she stares,
Glittering through her bristled hairs.
Rend her! Pierce her to the hilt!
She is Murder: have her out!
What! this little fist, as big
As the southern summer fig!
She is Madness, none may doubt.   20
Death, who dares deny her guilt!
Death, who says his blood she spilt!
        Make the bed for Attila!

XXIII

Torch and lamp and sunset-red
Fell three-fingered on the bed.
In the torch the beard-hair scant
With the great breast seemed to pant:

In the yellow lamp the limbs
Wavered, as the lake-flower swims:
In the sunset red the dead
Dead avowed him, dry blood-red.

XXIV

Hatred of that abject slave,
Earth, was in each chieftain's heart.
Earth has got him, whom God gave,
Earth may sing, and earth shall smart!
  Attila, my Attila!

XXV

Thus their prayer was raved and ceased.
Then had Vengeance of her feast
Scent in their quick pang to smite
Which they knew not, but huge pain
Urged them from some victim slain
Swift, and blotted from the sight.
Each at each, a crouching beast,
Glared, and quivered for the word.
Each at each, and all on that,
Humped and grinning like a cat,   10
Head-bound with its bridal-wreath.
Then the bitter chamber heard
Vengeance in a cauldron seethe.
Hurried counsel rage and craft
Yelped to hungry men, whose teeth
Hard the grey lip-ringlet gnawed,
Gleaming till their fury laughed.
With the steel-hilt in the clutch,
Eyes were shot on her that froze
In their blood-thirst overawed;   20
Burned to rend, yet feared to touch.
She that was his nuptial rose,
She was of his heart's blood clad:

XXIII *after 8, NQ:* Make the bed for Attila!

Oh! the last of him she had!—
Could a little fist as big
As the southern summer fig,
Push a dagger's point to pierce
Ribs like those? Who else! They glared
Each at each. Suspicion fierce
Many a black remembrance bared.   30
    Attila, my Attila!
Death, who dares deny her guilt!
Death, who says his blood she spilt!
Traitor he, who stands between!
Swift to hell, who harms the Queen!
She, the wild contention's cause,
Combed her hair with quiet paws.
    Make the bed for Attila!

XXVI

Night was on the host in arms.
Night, as never night before,
Hearkened to an army's roar
Breaking up in snaky swarms:
Torch and steel and snorting steed,
Hunted by the cry of blood,
Cursed with blindness, mad for day.
Where the torches ran a flood,
Tales of him and of the deed
Showered like a torrent spray.   10
Fear of silence made them strive
Loud in warrior-hymns that grew
Hoarse for slaughter yet unwreaked.
Ghostly Night across the hive,
With a crimson finger drew
Letters on her breast and shrieked.
Night was on them like the mould

XXV.28 glared] stared *proof*

On the buried half alive.
Night, their bloody Queen, her fold
Wound on them and struck them through.   20
    Make the bed for Attila!

XXVII

Earth has got him whom God gave,
Earth may sing, and earth shall smart!
None of earth shall know his grave.
They that dig with Death depart.
    Attila, my Attila!

XXVIII

Thus their prayer was raved and passed:
Passed in peace their red sunset:
Hewn and earthed those men of sweat
Who had housed him in the vast,
Where no mortal might declare,
There lies he—his end was there!
    Attila, my Attila!

XXIX

Kingless was the army left:
Of its head the race bereft.
Every fury of the pit
Tortured and dismembered it.
Lo, upon a silent hour,
When the pitch of frost subsides,
Danube with a shout of power
Loosens his imprisoned tides:
Wide around the frighted plains
Shake to hear his riven chains,   10
Dreadfuller than heaven in wrath,
As he makes himself a path:
High leap the ice-cracks, towering pile

Floes to bergs, and giant peers
Wrestle on a drifted isle;
Island on ice-island rears;
Dissolution battles fast:
Big the senseless Titans loom,
Through a mist of common doom
Striving which shall die the last: 20
Till a gentle-breathing morn
Frees the stream from bank to bank.
So the Empire built of scorn
Agonized, dissolved and sank.
Of the Queen no more was told
Than of leaf on Danube rolled.
          Make the bed for Attila!

Aneurin's Harp

In the *Fortnightly* the poem had this footnote: "ANEURIN: pronounced
An*ai*rin; as sharp as the German *eu--oi* in verse."

I

Prince of Bards was old Aneurin;
He the grand Gododin sang;
All his numbers threw such fire in,
Struck his harp so wild a twang;—
Still the wakeful Briton borrows
Wisdom from its ancient heat:
Still it haunts our source of sorrows,
Deep excess of liquor sweet!

THE NUPTIALS OF ATTILA

XXIX.26 of] a *NQ*

ANEURIN'S HARP

Previously printed in the Fortnightly 4 (*1 September 1868*).

II

Here the Briton, there the Saxon,
Face to face, three fields apart,
Thirst for light to lay their thwacks on
Each the other with good heart.
Dry the Saxon sits, 'mid dinful
Noise of iron knits his steel:
Fresh and roaring with a skinful,
Britons round the hirlas reel.

III

Yellow flamed the meady sunset;
Red runs up the flag of morn.
Signal for the British onset
Hiccups through the British horn.
Down these hillmen pour like cattle
Sniffing pasture: grim below,
Showing eager teeth of battle,
In his spear-heads lies the foe.

IV

—Monster of the sea! we drive him
   Back into his hungry brine.
—You shall lodge him, feed him, wive him.
   Look on us; we stand in line.
—Pale sea-monster! foul the waters
   Cast him; foul he leaves our land.
—You shall yield us land and daughters:
   Stay the tongue, and try the hand.

V

Swift as torrent-streams our warriors,
Tossing torrent lights, find way;
Burst the ridges, crowd the barriers,
Pierce them where the spear-heads play;

Turn them as the clods in furrow,
Top them like the leaping foam;
Sorrow to the mother, sorrow,
Sorrow to the wife at home!

VI

Stags, they butted; bulls, they bellowed;
Hounds, we baited them; oh, brave!
Every second man, unfellowed,
Took the strokes of two, and gave.
Bare as hop-stakes in November's
Mists they met our battle-flood:
Hoary-red as Winter's embers
Lay their dead lines done in blood.

VII

Thou, my Bard, didst hang thy lyre in
Oak-leaves, and with crimson brand
Rhythmic fury spent, Aneurin;
Songs the churls could understand:
Thrumming on their Saxon sconces
Straight, the invariable blow,
Till they snorted true responses.
Ever thus the Bard they know!

VIII

But ere nightfall, harper lusty!
When the sun was like a ball
Dropping on the battle dusty,
What was yon discordant call?
Cambria's old metheglin demon
Breathed against our rushing tide;
Clove us midst the threshing seamen:—
Gashed, we saw our ranks divide!

IX

Britain then with valedictory
Shriek veiled off her face and knelt.
Full of liquor, full of victory,
Chief on chief old vengeance dealt.
Backward swung their hurly-burly;
None but dead men kept the fight.
They that drink their cup too early,
Darkness they shall see ere night.

X

Loud we heard the yellow rover
Laugh to sleep, while we raged thick,
Thick as ants the ant-hill over,
Asking who has thrust the stick.
Lo, as frogs that Winter cumbers
Meet the Spring with stiffen'd yawn,
We from our hard night of slumbers,
Marched into the bloody dawn.

XI

Day on day we fought, though shattered;
Pushed and met repulses sharp,
Till our Raven's plumes were scattered:
All, save old Aneurin's harp.
Hear it wailing like a mother
O'er the strings of children slain!
He in one tongue, in another,
Alien, I; one blood, yet twain.

XII

Old Aneurin! droop no longer.
That squat ocean-scum, we own,
Had fine stoutness, made us stronger,
Brought us much-required backbone:

Claimed of Power their dues, and granted
Dues to Power in turn, when rose
Mightier rovers; they that planted
Sovereign here the Norman nose.

XIII

Glorious men, with heads of eagles,
Chopping arms, and cupboard lips;
Warriors, hunters, keen as beagles,
Mounted aye on horse or ships.
Active, being hungry creatures;
Silent, having nought to say:
High they raised the lord of features,
Saxon-worshipped to this day.

XIV

Hear its deeds, the great recital!
Stout as bergs of Arctic ice
Once it led, and lived; a title
Now it is, and names its price.
This our Saxon brothers cherish:
This, when by the worth of wits
Lands are reared aloft, or perish,
Sole illumes their lucre-pits.

XV

Know we not our wrongs, unwritten
Though they be, Aneurin? Sword,
Song, and subtle mind, the Briton
Brings to market, all ignored.
'Gainst the Saxon's bone impinging,
Still is our Gododin played;
Shamed we see him humbly cringing
In a shadowy nose's shade.

XVI

Bitter is the weight that crushes
Low, my Bard, thy race of fire.
Here no fair young future blushes
Bridal to a man's desire.
Neither chief, nor aim, nor splendour
Dressing distance, we perceive.
Neither honour, nor the tender
Bloom of promise, morn or eve.

XVII

Joined we are; a tide of races
Rolled to meet a common fate;
England clasps in her embraces
Many: what is England's state?
England her distended middle
Thumps with pride as Mammon's wife;
Says that thus she reads thy riddle,
Heaven! 'tis heaven to plump her life.

XVIII

O my Bard! a yellow liquor,
Like to that we drank of old—
Gold is her metheglin beaker,
She destruction drinks in gold.
Warn her, Bard, that Power is pressing
Hotly for his dues this hour;
Tell her that no drunken blessing
Stops the onward march of Power.

XIX

Has she ears to take forewarnings
She will cleanse her of her stains,
Feed and speed for braver mornings
Valorously the growth of brains.

Power, the hard man knit for action,
Reads each nation on the brow.
Cripple, fool, and petrifaction,
Fall to him—are falling now!

France

DECEMBER 1870

GM's letters from the time of the beginning of the Franco-Prussian War, July 19, 1870, show how he agonized over this conflict. His two years' schooling in Germany and his devotion to German poets had given him many favorable insights into the German character, but on the whole he sided with France. He would have liked to be a war correspondent, as he had been for the brief war between Italy and Austria in 1866, but no correspondents were allowed (letter to John Morley, July 21).

By December 7 he was almost ready to send his ode to the *Fortnightly* and wrote John Morley (see headnote, p. 296): "Now to business—I have a Grand Ode to France—called simply 'France 1870': from my point of view of sympathy and philosophy; which I think is ours. Latterly I have felt poetically weakened by the pressure of philosophical reflection, but this is going, and a fuller strength comes of it, for I believe I am within the shadow of the Truth, and as it's my nature to sing I may now do well."

The idea of writing an ode on France and her affairs may have been suggested by Swinburne's *Ode on the Proclamation of the French Republic, September 4th, 1870*. This ode was written in three days, September 5–7, and was published as a pamphlet (London: F. S. Ellis, 1870) (see *Works*, Bonchurch edition, 20:96–97).

I

We look for her that sunlike stood
Upon the forehead of our day,
An orb of nations, radiating food
For body and for mind alway.

FRANCE, DECEMBER 1870

Previously printed in the Fortnightly *15 (1 January 1871) and reprinted in* Odes in Contribution to the Song of French History (*1898*).

F VIII not reprinted in 1887
F IX = VIII 1887
F X = IX 1887
F XI = X 1887
F XII, XIII, XIV, XV not reprinted in 1887
F XVI = XI 1887

Where is the Shape of glad array;
The nervous hands, the front of steel,
The clarion tongue? Where is the bold proud face?
We see a vacant place;
We hear an iron heel.

II

O she that made the brave appeal
For manhood when our time was dark,
And from our fetters drove the spark
Which was as lighting to reveal
New seasons, with the swifter play
Of pulses, and benigner day;
She that divinely shook the dead
From living man; that stretched ahead
Her resolute forefinger straight,
And marched toward the gloomy gate   10
Of earth's Untried, gave note, and in
The good name of Humanity
Called forth the daring vision! she,
She likewise half corrupt of sin,
Angel and Wanton! can it be?
Her star has foundered in eclipse,
The shriek of madness on her lips;
Shreds of her, and no more, we see.
There is horrible convulsion, smothered din,
As of one that in a grave-cloth struggles to be free.   20

III

Look not for spreading boughs
On the riven forest tree.
Look down where deep in blood and mire
Black thunder plants his feet and ploughs

II.3 drove] struck F
II.10 toward] towards F
II.19 horrible] a horrible F
III.1 for] on F
III.2 On] For F

The soil for ruin: that is France:
Still thrilling like a lyre,
Amazed to shivering discord from a fall
Sudden as that the lurid hosts recall
Who met in heaven the irreparable mischance.
O that is France!   10
The brilliant eyes to kindle bliss,
The shrewd quick lips to laugh and kiss,
Breasts that a sighing world inspire,
And laughter-dimpled countenance
Where soul and senses caught desire!

IV

Ever invoking fire from heaven, the fire
Has grasped her, unconsumeable, but framed
For all the ecstasies of suffering dire.
Mother of Pride, her sanctuary shamed:
Mother of Delicacy, and made a mark
For outrage: Mother of Luxury, stripped stark:
Mother of Heroes, bondsmen: thro' the rains,
Across her boundaries, lo the league-long chains!
Fond Mother of her martial youth; they pass,
Are spectres in her sight, are mown as grass!   10
Mother of Honour, and dishonoured: Mother
Of Glory, she condemned to crown with bays
Her victor, and be fountain of his praise.
Is there another curse? There is another:
Compassionate her madness: is she not
Mother of Reason? she that sees them mown
Like grass, her young ones! Yea, in the low groan
And under the fixed thunder of this hour
Which holds the animate world in one foul blot
Tranced circumambient while relentless Power   20

III.15 Where] Whence *F*
IV.2 grasped] seized *F*   uncomsumeable] *1887*; unconsumable *F, 1898, de L*
IV.10 Are] They are *F*

Beaks at her heart and claws her limbs down-thrown,
She, with the plungeing lightnings overshot,
With madness for an armour against pain,
With milkless breasts for little ones athirst,
And round her all her noblest dying in vain,
Mother of Reason is she, trebly cursed,
To feel, to see, to justify the blow;
Chamber to chamber of her sequent brain
Gives answer of the cause of her great woe,
Inexorably echoing thro' the vaults,   30
''Tis thus they reap in blood, in blood who sow:
'This is the sum of self-absolvëd faults.'
Doubt not that thro' her grief, with sight supreme,
Thro' her delirium and despair's last dream,
Thro' pride, thro' bright illusion and the brood
Bewildering of her various Motherhood,
The high strong light within her, tho' she bleeds,
Traces the letters of returned misdeeds.
She sees what seed long sown, ripened of late,
Bears this fierce crop; and she discerns her fate   40
From origin to agony, and on
As far as the wave washes long and wan
Off one disastrous impulse: for of waves
Our life is, and our deeds are pregnant graves
Blown rolling to the sunset from the dawn.

                              v

Ah, what a dawn of splendour, when her sowers
Went forth and bent the necks of populations
And of their terrors and humiliations
Wove her the starry wreath that earthward lowers
Now in the figure of a burning yoke!
Her legions traversed North and South and East,
Of triumph they enjoyed the glutton's feast:
They grafted the green sprig, they lopped the oak.
They caught by the beard the tempests, by the scalp
The icy precipices, and clove sheer through   10

The heart of horror of the pinnacled Alp,
Emerging not as men whom mortals knew.
They were the earthquake and the hurricane,
The lightnings and the locusts, plagues of blight,
Plagues of the revel: they were Deluge rain,
And dreaded Conflagration; lawless Might.
Death writes a reeling line along the snows,
Where under frozen mists they may be tracked,
Who men and elements provoked to foes,
And Gods: they were of god and beast compact: 20
Abhorred of all. Yet, how they sucked the teats
Of Carnage, thirsty issue of their dam,
Whose eagles, angrier than their oriflamme,
Flushed the vext earth with blood, green earth forgets.
The gay young generations mask her grief;
Where bled her children hangs the loaded sheaf.
Forgetful is green earth; the Gods alone
Remember everlastingly: they strike
Remorselessly, and ever like for like.
By their great memories the Gods are known.   30

VI

They are with her now, and in her ears, and known.
'Tis they that cast her to the dust for Strength,
Their slave, to feed on her fair body's length,
That once the sweetest and the proudest shone;
Scoring for hideous dismemberment
Her limbs, as were the anguish-taking breath
Gone out of her in the insufferable descent
From her high chieftainship; as were she death,
Who hears a voice of justice, feels the knife
Of torture, drinks all ignominy of life.   10
They are with her, and the painful Gods might weep,
If ever rain of tears came out of heaven
To flatter Weakness and bid Conscience sleep,
Viewing the woe of this Immortal, driven

VI.13 Conscience] *1887, 1898*; conscience *misp. de L*

For the soul's life to drain the maddening cup
Of her own children's blood implacably:
Unsparing even as they to furrow up
The yellow land to likeness of a sea:
The bountiful fair land of vine and grain,
Of wit and grace and ardour, and strong roots,   20
Fruits perishable, imperishable fruits;
Furrowed to likeness of the dim grey main
Behind the black obliterating cyclone.

                              VII

Behold, the Gods are with her, and are known.
Whom they abandon misery persecutes
No more: them half-eyed apathy may loan
The happiness of pitiable brutes.
Whom the just Gods abandon have no light,
No ruthless light of introspective eyes
That in the midst of misery scrutinize
The heart and its iniquities outright.
They rest, they smile and rest; have earned perchance
Of ancient service quiet for a term;   10
Quiet of old men dropping to the worm;
And so goes out the soul. But not of France.
She cries for grief, and to the Gods she cries,
For fearfully their loosened hands chastize,
And icily they watch the rod's caress
Ravage her flesh from scourges merciless,
But she, inveterate of brain, discerns
That Pity has as little place as Joy
Among their roll of gifts; for Strength she yearns,
For Strength, her idol once, too long her toy.   20
Lo, Strength is of the plain root-Virtues born:
Strength shall ye gain by service, prove in scorn,

VII.4 pitiable] the pitiable *F*
VII.9 have] they have *F*
VII.15 icily] mercilessly *F*

Train by endurance, by devotion shape.
Strength is not won by miracle or rape.
It is the offspring of the modest years,
The gift of sire to son, thro' those firm laws
Which we name Gods; which are the righteous cause,
The cause of man, and manhood's ministers.
Could France accept the fables of her priests,
Who blest her banners in this game of beasts,   30
And now bid hope that heaven will intercede
To violate its laws in her sore need,
She would find comfort in their opiates:
Mother of Reason! can she cheat the Fates?
Would she, the champion of the open mind,
The Omnipotent's prime gift—the gift of growth—
Consent even for a night-time to be blind,
And sink her soul on the delusive sloth,
For fruits ethereal and material, both,
In peril of her place among mankind?   40
The Mother of the many Laughters might
Call one poor shade of laughter in the light
Of her unwavering lamp to mark what things
The world puts faith in, careless of the truth:
What silly puppet-bodies danced on strings,
Attached by credence, we appear in sooth,
Demanding intercession, direct aid,
When the whole tragic tale hangs on a broken blade!

She swung the sword for centuries; in a day
It slipped her, like a stream cut off from source.   50
She struck a feeble hand, and tried to pray,
Clamoured of treachery, and had recourse
To drunken outcries in her dream that Force
Needed but hear her shouting to obey.

VII.26 firm] sound *F*
VII.36 prime] first *F*
VII.48 broken] forfeit *F*
VII.50 cut off from] out from its *F*
VII.54 hear] to hear *F*

Was she not formed to conquer? The bright plumes
Of crested vanity shed graceful nods:
Transcendent in her foundries, Arts and looms,
Had France to fear the vengeance of the Gods?
Her faith was on her battle-roll of names
Sheathed in the records of old war; with dance   60
And song she thrilled her warriors and her dames,
Embracing her Dishonour: gave him France
From head to foot, France present and to come,
So she might hear the trumpet and the drum—
Bellona and Bacchante! rushing forth
On yon stout marching Schoolmen of the North.

Inveterate of brain, well knows she why
Strength failed her, faithful to himself the first:
Her dream is done, and she can read the sky,
And she can take into her heart the worst   70
Calamity to drug the shameful thought
Of days that made her as the man she served
A name of terror, but a thing unnerved:
Buying the trickster, by the trickster bought,
She for dominion, he to patch a throne.

VIII

Henceforth of her the Gods are known,
Open to them her breast is laid.
Inveterate of brain, heart-valiant,
Never did fairer creature pant
Before the altar and the blade!

VII.59 faith was on her] Gods were then the *F*
VII.62 Dishonour] Dishonourer *F, 1887*
VII.66 yon] those *F*
See Supplementary Textual Notes.
Part VIII is part IX in F.

IX

Swift fall the blows, and men upbraid,
And friends give echo blunt and cold,
The echo of the forest to the axe.
Within her are the fires that wax
For resurrection from the mould.

X

She snatched at heaven's flame of old,
And kindled nations: she was weak:
Frail sister of her heroic prototype,
The Man; for sacrifice unripe,
She too must fill a Vulture's beak.
Deride the vanquished, and acclaim
The conqueror, who stains her fame,
Still the Gods love her, for that of high aim
Is this good France, the bleeding thing they stripe.

XI

She shall rise worthier of her prototype
Thro' her abasement deep; the pain that runs
From nerve to nerve some victory achieves.
They lie like circle-strewn soaked Autumn-leaves
Which stain the forest scarlet, her fair sons!
And of their death her life is: of their blood
From many streams now urging to a flood,
No more divided, France shall rise afresh.
Of them she learns the lesson of the flesh:—

X.6–9 *not in F XI*

The lesson writ in red since first Time ran,   10
A hunter hunting down the beast in man:
That till the chasing out of its last vice,
The flesh was fashioned but for sacrifice.

Immortal Mother of a mortal host!
Thou suffering of the wounds that will not slay,
Wounds that bring death but take not life away!—
Stand fast and hearken while thy victors boast:
Hearken, and loathe that music evermore.
Slip loose thy garments woven of pride and shame:
The torture lurks in them, with them the blame   20
Shall pass to leave thee purer than before.
Undo thy jewels, thinking whence they came,
For what, and of the abominable name
Of her who in imperial beauty wore.

O Mother of a fated fleeting host
Conceived in the past days of sin, and born
Heirs of disease and arrogance and scorn,
Surrender, yield the weight of thy great ghost,
Like wings on air, to what the heavens proclaim
With trumpets from the multitudinous mounds   30
Where peace has filled the hearing of thy sons:
Albeit a pang of dissolution rounds
Each new discernment of the undying ones,
Do thou stoop to these graves here scattered wide
Along thy fields, as sunless billows roll;
These ashes have the lesson for the soul.

Between 1887 XI.13 and XI.14 in F XVI:

        Cast hence the slave's delights, the wanton's lures,
        O France! and of thy folly pay full price;
        The limitary nature that immures
        A spirit dulled in clay shall break, as thrice
        It has broken on a night of blood and tears,
        To give thy ghost free breath, and joy thy peers.

XI.34 *F:* Stoop to these graves here scattered thick and wide

'Die to thy Vanity, and strain thy Pride,
Strip off thy Luxury: that thou may'st live,
Die to thyself,' they say, 'as we have died
From dear existence and the foe forgive,   40
Nor pray for aught save in our little space
To warm good seed to greet the fair earth's face.'
O Mother! take their counsel, and so shall
The broader world breathe in on this thy home,
Light clear for thee the counter-changing dome,
Strength give thee, like an ocean's vast expanse
Off mountain cliffs, the generations all,
Not whirling in their narrow rings of foam,
But as a river forward. Soaring France!
Now is Humanity on trial in thee: 50
Now may'st thou gather humankind in fee:
Now prove that Reason is a quenchless scroll;
Make of calamity thine aureole,
And bleeding lead us thro' the troubles of the sea.

Men and Man

I

Men the Angels eyed;
And here they were wild waves,
And there as marsh descried,
Men the Angels eyed,
And liked the picture best
Where they were greenly dressed
In brotherhood of graves.

FRANCE, DECEMBER 1870

XI.37 strain] to *F*
XI.38 Strip off] And to *F*
XI.42 warm] warn *misp.* Odes (*1898*), *de L; corr. errata, de L 1911*
XI.49 as] like *F*
XI *between 51 and 52 F*: Fire lift thee to the heights meridional,
XI.54 lead] *F, 1887;* head *probable misp. 1898, de L*

II

Man the Angels marked:
He led a host through murk,
On fearful seas embarked,
Man the Angels marked;
To think without a nay,
That he was good as they,
And help him at his work.

III

Man and Angels, ye
A sluggish fen shall drain,
Shall quell a warring sea.
Man and Angels, ye,
Whom stain of strife befouls,
A light to kindle souls
Bear radiant in the stain.

The Last Contention

I

Young captain of a crazy bark!
O tameless heart in battered frame!
Thy sailing orders have a mark,
    And hers is not the name.

II

For action all thine iron clanks
In cravings for a splendid prize;
Again to race or bump thy planks
    With any flag that flies.

III

Consult them; they are eloquent
For senses not inebriate.
They trust thee on the star intent,
    That leads to land their freight.

IV

And they have known thee high peruse
The heavens, and deep the earth, till thou
Didst into the flushed circle cruise
    Where reason quits the brow.

V

Thou animatest ancient tales,
To prove our world of linear seed:
Thy very virtue now assails,
    A tempter to mislead.

VI

But thou hast answer: I am I;
My passion hallows, bids command:
And she is gracious, she is nigh:
    One motion of the hand!

VII

It will suffice; a whirly tune
These winds will pipe, and thou perform
The nodded part of pantaloon
    In thy created storm.

VIII

Admires thee Nature with much pride;
She clasps thee for a gift of morn,
Till thou art set against the tide,
    And then beware her scorn.

IX

Sad issue, should that strife befall
Between thy mortal ship and thee!
It writes the melancholy scrawl
    Of wreckage over sea.

X

This lady of the luting tongue,
The flash in darkness, billow's grace,
For thee the worship; for the young
    In muscle the embrace.

XI

Soar on thy manhood clear from those
Whose toothless Winter claws at May,
And take her as the vein of rose
    Athwart an evening grey.

Periander

    J. M. S. Tompkins in "Meredith's *Periander*" (*Review of English Studies*, n.s. 11 [August 1960]) gives Book 3 of Herodotus' *History* as GM's source. She finds in the poem an imaginative apotheosis of GM's estrangement from his older son Arthur who bore a striking resemblance to his mother, Mary Peacock Meredith (see I. 4, V. 3, XVIII. 2–4).

I

How died Melissa none dares shape in words.
A woman who is wife despotic lords
Count faggot at the question, Shall she live!
Her son, because his brows were black of her,
Runs barking for his bread, a fugitive,
And Corinth frowns on them that feed the cur.

PERIANDER

See Supplementary Textual Notes.

II

There is no Corinth save the whip and curb
Of Corinth, high Periander; the superb
In magnanimity, in rule severe.
Up on his marble fortress-tower he sits,
The city under him: a white yoked steer,
That bears his heart for pulse, his head for wits.

III

Bloom of the generous fires of his fair Spring
Still coloured him when men forbore to sting;
Admiring meekly where the ordered seeds
Of his good sovereignty showed gardens trim;
And owning that the hoe he struck at weeds
Was author of the flowers raised face to him.

IV

His Corinth, to each mood subservient
In homage, made he as an instrument
To yield him music with scarce touch of stops.
He breathed, it piped; he moved, it rose to fly:
At whiles a bloodhorse racing till it drops;
At whiles a crouching dog, on him all eye.

V

His wisdom men acknowledged; only one,
The creature, issue of him, Lycophron,
That rebel with his mother in his brows,
Contested: such an infamous would foul
Pirene! Little heed where he might house
The prince gave, hearing: so the fox, the owl!

VI

To prove the Gods benignant to his rule,
The years, which fasten rigid whom they cool,
Reviewing, saw him hold the seat of power.

A grey one asked: Who next? nor answer had:
One greyer pointed on the pallid hour
To come: a river dried of waters glad.

VII

For which of his male issue promised grip
To stride yon people, with the curb and whip?
This Lycophron! he sole, the father like,
Fired prospect of a line in one strong tide,
By right of mastery; stern will to strike;
Pride to support the stroke: yea, Godlike pride!

VIII

Himself the prince beheld a failing fount.
His line stretched back unto its holy mount:
The thirsty onward waved for him no sign.
Then stood before his vision that hard son.
The seizure of a passion for his line
Impelled him to the path of Lycophron.

IX

The youth was tossing pebbles in the sea;
A figure shunned along the busy quay,
Perforce of the harsh edict for who dared
Address him outcast. Naming it, he crossed
His father's look with look that proved them paired
For stiffness, and another pebble tossed.

X

An exile to the Island ere nightfall
He passed from sight, from the hushed mouths of all.
It had resemblance to a death: and on,
Against a coast where sapphire shattered white,
The seasons rolled like troops of billows blown
To spraymist. The prince gazed on capping night.

XI

Deaf Age spake in his ear with shouts: Thy son!
Deep from his heart Life raved of work not done.
He heard historic echoes moan his name,
As of the prince in whom the race had pause;
Till Tyranny paternity became,
And him he hated loved he for the cause.

XII

Not Lycophron the exile now appeared,
But young Periander, from the shadow cleared,
That haunted his rebellious brows. The prince
Grew bright for him; saw youth, if seeming loth,
Return: and of pure pardon to convince,
Despatched the messenger most dear with both.

XIII

His daughter, from the exile's Island home,
Wrote, as a flight of halcyons o'er the foam,
Sweet words: her brother to his father bowed;
Accepted his peace-offering, and rejoiced.
To bring him back a prince the father vowed,
Commanded man the oars, the white sails hoist.

XIV

He waved the fleet to strain its westward way
On to the sea-hued hills that crown the bay:
Soil of those hospitable islanders
Whom now his heart, for honour to his blood,
Thanked. They should learn what boons a prince confers
When happiness enjoins him gratitude!

XV

In watch upon the offing, worn with haste
To see his youth revived, and, close embraced,
Pardon who had subdued him, who had gained

Surely the stoutest battle between two
Since Titan pierced by young Apollo stained
Earth's breast, the prince looked forth, himself looked
    through.

XVI

Errors aforetime unperceived were bared,
To be by his young masterful repaired:
Renewed his great ideas gone to smoke;
His policy confirmed amid the surge
Of States and people fretting at his yoke.
And lo, the fleet brown-flocked on the sea-verge!

XVII

Oars pulled: they streamed in harbour; without cheer
For welcome shadowed round the heaving bier.
They, whose approach in such rare pomp and stress
Of numbers the free islanders dismayed
At Tyranny come masking to oppress,
Found Lycophron this breathless, this lone-laid.

XVIII

Who smote the man thrown open to young joy?
The image of the mother of his boy
Came forth from his unwary breast in wreaths,
With eyes. And shall a woman, that extinct,
Smite out of dust the Powerful who breathes?
Her loved the son; her served; they lay close-linked!

XIX

Dead was he, and demanding earth. Demand
Sharper for vengeance of an instant hand,
The Tyrant in the father heard him cry,
And raged a plague; to prove on free Hellenes
How prompt the Tyrant for the Persian dye;
How black his Gods behind their marble screens.

Solon

In this poem Solon, the poet and law-maker, who became an archon of Athens in 594 B.C. is seen as an old man, after his cousin Peisistratus, the Tyrant of the poem, had seized the Acropolis (560 B.C.). Solon had warned the people against this usurpation, and after it had taken place he urged them to fight against the new tyranny. Failing to arouse them, he continued writing poems that reproached them for their timidity. It was to the credit of Peisistratus that he left the "great man of Athens" (I. 2) unpunished. Plutarch accounts for this leniency in the first paragraph of John Dryden's translation of his *Life of Solon*: "Solon's mother . . . was a cousin of the mother of Peisistratus. And the two men were at first great friends, largely because of their kinship, and largely because of the youthful beauty of Peisistratus, with whom, as some say, Solon was passionately in love. And this may be the reason why, in later years, when they were at variance about matters of state, their enmity did not bring with it any harsh or savage feelings, but their former amenities lingered in their spirits."

I

The Tyrant passed, and friendlier was his eye
On the great man of Athens, whom for foe
He knew, than on the sycophantic fry
That broke as waters round a galley's flow,
Bubbles at prow and foam along the wake.
Solidity the Thunderer could not shake,
Beneath an adverse wind still stripping bare,
His kinsman, of the light-in-cavern look,
From thought drew, and a countenance could wear
Not less at peace than fields in Attic air   10
Shorn, and shown fruitful by the reaper's hook.

II

Most enviable so; yet much insane
To deem of minds of men they grow! these sheep,
By fits wild horses, need the crook and rein;
Hot bulls by fits, pure wisdom hold they cheap,
My Lawgiver, when fiery is the mood.

MS: Huntington HM6767, *fair copy of stanzas I–III; working drafts of IV–V. Variants are from this MS.*
I.10 Attic] Summer
II.4 Hot bulls by fits, pure] By fits hot bulls, mild *or* pure

For ones and twos and threes thy words are good;
For thine own government are pillars: mine
Stand acts to fit the herd; which has quick thirst,
Rejecting elegiacs, though they shine
On polished brass, and, worthy of the Nine,   10
In showering columns from their fountain burst.

III

Thus museful rode the Tyrant, princely plumed,
To his high seat upon the sacred rock:
And Solon, blank beside his rule, resumed
The meditation which that passing mock
Had buffeted awhile to sallowness.
He little loved the man, his office less,
Yet owned him for a flower of his kind.
Therefore the heavier curse on Athens he!
The people grew not in themselves, but blind,
Accepted sight from him, to him resigned   10
Their hopes of stature, rootless as at sea.

IV

As under sea lay Solon's work, or seemed
By turbid shore-waves beaten day by day;
Defaced, half formless, like an image dreamed,
Or child that fashioned in another clay
Appears, by strangers' hands to home returned.
But shall the Present tyrannize us? earned

II.7 pillars] fruitful
II.8 Stand acts to fit] Commend them to *or* Are acts to fit
III.1 rode] passed *del.*
III.3 blank beside his rule] whom his work *or* rule [had wrecked *del.*] made blank
III.6 He little loved the man] He loved the Tyrant not *del.*
III.7 him for] the man *del.*
III.10 sight] eyes
IV.5 home] us *del.*

It was in some way, justly says the sage.
One sees not how, while husbanding regrets;
While tossing scorn abroad from righteous rage,
High vision is obscured; for this is age   10
When robbed—more infant than the babe it frets!

v

Yet see Athenians treading the black path
Laid by a prince's shadow! well content
To wait his pleasure, shivering at his wrath:
They bow to their accepted Orient
With offer of the all that renders bright:
Forgetful of the growth of men to light,
As creatures reared on Persian milk they bow.
Unripe! unripe! The times are overcast.
But still may they who sowed behind the plough
True seed fix in the mind an unborn Now   10
To make the plagues afflicting us things past.

IV.7 justly says the sage] must the sage avow *dr. 1*; justly says] this *or* so far bows
IV.8 *dr. 1*: Nay, that black tyrant shall be overcast.   how] where *dr. 2*
IV.9 *dr. 1*: Faith in the good seed sown behind the plough,   tossing scorn abroad]
scattering reproach *dr. 2*
IV.10 *dr. 1*: Shall ripen for our roseate minds a *or* Now roseate minds a [living *del.*]
blooming
       dr. 2: [Is never vision clear: *del.*] Clear vision is obscured: for sober age,
IV.11 *dr. 1*: To make the plagues afflicting us things past.
       dr. 2: [When robbed *del.*] Robbed of the dues of labour, childlike frets
V.1 see Athenians] there is Athens *del.*
V.2 Laid by] Behind *del.* Flung by   well] too *del.*
V.3 shivering] shiver
V.4 And bow to [their *del.*] effulgent Orient,
V.6 of the growth of men] how free men are reared *or* grown
V.7 As if on Persian milk sustained *or* upreared *or* As creatures reared on Persian milk
they bow.
V.9 Faith in the &c [*MS breaks off*]; see *dr. 1, IV.9–11*

Bellerophon

I

Maimed, beggared, grey; seeking an alms; with nod
Of palsy doing task of thanks for bread;
     Upon the stature of a God,
He whom the Gods have struck bends low his head.

II

Weak words he has, that slip the nerveless tongue
Deformed, like his great frame: a broken arc:
     Once radiant as the javelin flung
Right at the centre breastplate of his mark.

III

Oft pausing on his white-eyed inward look,
Some undermountain narrative he tells,
     As gapped by Lykian heat the brook
Cut from the source that in the upland swells.

MSS: Huntington HM6768, *four fragments. Frag. A, early draft, fair copy corrected of stanzas III–IV, VIII numbered v, IX insertion numbered vi, V numbered vi* [sic], *VI numbered vii, VII numbered viii, XII numbered ix; frag. B, later draft, fair copy corrected of stanzas I–IV, V.1–2,* [space for vi], *VIII numbered vii, IX numbered viii, XI numbered ix,* [space left for x], *XII numbered xi; frag. C, working draft of XI unnumbered, verso of leaf 3; frag. D, fair copy corrected of X numbered xi, XI numbered xii,* [space left for xiii]. *Variants are from these fragments.*

I.1 Maimed] Lamed *frag. B*
II.1 has] hath *frag. B*
II.2 broken arc] broken bow *del.;* shattered arc *frag. B*
II.4 his mark] the foe *del. frag. B*
III.1 Oft] Now *frags. A, B*
III.2 Some undermountain narrative] For thought, some toothless history *frag. A;* narrative] history *frag. B*
III.4 upland] mountain *frag. A*

IV

The cottagers who dole him fruit and crust,
With patient inattention hear him prate:
　　And comes the snow, and comes the dust,
Comes the old wanderer, more bent of late.

V

A crazy beggar grateful for a meal
Has ever of himself a world to say.
　　For them he is an ancient wheel
Spinning a knotted thread the livelong day.

VI

He cannot, nor do they, the tale connect;
For never singer in the land had been
　　Who him for theme did not reject:
Spurned of the hoof that sprang the Hippocrene.

VII

Albeit a theme of flame to bring them straight
The snorting white-winged brother of the wave,
　　They hear him as a thing by fate
Cursed in unholy babble to his grave.

VIII

As men that spied the wings, that heard the snort,
Their sires have told; and of a martial prince
　　Bestriding him; and old report
Speaks of a monster slain by one long since.

Stanza IV frag. A:
　　　　　　They know him on these plains Aleïan,
　　　　　　The cottagers who dole him fruit & crust:
　　　　　　　They know [him] for a luckless man
　　　　　　Famed for wild riding, & left prone in dust,
V.4 knotted] draggled *frag. A vi*
VII.2 snorting white-winged horse & *frag. A viii*
VIII.1 *frag. A v*: Their sires of a strange horse with wings & snort;
　　　frag. B vii: Their sires of a bright horse with wings & snort
VIII.2 Their sires] Of fire *frags. A, B*

IX

There is that story of the golden bit
By Goddess given to tame the lightning steed:
    A mortal who could mount, and sit
Flying, and up Olympus midway speed.

X

He rose like the loosed fountain's utmost leap;
He played the star at span of heaven right o'er
    Men's heads: they saw the snowy steep,
Saw the winged shoulders: him they saw not more.

XI

He fell: and says the shattered man, I fell:
And sweeps an arm the height an eagle wins;
    And in his breast a mouthless well
Heaves the worn patches of his coat of skins.

XII

Lo, this is he in whom the surgent springs
Of recollections richer than our skies
    To feed the flow of tuneful strings,
Show but a pool of scum for shooting flies.

IX.1 the] a *del. frag. A vi*
IX.2 the] a *del. frag. A vi*
IX.3 A] The *del. frag. A vi*
IX.4 up Olympus midway] & to Olympus nigh did *frag. A vi*
Stanza X frag. D:
        He rose like the great fountain's utmost fling *or* leap,
        And played the star at span of heaven, before
            The eyes of men *or* men's eyes; they saw him spring *or* the steep
        Sheer to the height; such thirst had he to soar. *or* Saw the winged
            flanks, but him they saw no more.
XI.1 the shattered] this broken *frags. C, B ix, D xii*
XI.2 *frag. C:* [So closes to resume till at his throat *del.*] And sweeps an arm the height
an eagle wins
XI.3 *frag. C:* The words are waters of a well [dusty [?] breast a well *del.* breast a word-
less *del.*] And in breast a mouthless well
XI.4 Heaves the worn] Shakes all the *frag. C;* Heaves all the *frag. B ix*
XII.1 Lo] And *frag. A ix*   surgent] fountain— *frag. A ix;* fountain— *del.* surgent
frag. B xi
XII.4 pool of scum for shooting] stagnant pool for dust *or* scum & *frag. A ix*

Phaéthôn

ATTEMPTED IN THE GALLIAMBIC MEASURE

GM's experiment with the Galliambic measure was probably prompted by the success of Tennyson's *Boädicea* in *Enoch Arden and Other Poems* (1864). Writing about this poem, Swinburne reported in letters of October that he had been flogged at Eton because his master was not satisfied with his experiment in Galliambics (Algernon C. Swinburne, *The Swinburne Letters*, ed. Cecil Y. Lang, 1 [New Haven: Yale University Press, 1959]: 110). On October 23, 1868, GM asked Augustus Jessopp whether he had seen "the poem of 'Phaëthon' done in Galliambics in the *Fortnightly Review* of last September a year back? To my mind they are near on the mark, but as the public is not near it I might as well have missed. Two or three lines want a correcting touch." The apparatus criticus shows that he retouched several lines before republishing the poem in 1887.

At the coming up of Phoebus the all-luminous charioteer,
Double-visaged stand the mountains in imperial multitudes,
And with shadows dappled men sing to him, Hail, O Beneficent!
For they shudder chill, the earth-vales, at his clouding, shudder to
 black;
In the light of him there is music thro' the poplar and river-sedge,
Renovation, chirp of brooks, hum of the forest—an ocean-song.
Never pearl from ocean-hollows by the diver exultingly,
In his breathlessness, above thrust, is as earth to Helios.

Previously printed in the Fortnightly *8 (1 September 1867).* Phaéthôn *is* Phaëthon *in* F.
1 the all-luminous charioteer] in his jubilant Orient *F*
Between 1 and 2 F:
  When his rays suffuse the fair face of the morn,
   and his chariot,
  All irradiating, upward curvets red to his sovereignty,
Between 3 and 4 F:
  Greeting him who makes them trustful, greeting him,
   O beneficent!
4 shudder to black] shuddering lost *F*
7 -hollows] -bottoms *F, 1887*

Who usurps his place there, rashest? Aphrodite's loved one it is!
To his son the flaming Sun-God, to the tender youth, Phaethon,   10
Rule of day this day surrenders as a thing hereditary,
Having sworn by Styx tremendous, for the proof of his parentage,
He would grant his son's petition, whatsoever the sign thereof.
Then, rejoiced, the stripling answered: 'Rule of day give me; give it
      me,
'Give me place that men may see me how I blaze, and
      transcendingly,
'I, divine, proclaim my birthright.' Darkened Helios, and his
      utterance
Choked prophetic: 'O half mortal!' he exclaimed in an agony,
'O lost son of mine! lost son! No! put a prayer for another thing:
'Not for this: insane to wish it, and to crave the gift impious!
'Cannot other gifts my godhead shed upon thee? miraculous   20
'Mighty gifts to prove a blessing, that to earth thou shalt be a joy?
'Gifts of healing, wherewith men walk as the Gods beneficently;
'As a God to sway to concord hearts of men, reconciling them;
'Gifts of verse, the lyre, the laurel, therewithal that thine origin
'Shall be known even as when *I* strike on the string'd shell with
      melody,
'And the golden notes, like medicine, darting straight to the
      cavities,
'Fill them up, till hearts of men bound as the billows, the ships
      thereon.'
Thus intently urged the Sun-God; but the force of his eloquence
Was the pressing on of sea-waves scattered broad from the rocks
      away.
What shall move a soul from madness? Lost, lost in delirium,   30
Rock-fast, the adolescent to his father, irreverent,
'By the oath! the oath! thine oath!' cried. The effulgent foreseër
      then,
Quivering in his loins parental, on the boy's beaming countenance
Looked and moaned, and urged him for love's sake, for sweet
      life's sake, to yield the claim,
To abandon his mad hunger, and avert the calamity.

16 and his] his, *F, 1887*

But he, vehement, passionate, called out: 'Let me show I am what
    I say,
'That the taunts I hear be silenced: I am stung with their
    whispering.
'Only, Thou, my Father, Thou tell how aloft the revolving wheels,
'How aloft the cleaving horse-crests I may guide peremptorily,
'Till I drink the shadows, fire-hot, like a flower celestial,   40
'And my fellows see me curbing the fierce steeds, the dear dew-
    drinkers:
'Yea, for this I gaze on life's light; throw for this any sacrifice.'

All the end foreseeing, Phoebus, to his oath irrevocable,
Bowed obedient, deploring the insanity pitiless.
Then the flame-outsnorting horses were led forth: it was so
    decreed.
They were yoked before the glad youth by his sister-ancillaries.
Swift the ripple ripples follow'd, as of aureate Helicon,
Down their flanks, while they impatient pawed desire of the
    distances,
And the bit with fury champed. Oh! unimaginable delight!
Unimagined speed and splendour in the circle of upper air!   50
Glory grander than the armed host upon earth singing victory!
Chafed the youth with their spirit súrcharged, as when blossom is
    shaken by winds,
Marked that labour by his sister Phaethontiades finished, quick
On the slope of the car his forefoot set assured: and the morning
    rose:
Seeing whom, and what a day dawned, stood the God, as in
    harvest fields,
When the reaper grasps the full sheaf and the sickle that severs it:
Hugged the withered head with one hand, with the other, to
    indicate
(If this woe might be averted, this immeasurable evil),

49 delight] glories *F, 1887*
Between 50 and 51 F, 1887: Higher, higher than the mountains, than the eagle fleeing
arrows!
52 when blossom] when the blossom *F*
Between 54 and 55 F: Pearl-breasted Eos, grey-eyed, quiet, true to men wishing her.

Laid the kindling course in view, told how the reins to manipulate:
Named the horses fondly, fearful, caution'd urgently between-
    whiles: 60
Their diverging tempers dwelt on, and their wantonness,
    wickedness,
That the voice of Gods alone held in restraint; but the voice of
    Gods;
None but Gods can curb. He spake: vain were the words: scarcely
    listening,
Mounted Phaethon, swinging reins loose, and, 'Behold me,
    companions,
'It is I here, I!' he shouted, glancing down with supremacy;
'Not to any of you was this gift granted ever in annals of men;
'I alone what only Gods can, I alone am governing day!'
Short the triumph, brief his rapture: see a hurricane suddenly
Beat the lifting billow crestless, roll it broken this way and that;—
At the leap on yielding ether, in despite of his reprimand,   70
Swayed tumultuous the fire-steeds, plunging reckless hither and
    yon;
Unto men a great amazement, all agaze at the Troubled East:—
Pitifully for mastery striving in ascension, the charioteer,
Reminiscent, drifts of counsel caught confused in his arid wits;
The reins stiff ahind his shoulder madly pulled for the mastery,
Till a thunder off the tense chords thro' his ears dinnèd horrible.
Panic seized him: fled his vision of inviolability;
Fled the dream that he of mortals rode mischances predominant;
And he cried, 'Had I petitioned for a cup of chill aconite,
'My descent to awful Hades had been soft, for now must I go   80
'With the curse by father Zeus cast on ambition immoderate.
'Oh, my sisters! Thou, my Goddess, in whose love I was enviable,
'From whose arms I rushed befrenzied, what a wreck will this
    body be,

62 held in restraint; but the voice of Gods;] could hold in check; but gods alone: *F*
63 can curb] restrain *F*
64 reins] the reins *F*
66 was this gift] has this been *F*
72 Troubled East] Orient *F, 1887*

That admired of thee stood rose-warm in the courts where thy
    mysteries
'Celebration had from me, me the most splendidly privileged!
'Never more shall I thy temple fill with incenses bewildering;
'Not again hear thy half-murmurs—I am lost!—never, never more.
'I am wrecked on seas of air, hurled to my death in a vessel of
    flame!
'Hither, sisters! Father, save me! Hither, succour me, Cypria!'

Now a wail of men to Zeus rang: from Olympus the Thunderer   90
Saw the rage of the havoc wide-mouthed, the bright car
    superimpending
Over Asia, Africa, low down; ruin flaming over the vales;
Light disastrous rising savage out of smoke inveterately;
Beast-black, conflagration like a menacing shadow move
With voracious roaring southward, where aslant, insufferable,
The bright steeds careered their parched way down an arc of the
    firmament.
For the day grew like to thick night, and the orb was its beacon-
    fire,
And from hill to hill of darkness burst the day's apparition forth.
Lo, a wrestler, not a God, stood in the chariot ever lowering:
Lo, the shape of one who raced there to outstrip the legitimate
    hours: 100
Lo, the ravish'd beams of Phoebus dragged in shame at the
    chariot-wheels:
Light of days of happy pipings by the mead-singing rivulets!
Lo, lo, increasing lustre, torrid breath to the nostrils; lo,
Torrid brilliancies thro' the vapours lighten swifter, penetrate them,
Fasten merciless, ruminant, hueless, on earth's frame crackling
    busily.
He aloft, the frenzied driver, in the glow of the universe,
Like the paling of the dawn-star withers visibly, he aloft:
Bitter fury in his aspect, bitter death in the heart of him.

94 conflagration] the conflagration *F, 1887*

Crouch the herds, contract the reptiles, crouch the lions under
    their paws.
White as metal in the furnace are the faces of humankind: 110
Inarticulate creatures of earth, dumb all await the ultimate shock.

To the bolt he launched, 'Strike dead, thou,' uttered Zeus, very
    terrible;
'Perish folly, clse 'tis man's fate'; and the bolt flew unerringly.
Then the kindler stooped; from the torch-car down the measureless
    altitudes
Leaned his rayless head, relinquished rein and footing, raised not
    a cry.
Like the flower on the river's surface when expanding it vanishes,
Gave his limbs to right and left, quenched: and so fell he
    precipitate,
Seen of men as a glad rain-fall, sending coolness yet ere it comes:
So he showered above them, shadowed o'er the blue archipelagoes,
O'er the silken-shining pastures of the continents and the isles;   120
So descending brought revival to the greenery of our earth.

Lither, noisy in the breezes now his sisters shivering weep,
By the river flowing smooth out to the vexed sea of Adria,
Where he fell, and where they suffered sudden change to the
    tremulous
Ever-wailful trees bemoaning him, a bruised purple cyclamen.

121 our] the *F*
122 Lither] Lithe and *F*

A READING OF EARTH
(1888)

Seed-Time

I

Flowers of the willow-herb are wool;
Flowers of the briar berries red;
Speeding their seed as the breeze may rule,
Flowers of the thistle loosen the thread.
Flowers of the clematis drip in beard,
Slack from the fir-tree youngly climbed;
Chaplets in air, flies foliage seared;
Heeled upon earth, lie clusters rimed.

II

Where were skies of the mantle stained
Orange and scarlet, a coat of frieze
Travels from North till day has waned,
Tattered, soaked in the ditch's dyes;
Tumbles the rook under grey or slate;
Else enfolding us, damps to the bone;
Narrows the world to my neighbour's gate;
Paints me Life as a wheezy crone.

MSS: Yale; Huntington HM6757, *fair copy.*

I.7 flies foliage] the leaves are *Y*
I.8 lie clusters] brown leaves *del.* the fallen *Y*; are the dead leaves *del. H*
II.3 day] light *Y*
II.4 soaked in the ditch's dyes] little the light of skies *del. Y*

III

Now seems none but the spider lord;
Star in circle his web waits prey,
Silvering bush-mounds, blue brushing sward;
Slow runs the hour, swift flits the ray.
Now to his thread-shroud is he nigh,
Nigh to the tangle where wings are sealed,
He who frolicked the jewelled fly;
All is adroop on the down and the weald.

IV

Mists more lone for the sheep-bell enwrap
Nights that tardily let slip a morn
Paler than moons, and on noontide's lap
Flame dies cold, like the rose late born.
Rose born late, born withered in bud!—
I, even I, for a zenith of sun
Cry, to fulfil me, nourish my blood:
O for a day of the long light, one!

V

Master the blood, nor read by chills,
Earth admonishes: Hast thou ploughed,
Sown, reaped, harvested grain for the mills,
Thou hast the light over shadow of cloud.
Steadily eyeing, before that wail
Animal-infant, thy mind began,
Momently nearer me: should sight fail,
Plod in the track of the husbandman.

IV.4 Flame dies cold] Cold flame dies *del. Y*
V.5 eyeing] noting *Y*
V.6 thy mind] mine eye *Y*

VI

Verily now is our season of seed,
Now in our Autumn; and Earth discerns
Them that have served her in them that can read,
Glassing, where under the surface she burns,
Quick at her wheel, while the fuel, decay,
Brightens the fire of renewal: and we?
Death is the word of a bovine day,
Know you the breast of the springing To-be.

Hard Weather

Bursts from a rending East in flaws
The young green leaflet's harrier, sworn
To strew the garden, strip the shaws,
And show our Spring with banner torn.
Was ever such virago morn?
The wind has teeth, the wind has claws.
All the wind's wolves through woods are loose,
The wild wind's falconry aloft.
Shrill underfoot the grassblade shrews,
At gallop, clumped, and down the croft   10
Bestrid by shadows, beaten, tossed;
It seems a scythe, it seems a rod.
The howl is up at the howl's accost;
The shivers greet and the shivers nod.

Is the land ship? we are rolled, we drive
Tritonly, cleaving hiss and hum;
Whirl with the dead, or mount or dive,
Or down in dregs, or on in scum.
And drums the distant, pipes the near,
And vale and hill are grey in grey,   20

HARD WEATHER
MSS: Yale, *relatively fair copy;* Huntington HM6758, *fair copy.*
8 wild wind's] wind's wild *Y*
20 in] through *del. Y*

As when the surge is crumbling sheer,
And sea-mews wing the haze of spray.
Clouds—are they bony witches?—swarms,
Darting swift on the robber's flight,
Hurry an infant sky in arms:
It peeps, it becks; 'tis day, 'tis night.
Black while over the loop of blue
The swathe is closed, like shroud on corse.
Lo, as if swift the Furies flew,
The Fates at heel at a cry to horse!   30

Interpret me the savage whirr:
And is it Nature scourged, or she,
Her offspring's executioner,
Reducing land to barren sea?
But is there meaning in a day
When this fierce angel of the air,
Intent to throw, and haply slay,
Can for what breath of life we bear,
Exact the wrestle? Call to mind
The many meanings glistening up   40
When Nature to her nurselings kind,
Hands them the fruitage and the cup!
And seek we rich significance
Not otherwise than with those tides
Of pleasure on the sunned expanse,
Whose flow deludes, whose ebb derides?

Look in the face of men who fare
Lock-mouthed, a match in lungs and thews
For this fierce angel of the air,
To twist with him and take his bruise.   50

21 when] where *H*
24 swift] stretched *Y*
26 'tis day, 'tis night] a swaddled light *Y*
29 Lo] 'Tis *Y*
41 nurselings] *spelling from H. The medial* e *was increasingly GM's practice.*

That is the face beloved of old
Of Earth, young mother of her brood:
Nor broken for us shows the mould
When muscle is in mind renewed:
Though farther from her nature rude,
Yet nearer to her spirit's hold:
And though of gentler mood serene,
Still forceful of her fountain-jet.
So shall her blows be shrewdly met,
Be luminously read the scene   60
Where Life is at her grindstone set,
That she may give us edgeing keen,
String us for battle, till as play
The common strokes of fortune shower.
Such meaning in a dagger-day
Our wits may clasp to wax in power.
Yea, feel us warmer at her breast,
By spin of blood in lusty drill,
Than when her honeyed hands caressed,
And Pleasure, sapping, seemed to fill.   70

Behold the life at ease; it drifts.
The sharpened life commands its course.
She winnows, winnows roughly; sifts,
To dip her chosen in her source:
Contention is the vital force,
Whence pluck they brain, her prize of gifts,
Sky of the senses! on which height,
Not disconnected, yet released,
They see how spirit comes to light,
Through conquest of the inner beast,   80
Which Measure tames to movement sane,
In harmony with what is fair.
Never is Earth misread by brain:
That is the welling of her, there

75 vital] torrent Y
84 welling] fountain Y

The mirror: with one step beyond,
For likewise is it voice; and more,
Benignest kinship bids respond,
When wail the weak, and them restore
Whom days as fell as this may rive,
While Earth sits ebon in her gloom,　　　　　　　90
Us atomies of life alive
Unheeding, bent on life to come.
Her children of the labouring brain,
These are the champions of the race,
True parents, and the sole humane,
With understanding for their base.
Earth yields the milk, but all her mind
Is vowed to thresh for stouter stock.
Her passion for old giantkind,
That scaled the mount, uphurled the rock,　　　　　　　100
Devolves on them who read aright
Her meaning and devoutly serve;
Nor in her starlessness of night
Peruse her with the craven nerve:
But even as she from grass to corn,
To eagle high from grubbing mole,
Prove in strong brain her noblest born,
The station for the flight of soul.

87 Benignest kinship] The *del.* A heart beneath it *Y*
88 wail] cry *Y*
89 days as fell] such a day *Y*
95 True parents, and the] The veritably *Y*
99 passion for old] early love of *del. Y*

The South-Wester

See headnote on *South-West Wind in the Woodland*, page 25.

Day of the cloud in fleets! O day
Of wedded white and blue, that sail
Immingled, with a footing ray
In shadow-sandals down our vale!—
And swift to ravish golden meads,
Swift up the run of turf it speeds,
Thy bright of head and dark of heel,
To where the hilltop flings on sky,
As hawk from wrist or dust from wheel,
The tiptoe scalers tossed to fly:—   10
Thee the last thunder's caverned peal
Delivered from a wailful night:
All dusky round thy cradled light,
Those brine-born issues, now in bloom
Transfigured, wreathed as raven's plume
And briony-leaf to watch thee lie:
Dark eyebrows o'er a dreamful eye
Nigh opening: till in the braid
Of purpled vapours thou wert rosed:
Till that new babe a Goddess maid   20
Appeared and vividly disclosed
Her beat of life: then crimson played
On edges of the plume and leaf:
Shape had they and fair feature brief,
The wings, the smiles: they flew the breast,
Earth's milk. But what imperial march
Their standards led for earth, none guessed
Ere upward of a coloured arch,
An arrow straining eager head
Lightened, and high for zenith sped.   30

See Supplementary Textual Notes.

Fierier followed; followed Fire.
Name the young lord of Earth's desire,
Whose look her wine is, and whose mouth
Her music! Beauteous was she seen
Beneath her midway West of South;
And sister was her quivered green
To sapphire of the Nereid eyes
On sea when sun is breeze; she winked
As they, and waved, heaved waterwise
Her flood of leaves and grasses linked: 40
A myriad lustrous butterflies
A moment in the fluttering sheen;
Becapped with the slate air that throws
The reindeer's antlers black between
Low-frowning and wide-fallen snows,
A minute after; hooded, stoled
To suit a graveside Season's dirge.
Lo, but the breaking of a surge,
And she is in her lover's fold,
Illumined o'er a boundless range   50
Anew: and through quick morning hours
The Tropic-Arctic counterchange
Did seem to pant in beams and showers.

But noon beheld a larger heaven;
Beheld on our reflecting field
The Sower to the Bearer given,
And both their inner sweetest yield,
Fresh as when dews were grey or first
Received the flush of hues athirst.
Heard we the woodland, eyeing sun,   60
As harp and harper were they one.
A murky cloud a fair pursued,
Assailed, and felt the limbs elude:
He sat him down to pipe his woe,
And some strange beast of sky became:
A giant's club withheld the blow;

A milky cloud went all to flame.
And there were groups where silvery springs
The ethereal forest showed begirt
By companies in choric rings,   70
Whom but to see made ear alert.
For music did each movement rouse,
And motion was a minstrel's rage
To have our spirits out of house,
And bathe them on the open page.

This was a day that knew not age.
Since flew the vapoury twos and threes
From western pile to eastern rack;
As on from peaks of Pyrenees
To Graians; youngness ruled the track.   80
When songful beams were shut in caves,
And rainy drapery swept across;
When the ranked clouds were downy waves,
Breast of swan, eagle, albatross,
In ordered lines to screen the blue,
Youngest of light was nigh, we knew.
The silver finger of it laughed
Along the narrow rift: it shot,
Slew the huge gloom with golden shaft,
Then haled on high the volumed blot,   90
To build the hurling palace, cleave
The dazzling chasm; the flying nests,
The many glory-garlands weave,
Whose presence not our sight attests
Till wonder with the splendour blent,
And passion for the beauty flown,
Make evanescence permanent,
The thing at heart our endless own.

Only at gathered eve knew we
The marvels of the day: for then   100
Mount upon mountain out of sea
Arose, and to our spacious ken

Trebled sublime Olympus round
In towering amphitheatre.
Colossal on enormous mound,
Majestic gods we saw confer.
They wafted the Dream-messenger
From off the loftiest, the crowned:
That Lady of the hues of foam
In sun-rays: who, close under dome,   110
A figure on the foot's descent,
Irradiate to vapour went,
As one whose mission was resigned;
Dispieced, undraped, dissolved to threads.
Melting she passed into the mind,
Where immortal with mortal weds.

Whereby was known that we had viewed
The union of our earth and skies
Renewed: nor less alive renewed
Than when old bards, in nature wise,   120
Conceived pure beauty given to eyes,
And with undyingness imbued.
Pageant of man's poetic brain,
His grand procession of the song,
It was; the Muses and their train;
Their God to lead the glittering throng;
At whiles a beat of forest gong;
At whiles a glimpse of Python slain.
Mostly divinest harmony,
The lyre, the dance. We could believe   130
A life in orb and brook and tree
And cloud: and still holds Memory
A morning in the eyes of eve.

The Thrush in February

In February 1885 GM was dreading the impending death from cancer
of his second wife, Marie Vulliamy Meredith.

I know him, February's thrush,
And loud at eve he valentines
On sprays that paw the naked bush
Where soon will sprout the thorns and bines.

Now ere the foreign singer thrills
Our vale his plain-song pipe he pours,
A herald of the million bills;
And heed him not, the loss is yours.

My study, flanked with ivied fir
And budded beech with dry leaves curled,   10
Perched over yew and juniper,
He neighbours, piping to his world:—

The wooded pathways dank on brown,
The branches on grey cloud a web,
The long green roller of the down,
An image of the deluge-ebb:—

And farther, they may hear along
The stream beneath the poplar row,
By fits, like welling rocks, the song
Spouts of a blushful Spring in flow.   20

But most he loves to front the vale
When waves of warm South-western rains
Have left our heavens clear in pale,
With faintest beck of moist red veins:

Previously printed in Macmillan's *52 (August 1885). Proof for* M *corrected by GM:* Yale.

Vermilion wings, by distance held
To pause aflight while fleeting swift:
And high aloft the pearl inshelled
Her lucid glow in glow will lift;

A little south of coloured sky;
Directing, gravely amorous,   30
The human of a tender eye
Through pure celestial on us:

Remote, not alien; still, not cold;
Unraying yet, more pearl than star;
She seems a while the vale to hold
In trance, and homelier makes the far.

Then Earth her sweet unscented breathes;
An orb of lustre quits the height;
And like broad iris-flags, in wreaths
The sky takes darkness, long ere quite.   40

His Island voice then shall you hear,
Nor ever after separate
From such a twilight of the year
Advancing to the vernal gate.

He sings me, out of Winter's throat,
The young time with the life ahead;
And my young time his leaping note
Recalls to spirit-mirth from dead.

Imbedded in a land of greed,
Of mammon-quakings dire as Earth's,   50
My care was but to soothe my need;
At peace among the littleworths.

39 broad] blue *1897*

To light and song my yearning aimed;
To that deep breast of song and light
Which men have barrenest proclaimed;
As 'tis to senses pricked with fright.

So mine are these new fruitings rich
The simple to the common brings;
I keep the youth of souls who pitch
Their joy in this old heart of things: 60

Who feel the Coming young as aye,
Thrice hopeful on the ground we plough;
Alive for life, awake to die;
One voice to cheer the seedling Now.

Full lasting is the song, though he,
The singer, passes: lasting too,
For souls not lent in usury,
The rapture of the forward view.

With that I bear my senses fraught
Till what I am fast shoreward drives.   70
They are the vessel of the Thought.
The vessel splits, the Thought survives.

Nought else are we when sailing brave,
Save husks to raise and bid it burn.
Glimpse of its livingness will wave
A light the senses can discern

Across the river of the death,
Their close. Meanwhile, O twilight bird
Of promise! bird of happy breath!
I hear, I would the City heard.   80

The City of the smoky fray;
A prodded ox, it drags and moans:
Its Morrow no man's child; its Day
A vulture's morsel beaked to bones.

It strives without a mark for strife;
It feasts beside a famished host:
The loose restraint of wanton life,
That threatened penance in the ghost!

Yet there our battle urges; there
Spring heroes many: issuing thence,   90
Names that should leave no vacant air
For fresh delight in confidence.

Life was to them the bag of grain,
And Death the weedy harrow's tooth.
Those warriors of the sighting brain
Give worn Humanity new youth.

Our song and star are they to lead
The tidal multitude and blind
From bestial to the higher breed
By fighting souls of love divined.   100

They scorned the ventral dream of peace,
Unknown in nature. This they knew:
That life begets with fair increase
Beyond the flesh, if life be true.

Just reason based on valiant blood,
The instinct bred afield would match
To pipe thereof a swelling flood,
Were men of Earth made wise in watch.

Though now the numbers count as drops
An urn might bear, they father Time. 110
She shapes anew her dusty crops;
Her quick in their own likeness climb.

Of their own force do they create;
They climb to light, in her their root.
Your brutish cry at muffled fate
She smites with pangs of worse than brute.

She, judge of shrinking nerves, appears
A Mother whom no cry can melt;
But read her past desires and fears,
The letters on her breast are spelt. 120

A slayer, yea, as when she pressed
Her savage to the slaughter-heaps,
To sacrifice she prompts her best:
She reaps them as the sower reaps.

But read her thought to speed the race,
And stars rush forth of blackest night:
You chill not at a cold embrace
To come, nor dread a dubious might.

Her double visage, double voice,
In oneness rise to quench the doubt. 130
This breath, her gift, has only choice
Of service, breathe we in or out.

Since Pain and Pleasure on each hand
Led our wild steps from slimy rock
To yonder sweeps of gardenland,
We breathe but to be sword or block.

109–24 *followed* 137–40 *in proof, order corr. GM for M*
115 Your] The *del.* That *corr. GM proof for M*
130 rise] hiss *del. GM proof for M*

The sighting brain her good decree
Accepts; obeys those guides, in faith,
By reason hourly fed, that she,
To some the clod, to some the wraith,   140

Is more, no mask; a flame, a stream.
Flame, stream, are we, in mid career
From torrent source, delirious dream,
To heaven-reflecting currents clear.

And why the sons of Strength have been
Her cherished offspring ever; how
The Spirit served by her is seen
Through Law; perusing love will show.

Love born of knowledge, love that gains
Vitality as Earth it mates,   150
The meaning of the Pleasures, Pains,
The Life, the Death, illuminates.

For love we Earth, then serve we all;
Her mystic secret then is ours:
We fall, or view our treasures fall,
Unclouded, as beholds her flowers

Earth, from a night of frosty wreck,
Enrobed in morning's mounted fire,
When lowly, with a broken neck,
The crocus lays her cheek to mire.   160

The Appeasement of Demeter

On October 27, 1886, GM wrote Mrs. Robert Louis Stevenson that he was "just finishing a poem 'The Appeasement of Demeter' that it is just possible Louis may like."

For GM's earlier treatment of the myth of Demeter, see page 222, *The Day of the Daughter of Hades*, part II.

I

Demeter devastated our good land,
In blackness for her daughter snatched below.
Smoke-pillar or loose hillock was the sand,
Where soil had been to clasp warm seed and throw
The wheat, vine, olive, ripe to Summer's ray.
Now whether night advancing, whether day,
              Scarce did the baldness show:
The hand of man was a defeated hand.

II

Necessity, the primal goad to growth,
Stood shrunken; Youth and Age appeared as one;
Like Winter Summer; good as labour sloth;
Nor was there answer wherefore beamed the sun,
Or why men drew the breath to carry pain.
High reared the ploughshare, broken lay the wain,
              Idly the flax-wheel spun
Unridered: starving lords were wasp and moth.

III

Lean grassblades losing green on their bent flags,
Sang chilly to themselves; lone honey-bees
Pursued the flowers that were not with dry bags;
Sole sound aloud the snap of sapless trees,

Previously printed in Macmillan's 56 *(September 1887). MS:* Yale, *fragment, stanza IX.*

More sharp than slingstones on hard breastplates hurled.
Back to first chaos tumbled the stopped world,
   Careless to lure or please.
A nature of gaunt ribs, an Earth of crags.

IV

No smile Demeter cast: the gloom she saw,
Well draped her direful musing; for in gloom,
In thicker gloom, deep down the cavern-maw,
Her sweet had vanished; liker unto whom,
And whose pale place of habitation mute,
She and all seemed where seasons, pledged for fruit
   Anciently, gaped for bloom:
Where hand of man was as a plucked fowl's claw.

V

The wrathful Queen descended on a vale,
That ere the ravished hour for richness heaved.
Iambe, maiden of the merry tale,
Beside her eyed the once red-cheeked, green-leaved.
It looked as if the Deluge had withdrawn.
Pity caught at her throat; her jests were gone.
   More than for her who grieved,
She could for this waste home have piped the wail.

VI

Iambe, her dear mountain-rivulet
To waken laughter from cold stones, beheld
A riven wheatfield cracking for the wet,
And seed like infant's teeth, that never swelled,
Apeep up flinty ridges, milkless round.
Teeth of the giants marked she where thin ground
   Rocky in spikes rebelled
Against the hand here slack as rotted net.

VII

The valley people up the ashen scoop
She beckoned, aiming hopelessly to win
Her Mistress in compassion of yon group
So pinched and wizened; with their aged grin,
For lack of warmth to smile on mouths of woe,
White as in chalk outlining little O
       Dumb, from a falling chin;
Young, old, alike half-bent to make the hoop.

VIII

Their tongues of birds they wagged, weak-voiced as when
Dark underwaters the recesses choke;
With cluck and upper quiver of a hen
In grasp, past pecking: cry before the croak.
Relentlessly their gold-haired Heaven, their fount
Bountiful of old days, heard them recount
       This and that cruel stroke:
Nor eye nor ear had she for piteous men.

IX

A figure of black rock by sunbeams crowned
Through stormclouds, where the volumed shades enfold
An earth in awe before the claps resound
And woods and dwellings are as billows rolled,
The barren Nourisher unmelted shed
Death from the looks that wandered with the dead
       Out of the realms of gold,
In famine for her lost, her lost unfound.

IX.2 the volumed] advancing *frag.*
IX.4 dwellings] dwelling *frag.*
IX.6 with] with *del.* for *frag.*
IX.7 Out of] Far from *del. frag.*
IX.8 *frag.*: And dry of tears, & thirsting, sought nor found.

X

Iambe from her Mistress tripped; she raised
The cattle-call above the moan of prayer;
And slowly out of fields their fancy grazed,
Among the droves, defiled a horse and mare:
The wrecks of horse and mare: such ribs as view
Seas that have struck brave ships ashore, while through
               Shoots the swift foamspit: bare
They nodded, and Demeter on them gazed.

XI

Howbeit the season of the dancing blood,
Forgot was horse of mare, yea, mare of horse:
Reversed, each head at either's flank, they stood.
Whereat the Goddess, in a dim remorse,
Laid hand on them, and smacked; and her touch pricked.
Neighing within, at either's flank they licked;
               Played on a moment's force
At courtship, withering to the crazy nod.

XII

The nod was that we gather for consent;
And mournfully amid the group a dame,
Interpreting the thing in nature meant,
Her hands held out like bearers of the flame,
And nodded for the negative sideways.
Keen at her Mistress glanced Iambe: rays
               From the Great Mother came:
Her lips were opened wide; the curse was rent.

XIII

She laughed: since our first harvesting heard none
Like thunder of the song of heart: her face,
The dreadful darkness, shook to mounted sun,
And peal on peal across the hills held chase.

She laughed herself to water; laughed to fire;
Laughed the torrential laugh of dam and sire
        Full of the marrowy race.
Her laughter, Gods! was flesh on skeleton.

XIV

The valley people huddled, broke, afraid,
Assured, and taking lightning in the veins,
They puffed, they leaped, linked hands, together swayed,
Unwitting happiness till golden rains
Of tears in laughter, laughter weeping, smote
Knowledge of milky mercy from that throat
        Pouring to heal their pains:
And one bold youth set mouth at a shy maid.

XV

Iambe clapped to see the kindly lusts
Inspire the valley people, still on seas,
Like poplar-tops relieved from stress of gusts,
With rapture in their wonderment; but these,
Low homage being rendered, ran to plough,
Fed by the laugh, as by the mother cow
        Calves at the teats they tease:
Soon drove they through the yielding furrow-crusts.

XVI

Uprose the blade in green, the leaf in red,
The tree of water and the tree of wood:
And soon among the branches overhead
Gave beauty juicy issue sweet for food.
O Laughter! beauty plumped and love had birth.
Laughter! O thou reviver of sick Earth!
        Good for the spirit, good
For body, thou! to both art wine and bread!

Earth and a Wedded Woman

I

The shepherd, with his eye on hazy South,
Has told of rain upon the fall of day.
But promise is there none for Susan's drouth,
That he will come, who keeps in dry delay.
The freshest of the village three years gone,
She hangs as the white field-rose hangs short-lived;
      And she and Earth are one
      In withering unrevived.
Rain! O the glad refresher of the grain!
And welcome waterspouts, had we sweet rain!   10

II

Ah, what is Marriage, says each pouting maid,
When she who wedded with the soldier hides
At home as good as widowed in the shade,
A lighthouse to the girls that would be brides:
Nor dares to give a lad an ogle, nor
To dream of dancing, but must hang and moan
      Her husband in the war,
      And she to lie alone.
Rain! O the glad refresher of the grain!
And welcome waterspouts, had we sweet rain!   10

III

They have not known; they are not in the stream;
Light as the flying seed-ball is their play,
The silly maids! and happy souls they seem;
Yet Grief would not change fates with such as they.

MS: Yale, *fair copy.*
I.1 hazy] the *del.* hazy *MS*
I.5 freshest] plumpest *MS*

They have not struck the roots which meet the fires
Beneath, and bind us fast with Earth, to know
  The strength of her desires,
  The sternness of her woe.
Rain! O the glad refresher of the grain!
And welcome waterspouts, had we sweet rain!   10

IV

Now, shepherd, see thy word, where without shower
A borderless low blotting Westward spreads.
The hall-clock holds the valley on the hour;
Across an inner chamber thunder treads;
The dead leaf trips, the tree-top swings, the floor
Of dust whirls, dropping lumped: near thunder speaks,
  And drives the dames to door,
  Their kerchiefs flapped at cheeks.
Rain! O the glad refresher of the grain!
And welcome waterspouts of blessed rain!   10

V

Through night, with bedroom window wide for air,
Lay Susan tranced to hear all heaven descend:
And gurgling voices came of Earth, and rare,
Past flowerful, breathings, deeper than life's end,
From her heaved breast of sacred common mould;
Whereby this lone-laid wife was moved to feel
  Unworded things and old
  To her pained heart appeal.
Rain! O the glad refresher of the grain!
And down in deluges of blessed rain!   10

VI

At morn she stood to live for ear and sight,
Love sky or cloud, or rose or grasses drenched.
A lureful devil, that in glow-worm light
Set languor writhing all its folds, she quenched.

But she would muse when neighbours praised her face,
Her services, and staunchness to her mate:
　　　Knowing by some dim trace,
　　　The change might bear a date.
Rain! O the glad refresher of the grain!
Thrice beauteous is our sunshine after rain!　　　　10

Mother to Babe

I

　　Fleck of sky you are,
　　Dropped through branches dark,
　　　　O my little one, mine!
　　Promise of the star,
　　Outpour of the lark;
　　　　Beam and song divine.

II

　　See this precious gift,
　　Steeping in new birth
　　　　All my being, for sign
　　Earth to heaven can lift,
　　Heaven descend on earth,
　　　　Both in one be mine!

III

　　Life in light you glass
　　When you peep and coo,
　　　　You, my little one, mine!
　　Brooklet chirps to grass,
　　Daisy looks in dew
　　　　Up to dear sunshine.

MOTHER TO BABE

Previously printed in the English Illustrated *37 (October 1886).*

Woodland Peace

Sweet as Eden is the air,
  And Eden-sweet the ray.
No Paradise is lost for them
Who foot by branching root and stem,
And lightly with the woodland share
  The change of night and day.

Here all say,
We serve her, even as I:
We brood, we strive to sky,
We gaze upon decay,   10
We wot of life through death,
How each feeds each we spy;
And is a tangle round,
Are patient; what is dumb,
We question not, nor ask
The silent to give sound,
The hidden to unmask,
The distant to draw near.

And this the woodland saith:
I know not hope or fear;   20
I take whate'er may come;
I raise my head to aspects fair,
From foul I turn away.

Sweet as Eden is the air,
  And Eden-sweet the ray.

Previously printed in the Fortnightly *14 (1 August 1870) as stanza vii of* In the Woods.
MS: Huntington HM6754, *fair copy.*

4 Who] That *F*; That *del.* Who *MS*
7 all] all things *F*
8 serve her] know not *F*
12–13 *not in F*
14 Are] We are *F*
16 *not in F*
20 or] nor *F*
22 aspects] all things *F*

The Question Whither

I

When we have thrown off this old suit,
    So much in need of mending,
To sink among the naked mute,
    Is that, think you, our ending?
We follow many, more we lead,
    And you who sadly turf us,
Believe not that all living seed
    Must flower above the surface.

II

Sensation is a gracious gift,
    But were it cramped to station,
The prayer to have it cast adrift,
    Would spout from all sensation.
Enough if we have winked to sun,
    Have sped the plough a season;
There is a soul for labour done,
    Endureth fixed as reason.

III

Then let our trust be firm in Good,
    Though we be of the fasting;
Our questions are a mortal brood,
    Our work is everlasting.
We children of Beneficence
    Are in its being sharers;
And Whither vainer sounds than Whence,
    For word with such wayfarers.

MS: Texas, *fair copy corrected. Variants are from this MS.*

II.8 Endureth] Endures as *del.*
III.3 Our] The *del.*
III.4 Our] The *del.*
III.5 We] The *del.*

Outer and Inner

I

From twig to twig the spider weaves
    At noon his webbing fine.
So near to mute the zephyrs flute
    That only leaflets dance.
The sun draws out of hazel leaves
    A smell of woodland wine.
I wake a swarm to sudden storm
    At any step's advance.

II

Along my path is bugloss blue,
    The star with fruit in moss;
The foxgloves drop from throat to top
    A daily lesser bell.
The blackest shadow, nurse of dew,
    Has orange skeins across;
And keenly red is one thin thread
    That flashing seems to swell.

III

My world I note ere fancy comes,
    Minutest hushed observe:
What busy bits of motioned wits
    Through antlered mosswork strive.
But now so low the stillness hums,
    My springs of seeing swerve,
For half a wink to thrill and think
    The woods with nymphs alive.

MS: Yale, *fair copy. Variants are from this MS.*

IV

I neighbour the invisible
So close that my consent
Is only asked for spirits masked
To leap from trees and flowers.
And this because with them I dwell
In thought, while calmly bent
To read the lines dear Earth designs
Shall speak her life on ours.

V

Accept, she says; it is not hard
In woods; but she in towns
Repeats, accept; and have we wept,
And have we quailed with fears,
Or shrunk with horrors, sure reward
We have whom knowledge crowns;
Who see in mould the rose unfold,
The soul through blood and tears.

Nature and Life

I

Leave the uproar: at a leap
Thou shalt strike a woodland path,
Enter silence, not of sleep,
Under shadows, not of wrath;
Breath which is the spirit's bath,

OUTER AND INNER

IV.8 & del.
V.2 in] of del.
V.3 have we] who has del.
V.4 have we] who has del.
V.5 sure] has del.

NATURE AND LIFE

MS: Huntington HM6755, *fair copy*.

In the old Beginnings find,
And endow them with a mind,
Seed for seedling, swathe for swathe.
That gives Nature to us, this
Give we her, and so we kiss.

II

Fruitful is it so: but hear
How within the shell thou art,
Music sounds; nor other near
Can to such a tremor start.
Of the waves our life is part;
They our running harvests bear:
Back to them for manful air,
Laden with the woodland's heart!
That gives Battle to us, this
Give we it, and good the kiss.   10

Dirge in Woods

GM wrote this poem when Justin Theodore Vulliamy, his father-in-law, died in 1870, and he would often quote it as one of his favorites (Sencourt, pp. 174–75).

The lyric bears a striking resemblance to Goethe's famous "*Über allen Gipfeln*" (John Bailey, "The Poetry of George Meredith," *Fortnightly*, n.s. 86 [July 1909]: 42).

A wind sways the pines,
      And below
Not a breath of wild air;
Still as the mosses that glow
On the flooring and over the lines
Of the roots here and there.

DIRGE IN WOODS
Previously printed in the Fortnightly *14 (1 August 1870) as stanza ix of* In the Woods.
4 Still] All still *F*

The pine-tree drops its dead;
They are quiet, as under the sea.
Overhead, overhead
Rushes life in a race,   10
As the clouds the clouds chase;
    And we go,
And we drop like the fruits of the tree,
      Even we,
      Even so.

A Faith on Trial

The experience commemorated in this poem took place on May 1, 1885.
Since mid-winter Marie Vulliamy Meredith had been dying of cancer of
the throat. On this May Day she was at Eastbourne, Sussex, while GM
was at their home, Flint Cottage, Box Hill, near Dorking, Surrey; "our
hill," (line 5) was Box Hill. Marie lived until September 17 (see "M.M.,"
p. 460).
    On 8 or 9 April 1899, GM told Edward Clodd that this poem was
"designed to depict the trend of modern thought" (*TLS-II*).

On the morning of May,
Ere the children had entered my gate
With their wreaths and mechanical lay,
A metal ding-dong of the date!
I mounted our hill, bearing heart
That had little of life save its weight:
The crowned Shadow poising dart
Hung over her: she, my own,
My good companion, mate,
Pulse of me: she who had shown   10
Fortitude quiet as Earth's
At the shedding of leaves. And around
The sky was in garlands of cloud,
Winning scents from unnumbered new births,
Pointed buds, where the woods were browned
By a mouldered beechen shroud;

A FAITH ON TRIAL
MS: Yale, *fair copy corrected. Proof*: Yale, *corrected by GM for the Edition de Luxe.*

Or over our meads of the vale,
Such an answer to sun as he,
Brave in his gold; to a sound,
None sweeter, of woods flapping sail,   20
With the first full flood of our year,
For their voyage on lustreful sea:
Unto what curtained haven in chief,
Will be writ in the book of the sere.
But surely the crew are we,
Eager or stamped or bowed;
Counted thinner at fall of the leaf.
Grief heard them, and passed like a bier.
Due Summerward, lo, they were set,
In volumes of foliage proud,   30
On the heave of their favouring tides,
And their song broadened out to the cheer
When a neck of the ramping surf
Rattles thunder a boat overrides.
All smiles ran the highways wet;
The worm drew its links from the turf;
The bird of felicity loud,
Spun high, and a South wind blew.
Weak out of sheath downy leaves
Of the beech quivered lucid as dew,   40
Their radiance asking, who grieves;
For nought of a sorrow they knew:
No space to the dread wrestle vowed,
No chamber in shadow of night.
At times as the steadier breeze
Flutter-huddled their twigs to a crowd,
The beam of them wafted my sight
To league-long sun upon seas:

21 With] O'er *del. MS*
22 lustreful] luminous *del. MS*
33 ramping] breaking *del. MS*
34 Rattles] Rolls *del. MS*
44 in shadow of] perpetual *del. MS*
45 as] to *del. MS*
47 beam] flash *del. MS*

The golden path we had crossed
Many years, till her birthland swung   50
Recovered to vision from lost,
A light in her filial glance.
And sweet was her voice with the tongue,
The speechful tongue of her France,
Soon at ripple about us, like rills
Ever busy with little: away
Through her Normandy, down where the mills
Dot at lengths a rivercourse, grey
As its bordering poplars bent
To gusts off the plains above.   60
Old stone château and farms,
Home of her birth and her love!
On the thread of the pasture you trace,
By the river, their milk, for miles,
Spotted once with the English tent,
In days of the tocsin's alarms,
To tower of the tallest of piles,
The country's surveyor breast-high.
Home of her birth and her love!
Home of a diligent race;   70
Thrifty, deft-handed to ply
Shuttle or needle, and woo
Sun to the roots of the pear
Frogging each mud-walled cot.
The elders had known her in arms.
There plucked we the bluet, her hue
Of the deeper forget-me-not;
Well wedding her ripe-wheat hair.

I saw, unsighting: her heart
I saw, and the home of her love   80
There printed, mournfully rent:
Her ebbing adieu, her adieu,

74 Frogging] Branched *del.* frogging *MS*
79 unsighting] unseeing *del. MS*

And the stride of the Shadow athwart.
For one of our Autumns there! ...
Straight as the flight of a dove
We went, swift winging we went.
We trod solid ground, we breathed air,
The heavens were unbroken. Break they,
The word of the world is adieu:
Her word: and the torrents are round, 90
The jawed wolf-waters of prey.
We stand upon isles, who stand:
A Shadow before us, and back,
A phantom the habited land.
We may cry to the Sunderer, spare
That dearest! he loosens his pack.
Arrows we breathe, not air.
The memories tenderly bound
To us are a drifting crew,
Amid grey-gapped waters for ground. 100
Alone do we stand, each one,
Till rootless as they we strew
Those deeps of the corse-like stare
At a foreign and stony sun.

Eyes had I but for the scene
Of my circle, what neighbourly grew.
If haply no finger lay out
To the figures of days that had been,
I gathered my herb, and endured;
My old cloak wrapped me about. 110
Unfooted was ground-ivy blue,
Whose rustic shrewd odour allured
In Spring's fresh of morning: unseen
Her favourite wood-sorrel bell
As yet, though the leaves' green floor
Awaited their flower, that would tell

Of a red-veined moist yestreen,
With its droop and the hues it wore,
When we two stood overnight
One, in the dark van-glow   120
On our hill-top, seeing beneath,
Our household's twinkle of light
Through spruce-boughs, gem of a wreath.

Budding, the service-tree, white
Almost as whitebeam, threw,
From the under of leaf upright,
Flecks like a showering snow
On the flame-shaped junipers green,
On the sombre mounds of the yew.
Like silvery tapers bright   130
By a solemn cathedral screen,
They glistened to closer view.
Turf for a rooks' revel striped,
Pleased those devourers astute.
Chorister blackbird and thrush
Together or alternate piped;
A free-hearted harmony large,
With meaning for man, for brute,
When the primitive forces are brimmed.
Like featherings hither and yon   140
Of aëry tree-twigs over marge,
To the comb of the winds, untrimmed,
Their measure is found in the vast.
Grief heard them, and stepped her way on.
She has but a narrow embrace.
Distrustful of hearing she passed.
They piped her young Earth's Bacchic rout;
The race, and the prize of the race;
Earth's lustihead pressing to sprout.

120 dark] dark's *1888*
124 Budding, the] Buds of the *del. MS*
133 rooks'] rook's *1888, corr. GM proof for de L*
139 the] his *del. MS*
140 featherings] the *del.* feathering *MS*
142 To the comb of the winds,] Discord only careless *del. MS*

But sight holds a soberer space.   150
Colourless dogwood low,
Curled up a twisted root,
Nigh yellow-green mosses, to flush
Redder than sun upon rocks,
When the creeper clematis-shoot
Shall climb, cap his branches, and show,
Beside veteran green of the box,
At close of the year's maple blush,
A bleeding greybeard is he,
Now hale in the leafage lush.   160
Our parasites paint us. Hard by,
A wet yew-trunk flashed the peel
Of our naked forefathers in fight;
With stains of the fray sweating free;
And him came no parasite nigh:
Firm on the hard knotted knee,
He stood in the crown of his dun;
Earth's toughest to stay her wheel:
Under whom the full day is night;
Whom the century-tempests call son,   170
Having striven to rend him in vain.

I walked to observe, not to feel,
Not to fancy, if simple of eye
One may be among images reaped
For a shift of the glance, as grain:
Profitless froth you espy
Ashore after billows have leaped.
I fled nothing, nothing pursued:
The changeful visible face
Of our Mother I sought for my food;   180
Crumbs by the way to sustain.
Her sentence I knew past grace.
Myself I had lost of us twain,
Once bound in mirroring thought.

160 hale] brave *del. MS*

She had flung me to dust in her wake;
And I, as your convict drags
His chain, by the scourge untaught,
Bore life for a goad, without aim.
I champed the sensations that make
Of a ruffled philosophy rags.   190
For them was no meaning too blunt,
Nor aspect too cutting of steel.
This Earth of the beautiful breasts,
Shining up in all colours aflame,
To them had visage of hags:
A Mother of aches and jests:
Soulless, heading a hunt
Aimless except for the meal.
Hope, with the star on her front;
Fear, with an eye in the heel;   200
Our links to a Mother of grace;
They were dead on the nerve, and dead
For the nature divided in three;
Gone out of heart, out of brain,
Out of soul: I had in their place
The calm of an empty room.
We were joined but by that thin thread,
My disciplined habit to see.
And those conjure images, those,
The puppets of loss or gain;   210
Not he who is bare to his doom;
For whom never semblance plays
To bewitch, overcloud, illume.
The dusty mote-images rose;
Sheer film of the surface awag:
They sank as they rose; their pain
Declaring them mine of old days.

187–88 *MS del.:* His chain, bore the burden & rough
190 ruffled] shaken *del. MS*
199 the] her *del. MS*   her] the *del. MS*
216 rose] sprang *del. MS*
217 Declaring] Confessed *del. MS*

Now gazed I where, sole upon gloom,
As flower-bush in sun-specked crag,
Up the spine of the double combe   220
With yew-boughs heavily cloaked,
A young apparition shone:
Known, yet wonderful, white
Surpassingly; doubtfully known,
For it struck as the birth of Light:
Even Day from the dark unyoked.
It waved like a pilgrim flag
O'er processional penitents flown
When of old they broke rounding yon spine:
O the pure wild-cherry in bloom!   230

For their Eastward march to the shrine
Of the footsore far-eyed Faith,
Was banner so brave, so fair,
So quick with celestial sign
Of victorious rays over death?
For a conquest of coward despair;—
Division of soul from wits,
And these made rulers;—full sure,
More starlike never did shine
To illumine the sinister field   240
Where our life's old night-bird flits.
I knew it: with her, my own,
Had hailed it pure of the pure;
Our beacon yearly: but strange
When it strikes to within is the known;
Richer than newness revealed.
There was needed darkness like mine.
Its beauty to vividness blown,
Drew the life in me forward, chased,
From aloft on a pinnacle's range,   250

218 gazed I] gazing del. MS
230 O the pure] The white del. MS
233 brave] pure del. MS

That hindward spidery line,
The length of the ways I had paced,
A footfarer out of the dawn,
To Youth's wild forest, where sprang,
For the morning of May long gone,
The forest's white virgin; she
Seen yonder; and sheltered me, sang;
She in me, I in her; what songs
The fawn-eared wood-hollows revive
To pour forth their tune-footed throngs;   260
Inspire to the dreaming of good
Illimitable to come:
She, the white wild cherry, a tree,
Earth-rooted, tangibly wood,
Yet a presence throbbing alive;
Nor she in our language dumb:
A spirit born of a tree;
Because earth-rooted alive:
Huntress of things worth pursuit
Of souls; in our naming, dreams.   270
And each unto other was lute,
By fits quick as breezy gleams.
My quiver of aims and desires
Had colour that she would have owned;
And if by humaner fires
Hued later, these held her enthroned:
My crescent of Earth; my blood
At the silvery early stir;
Hour of the thrill of the bud
About to burst, and by her   280
Directed, attuned, englobed:
My Goddess, the chaste, not chill;

259 fawn] cock *del. MS*
260 their] *added MS*
262 *added MS*
266 *added MS*
272 fits] turns *del. MS*
275 humaner] our humaner *MS, 1888, corr. GM proof for de L*

Choir over choir white-robed;
White-bosomed fold within fold:
For so could I dream, breast-bare,
In my time of blooming; dream still
Through the maze, the mesh, and the wreck,
Despite, since manhood was bold,
The yoke of the flesh on my neck.
She beckoned, I gazed, unaware   290
How a shaft of the blossoming tree
Was shot from the yew-wood's core.
I stood to the touch of a key
Turned in a fast-shut door.

They rounded my garden, content,
The small fry, clutching their fee,
Their fruit of the wreath and the pole;
And, chatter, hop, skip, they were sent,
In a buzz of young company glee,
Their natural music, swift shoal   300
To the next easy shedders of pence.
Why not? for they had me in tune
With the hungers of my kind.

Do readings of earth draw thence,
Then a concord deeper than cries
Of the Whither whose echo is Whence,
To jar unanswered, shall rise
As a fountain-jet in the mind
Bowed dark o'er the falling and strewn.

———————

291 a] the *del. MS*   the blossoming tree] a message for me *del. MS*
305 Then a] A *del. MS*
308 in] to *del. MS*

Unwitting where it might lead,   310
How it came, for the anguish to cease,
And the Questions that sow not nor spin,
This wisdom, rough-written, and black,
As of veins that from venom bleed,
I had with the peace within;
Or patience, mortal of peace,
Compressing the surgent strife
In a heart laid open, not mailed,
To the last blank hour of the rack,
When struck the dividing knife: 320
When the hand that never had failed
In its pressure to mine hung slack.

But this in myself did I know,
Not needing a studious brow,
Or trust in a governing star,
While my ears held the jangled shout
The children were lifting afar:
That natures at interflow
With all of their past and the now,
Are chords to the Nature without,   330
Orbs to the greater whole:
First then, not utterly then
Till our lord of sensations at war,
The rebel, the heart, yields place
To brain, each prompting the soul.
Thus our dear Earth we embrace
For the milk, her strength to men.

And crave we her medical herb,
We have but to see and hear,
Though pierced by the cruel acerb,   340
The troops of the memories armed

317 *added MS*
320 *added MS*
323 did I know] I had known *del. MS*
336 Thus our] Only thus *del. MS*

Hostile to strike at the nest
That nourished and flew them warmed.
Not she gives the tear for the tear.
Weep, bleed, rave, writhe, be distraught,
She is moveless. Not of her breast
Are the symbols we conjure when Fear
Takes leaven of Hope. I caught,
With Death in me shrinking from Death,
As cold from cold, for a sign   350
Of the life beyond ashes: I cast,
Believing the vision divine,
Wings of that dream of my Youth
To the spirit beloved: 'twas unglassed
On her breast, in her depths austere:
A flash through the mist, mere breath,
Breath on a buckler of steel.
For the flesh in revolt at her laws,
Neither song nor smile in ruth,
Nor promise of things to reveal,   360
Has she, nor a word she saith:
We are asking her wheels to pause.
Well knows she the cry of unfaith.
If we strain to the farther shore,
We are catching at comfort near.
Assurances, symbols, saws,
Revelations in Legends, light
To eyes rolling darkness, these
Desired of the flesh in affright,
For the which it will swear to adore,   370
She yields not for prayers at her knees;
The woolly beast bleating will shear.

343 warmed] & *del.* warmed *MS*
353 Wings] A wing *del. MS*
360 *added MS*
365 We are] As in *del. MS*
368 To] For *del. MS*
370 it will] they have *del. MS*
371 yields] deals *del. MS*

These are our sensual dreams;
Of the yearning to touch, to feel
The dark Impalpable sure,
And have the Unveiled appear;
Whereon ever black she beams,
Doth of her terrible deal,
She who dotes over ripeness at play,
Rosiness fondles and feeds,   380
Guides it with shepherding crook,
To her sports and her pastures alway.
Not she gives the tear for the tear:
Harsh wisdom gives Earth, no more;
In one the spur and the curb:
An answer to thoughts or deeds;
To the Legends an alien look;
To the Questions a figure of clay.
Yet we have but to see and hear,
Crave we her medical herb.   390

For the road to her soul is the Real:
The root of the growth of man:
And the senses must traverse it fresh
With a love that no scourge shall abate,
To reach the lone heights where we scan
In the mind's rarer vision this flesh;
In the charge of the Mother our fate;
Her law as the one common weal.

We, whom the view benumbs,
We, quivering upward, each hour   400
Know battle in air and in ground
For the breath that goes as it comes,

374 yearning] something *del. MS*
376 *added MS*
378 *added MS*   of her terrible] her most *del.* terrible *MS*
381–83 *added MS*
384 Harsh] Black *del. MS*
394 shall] can *del. MS*
401 Know] Do *del. MS*

For the choice between sweet and sour,
For the smallest grain of our worth:
And he who the reckoning sums,
Finds nought in his hand save Earth.
Of Earth are we stripped or crowned.
The fleeting Present we crave,
Barter our best to wed,
In hope of a cushioned bower,   410
What is it but Future and Past
Like wind and tide at a wave!
Idea of the senses, bred
For the senses to snap and devour:
Thin as the shell of a sound
In delivery, withered in light.
Cry we for permanence fast,
Permanence hangs by the grave;
Sits on the grave green-grassed,
On the roll of the heaved grave-mound.   420
By Death, as by Life, are we fed:
The two are one spring; our bond
With the numbers; with whom to unite
Here feathers wings for beyond:
Only they can waft us in flight.
For they are Reality's flower.
Of them, and the contact with them,
Issues Earth's dearest daughter, the firm
In footing, the stately of stem;
Unshaken though elements lour;   430
A warrior heart unquelled;
Mirror of Earth, and guide
To the Holies from sense withheld:
Reason, man's germinant fruit.
She wrestles with our old worm
Self in the narrow and wide:

403 *added MS*
425 *added MS*
434 *added MS*

Relentless quencher of lies,
With laughter she pierces the brute;
And hear we her laughter peal,
'Tis Light in us dancing to scour   440
The loathed recess of his dens;
Scatter his monstrous bed,
And hound him to harrow and plough.
She is the world's one prize;
Our champion, rightfully head;
The vessel whose piloted prow,
Though Folly froth round, hiss and hoot,
Leaves legible print at the keel.
Nor least is the service she does,
That service to her may cleanse   450
The well of the Sorrows in us;
For a common delight will drain
The rank individual fens
Of a wound refusing to heal
While the old worm slavers its root.

I bowed as a leaf in rain;
As a tree when the leaf is shed
To winds in the season at wane:
And when from my soul I said,
May the worm be trampled: smite,   460
Sacred Reality! power
Filled me to front it aright.
I had come of my faith's ordeal.

It is not to stand on a tower
And see the flat universe reel;
Our mortal sublimities drop
Like raiment by glisterlings worn,

437 *added MS*
443–48 *added MS*
446 piloted] pilotted *MS*
457–58 *added MS*
465 flat] wide *del. MS*

At a sweep of the scythe for the crop.
Wisdom is won of its fight,
The combat incessant; and dries   470
To mummywrap perching a height.
It chews the contemplative cud
In peril of isolate scorn,
Unfed of the onward flood.
Nor view we a different morn
If we gaze with the deeper sight,
With the deeper thought forewise:
The world is the same, seen through;
The features of men are the same.
But let their historian new,   480
In the language of nakedness write,
Rejoice we to know not shame,
Not a dread, not a doubt: to have done
With the tortures of thought in the throes,
Our animal tangle, and grasp
Very sap of the vital in this:
That from flesh unto spirit man grows
Even here on the sod under sun:
That she of the wanton's kiss
Broken through with the bite of an asp,   490
Is Mother of simple truth,
Relentless quencher of lies;
Eternal in thought; discerned
In thought mid-ferry between
The Life and the Death, which are one,
As our breath in and out, joy or teen.
She gives the rich vision to youth,
If we will, of her prompting wise;
Or men by the lash made lean,
Who in harness the mind subserve,   500

469–74 *added MS*
477 *added MS*
482 Rejoice we] ̓Our gain is *del. MS*
497 the] a *del. MS*
500 *added MS*

Their title to read her have earned;
Having mastered sensation—insane
At a stroke of the terrified nerve;
And out of the sensual hive,
Grown to the flower of brain;
To know her a thing alive,
Whose aspects mutably swerve,
Whose laws immutably reign.
Our sentencer, clother in mist,
Her morn bends breast to her noon,   510
Noon to the hour dark-dyed,
If we will, of her promptings wise:
Her light is our own if we list.
The Legends that sweep her aside,
Crying loud for an opiate boon,
To comfort the human want,
From the bosom of magical skies,
She smiles on, marking their source:
They read her with infant eyes.
Good ships of morality they,   520
For our crude developing force;
Granite the thought to stay,
That she is a thing alive
To the living, the falling and strewn.
But the Questions, the broods that haunt
Sensation insurgent, may drive,
The way of the channelling mole,
Head in a ground-vault gaunt

503 of] *MS*; on *1888*
504 *added MS*
505 Grown] And *del.* grown *MS*
509 *added MS*
510 bends] will *del.* bend *MS·*
513 *added MS*
518 marking] eyeing *del. MS*
521 *added MS*   our] the *del. MS*
522 Granite] Through *del.* Yet *del.* granite *MS*

As your telescope's skeleton moon.
Barren comfort to these will she dole;   530
Dead is her face to their cries.
Intelligence pushing to taste,
A lesson from beasts might heed.
They scatter a voice in the waste,
Where any dry swish of a reed
By grey-glassy water replies.

'They see not above or below;
'Farthest are they from my soul,'
Earth whispers: 'they scarce have the thirst,
'Except to unriddle a rune;   540
'And I spin none; only show,
'Would humanity soar from its worst,
'Winged above darkness and dole,
'How fresh unto spirit must grow.
'Spirit raves not for a goal.
'Shapes in man's likeness hewn,
'Desires not; neither desires
'The Sleep or the Glory: it trusts;
'Uses my gifts, yet aspires;
'Dreams of a higher than it.   550
'The dream is an atmosphere;
'A scale still ascending to knit
'The clear to the loftier Clear.
''Tis Reason herself, tiptoe
'At the ultimate bound of her wit,
'On the verges of Night and Day.
'But is it a dream of the lusts,
'To my dustiest 'tis decreed;

530–36 *added MS*
532 pushing] striving *del. MS*
533 A lesson from beasts] Instinct of babes *MS*
543 *added MS*
552 still ascending] ever mounting *del. MS*
553 to] with *del. MS*
557–59 *added MS*

'And them that so shuffle astray,
'I touch with no key of gold   560
'For the wealth of the secret nook;
'Though I dote over ripeness at play,
'Rosiness fondle and feed,
'Guide it with shepherding crook
'To my sports and my pastures alway.
'The key will shriek in the lock,
'The door will rustily hinge,
'Will open on features of mould,
'To vanish corrupt at a glimpse,
'And mock as the wild echoes mock,   570
'Soulless in mimic, doth Greed
'Or the passion for fruitage tinge
'That dream, for your parricide imps
'To wing through the body of Time,
'Yourselves in slaying him slay.
'Much are you shots of your prime,
'You men of the act and the dream:
'And please you to fatten a weed
'That perishes, pledged to decay,
''Tis dearth in your season of need,   580
'Down the slopes of the shoreward way;—
'Nigh on the misty stream,
'Where Ferryman under his hood,
'With a call to be ready to pay
'The small coin, whitens red blood.
'But the young ethereal seed
'Shall bring you the bread no buyer
'Can have for his craving supreme;
'To my quenchless quick shall speed
'The soul at her wrestle rude   590

564–65 *added MS*
565 my] the *del. MS*   my] the *del. MS*
567 rustily] rutedly *MS*
571 doth] did *MS*
582 *added MS*
589 *added MS*
590 The] When *del.* the *MS*   her *added MS*

'With devil, with angel more dire;
'With the flesh, with the Fates, enringed.
'The dream of the blossom of Good,
'Is your banner of battle unrolled
'In its waver and current and curve
'(Choir over choir white-winged,
'White-bosomed fold within fold):
'Hopeful of victory most
'When hard is the task to sustain
'Assaults of the fearful sense   600
'At a mind in desolate mood
'With the Whither, whose echo is Whence;
'And humanity's clamour, lost, lost;
'And its clasp of the staves that snap;
'And evil abroad, as a main
'Uproarious, bursting its dyke.
'For back do you look, and lo,
'Forward the harvest of grain!—
'Numbers in council, awake
'To love more than things of my lap,   610
'Love me; and to let the types break,
'Men be grass, rocks rivers, all flow;
'All save the dream sink alike
'To the source of my vital in sap:
'Their battle, their loss, their ache,
'For my pledge of vitality know.
'The dream is the thought in the ghost;
'The thought sent flying for food;
'Eyeless, but sprung of an aim
'Supernal of Reason, to find   620
'The great Over-Reason we name
'Beneficence: mind seeking Mind.
'Dream of the blossom of Good,
'In its waver and current and curve,

594 banner of battle] battle a flag del. MS
595 added MS
598 Hopeful] Conscious del. MS

'With the hopes of my offspring enscrolled!
'Soon to be seen of a host
'The flag of the Master I serve!
'And life in them doubled on Life,
'As flame upon flame, to behold,
'High over Time-tumbled sea,   630
'The bliss of his headship of strife,
'Him through handmaiden me.'

Change in Recurrence

I

I stood at the gate of the cot
Where my darling, with side-glance demure,
Would spy, on her trim garden-plot,
The busy wild things chase and lure.
For these with their ways were her feast
They had surety no enemy lurked.
Their deftest of tricks to their least,
She gathered in watch as she worked.

II

When berries were red on her ash,
The blackbird would rifle them rough,
Till the ground underneath looked a gash,
And her rogue grew the round of a chough.
The squirrel cocked ear o'er his hoop,
Up the spruce, quick as eye, trailing brush.
She knew any tit of the troop
All as well as the snail-tapping thrush.

CHANGE IN RECURRENCE

MS: Yale, *fair copy*.

III

I gazed: 'twas the scene of the frame,
With the face, the dear life for me, fled.
No window a lute to my name,
No watcher there plying the thread.
But the blackbird hung pecking at will;
The squirrel from cone hopped to cone;
The thrush had a snail in his bill,
And tap-tapped the shell hard on a stone.

Hymn to Colour

I

With Life and Death I walked when Love appeared,
And made them on each side a shadow seem.
Through wooded vales the land of dawn we neared,
Where down smooth rapids whirls the helmless dream
To fall on daylight; and night puts away
      Her darker veil for grey.

II

In that grey veil green grassblades brushed we by;
We came where woods breathed sharp, and overhead
Rocks raised clear horns on a transforming sky:
Around, save for those shapes, with him who led
And linked them, desert varied by no sign
      Of other life than mine.

III

By this the dark-winged planet, raying wide,
From the mild pearl-glow to the rose upborne,
Drew in his fires, less faint than far descried,
Pure-fronted on a stronger wave of morn:
And those two shapes the splendour interweaved,
      Hung web-like, sank and heaved.

IV

Love took my hand when hidden stood the sun
To fling his robe on shoulder-heights of snow.
Then said: There lie they, Life and Death in one.
Whichever is, the other is: but know,
It is thy craving self that thou dost see,
          Not in them seeing me.

V

Shall man into the mystery of breath,
From his quick beating pulse a pathway spy?
Or learn the secret of the shrouded death,
By lifting up the lid of a white eye?
Cleave thou thy way with fathering desire
          Of fire to reach to fire.

VI

Look now where Colour, the soul's bridegroom, makes
The house of heaven splendid for the bride.
To him as leaps a fountain she awakes,
In knotting arms, yet boundless: him beside,
She holds the flower to heaven, and by his power
          Brings heaven to the flower.

VII

He gives her homeliness in desert air,
And sovereignty in spaciousness; he leads
Through widening chambers of surprise to where
Throbs rapture near an end that aye recedes,
Because his touch is infinite and lends
          A yonder to all ends.

VIII

Death begs of Life his blush; Life Death persuades
To keep long day with his caresses graced.
He is the heart of light, the wing of shades,

The crown of beauty: never soul embraced
Of him can harbour unfaith; soul of him
    Possessed walks never dim.

IX

Love eyed his rosy memories: he sang:
O bloom of dawn, breathed up from the gold sheaf
Held springing beneath Orient! that dost hang
The space of dewdrops running over leaf;
Thy fleetingness is bigger in the ghost
    Than Time with all his host!

X

Of thee to say behold, has said adieu:
But love remembers how the sky was green,
And how the grasses glimmered lightest blue;
How saint-like grey took fervour: how the screen
Of cloud grew violet; how thy moment came
    Between a blush and flame.

XI

Love saw the emissary eglantine
Break wave round thy white feet above the gloom;
Lay finger on thy star; thy raiment line
With cherub wing and limb; wed thy soft bloom,
Gold-quivering like sunrays in thistle-down,
    Earth under rolling brown.

XII

They do not look through love to look on thee,
Grave heavenliness! nor know they joy of sight,
Who deem the wave of rapt desire must be
Its wrecking and last issue of delight.
Dead seasons quicken in one petal-spot
    Of colour unforgot.

XIII

This way have men come out of brutishness
To spell the letters of the sky and read
A reflex upon earth else meaningless.
With thee, O fount of the Untimed! to lead;
Drink they of thee, thee eyeing, they unaged
        Shall on through brave wars waged.

XIV

More gardens will they win than any lost;
The vile plucked out of them, the unlovely slain.
Not forfeiting the beast with which they are crossed,
To stature of the Gods will they attain.
They shall uplift their Earth to meet her Lord,
        Themselves the attuning chord!

XV

The song had ceased; my vision with the song.
Then of those Shadows, which one made descent
Beside me I knew not: but Life ere long
Came on me in the public ways and bent
Eyes deeper than of old: Death met I too,
        And saw the dawn glow through.

Meditation under Stars

What links are ours with orbs that are
        So resolutely far:
The solitary asks, and they
Give radiance as from a shield:

MEDITATION UNDER STARS

MSS: Yale. *MS 1, fair copy corrected; MS 2, fair copy, lines 1–56.*
2 far:] far? *MS 1*
3–6 *not in MS 1, instead:*
                Defended by their radiance they
                Shut out all eyes alway;

Still at the death of day,
The seen, the unrevealed.
Implacable they shine
To us who would of Life obtain
An answer for the life we strain,
To nourish with one sign.   10
Nor can imagination throw
The penetrative shaft: we pass
The breath of thought, who would divine
If haply they may grow
As Earth; have our desire to know;
If life comes there to grain from grass,
And flowers like ours of toil and pain;
Has passion to beat bar,
Win space from cleaving brain;
The mystic link attain,   20
Whereby star holds on star.

Those visible immortals beam
Allurement to the dream:
Ireful at human húngers brook
No question in the look.
For ever virgin to our sense,
Remote they wane to gaze intense:
Prolong it, and in ruthlessness they smite
The beating heart behind the ball of sight:

8–10 *not in MS 1*
8 who] that *del. MS 2*
12 The] One *MS 1*
14 *MS 1:* With out endowments if they grow
15 Earth] we *MS 1*
19 from] for *MS 1*
21 holds on] touches *or* holds on *MS 1*
24 Ireful] In ire *del. MS 1*
27 Remote] Dimmer *del. MS 1*
28 in ruthlessness] remorselessly *MS 1*

Till we conceive their heavens hoar,   30
Those lights they raise but sparkles frore,
And Earth, our blood-warm Earth, a shuddering prey
To that frigidity of brainless ray.

Yet space is given for breath of thought
Beyond our bounds when musing: more
When to that musing love is brought,
And love is asked of love's wherefore.
'Tis Earth's, her gift; else have we nought:
Her gift, her secret, here our tie.
And not with her and yonder sky?   40
Bethink you: were it Earth alone
Breeds love, would not her region be
        The sole delight and throne
        Of generous Deity?

To deeper than this ball of sight
Appeal the lustrous people of the night.
Fronting yon shoreless, sown with fiery sails,
        It is our ravenous that quails,
Flesh by its craven thirsts and fears distraught.
        The spirit leaps alight,   50
        Doubts not in them is he,
The binder of his sheaves, the sane, the right:
Of magnitude to magnitude is wrought,
To feel it large of the great life they hold:
In them to come, or vaster intervolved,
The issues known in us, our unsolved solved:

31 Those] The *MS 1*
36 that] such *MS 1*
40 and] to *MS 1*
45 this] our *MS 1*
52 *not in MS 1*
54 To feel it large of the great] To read & feel one with the *MS 1*; To read & feel it of
the *del. MS 2*

That there with toil Life climbs the self-same Tree,
Whose roots enrichment have from ripeness dropped.
So may we read and little find them cold:
Let it but be the lord of Mind to guide   60
Our eyes; no branch of Reason's growing lopped;
Nor dreaming on a dream; but fortified
By day to penetrate black midnight; see,
Hear, feel, outside the senses; even that we,
The specks of dust upon a mound of mould,
We who reflect those rays, though low our place,
　　　To them are lastingly allied.
So may we read, and little find them cold:
Not frosty lamps illumining dead space,
Not distant aliens, not senseless Powers.   70
The fire is in them whereof we are born;
The music of their motion may be ours.
Spirit shall deem them beckoning Earth and voiced
Sisterly to her, in her beams rejoiced.
Of love, the grand impulsion, we behold
　　　The love that lends her grace
　　　Among the starry fold.
Then at new flood of customary morn,
　　　Look at her through her showers,
　　　Her mists, her streaming gold,   80
A wonder edges the familiar face:
She wears no more that robe of printed hours;
Half strange seems Earth, and sweeter than her flowers.

58–67 *not in MS 1, instead:*
　　　　　　Whose roots are nourished of the rich brain-mould
　　　　　　Dropped from the anguish of a warrior race,
　　　　　　At quick pulsation with felicity.
73 deem] know *MS 1*
74 beams] rays *MS 1*
76 lends] gives *MS 1*　　　grace] place *MS 1*
79 *MS 1:* Look on her through [her *del.*] the showers
80 *MS 1:* [Her *del.*] The mists, [her *del.*] the sheeted gold,
81 the] her *del. MS 1*
83 seems Earth] she seems *MS 1*

Woodman and Echo

This poem repudiates a single, sentimental line in the early notebook, NB A, [p. 3]: "Echo hears the woodmans axe & answers it in anguish."

Close Echo hears the woodman's axe,
To double on it, as in glee,
With clap of hands, and little lacks
Of meaning in her repartee.
For all shall fall,
As one has done,
The tree of me,
Of thee the tree;
And unto all
The fate we wait   10
Reveals the wheels
Whereon we run:
We tower to flower,
We spread the shade,
We drop for crop,
At length are laid;
Are rolled in mould,
From chop and lop:
And are we thick in woodland tracks,
Or tempting of our stature we,   20
The end is one, we do but wax
For service over land and sea.
So, strike! the like
Shall thus of us,

MS: Huntington HM6770, *fair copy, title: "The Woodman."*
7 of] in *MS*
8 Of] In *MS*
9–18 *not in MS*
19–21 *MS:*

> And howsoever high we wax,
> A stroke will come to tell us we
> Have ended in the woodland tracks,

23–25 *not in MS*

My brawny woodman, claim the tax.
　　Nor foe thy blow,
　　Though wood be good,
And shriekingly the timber cracks:
　　The ground we crowned
　　Shall speed the seed   30
Of younger into swelling sacks.

　　For use he hews,
　　To make awake
The spirit of what stuff we be:
　　Our earth of mirth
　　And tears he clears
For braver, let our minds agree;
　　And then will men
　　Within them win
An Echo clapping harmony.   40

The Wisdom of Eld

We spend our lives in learning pilotage,
And grow good steersmen when the vessel's crank!
Gap-toothed he spake, and with a tottering shank
Sidled to gain the sunny bench of Age.
It is the sentence which completes that stage;
A testament of wisdom reading blank.

WOODMAN AND ECHO

29–37 *MS:*

For use he hews,	[*Cf. line 32*]
To make awake	[*Cf. line 33*]
The spirit of what stuff we be.	[*Cf. line 34*]
This ground we crowned	[*Cf. line 29*]
Shall speed the seed	[*Cf. line 30*]
Of brighter into swelling sacks;	[*Cf. line 31*]
This earth of mirth	[*Cf. line 35*]
And tears he clears	[*Cf. line 36*]
For garden, let our minds agree.	[*Cf. line 37*]

38–40 *not in MS*
40 An] And *misp. 1888, de L; corr. GM letter to G. W. Foote, February 25, 1889, corr. errata, de L 1911*

The seniors of the race, on their last plank,
Pass mumbling it as nature's final page.
These, bent by such experience, are the band
Who captain young enthusiasts to maintain   10
What things we view, and Earth's decree withstand,
Lest dreaded Change, long dammed by dull decay,
Should bring the world a vessel steered by brain,
And ancients musical at close of day.

Earth's Preference

Earth loves her young: a preference manifest:
She prompts them to her fruits and flower-beds;
Their beauty with her choicest interthreads,
And makes her revel of their merry zest.
As in our East much were it in our West,
If men had risen to do the work of heads.
Her gabbling grey she eyes askant, nor treads
The ways they walk; by what they speak oppressed.
How wrought they in their zenith? 'Tis not writ;
Not all; yet she by one sure sign can read: 10
Have they but held her laws and nature dear,
They mouth no sentence of inverted wit.
More prizes she her beasts than this high breed
Wry in the shape she wastes her milk to rear.

Society

Historic be the survey of our kind,
And how their brave Society took shape.
Lion, wolf, vulture, fox, jackal and ape,
The strong of limb, the keen of nose, we find,
Who, with some jars in harmony, combined,
Their primal instincts taming, to escape

The brawl indecent, and hot passions drape.
Convenience pricked conscience, that the mind.
Thus entered they the field of milder beasts,
Which in some sort of civil order graze, 10
And do half-homage to the God of Laws.
But are they still for their own ravenous feasts,
Earth gives the edifice they build no base:
They spring another flood of fangs and claws.

Winter Heavens

Sharp is the night, but stars with frost alive
Leap off the rim of earth across the dome.
It is a night to make the heavens our home
More than the nest whereto apace we strive.
Lengths down our road each fir-tree seems a hive,
In swarms outrushing from the golden comb.
They waken waves of thoughts that burst to foam:
The living throb in me, the dead revive.
Yon mantle clothes us: there, past mortal breath,
Life glistens on the river of the death. 10
It folds us, flesh and dust; and have we knelt,
Or never knelt, or eyed as kine the springs
Of radiance, the radiance enrings:
And this is the soul's haven to have felt.

WINTER HEAVENS

6 In] *1888;* It *de L; corr. errata, de L 1911*

Epitaphs

M. M.

Marie Vulliamy Meredith died on September 17, 1885, and was buried in the cemetery at Dorking (see p. 428, headnote to *A Faith on Trial*).

> Who call her Mother and who calls her Wife
> Look on her grave and see not Death but Life.

The Lady C. M.

Lady Caroline Maxse, the mother of GM's great friend Frederick A. Maxse (see p. xxxii), died on January 21, 1886, and GM sent this epitaph to Maxse the next day. He had always had the greatest reverence and affection for her. Enclosing the lines, he wrote: "I have written four lines for epitaph—and you can toss them aside. It seems to me that they give an expression of her."

> To them that knew her, there is vital flame
> In these the simple letters of her name.
> To them that knew her not, be it but said,
> So strong a spirit is not of the dead.

J. C. M.

James Cotter Morison (see p. xxxiii) had died on February 26, 1888. John Morley quoted this epitaph approvingly in his dazzling account of Morison, in *Recollections*, 1:11.

Edward Clodd described Morison's funeral and Meredith's comments on it:

J. C. M.

MS: Huntington HM7472, *fair copy.*

On the first of March, 1888, a day so bleak that a tent was pitched over the grave to protect the mourners, Morison was buried in Kensal Green Cemetery. Among the sparse company, which included Lord Morley, was George Meredith, who took me, after the ceremony, to lunch at the Garrick Club. He talked of the mockery of the Burial Service which had been read in full over the remains of a man who lived and died an unbeliever, and whose last book was a trenchant attack on Christianity [*The Service of Man: An Essay towards the Religion of the Future* (1887)]. And he said that if we did not give directions to the contrary, words, all unmeaning to those who die outside the Christian pale, will be spoken at our graveside. These directions he himself omitted to give (p. 116).

> A fountain of our sweetest, quick to spring
> In fellowship abounding, here subsides:
> And never passage of a cloud on wing
> To gladden blue forgets him; near he hides.

Islet the Dachs

Frederick A. Maxse's older brother, Sir Henry Berkeley Fitzhardinge Maxse, governor of Heligoland from 1864 to 1881, undoubtedly was the donor of Islet. In 1886 Frederick gave GM another dachshund. GM reported the gift in a letter to his daughter, July 24, "It is the dearest little Dachs, from the Admiral, of a smooth, glossy full brown; exactly like Isly in shape, with the greyhound's back and belly, the escutcheon, fine tail, big paws, pretty face, full of fun and inquiry."

> Our Islet out of Helgoland, dismissed
> From his quaint tenement, quits hates and loves.
> There lived with us a wagging humourist
> In that hound's arch dwarf-legged on boxing-gloves.

J. C. M.

4 near he] he but *del. MS*

ISLET THE DACHS

MS: Huntington, *pasted verso of* HM7472 *and* 7473, *no title.*

2 quits hates and loves] here owns the laws *MS*
3–4 *MS:*
>   Would you have known a wagging humourist
>   He stood in that bounds arch on dwarf-leg paws

Gordon of Khartoum

Having withstood a ten-month siege by the Mahdi at Khartoum, Gen. Charles George Gordon finally was killed on January 26, 1885.

Of men he would have raised to light he fell:
In soul he conquered with those nerveless hands.
His country's pride and her abasement knell
The Man of England circled by the sands.

The Emperor Frederick of Our Time

Frederick III, king of Prussia and German emperor, politically a Liberal, died on June 15, 1888, having reigned only ninety-nine days after the death of his father, the emperor William I. GM's title suggests a comparison with Frederick II, "the Great" (1712–86), who was a scholar and patron of the arts.

With Alfred and St. Louis he doth win
Grander than crowned head's mortuary dome:
His gentle heroic manhood enters in
The ever-flowering common heart for home.

The Year's Sheddings

The varied colours are a fitful heap:
They pass in constant service though they sleep;
The self gone out of them, therewith the pain:
Read that, who still to spell our earth remain.

GORDON OF KHARTOUM
MS: Huntington HM7473, *fair copy, title: "The Latest Hero" del.*
THE EMPEROR FREDERICK OF OUR TIME
MS: Huntington HM7474, *fair copy.*
4 ever-flowering] universal *MS*
THE YEAR'S SHEDDINGS
MS: Huntington HM7475, *fair copy.*

THE SAGE ENAMOURED AND THE HONEST LADY
(1892)

The full title of this volume was *Modern Love, A Reprint, to which is added The Sage Enamoured and the Honest Lady.* However, in the present edition the text of *Modern Love* is not reprinted from *Modern Love* (1862).

The Sage Enamoured and the Honest Lady

The "Lady" was Hilda de Longueuil, a Canadian cousin of GM's neighbors the Grant Allens, who received a visit from her in the autumn of 1886. She was twenty-four years old, beautiful, intelligent, and miserable over a catastrophic love affair. When she left the Allens for southern France, GM continued to show his admiration for her by writing long letters intended to help her face life anew (LS, pp. 269–70). See page 865, *Hilda's Morning and Evening Dose of Rhyme.*

Evidently GM's son, William Maxse, got wind of this attachment and wrote his father "bluntly," because GM replied on January 24, 1887, flatly denying the report. But three days later he undertook an "explanation" of the gossip. "I live much alone, and not having an idle mind, have of late conversed heavily with the dead; but as I have also a poetical temperament, I am susceptible to forms and shows of life, and one appeared in the person of a lady, who drew me up to daylight, as to the animation she created." He went on to say that she was half his age, and that he would always "entertain" "special" and "fervent" "admiration" for her. "She [was] out of England," and he might not see her within the year. "My trick of speaking out my admirations and seeking pleasure with those who cause them, gave the gossips cue."

MSS: Yale. Fair copy, including instructions to printer; frag. A, IV.143–184; frag. B, passage for insertion after IV.172; frag. C, draft for frag. A, IV.177–84; frag. D, part V; frag. E, revision of V.1–33.

I

One fairest of the ripe unwedded left
Her shadow on the Sage's path; he found,
By common signs, that she had done a theft.
He could have made the sovereign heights resound
With questions of the wherefore of her state:
He on far other but an hour before
Intent. And was it man, or was it mate,
That she disdained? or was there haply more?

About her mouth a placid humour slipped
The dimple, as you see smooth lakes at eve   10
Spread melting rings where late a swallow dipped.
The surface was attentive to receive,
The secret underneath enfolded fast.
She had the step of the unconquered, brave,
Not arrogant; and if the vessel's mast
Waved liberty, no challenge did it wave.

Her eyes were the sweet world desired of souls,
With something of a wavering line unspelt.
They held the look whose tenderness condoles
For what the sister in the look has dealt   20
Of fatal beyond healing; and her tones
A woman's honeyed amorous outvied,
As when in a dropped viol the wood-throb moans
Among the sobbing strings, that plain and chide
Like infants for themselves, less deep to thrill
Than those rich mother-notes for them breathed round.
Those voices are not magic of the will
To strike love's wound, but of love's wound give sound,
Conveying it; the yearnings, pains and dreams.
They waft to the moist tropics after storm,   30
When out of passion spent thick incense steams,
And jewel-belted clouds the wreck transform.

Was never hand on brush or lyre to paint
Her gracious manners, where the nuptial ring
Of melody clasped motion in restraint:
The reed-blade with the breeze thereof may sing.

With such endowments armed was she and decked
To make her spoken thoughts eclipse her kind;
Surpassing many a giant intellect,
The marvel of that cradled infant mind.   40
It clenched the tiny fist, it curled the toe;
Cherubic laughed, enticed, dispensed, absorbed;
And promised in fair feminine to grow
A Sage's match and mate, more heavenly orbed.

II

Across his path the spouseless Lady cast
Her shadow, and the man that thing became.
His youth uprising called his age the Past.
This was the strong grey head of laurelled name,
And in his bosom an inverted Sage
Mistook for light of morn the light which sank.
But who while veins run blood shall know the page
Succeeding ere we turn upon our blank?
Comes Beauty with her tale of moon and cloud,
Her silvered rims of mystery pointing in   10
To hollows of the half-veiled unavowed,
Where beats her secret life, grey heads will spin
Quick as the young, and spell those hieroglyphs
Of phosphorescent dusk devoutly bent;
They drink a cup to whirl on dizzier cliffs
For their shamed fall, which asks, why was she sent!
Why, and of whom, and whence; and tell they truth,
The legends of her mission to beguile?

Hard likeness to the toilful apes of youth,
He bore at times, and tempted the sly smile;   20
And not on her soft lips was it descried.
She stepped her way benevolently grave:

Nor sign that Beauty fed her worm of pride,
By tossing victim to the courtier knave,
Let peep, nor of the naughty pride gave sign.
Rather 'twas humbleness in being pursued,
As pilgrim to the temple of a shrine.
Had he not wits to pierce the mask he wooed?
All wisdom's armoury this man could wield;
And if the cynic in the Sage it pleased,   30
Traverse her woman's curtain and poor shield,
For new example of a world diseased;
Showing her shrineless, not a temple, bare;
A curtain ripped to tatters by the blast.
Yet she most surely to this man stood fair:
He worshipped like the young enthusiast,
Named simpleton or poet. Did he read
Right through, and with the voice she held reserved
Amid her vacant ruins jointly plead?

Compassion for the man thus noble nerved   40
The pity for herself she felt in him,
To wreak a deed of sacrifice, and save;
At least, be worthy. That our soul may swim,
We sink our heart down bubbling under wave.
It bubbles till it drops among the wrecks.
But, ah! confession of a woman's breast:
She eminent, she honoured of her sex!
Truth speaks, and takes the spots of the confessed,
To veil them. None of women, save their vile,
Plays traitor to an army in the field.   50
The cries most vindicating most defile.
How shall a cause to Nature be appealed,
When, under pressure of their common foe,
Her sisters shun the Mother and disown,
On pain of his intolerable crow
Above the fiction, built for him, o'erthrown?
Irrational he is, irrational
Must they be, though not Reason's light shall wane

In them with ever Nature at close call,
Behind the fiction torturing to sustain;   60
Who hear her in the milk, and sometimes make
A tongueless answer, shivered on a sigh:
Whereat men dread their lofty structure's quake
Once more, and in their hosts for tocsin ply
The crazy roar of peril, leonine
For injured majesty. That sigh of dames
Is rare and soon suppressed. Not they combine
To shake the structure sheltering them, which tames
Their lustier if not wilder: fixed are they,
In elegancy scarce denoting ease;   70
And do they breathe, it is not to betray
The martyr in the caryatides.
Yet here and there along the graceful row
Is one who fetches breath from deeps, who deems,
Moved by a desperate craving, their old foe
May yield a trustier friend than woman seems,
And aid to bear the sculptured floral weight
Massed upon heads not utterly of stone:
May stamp endurance by expounding fate.

She turned to him, and, This you seek is gone;   80
Look in, she said, as pants the furnace, brief,
Frost-white. She gave his hearing sight to view
The silent chamber of a brown curled leaf:
Thing that had throbbed ere shot black lightning through.
No further sign of heart could he discern:
The picture of her speech was winter sky;
A headless figure folding a cleft urn,
Where tears once at the overflow were dry.

III

So spake she her first utterance on the rack.
It softened torment, in the funeral hues
Round wan Romance at ebb, but drove her back
To listen to herself, herself accuse

Harshly as Love's imperial cause allowed.
She meant to grovel, and her lover praised
So high o'er the condemnatory crowd,
That she perforce a fellow phoenix blazed.

The picture was of hand fast joined to hand,
Both pushed from angry skies, their grasp more pledged   10
Under the threatened flash of a bright brand
At arm's length up, for severing action edged.

Why, then Love's Court of Honour contemplate;
And two drowned shorecasts, who, for the life esteemed
Above their lost, invoke an advocate
In passion's purity, thereby redeemed.

Redeemed, uplifted, glimmering on a throne,
The woman stricken by an arrow falls.
His advocate she can be, not her own,
If, Traitress to thy sex! one sister calls.   20

Have we such scenes of drapery's mournfulness
On Beauty's revelations, witched we plant,
Over the fair shape humbled to confess,
An angel's buckler, with loud choric chant.

IV

No knightly sword to serve, nor harp of bard,
The lady's hand in her physician's knew.
She had not hoped for them as her award,
When zig-zag on the tongue electric flew
Her charge of counter-motives, none impure:
But muteness whipped her skin. She could have said,
Her free confession was to work his cure,
Show proofs for why she could not love or wed.

Were they not shown? His muteness shook in thrall
Her body on the verge of that black pit   10
Sheer from the treacherous confessional,
Demanding further, while perusing it.

Slave is the open mouth beneath the closed.
She sank; she snatched at colours; they were peel
Of fruit past savour, in derision rosed.
For the dark downward then her soul did reel.
A press of hideous impulse urged to speak:
A novel dread of man enchained her dumb.
She felt the silence thicken, heard it shriek,
Heard Life subsiding on the eternal hum: 20
Welcome to women, when, between man's laws
And Nature's thirsts, they, soul from body torn,
Give suck at breast to a celestial cause,
Named by the mouth infernal, and forsworn.

Nathless her forehead twitched a sad content,
To think the cure so manifest, so frail
Her charm remaining. Was the curtain's rent
Too wide? he but a man of that herd male?
She saw him as that herd of the forked head
Butting the woman harrowed on her knees,   30
Clothed only in life's last devouring red.
Confession at her fearful instant sees
Judicial Silence write the devil fact
In letters of the skeleton: at once,
Swayed on the supplication of her act,
The rabble reading, roaring to denounce,
She joins. No longer colouring, with skips
At tangles, picture that for eyes in tears
Might swim the sequence, she addressed her lips
To do the scaffold's office at his ears.   40

Into the bitter judgement of that herd
On women, she, deeming it present, fell.
Her frenzy of abasement hugged the word

They stone with, and so pile their citadel
To launch at outcasts the foul levin bolt.
As had he flung it, in her breast it burned.
Face and reflect it did her hot revolt
From hardness, to the writhing rebel turned;
Because the golden buckler was withheld,
She to herself applies the powder-spark,   50
For joy of one wild demon burst ere quelled,
Perishing to astound the tyrant Dark.

She had the Scriptural word so scored on brain,
It rang through air to sky, and rocked a world
That danced down shades the scarlet dance profane;
Most women! see! by the man's view dustward hurled,
Impenitent, submissive, torn in two.
They sink upon their nature, the unnamed,
And sops of nourishment may get some few,
In place of understanding scourged and shamed.   60

Barely have seasoned women understood
The great Irrational, who thunders power,
Drives Nature to her primitive wild wood,
And courts her in the covert's dewy hour;
Returning to his fortress nigh night's end,
With execration of her daughters' lures.
They help him the proud fortress to defend,
Nor see what front it wears, what life immures,
The murder it commits; nor that its base
Is shifty as a huckster's opening deal   70
For bargain under smoothest market face,
While Gentleness bids frigid Justice feel,
Justice protests that Reason is her seat;
Elect Convenience, as Reason masked,
Hears calmly cramped Humanity entreat;
Until a sentient world is overtasked,
And rouses Reason's fountain-self: she calls
On Nature; Nature answers: Share your guilt
In common when contention cracks the walls
Of the big house which not on me is built.   80

The Lady said as much as breath will bear;
To happier sisters inconceivable:
Contemptible to veterans of the fair,
Who show for a convolving pearly shell,
A treasure of the shore, their written book.
As much as woman's breath will bear and live,
Shaped she to words beneath a knotted look,
That held as if for grain the summing sieve.

Her judge now brightened without pause, as wakes
Our homely daylight after dread of spells.   90
Lips sugared to let loose the little snakes
Of slimy lustres ringing elfin bells
About a story of the naked flesh,
Intending but to put some garment on,
Should learn, that in the subject they enmesh,
A traitor lurks and will be known anon.
Delusion heating pricks the torpid doubt,
Stationed for index down an ancient track:
And ware of it was he while she poured out,
A broken moon on forest-waters black.   100

Though past the stage where midway men are skilled
To scan their senses wriggling under plough,
When yet to the charmed seed of speech distilled,
Their hearts are fallow, he, and witless how,
Loathing, had yielded, like bruised limb to leech,
Not handsomely; but now beholding bleed
Soul of the woman in her prostrate speech,
The valour of that rawness he could read.
Thence flashed it, as the crimson currents ran
From senses up to thoughts, how she had read   110
Maternally the warm remainder man
Beneath his crust, and Nature's pity shed,
In shedding dearer than heart's blood to light
His vision of the path mild Wisdom walks.
Therewith he could espy Confession's fright;
Her need of him: these flowers grow on stalks;

They suck from soil, and have their urgencies
Beside and with the lovely face mid leaves.
Veins of divergencies, convergencies,
Our botanist in womankind perceives;   120
And if he hugs no wound, the man can prize
That splendid consummation and sure proof
Of more than heart in her, who might despise,
Who drowns herself, for pity up aloof
To soar and be like Nature's pity: she
Instinctive of what virtue in young days
Had served him for his pilot-star on sea,
To trouble him in haven. Thus his gaze
Came out of rust, and more than the schooled tongue
Was gifted to encourage and assure.   130
He gave her of the deep well she had sprung;
And name it gratitude, the word is poor.
But name it gratitude, is aught as rare
From sex to sex? And let it have survived
Their conflict, comes the peace between the pair,
Unknown to thousands husbanded and wived:
Unknown to Passion, generous for prey:
Unknown to Love, too blissful in a truce.
Their tenderest of self did each one slay;
His cloak of dignity, her fleur de luce;   140
Her lily flower, and his abolla cloak,
Things living, slew they, and no artery bled.
A moment of some sacrificial smoke,
They passed, and were the dearer for their dead.

He learnt how much we gain who make no claims.
A nightcap on his flicker of grey fire,
Was thought of her sharp shudder in the flames,
Confessing; and its conjured image dire,
Of love, the torrent on the valley dashed;
The whirlwind swathing tremulous peaks; young force,   150

IV.145 gain] have *frag. A*
IV.148 image] vision *frag. A*
IV.150 young] the *frag. A*

Visioned to hold corrected and abashed
Our senile emulous; which rolls its course
Proud to the shattering end; with these few last
Hot quintessential drops of bryony juice,
Squeezed out in anguish: all of that once vast!
And still, though having skin for man's abuse,
Though no more glorying in the beauteous wreath
Shot skyward from a blood at passionate jet,
Repenting but in words, that stand as teeth
Between the vivid lips; a vassal set;   160
And numb, of formal value. Are we true
In nature, never natural thing repents;
Albeit receiving punishment for due,
Among the group of this world's penitents;
Albeit remorsefully regretting, oft
Cravenly, while the scourge no shudder spares.

Our world believes it stabler if the soft
Are whipped to show the face repentance wears.
Then hear it, in a moan of atheist gloom,
Deplore the weedy growth of hypocrites;   170
Count Nature devilish, and accept for doom
The chasm between our passions and our wits!

IV.151 Visioned] Enough *frag. A*
IV.155 Squeezed out in] Expressed in *frag. A*
IV.160 a vassal] an ordered *frag. A*
IV.166 while] when *frag. A*
IV.168 Are whipped to show the face] Are stamped with features which *frag. A*
IV.169 a] its *frag. A*

For insertion after frag. A, IV.172, frag. B:

> She sees an ailing world, off her good road
> Of health, in search of magic herbs astray:
> Its aimless wisdom, conscious of a good,
> To chasten crudeness, or to prop decay;
> Or supplicate for some immediate needs,
> The Power it dreads as evil's origin.
> Behold, on fitful tides it flows, recedes;
> Awaiting sin's extremes to cure the sin:
> Affecting lunar whiteness, Alpine pride;   [9–12 cf. IV.173–76]
> Betraying lunar spots; it will not flow   10
> With Nature's glacier-conscience, purified.
> By witness of the streak it wears, below.

Affecting lunar whiteness, patent snows,
It trembles at betrayal of a sore.
Hers is the glacier-conscience, to expose
Impurities for clearness at the core.

She to her hungered thundering in breast,
Ye shall not starve, not feebly designates
The world repressing as a life repressed,
Judged by the wasted martyrs it creates.   180

How Sin, amid the shades Cimmerian,
Repents, she points for sight: and she avers,
The hoofed half-angel in the Puritan
Nigh reads her when no brutish wrath deters.

Sin against immaturity, the sin
Of ravenous excess, what deed divides
Man from vitality; these bleed within;
Bleed in the crippled relic that abides.
Perpetually they bleed; a limb is lost,
A piece of life, the very spirit maimed.   190
But culprit who the law of man has crossed
With Nature's, dubiously within is blamed;
Despite our cry at cutting of the whip,
Our shiver in the night when numbers frown
We but bewail a broken fellowship,
A sting, an isolation, a fall'n crown.

Abject of sinners is that sensitive,
The flesh, amenable to stripes, miscalled
Incorrigible: such title do we give
To the poor shrinking stuff wherewith we are walled;   200

IV.177 in] through the *frag. A, frag. C*
IV.179 as] for *frag. A*;   for *or* as *frag. C*
IV.180 Judged by the wasted] Condemned in the white *frag. A*;   And poorer for the
del. Condemned in the white *frag. C*
After IV.180 frag. C:
    They serve it, for they will not scratch in food:
    They leave it to the choice twixt meat & bone.
frag. C: The health of life, unknown till she is known.
frag. C: The hoofed half-angel in the Puritan   [*Cf. line 183*]
IV.193 of] off *misp. 1892, 1894*

And taking it for Nature, place in ban
Our Mother, as a Power wanton-willed,
The shame and baffler of the soul of man,
The recreant, reptilious. Do thou build
Thy mind on her foundations in earth's bed;
Behold man's mind the child of her keen rod,
For teaching how the wits and passions wed
To rear that temple of the credible God;
Sacred the letters of her laws, and plain,
Will shine, to guide thy feet and hold thee firm: 210
Then, as a pathway through a field of grain,
Man's laws appear the blind progressive worm,
That moves by touch, and thrust of linking rings
The which to endow with vision, lift from mud
To level of their nature's aims and springs,
Must those, the twain beside our vital flood,
Now on opposing banks, the twain at strife
(Whom the so rosy ferryman invites
To junction, and mid-channel over Life,
Unmasked to the ghostly, much asunder smites),   220
Instruct in deeper than Convenience,
In higher than the harvest of a year.
Only the rooted knowledge to high sense
Of heavenly can mount, and feel the spur
For fruitfullest advancement, eye a mark
Beyond the path with grain on either hand,
Help to the steering of our social Ark
Over the barbarous waters unto land.

For us the double conscience and its war,
The serving of two masters, false to both,   230
Until those twain, who spring the root and are
The knowledge in division, plight a troth
Of equal hands: nor longer circulate
A pious token for their current coin,
To growl at the exchange; they, mate and mate,
Fair feminine and masculine shall join
Upon an upper plane, still common mould,
Where stamped religion and reflective pace

A statelier measure, and the hoop of gold
Rounds to horizon for their soul's embrace.   240
Then shall those noblest of the earth and sun
Inmix unlike to waves on savage sea.
But not till Nature's laws and man's are one,
Can marriage of the man and woman be.

                                        V

He passed her through the sermon's dull defile.
Down under billowy vapour-gorges heaved
The city and the vale and mountain-pile.
She felt strange push of shuttle-threads that weaved.

A new land in an old beneath her lay;
And forth to meet it did her spirit rush,
As bride who without shame has come to say,
Husband, in his dear face that caused her blush.

A natural woman's heart, not more than clad
By station and bright raiment, gathers heat   10
From nakedness in trusted hands: she had
The joy of those who feel the world's heart beat,
After long doubt of it as fire or ice;
Because one man had helped her to breathe free;
Surprised to faith in something of a price
Past the old charity in chivalry:—

V.1 dull] dark *del. frag.* D
V.2–32 *not in frag.* D, *instead:*
            A liberal air beyond rang welcome-peals.
            A spacious country belled to reconcile
            Her mind's & fortune's intervolved ordeals.
            The rocks had frowns whereunder wisdom hung;
            The meads shook their green aprons in the dance;
            The flashing waters pitched a songful tongue.
            Less did she deem herself the child of chance.

Our first wild step to right the loaded scales
Displaying women shamefully outweighed.
The wisdom of humaneness best avails
For serving justice till that fraud is brayed.   20

Her buried body fed the life she drank.
And not another stripping of her wound!
The startled thought on black delirium sank,
While with her gentle surgeon she communed,
And woman's prospect of the yoke repelled.
Her buried body gave her flowers and food;
The peace, the homely skies, the springs that welled;
Love, the large love that folds the multitude.

Soul's chastity in honesty, and this
With beauty, made the dower to men refused.   30
And little do they know the prize they miss;
Which is their happy fortune! Thus he mused.

For him, the cynic in the Sage had play
A hazy moment, by a breath dispersed;
To think, of all alive most wedded they,
Whom time disjoined! He needed her quick thirst
For renovated earth: on earth she gazed,
With humble aim to foot beside the wise.
Lo, where the eyelashes of night are raised
Yet lowly over morning's pure grey eyes.   40

V.18 Displaying] Exposing *frag. E*
V.19 The wisdom in humaneness *line not completed, frag. E*
V.20 *not in frag. E, instead a space*
V.33 had] made *frag. D*   For him, the cynic in the Sage [*blank*] *frag. E*
V.34 hazy] misty *frag. D*   by] that *frag. D*
V.37–38 *not in frag. D*
V.39 the] dark *del. frag. D*

Love is winged for two

Love is winged for two,
In the worst he weathers,
When their hearts are tied;
But if they divide,
O too true!
Cracks a globe, and feathers, feathers,
Feathers all the ground bestrew.

I was breast of morning sea,
Rosy plume on forest dun,
I the laugh in rainy fleeces,　　　　　　　　　10
　　While with me
　　She made one.
Now must we pick up our pieces,
For that then so winged were we.

Ask, is Love divine

Ask, is Love divine,
Voices all are, ay.
Question for the sign,
There's a common sigh.
Would we through our years,
Love forego,
Quit of scars and tears?
Ah, but no, no, no!

LOVE IS WINGED FOR TWO

MS: Yale, *fair copy, including instructions to printer.*
2 he] of *MS*
11 While] Ere & while *MS*

ASK, IS LOVE DIVINE

MS: Yale, *fair copy, including instructions to printer.*

Joy is fleet

Since *Joy is fleet* is rewritten from a lyric in an early notebook, it is probable that the two preceding lyrics come from the same source, taken from among the many torn-out leaves.

> Joy is fleet,
> Sorrow slow.
> Love so sweet,
> Sorrow will sow.
> Love, that has flown
> Ere day's decline,
> Love to have known,
> Sorrow, be mine!

The Lesson of Grief

> Not ere the bitter herb we taste,
> Which ages thought of happy times,
> To plant us in a weeping waste,
> Rings with our fellows this one heart
>   Accordant chimes.

JOY IS FLEET

MSS: Yale. NB B, *[p. 34]; fair copy, including instructions to printer.*
NB B:

> Love is fleet
> And sorrow slow
> Love so sweet
> With [sic] sorrow sow.
>
> Love is the Dawn
> Comes unto all:
> Love is long gone
> Ere even fall.

THE LESSON OF GRIEF

MS: Yale, *fair copy.*

When I had shed my glad year's leaf,
I did believe I stood alone,
Till that great company of Grief
Taught me to know this craving heart
      For not my own.

POEMS: THE EMPTY PURSE,
WITH ODES TO THE COMIC SPIRIT,
TO YOUTH IN MEMORY, AND VERSES
(1892)

Wind on the Lyre

GM had written his old friend Frederick Greenwood, editor of the
Anti-Jacobin, on November 30, 1891: "Here is a twitter of song for your
Anty-J., if you care to have it, just to show you my heart is warm. . . ."

That was the chirp of Ariel
You heard, as overhead it flew,
The farther going more to dwell,
And wing our green to wed our blue;
But whether note of joy or knell,
Not his own Father-singer knew;
Nor yet can any mortal tell,
Save only how it shivers through;
The breast of us a sounded shell,
The blood of us a lighted dew.   10

Previously printed in the Anti-Jacobin 45 (5 December 1891): *MBF failed to note this
appearance of the poem. MSS:* Huntington HM7465. *MS 1, working draft, title: "Clear
Singing"; MS 2, fair copy.*

1 chirp] note *MS 1*
3 The] And *MS 1*   to] did *MS 1*   dwell] swell *A-J*
4 *MS 1:* To wed the *or* knit our *or* The more to knit the green fields with the blue;
7 any mortal] one among us *or* any mortal *MS 1*

The Youthful Quest

His Lady queen of woods to meet,
    He wanders day and night:
The leaves have whisperings discreet,
    The mossy ways invite.

Across a lustrous ring of space,
    By covert hoods and caves,
Is promise of her secret face
    In film that onward waves.

For darkness is the light astrain,
    Astrain for light the dark.   10
A grey moth down a larches' lane
    Unwinds a ghostly spark.

Her lamp he sees, and young desire
    Is fed while cloaked she flies.
She quivers shot of violet fire
    To ash at look of eyes.

MSS: Huntington HM7466. *MS 1, working draft, title:* "*Quest of Youth*"; *MS 2*, fair copy.

1 His Lady queen of] Our lady of the *MS 1*
2 He wanders] I wander *MS 1*
3 The] Her *MS 1*
4 The] Her *MS 1*
5 Across] I cross *MS 1*
6 *MS 1:* Through coverts breathing low
7 Is promise] The marvel *MS 1*
8 *MS 1:* Nor light nor dark will show.
9 *MS 1:* The light is all for Earth astrain, *del.* For dark the light is all astrain,
10 Astrain] Athirst *MS 1*
11 A grey moth down] There flits along *MS 1*
12 Unwinds] A moth, *MS 1*
13 *MS 1:* Her lamp it is, & my desire   Her lamp he sees] He sees her lamp *del.* Her lamp he sees *MS 2*
14 Is fed while] As on it flies *del. MS 1*
15 *MS 1:* I know that she would pass in fire

The Empty Purse
A SERMON TO OUR LATER PRODIGAL SON

The origin of *The Empty Purse* is found, about forty years before its publication, in NB B, [p. 37]. Here GM wrote:

THE STUDENT TO HIS EMPTY PURSE

A [Fledgling wanting *del.*] bird stript of its feathers,
    A Fish without fin,
Is he who holds the Empty Purse—
Is he who lives to lack, and curse
    The thing that was within.—
For O! it gave the world a glow:
And ah! it taught the blood to flow.
And 'tis the trick o' the Serpent
    To slip & leave its skin.

2

    But let me read [the Sermon *del.*] what's written
    With Memory's mocking elves.
Still cheerful as a Winter wren,
We cry: you've taught us much of men,
    But little of ourselves!
So here's the toughest lesson last:
And, Empty Purse! when that is pass'd,
    You will have taught *or* probed us deeper
    Than all the dusty *or* volumed shelves.

GM evidently was determined to retrieve the first two lines of these early verses. He began *The Empty Purse* with the same metaphors (MS 1, line 1) and finally perfected his wording in line 330. These *lignes données*, to dignify the inception of *The Empty Purse*, are from *The Comedy of Errors*. Dromio of Syracuse: "Ay, when fowls have no feathers and fish have no fin." Dromio of Ephesus: "For a fish without a fin, there's a fowl without a feather" (3. 1. 79, 82).

In the volume of Robert Southey's *Common-place Book* published in 1850 there is a list of "Subjects for Poemlings," probably dating from 1799, among which is "Meditations on an empty purse" (ed. John Wood, 4th ser. [London: Longman], pp. 20–21). The date of the publication of this volume may help date the early fragment.

Subtitle. The parable of the prodigal son: Luke 15:11–32.

See Supplementary Textual Notes.

Thou, run to the dry on this wayside bank,
Too plainly of all the propellers bereft!
    Quenched youth, and is that thy purse?
Even such limp slough as the snake has left
Slack to the gale upon spikes of whin,
For cast-off coat of a life gone blank
In its frame of a grin at the seeker, is thine;
    And thine to crave and to curse
    The sweet thing once within.
Accuse him: some devil committed the theft,   10
    Which leaves of the portly a skin,
    No more; of the weighty a whine.

Pursue him: and first, to be sure of his track,
Over devious ways that have led to this,
    In the stream's consecutive line,
    Let memory lead thee back
To where waves Morning her fleur-de-lys,
Unflushed at the front of the roseate door
Unopened yet: never shadow there
    Of a Tartarus lighted by Dis   20
    For souls whose cry is, alack!
An ivory cradle rocks, apeep
Through his eyelashes' laugh, a breathing pearl.

There the young chief of the animals wore
A likeness to heavenly hosts, unaware
Of his love of himself; with the hours at leap.
In a dingle away from a rutted highroad,
Around him the earliest throstle and merle,
Our human smile between milk and sleep,
    Effervescent of Nature he crowed.   30
Fair was that season; furl over furl
The banners of blossom; a dancing floor
This earth; very angels the clouds; and fair
Thou on the tablets of forehead and breast:
Careless, a centre of vigilant care.

Thy mother kisses an infant curl.
The room of the toys was a boundless nest,
    A kingdom the field of the games,
    Till entered the craving for more,
    And the worshipped small body had aims.   40
A good little idol, as records attest,
When they tell of him lightly appeased in a scream
By sweets and caresses: he gave but sign,
That the heir of a purse-plumped dominant race,
Accustomed to plenty, not dumb would pine.
Almost magician, his earliest dream
    Was lord of the unpossessed
    For a look; himself and his chase,
    As on puffs of a wind at whirl,
    Made one in the wink of a gleam.   50
    She kisses a locket curl,
She conjures to vision a cherub face,
    When her butterfly counted his day
    All meadow and flowers, mishap
    Derided, and taken for play
    The fling of an urchin's cap.

When her butterfly showed him an eaglet born,
    For preying too heedlessly bred,
    What a heart clapped in thee then!
    With what fuller colours of morn!   60
And high to the uttermost heavens it flew,
    Swift as on poet's pen.
    It flew to be wedded, to wed
    The mystery scented around:
    Issue of flower and dew,
    Issue of light and sound:
    Thinner than either; a thread
    Spun of the dream they threw
    To kindle, allure, evade.
It ran the sea-wave, the garden's dance,   70

To the forest's dark heart down a dappled glade;
    Led on by a perishing glance,
    By a twinkle's eternal waylaid.
Woman, the name was, when she took form;
Sheaf of the wonders of life. She fled,
Close imaged; she neared, far seen. How she made
Palpitate earth of the living and dead!
Did she not show thee the world designed
Solely for loveliness? Nested warm,
The day was the morrow in flight. And for thee,   80
She muted the discords, tuned, refined;
Drowned sharp edges beneath her cloak.
Eye of the waters, and throb of the tree,
Sliding on radiance, winging from shade,
With her witch-whisper o'er ruins, in reeds,
She sang low the song of her promise delayed;
Beckoned and died, as a finger of smoke
Astream over woodland. And was not she
History's heroines white on storm?
Remember her summons to valorous deeds.   90
Shone she a lure of the honey-bag swarm,
Most was her beam on the knightly: she led
For the honours of manhood more than the prize;
    Waved her magnetical yoke
    Whither the warrior bled,
    Ere to the bower of sighs.
And shy of her secrets she was; under deeps
Plunged at the breath of a thirst that woke
The dream in the cave where the Dreaded sleeps.

Away over heaven the young heart flew,   100
And caught many lustres, till some one said
(Or was it the thought into hearing grew?),
    Not thou as commoner men!
    Thy stature puffed and it swayed,
    It stiffened to royal-erect;

A brassy trumpet brayed;
A whirling seized thy head;
The vision of beauty was flecked.
Note well the how and the when,
The thing that prompted and sped.   110

Thereanon the keen passions clapped wing,
    Fixed eye, and the world was prey.
No simple world of thy greenblade Spring,
    Nor world of thy flowerful prime
    On the topmost Orient peak
    Above a yet vaporous day.
    Flesh was it, breast to beak:
A four-walled windowless world without ray,
Only darkening jets on a river of slime,
Where harsh over music as woodland jay,   120
    A voice chants, Woe to the weak!
    And along an insatiate feast,
    Women and men are one
    In the cup transforming to beast.

Magian worship they paid to their sun,
Lord of the Purse! Behold him climb.
    Stalked ever such figure of fun
For monarch in great-grin pantomime?
See now the heart dwindle, the frame distend;
The soul to its anchorite cavern retreat,   130
From a life that reeks of the rotted end;
While he—is he pictureable? replete,
Gourd-like swells of the rank of the soil,
    Hollow, more hollow at core.
    And for him did the hundreds toil
    Despised; in the cold and heat,
    This image ridiculous bore
    On their shoulders for morsels of meat!

Gross, with the fumes of incense full,
With parasites tickled, with slaves begirt,   140
He strutted, a cock, he bellowed, a bull,
    He rolled him, a dog, in dirt.
And dog, bull, cock, was he, fanged, horned, plumed;
Original man, as philosophers vouch;
Carnivorous, cannibal; length-long exhumed,
Frightfully living and armed to devour;
The primitive weapons of prey in his pouch;
    The bait, the line and the hook:
    To feed on his fellows intent.
    God of the Danaé shower,   150
    He had but to follow his bent.
He battened on fowl not safely hutched,
    On sheep astray from the crook;
    A lure for the foolish in fold:
    To carrion turning what flesh he touched.
    And O the grace of his air,
    As he at the goblet sips,
    A centre of girdles loosed,
    With their grisly label, Sold!
Credulous hears the fidelity swear,   160
Which has roving eyes over yielded lips:
To-morrow will fancy himself the seduced,
    The stuck in a treacherous slough,
Because of his faith in a purchased pair,
    False to a vinous vow.

In his glory of banquet strip him bare,
    And what is the creature we view?
Our pursy Apollo Apollyon's tool;
    A small one, still of the crew
    By serpent Apollyon blest: 170
His plea in apology, blindfold Fool.
A fool surcharged, propelled, unwarned;
    Not viler, you hear him protest:
Of a popular countenance not incorrect.
But deeds are the picture in essence, deeds

Paint him the hooved and horned,
Despite the poor pother he pleads,
And his look of a nation's elect.

We have him, our quarry confessed!
And scan him: the features inspect   180
Of that bestial multiform: cry,
Corroborate I, O Samian Sage!
The book of thy wisdom, proved
On me, its last hieroglyph page,
Alive in the horned and hooved?
Thou! will he make reply.

Thus has the plenary purse
Done often: to do will engage
Anew upon all of thy like, or worse.

And now is thy deepest regret   190
To be man, clean rescued from beast:
From the grip of the Sorcerer, Gold,
Celestially released.

But now from his cavernous hold,
Free may thy soul be set,
As a child of the Death and the Life, to learn,
Refreshed by some bodily sweat,
The meaning of either in turn,
What issue may come of the two:—
A morn beyond mornings, beyond all reach   200
Of emotional arms at the stretch to enfold:
A firmament passing our visible blue.
To those having nought to reflect it,'tis nought;
To those who are misty, 'tis mist on the beach
From the billow withdrawing; to those who see
Earth, our mother, in thought,
Her spirit it is, our key.

Ay, the Life and the Death are her words to us here,
Of one significance, pricking the blind.
This is thy gain now the surface is clear: 210
To read with a soul in the mirror of mind,
Is man's chief lesson.—Thou smilest! I preach!
    Acid smiling, my friend, reveals
Abysses within; frigid preaching a street
      Paved unconcernedly smooth
      For the lecturer straight on his heels,
      Up and down a policeman's beat;
      Bearing tonics not labelled to soothe.
Thou hast a disgust of the sermon in rhyme.
It is not attractive in being too chaste. 220
The popular tale of adventure and crime
Would equally sicken an overdone taste.
So, then, onward. Philosophy, thoughtless to soothe,
Lifts, if thou wilt, or there leaves thee supine.

Thy condition, good sooth, has no seeming of sweet;
It walks our first crags, it is flint for the tooth,
    For the thirsts of our nature brine.
But manful has met it, manful will meet.
And think of thy privilege: supple with youth,
      To have sight of the headlong swine, 230
      Once fouling thee, jumping the dips!
      As the coin of thy purse poured out:
      An animal's holiday past:
And free of them thou, to begin a new bout;
To start a fresh hunt on a resolute blast:
No more an imp-ridden to bournes of eclipse:
Having knowledge to spur thee, a gift to compare;
Rubbing shoulder to shoulder, as only the book
Of the world can be read, by necessity urged.
For witness, what blinkers are they who look 240
From the state of the prince or the millionnaire!
      They see but the fish they attract,
      The hungers on them converged;

And never the thought in the shell of the act,
    Nor ever life's fangless mirth.
But first, that the poisonous of thee be purged,
    Go into thyself, strike Earth.
She is there, she is felt in a blow struck hard.
Thou findest a pugilist countering quick,
Cunning at drives where thy shutters are barred;   250
Not, after the studied professional trick,
Blue-sealing; she brightens the sight. Strike Earth,
Antaeus, young giant, whom fortune trips!
    And thou com'st on a saving fact,
    To nourish thy planted worth.
Be it clay, flint, mud, or the rubble of chips,
Thy roots have grasp in the stern-exact:
The redemption of sinners deluded! the last
    Dry handful, that bruises and saves.
To the common big heart are we bound right fast,   260
    When our Mother admonishing nips
    At the nakedness bare of a clout,
    And we crave what the commonest craves.

    This wealth was a fortress-wall,
Under which grew our grim little beast-god stout;
Self-worshipped, the foe, in division from all;
With crowds of illogical Christians, no doubt;
    Till the rescuing earthquake cracked.
    Thus are we man made firm;
    Made warm by the numbers compact.   270
We follow no longer a trumpet-snout,
    At a trot where the hog is tracked,
    Nor wriggle the way of the worm.

    Thou wilt spare us the cynical pout
At humanity: sign of a nature bechurled.
    No stenchy anathemas cast
    Upon Providence, women, the world.

Distinguish thy tempers and trim thy wits.
The purchased are things of the mart, not classed
Among resonant types that have freely grown.   280

Thy knowledge of women might be surpassed:
As any sad dog's of sweet flesh when he quits
    The wayside wandering bone!
No revilings of comrades as ingrates: thee
The temper, misleader, and criminal (screened
    By laws yet barbarous) own.
If some one performed Fiend's deputy,
    He was for awhile the Fiend.

        Still, nursing a passion to speak,
As the punch-bowl does, in the moral vein,   290
    When the ladle has finished its leak,
And the vessel is loquent of nature's inane,
    Hie where the demagogues roar
Like a Phalaris bull, with the victim's force:
    Hurrah to their jolly attack
    On a City that smokes of the Plain;
    A city of sin's death-dyes,
    Holding revel of worms in a corse;
    A city of malady sore,
    Over-ripe for the big doom's crack: 300
    A city of hymnical snore;
    Connubial truths and lies
    Demanding an instant divorce,
    Clean as the bright from the black.
It were well for thy system to sermonize.
There are giants to slay, and they call for their Jack.

        Then up stand thou in the midst:
        Thy good grain out of thee thresh,
        Hand upon heart: relate
        What things thou legally didst   310
        For the Archseducer of flesh.

Omitting the murmurs at women and fate,
    Confess thee an instrument armed
    To be snare of our wanton, our weak,
    Of all by the sensual charmed.
For once shall repentance be done by the tongue:
    Speak, though execrate, speak
    A word on grandmotherly Laws
    Giving rivers of gold to our young,
    In the days of their hungers impure;   320
    To furnish them beak and claws,
    And make them a banquet's lure.

    Thou the example, saved
Miraculously by this poor skin!
    Thereat let the Purse be waved:
The snake-slough sick of the snaky sin:
A devil, if devil as devil behaved
Ever, thou knowest, look thou but in,
Where he shivers, a culprit fettered and shaved;
O a bird stripped of feather, a fish clipped of fin!   330

And commend for a washing the torrents of wrath,
Which hurl at the foe of the dearest men prize,
    Rough-rolling boulders and froth.
Gigantical enginery they can command,
For the crushing of enemies not of great size:
    But hold to thy desperate stand.
Men's right of bequeathing their all to their own
(With little regard for the creatures they squeezed);
Their mill and mill-water and nether mill-stone
Tied fast to their infant; lo, this is the last   340
Of their hungers, by prudent devices appeased.
The law they decree is their ultimate slave;
Wherein we perceive old Voracity glassed.
It works from their dust, and it reeks of their grave.
Point them to greener, though Journals be guns;
To brotherly fields under fatherly skies;

Where the savage still primitive learns of a debt
He has owed since he drummed on his belly for war;
And how for his giving, the more will he get;
For trusting his fellows, leave friends round his sons: 350
Till they see, with the gape of a startled surprise,
Their adored tyrant-monster a brute to abhor,
The sun of their system a father of flies!

So, for such good hope, take their scourge unashamed;
'Tis the portion of them who civilize,
    Who speak the word novel and true:
How the brutish antique of our springs may be tamed,
Without loss of the strength that should push us to flower;
How the God of old time will act Satan of new,
If we keep him not straight at the higher God aimed;   360
For whose habitation within us we scour
This house of our life; where our bitterest pains
Are those to eject the Infernal, who heaps
Mire on the soul. Take stripes or chains;
    Grip at thy standard reviled.
And what if our body be dashed from the steeps?
    Our spoken in protest remains.
    A young generation reaps.

The young generation! ah, there is the child
Of our souls down the Ages! to bleed for it, proof   370
That souls we have, with our senses filed,
    Our shuttles at thread of the woof.
    May it be braver than ours,
To encounter the rattle of hostile bolts,
To look on the rising of Stranger Powers.
May it know how the mind in expansion revolts
From a nursery Past with dead letters aloof,
And the piping to stupor of Precedents shun,
In a field where the forefather print of the hoof
Is not yet overgrassed by the watering hours,   380
And should prompt us to Change, as to promise of sun,
    Till brain-rule splendidly towers.

For that large light we have laboured and tramped
Thorough forests and bogland, still to perceive
    Our animate morning stamped
    With the lines of a sombre eve.

A timorous thing ran the innocent hind,
When the wolf was the hypocrite fang under hood,
    The snake a lithe lurker up sleeve,
    And the lion effulgently ramped.   390
Then our forefather hoof did its work in the wood,
    By right of the better in kind.
But now will it breed yon bestial brood
Three-fold thrice over, if bent to bind,
    As the healthy in chains with the sick,
Unto despot usage our issuing mind.
It signifies battle or death's dull knell.

Precedents icily written on high,
Challenge the Tentatives hot to rebel.
Our Mother, who speeds her bloomful quick   400
For the march, reads which the impediment well.
She smiles when of sapience is their boast.
O loose of the tug between blood run dry
And blood running flame may our offspring run!
May brain democratic be king of the host!
Less then shall the volumes of History tell
Of the step in progression, the slip in relapse,
That counts us a sand-slack inch hard won
Beneath an oppressive incumbent perhaps.

Let the senile lords in a parchment sky,   410
And the generous turbulents drunken of morn,
    Their battle of instincts put by,
    A moment examine this field:
On a Roman street cast thoughtful eye,
Along to the mounts from the bog-forest weald.
It merits a glance at our history's maps,
To see across Britain's old shaggy unshorn,

Through the Parties in strife internecine, foot
The ruler's close-reckoned direct to the mark.
From the head ran the vanquisher's orderly route,   420
In the stride of his forts through the tangle and dark.
From the head runs the paved firm way for advance,
And we shoulder, we wrangle! The light on us shed,
Shows dense beetle blackness in swarm, lurid Chance,
The Goddess of gamblers, above. From the head,
Then when it worked for the birth of a star
Fraternal with heaven's in beauty and ray,
Sprang the Acropolis. Ask what crown
Comes of our tides of the blood at war,
For men to bequeath generations down!   430
And ask what thou wast when the Purse was brimmed:
What high-bounding ball for the Gods at play:
A Conservative youth! who the cream-bowl skimmed,
Desiring affairs to be left as they are.

So, thou takest Youth's natural place in the fray,
    As a Tentative, combating Peace,
    Our lullaby word for decay.—
    There will come an immediate decree
In thy mind for the opposite party's decease,
    If he bends not an instant knee.   440
Expunge it: extinguishing counts poor gain.
    And accept a mild word of police:—
    Be mannerly, measured; refrain
From the puffings of him of the bagpipe cheeks.
Our political, even as the merchant main,
    A temperate gale requires
    For the ship that haven seeks;
Neither God of the winds nor his bellowsy squires.

    Then observe the antagonist, con
His reasons for rocking the lullaby word.   450
You stand on a different stage of the stairs.
He fought certain battles, yon senile lord.

In the strength of thee, feel his bequest to his heirs.
We are now on his inches of ground hard won,
For a perch to a flight o'er his resting fence.

Does it knock too hard at thy head if I say,
    That Time is both father and son?
Tough lesson, when senses are floods over sense!—
    Discern the paternal of Now
    As the Then of thy present tense.   460
    You may pull as you will either way,
    You can never be other than one.
    So, be filial. Giants to slay,
    Demand knowing eyes in their Jack.
There are those whom we push from the path with respect.
Bow to that elder, though seeing him bow
To the backward as well, for a thunderous back
Upon thee. In his days he was not all wrong.
Unto some foundered zenith he strove, and was wrecked.
He scrambled to shore with a worship of shore.   470
The Future he sees as the slippery murk;
The Past as his doctrinal library lore.
He stands now the rock to the wave's wild wash.
Yet thy lumpish antagonist once did work
    Heroical, one of our strong.
His gold to retain and his dross reject,
Engage him, but humour, not aiming to quash.
    Detest the dead squat of the Turk,
    And suffice it to move him along.

    Drink of faith in the brains a full draught   480
    Before the oration: beware
    Lest rhetoric moonily waft
    Whither horrid activities snare.
    Rhetoric, juice for the mob
    Despising more luminous grape,
    Oft at its fount has it laughed
    In the cataracts rolling for rape
    Of a Reason left single to sob!

'Tis known how the permanent never is writ
In blood of the passions: mercurial they,   490
Shifty their issue: stir not that pit
    To the game our brutes best play.

But with rhetoric loose, can we check man's brute?
Assemblies of men on their legs invoke
Excitement for wholesome diversion: there shoot
Electrical sparks between their dry thatch
And thy waved torch, more to kindle than light.
'Tis instant between you: the trick of a catch
    (To match a Batrachian croak)
Will thump them a frenzy or fun in their veins.   500
Then may it be rather the well-worn joke
Thou repeatest, to stop conflagration, and write
Penance for rhetoric. Strange will it seem,
When thou readest that form of thy homage to brains!

    For the secret why demagogues fail,
Though they carry hot mobs to the red extreme,
    And knock out or knock in the nail
    (We will rank them as flatly sincere,
    Devoutly detesting a wrong,
Engines o'ercharged with our human steam),   510
Question thee, seething amid the throng.
And ask, whether Wisdom is born of blood-heat;
Or of other than Wisdom comes victory here;—
Aught more than the banquet and roundelay,
That is closed with a terrible terminal wail,
    A retributive black ding-dong?
And ask of thyself: This furious Yea
    Of a speech I thump to repeat,
    In the cause I would have prevail,
    For seed of a nourishing wheat,   520
    Is it accepted of Song?
    Does it sound to the mind through the ear,
Right sober, pure sane? has it disciplined feet?
    Thou wilt find it a test severe;

Unerring whatever the theme.
Rings it for Reason a melody clear,
   We have bidden old Chaos retreat;
   We have called on Creation to hear;
All forces that make us are one full stream.

Simple islander! thus may the spirit in verse,   530
Showing its practical value and weight,
Pipe to thee clear from the Empty Purse,
Lead thee aloft to that high estate.—
   The test is conclusive, I deem:
   It embraces or mortally bites.
   We have then the key-note for debate:
   A Senate that sits on the heights
   Over discords, to shape and amend.

   And no singer is needed to serve
   The musical God, my friend.   540
Needs only his law on a sensible nerve:
A law that to Measure invites,
   Forbidding the passions contend.

   Is it accepted of Song?
   And if then the blunt answer be Nay,
Dislink thee sharp from the ramping horde,
Slaves of the Goddess of hoar-old sway,
   The Queen of delirous rites,
Queen of those issueless mobs, that rend
For frenzy the strings of a fruitful accord,   550
Pursuing insensate, seething in throng,
Their wild idea to its ashen end.
Off to their Phrygia, shriek and gong,
Shorn from their fellows, behold them wend!

   But thou, should the answer ring Ay,
   Hast warrant of seed for thy word:
   The musical God is nigh
To inspirit and temper, tune it, and steer
   Through the shoals: is it worthy of Song,

There are souls all woman to hear,   560
Woman to bear and renew.
For he is the Master of Measure, and weighs,
    Broad as the arms of his blue,
    Fine as the web of his rays,
Justice, whose voice is a melody clear,
The one sure life for the numbered long.
    From him are the brutal and vain,
    The vile, the excessive, out-thrust:
He points to the God on the upmost throne:
    He is the saver of grain,   570
    The sifter of spirit from dust.
He, Harmony, tells how to Measure pertain
    The virilities: Measure alone
    Has votaries rich in the male:
    Fathers embracing no cloud,
    Sowing no harvestless main:
Alike by the flesh and the spirit endowed
To create, to perpetuate; woo, win, wed;
Send progeny streaming, have earth for their own,
Over-run the insensates, disperse with a puff   580
    Simulacra, though solid they sail,
    And seem such imperial stuff:
    Yes, the living divide off the dead.

    Then thou with thy furies outgrown,
Not as Cybele's beast will thy head lash tail
So præter-determinedly thermonous,
    Nor thy cause be an Attis far fled.
    Thou under stress of the strife,
    Shalt hear for sustainment supreme,
    The cry of the conscience of Life: 590
    Keep the young generations in hail,
    And bequeath them no tumbled house!

    There hast thou the sacred theme,
    Therein the inveterate spur,
    Of the Innermost. See her one blink

In vision past eyeballs. Not thee
She cares for, but us. Follow her.
Follow her, and thou wilt not sink.
With thy soul the Life espouse:
This Life of the visible, audible, ring   600
With thy love tight about; and no death will be;
    The name be an empty thing,
    And woe a forgotten old trick:
And battle will come as a challenge to drink;
As a warrior's wound each transient sting.
She leads to the Uppermost link by link;
Exacts but vision, desires not vows.
Above us the singular number to see;
The plural warm round us; ourself in the thick,
A dot or a stop: that is our task;   610
Her lesson in figured arithmetic,
For the letters of Life behind its mask;
Her flower-like look under fearful brows.

As for thy special case, O my friend, one must think
Massilia's victim, who held the carouse
    For the length of a carnival year,
Knew worse: but the wretch had his opening choice.
For thee, by our law, no alternatives were:
Thy fall was assured ere thou camest to a voice.

He cancelled the ravaging Plague,   620
With the roll of his fat off the cliff.
Do thou with thy lean as the weapon of ink,
Though they call thee an angler who fishes the vague
    And catches the not too pink,
Attack one as murderous, knowing thy cause
Is the cause of community. Iterate,
Iterate, iterate, harp on the trite:
Our preacher to win is the supple in stiff:
Yet always in measure, with bearing polite:
The manner of one that would expiate   630

His share in grandmotherly Laws,
Which do the dark thing to destroy,
Under aspect of water so guilelessly white
For the general use, by the devils befouled.

Enough, poor prodigal boy!
Thou hast listened with patience; another had howled.
Repentance is proved, forgiveness is earned.
And 'tis bony: denied thee thy succulent half
Of the parable's blessing to swineherd returned:
A Sermon thy slice of the Scriptural calf!   640

By my faith, there is feasting to come,
Not the less, when our Earth we have seen
Beneath and on surface, her deeds and designs:
Who gives us the man-loving Nazarene,
The martyrs, the poets, the corn and the vines.
By my faith in the head, she has wonders in loom;
Revelations, delights. I can hear a faint crow
Of the cock of fresh mornings, far, far, yet distinct;
    As down the new shafting of mines,
    A cry of the metally gnome.   650
    When our Earth we have seen, and have linked
With the home of the Spirit to whom we unfold,
Imprisoned humanity open will throw
Its fortress gates, and the rivers of gold
    For the congregate friendliness flow.
Then the meaning of Earth in her children behold:
Glad eyes, frank hands, and a fellowship real:
And laughter on lips, as the birds' outburst
At the flooding of light. No robbery then
The feast, nor a robber's abode the home,   660
For a furnished model of our first den!
    Nor Life as a stationed wheel;
Nor History written in blood or in foam,
For vendetta of Parties in cursing accursed.

The God in the conscience of multitudes feel,
    And we feel deep to Earth at her heart,
    We have her communion with men,
    New ground, new skies for appeal.
Yield into harness thy best and thy worst;
Away on the trot of thy servitude start,   670
Through the rigours and joys and sustainments of air.
If courage should falter, 'tis wholesome to kneel.
Remember that well, for the secret with some,
Who pray for no gift, but have cleansing in prayer,
And free from impurities tower-like stand.
I promise not more, save that feasting will come
To a mind and a body no longer inversed:
The sense of large charity over the land,
Earth's wheaten of wisdom dispensed in the rough,
And a bell ringing thanks for a sustenance meal   680
    Through the active machine: lean fare,
But it carries a sparkle! And now enough,
    And part we as comrades part,
To meet again never or some day or soon.

Our season of drought is reminder rude:—
    No later than yesternoon,
    I looked on the horse of a cart,
    By the wayside water-trough.
How at every draught of his bride of thirst
His nostrils widened! The sight was good: 690
    Food for us, food, such as first
    Drew our thoughts to earth's lowly for food.

Jump-to-Glory Jane

The first mention of this poem is on July 29, 1889. On that date GM wrote to William Sharp ("Fiona Macleod") that if some editor made application for the poem he should have it. "It being understood that the work is to be approved before acceptance, I never take offence at an Editor's refusal." The poem was quickly accepted by Harry Quilter for the *Universal Review*. On August 15, 1889, GM wrote Quilter about the possibility of its being illustrated by Linley Sambourne: "Sambourne is excellent for Punch, he might hit the mean. Whoever does it should be warned against giving burlesque outlines. It is a grave narration of events in English country (?life) [*sic*]. Jane, though a jumping, is a thoughtful woman. She has discovered that the circulation of the blood is best brought about by a continual exercise, and conduces to happy sensations, which are to her as the being of angels in her frame. She has wistful eyes in a touching, but bony face."

Sambourne could not do the drawing, and neither could Bernard Partridge, so the poem went into the *Universal Review* unillustrated. No sooner had the poem appeared in the *Review* than it was pirated in an issue of fifty copies, "privately printed for friends." Three years later, on November 15, 1892, GM wrote that he had never seen this leaflet: "Of course it is piratical; whether issued by a lunatic or a profoundly speculative Yankee, I cannot decide. 'Printed for friends only' is very amusing. The reason why a poem of a writer whose verse is not popular should have been selected for fraudulent publication is not clearly seen. I trust all is right concerning it" (MBF, pp. 87–88).

Another piracy of a kind was committed by Harry Quilter himself. Disappointed in his hopes of having the poem illustrated for the *Universal Review*, he secured the services of Laurence Housman and produced an elegant little book in October 1892, the same month that the poem appeared in the volume, *The Empty Purse*. GM was annoyed by this venture, but allowed Quilter to go through with it, as he wrote to Norman MacColl, editor of the *Athenaeum*, on September 28, 1892, "for the sake of peace." In this letter he summarized the poem: "The poem is called, 'Jump-to-Glory Jane,' who founds in our advanced community a sect inflated by the idea that by jumping high and high we take the best way for getting to

Previously printed in the Universal Review *5 (15 October 1889); piratically printed 1889; published with introductory notes by Harry Quilter and forty-four designs by Lawrence [sic] Housman 1892. MSS: Robert L. Taylor. MS 1, working draft, stanzas XXXIV–XXXVI missing; frag. B, single leaf numbered 13 from another draft, stanzas XXVIII.5–XXX.4, XXXI, numbered xxix, xxx, xxx (sic). Yale. MS 2, fair copy; frag. A, early draft, incomplete, stanzas unnumbered, title: "Jane the Jumper"; frag. C, single leaf numbered 13, stanza XXXIV numbered xxxv, XXXV–XXXVI unnumbered. Frag. C at Yale is apparently the last leaf of MS 1 in Mr. Taylor's possession.*

HIM; and so they go across country, until she meets a Bishop, who is in his blindness about to bless the wicked meats and drinks of his friend the squire's feast to tenants. She and thirty of her followers jump at him to convert him. She fails and dies, of a broken heart, some think, but it is hardly possible to know, as the jumpers do not speak."

An earlier letter to Quilter (September 10, 1889) clearly indicates the inspiration of the poem: "Yes, they are a Satire, but one of the pictures of our England as well. Remember Mrs. Girling and her following, and the sensations of Jane with her blood at the spin with activity, warranted her feeling of exaltation." Mrs. Mary Anne (Clouting) Girling (1827–86) was a religious fanatic, who believed herself an incarnation of the deity and acquired stigmata on her hands, feet, and side. (GM's humble Jane had no such illusions.) Mrs. Girling's followers called themselves "Children of God," though they were publicly and erroneously known as "Shakers." Laurence Housman's novel *The Sheepfold* (1918) was based on Mrs. Girling and her band, and his illustrations in *Jump-to-Glory Jane* well reflect what is known of them. The chief resemblances between them and GM's Jane and her followers are the austerity of their lives and their habit of dancing. There is an interesting account of the "Children of God" in a paper by T. A. Wylie, read before the Milford-on-Sea Record Society on October 18, 1926. Wylie reported that they were nick-named "Shakers," "because of their habit of dancing when moved by the Spirit of God in their religious services. . . . Chiefly with a view to economy and partly to avoid giving rise to . . . feelings of jealously [*sic*] . . . , Mrs. Girling required all the women to dress alike on Sundays in simply made white dresses, and the girls wore their hair hanging down their backs. . . . This gave them a rather fantastic appearance when singing and dancing. . . ." An old woman who had been an early follower of Mrs. Girling became so excited when telling Wylie about her youthful experiences that she "jumped out of her arm-chair and commenced to show me how they danced when moved by 'the Holy Spirit'" (*Milford-on-Sea Record Society*, 5:29, 36).

I

A revelation came on Jane,
The widow of a labouring swain:
And first her body trembled sharp,
Then all the woman was a harp
With winds along the strings; she heard,
Though there was neither tone nor word.

I.4 Then all the woman was] And then her soul was like *frag. A*
I.6 *frag. A del.:* And knew, though there was never *or* not a word.

II

For past our hearing was the air,
Beyond our speaking what it bare,
And she within herself had sight
Of heaven at work to cleanse outright,
To make of her a mansion fit
For angel hosts inside to sit.

III

They entered, and forthwith entranced,
Her body braced, her members danced;
Surprisingly the woman leapt;
And countenance composed she kept;
As gossip neighbours in the lane
Declared, who saw and pitied Jane.

IV

These knew she had been reading books,
The which was witnessed by her looks
Of late: she had a mania
For mad folk in America,
And said for sure they led the way,
But meat and beer were meant to stay.

V

That she had visited a fair,
Had seen a gauzy lady there,
Alive with tricks on legs alone,

II.1 our] the *del. frag. A*   the] that *frag. A*
II.2 Beyond our] And past the *del. frag. A*
II.3 And] But *or* And *frag. A*
II.5 To] And *del. frag. A*
II.6 *frag. A:* For angels to inhabit it *or* For angel hosts inside to sit
III.2 braced] swayed *frag. A, MS 1*
III.6 Declared] Affirmed *del. frag. A*
V.2 Had] And *or* Had *frag. A*   gauzy] spangled *frag. A, MS 1*
V.3 Alive with tricks on] Who did her tricks with *frag. A, MS 1*

As good as wings, was also known:
And longwhiles in a sullen mood,
Before her jumping, Jane would brood.

VI

A good knee's height, they say, she sprang;
Her arms and feet like those who hang:
As if afire the body sped,
And neither pair contributed.
She jumped in silence: she was thought
A corpse to resurrection caught.

VII

The villagers were mostly dazed;
They jeered, they wondered, and they praised.
'Twas guessed by some she was inspired,
And some would have it she had hired
An engine in her petticoats,
To turn their wits and win their votes.

V.4–6 *frag. A:*

> Resembling wings, was likewise known:
> And often in a pensive fit,
> Until her jumping Jane would sit.

V.4 also] likewise *del. MS 1*
V.5 longwhiles] often *del. MS 1*   sullen] sulky *MS 1*

Stanzas VI–IX not in frag. A

VI.1 *MS 1:* By measurement three feet she sprang, *or* Three feet, they say, the woman sprang
VI.2 Her arms and feet] With hands & legs *or* And at her ease, *MS 1*
VI.3–6 *MS 1:*

> Or decent for the coffin set: *or* grave are set:
> And in her second week she met
> Old Gaffer Green, that home did hop,
> *Del.:* Like Jane herself, & scarce could stop.
> Oft calling on himself to stop [.]

Stanza VII not in MS 1

VIII

Her first was Winny Earnes, a kind
Of woman not to dance inclined;
But she went up, entirely won,
Ere Jump-to-glory Jane had done;
And once a vixen wild for speech,
She found the better way to preach.

IX

No long time after, Jane was seen
Directing jumps at Daddy Green;
And that old man, to watch her fly,
Had eyebrows made of arches high;
Till homeward he likewise did hop,
Oft calling on himself to stop!

X

It was a scene when man and maid,
Abandoning all other trade,
And careless of the call to meals,
Went jumping at the woman's heels.
By dozens they were counted soon,
Without a sound to tell their tune.

XI

Along the roads they came, and crossed
The fields, and o'er the hills were lost,
And in the evening reappeared;

VIII.1 Her first] The next *MS 1*   Winny] Biddy *MS 1*
VIII.5 vixen] creature *MS 1*
Stanza IX; cf. stanza VI, MS 1
Stanza X, stanza vii, MS 1
X.1 scene] sight *frag. A*
Stanza XI, also numbered vii, MS 1
XI.2 hills] hill *frag. A*

Then short like hobbled horses reared,
And down upon the grass they plumped:
Alone their Jane to glory jumped.

XII

At morn they rose, to see her spring
All going as an engine thing;
And lighter than the gossamer
She led the bobbers following her,
Past old acquaintances, and where
They made the stranger stupid stare.

XIII

When turnips were a filling crop,
In scorn they jumped a butcher's shop:
Or, spite of threats to flog and souse,
They jumped for shame a public-house:
And much their legs were seized with rage
If passing by the vicarage.

XIV

The tightness of a hempen rope
Their bodies got; but laundry soap
Not handsomer can rub the skin

XI.4 Then] And *or* Then *MS 1*   like] as *del. frag. A*
XI.5 And] Till *frag. A, MS 1*
XI.6 *frag. A:* And only Jane, their leader, jumped.   And only] While none but *MS 1*

Stanza XII, stanza viii, MS 1

XII.2 All going] Unwearied *frag. A, MS 1*
XII.4 bobbers] dancers *frag. A*

Stanza XIII, stanza ix, MS 1

XIII.1–2 *reverse order, corrected frag. A*
XIII.1 *frag. A:* When turnips did their empty stop:
XIII.2 In scorn they jumped] Sometimes they danced *frag. A*; They jumped to scorn *del.*
MS 1
XIII.4 jumped for] danced to *frag. A*

Stanza XIV after XVI, frag. A; Stanza XIV, stanza x, MS 1

XIV.1 tightness] leanness *frag. A, MS 1*
XIV.3 rub] make *frag. A*; wash *del. MS 2*

For token of the washed within.
Occasionally coughers cast
A leg aloft and coughed their last.

XV

The weaker maids and some old men,
Requiring rafters for the pen
On rainy nights, were those who fell.
The rest were quite a miracle,
Refreshed as you may search all round
On Club-feast days and cry, Not found!

XVI

For these poor innocents, that slept
Against the sky, soft women wept:
For never did they any theft;
'Twas known when they their camping left,
And jumped the cold out of their rags;
In spirit rich as money-bags.

XVII

They jumped the question, jumped reply;
And whether to insist, deny,
Reprove, persuade, they jumped in ranks

XIV.4 For] In *frag. A*
XIV.5 Occasionally] Though there were many *frag. A*; Yet many were the *or*
Occasionally *MS 1*

Stanza XV, stanza xi, MS 1

XV.2 Requiring rafters for] Who needed rafters o'er *frag. A*
XV.3 rainy] frosty *frag. A*
XV.4 quite] like *frag. A*
XV.6 days and cry] day, & say *frag. A*; days & say *MS 1*

Stanza XVI after XIII, frag. A; stanza xii, MS 1

XVI.1 that] who *frag. A*
XVI.5 jumped] danced *frag. A*

Stanza XVII, stanza xiii, MS 1

XVII.1 *frag. A:* They danced their question, danced reply,
XVII.2 insist] assert *frag. A*
XVII.3 jumped] danced *frag. A*

Or singly, straight the arms to flanks,
And straight the legs, with just a knee
For bending in a mild degree.

XVIII

The villagers might call them mad;
An endless holiday they had,
Of pleasure in a serious work:
They taught by leaps where perils lurk,
And with the lambkins practised sports
For 'scaping Satan's pounds and quarts.

XIX

It really seemed on certain days,
When they bobbed up their Lord to praise,
And bobbing up they caught the glance
Of light, our secret is to dance,
And hold the tongue from hindering peace;
To dance out preacher and police.

XX

Those flies of boys disturbed them sore
On Sundays and when daylight wore:
With withies cut from hedge or copse,

XVII.5 just a] merely *frag. A*

Stanza XVIII, stanza xiv, MS 1

XVIII.3 serious work] business high *frag. A, MS 1*
XVIII.4 by leaps where perils lurk] in leaps the way we fly *frag. A, MS 1*   where] when
UR

Stanza XIX, stanza xv, MS 1

XIX.2 bobbed up] went forth *del. frag. A*
XIX.5 hold] keep *frag. A*

Between stanzas XIX and XX, frag. A:

> Now Jane, whom many took for mad *or* crazed,
> A face of such composure had,
> With gentle eyes, that shot a spark
> When she went springing to the lark

Stanza XX, stanza xvi, MS 1

XX.1 disturbed] pursued *frag. A*; pursued *del.* assailed *MS 1*
XX.3–4 *reverse order frag. A; reverse order, corr. MS 1*
XX.3 cut] plucked *frag. A*

They treated them as whipping-tops,
And flung big stones with cruel aim;
Yet all the flock jumped on the same.

XXI

For what could persecution do
To worry such a blessed crew,
On whom it was as wind to fire,
Which set them always jumping higher?
The parson and the lawyer tried,
By meek persistency defied.

XXII

But if they bore, they could pursue
As well, and this the Bishop too;
When inner warnings proved him plain
The chase for Jump-to-glory Jane.
She knew it by his being sent
To bless the feasting in the tent.

XXIII

Not less than fifty years on end,
The Squire had been the Bishop's friend:
And his poor tenants, harmless ones,

XX.4 They] And *frag. A*   as] like *frag. A*
XX.5 And] They *frag. A*
XX.6 Yet all the flock] But all the troop *frag. A, MS 1*

Stanza XXI, stanza xvii, MS 1

XXI.5 and the] & the *del.* squire, & *del. MS 1*
XXI.6 By meek persistency] To hunt them down, & were *del. MS 1*

Stanza XXII, stanza xviii, MS 1

XXII.1–2 *MS 1 del.:*

> A line of thirty at her heels
> Who never knew the hour for meals,

XXII.1 But if they bore] If they could bear *or* But if they bore *MS 1*
XXII.3 inner warnings proved] private warnings [made *del.*] showed *del. MS 1*
XXII.5 She] Who *del. MS 1*

Stanza XXIII, stanza xix, MS 1

XXIII.1 *MS 1:* For fifteen dozen it was laid.   fifty] sixty *MS 2*

With souls to save! fed not on buns,
But angry meats: she took her place
Outside to show the way to grace.

XXIV

In apron suit the Bishop stood;
The crowding people kindly viewed.
A gaunt grey woman he saw rise
On air, with most beseeching eyes:
And evident as light in dark
It was, she set to him for mark.

XXV

Her highest leap had come: with ease
She jumped to reach the Bishop's knees:
Compressing tight her arms and lips,
 She sought to jump the Bishop's hips:
Her aim flew at his apron-band,
That he might see and understand.

XXIII.2–4 *MS 1:*

> The squire's dear daughter he had made
> A wife with [holy words, & sweet *del.*] words of binding sweet:
> The people next to beer & meat.

XXIII.5 But angry meats:] Outside the tent *MS 1*
XXIII.6 Outside to show the way] To show him shorter cuts *MS 1*

Stanza XXIV, stanza xx, MS 1

XXIV.1 *MS 1 del.:* The Bishop stood in apron suit;
XXIV.2 *MS 1 del.:* He saw the jumper[s *del.*] jumping mute *or* And kindly wise the crow
[*sic*]   crowding people] outside crowders *MS 1*
XXIV.3 *MS 1:* He saw a grey gaunt woman rise *or* A grey gaunt woman he saw rise
XXIV.4 On air, with] With soft & *MS 1*

Stanza XXV, stanza xxi, MS 1

XXV.1 Her highest leap] Occasion now *MS 1*
XXV.4 sought to jump] jumped to nigh *MS 1*
XXV.5–6 *reverse order corr. MS 1*
XXV.5 Her aim flew at] She almost jumped *MS 1*

XXVI

The mild inquiry of his gaze
Was altered to a peaked amaze,
At sight of thirty in ascent;
To gain his notice clearly bent:
And greatly Jane at heart was vexed
By his ploughed look of mind perplexed.

XXVII

In jumps that said, Beware the pit!
More eloquent than speaking it—
That said, Avoid the boiled, the roast;
The heated nose on face of ghost,
Which comes of drinking: up and o'er
The flesh with me! did Jane implore.

XXVIII

She jumped him high as huntsmen go
Across the gate; she jumped him low,
To coax him to begin and feel

Stanza XXVI, stanza xxii, MS 1

XXVI.1–3 *MS 1 del.:*

> His gaze of mild inquiry vexed *or* He gazed around
> Her fiery zeal
> The sweat was pouring from her skin

XXVI.3 in ascent;] on the strain *MS 1*
XXVI.4 *MS 1:* To spring with Jump-to-Glory Jane;
XXVI.5 *MS 1:* [And much his look of mind perplexed, *del.*] And much her hope to win
was vexed   Jane at heart was] was her spirit *MS 2*
XXVI.6 *MS 1 del.:* Her hunger to convert him vexed.

Stanza XXVII, stanza xxiii, MS 1

XXVII.4 *MS 1 del.:* The devil's draught, for making[?] toast[?];—   heated] ruddy
del. lobster *del.* hot[?] red *del.* angry *del. MS 1*
XXVII.5 *MS 1 del.:* And up with me, all sinners oer,   Which] That *MS 1*   of] of
del. from *MS 1*
XXVII.6 The flesh with me] With me to bliss *del. MS 1*

Stanza XXVIII, stanza xxiv, MS 1

XXVIII.1 *MS 1:* She jumped him fast to make him feel *or* She jumped him fast, she
jumped him slow
XXVIII.2 *MS 1:* And cast his earthly pride as peel *or* She jumped him high as huntsmen
go

His infant steps returning, peel
His mortal pride, exposing fruit,
And off with hat and apron suit.

XXIX

We need much patience, well she knew,
And out and out, and through and through,
When we would gentlefolk address,
However we may seek to bless:
At times they hide them like the beasts
From sacred beams; and mostly priests.

XXX

He gave no sign of making bare,
Nor she of faintness or despair.
Inflamed with hope that she might win,

XXVIII.3–4 *MS 1:*

> Across the gate, that he might feel
> And strip his mortal pride as peel

XXVIII.5–6 *MS 1 del.:*

> Throw off the fruit; *or* Exposing fruit
> To reason with his *or* To wean him from the love of show:
> And high she jumped his mortal fat
> From [apron, gaiters *del.*] gaiters apron, tie & hat.

XXVIII *MS 1, margin:*

> Her meaning was, that he should heave
> His darkness off, & her perceive,

XXVIII *MS 1, interlinear: final version of stanza*

Stanza XXIX, stanza xxx, MS 1; numbering jumps from xxiv to xxx

XXIX.1–2, 4–3 reverse order, corrected MS 1

XXIX.1 need much] must have *MS 1*
XXIX.3 we would gentlefolk] gentlefolk we would *frag. B*
XXIX.3–4 *reverse order MS 1*
XXIX.5–6 *MS 1:*

> For they are thicker than the beasts
> To signs *or* glimpse of light: and woe for *or* chiefly priests!

XXIX.6 sacred] holy light *del.* holy beams *frag. B*

Stanza XXX, stanza xxxi, MS 1; xxx, frag. B

XXX.1 *MS 1, del.:* Her passion with her patience   He gave no sign] No sign [he gave *del.*] gave he *MS 1*; No sign gave he *frag. B*
XXX.2 faintness] weakness *del. MS 1*
XXX.3 *MS 1 del.:* But burning with the hope to win   hope] thoughts *MS 1*   that she might] that prize to *del. frag. B*

If she but coaxed him to begin,
She used all arts for making fain;
The mother with her babe was Jane.

XXXI

Now stamped the Squire, and knowing not
Her business, waved her from the spot.
Encircled by the men of might,
The head of Jane, like flickering light,
As in a charger, they beheld
Ere she was from the park expelled.

XXXII

Her grief, in jumps of earthly weight,
Did Jane around communicate:
For that the moment when began
The holy but mistaken man,
In view of light, to take his lift,
They cut him from her charm adrift!

XXX.4 she but coaxed] she might coax *del.* once she coaxed *MS 1*; once she coaxed
frag. B
XXX.5–6 *MS 1:*

> In Jane the mother & the more
> Than Earthly bade her still implore.

Stanza XXXI, stanza xxxii, MS 1; xxx [sic], *frag. B*
XXXI.1–2 *MS 1:*

> The squire he waved her from the spot;
> Her urgent business he knew not.

XXXI.1 Now stamped the Squire] The Squire he stamped *frag. B*
XXXI.3–4 *reverse order, frag. B*
XXXI.4 The head of Jane] [The *del.*] Her jumping head *MS 1*
XXXI.5 They saw *del. MS 1*   charger] salver *MS 1, frag. B*
XXXI.6 expelled] excpelled *MS 1*

Stanza XXXII, stanza xxxiii, MS 1
XXXII.1–2 *MS 1:*

> Her grief, though without *or* with not a word to say,
> Did Jane unto her friends convey:

XXXII.5 In view of light] To see the light *del. MS 1*
XXXII.6 *MS 1:* They snapped her charm & let him drift.

XXXIII

And he was lost: a banished face
For ever from the ways of grace,
Unless pinched hard by dreams in fright.
They saw the Bishop's wavering sprite
Within her look, at come and go,
Long after he had caused her woe.

XXXIV

Her greying eyes (until she sank
At Fredsham on the wayside bank,
Like cinder heaps that whitened lie
From coals that shot the flame to sky)
Had glassy vacancies, which yearned
For one in memory discerned.

Stanza XXXIII, stanza xxxiv, MS 1

XXXIII.1–3 *MS 1 del.:*

> [The *del.*] A rumour that she saw him move
> The leg which doth adhesion prove,
> Past wavering

XXXIII.3 *MS 1:* So near to it, [in view of *del.*] beneath its light!
XXXIII.4 They saw] She held *MS 1*
XXXIII.6 her] that *MS 1*
XXXIV.1 *frag. C:* Her eyes (until she jumped & sank
XXXIV.2 on] by *frag. C*
XXXIV.3 *frag. C:* [As white as pearls *del.*] reserved the seat   *Del.:* And lay like whitened cinder heaps) Like some white cinders kept the seat *or* like cinderheaps and whitened lie,
XXXIV.4 *frag. C:* For him she hoped again to meet. *or* From coals that shoot the flames on high
XXXIV.5 *frag. C del.:* And teach the way, past mortal doubt. They had [a vacancy *del.*] Had longing vacancies, not dim,   *MS 2:* Had longing vacancies that would
XXXIV.6 *frag. C del.:* Was never frame so quite burnt *or* body so burnt out! But throwing beams far out, for him. *MS 2:* Have drawn him to her for his good.

After stanza XXXIV, stanza xxxv, frag. C del.:

> She scarcely ate of turnips now.
> It seemed as if she made a vow
> To conjure him to her

XXXV

May those who ply the tongue that cheats,
And those who rush to beer and meats,
And those whose mean ambition aims
At palaces and titled names,
Depart in such a cheerful strain
As did our Jump-to-glory Jane!

XXXVI

Her end was beautiful: one sigh.
She jumped a foot when it was nigh.
A lily in a linen clout
She looked when they had laid her out.
It is a lily-light she bears
For England up the ladder-stairs.

Odes

To the Comic Spirit

Compare GM's "Essay on the Idea of Comedy and of the Uses of the Comic Spirit," delivered as a lecture at the London Institution on February 1, 1877, printed in the *New Quarterly*, April 1877, and first published in book form (London: Constable) in 1897.

JUMP-TO-GLORY JANE

XXXV.2 rush] fly *del. frag. C*
XXXVI.2–4 *frag. C:*

> So may all good ones hope to die.
> For human ills she had the cure
> If men [?] will prudently abjure

XXXVI.3 *frag. C, MS 2:* Of her salvation ne'er in doubt:
XXXVI.4 *frag. C, MS 2:* The doctor said, she seemed burnt out.
XXXVI.5 *frag. C, MS 2:* But she cast light, 'tis understood,
XXXVI.6 *frag. C:* [May *del.*] That still may do old England good   *MS 2*: By this, may do Old England good.

TO THE COMIC SPIRIT

MSS: Huntington HM 7469, *title: "To the Comic Spirit." MS 1, late draft; MS 2, fair copy for printer.*

Sword of Common Sense!—
Our surest gift: the sacred chain
Of man to man: firm earth for trust
In structures vowed to permanence:—
Thou guardian issue of the harvest brain!
Implacable perforce of just;
With that good treasure in defence,
Which is our gold crushed out of joy and pain
Since first men planted foot and hand was king:
Bright, nimble of the marrow-nerve   10
To wield thy double edge, retort
Or hold the deadlier reserve,
And through thy victim's weapon sting:
Thine is the service, thine the sport
This shifty heart of ours to hunt
Across its webs and round the many a ring
Where fox it is, or snake, or mingled seeds
Occasion heats to shape, or the poor smoke
Struck from a puff-ball, or the troughster's grunt;—
Once lion of our desert's trodden weeds;   20
And but for thy straight finger at the yoke,
Again to be the lordly paw,
Naming his appetites his needs,
Behind a decorative cloak:
Thou, of the highest, the unwritten Law
We read upon that building's architrave
In the mind's firmament, by men upraised
With sweat of blood when they had quitted cave
For fellowship, and rearward looked amazed,
Where the prime motive gapes a lurid jaw,   30
Thou, soul of wakened heads, art armed to warn,
Restrain, lest we backslide on whence we sprang,
Scarce better than our dwarf beginning shoot,
Of every gathered pearl and blossom shorn;

MS 1, p. 1, margin, del.:

Satire [?] to the fevered is thy goal;
Be the self-caressing tearful once allowed [?]

Through thee, in novel wiles to win disguise,
Seen are the pits of the disruptor, seen
His rebel agitation at our root:
Thou hast him out of hawking eyes;
Nor ever morning of the clang
Young Echo sped on hill from horn   40
In forest blown when scent was keen
Off earthy dews besprinkling blades
Of covert grass more merrily rang
The yelp of chase down alleys green,
Forth of the headlong-pouring glades,
Over the dappled fallows wild away,
Than thy fine unaccented scorn
At sight of man's old secret brute,
Devout for pasture on his prey,
Advancing, yawning to devour;   50
With step of deer, with voice of flute,
Haply with visage of the lily flower.

Let the cock crow and ruddy morn
His handmaiden appear! Youth claims his hour.
The generously ludicrous
Espouses it. But see we sons of day,
On whom Life leans for guidance in our fight,
Accept the throb for lord of us;
For lord, for the main central light
That gives direction, not the eclipse;   60
Or dost thou look where niggard Age,
Demanding reverence for wrinkles, whips
A tumbled top to grind a wolf's worn tooth;—
Hoar despot on our final stage,
In dotage of a stunted Youth;—
Or it may be some venerable sage,
Not having thee awake in him, compact
Of wisdom else, the breast's old tempter trips;

67 awake] alive [?] *del. MS 1*

Or see we ceremonial state,
Robing the gilded beast, exact   70
Abjection, while the crackskull name of Fate
Is used to stamp and hallow printed fact;
A cruel corner lengthens up thy lips;
These are thy game wherever men engage:
These and, majestic in a borrowed shape,
The major and the minor potentate,
Creative of their various ape;—
The tiptoe mortals triumphing to write
Upon a perishable page
An inch above their fellows' height;—   80
The criers of foregone wisdom, who impose
Its slough on live conditions, much for the greed
Of our first hungry figure wide agape;—
Call up thy hounds of laughter to their run.
These, that would have men still of men be foes,
Eternal fox to prowl and pike to feed;
Would keep our life the whirly pool
Of turbid stuff dishonouring History;
The herd the drover's herd, the fool the fool,
Ourself our slavish self's infernal sun: 90
These are the children of the heart untaught
By thy quick founts to beat abroad, by thee
Untamed to tone its passions under thought,
The rich humaneness reading in thy fun.
Of them a world of coltish heels for school,
We have; a world with driving wrecks bestrewn.

'Tis written of the Gods of human mould,
Those Nectar Gods, of glorious stature hewn
To quicken hymns, that they did hear incensed,
Satiric comments overbold,   100
From one whose part was by decree
The jester's; but they boiled to feel him bite.

70 Robing] Robeing *MS 1*
81 foregone] past *MS 1, MS 2*

Better for them had they with Reason fenced
Or smiled corrected! They in the great Gods' might,
Their prober crushed, as fingers flea.
Crumbled Olympus when the sovereign sire
His fatal kick to Momus gave, albeit
Men could behold the sacred Mount aspire,
The Satirist pass by on limping feet.
Those Gods who saw the ejected laugh alight   110
Below, had then their last of airy glee;
They in the cup sought Laughter's drownèd sprite,
Fed to dire fatness off uncurbed conceit.
Eyes under saw them waddle on their Mount,
And drew them down; to flattest earth they rolled.
This know we veritable. O Sage of Mirth!
Can it be true, the story men recount
Of the fall'n plight of the great Gods on earth?
How they being deathless, though of human mould,
With human cravings, undecaying frames,   120
Must labour for subsistence; are a band
Whom a loose-cheeked, wide-lipped gay cripple leads
At haunts of holiday on summer sand:
And lightly he will hint to one that heeds,
Names in pained designation of them, names
Ensphered on blue skies and on black, which twirl
Our hearing madly from our seeing dazed,
Add Bacchus unto both; and he entreats
(His baby dimples in maternal chaps
Running wild labyrinths of line and curl)   130
Compassion for his masterful Trombone,
Whose thunder is the brass of how he blazed
Of old: for him of the mountain-muscle feats,
Who guts a drum to fetch a snappish groan:

Between 113 and 114 MS 1 del.:

> Ah, for that woeful shattering kick!
> Their breasts of the thrice-mortal girth.
> Contracted: nought to broaden, none to prick!

122 wide-] long *del. MS 1*
133 Of old] Before *del. MS 1*

For his fierce bugler horning onset, whom
A truncheon-battered helmet caps. . . .
The creature is of earnest mien
To plead a sorrow darker than the tomb.
His Harp and Triangle, in tone subdued,
He names; they are a rayless red and white;   140
The dawn-hued libertine, the gibbous prude.
And, if we recognize his Tambourine,
He asks; exhausted names her: she has become
A globe in cupolas; the blowziest queen
Of overflowing dome on dome;
Redundancy contending with the tight,
Leaping the dam! He fondly calls, his girl,
The buxom tripper with the goblet-smile,
Refreshful. O but now his brows are dun,
Bunched are his lips, as when distilling guile,   150
To drop his venomous: the Dame of dames,
Flower of the world, that honey one,
She of the earthly rose in the sea-pearl,
To whom the world ran ocean for her kiss;
He names her, as a worshipper he names,
And indicates with a contemptuous thumb.
The lady meanwhile lures the mob, alike
Ogles the bursters of the horn and drum.
Curtain her close! her open arms
Have suckers for beholders: she to this?   160
For that she could not, save in fury, hear
A sharp corrective utterance flick
Her idle manners, for the laugh to strike
Beauty so breeding beauty, without peer
Above the snows, among the flowers? She reaps
This mouldy garner of the fatal kick?
Gross with the sacrifice of Circe-swarms,
Astarte of vile sweets that slay, malign,

142 And] Then *del. MS 1*
159 her] those[?] *del. MS 2*

From Greek resplendent to Phoenician foul,
The trader in attractions sinks, all brine   170
To thoughts of taste; is't love?—bark, dog! hoot, owl!
And she is blushless: ancient worship weeps.
Suicide Graces dangle down the charms
Sprawling like gourds on outer garden-heaps.
She stands in her unholy oily leer
A statue losing feature, weather-sick
Mid draggled creepers of twined ivy sere.
The curtain cried for magnifies to see!—
We cannot quench our one corrupting glance:
The vision of the rumour will not flee.   180
Doth the Boy own such Mother?—shoot his dart
To bring her, countless as the crested deeps,
Her subjects of the uncorrected heart?
False is that vision, shrieks the devotee;
Incredible, we echo; and anew
Like a far growling lightning-cloud it leaps.
Low humourist this leader seems; perchance
Pitched from his University career,
Adept at classic fooling. Yet of mould
Human those Gods were: deathless too: 190
On high they not as meditatives paced:
Prodigiously they did the deeds of flesh:
Descending, they would touch the lowest here:
And she, that lighted form of blue and gold,
Whom the seas gave, all earth, all earth embraced;
Exulting in the great hauls of her mesh;
Desired and hated, desperately dear;
Most human of them was. No more pursue!
Enough that the black story can be told.
It preaches to the eminently placed: 200

169 resplendent] irradiate *MS 1, MS 2*
173–78 *MS 1, MS 2, order: 175–78, 173–74*
177 twined ivy sere] sere ivy-twine *del. MS 1*
180 The vision of the rumour] Though be a rumour, brought[?], *del. MS 1*
182 bring] fetch[?] *del. MS 1*
198 No more pursue] Pursue no more *del. MS 1*

For whom disastrous wreckage is nigh due,
Paints omen. Truly they our throbber had;
The passions plumping, passions playing leech,
Cunning to trick us for the day's good cheer.
Our uncorrected human heart will swell
To notions monstrous, doings mad
As billows on a foam-lashed beach;
Borne on the tides of alternating heats,
Will drug the brain, will doom the soul as well;
Call the closed mouth of that harsh final Power   210
To speak in judgement: Nemesis, the fell:
Of those bright Gods assembled, offspring sour;
The last surviving on the upper seats;
As with men Reason when their hearts rebel.

Ah, what a fruitless breeder is this heart,
Full of the mingled seeds, each eating each.
Not wiser of our mark than at the start,
It surges like the wrath-faced father Sea
To countering winds; a force blind-eyed,
On endless rounds of aimless reach;   220
Emotion for the source of pride,
The grounds of faith in fixity
Above our flesh; its cravings urging speech,
Inspiring prayer; by turns a lump
Swung on a time-piece, and by turns
A quivering energy to jump
For seats angelical: it shrinks, it yearns,
Loves, loathes; is flame or cinders; lastly cloud
Capping a sullen crater: and mankind
We see cloud-capped, an army of the dark,   230
Because of thy straight leadership declined;
At heels of this or that delusive spark:

202 omen] warning *del. MS 1*
213 the] their *del. MS 1*
223 urging] urgeing *MS 1*
224 Inspiring] Inspireing *del. MS 1*
228 Loves, loathes] Loathes, loves *del. MS 1*

Now when the multitudinous races press
Elbow to elbow hourly more,
A thickened host; when now we hear aloud
Life for the very life implore
A signal of a visioned mark;
Light of the mind, the mind's discourse,
The rational in graciousness,
Thee by acknowledgement enthroned,   240
To tame and lead that blind-eyed force
In harmony of harness with the crowd,
For payment of their dues; as yet disowned,
Save where some dutiful lone creature, vowed
To holy work, deems it the heart's intent;
Or where a silken circle views it cowled,
The seeming figure of concordance, bent
On satiating tyrant lust
Or barren fits of sentiment.

Thou wilt not have our paths befouled   250
By simulation; are we vile to view,
The heavens shall see us clean of our own dust,
Beneath thy breezy flitting wing:
They make their mirror upon faces true;
And where they win reflection, lucid heave
The under tides of this hot heart seen through.
Beneficently wilt thou clip
All oversteppings of the plumed,
The puffed, and bid the masker strip,
And into the crowned windbag thrust,   260
Tearing the mortal from the vital thing,
A lightning o'er the half-illumed,
Who to base brute-dominion cleave,
Yet mark effects, and shun the flash,
Till their drowsed wits a beam conceive,
To spy a wound without a gash,

239 in] of *del. MS 1*
243 their] its *MS 1, MS 2*

The magic in a turn of wrist,
And how are wedded heart and head regaled
When Wit o'er Folly blows the mort,
And their high note of union spreads   270
Wide from the timely word with conquest charged;
Victorious laughter, of no loud report,
If heard; derision as divinely veiled
As terrible Immortals in rose-mist,
Given to the vision of arrested men:
Whereat they feel within them weave
Community its closer threads,
And are to our fraternal state enlarged;
Like warm fresh blood is their enlivened ken:
They learn that thou art not of alien sort,   280
Speaking the tongue by vipers hissed,
Or of the frosty heights unscaled,
Or of the vain who simple speech distort,
Or of the vapours pointing on to nought
Along cold skies; though sharp and high thy pitch:
As when sole homeward the belated treads,
And hears aloft a clamour wailed,
That once had seemed the broomstick witch
Horridly violating cloud for drought:
He from the rub of minds dispersing fears,   290
Hears migrants marshalling their midnight train;
Homeliest order in black sky appears,
Not less than in the lighted village steads.
So do those half-illumed wax clear to share
A cry that is our common voice; the note
Of fellowship upon a loftier plane,
Above embattled castle-wall and moat;
And toning drops as from pure heaven it sheds.
So thou for washing a phantasmal air,
For thy sweet singing keynote of the wise,   300

283 simple] simply *del. MS 1*
290 from] in *del. MS 2*
298 toning drops] toneing dew *MS 1, MS 2*; toning *1892, de L*
300–303 *MS 1: del.:* For the sweet laughter, keynote of the wise,

Laughter—the joy of Reason seeing fade
Obstruction into Earth's renewing beds,
Beneath the stroke of her good servant's blade—
Thenceforth art as their earth-star hailed;
Gain of the years, conjunction's prize.
The greater heart in thy appeal to heads,
They see, thou Captain of our civil Fort!
By more elusive savages assailed
On each ascending stage; untired
Both inner foe and outer to cut short,   310
And blow to chaff pretenders void of grist:
Showing old tiger's claws, old crocodile's
Yard-grin of eager grinders, slim to sight,
Like forms in running water, oft when smiles,
When pearly tears, when fluent lips delight:
But never with the slayer's malice fired:
As little as informs an infant's fist
Clenched at the sneeze! Thou wouldst but have us be
Good sons of mother soil, whereby to grow
Branching on fairer skies, one stately tree;   320
Broad of the tilth for flowering at the Court:
Which is the tree bound fast to wave its tress;
Of strength controlled sheer beauty to bestow.
Ambrosial heights of possible acquist,
Where souls of men with soul of man consort,
And all look higher to new loveliness
Begotten of the look: thy mark is there;
While on our temporal ground alive,
Rightly though fearfully thou wieldest sword,
Of finer temper now a numbered learn   330
That they resisting thee themselves resist;
And not thy bigger joy to smite and drive,
Prompt the dense herd to butt, and set the snare
Witching them into pitfalls for hoarse shouts.

320 skies] heavens[?] *del. MS 1*
323 sheer] pure *del. MS 1*
330 a numbered] the numbers *del. MS 1*

More now, and hourly more, and of the Lord
Thou lead'st to, doth this rebel heart discern,
When pinched ascetic and red sensualist
Alternately recurrent freeze or burn,
And of its old religions it has doubts.
It fears thee less when thou hast shown it bare;   340
Less hates, part understands, nor much resents,
When the prized objects it has raised for prayer,
For fitful prayer;—repentance dreading fire,
Impelled by aches; the blindness which repents
Like the poor trampled worm that writhes in mire;—
Are sounded by thee, and thou darest probe
Old Institutions and Establishments,
Once fortresses against the floods of sin,
For what their worth; and questioningly prod
For why they stand upon a racing globe,   350
Impeding blocks, less useful than the clod;
Their angel out of them, a demon in.

This half-enlightened heart, still doomed to fret,
To hurl at vanities, to drift in shame
Of gain or loss, bewailing the sure rod,
Shall of predestination wed thee yet.
Something it gathers of what things should drop
At entrance on new times; of how thrice broad
The world of minds communicative; how
A straggling Nature classed in school, and scored   360
With stripes admonishing, may yield to plough
Fruitfullest furrows, nor for waxing tame
Be feeble on an Earth whose gentler crop
Is its most living, in the mind that steers,
By Reason led, her way of tree and flame,

344 aches] pain *del. MS 1*
345 that writhes] atwist *del. MS 1*
346 sounded by] questioned of *del. MS 1*
350 racing] rolling *del. MS 1*; racing *1892, de L*
354 To] And *del. MS 1*   to] & *del. MS 1*

Beyond the genuflexions and the tears;
Upon an Earth that cannot stop,
Where upward is the visible aim,
And ever we espy the greater God,
For simple pointing at a good adored: 370
Proof of the closer neighbourhood. Head on,
Sword of the many, light of the few! untwist
Or cut our tangles till fair space is won
Beyond a briared wood of austere brow,
Relieved of discord by thy timely word
At intervals refreshing life: for thou
Art verily Keeper of the Muse's Key;
Thyself no vacant melodist;
On lower land elective even as she;
Holding, as she, all dissonance abhorred;   380
Advising to her measured steps in flow;
And teaching how for being subjected free
Past thought of freedom we may come to know
The music of the meaning of Accord.

Youth in Memory

Days, when the ball of our vision
Had eagles that flew unabashed to sun;
When the grasp on the bow was decision,
And arrow and hand and eye were one;

TO THE COMIC SPIRIT

366 Beyond the] Upward. The del. MS 1
367 Upon] Be feeble on del. MS 1
368 visible aim] the way of tree & flower del. MS 1
380 not in MS 1
383 thought of freedom we may] aim at liberty we del. MS 1

YOUTH IN MEMORY

MSS: Huntington HM470, fair copy for printer, lines 218–21 missing. Yale, leaf numbered 13, lines 218–21 (the leaf at Yale is that missing from Huntington). Variants are from these MSS, except for line 173 q.v.
3 grasp] hand del.
4 And] When del.

When the Pleasures, like waves to a swimmer,
Came heaving for rapture ahead!—
Invoke them, they dwindle, they glimmer
As lights over mounds of the dead.

Behold the winged Olympus, off the mead,
With thunder of wide pinions, lightning speed,   10
Wafting the shepherd-boy through ether clear,
To bear the golden nectar-cup.
So flies desire at view of its delight,
When the young heart is tiptoe perched on sight.
We meanwhile who in hues of the sick year,
The Spring-time paint to prick us for our lost,
Mount but the fatal half way up—
Whereon shut eyes! This is decreed,
For Age that would to youthful heavens ascend,
By passion for the arms' possession tossed,   20
It falls the way of sighs and hath their end;
A spark gone out to more sepulchral night.
Good if the arrowy eagle of the height,
Be then the little bird that hops to feed.

Lame falls the cry to kindle days
Of radiant orb and daring gaze.
It does but clank our mortal chain.
For Earth reads through her felon old,
The many-numbered of her fold,
Who forward tottering backward strain,   30
And would be thieves of treasure spent,
With their grey season soured.
She could write out their history in their thirst
To have again the much devoured,
And be the bud at burst;
In honey fancy join the flow,

10 With] In
12 To bear] To bear aloft *del.*
15 sick] dead *del.*
16 Spring] seed[?] *del.*

Where Youth swims on as once they went,
All choiric for spontaneous glee
Of active eager lungs and thews;
They now bared roots beside the river bent;   40
Whose privilege themselves to see;
Their place in yonder tideway know;
The current glass peruse;
The depths intently sound;
And sapped by each returning flood,
Accept for monitory nourishment,
Those worn roped features under crust of mud,
Reflected in the silvery smooth around:
Not less the branching and high singing tree,
A home of nests, a landmark and a tent,   50
Until their hour for losing hold on ground.
Even such good harvest of the things that flee,
Earth offers her subjected, and they choose
Rather of Bacchic Youth one beam to drink,
And warm slow marrow with the sensual wink.
So block they at her source the Mother of the Muse.

Who cheerfully the little bird becomes,
Without a fall, and pipes for peck at crumbs,
May have her dolings to the lightest touch;
As where some cripple muses by his crutch,   60
Unwitting that the spirit in him sings:
'When I had legs, then had I wings,
As good as any born of eggs,
To feed on all aërial things,
When I had legs!'
And if not to embrace he sighs,
She gives him breath of Youth awhile,
Perspective of a breezy mile,
Companionable hedgeways, lifting skies;
Scenes where his nested dreams upon their hoard   70

48 silvery] brightly *del.*
66 not] not vainly *del.*

Brooded, or up to empyrean soared:
Enough to link him with a dotted line.
But cravings for an eagle's flight,
To top white peaks and serve wild wine
Among the rosy undecayed,
Bring only flash of shade
From her full throbbing breast of day in night.
By what they crave are they betrayed:
And cavernous is that young dragon's jaw,
Crimson for all the fiery reptile saw   80
In time now coveted, for teeth to flay,
Once more consume, were Life recurrent May.
They to their moment of drawn breath,
Which is the life that makes the death,
The death that makes ethereal life would bind:
The death that breeds the spectre do they find.
Darkness is wedded and the waste regrets
Beating as dead leaves on a fitful gust,
By souls no longer dowered to climb
Beneath their pack of dust,   90
Whom envy of a lustrous prime,
Eclipsed while yet invoked, besets,
And dooms to sink and water sable flowers,
That never gladdened eye or loaded bee.
Strain we the arms for Memory's hours,
We are the seized Persephone.

Responsive never to the soft desire
For one prized tune is this our chord of life.
'Tis clipped to deadness with a wanton knife,
In wishes that for ecstasies aspire.   100
Yet have we glad companionship of Youth,
Elysian meadows for the mind,

79 cavernous] red to men *del.*
80 Crimson] Agape *del.*
82 consume] to rend *del.*
87 waste] wild[?] *del.*

Dare we to face deeds done, and in our tomb
Filled with the part-coloured bloom
Of loved and hated, grasp all human truth
Sowed by us down the mazy paths behind.
To feel that heaven must we that hell sound through:
Whence comes a line of continuity,
That brings our middle station into view,
Between those poles; a novel Earth we see,   110
In likeness of us, made of banned and blest;
The sower's bed, but not the reaper's rest:
An Earth alive with meanings, wherein meet
Buried, and breathing, and to be.
Then of the junction of the three,
Even as a heart in brain, full sweet
May sense of soul, the sum of music, beat.

Only the soul can walk the dusty track
Where hangs our flowering under vapours black,
And bear to see how these pervade, obscure,   120
Quench recollection of a spacious pure.
They take phantasmal forms, divide, convolve,
Hard at each other point and gape,
Horrible ghosts! in agony dissolve,
To reappear with one they drape
For criminal, and, Father! shrieking name,
Who such distorted issue did beget.
Accept them, them and him, though hiss thy sweat
Off brow on breast, whose furnace flame
Has eaten, and old Self consumes.   130
Out of the purification will they leap,
Thee renovating while new light illumes
The dusky web of evil, known as pain,
That heavily up healthward mounts the steep;
Our fleshly road to beacon-fire of brain:

111 In likeness of us, made] As likeness in us, drawn[?] *del.*
113 An Earth alive] Alive *del.*

Midway the tameless oceanic brute
Below, whose heave is topped with foam for fruit,
And the fair heaven reflecting inner peace
On righteous warfare, that asks not to cease.

Forth of such passage through black fire we win   140
Clear hearing of the simple lute,
Whereon, and not on other, Memory plays
For them who can in quietness receive
Her restorative airs: a ditty thin
As note of hedgerow bird in ear of eve,
Or wave at ebb, the shallow catching rays
On a transparent sheet, where curves a glass
To truer heavens than when the breaker neighs
Loud at the plunge for bubbly wreck in roar.
Solidity and bulk and martial brass,   150
Once tyrants of the senses, faintly score
A mark on pebbled sand or fluid slime,
While present in the spirit, vital there,
Are things that seemed the phantoms of their time;
Eternal as the recurrent cloud, as air
Imperative, refreshful as dawn-dew.
Some evanescent hand on vapour scrawled
Historic of the soul, and heats anew
Its coloured lines where deeds of flesh stand bald.
True of the man, and of mankind 'tis true.   160
Did we stout battle with the Shade, Despair,
Our cowardice, it blooms; or haply warred
Against the primal beast in us, and flung;
Or cleaving mists of Sorrow, left it starred
Above self-pity slain: or it was Prayer
First taken for Life's cleanser; or the tongue
Spake for the world against this heart; or rings
Old laughter, from the founts of wisdom sprung;
Or clap of wing of joy, that was a throb

140 Forth] Now *del.*
144 ditty] piping *del.*

From breast of Earth, and did no creature rob: 170
These quickening live. But deepest at her springs,
Most filial, is an eye to love her young.
And had we it, to see with it, alive
Is our lost garden, flower, bird and hive.
Blood of her blood, aim of her aim, are then
The green-robed and grey-crested sons of men:
She tributary to her aged restores
The living in the dead; she will inspire
Faith homelier than on the Yonder shores,
Abhorring these as mire,   180
Uncertain steps, in dimness gropes,
With mortal tremours pricking hopes,
And, by the final Bacchic of the lusts
Propelled, the Bacchic of the spirit trusts:
A fervour drunk from mystic hierophants;
Not utterly misled, though blindly led,
Led round fermenting eddies. Faith she plants
In her own firmness as our midway road:
Which rightly Youth has read, though blindly read;
Her essence reading in her toothsome goad;   190
Spur of bright dreams experience disenchants.
But love we well the young, her road midway
The darknesses runs consecrated clay.
Despite our feeble hold on this green home,
And the vast outer strangeness void of dome,
Shall we be with them, of them, taught to feel,
Up to the moment of our prostrate fall,
The life they deem voluptuously real,
Is more than empty echo of a call,
Or shadow of a shade, or swing of tides;   200
As brooding upon age, when veins congeal,

173 to] still *MS, 1892*
183 final] paler *del.*
191 Spur of] Whence the *del.*
193 darknesses runs] darkness runs a *del.*

Grey palsy nods to think. With us for guides,
Another step above the animal,
To views in Alpine thought are they helped on.
Good if so far we live in them when gone!

And there the arrowy eagle of the height,
Becomes the little bird that hops to feed,
Glad of a crumb, for tempered appetite
To make it wholesome blood and fruitful seed.
Then Memory strikes on no slack string,   210
Nor sectional will varied Life appear:
Perforce of soul discerned in mind, we hear
Earth with her Onward chime, with Winter Spring.
And ours the mellow note, while sharing joys
No more subjecting mortals who have learnt
To build for happiness on equipoise,
The Pleasures read in sparks of substance burnt;
Know in our seasons an integral wheel,
That rolls us to a mark may yet be willed.
This, the truistic rubbish under heel   220
Of all the world, we peck at and are filled.

208 tempered] modest *del.*
216 To build for happiness] That happiness is built *del.*
218–21 *not in MS; leaf, at Y.*

Verses

Penetration and Trust

I

Sleek as a lizard at round of a stone,
The look of her heart slipped out and in.
Sweet on her lord her soft eyes shone,
As innocents clear of a shade of sin.

II

He laid a finger under her chin,
His arm for her girdle at waist was thrown:
Now, what will happen and who will win,
With me in the fight and my lady lone?

III

He clasped her, clasping a shape of stone;
Was fire on her eyes till they let him in.
Her breast to a God of the daybeams shone,
And never a corner for serpent sin.

IV

Tranced she stood, with a chattering chin;
Her shrunken form at his feet was thrown:
At home to the death my lord shall win,
When it is no tyrant who leaves me lone!

MSS: Huntington HM7471. *MS 1, late draft; MS 2, fair copy.*
I.2 look] thought *MS 1, MS 2*
I.3 Sweet on her lord] While sweet upon him *del.* But sweet on her lord *MS 1*   Sweet]
And sweet *del. MS 2*
II.1 under] beneath *MS 1, MS 2*
II.2 His arm for her girdle at] And an arm about her *MS 1*
II.4 *MS 1:* When I'm in the fight & my wife is lone?
III.1 clasped] hugged *or* clasped *MS 1*   clasping] hugging *or* clasping *MS 1*
III.2 *MS 1:* Till her eyes met his to let them in.
III.3 *MS 1:* [Thus[?] she *del.*] She knew by the fire that through her shone,
III.4 *MS 1:* He was no dupe of the brooded sin.   serpent] brooded *del. MS 2*
IV.1 Tranced] Sudden *MS 1*

Night of Frost in May

Night of Frost in May was salvaged from an unpublished poem in two parts, "The Poet's Night," written—on the evidence of handwriting—about 1890. The second part is given in the Supplementary Textual Notes.

> With splendour of a silver day,
> A frosted night had opened May:
> And on that plumed and armoured night,
> As one close temple hove our wood,
> Its border leafage virgin white.
> Remote down air an owl hallooed.
> The black twig dropped without a twirl;
> The bud in jewelled grasp was nipped;
> The brown leaf cracked a scorching curl;
> A crystal off the green leaf slipped.   10
> Across the tracks of rimy tan,
> Some busy thread at whiles would shoot;
> A limping minnow-rillet ran,
> To hang upon an icy foot.
>
> In this shrill hush of quietude,
> The ear conceived a severing cry.
> Almost it let the sound elude,
> When chuckles three, a warble shy,
> From hazels of the garden came,
> Near by the crimson-windowed farm.   20
> They laid the trance on breath and frame,
> A prelude of the passion-charm.

PENETRATION AND TRUST

IV.3 to the death] & abroad *del. MS 1*   shall] will *del. MS 1*
IV.4 When] If *MS 1*

NIGHT OF FROST IN MAY

See Supplementary Textual Notes.

Then soon was heard, not sooner heard
Than answered, doubled, trebled, more,
Voice of an Eden in the bird
Renewing with his pipe of four
The sob: a troubled Eden, rich
In throb of heart: unnumbered throats
Flung upward at a fountain's pitch,
The fervour of the four long notes,   30
That on the fountain's pool subside,
Exult and ruffle and upspring:
Endless the crossing multiplied
Of silver and of golden string.
There chimed a bubbled underbrew
With witch-wild spray of vocal dew.

It seemed a single harper swept
Our wild wood's inner chords and waked
A spirit that for yearning ached
Ere men desired and joyed or wept.   40
Or now a legion ravishing
Musician rivals did unite
In love of sweetness high to sing
The subtle song that rivals light;
From breast of earth to breast of sky:
And they were secret, they were nigh:
A hand the magic might disperse;
The magic swung my universe.

Yet sharpened breath forbade to dream,
Where all was visionary gleam;   50
Where Seasons, as with cymbals, clashed;
And feelings, passing joy and woe,
Churned, gurgled, spouted, interflashed,
Nor either was the one we know:
Nor pregnant of the heart contained
In us were they, that griefless plained,
That plaining soared; and through the heart

Struck to one note the wide apart:—
A passion surgent from despair;
A paining bliss in fervid cold;   60
Off the last vital edge of air,
Leap heavenward of the lofty-souled,
For rapture of a wine of tears;
As had a star among the spheres
Caught up our earth to some mid-height
Of double life to ear and sight,
She giving voice to thought that shines
Keen-brilliant of her deepest mines;
While steely drips the rillet clinked,
And hoar with crust the cowslip swelled.   70

Then was the lyre of earth beheld,
Then heard by me: it holds me linked;
Across the years to dead-ebb shores
I stand on, my blood-thrill restores.
But would I conjure into me
Those issue notes, I must review
What serious breath the woodland drew;
The low throb of expectancy;
How the white mother-muteness pressed
On leaf and meadow-herb; how shook,   80
Nigh speech of mouth, the sparkle-crest
Seen spinning on the bracken-crook.

The Teaching of the Nude

I

A Satyr spied a Goddess in her bath,
Unseen of her attendant nymphs: none knew.
Forthwith the creature to his fellows drew,
And looking backward on the curtained path,
He strove to tell; he could but heave a breast
Too full, and point to mouth, with failing leers:
Vainly he danced for speech, he giggled tears,
Made as if torn in two, as if tight pressed,
As if cast prone; then fetching whimpered tunes
For words, flung heel and set his hairy flight   10
Through forest-hollows, over rocky height.
The green leaves buried him three rounds of moons.
A senatorial Satyr named what herb
Had hurried him outrunning reason's curb.

II

'Tis told how when that hieaway unchecked,
To dell returned, he seemed of tempered mood:
Even as the valley of the torrent rude,
The torrent now a brook, the valley wrecked.
In him, to hale him high or hurl aheap,

Previously printed in the Athenaeum *100 (17 August 1892). MSS:* Houghton, Lowell
1567. 15, *fair copy;* Huntington HM 6759, *fair copy corrected.*
I.1 in] by *Ho*
I.2 her attendant] all her sacred *del. H*
I.3 the] that *MSS*
I.4 *MSS:* And ever looking backward on the path,
I.6 mouth] tongue *Ho*
I.7 speech] words *Ho*
I.9 cast] laid *Ho*
I.10 words] speech *Ho*
I.14 *Ho:* Had driven the wretch to overrun his curb. *H del.:* Had driven him to outrun
his reason's curb.
II.1 'Tis told] They tell *MSS, Ath.*
II.2 tempered mood] moderate blood *Ho*; quiet mood *H*
II.3 rude] flood *MSS*
II.5 hurl aheap] cast on heap *Ho*; cast aheap *H, Ath.*

Goddess and Goatfoot hourly wrestled sore;
Hourly the immortal prevailing more:
Till one hot noon saw Meliboeus peep
From thicket-sprays to where his full-blown dame,
In circle by the lusty friskers gripped,   10
Laughed the showered rose-leaves while her limbs
    were stripped.
She beckoned to our Satyr, and he came.
Then twirled she mounds of ripeness, wreath of arms.
His hoof kicked up the clothing for such charms.

Breath of the Briar

I

O briar-scents, on yon wet wing
Of warm South-west wind brushing by,
You mind me of the sweetest thing
That ever mingled frank and shy:
When she and I, by love enticed,
Beneath the orchard-apples met,
In equal halves a ripe one sliced,
And smelt the juices ere we ate.

II

That apple of the briar-scent,
Among our lost in Britain now,
Was green of rind, and redolent
Of sweetness as a milking cow.
The briar gives it back, well nigh
The damsel with her teeth on it;
Her twinkle between frank and shy,
My thirst to bite where she had bit.

THE TEACHING OF THE NUDE
II.11 rose-leaves] rose-leaf *H*

PART I: POEMS COLLECTED BY MEREDITH

Empedocles

I

He leaped. With none to hinder,
Of Aetna's fiery scoriae
In the next vomit-shower, made he
    A more peculiar cinder.
And this great Doctor, can it be,
He left no saner recipe
For men at issue with despair?
Admiring, even his poet owns,
While noting his fine lyric tones,
The last of him was heels in air!   10

II

    Comes Reverence, her features
Amazed to see high Wisdom hear,
With glimmer of a faunish leer,
    One mock her pride of creatures.
Shall such sad incident degrade
A stature casting sunniest shade?
O Reverence! let Reason swim;
Each life its critic deed reveals;
And him reads Reason at his heels,
If heels in air the last of him!   10

Previously printed in the Anti-Jacobin *46 (12 December 1891). MS:* Yale, *fair copy.*
II.9 And him] And his *A-J*

To Colonel Charles

(DYING GENERAL C. B. B.)

GM may have thought that his good friend Maj. Gen. Charles Booth Brackenbury (1831–90) was "dying" in the winter of 1887 or during an illness in the late winter of 1889 (Cline, Letter 1181)—the only explanation, and a poor one, for the subtitle added in 1892. But according to the *Annual Register* he died suddenly from apoplexy on June 20, 1890. Like Frederick A. Maxse (see p. xxxii), he had been a hero of the Crimean War, receiving both English and Turkish medals after the fall of Sebastopol.

Apparently he and GM first met at the Hotel Vittoria in Venice during the summer of 1866 at the end of the Seven Weeks War. Brackenbury, as war correspondent for the *Times*, and GM, as war correspondent for the *Morning Post*, were waiting, among others, "to witness the festivities celebrating the province's [Venetia's] freedom . . ." (LS, p. 156).

As correspondent for the *Times*, Brackenbury accompanied "Prince Frederick Charles in the campaign of Le Mans, 1870–71; and in the Russo-Turkish war, . . . he crossed the Balkans with Gourko" (*DNB*). He was a serious student of warfare, with many publications to his credit, one of which was the life of *Frederick the Great* (1884), written for the series of *Military Biographies*. Brackenbury was promoted to the rank of colonel in the Royal Artillery, 1882, and to the temporary rank of Major General in 1889, following his appointment as Director of Artillery Studies at Woolwich.

GM had a great interest in military affairs, and in this poem, as elsewhere, favored greater preparedness on the part of England.

I

An English heart, my commandant,
A soldier's eye you have, awake
To right and left; with looks askant
On bulwarks not of adamant,
Where white our Channel waters break.

Previously printed in the Pall Mall Gazette, *16 February 1887, title:* To Colonel Charles. *MSS: Huntington HM6762, untitled MS of "The Two Masks," containing stanzas I, II.1, and an intervening stanza, verso of leaf 2. Yale, working draft, untitled.*

I.1 An English] A soldier's *or* An English *H*
I.2 awake] on guard *H*
I.3–4 *H, reverse order*
I.3 *H:* Along our [Southern *del.*] cliffs will look askant,
I.4 On] For *H*
I.5 *H:* Where Channel waters do their ward.   white] grey *del. Y*

II

Where Grisnez winks at Dungeness ·
Across the ruffled strip of salt,
You look, and like the prospect less.
On men and guns would you lay stress,
To bid the Island's foemen halt.

III

While loud the Year is raising cry
At birth to know if it must bear
In history the bloody dye,
An English heart, a soldier's eye,
For the old country first will care.

IV

And how stands she, artillerist,
Among the vapours waxing dense,
With cannon charged? 'Tis hist! and hist!
And now she screws a gouty fist,
And now she counts to clutch her pence.

Between stanzas I and II, H:

       The country *or* Old England seems a drifting log,
       A stationed fort is yon armed France.
       The days ahead are dark in fog,
       And growls the military dog
       To warn his master, 'ware the chance!

Before III.1: along the strip of salt *H*

III.1 While loud] Now while *Y*
III.3 bloody] crimson *or* bloody *Y*
IV.1 *Y del.:* And how, among their vapours dense,
IV.2 *Y del.:* With cannon charged, artillerist,
IV.4 she screws a gouty] a paralytic *Y*
IV.5 And now she counts to clutch] She clutches; now she counts *or* And now she counts
to clutch her pence. *Y*

V

With shudders chill as aconite,
The couchant chewer of the cud
Will start at times in pussy fright
Before the dogs, when reads her sprite
The streaks predicting streams of blood.

VI

She thinks they may mean something; thinks
They may mean nothing: haply both.
Where darkness all her daylight drinks,
She fain would find a leader lynx,
Not too much taxing mental sloth.

VII

Cleft like the fated house in twain,
One half is, Arm! and one, Retrench!
Gambetta's word on dull MacMahon:
'The cow that sees a passing train':
So spies she Russian, German, French.

Stanza V Y del.:

> At whiles a hare in panic flight;
> At whiles the chewer of the cud;
> By turns these rounding waters white
> Are brandy or chill aconite
> To her

V.1 *Y:* She starts, a hare in panic flight!
V.2 The couchant] She couches, *Y*
V.3 *Y:* [And chill she is *del.*] With shudders chill as aconite,
V.4 *Y:* Or hot as brandy, [mounts *del.*] reads her sprite
V.5 predicting] before the *Y*
VI.2 haply both] both may mean *Y*
VI.3 *Y:* The coin upon her counter clinks
VI.4 She fain would find] Alarmedly: *Y*
VI.5 *Y:* [?] to see when nought of day is seen
VII.1 *Y:* Divided like the houses doomed, [wilful blind *del.*]
VII.2 is] cried *Y*
VII.3 *Y:* Where last a warning omen boomed,
VII.4 *Y:* She looks with hate in dread resumed,
VII.5 So spies she] By turns on *Y*

VIII

She? no, her weakness: she unbraced
Among those athletes fronting storms!
The muscles less of steel than paste,
Why, they of nature feel distaste
For flash, much more for push, of arms.

IX

The poet sings, and well know we,
That 'iron draws men after it.'
But towering wealth may seem the tree
Which bears the fruit *Indemnity*,
And draw as fast as battle's fit,

X

If feeble be the hand on guard,
Alas, alas! And nations are
Still the mad forces, though the scarred.
Should they once deem our emblem Pard
Wagger of tail for all save war;—

XI

Mechanically screwed to flail
His flanks by Presses conjuring fear;—
A money-bag with head and tail;—
Too late may valour then avail!
As you beheld, my cannonier,

XII

When with the staff of Benedek,
On the plateau of Königgrätz,
You saw below that wedgeing speck;
Foresaw proud Austria rammed to wreck,
Where Chlum drove deep in smoky jets.

XII.3 below that wedgeing speck] as from the vessels deck *or* that dubious wedging [*sic*]
speck *Y*
XII.4 Foresaw proud] His gallant *del. Y*
XII.5 drove deep] the wedge *del. Y*

England before the Storm

On December 9, 1891, GM wrote Frederick Greenwood, editor of the *Anti-Jacobin* at the time, that he had been writing these verses for Greenwood's paper when Norman MacColl of the *Athenaeum*, came in from Burford, listened to them, and bore them off.

In the autumn of 1891 England was not threatened with war. The poem is one of GM's perpetual admonitions.

I

The day that is the night of days,
With cannon-fire for sun ablaze,
We spy from any billow's lift;
And England still this tidal drift!
Would she to sainted forethought vow
A space before the thunders flood,
That martyr of its hour might now
Spare her the tears of blood.

II

Asleep upon her ancient deeds,
She hugs the vision plethora breeds,
And counts her manifold increase
Of treasure in the fruits of peace.
What curse on earth's improvident,
When the dread trumpet shatters rest,
Is wreaked, she knows, yet smiles content
    As cradle rocked from breast.

III

She, impious to the Lord of Hosts,
The valour of her offspring boasts,
Mindless that now on land and main
His heeded prayer is active brain.

Previously printed in the Athenaeum *98 (5 December 1891). MS:* Yale, *stanzas I and IV.*

1.2 *MS:* Illumined under powder-blaze *or* With cannon fire for sun ablaze.

No more great heart may guard the home,
Save eyed and armed and skilled to cleave
Yon swallower wave with shroud of foam,
    We see not distant heave.

IV

They stand to be her sacrifice,
The sons this mother flings like dice,
To face the odds and brave the Fates;
As in those days of starry dates,
When cannon cannon's counterblast
Awakened, muzzle muzzle bowled,
And high in swathe of smoke the mast
    Its fighting rag outrolled.

Tardy Spring

Now the North wind ceases,
The warm South-west awakes;
Swift fly the fleeces,
Thick the blossom-flakes.

Now hill to hill has made the stride,
And distance waves the without end:
Now in the breast a door flings wide;
Our farthest smiles, our next is friend.
And song of England's rush of flowers
Is this full breeze with mellow stops,   10
That spins the lark for shine, for showers;

ENGLAND BEFORE THE STORM

Stanza IV MS del.:

    Her sons are here
    Prompt at a call to pay the price
    Of sloth & be her sacrifice,
    To face the odds & brave the Fates,

IV.4 starry] glorious *del. MS*

TARDY SPRING

Previously printed in the Illustrated London News *2722 (20 June 1891). MS: Ashley 3636, fair copy leaf 1: facsimile in MBF facing p. 204.*

He drinks his hurried flight, and drops.
The stir in memory seem these things,
Which out of moistened turf and clay,
Astrain for light push patient rings,
Or leap to find the waterway.
'Tis equal to a wonder done,
Whatever simple lives renew
Their tricks beneath the father sun,
As though they caught a broken clue: 20
So hard was earth an eyewink back;
But now the common life has come,
The blotting cloud a dappled pack,
The grasses one vast underhum.
A City clothed in snow and soot,
With lamps for day in ghostly rows,
Breaks to the scene of hosts afoot,
The river that reflective flows:
And there did fog down crypts of street
Play spectre upon eye and mouth:—   30
Their faces are a glass to greet
This magic of the whirl for South.
A burly joy each creature swells
With sound of its own hungry quest;
Earth has to fill her empty wells,
And speed the service of the nest;
The phantom of the snow-wreath melt,
That haunts the farmer's look abroad,
Who sees what tomb a white night built,
Where flocks now bleat and sprouts the clod.   40
For iron Winter held her firm;
Across her sky he laid his hand;
And bird he starved, he stiffened worm;
A sightless heaven, a shaven land.

27 Breaks] Cracks *MS, ILN*

Her shivering Spring feigned fast asleep,
The bitten buds dared not unfold:
We raced on roads and ice to keep
Thought of the girl we love from cold.

But now the North wind ceases,
The warm South-west awakes,   50
The heavens are out in fleeces,
And earth's green banner shakes.

48 Thought of the girl] The thought of her *MS, ILN*

ODES IN CONTRIBUTION
TO THE SONG OF FRENCH HISTORY
(1898)

The Revolution

On September 28, 1896, GM wrote to the poet and essayist Alice
Meynell that the "'French Revolution' [was] done" and that he had
"started on 'Napoleon.'" He read this ode to Edward Clodd on 16 or
17 January 1897, "one of three of which the others are unfinished"
(*TLS-II*).

I

Not yet had History's Ætna smoked the skies,
And low the Gallic Giantess lay enchained,
While overhead in ordered set and rise,
Her kingly crowns immutably defiled;
Effulgent on funereal piled
Across the vacant heavens, and distrained
Her body, mutely, even as earth, to bear;
Despoiled the tomb of hope, her mouth of air.

II

Through marching scores of winters racked she lay,
Beneath a hoar-frost's brilliant crust;
Whereon the jewelled flies that drained
Her breasts disported in a glistering spray;

Previously printed in Cosmopolis 9 (*March 1898*). *MS:* Huntington HM6760, *copy for*
typist, title: "*The French Revolution: An Ode.*"

She, the land's fount of fruits, enclosed with dust;
By good and evil angels fed, sustained
In part to curse, in part to pray,
Sucking the dubious rumours, till men saw
The throbs of her charged heart before the Just,
So worn the harrowed surface had become: 10
And still they deemed the dance above was Law,
Amort all passion in a rebel dumb.

                              III

Then on the unanticipated day,
Earth heaved, and rose a veinous mound
To roar of the underfloods; and off it sprang,
Ravishing as red wine in woman's form,
A splendid Mænad, she of the delirious laugh,
Her body twisted flames with the smoke-cap crowned;
She of the Bacchic foot; the challenger to the fray,
Bewitchment for the embrace; who sang, who sang
Intoxication to her swarm,
Revolved them, hair, voice, feet, in her carmagnole,   10
As with a stroke she snapped the Royal staff,
Dealt the awaited blow on gilt decay
(O ripeness of the time! O Retribution sure,
If but our vital lamp illume us to endure!)
And, like a glad releasing of her soul,
Sent the word Liberty up to meet the midway blue,
Her bridegroom in descent to her; and they joined,
In the face of men they joined: attest it true,
The million witnesses, that she
For ages lying beside the mole,   20
Was on the unanticipated miracle day
Upraised to midway heaven and, as to her goal
Enfolded, ere the Immaculate knew
What Lucifer of the Mint had coined

III.2 heaved] cracked *MS*
III.21 the] her *del. MS*
III.23 the] that bright *del. MS*

His bride's adulterate currency
Of burning love corrupt of an infuriate hate;
She worthy, she unworthy; that one day his mate:
His mate for that one day of the unwritten deed.
Read backward on the hoar-frost's brilliant crust;
Beneath it read.   30
Athirst to kiss, athirst to slay, she stood,
A radiance fringed with grim affright;
For them that hungered, she was nourishing food,
For those who sparkled, Night.
Read in her heart, and how before the Just
Her doings, her misdoings, plead.

                                    IV

Down on her leap for him the young Angelical broke
To husband a resurgent France:
From whom, with her dethroning stroke,
Dishonour passed; the dalliance,
That is occasion's yea or nay,
In issues for the soul to pay,
Discarded; and the cleft 'twixt deed and word,
The sinuous lie which warbles the sweet bird,
Wherein we see old Darkness peer,
Cold Dissolution beck, she had flung hence;   10
And hence the talons and the beak of prey;
Hence all the lures to silken swine
Thronging the troughs of indolence;
With every sleek convolvement serpentine;
The pride in elfin arts to veil an evil leer,
And bid a goatfoot trip it like a fay.
He clasped in this revived, uprisen France,
A valorous dame, of countenance
The lightning's upon cloud: unlit as yet
On brows and lips the lurid shine   20
Of seas in the night-wind's whirl; unstirred
Her pouch of the centuries' injuries compressed;

IV.11 *not in MS*

The shriek that tore the world as yet unheard:
Earth's animate full flower she looked, intense
For worship, wholly given him, fair
Adoring or desiring; in her bright jet,
Earth's crystal spring to sky: Earth's warrior Best
To win Heaven's Pure up that midway
We vision for new ground, where sense
And spirit are one for the further flight; breast-bare,   30
Bare-limbed; nor graceless gleamed her disarray
In scorn of the seductive insincere,
But martially nude for hot Bellona's play,
And amorous of the loftiest in her view.

V

She sprang from dust to drink of earth's cool dew,
The breath of swaying grasses share,
Mankind embrace, their weaklings rear,
At wrestle with the tyrannic strong;
Her forehead clear to her mate, virgin anew,
As immortals may be in the mortal sphere.
Read through her launching heart, who had lain long
With Earth and heard till it became her own,
Our good Great Mother's eve and matin song:
The humming burden of Earth's toil to feed   10
Her creatures all, her task to speed their growth,
Her aim to lead them up her pathways, shown
Between the Pains and Pleasures; warned of both,
Of either aided on their hard ascent.
Now when she looked with love's benign delight
After great ecstasy, along the plains,
What foulest impregnation of her sight
Transformed the scene to multitudinous troops
Of human sketches, quaver-figures, bent,
As were they winter sedges, broken hoops,   20

V.4 At wrestle] Do battle *del. MS*

Dry udders, vineless poles, worm-eaten posts,
With features like the flowers defaced by deluge rains?
Recked she that some perverting devil had limned
Earth's proudest to spout scorn of the Maker's hand,
Who could a day behold these deathly hosts.
And see, decked, graced, and delicately trimmed
A ribanded and gemmed elected few,
Sanctioned, of milk and honey starve the land:—
Like melody in flesh, its pleasant game
Olympianwise perform, cloak but the shame:					30
Beautiful statures; hideous,
By Christian contrast; pranked with golden chains,
And flexile where is manhood straight;
Mortuaries where warm should beat
The brotherhood that keeps blood sweet:
Who dared in cantique impious,
Proclaim the Just, to whom was due
Cathedral gratitude in the pomp of state,
For that on those lean outcasts hung the sucker Pains,
On these elect the swelling Pleasures grew.					40
Surely a devil's land when that meant death for each!
Fresh from the breast of Earth, not thus,
With all the body's life to plump the leech,
Is Nature's way, she knew. The abominable scene
Spat at the skies; and through her veins,
To cloud celestially sown,
Ran venom of what nourishment
Her dark sustainer subterrene
Supplied her, stretched supine on the rack,

V.21 *MS del.:* Bodies decaying[?], dry udders, wormy posts,
V.23 Recked she] She recked *MS*
V.24 of] on *MS*
V.26 see] lo[?] *del. MS*
V.28 starve] starved *del. MS*
V.30 perform] performed *del. MS*   cloak but] & cloaking *del. MS*
V.37 Proclaim] Praising *del. MS*
V.39 For that on] From *del. MS*
V.40 On] For *del. MS*
V.43 life] blood *del. MS*

Alive in the shrewd nerves, the seething brains,   50
Under derisive revels, prone
As one clamped fast, with the interminable senseless blent.

VI

Now was her face white waves in the tempest's sharp flame-blink;
Her skies shot black.
Now was it visioned infamy to drink
Of earth's cool dew, and through the vines
Frolic in pearly laughter with her young,
Watching the healthful, natural, happy signs
Where hands of lads and maids like tendrils clung,
After their sly shy ventures from the leaf,
And promised bunches. Now it seemed
The world was one malarious mire,   10
Crying for purification: chief
This land of France. It seemed
A duteous desire
To drink of life's hot flood, and the crimson streamed.

VII

She drank what makes man demon at the draught.
Her skies lowered black,
Her lover flew,
There swept a shudder over men.
Her heavenly lover fled her, and she laughed,
For laughter was her spirit's weapon then.
The Infernal rose uncalled, he with his crew.

VIII

As mighty thews burst manacles, she went mad:
Her heart a flaring torch usurped her wits.
Such enemies of her next-drawn breath she had!
To tread her down in her live grave beneath

V.50 seething brains] brains afire *del. MS*
VI.1 sharp flame-] fiery *del. MS*
VI.8 their sly] sly pushes *del. MS*
VIII.4 live] old *del. MS*

Their dancing floor sunned blind by the Royal wreath,
They ringed her steps with crafty prison pits.
Without they girdled her, made nest within.
There ramped the lion, here entrailed the snake.
They forced the cup to her lips when she drank blood;
Believing it, in the mother's mind at strain,   10
In the mother's fears, and in young Liberty's wail
Alarmed, for her encompassed children's sake;
The sole sure way to save her priceless bud.
Wherewith, when power had gifted her to prevail,
Vengeance appeared as logically akin.
Insanely rational they; she rationally insane;
And in compute of sin, was hers the appealing sin.

IX

Amid the plash of scarlet mud
Stained at the mouth, drunk with our common air,
Not lack of love was her defect;
The Fury mourned and raged and bled for France;
Breathing from exultation to despair
At every wild-winged hope struck by mischance
Soaring at each faint gleam o'er her abyss.
Heard still, to be heard while France shall stand erect,
The frontier march she piped her sons, for where
Her crouching outer enemy camped,   10
Attendant on the deadlier inner's hiss.
She piped her sons the frontier march, the wine
Of martial music, History's cherished tune;
And they, the saintliest labourers that aye
Dropped sweat on soil for bread, took arms and tramped;
High-breasted to match men or elements,
Or Fortune, harsh schoolmistress with the undrilled:
War's ragged pupils; many a wavering line,

VIII.13 *not in MS*
VIII.17 appealing] magnanimous[?] *del. MS*
IX.1 scarlet] crimson *MS*
Between IX.2 and IX.3 MS del.: Amid the plash of scarlet mud
IX.17 with] for *del. MS*

Torn from the dear fat soil of champaigns hopefully tilled,
Torn from the motherly bowl, the homely spoon,   20
To jest at famine, ply
The novel scythe, and stand to it on the field;
Lie in the furrows, rain-clouds for their tents;
Fronting the red artillery straighten spine;
Buckle the shiver at sight of comrades strewn;
Over an empty platter affect the merrily filled;
Die, if the multiple hazards around said die;
Downward measure a foeman mightily sized;
Laugh at the legs that would run for a life despised;
Lyrical on into death's red roaring jaw-gape, steeled   30
Gaily to take of the foe his lesson, and give reply.
Cheerful apprentices, they shall be masters soon!

X

Lo, where hurricane flocks of the North-wind rattle their thunder
Loud through a night, and at dawn comes change to the great
    South-west,
Hounds are the hounded in clouds, waves, forests, inverted the race:
Lo, in the day's young beams the colossal invading pursuers
Burst upon rocks and were foam;
Ridged up a torrent crest;
Crumbled to ruin, still gazing a glacial wonder;
Turned shamed feet toe to heel on their track at a panic pace.
Yesterday's clarion cock scudded hen of the invalid comb;
They, the triumphant tonant towering upper, were under;   10
They, violators of home, dared hope an inviolate home;
They that had stood for the stroke were the vigorous hewers;
Quick as the trick of the wrist with the rapier, they the pursuers.
Heavens and men amazed heard the arrogant crying for grace;
Saw the once hearth-reek rabble the scourge of an army dispieced;
Saw such a shift of the hunt as when Titan Olympus clomb.
Fly! was the sportsman's word; and the note of the quarry rang, Chase!

IX.26–28 *order in MS:* 27, 28, 26
X.4 colossal] pursuers *del. MS*
X.9 cock] cocks *del. MS*   hen] hens *del. MS*
X.15 hearth-reek] impure *del. MS*

XI

Banners from South, from East,
Sheaves of pale banners drooping hole and shred;
The captive brides of valour, Sabine Wives
Plucked from the foeman's blushful bed,
For glorious muted battle-tongues
Of deeds along the horizon's red,
At cost of unreluctant lives;
Her toilful heroes homeward poured,
To give their fevered mother air of the lungs.
She breathed, and in the breathing craved.   10
Environed as she was, at bay,
Safety she kissed on her drawn sword,
And waved for victory, for fresh victory waved:
She craved for victory as her daily bread;
For victory as her daily banquet raved.

XII

Now had her glut of vengeance left her grey
Of blood, who in her entrails fiercely tore
To clutch and squeeze her snakes; herself the more
Devitalizing: red was her Auroral ray;
Desired if but to paint her pallid hue.
The passion for that young horizon red,
Which dowered her with the flags, the blazing fame,
Like dotage of the past-meridian dame
For some bright Sungod adolescent, swelled
Insatiate, to the voracious grew,   10
The glutton's inward raveners bred;
Till she, mankind's most dreaded, most abhorred,

XI.6 along the] on the far *del. MS*
XI.8 toilful] tireless *MS, Cos*
XI.15 raved] craved *del. MS*
Section XII part of XI in MS; XIII numbered xii.

Witless in her demands on Fortune, asked,
As by the weaving Fates impelled,
To have the thing most loathed, the iron lord,
Controller and chastiser, under Victory masked.

XIII

Banners from East, from South.
She hugged him in them, feared the scourge they meant,
Yet blindly hugged, and hungering built his throne.
So may you see the village innocent,
With curtsey of shut lids and open mouth.
In act to beg for sweets expect a loathly stone:
See furthermore the Just in his measures weigh
Her sufferings and her sins, dispense her meed.
False to her bridegroom lord of the miracle day,
She fell: from his ethereal home observed   10
Through love, grown alien love, not moved to plead
Against the season's fruit for deadly Seed,
But marking how she had aimed, and where she swerved,
Why suffered, with a sad consenting thought.
Nor would he shun her sullen look, nor monstrous hold
The doer of the monstrous; she aroused,
She, the long tortured, suddenly freed, distraught,
More strongly the divine in him than when
Joy of her as she sprang from mould
Drew him the midway heavens adown   20
To clasp her in his arms espoused
Before the sight of wondering men,
And put upon the day a deathless crown.
The veins and arteries of her, fold in fold,
His alien love laid open, to divide
The martyred creature from her crimes; he knew

XII.13 *MS del.:* In her demands on Fortune, witless asked.
Between XII.13 and XII.14 line XII.16 del. MS
XII.15 *MS del.:* Her most loathed[?] & hated, the stern lord,
XIII.7 measures] measure *MS*
XIII.8 dispense her] & give the *del. MS*
XIII.21 clasp] fold *del. MS*

What cowardice in her valour could reside;
What strength her weakness covered; what abased
Sublimity so illumining, and what raised
This wallower in old slime to noblest heights,   30
Up to the union on the midway blue:—
Day that the celestial grave Recorder hangs
Among dark History's nocturnal lights,
With vivid beams indicative to the quick
Of all who have felt the vaulted body's pangs
Beneath a mind in hopeless soaring sick.
She had forgot how, long enslaved, she yearned
To the one helping hand above;
Forgot her faith in the Great Undiscerned,
Whereof she sprang aloft to her Angelical love   40
That day: and he, the bright day's husband, still with love,
Though alien, though to an upper seat retired,
Beheld a wrangling heart, as 'twere her soul
On eddies of wild waters cast;
In wilderness division; fired
For domination, freedom, lust,
The Pleasures; lo, a witch's snaky bowl
Set at her lips; the blood-drinker's madness fast
Upon her; and therewith mistrust,
Most of herself: a mouth of guile.   50
Compassionately could he smile,
To hear the mouth disclaiming God,
And clamouring for the Just!
Her thousand impulses, like torches, coursed
City and field; and pushed abroad
O'er hungry waves to thirsty sands,
Flaring at further; she had grown to be

XIII.35 vaulted] buried *del. MS*
XIII.37 forgot how, long] forgotten how *del. MS*
XIII.39 Forgot her] Her *del. MS*
XIII.42 retired] withdrawn *del. MS*
XIII.52 disclaiming] denying *MS*
XIII.56 hungry] tameless *MS, Cos*

The headless with the fearful hands;
To slaughter, else to suicide enforced.
But he, remembering how his love began,   60
And of what creature, pitied when was plain
Another measure of captivity
The need for strap and rod:
The penitential prayers again;
Again the bitter bowing down to dust;
The burden on the flesh for who disclaims the God
The answer when is call upon the Just.
Whence her lost virtue had found refuge strode
Her Master, saying, "I only; I who can!"
And echoed round her army, now her chain.   70
So learns the nation closing Anarch's reign,
That she had been in travail of a Man.

Napoléon

From the time that GM first reported to Alice Meynell that he had
started this poem, September 28, 1896, he alluded to it an extraordinary
number of times in his letters. It was "a big thing" in which Mrs. Walter
Palmer inspired him, October 1, 1896. By December 2, 1896, he was
midway. By the end of January, 1897, he reported that Fernand Ortmans,
editor of *Cosmopolis*, had visited him and wanted all three odes (*The
Revolution* and *Alsace-Lorraine* as well). On February 10, 1897, GM wrote
Mrs. Palmer that he was under the stress "of finishing the 'Napoléon.'"

He finally sent *Napoléon* to Alice Meynell on June 13, 1897, with a
statement of his problem in writing it: "Remember that it is an Ode of
History, which presents us with gross matter, and I must deal it out, to
be true to the subject. I have been tempted by the rhetorical—History's
pitfall for the Muse. I have avoided this as much as I could, even in the
Portrait, where antithesis invited strongly and was not always to be

THE REVOLUTION

XIII.66 disclaims] denies *MS*
XIII.69 master, saying] lord who said *del. MS*
XIII.71 So learns the nation closing] So might she learn at close of *MS*
XIII.72 had] had *or* has *MS*; has *Cos, 1898*

NAPOLÉON

Previously printed in Cosmopolis 10 (*April 1898*). *MSS:* Huntington HM6753. *Copy for
typist; corrected TS.*

shunned." According to a letter of December 6, 1897, he did not send *Alsace-Lorraine* to Mrs. Meynell because she had been shaken by *Napoléon*. All three odes were ready for Ortmans that month. He wrote of them to Frederick Greenwood, January 3, 1898: "You will think the Odes are long. But they do not dawdle, for the tussle between the soul of France and the Napoleonic grip has to be shown."

It is interesting to note that GM told Lady Ulrica Duncombe, December 1, 1900, that the "only true reading" of Napoleon was "to be had from the Mémoires of his Captains. I have them all. . . ."

GM was convinced that he had portrayed Napoleon correctly. A French admirer, Constantin Photiadès, recalled that when he had interviewed GM at length in September 1908, the latter asked him whether he had read the *Ode to Napoleon*. "I reply in the affirmative; but that I was particularly moved by the piece entitled, *France, December*, 1870, published at the time of our defeat, and so pulsating with affection. His reply is suggestive of some slight disappointment: 'Without doubt, it is the most successful and the most perfect; but the other touches me more, because I flatter myself that I have accurately drawn the character of Napoleon, and clearly stated that his genius was in absolute contradiction to the traditional genius of France'" (*George Meredith, His Life, Genius & Teaching*, rendered into English by Arthur Price [London: Constable, 1913], pp. 18–19).

On November 15, 1908, GM wrote Clement K. Shorter about some books he had been reading on Napoleon, and added: "I still think my portrait of him in the Ode 'Napoléon' is right. . . . The action and counteraction of Napoléon and France each on the other, are presented."

Mona E. Mackay in *Meredith et la France*, after listing some of the memoirs about Napoleon and his aides that were in GM's library, attests to the accurate historical details of this ode ([Paris: Boivin, 1937], pp. 200–01).

I

Cannon his name,
Cannon his voice, he came.
Who heard of him heard shaken hills,
An earth at quake, to quiet stamped;
Who looked on him beheld the will of wills,
The driver of wild flocks where lions ramped:
Beheld War's liveries flee him, like lumped grass
Nid-nod to ground beneath the cuffing storm;
While laurelled over his Imperial form,
Forth from her bearded tube of lacquey brass,   10

Reverberant notes and long blew volant Fame.
Incarnate Victory, Power manifest,
Infernal or God-given to mankind,
On the quenched volcano's cusp did he take stand,
A conquering army's height above the land,
Which calls that army offspring of its breast,
And sees it mid the starry camps enshrined;
His eye the cannon's flame,
The cannon's cave his mind.

II

To weld the nation in a name of dread,
And scatter carrion flies off wounds unhealed,
The Necessitated came, as comes from out
Electric ebon lightning's javelin-head,
Threatening annihilation in the revealed
Founts of our being; terrible with doubt,
With radiance restorative. At one stride
Athwart the Law he stood for sovereign sway.
That Soliform made featureless beside
His brilliancy who neighboured: vapour they;   10
Vapour what postured statutes barred his tread.
On high in amphitheatre field on field,
Italian, Egyptian, Austrian,
Far heard and of the carnage discord clear,
Bells of his escalading triumphs pealed
In crashes on a choral chant severe,
Heraldic of the authentic Charlemagne,
Globe, sceptre, sword, to enfold, to rule, to smite,
Make unity of the mass,
Coherent or refractory, by his might.   20

Forth from her bearded tube of lacquey brass,
Fame blew, and tuned the jangles, bent the knees
Rebellious or submissive; his decrees
Were thunder in those heavens and compelled:

I.11 Reverberant] The *del.* reverberant *MS*
II.11 statutes] statues *de L; corr. errata, de L 1911*

Such as disordered earth, eclipsed of stars,
Endures for sign of Order's calm return,
Whereunto she is vowed; and his wreckage-spars,
His harried ships, old riotous Ocean lifts alight,
Subdued to splendour in his delirant churn.
Glory suffused the accordant, quelled,   30
By magic of high sovereignty, revolt:
And he, the reader of men, himself unread;
The name of hope, the name of dread;
Bloom of the coming years or blight;
An arm to hurl the bolt
With aim Olympian; bore
Likeness to Godhead. Whither his flashes hied
Hosts fell; what he constructed held rock-fast.
So did earth's abjects deem of him that built and clove.
Torch on imagination, beams he cast,   40
Whereat they hailed him deified:
If less than an eagle-speeding Jove, than Vulcan more.
Or it might be a Vulcan-Jove,
Europe for smithy, Europe's floor
Lurid with sparks in evanescent showers,
Loud echo-clap of hammers at all hours,
Our skies the reflex of its furnace blast.

III

On him the long enchained, released
For bride of the miracle day up the midway blue;
She from her heavenly lover fallen to serve for feast
Of rancours and raw hungers; she, the untrue,
Yet pitiable, not despicable, gazed.
Fawning her body bent, she gazed
With eyes the moonstone portals to her heart:
Eyes magnifying through hysteric tears
This apparition, ghostly for belief;
Demoniac or divine, but sole   10

II.26 calm] sure[?] del. MS
II.36 Olympian] of the Deathly del. MS

Over earth's mightiest written Chief;
Earth's chosen, crowned, unchallengeable upstart:
The trumpet word to awake, transform, renew;
The arbiter of circumstance;
High above limitations, as the spheres.
Nor ever had heroical Romance,
Never ensanguined History's lengthened scroll,
Shown fulminant to shoot the levin dart
Terrific as this man, by whom upraised,
Aggrandized and begemmed, she outstripped her peers;   20
Like midnight's levying brazier-beacon blazed
Defiant to the world, a rally for her sons,
Day of the darkness; this man's mate; by him,
Cannon his name,
Rescued from vivisectionist and knave,
Her body's dominators and her shame;
By him with the rivers of ranked battalions, brave
Past mortal, girt: a march of swords and guns
Incessant; his proved warriors; loaded dice
He flung on the crested board, where chilly Fears   30
Behold the Reaper's ground, Death sitting grim,
Awatch for his predestined ones,
Mid shrieks and torrent-hooves; but these,
Inebriate of his inevitable device,
Hail it their hero's wood of lustrous laurel-trees,
Blossom and fruit of fresh Hesperides,
The boiling life-blood in their cheers.
Unequalled since the world was man they pour
A spiky girdle round her; these, her sons,
His cataracts at smooth holiday, soon to roar   40
Obstruction shattered at his will or whim:
Kind to her ear as quiring Cherubim,
And trampling earth like scornful mastodons.

III.13 awake] arrest *del. MS*
III.20 outstripped her] eclipsed all[?] *del. MS*
III.21 brazier-] brasier- *MS*
III.34 inevitable] dread[?] *del.* sure *del. MS*
III.39 A spiky girdle] Bright spiky girdles *del. MS*
III.41 Obstruction shattered] Whelming obstruction *del. MS*

IV

The flood that swept her to be slave
Adoring, under thought of being his mate,
These were, and unto the visibly unexcelled,
As much of heart as abjects can she gave,
Or what of heart the body bears for freight
When Majesty apparent overawes;
By the flash of his ascending deeds upheld,
Which let not feminine pride in him have pause
To question where the nobler pride rebelled.
She read the hieroglyphic on his brow,   10
Felt his firm hand to wield the giant's mace;
Herself whirled upward in an eagle's claws,
Past recollection of her earthly place;
And if cold Reason pressed her, called him Fate;
Offering abashed the servile woman's vow.
Delirium was her virtue when the look
At fettered wrists and violated laws
Faith in a rectitude Supernal shook,
Till worship of him shone as her last rational state,
The slave's apology for gemmed disgrace.   20
Far in her mind that leap from earth to the ghost
Midway on high; or felt as a troubled pool;
Or as a broken sleep that hunts a dream half lost,
Arrested and rebuked by the common school
Of daily things for truancy. She could rejoice
To know with wakeful eyeballs Violence
Her crowned possessor, and, on every sense
Incumbent, Fact, Imperial Fact, her choice,
In scorn of barren visions, aims at a glassy void.
Who sprang for Liberty once, found slavery sweet;   30
And Tyranny on alert subservience buoyed,
Spurred a blood-mare immeasureably fleet
To shoot the transient leagues in a passing wink,

IV.5 freight] weight *MS*
IV.10 hieroglyphic] [?] writing *del. MS*
Between IV.11 and IV.12 line IV.15 del. MS
IV.12–13 *not in MS; added in TS*

Prompt for the glorious bound at the fanged abyss's brink.
Scarce felt she that she bled when battle scored
On riddled flags the further conjured line;
From off the meteor gleam of his waved sword
Reflected bright in permanence: she bled
As the Bacchante spills her challengeing wine
With whirl o' the cup before the kiss to lip;   40
And bade drudge History in his footprints tread,
For pride of sword-strokes o'er slow penmanship:
Each step of his a volume: his sharp word
The shower of steel and lead
Or pastoral sunshine.

                                    V

Persistent through the brazen chorus round
His thunderous footsteps on the foeman's ground,
A broken carol of wild notes was heard,
As when an ailing infant wails a dream.
Strange in familiarity it rang:
And now along the dark blue vault might seem
Winged migratories having but heaven for home,
Now the lone sea-bird's cry down shocks of foam,
Beneath a ruthless paw the captive's pang.

It sang the gift that comes from God   10
To mind of man as air to lung.
So through her days of under sod
Her faith unto her heart had sung,
Like bedded seed by frozen clod,

IV.21 Far in] Lost to *del. MS*   ghost] gleam *del. MS*
IV.23 dream half lost] formless[?] dream *del. MS*
IV.24 rebuked] reproved *del. MS*
IV.38 bright in] in[?] glad *del. MS*
V.10 gift] thing *del. MS*
V.11 as] like *del. MS*

With view of wide-armed heaven and buds at burst
And midway up, Earth's fluttering little lyre.
Even for a glimpse, for even a hope in chained desire
The vision of it watered thirst.

VI

But whom those errant moans accused
As Liberty's murderous mother, cried accursed,
France blew to deafness: for a space she mused;
She smoothed a startled look, and sought,
From treasuries of the adoring slave,
Her surest way to strangle thought;
Picturing her dread lord decree advance
Into the enemy's land; artillery, bayonet, lance;
His ordering fingers point the dial's to time their ranks:
Himself the black storm-cloud, the tempest's bayonet-glaive.   10
Like foam-heads of a loosened freshet bursting banks,
By mount and fort they thread to swamp the sluggard plains.
Shines his gold-laurel sun, or cloak connivent rains.
They press to where the hosts in line and square throng mute;
He watchful of their form, the Audacious, the Astute;
Eagle to grip the field; to work his craftiest, fox.
From his brief signal, straight the stroke of the leveller falls;
From him those opal puffs, those arcs with the clouded balls:
He waves, and the voluble scene is a quagmire shifting blocks;
They clash, they are knotted, and now 'tis the deed of the
     axe on the log;   20
Here away moves a spiky woodland, and yon away sweep
Rivers of horse torrent-mad to the shock, and the heap over
     heap
Right through the troughed black lines turned to bunches or
     shreds, or a fog
Rolling off sunlight's arrows. Not mightier Phœbus in ire,
Nor deadlier Jove's avengeing right hand, than he of the brain

V.15 view of wide-armed] views of *del. MS*
V.17 a hope in chained] the hope in blind *del. MS*
VI.12 swamp the sluggard] [?] swamp the *del. MS*
VI.13 cloak] cloaks *del. MS*

Keen at an enemy's mind to encircle and pierce and constrain,
Muffling his own for a fate-charged blow very Gods may
    admire.
Sure to behold are his eagles on high where the conflict raged.
Rightly, then, should France worship, and deafen the disaccord
Of those who dare withstand an irresistible sword   30
To thwart his predestined subjection of Europe. Let them
    submit!
She said it aloud, and heard in her breast, as a singer caged,
With the beat of wings at bars, Earth's fluttering little lyre.
No more at midway heaven, but liker midway to the pit:
Not singing the spirally upward of rapture, the downward of
    pain
Rather, the drop sheer downward from pressure of
    merciless weight.

Her strangled thought got breath, with her worship held
    debate;
To yield and sink, yet eye askant the mark she had missed.
Over the black-blue rollers of that broad Westerly main,
Steady to sky, the light of Liberty glowed   40
In a flaming pillar, that cast on the troubled waters a road
For Europe to cross, and see the thing lost subsist.
For there 'twas a shepherd led his people, no butcher of
    sheep;
Firmly there the banner he first upreared,
Stands to rally; and nourishing grain do his children reap
From a father beloved in life, in his death revered.
Contemplating him and his work, shall a skyward glance
Clearer sight of our dreamed and abandoned obtain;
Nay, but as if seen in station above the Republic, France
Had view of her one-day's heavenly lover again;   50

VI.27 *MS del.:* By muffling his own for a fatal[?] blow that the Gods admire.
Between VI.27 and VI.28 a break, MS, TS
VI.30 dare] *Cos, 1898;* dared *MS, TS*
VI.45 children] people *del. MS*
VI.50 view] glimpse *del. MS*

Saw him amid the bright host looking down on her; knew
    she had erred,
Knew him her judge, knew yonder the spirit preferred;
Yonder the base of the summit she strove that day to ascend,
Ere cannon mastered her soul, and all dreams had end.

VII

Soon felt she in her shivered frame
A bodeful drain of blood illume
Her wits with frosty fire to read
The dazzling wizard who would have her bleed
On fruitless marsh and snows of spectral gloom
For victory that was victory scarce in name.
Husky his clarions laboured, and her sighs
O'er slaughtered sons were heavier than the prize;
Recalling how he stood by Frederic's tomb,
With Frederic's country underfoot and spurned: 10
There meditated; till her hope might guess,
Albeit his constant star prescribe success,
The savage strife would sink, the civil aim
To head a mannered world breathe zephyrous
Of morning after storm; whereunto she yearned;
And Labour's lovely peace, and Beauty's courtly bloom,
The mind in strenuous tasks hilarious.
At such great height, where hero hero topped,
Right sanely should the Grand Ascendant think
No further leaps at the fanged abyss's brink   20
True Genius takes: be battle's dice-box dropped!

She watched his desert features, hung to hear
The honey words desired, and veiled her face;
Hearing the Seaman's name recur
Wrathfully, thick with a meaning worse

VI.52 knew] & *del. MS*
VII.1 Soon] Now *del. MS*
VII.5 spectral] wintry *MS*
VII.7 Husky his clarions laboured] Faint blew[?] *del.* Faint pealed his wonted clarions
del. MS
VII.19 should] would *del. MS*   Grand] young *del. MS*
VII.21 True Genius takes] Should Genius take *del. MS*

Than call to the march: for that inveterate Purse
Could kindle the extinct, inform a vacant place,
Conjure a heart into the trebly felled.
It squeezed tne globe, insufferably swelled
To feed insurgent Europe: rear and van   30
Were haunted by the amphibious curse;
Here flesh, there phantom, livelier after rout:
The Seaman piping aye to the rightabout,
Distracted Europe's Master, puffed remote
Those Indies of the swift Macedonian,
Whereon would Europe's Master somewhiles doat,
In dreamings on a docile universe
Beneath an immarcessible Charlemagne.

Nor marvel France should veil a seer's face,
And call on darkness as a blest retreat.   40
Magnanimously could her iron Emperor
Confront submission: hostile stirred to heat
All his vast enginery, allowed no halt
Up withered avenues of waste-blood war,
To the pitiless red mounts of fire afume,
As 'twere the world's arteries opened! Woe the race!
Ask wherefore Fortune's vile caprice should balk
His panther spring across the foaming salt,
From martial sands to the cliffs of pallid chalk!
There is no answer: seed of black defeat   50
She then did sow, and France nigh unto death foredoom.

See since that Seaman's epicycle sprite
Engirdle, lure and goad him to the chase
Along drear leagues of crimson spotting white
With mother's tears of France, that he may meet
Behind suborned battalions, ranked as wheat

VII.31 the amphibious curse] these[?] gatherings to disperse *del. MS*
VII.33 The] That *del. MS*
VII.38 an] the more *MS*   immarcessible] magnificent[?] *del. MS*
VII.43 allowed] & allowed *del. MS*
VII.44 withered] the withered *del. MS*
VII.45 *not in MS; added in TS*
VII.46 As 'twere] Like *del. MS*

Where peeps the weedy poppy, him of the sea;
Earth's power to baffle Ocean's power resume;
Victorious army crown o'er Victory's fleet;
And bearing low that Seaman upon knee,   60
Stay the vexed question of supremacy,
Obnoxious in the vault by Frederic's tomb.

VIII

Poured streams of Europe's veins the flood
Full Rhine or Danube rolls off morning-tide
Through shadowed reaches into crimson-dyed:
And Rhine and Danube knew her gush of blood
Down the plucked roots the deepest in her breast.
He tossed her cordials, from his laurels pressed.
She drank for dryness thirstily, praised his gifts.
The blooded frame a powerful draught uplifts,
Writhed the devotedness her voice rang wide
In cries ecstatic, as of the martyr-Blest,   10
Their spirits issuing forth of bodies racked,
And crazy chuckles, with life's tears at feud;
While near her heart the sunken sentinel
Called Critic marked, and dumb in awe reviewed
This torture, this anointed, this untracked
To mortal source, this alien of his kind;
Creator, slayer, conjuror, Solon-Mars,
The cataract of the abyss, the star of stars;
Whose arts to lay the senses under spell
Aroused an insurrectionary mind.   20

IX

He, did he love her? France was his weapon, shrewd
At edge, a wind in onset: he loved well
His tempered weapon, with the which he hewed
Clean to the ground impediments, or hacked,

VIII.3 Through] Down del. MS
VIII.5 Down] From del. MS
VIII.13 near] down[?] del. MS
VIII.14 marked] wakened[?] del. MS

Sure of the blade that served the great man-miracle.
He raised her, robed her, gemmed her for his bride,
Did but her blood in blindness given exact.
Her blood she gave, was blind to him as guide:
She quivered at his word, and at his touch
Was hound or steed for any mark he espied.   10
He loved her more than little, less than much.
The fair subservient of Imperial Fact
Next to his consanguineous was placed
In ranked esteem; above the diurnal meal,
Vexatious carnal appetites above,
Above his hoards, while she Imperial Fact embraced,
And rose but at command from under heel.
The love devolvent, the ascension love,
Receptive or profuse, were fires he lacked,
Whose marrow had expelled their wasteful sparks;   20
Whose mind, the vast machine of endless haste,
Took up but solids for its glowing seal.
The hungry love, that fish-like creatures feel,
Impelled for prize of hooks, for prey of sharks,
His night's first quarter sicklied to distaste,
In warm enjoyment barely might distract.
A head that held an Europe half devoured,
Taste in the blood's conceit of pleasure soured.
Nought save his rounding aim, the means he plied,
Death for his cause, to him could point appeal.   30
His mistress was the thing of uses tried.
Frigid the netting smile on whom he wooed,
But on his Policy his eye was lewd.
That sharp long zig-zag into distance brooked
No foot across; a shade his ire provoked.
The blunder or the cruelty of a deed,

IX.20 wasteful] early *MS*
IX.21 mind] head *del. MS*   endless] tireless *MS, TS, Cos*

His Policy imperative could plead.
He deemed nought other precious, nor knew he
Legitimate outside his Policy.
Men's lives and works were due, from their birth's date,   40
To the State's shield and sword, himself the State.
He thought for them in mass, as Titan may;
For their pronounced well-being bade obey;
O'er each obstructive thicket thunderclapped,
And straight their easy road to market mapped.

Watched Argus to survey the huge preserves
He held or coveted; Mars was armed alert
At sign of motion; yet his brows were murk,
His gorge would surge, to see the butcher's work,
The Reaper's field; a sensitive in nerves.   50
He rode not over men to do them hurt.
As one who claimed to have for paramour
Earth's fairest form, he dealt the cancelling blow;
Impassioned, still impersonal; to ensure
Possession; free of rivals, not their foe.

IX.37 imperative could plead] necessitous decreed *MS*
After IX.37 MS:

> A God and Devil yoked in him appear
> Drawing him on, his will for charioteer.
> In him, with Laws he trampled, Laws he coined,
> Lycurgus and a Bandit Frate joined.

IX.38–45 *not in MS; added in TS*

Between IX.45 and IX.46 TS:

> Transcendent and adept devise and rear
> Yoked to his car, his will for charioteer.
> In him, with Laws he trampled, Laws he coined,
> Lycurgus and a bandit Frate joined.
> Around the brain which spun a concrete globe,
> Imagination was its cloudy robe,
> Used by him for a leaven or a brand
> To swell the sluggish, light the fires he fanned.

IX.46 survey] protect *MS*
IX.47 armed alert] fore defied *del. MS*
IX.48 sign of] any signal *del. MS*
IX.51 rode] drove *del. MS*
IX.53 dealt] struck *MS*

The common Tyrant's frenzies, rancour, spites,
He knew as little as men's claim on rights.
A kindness for old servants, early friends,
Was constant in him while they served his ends;
And if irascible, 'twas the moment's reek   60
From fires diverted by some gusty freak.
His Policy the act which breeds the act
Prevised, in issues accurately summed
From reckonings of men's tempers, terrors, needs:—
That universal army, which he leads
Who builds Imperial on Imperious Fact.
Within his hot brain's hammering workshop hummed
A thousand furious wheels at whirr, untired
As Nature in her reproductive throes;
And did they grate, he spake, and cannon fired: 70
The cause being aye the incendiary foes
Proved by prostration culpable. His dispense
Of Justice made his active conscience;
His passive was of ceaseless labour formed.
So found this Tyrant sanction and repose;
Humanly just, inhumanly unwarmed.

Preventive fencings with the foul intent
Occult, by him observed and foiled betimes,
Let fool historians chronicle as crimes.
His blows were dealt to clear the way he went: 80
Too busy sword and mind for needless blows.
The mighty bird of sky minutest grains
On ground perceived; in heaven but rays or rains;
In humankind diversities of masks,
For rule of men the choice of bait or goads.

IX.56 rancour] rancours *del. MS*
IX.57 claim] claims *MS, TS*
IX.58–61 *not in MS; added in TS*
IX.62 which] that *MS*
IX.64 terrors] passions *del. MS*
IX.78 observed] perceived *del. MS*

The statesman steered the despot to large tasks;
The despot drove the statesman on short roads.
For Order's cause he laboured, as inclined
A soldier's training and his Euclid mind.
His army unto men he could present   90
As model of the perfect instrument.

That creature, woman, was the sofa soft,
When warriors their dusty armour doffed,
And read their manuals for the making truce
With rosy frailties framed to reproduce.
He farmed his land, distillingly alive
For the utmost extract he might have and hive,
Wherewith to marshal force; and in like scheme,
Benign shone Hymen's torch on young love's dream.
Thus to be strong was he beneficent;   100
A fount of earth, likewise a firmament.

The disputant in words his eye dismayed:
Opinions blocked his passage. Rent
Were Councils with a gesture; brayed
By hoarse camp-phrase what argument
Dared interpose to waken spleen
In him whose vision grasped the unseen,
Whose counsellor was the ready blade,
Whose argument the cannonade.
He loathed his land's divergent parties, loth   110
To grant them speech, they were such idle troops;
The friable and the grumous, dizzards both.
Men were good sticks his mastery wrought from hoops;
Some serviceable, none credible on oath.

IX.86 large] hard *del. MS*
IX.90–95 *not in MS; added in TS*
IX.90 *TS del.:* His army to mankind did he present
IX.92 the] a *del. TS*
IX.94 for the making] to make *del. TS*
IX.95 rosy] tameless[?] *del. TS*
IX.102 eye] look *del. MS*
IX.104 a] sharp *del. MS*

The silly preference they nursed to die
In beds he scorned, and led where they should lie.
If magic made them pliable for his use,
Magician he could be by planned surprise.
For do they see the deuce in human guise,
As men's acknowledged head appears the deuce,   120
And they will toil with devilish craft and zeal.
Among them certain vagrant wits that had
Ideas buzzed; they were the feebly mad;
Pursuers of a film they hailed ideal;
But could be dangerous fire-flies for a brain
Subdued by fact, still amorous of the inane.
With a breath he blew them out, to beat their wings
The way of such transfeminated things,
And France had sense of vacancy in Light.

That is the soul's dead darkness, making clutch   130
Wild hands for aid at muscles within touch;
Adding to slavery's chain the stringent twist;
Even when it brings close surety that aright
She reads her Tyrant through his golden mist;
Perceives him fast to a harsher Tyrant bound;
Self-ridden, self-hunted, captive of his aim;
Material grandeur's ape, the Infernal's hound;
Enormous, with no infinite around;
No starred deep sky, no Muse, or lame
The dusty pattering pinions,   140
The voice as through the brazen tube of Fame.

X

Hugest of engines, a much limited man,
She saw the Lustrous, her great lord, appear
Through that smoked glass her last privation brought

IX.115 nursed] had[?] *del. MS*
IX.116 led] showed *del. MS*
IX.119 do] when *del. MS*
IX.126 inane] insane *MS*
Before X.1 MS del.:
                    France owned a lord; in their own likeness owned
                    The unmannered, graceless [?] [?]

To point her critic eye and spur her thought:
A heart but to propel Leviathan;
A spirit that breathed but in earth's atmosphere.
Amid the plumed and sceptred ones
Irradiatingly Jovian,
The mountain tower capped by the floating cloud;
A nursery screamer where dialectics ruled: 10
Mannerless, graceless, laughterless, unlike
Herself in all, yet with such power to strike,
That she the various features she could scan,
Dared not to sum, though seeing: and befooled
By power which beamed omnipotent, she bowed,
Subservient as roused echo round his guns.
Invulnerable Prince of Myrmidons,
He sparkled, by no sage Athene schooled.
Partly she read her riddle, stricken and pained;
But irony, her spirit's tongue, restrained.   20
The Critic, last of vital in the proud
Enslaved, when most detectively endowed,
Admired how irony's venom off him ran,
Like rain-drops down a statue cast in bronze:
Whereby of her keen rapier disarmed,
Again her chant of eulogy began,
Protesting, but with slavish senses charmed.

Her warrior, chief among the valorous great
In arms he was, dispelling shades of blame,
With radiance palpable in fruit and weight.   30
Heard she reproach, his victories blared response;
His victories bent the Critic to acclaim,
As with fresh blows upon a ringing sconce.
Or heard she from scarred ranks of jolly growls,

X.1–10 *MS, 6-line draft del.: lines 1, 2 & 7, 8–10*
  2 & 7 She saw her Master: mid the sceptred ones,
  9 The] A   by] with
X.17–18 *not in MS; added in TS*
X.25–27 *not in MS; added in TS*
X.30 *not in MS; added in TS*
X.31 reproach] the word *MS*   blared] roused[?] *del. MS*
X.33–38 *not in MS; added in TS*

His veterans dwarf their reverence and, like owls,
Laugh in the pitch of discord, to exalt
Their idol for some genial trick or fault,
She, too, became his marching veteran.
Again she took her breath from them who bore
His eagles through the tawny roar,   40
And murmured at a peaceful state,
That bred the title charlatan,
As missile from the mouth of hate,
For one the daemon fierily filled and hurled,
Cannon his name,
Shattering against a barrier world;
Her supreme player of man's primaeval game.

The daemon filled him, and he filled her sons;
Strung them to stature over human height,
As march the standards down the smoky fight;   50
Her cherubim, her towering mastodons!
Directed vault or breach, break through
Earth's toughest, seasons, elements, tame;
Dash at the bulk the sharpened few;
Count death the smallest of their debts:
Show that the will to do,
Is masculine and begets!

These princes unto him the mother owed;
These jewels of manhood that rich hand bestowed.
What wonder, though with wits awake   60
To read her riddle, for these her offspring's sake;—
And she, before high heaven adulteress,
The lost to honour, in his glory clothed,

X.41 murmured] fretted *MS*
X.52 Directed] Commanded *del. MS*
X.60 though] if *MS*
X.62 And she] And she *del.* She, too *MS*

Else naked, shamed in sight of men, self-loathed;—
That she should quench her thought, nor worship less
Than ere she bled on sands or snows and knew
The slave's alternative, to worship or to rue!

XI

Bright from the shell of that much limited man,
Her hero, like the falchion out of sheath,
Like soul that quits the tumbled body, soared:
And France, impulsive, nuptial with his plan,
Albeit the Critic fretting her, adored
Once more. Exultingly her heart went forth,
Submissive to his mind and mood,
The way of those pent-eyebrows North;
For now was he to win the wreath
Surpassing sunniest in camp or Court;   10
Next, as the blessed harvest after years of blight,
Sit, the Great Emperor, to be known the Good!

Now had the Seaman's volvent sprite,
Lean from the chase that barked his contraband,
A beggared applicant at every port,
To strew the profitless deeps and rot beneath,
Slung northward, for a hunted beast's retort
On sovereign power; there his final stand,
Among the perjured Scythian's shaggy horde,
The hydrocephalic aërolite   20
Had taken; flashing thence repellent teeth,
Though Europe's Master Europe's Rebel banned
To be earth's outcast, ocean's lord and sport.

X.65 That she should quench her thought] Should quench her speaking[?] mind
del. MS
X.66 or] & *del. MS*
XI.5 Albeit] Though with *MS*
XI.11 Next] Then *del.* Soon *del. MS*
XI.17 for a hunted beast's retort] [?] his final stand *del. MS*
XI.21 repellent] defiant *del. MS*

Unmoved might seem the Master's taunted sword.
Northward his dusky legions nightly slipped,
As on the map of that all-provident head;
He luting Peace the while, like morning's cock
The quiet day to round the hours for bed;
No pastoral shepherd sweeter to his flock.
Then Europe first beheld her Titan stripped.   30
To what vast length of limb and mounds of thews,
How trained to scale the eminences, pluck
The hazards for new footing, how compel
Those timely incidents by men named luck,
Through forethought that defied the Fates to choose
Her grovelling admiration had not yet
Imagined of the great man-miracle;
And France recounted with her comic smile,
Duplicities of Court and Cabinet,
The silky female of his male in guile,   40
Wherewith her two-faced Master could amuse
A dupe he charmed in sunny beams to bask,
Before his feint for camisado struck
The lightning moment of the cast-off mask.

Splendours of earth repeating heaven's at set
Of sun down mountain cloud in masses arched;
Since Asia upon Europe marched,
Unmatched the copious multitudes; unknown
To Gallia's over-runner, Rome's inveterate foe,
Such hosts; all one machine for overthrow,   50
Coruscant from the Master's hand, compact
As reasoned thoughts in the Master's head; were shown
Yon lightning moment when his acme might

XI.24 might seem] appeared *del. MS*

Between XI.37 and XI.38 MS del.: Whose grandeur gave her [?]

XI.40 male] masculine *del. MS*
XI.43 Before] Until *del. MS*
XI.45 repeating] outvieing *MS*
XI.51 Coruscant from] Directed by *del. MS*
XI.52 reasoned thoughts] signs *del. MS*

Blazed o'er the stream that cuts the sandy tract
Borussian from Sarmatia's famished flat;
The century's flower; and off its pinnacled throne,
Rayed servitude on Europe's ball of sight.

XII

Behind the Northern curtain-folds he passed.
There heard hushed France her muffled heart beat fast
Against the hollow ear-drum, where she sat
In expectation's darkness, until cracked
The straining curtain-seams: a scaly light
Was ghost above an army under shroud.
Imperious on Imperial Fact
Incestuously the incredible begat.
His veterans and auxiliaries,
The trained, the trustful, sanguine, proud,   10
Princely, scarce numerable to recite,—
Titanic of all Titan tragedies!—
That Northern curtain took them, as the seas
Gulp the great ships to give back shipmen white.

Alive in marble, she conceived in soul,
With barren eyes and mouth, the mother's loss;
The bolt from her abandoned heaven sped;
The snowy army rolling knoll on knoll
Beyond horizon, under no blest Cross:
By the vulture dotted and engarlanded.   20

Was it a necromancer lured
To weave his tense betraying spell?
A Titan whom our God endured
Till he of his foul hungers fell,

XII.2 There heard hushed France her muffled] And there France heard her active
del. MS
XII.5 scaly] dubious[?] *del. MS*
XII.6 Was ghost above] Hung ghostly on *del. MS*
XII.21–25 *not in MS; added in TS*

By all his craft and labour scourged?
A deluge Europe's liberated wave,
Pæan to sky, leapt over that vast grave.
Its shadow-points against her sacred land converged.
And him, her yoke-fellow, her black lord, her fate,
In doubt, in fevered hope, in chills of hate,   30
That tore her old credulity to strips,
Then pressed the auspicious relics on her lips,
His withered slave for foregone miracles urged.
And he, whom now his ominous halo's round,
A three parts blank decrescent sickle, crowned,
Prodigious in catastrophe, could wear
The realm of Darkness with its Prince's air;
Assume in mien the resolute pretence
To satiate an hungered confidence,
Proved criminal by the sceptic seen to cower   40
Beside the generous face of that frail flower.

XIII

Desire and terror then had each of each:
His crown and sword were staked on the magic stroke;
Her blood she gave as one who loved her leech;
And both did barter under union's cloak.
An union in hot fever and fierce need
Of either's aid, distrust in trust did breed.
Their traffic instincts hooded their live wits
To issues. Never human fortune throve
On such alliance. Viewed by fits,
From Vulcan's forge a hovering Jove   10
Evolved. The slave he dragged the Tyrant drove.
Her awe of him his dread of her invoked:
His nature with her shivering faith ran yoked.

XII.32 Then] And *del. MS*
XII.39 an] her *del. TS*
XII.41 frail] false *MS*
XIII.9 Viewed] Dim *MS*
XIII.10 From] In[?] *del. MS*
XIII.11 Evolved] Appeared *del. MS*

What wisdom counselled, Policy declined;
All perils dared he save the step behind.
Ahead his grand initiative becked:
One spark of radiance blurred, his orb was wrecked.
Stripped to the despot upstart, for success
He raged to clothe a perilous nakedness.
He would not fall, while falling; would not be taught,   20
While learning; would not relax his grasp on aught
He held in hand, while losing it; pressed advance,
Pricked for her lees the veins of wasted France;
Who, had he stayed to husband her, had spun
The strength he taxed unripened for his throw,
In vengeful casts calamitous,
On fields where palsying Pyrrhic laurels grow,
The luminous the ruinous.
An incalescent scorpion,
And fierier for the mounded cirque   30
That narrowed at him thick and murk,
This gambler with his genius
Flung lives in angry volleys, bloody lightnings, flung
His fortunes to the hosts he stung,
With victories clipped his eagle's wings.
By the hands that built him up was he undone:
By the star aloft, which was his ram's-head will
Within; by the toppling throne the soldier won;
By the yeasty ferment of what once had been,
To cloud a rational mind for present things;   40
By his own force, the suicide in his mill.
Needs never God of Vengeance intervene
When giants their last lesson have to learn.
Fighting against an end he could discern,
The chivalry whereof he had none,

XIII.18–19 *not in MS; added in TS*
XIII.26 vengeful] repercussent *MS, TS, Cos*
XIII.35 eagle's] eagles' *MS, TS*
XIII.41 *not in MS; added in TS*
XIII.42 God of Vengeance] those bright heavens to *del.* the angelical *MS*
XIII.43 their last lesson have] have their latest task *MS*

He called from his worn slave's abundant springs:
Not deigning spousally entreat
That ever blinded by his martial skill,
But harsh to have her worship counted out
In human coin, her vital rivers drained,　　　　　　　　50
Her infant forests felled, commanded die
The decade thousand deaths for his Imperial seat,
Where throning he her faith in him maintained;
Bound Reason to believe delayed defeat
Was triumph; and what strength in her remained
To head against the ultimate foreseen rout,
Insensate taxed; of his impenitent will,
Servant and sycophant: without ally,
In Python's coils, the Master Craftsman still;
The smiter, panther springer, trapper sly,　　　　　　　60
The deadly wrestler at the crucial bout,
The penetrant, the tonant, tower of towers,
Striking from black disaster starry showers.
Her supreme player of man's primaeval game,
He won his harnessed victim's rapturous shout,
When every move was mortal to her frame,
Her prayer to life that stricken he might lie,
She to exchange his laurels for earth's flowers.

The innumerable whelmed him, and he fell:
A vessel in mid-ocean under storm.　　　　　　　　70
Ere ceased the lullaby of his passing bell,
He sprang to sight, in human form
Revealed, from no celestial aids:
The shades enclosed him, and he fired the shades.

Cannon his name,
Cannon his voice, he came.
The fount of miracles from drought-dust arose,

XIII.56 ultimate foreseen] dusky ultimate *MS*
XIII.57 Insensate] Relentless *MS, TS, Cos*
XIII.65 his] the *MS*
XIII.71 passing] burial[?] *del. MS*
XIII.72 in human form] from no celestials aids *del. MS*

Amazing even on his Imperial stage,
Where marvels lightened through the alternate hours
And winged o'er human earth's heroical shone.   80
Into the press of cumulative foes,
Across the friendly fields of smoke and rage,
A broken structure bore his furious powers;
The man no more, the Warrior Chief the same;
Match for all rivals; in himself but flame
Of an outworn lamp, to illumine nought anon.
Yet loud as when he first showed War's effete
Their Schoolman off his eagre mounted high,
And summoned to subject who dared compete,
The cannon in the name Napoleon   90
Discoursed of sulphur earth to curtained sky.

So through a tropic day a regnant sun,
Where armies of assailant vapours thronged,
His glory's trappings laid on them: comes night,
Enwraps him in a bosom quick of heat
From his anterior splendours, and shall seem
Day instant, Day's own lord in the furnace gleam,
The virulent quiver on ravished eyes prolonged,
When severed darkness, all flaminical bright,
Slips vivid eagles linked in rapid flight;   100
Which bring at whiles the lionly far roar,
As wrestled he with manacles and gags,

XIII.77 *MS:* The wondrous apparition rose, *TS:* The fount of miracles from drought-dust arose
XIII.83 structure] engine *del. MS*   furious] quenchless *MS, TS*
Between XIII.84 and XIII.85 MS: His presence & illusion: here, & gone. *del. TS*
XIII.86 an outworn lamp, to illumine] outworn lamp, to lighten *del. MS*
XIII.87 Yet loud as] Louder than *del. MS*   showed] read *MS*
XIII.88 Schoolman] lesson *MS*   eagre] eagle *misp. GMT*
XIII.89 subject] reprove *MS*
XIII.91 *MS del.:* Discoursed of [?] earth to shaken clouded sky.
XIII.94 comes] till *MS*
XIII.95 Enwraps] Enwrapped *del. MS*
XIII.96 shall] might *del.* may *MS*
XIII.100 Slips] Slipped *del. MS*
XIII.101 bring] made *del. MS*   lionly far] distant[?] *del. MS*

To speed across a cowering world once more,
Superb in ordered floods, his lordly flags.
His name on silence thundered, on the obscure
Lightened; it haunted morn and even-song:
Earth of her prodigy's extinction long,
With shudderings and with thrillings, hung unsure.

Snapped was the chord that made the resonant bow,
In France, abased and like a shrunken corse;   110
Amid the weakest weak, the lowest low,
From the highest fallen, stagnant off her source;
Condemned to hear the nations' hostile mirth;
See curtained heavens, and smell a sulphurous earth;
Which told how evermore shall tyrant Force
Beget the greater for its overthrow.
The song of Liberty in her hearing spoke
A foreign tongue; Earth's fluttering little lyre
Unlike, but like the raven's ravening croak.
Not till her breath of being could aspire   120
Anew, this loved and scourged of Angels found
Our common brotherhood in sight and sound:
When mellow rang the name Napoleon,
And dim aloft her young Angelical waved.
Between ethereal and gross to choose,
She swung; her soul desired, her senses craved.
They pricked her dreams, while oft her skies were dun
Behind o'ershadowing foemen: on a tide
They drew the nature having need of pride
Among her fellows for its vital dues: 130
He seen like some rare treasure-galleon,
Hull down, with masts against the Western hues.

XIII.103 speed] march *del. MS*
XIII.104 Superb in ordered floods] Magnificent in force *del. MS*
XIII.111 Amid] Among *del. MS*
XIII.114 a sulphurous] the sulphur *del. MS*
XIII.116 Beget] Create *MS*
XIII.125 ethereal] etherial *MS, TS*
XIII.126 swung] hung *MS*
XIII.130 Among] Amid *del. MS*   vital] natural *del. MS*

Alsace-Lorraine

I

The sister Hours in circles linked,
Daughters of men, of men the mates,
Are gone on flow with the day that winked,
With the night that spanned at golden gates.
Mothers, they leave us, quickening seed;
They bear us grain or flower or weed,
As we have sown; is nought extinct
For them we fill to be our Fates.
Life of the breath is but the loan;
Passing death what we have sown.   10

Pearly are they till the pale inherited stain
Deepens in us, and the mirrors they form on their flow,
Darken to feature and nature: a volumed chain,
Sequent of issue, in various eddies they show.
Theirs is the Book of the River of Life, to read
Leaf by leaf by reapers of long-sown seed:
There doth our shoot up to light from a spiriting sane,
Stand as a tree whereon numberless clusters grow:
Legible there how the heart, with its one false move,
Cast Eurydice pallor on all we love.   20

Our fervid heart has filled that Book in chief;
Our fitful heart a wild reflection views;
Our craving heart of passion suckling grief,
Disowns the author's work it must peruse;

Previously printed in Cosmopolis *10 (May 1898). MSS:* Huntington HM6756, *title:* "*Alsace-Lorraine: An Ode.*" *Copy for typist; corrected TS;* Texas, *later corrected TS.*

I.3 on] or *misp. TSS*
I.12 form] build *del. MS*
I.16 reapers] the reapers *del. MS*
I.20 all we] all [that *del.*] we *MS*
I.21 Our] The *del. MS*
I.22 Our] This *del. MS*
I.23 Our] This *del. MS*

Inconscient in its leap to wreak the deed,
A round of harvests red from crimson seed,
It marks the current Hours show leaf by leaf,
And rails at Destiny; nor traces clues;
Though sometimes it may think what novel light
Will strike their faces when the mind shall write.   30

II

Succourful daughters of men are the rosed and starred
Revolving Twelves in their fluent germinal rings,
Despite the burden to chasten, abase, depose.
Fallen on France, as the sweep of scythe over sward,
They breathed in her ear their voice of the crystal springs,
That run from a twilight rise, from a twilight close,
Through alternate beams and glooms, rejoicingly young.
Only to Earth's best loved, at the breathless turns
Where Life in fold of the Shadow reclines unstrung,
And a ghostly lamp of their moment's union burns,   10
Will such pure notes from the fountain-head be sung.

Voice of Earth's very soul to the soul she would see renewed:
A song that sought no tears, that laid not a touch on the breast
Sobbing aswoon and, like last foxgloves' bells upon ferns
In sandy alleys of woodland silence, shedding to bare.
Daughters of Earth and men, they piped of her natural brood;
Her patient helpful four-feet; wings on the flit or in nest;
Paws at our old-world task to scoop a defensive lair;
Snouts at hunt through the scented grasses; enhavened scuts

I.25 in] *TS H, Cos;* of *MS, TS T, 1898*
I.30 Will] Would *del. MS*
II.3 the] their *del. MS*   chasten] strengthen *del. MS*
II.7 Through alternate] Thorough the *del. MS*
II.9 fold] the *del.* fold *MS*
II.10 a] the *del. MS*
II.11 such] those *del. MS*   fountain-head] primal fount *MS, TSS, Cos*
II.14 foxgloves'] foxglove *MS;* foxgloves *TSS*
II.15 shedding] stripping *del. MS*
II.16 men] of *del.* men *MS*
II.17 wings] birds *del.* wings *MS*

Flashing escape under show of a laugh nigh the mossed
    burrow-mouth.   20
Sack-like droop bronze pears on the nailed branch-frontage
    of huts,
To greet those wedded toilers from acres where sweat is a
    shower.
Snake, cicada, lizard, on lavender slopes up South,
Pant for joy of a sunlight driving the fielders to bower.
Sharpened in silver by one chance breeze is the olive's grey;
A royal-mantle floats, a red fritillary hies;
The bee, for whom no flower of garden or wild has nay,
Noises, heard if but named, so hot is the trade he plies.
Processions beneath green arches of herbage, the long
    colonnades;
Laboured mounds that a foot or a wanton stick may subvert;   30
Homely are they for a lowly look on bedewed grass-blades,
On citied fir-droppings, on twisted wreaths of the worm in
    dirt.

Does nought so loosen our sight from the despot heart, to
    receive
Balm of a sound Earth's primary heart at its active beat:
The motive, yet servant of energy; simple as morn and eve;
Treasureless, fetterless; free of the bonds of a great conceit:
Unwounded even by cruel blows on a body that writhes;
Nor whimpering under misfortune; elusive of obstacles; prompt
To quit any threatened familiar domain seen doomed by the
    scythes;
Its day's hard business done, the score to the good accompt.   40

II.20 under] with *del. MS*   show] glint *del. MS*
II.21 Sack-like droop] Heavily sweet *del. MS*
II.25 in] to *del. MS*
II.28 named] imaged *del. MS*
II.32 citied] piled *del.* staged *del. MS*   droppings] sheddings *del. MS*
II.39 To quit any threatened familiar] At a signal to quit a threatened *del. MS*
II.40 Its] Their *del. MS*   [?] the [glad *del.*] score *MS*

Creatures of forest and mead, Earth's essays in being, all kinds
Bound by the navel-knot to the Mother, never astray,
They in the ear upon ground will pour their intuitive minds,
Cut man's tangles for Earth's first broad rectilinear way:
Admonishing loftier reaches, the rich adventurous shoots,
Pushes of tentative curves, embryonic upwreathings in air;
Not always the sprouts of Earth's root-Laws preserving her
    brutes;
Oft but our primitive hungers licentious in fine and fair.

Yet the like aërial growths may chance be the delicate sprays,
Infant of Earth's most urgent in sap, her fierier zeal   50
For entry on Life's upper fields: and soul thus flourishing
    pays
The martyr's penance, mark for brutish in man to heel.

Her, from a nerveless well among stagnant pools of the dry,
Through her good aim at divine, shall commune with Earth
    remake;
Fraternal unto sororial, her, where abashed she may lie,
Divinest of man shall clasp; a world out of darkness awake,
As it were with the Resurrection's eyelids uplifted, to see
Honour in shame, in substance the spirit, in that dry fount
Jets of the songful ascending silvery-bright water-tree
Spout, with our Earth's unbaffled resurgent desire for the
    mount,   60
Though broken at intervals, clipped, and barren in seeming
    it be.

II.43 in the ear upon ground will pour] to a studious thought will yield *del. MS*
II.48 our] the *del. MS*
II.49 the like from] *del.* among *del. MS*
II.50 fierier] fieriest *del. MS*
II.51 and soul thus flourishing] & whoso beareth them *del. MS*
II.53 Her] Them *del. MS*
II.54 her] their *del. MS*
II.55 her] them *del. MS*   she may] they *del. MS*
II.56 of man] in man *del. MS*
II.57 see] know *del. MS*
II.60 unbaffled resurgent] incessant unbaffled *del. MS*
II.61 it] she *del. MS*

For this at our nature arises rejuvenescent from Earth,
However respersive the blow and nigh on infernal the fall,
The chastisement drawn down on us merited: are we of worth
Amid our satanic excrescences, this, for the less than a call,
Will Earth reprime, man cherish; the God who is in us and
    round,
Consenting, the God there seen. Impiety speaks despair;
Religion the virtue of serving as things of the furrowy ground,
Debtors for breath while breath with our fellows in service
    we share.
Not such of the crowned discrowned   70
Can Earth or humanity spare;
Such not the God let die.

III

Eastward of Paris morn is high;
And darkness on that Eastward side
The heart of France beholds: a thorn
Is in her frame where shines the morn:
A rigid wave usurps her sky,
With eagle crest and eagle-eyed
To scan what wormy wrinkles hint
Her forces gathering: she the thrown
From station, lopped of an arm, astounded, lone,
Reading late History as a foul misprint: 10
Imperial, Angelical,
At strife commingled in her frame convulsed;
Shame of her broken sword, a ravening gall;
Pain of the limb where once her warm blood pulsed;
These tortures to distract her underneath
Her whelmed Aurora's shade. But in that space
When lay she dumb beside her trampled wreath,
Like an unburied body mid the tombs,

II.68 furrowy] furrowed *del. MS*
II.69 our] their *del. MS*   we] they *del. MS*
III.5 rigid] monster[?] *del. MS*
III.6 crest] crest outspread *del. MS*
III.9 From station] Uprisen *del. MS*

Feeling against her heart life's bitter probe
For life, she saw how children of her race,   20
The many sober sons and daughters, plied,
By cottage lamplight through the water-globe,
By simmering stew-pots, by the serious looms,
Afield, in factories, with the birds astir,
Their nimble feet and fingers; not denied
Refreshful chatter, laughter, galliard songs.
So like Earth's indestructible they were,
That wrestling with its anguish rose her pride,
To feel where in each breast the thought of her,
On whom the circle Hours laid leaded thongs,   30
Was constant; spoken sometimes in low tone
At lip or in a fluttered look,
A shortened breath: and they were her loved own;
Nor ever did they waste their strength with tears,
For pity of the weeper, nor rebuke,
Though mainly they were charged to pay her debt,
The Mother having conscience in arrears;
Ready to gush the flood of vain regret,
Else hearken to her weaponed children's moan
Of stifled rage invoking vengeance: hell's,   40
If heaven should fail the counter-wave that swells
In blood and brain for retribution swift.
Those helped not: wings to her soul were these who yet
Could welcome day for labour, night for rest,
Enrich her treasury, built of cheerful thrift,
Of honest heart, beyond all miracles;
And likened to Earth's humblest were Earth's best.

IV

Brooding on her deep fall, the many strings
Which formed her nature set a thought on Kings,
As aids that might the low-laid cripple lift;
And one among them hummed devoutly leal,

III.31 constant; spoken] dear & *del.* shown as *del. MS*
III.43 Those] These *del. MS*   these] those *del. MS*
IV.3 low-laid] wounded *del. MS*

While passed the sighing breeze along her breast.
Of Kings by the festive vanquishers rammed down
Her gorge since fell the Chief, she knew their crown;
Upon her through long seasons was its grasp,
For neither soul's nor body's weal;
As much bestows the robber wasp,   10
That in the hanging apple makes a meal,
And carves a face of abscess where was fruit
Ripe ruddy. They would blot
Her radiant leap above the slopes acute,
Off summit to celestial; impute
The wanton's aim to her divinest shot;
Bid her walk History backward over gaps;
Abhor the day of Phrygian caps;
Abjure her guerdon, execrate herself;
The Hapsburg, Hohenzollern, Guelph,   20
Admire repentant; reverently prostrate
Her person unto the belly-god; of whom
Is inward plenty and external bloom;
Enough of pomp and state
And carnival to quench
The breast's desires of an intemperate wench,
The head's ideas beyond legitimate.

She flung them: she was France: nor with far frown
Her lover from the embrace of her refrained:
But in her voice an interwoven wire,   30
The exultation of her gross renown,
Struck deafness at her heavens, and they waned
Over a look ill-gifted to aspire.

IV.5 While] Till del. MS
IV.6 vanquishers] victor lords del. MS
IV.8 Upon] About[?] del. MS   through] for del. MS
IV.12 carves] paints del. MS
IV.15 Off] Of misp. de L; corr. errata, de L 1911
IV.19 Abjure] Renounce del. MS
IV.28 far] out del. MS
IV.33 Over] Above del. MS

Wherefore, as in abandonment, irate,
The intemperate summoned up her trumpet days,
Her treasure-galleon's wondrous freight.
The cannon-name she sang and shrieked; transferred
Her soul's allegiance; o'er the Tyrant slurred,
Tranced with the zeal of her first fawning gaze,
To clasp his trophy flags and hail him Saint.   40

V

She hailed him Saint:
And her Jeanne unsainted, foully sung!
The virgin who conceived a France when funeral glooms
Across a land aquake with sharp disseverance hung:
Conceived, and under stress of battle brought her forth;
Crowned her in purification of feud and foeman's taint;
Taught her to feel her blood her being, know her worth,
Have joy of unity: the Jeanne bescreeched, bescoffed,
Who flamed to ashes, flew up wreaths of faggot fumes;
Through centuries a star in vapour-folds aloft.   10

For her people to hail her Saint,
Were no lifting of her, Earth's gem,
Earth's chosen, Earth's throb on divine:
In the ranks of the starred she is one,
While man has thought on our line:
No lifting of her, but for them,
Breath of the mountain, beam of the sun
Through mist, out of swamp-fires' lures release,
Youth on the forehead, the rough right way
Seen to be footed: for them the heart's peace,   20
By the mind's war won for a permanent miracle day.

IV.34 in] an *misp. 1898, de L; corr. errata, de L 1911*
IV.39 Tranced with the zeal] As[?] in the time of *del. MS*
V.2 And her Jeanne] Saint! And her Jeanne had lain *del. MS*
V.8 *MS del.:*

> Have joy of unity; from emblems to[?] aloft
> Take step asserted: the Jeanne bescreeched, bescoffed,

V.10 Through] For *del. MS*
V.15 on] of *del. MS*

Her arms below her sword-hilt crossed,
The heart of that high-hallowed Jeanne
Into the furnace-pit she tossed
Before her body knew the flame,
And sucked its essence: warmth for righteous work,
An undivided power to speed her aim.
She has no self but France: the sainted man
No France but self. Him warrior and clerk,
Free of his iron clutch; and him her young,   30
In whirled imagination mastodonized;
And him her penmen, him her poets; all
For the visioned treasure-galleon astrain;
Sent zenithward on bass and treble tongue,
Till solely through his glory France was prized.
She who had her Jeanne;
The child of her industrious;
Earth's truest, earth's pure fount from the main;
And she who had her one day's mate,
In the soul's view illustrious   40
Past blazonry, her Immaculate;
Those hours of slavish Empire would recall;
Thrill to the rattling anchor-chain
She heard upon a day in "I who can";
Start to the softened, tremulous bugle-blare
Of that Caesarean Italian
Across the storied fields of trampled grain,
As to a Vercingetorix of old Gaul
Blowing the rally against a Caesar's reign.
Her soul's protesting sobs she drowned to swear   50
Fidelity unto the sainted man,
Whose nimbus was her crown; and be again
The foreigner in Europe, known of none,

V.32 penmen, him] many writers, & him *del. MS*
V.42 Those hours] Those days *MS*; These days *TS H*
V.44 upon a day] of old *MS, TSS*
V.45 Start] Thrill *MS*
V.46 Caesarian] Corsican *del. typing error TS T*

None knowing; sight to dazzle, voice to stun.
Rearward she stepped, with thirst for Europe's van;
The dream she nursed a snare,
The flag she bore a pall.

VI

In Nature is no rearward step allowed.
Hard on the rock Reality do we dash
To be shattered, if the material dream propels.
The worship to departed splendour vowed
Conjured a simulacrum, wove her lash,
For the slow measure timed her peal of bells.

Thereof was the cannon-name a mockery round her hills;
For the will of wills,
Its flaccid ape,
Weak as the final echo off a giant's bawl: 10
Napoleon for disdain,
His banner steeped in crape.
Thereof the barrier of Alsace-Lorraine;
The frozen billow crested to its fall;
Dismemberment; disfigurement;
Her history blotted; her proud mantle rent;
And ever that one word to reperuse,
With eyes behind a veil of fiery dews;
Knelling the spot where Gallic soil defiled,
Showed her sons' valour as a frenzied child   20
In arms of the mailed man.
Word that her mind must bear, her heart put under ban,
Lest burst it: unto her eyes a ghost,
Incredible though manifest: a scene
Stamped with her new Saint's name: and all his host
A wattled flock the foeman's dogs between!

VI.6 the slow measure] slower measures *del. MS*
VI.18 a] the *del. MS*
VI.19 the] that *del. MS*

VII

Mark where a credible ghost pulls bridle to view that bare
Corpse of a field still reddening cloud, and alive in its throes
Beneath her Purgatorial Saint's evocative stare:
Brand on his name, the gulf of his glory, his Legend's close.
A lustreless Phosphor heading for daybeam Night's dead-born,
His underworld eyeballs grip the cast of the land for a fray
Expugnant; swift up the heights, with the Victor's instinctive
    scorn
Of the trapped below, he rides; he beholds, and a two-fold grey,
Even as the misty sun growing moon that a frost enrings,
Is shroud on the shrouded; he knows him there in the
    helmeted ranks.   10
The golden eagles flap lame wings,
The black double-headed are round their flanks.

He is there in midst of the pupils he harried to brain-awake,
    trod into union; lo,
These are his Epic's tutored Dardans, yon that Rhapsode's
    Achaeans to know.
Nor is aught of an equipollent conflict seen, nor the weaker's
    flashed device;
Headless is offered a breast to beaks deliberate, formal,
    assured, precise.
Ruled by the mathematician's hand, they solve their problem,
    as on a slate.
This is the ground foremarked, and the day; their leader
    modestly hazarded date.
His helmeted ranks might be draggers of pools or reapers of
    plains for the warrior's guile
Displayed; they haul, they rend, as in some orderly office
    mercantile.   20

VII.7 Expugnant] Decisive *del. MS*   Victor's] conqueror's *del. MS*
VII.10 Is shroud on the shrouded; he knows him] His presence [?] [?] [?] he is *del. MS*
VII.13 lo] these *del. MS*
VII.14 These are] Are *del. MS* yon] yonder *del. MS*   Rhapsode's] Rhapsody's *del. MS*
VII.15 seen] shown *del. MS*
VII.18 hazarded] named the *del. MS*

And a timed artillery speaks full-mouthed on a stuttering
    feeble reduced to nought.
Can it be France, an army of France, tricked, netted,
    convulsive, all writhen caught?

Arterial blood of an army's heart outpoured, the Grey
    Observer sees:
A forest of Francc in thunder comes, like a landslide hurled
    off her Pyrenees.
Torrent and forest ramp, roll, sling on for a charge against iron,
    reason, Fate;
It is gapped through the mass midway, bare ribs and dust
    ere the helmeted feel its weight.
So the blue billow white-plumed is plunged upon shingle to
    screaming withdrawal, but snatched,
Waved is the laurel eternal yielded by Death o'er the waste of
    brave men outmatched.
The France of the fury was there, the thing he had wielded,
    whose honour was dearer than life;
The Prussia despised, the harried, the trodden, was here; his
    pupil, the scholar in strife.   30

He haled to heel, in a spasm of will,
From sleep or debate, a mannikin squire
With head of a merlin hawk and quill
Acrow on an ear. At him rained fire
From a blast of eyeballs hotter than speech,
To say what a deadly poison stuffed
The France here laid in her bloody ditch,
Through the Legend passing human puffed.

VII.21 timed] grand *MS, TS H*   full-mouthed] its will *del.* command *del. MS*
VII.22 Can] But can *del. MS*
VII.23 an] her *del. TSS*
VII.25 *MS del.:* Then indeed tis red forest across for a charge against iron, & reason, &
Hate
VII.31 haled] drew *del. MS*
VII.32 sleep or debate] bed & sleep *del. MS*
VII.34 Acrow on] Bestriding *del.* Cocked on *del. MS*
VII.36 a] *not in MS, TS H*   stuffed] had stuffed *MS, TS H;* had *del. TS T*

Credible ghost of the field which from him descends,
Each dark anniversary day will its father return,   40
Haling his shadow to spy where the Legend ends,
That penman trumpeter's part in the wreck discern.

There, with the cup it presents at her lips, she stands,
France, with her future staked on the word it may pledge.
The vengeance urged of desire a reserve countermands;
The patience clasped totters hard on the precipice-edge.

Lopped of an arm, mother love for her own springs quick,
To curdle the milk in her breasts for the young they feed,
At thought of her single hand, and the lost so nigh.
Mother love for her own, who raised her when she lay sick   50
Nigh death, and would in like fountains fruitlessly bleed,
Withholds the fling of her heart on the further die.

Of love is wisdom. Is it great love, then wise
Will our wild heart be, though whipped unto madness more
By its mentor's counselling voice than thoughtfully reined.
Desire of the wave for the shore,
Passion for one last agony under skies,
To make her heavens remorseful, she restrained.

VIII

On her lost arm love bade her look;
On her one hand to meditate;
The tumult of her blood abate;
Disaster face, derision brook:
Forbade the page of her Historic Muse,
Until her demon his last hold forsook,
And smoothly, with no countenance of hate,
Her conqueror she could scan to measure. Thence

VII.41 Haling] defying[?] del. MS
VII.46 hard on] near[?] to del. MS
VII.52 Withholds the] Restrains the mad del. MS
VII.57 under [the del.] skies MS
VIII.8 to] & MS

The strange new Winter stream of ruling sense,
Cold, comfortless, but braced to disabuse,   10
Ran through the mind of this most lowly laid;
From the top billow of victorious War,
Down in the flagless troughs at ebb and flow;
A wreck; her past, her future, both in shade.

She read the things that are;
Reality unaccepted read
For sign of the distraught, and took her blow
To brain; herself read through;
Wherefore her predatory Glory paid
Napoleon ransom knew.   20
Her nature's many strings hot gusts did jar
Against the note of reason uttered low,
Ere passionate with duty she might wed,
Compel the bride's embrace of her stern groom.
Joined at an altar liker to the tomb,
Nest of the Furies their first nuptial bed,
They not the less were mated and proclaimed
The rational their issue. Then she rose.

See how the rush of southern Springtide glows
Oceanic in the chariot-wheel's ascent,   30
Illuminated with one breath. The maimed,
Torn, tortured, winter-visaged, suddenly
Had stature; to the world's wonderment,
Fair features, grace of mien, nor least
The comic dimples round her April mouth,
Sprung of her intimate humanity.
She stood before mankind the very South
Rapt out of frost to flowery drapery;
Unshadowed save when somewhiles she looked East.

VIII.15 She] Like woman[?] she *del. MS*
VIII.21 hot gusts did] would[?] hot gusts *del.* did hot gusts *del. MS*
VIII.22 Against the] The *del. MS*
VIII.23 might] must[?] *del. MS*
VIII.27 proclaimed] made known *del. MS*
VIII.29 how] where *MS, TS H*
VIII.32 visaged] faced *del. MS*   suddenly] immediately[?] *del. MS*

IX

Let but the rational prevail,
Our footing is on ground though all else fail:
Our kiss of Earth is then a plight
To walk within her Laws and have her light.
Choice of the life or death lies in ourselves;
There is no fate but when unreason lours.
This Land the cheerful toiler delves,
The thinker brightens with fine wit,
The lovelier grace as lyric flowers,
Those rosed and starred revolving Twelves   10
Shall nurse for effort infinite
While leashed to brain the heart of France the Fair
Beats tempered music and its lead subserves.
Washed from her eyes the Napoleonic glare,
Divinely raised by that in her divine,
Not the clear sight of Earth's blunt actual swerves
When her lost look, as on a wave of wine,
Rolls Eastward, and the mother-flag descries
Caress with folds and curves
The fortress over Rhine,   20
Beneath the one tall spire.
Despite her brooding thought, her nightlong sighs,
Her anguish in desire,
She sees, above the brutish paw
Alert on her still quivering limb—
As little in past time she saw,
Nor when dispieced as prey,
As victrix when abhorred—
A Grand Germania, stout on soil;
Audacious up the ethereal dim;   30
The forest's Infant; the strong hand for toil;
The patient brain in twilights when astray;

IX.1 Let] If del. MS
IX.6 lours] lowers MS, TSS
IX.14 Washed] Plucked MS, TS H
IX.16 blunt] hard del. MS
XI.20 fortress] tall spire del. MS

Shrewdest of heads to foil and counterfoil;
The sceptic and devout; the potent sword;
With will and armed to help in hewing way
For Europe's march; and of the most golden chord
Of the Heliconian lyre
Excellent mistress. Yea, she sees, and can admire;
Still seeing in what walks the Gallia leads;
And with what shield upon Alsace-Lorraine   40
Her wary sister's doubtful look misreads
A mother's throbs for her lost: so loved: so near:
Magnetic. Hard the course for her to steer,
The leap against the sharpened spikes restrain.

For the belted Overshadower hard the course,
On whom devolves the spirit's touchstone, Force:
Which is the strenuous arm, to strike inclined,
That too much adamantine makes the mind;
Forgets it coin of Nature's rich Exchange;
Contracts horizons within present sight: 50
Amalekite to-day, across its range
Indisputable; to-morrow Simeonite.

                              X

The mother who gave birth to Jeanne;
Who to her young Angelical sprang;
Who lay with Earth and heard the notes she sang,
And heard her truest sing them; she may reach
Heights yet unknown of nations; haply teach
A thirsting world to learn 'tis "she who can."

She that in History's Heliaea pleads
The nation flowering conscience o'er the beast;
With heart expurged of rancour, tame of greeds;
With the winged mind from fang and claw released;—   10

IX.27 dispieced] despoiled *del. MS*
IX.30 ethereal] aetherial *MS, TS H*; etherial *TS T*
IX.36 and of] of *MS, TS H*
IX.42 A mother's throbs for] The mother's yearning wants *del. MS*
X.7 Heliaea] Heliaia *MS, TS H*

Will such a land be seen? It will be seen;—
Shall stand adjudged our foremost and Earth's Queen.
Acknowledgement that she of God proceeds
The invisible makes visible, as his priest,
To her is yielded by a world reclaimed.
And stands she mutilated, fancy-shamed,
Yet strong in arms, yet strong in self-control,
Known valiant, her maternal throbs repressed,
Discarding vengeance, Giant with a soul;—
My faith in her when she lay low   20
Was fountain; now as wave at flow
Beneath the lights, my faith in God is best;—
On France has come the test
Of what she holds within
Responsive to Life's deeper springs.
She above the nations blest
In fruitful and in liveliest,
In all that servant earth to heavenly bidding brings,
The devotee of Glory, she may win
Glory despoiling none, enrich her kind,   30
Illume her land, and take the royal seat
Unto the strong self-conqueror assigned.

But ah, when speaks a loaded breath the double name,
Humanity's old Foeman winks agrin.
Her constant Angel eyes her heart's quick beat,
The thrill of shadow coursing through her frame,
Like wind among the ranks of amber wheat.
Our Europe, vowed to unity or torn,
Observes her face, as shepherds note the morn,
And in a ruddy beacon mark an end   40
That for the flock in their grave hearing rings.
Specked overhead the imminent vulture wings

X.12 stand] be *del. MS*
X.33 ah, when speaks a loaded breath] does a whisper speak *del.* ah, when speaks a
whispered breath *MS*
X.40 in a ruddy beacon] is it grey[?] or ruddy *del. MS*
X.42 Specked] High *del.* Dark *del. MS*

At poise, one fatal movement indiscreet,
Sprung from the Ætna passions' mad revolts,
Draws down; the midnight hovers to descend;
And dire as Indian noons of ulcer heat
Anticipating tempest and the bolts,
Hangs curtained terrors round our next day's door,
Death's emblems for the breast of Europe flings;
The breast that waits a spark to fire her store.   50
Shall, then, the great vitality, France,
Signal the backward step once more;
Again a Goddess Fortune trace
Amid the Deities, and pledge to chance
One whom we never could replace?
Now may she tune her nature's many strings
To noble harmony, be seen, be known.

It was the foreign France, the unruly, feared;
Little for all her witcheries endeared;
Theatrical of arrogance, a sprite   60
With gaseous vapours overblown,
In her conceit of power ensphered,
Foredoomed to violate and atone;
Her the grim conqueror's iron might
Avengeing clutched, distrusting rent;
Not that sharp intellect with fire endowed
To cleave our webs, run lightnings through our cloud;
Not virtual France, the France benevolent,
The chivalrous, the many-stringed, sublime
At intervals, and oft in sweetest chime;   70
Though perilously instrument,
A breast for any having godlike gleam.
This France could no antagonist disesteem,
To spurn at heel and confiscate her brood.

X.45 the midnight] in cloud; it *del. MS*
X.48 our] the *misp. GMT*
X.53 trace] place[?] *del. MS*; raise *MS, TS H*
X.65 Avengeing] Avenging *MS, TSS*
X.67 run lightnings through] be lightning of *del. MS*

Albeit a waverer between heart and mind,
And laurels won from sky or plucked from blood,
Which wither all the wreath when intertwined,
This cherishable France she may redeem.
Beloved of Earth, her heart should feel at length
How much unto Earth's offspring it doth owe.   80
Obstructions are for levelling, have we strength;
'Tis poverty of soul conceives a foe.
Rejected be the wrath that keeps unhealed
Her panting wound; to higher Courts appealed
The wrongs discerned of higher: Europe waits:
She chooses God or gambles with the Fates.
Shines the new Helen in Alsace-Lorraine,
A darker river severs Rhine and Rhone,
Is heard a deadlier Epic of the twain;
We see a Paris burn   90
Or France Napoleon.

For yet he breathes whom less her heart forswears
While trembles its desire to thwart her mind:
The Tyrant lives in Victory's return.
What figure with recurrent footstep fares
Around those memoried tracks of scarlet mud,
To sow her future from an ashen urn
By lantern-light, as dragons' teeth are sown?
Of bleeding pride the piercing seër is blind.
But, cleared her eyes of that ensanguined scud   100
Distorting her true features, to be shown
Benignly luminous, one who bears
Humanity at breast, and she might learn
How surely the excelling generous find
Renouncement is possession. Sure

X.85 discerned] observed[?] del. MS
X.92 yet he breathes] still he lives del. MS
X.99 MS del.: 'Tis vengeance holds the piercing seër blind.
X.101 Distorting] Obscuring del. MS
X.103 might] will del. MS

As light enkindles light when heavenly earthly mates,
The flame of pure immits the flame of pure,
Magnanimous magnanimous creates.
So to majestic beauty stricken rears
Hard-visaged rock against the risen glow;   110
And men are in the secret with the spheres,
Whose glory is celestially to bestow.

Now nation looks to nation, that may live
Their common nurseling, like the torrent's flower,
Shaken by foul Destruction's fast-piled heap.
On France is laid the proud initiative
Of sacrifice in one self-mastering hour,
Whereby more than her lost one will she reap;
Perchance the very lost regain,
To count it less than her superb reward.   120
Our Europe, where is debtor each to each,
Pass measure of excess, and war is Cain,
Fraternal from the Seaman's beach,
From answering Rhine in grand accord,
From Neva beneath Northern cloud,
And from our Transatlantic Europe loud,
Will hail the rare example for their theme;
Give response, as rich foliage to the breeze;
In their entrusted nurseling know them one:
Like a brave vessel under press of steam,   130
Abreast the winds and tides, on angry seas,
Plucked by the heavens forlorn of present sun,
Will drive through darkness, and, with faith supreme,
Have sight of haven and the crowded quays.

X.113 *MS del.:* On France the nations look, that she may live
X.114 common nurseling] nurseling, shaken *del. MS*
X.115 Shaken by] By *del. MS*   fast-piled] ever-piling *del. MS*

Between X.117 and X.118 MS del.: The great example it is here to give,

X.120 To] And *del. MS*
X.125 beneath] under *del. MS*
X.127 rare] great *del. MS*
X.129 their] its *MS*   them] it *MS*

Invitation to the Country

Now 'tis Spring on wood and wold,
Early Spring that shivers with cold,
But gladdens, and gathers, day by day,
A lovelier hue, a warmer ray,
A sweeter song, a dearer ditty;
Ouzel and throstle, new-mated and gay,
Singing their bridals on every spray—
Oh, hear them, deep in the songless City!
Cast off the yoke of toil and smoke,
As Spring is casting winter's grey,   10
As serpents cast their skins away:
And come, for the Country awaits thee with pity
And longs to bathe thee in her delight,

Previously printed in Fraser's 44 *(August 1851). MSS:* Yale. NB A, *[p. 27]; corrected TS for* "*Scattered Poems.*"

Before 1 MS, F; TS del.:

> There's a charm in all weathers with thee, my friend!
> And a meadow unreap'd by the bee, my friend,
> Is a very good image of me, my friend,
> While my wishes all flower for thee, my friend!

2 that] who *MS, F*
4 hue, a] hue and a *MS, F*
5 A sweeter song] And a sweeter song & *MS, F*
10–11 *not in MS*

Between 11 and 12 F; TS del.: No serpent—but of a dye as bright!

And take a new joy in thy kindling sight;
And I no less, by day and night,
Long for thy coming, and watch for, and wait thee,
And wonder what duties can thus belate thee.

Dry-fruited firs are dropping their cones,
And vista'd avenues of pines
Take richer green, give fresher tones,   20
As morn after morn the glad sun shines.

Primrose tufts peep over the brooks,
Fair faces amid moist decay!
The rivulets run with the dead leaves at play,
The leafless elms are alive with the rooks.

Over the meadows the cowslips are springing,
The marshes are thick with king-cup gold,
Clear is the cry of the lambs in the fold,
The skylark is singing, and singing, and singing.

Soon comes the cuckoo when April is fair,   30
And her blue eye the brighter the more it may weep:
The frog and the butterfly wake from their sleep,
Each to its element, water and air.

Mist hangs still on every hill,
And curls up the valleys at eve; but noon
Is fullest of Spring; and at midnight the moon
Gives her westering throne to Orion's bright zone,
As he slopes o'er the darkened world's repose;
And a lustre in eastern Sirius glows.

16 watch for] wish thee *MS*; watch thee *F*
22–33 *not in MS*
36 fullest] full *MS, F*
38 darkened] mighty *MS*

Come, in the season of opening buds; 40
Come, and molest not the otter that whistles
Unlit by the moon, 'mid the wet winter bristles
Of willow, half-drowned in the fattening floods.
Let him catch his cold fish without fear of a gun,
And the stars shall shield him, and thou wilt shun!
And every little bird under the sun
Shall know that the bounty of Spring doth dwell
In the winds that blow, in the waters that run,
And in the breast of man as well.

After 39 MS, F, TS:

Come, while [ere *MS*] the larches burst bud, and the palm
Sheds its white down, ere [and *MS*] the odorous balm
Of flowers has wasted its first keen sense
Of Elysian air, and pastoral sweetness,
Which fills us with godlike power intense,
To enjoy the wise insight to [of *MS*] nature's completeness.

F, TS continue:

Come, like a flower, and grow in the rains!
While the fields are preparing the sweet May-mirth.
Feel the yearning of Summer below the green earth,
That March foretells, and April feigns.

41 molest] regret *MS, F, TS*
45 And the stars shall shield him] The stars are his shield *MS* wilt] shalt *F*
46–49 *not in MS*
48 in] and *F*

After 49 and a space, TS del.:

There's a charm in all weathers with thee, my friend!
And a meadow unreap'd by the bee, my friend,
Is a very good image of me, my friend,
While my wishes all flower for thee, my friend!

The Sweet o' the Year

The title and refrain come from the song "When daffodils begin to peer," in Shakespeare's *Winter's Tale*, 4. 3. 3.

Now the frog, all lean and weak,
　　Yawning from his famished sleep,
Water in the ditch doth seek,
　　　Fast as he can stretch and leap:
　　　　Marshy king-cups burning near,
　　　　Tell him 'tis the sweet o' the year.

Now the ant works up his mound
　　In the mouldered piny soil,
And above the busy ground
　　　Takes the joy of earnest toil:
　　　　Dropping pine-cones, dry and sere,
　　　　Warn him 'tis the sweet o' the year.

Now the chrysalis on the wall
　　Cracks, and out the creature springs,
Raptures in his body small,
　　　Wonders on his dusty wings:
　　　　Bells and cups, all shining clear,
　　　　Show him 'tis the sweet o' the year.

Now the brown bee, wild and wise,
　　Hums abroad, and roves and roams,
Storing in his wealthy thighs
　　　Treasure for the golden combs:
　　　　Dewy buds and blossoms dear
　　　　Whisper 'tis the sweet o' the year.

Previously printed in Fraser's 45 *(June 1852). MSS:* Berg; Yale, *corrected TS for* "*Scattered Poems.*"

4 stretch and leap] crawl and creep *MS*, *F* stretch and leap *TS*
5 king-cups] Ringcups *MS*; ring-cups *F*
10 earnest] sunny *MS*
15 Raptures] Rapture *MS*
24 Whisper 'tis] Fill him with *MS*

Now the merry maids so fair
   Weave the wreaths and choose the queen,
Blooming in the open air,
   Like fresh flowers upon the green;
     Spring, in every thought sincere,
     Thrills them with the sweet o' the year.   30

Now the lads, all quick and gay,
   Whistle to the browsing herds,
Or in the twilight pastures grey
   Learn the use of whispered words:
     First a blush, and then a tear,
     And then a smile, i' the sweet o' the year.

Now the May-fly and the fish
   Play again from noon to night;
Every breeze begets a wish,
   Every motion means delight: 40
     Heaven high over heath and mere,
     Crowns with blue the sweet o' the year.

Now all Nature is alive,
   Bird and beetle, man and mole;
Bee-like goes the human hive,
   Lark-like sings the soaring soul:
     Hearty faith and honest cheer
     Welcome in the sweet o' the year.

Between 24 and 25 MS:
   Now the serpent casts his Skin
     Gliding [like a stealthy dawn. *del.*] thro' the grasses wan.
   Now the cygnet brown and thin,
     Changes to the snowy swan:
      Whiter than the foaming wier,
      Swims she in the sweet o' the year.

46 sings] soars *del. MS*   soaring] human *del. MS*

The Song of Courtesy

On June 4, [1859] GM wrote to Samuel Lucas that he hoped John E. Millais might illustrate this poem "unless the mention of 'bride-beds' be thought too strong for our virtuous public." It was illustrated by John Tenniel. GM protested to Lucas [July 7, 1859] about the garbled printing of the last three lines. "By the way, your cutting short the concluding triplet of 'Sir Gawain' was a mistake. I seem to end in a caper, and perform an *entrechat*, instead of going off with a certain sedateness." He must have been writing about the poem in proof, because the lines appear in *Once a Week*. Cline gives the variant in Letter 48, note 5.

GM could have found the fragmentary ballad *The Marriage of Sir Gawain* in many collections of ballads.

I

When Sir Gawain was led to his bridal-bed,
By Arthur's knights in scorn God-sped:—
How, think you, he felt?
          O the bride within
Was yellow and dry as a snake's old skin;
          Loathly as sin!
          Scarcely faceable,
          Quite unembraceable;
With a hog's bristle on a hag's chin!—
Gentle Gawain felt as should we,   10
Little of Love's soft fire knew he:
But he was the Knight of Courtesy.

II

When that evil lady he lay beside
Bade him turn to greet his bride,
What, think you, he did?
          O, to spare her pain,
And let not his loathing her loathliness vain
          Mirror too plain,

Previously printed in Once a Week *1 (9 July 1859). MS:* Yale, *TS corrected by GM for* "*Scattered Poems.*"
II.2 greet] welcome *OaW*

Sadly, sighingly,
Almost dyingly,
Turned he and kissed her once and again.
Like Sir Gawain, gentles, should we?   10
Silent, all! But for pattern agree
There's none like the Knight of Courtesy.

III

Sir Gawain sprang up amid laces and curls:
Kisses are not wasted pearls:—
What clung in his arms?
O, a maiden flower,
Burning with blushes the sweet bride-bower,
Beauty her dower!
Breathing perfumingly,
Shall I live bloomingly,
Said she, by day, or the bridal hour?
Thereat he clasped her, and whispered he,   10
Thine, rare bride, the choice shall be.
Said she, Twice blest is Courtesy!

IV

Of gentle Sir Gawain they had no sport,
When it was morning in Arthur's court;
What, think you, they cried?
Now, life and eyes!
This bride is the very Saint's dream of a prize,
Fresh from the skies!
See ye not, Courtesy
Is the true Alchemy,
Turning to gold all it touches and tries?
Like the true knight, so may we   10
Make the basest that there be
Beautiful by Courtesy!

IV.10 so may] may *OaW*; so may *TS*
IV.11 that there be] that be *OaW*; that there be *TS*
IV.12 Beautiful] Beautiful ever *OaW*; Beautiful *TS*

The Three Maidens

Except for the addition of a refrain, the form of this poem imitates Uhland's famous ballad of *Der Wirthin Töchterlein* (Galland, p. 220), translated by GM a decade earlier. For *The Landlady's Daughter*, see page 811. GM wrote to Lucas [July 7, 1859] that he thought the poem might "pass."

There were three maidens met on the highway;
    The sun was down, the night was late:
And two sang loud with the birds of May,
    O the nightingale is merry with its mate.

Said they to the youngest, Why walk you there so still?
    The land is dark, the night is late:
O, but the heart in my side is ill,
    And the nightingale will languish for its mate.

Said they to the youngest, Of lovers there is store;
    The moon mounts up, the night is late: 10
O, I shall look on man no more,
    And the nightingale is dumb without its mate.

Said they to the youngest, Uncross your arms and sing:
    The moon mounts high, the night is late:
O my dear lover can hear no thing,
    And the nightingale sings only to its mate.

They slew him in revenge, and his true-love was his lure:
    The moon is pale, the night is late:
His grave is shallow on the moor;
    O the nightingale is dying for its mate.   20

Previously printed in Once a Week *1 (30 July 1859). MS:* Yale, *TS for* " *Scattered Poems.*"
11 on man no] *possible misp. TS* on no man *OaW*

His blood is on his breast, and the moss-roots at his hair:
     The moon is chill, the night is late:
But I will lie beside him there:
     O the nightingale is dying for its mate.

The Crown of Love

This poem is a brief retelling of the story of the *Deux Amants* by the
twelfth-century poet Marie de France (Galland, p. 219).

O might I load my arms with thee,
     Like that young lover of Romance
Who loved and gained so gloriously
     The fair Princess of France!

Because he dared to love so high,
     He, bearing her dear weight, shall speed
To where the mountain touched on sky:
     So the proud king decreed.

Unhalting he must bear her on,
     Nor pause a space to gather breath,   10
And on the height she will be won;—
     And she was won in death!

THE THREE MAIDENS
After 24 OaW, TS:
          Farewell, all my happy friends, and my parents kiss for me;
               The morn is near, the night is late:
          He bids me come, and quiet be,
               O the nightingale is dying for its mate.

THE CROWN OF LOVE
Previously printed in Once a Week *2 (31 December 1859). MSS:* Yale. NB B, [p. 44],
first two stanzas; TS for "Scattered Poems."
Stanza 2 MS:
                    "Sir gallant! to yon mountain's height
                    Del.: Without a halt bear up her weight
                    Without a halt her burden bring:
               And she you love is yours by right
                    Of Conquest, spake the King.

6 shall] must *OaW*
7 on] the *OaW*   the *del. TS, corr. GM proof de L*
11 will] would *OaW*

Red the far summit flames with morn,
    While in the plain a glistening Court
Surrounds the king who practised scorn
    Through such a mask of sport.

She leans into his arms; she lets
    Her lovely shape be clasped: he fares.
God speed him whole! The knights make bets:
    The ladies lift soft prayers.   20

O have you seen the deer at chase?
    O have you seen the wounded kite?
So boundingly he runs the race,
    So wavering grows his flight.

—My lover! linger here, and slake
    Thy thirst, or me thou wilt not win.
—Scc'st thou the tumbled heavens? they break!
    They beckon us up and in.

—Ah, hero-love! unloose thy hold:
    O drop me like a curséd thing.   30
—See'st thou the crowded swards of gold?
    They wave to us Rose and Ring.

—O death-white mouth! O cast me down!
    Thou diest? Then with thee I die.
—See'st thou the angels with their Crown?
    We twain have reached the sky.

35 their] a *OaW*

Lines to a Friend Visiting America

GM's friend who was visiting America in the autumn of 1867 was John Morley; see the sonnet *To J. M.* and headnote, page 296. GM assumed editorial duties for the *Fortnightly* during the three months of Morley's absence.

I

Now farewell to you! you are
One of my dearest, whom I trust:
Now follow you the Western star,
And cast the old world off as dust.

II

From many friends adieu! adieu!
The quick heart of the word therein.
Much that we hope for hangs with you:
We lose you, but we lose to win.

III

The beggar-king, November, frets:
His tatters rich with Indian dyes
Goes hugging: we our season's debts
Pay calmly, of the Spring forewise.

IV

We send our worthiest; can no less,
If we would now be read aright,—
To that great people who may bless
Or curse mankind: they have the might.

V

The proudest seasons find their graves,
And we, who would not be wooed, must court.
We have let the blunderers and the waves
Divide us, and the devil had sport.

Previously printed in the Fortnightly 8 (*1 December 1867*). MS: Yale, TS for " Scattered Poems."

VI

The blunderers and the waves no more
Shall sever kindred sending forth
Their worthiest from shore to shore
For welcome, bent to prove their worth.

VII

Go you and such as you afloat,
Our lost kinsfellowship to revive.
The battle of the antidote
Is tough, though silent: may you thrive!

VIII

I, when in this North wind I see
The straining red woods blown awry,
Feel shuddering like the winter tree,
All vein and artery on cold sky.

IX

The leaf that clothed me is torn away;
My friend is as a flying seed.
Ay, true; to bring replenished day
Light ebbs, but I am bare, and bleed.

X

What husky habitations seem
These comfortable sayings! they fell,
In some rich year become a dream:—
So cries my heart, the infidel! . . .

XI

Oh! for the strenuous mind in quest,
Arabian visions could not vie
With those broad wonders of the West,
And would I bid you stay? Not I!

XII

The strange experimental land
Where men continually dare take
Niagara leaps;—unshattered stand
'Twixt fall and fall;—for conscience' sake,

XIII

Drive onward like a flood's increase;—
Fresh rapids and abysms engage;—
(We live—we die) scorn fireside peace,
And, as a garment, put on rage,

XIV

Rather than bear God's reprimand,
By rearing on a full fat soil
Concrete of sin and sloth;—this land,
You will observe it coil in coil.

XV

The land has been discover'd long,
The people we have yet to know;
Themselves they know not, save that strong
For good and evil still they grow.

XVI

Nor know they us. Yea, well enough
In that inveterate machine
Through which we speak the printed stuff
Daily, with voice most hugeous, mien

XVII

Tremendous:—as a lion's show
The grand menagerie paintings hide:
Hear the drum beat, the trombones blow!
The poor old Lion lies inside! . . .

XVIII

It is not England that they hear,
But mighty Mammon's pipers, trained
To trumpet out his moods, and stir
His sluggish soul: *her* voice is chained:

XIX

Almost her spirit seems moribund!
O teach them, 'tis not she displays
The panic of a purse rotund,
Eternal dread of evil days,—

XX

That haunting spectre of success
Which shows a heart sunk low in the girths:
Not England answers nobleness,—
'Live for thyself: thou art not earth's.'

XXI

Not she, when struggling manhood tries
For freedom, air, a hopefuller fate,
Points out the planet, Compromise,
And shakes a mild reproving pate:

XXII

Says never: 'I am well at ease,
My sneers upon the weak I shed:
The strong have my cajoleries:
And those beneath my feet I tread.'

XXIII

Nay, but 'tis said for her, great Lord!
The misery's there! The shameless one
Adjures mankind to sheathe the sword,
Herself not yielding what it won:—

XXIV

Her sermon at cock-crow doth preach,
On sweet Prosperity—or greed.
'Lo! as the beasts feed, each for each,
God's blessings let us take, and feed!'

XXV

Ungrateful creatures crave a part—
She tells them firmly she is full;
Lest sheared sheep hurt her tender heart
With bleating, stops her ears with wool:—

XXVI

Seized sometimes by prodigious qualms
(Nightmares of bankruptcy and death),—
Showers down in lumps a load of alms,
Then pants as one who has lost a breath;

XXVII

Believes high heaven, whence favours flow,
Too kind to ask a sacrifice
For what it specially doth bestow:—
Gives *she*, 'tis generous, cheese to mice.

XXVIII

She saw the young Dominion strip
For battle with a grievous wrong,
And curled a noble Norman lip,
And looked with half an eye sidelong;

XXIX

And in stout Saxon wrote her sneers,
Denounced the waste of blood and coin,
Implored the combatants, with tears,
Never to think they could rejoin.

XXVIII.3 curled] aped *F*

XXX

Oh! was it England that, alas!
Turned sharp the victor to cajole?
Behold her features in the glass:
A monstrous semblance mocks her soul!

XXXI

A false majority, by stealth,
Have got her fast, and sway the rod:
A headless tyrant built of wealth,
The hypocrite, the belly-God.

XXXII

To him the daily hymns they raise:
His tastes are sought: his will is done:
He sniffs the putrid steam of praise,
Place for true England here is none!

XXXIII

But can a distant race discern
The difference 'twixt her and him?
My friend, that will you bid them learn.
He shames and binds her, head and limb.

XXXIV

Old wood has blossoms of this sort.
Though sound at core, she is old wood.
If freemen hate her, one retort
She has; but one!—'You are my blood.'

XXXV

A poet, half a prophet, rose
In recent days, and called for power.
I love him; but his mountain prose—
His Alp and valley and wild flower—

XXXI.4 The the] A a *F*; The the *TS*

XXXVI

Proclaimed our weakness, not its source.
What medicine for disease had he?
Whom summoned for a show of force?
Our titular aristocracy!

XXXVII

Why, these are great at City feasts;
From City riches mainly rise:
'Tis well to hear them, when the beasts
That die for us they eulogize!

XXXVIII

But these, of all the liveried crew
Obeisant in Mammon's walk,
Most deferent ply the facial screw,
The spinal bend, submissive talk.

XXXIX

Small fear that they will run to books
(At least the better form of seed)!
I, too, have hoped from their good looks,
And fables of their Northman breed;—

XL

Have hoped that they the land would head
In acts magnanimous; but, lo,
When fainting heroes beg for bread
They frown: where they are driven they go.

XXXVII.4 eulogize] eulogise *F*; eulogize *TS*
Between stanzas XXXVIII and XXXIX F; TS del.:
>   It is their pride that they have long
>   Consented to be harmless quite.
>   Conciliation is their song
>   At home, and peace abroad, and night.

XLI

Good health, my friend! and may your lot
Be cheerful o'er the Western rounds.
This butter-woman's market-trot
Of verse is passing market-bounds.

XLII

Adieu! the sun sets; he is gone.
On banks of fog faint lines extend:
Adieu! bring back a braver dawn
To England, and to me my friend.

On the Danger of War

The title refers to the danger of a war with Russia over the northwestern frontier of Afghanistan. In 1883 the British had formally renewed their promise to come to the aid of the "Amir in case of unprovoked aggression." In 1884 a joint British and Russian commission was unsuccessful in trying to settle the boundary, and on March 30, 1885, "the apprehended collision occurred. The Afghans occupied a position from which they refused to withdraw, and in the battle which ensued they were driven out of Penjdeh with a loss of life estimated at five hundred." Gladstone considered this attack an "unprovoked aggression" and set about raising money for a war with Russia. By May the king of Denmark was agreed upon as arbitrator, but the British public, as indicated in GM's sonnet, still clamored for war. The border was settled by Protocol in September. (William Habberton, *Anglo-Russian Relations Concerning Afghanistan 1837–1907*, Illinois Studies in the Social Sciences, vol. 21, no. 4 [Urbana, 1937], pp. 49–56).

Avert, High Wisdom, never vainly wooed,
This threat of War, that shows a land brain-sick
When nations gain the pitch where rhetoric
Seems reason they are ripe for cannon's food.
Dark looms the issue though the cause be good,
But with the doubt 'tis our old devil's trick.

ON THE DANGER OF WAR

Previously printed in the Pall Mall Gazette *41 (1 May 1885), and in Cline, Letter 899. Maxse Papers;* Yale, *TS for "Scattered Poems."*
5 the cause] a cause *letter*

O now the down-slope of the lunatic
Illumine lest we redden of that brood.
For not since man in his first view of thee
Ascended to the heavens giving sign   10
Within him of deep sky and sounded sea,
Did he unforfeiting thy laws transgress;
In peril of his blood his ears incline
To drums whose loudness is their emptiness.

To Cardinal Manning

Cardinal Manning had supported William Thomas Stead, editor of the
Pall Mall Gazette, in his attack on the government's toleration of the
white slave trade. For this Manning was denounced by his fellow
Catholics. Manning subscribed to the Stead Defense Fund and attended
the trial in which Stead was sentenced to a brief prison term in 1885.

I, wakeful for the skylark voice in men,
Or straining for the angel of the light,
Rebuked am I by hungry ear and sight,
When I behold one lamp that through our fen
Goes hourly where most noisome; hear again
A tongue that loathsomeness will not affright
From speaking to the soul of us forthright
What things our craven senses keep from ken.
This is the doing of the Christ; the way
He went on earth; the service above guile   10
To prop a tyrant creed: it sings, it shines;
Cries to the Mammonites: Allay, allay
Such misery as by these present signs
Brings vengeance down; nor them who rouse revile.

TO CARDINAL MANNING

Previously printed in the Pall Mall Gazette *44 (5 November 1886). MS:* Yale, TS *for*
"*Scattered Poems.*"

To Children

(FOR TYRANTS)

I

Strike not thy dog with a stick!
   I did it yesterday:
Not to undo though I gained
The Paradise: heavy it rained
   On Kobold's flanks, and he lay.

II

Little Bruno, our long-ear pup,
   From his hunt had come back to my heel.
I heard a sharp worrying sound,
And Bruno foamed on the ground,
   With Koby as making a meal.

III

I did what I could not undo
   Were the gates of the Paradise shut
Behind me: I deemed it was just.
I left Koby crouched in the dust,
   Some yards from the woodman's hut.

IV

He bewhimpered his welting, and I
   Scarce thought it enough for him: so,
By degrees, through the upper box-grove,
Within me an old story hove,
   Of a man and a dog: you shall know.

Previously printed in the English Illustrated 4 (*December 1887*). *MS:* Yale, *TS for "Scattered Poems."*

V

The dog was of novel breed,
  The Shannon retriever, untried:
His master, an old Irish lord,
In an oaken armchair snored
  At midnight, whisky beside.

VI

Perched up a desolate tower,
  Where the black storm-wind was a whip
To set it nigh spinning, these two
Were alone, like the last of a crew,
  Outworn in a wave-beaten ship.

VII

The dog lifted muzzle, and sniffed;
  He quitted his couch on the rug,
Nose to floor, nose aloft; whined, barked;
And finding the signals unmarked,
  Caught a hand in a death-grapple tug.

VIII

He pulled till his master jumped
  For fury of wrath, and laid on
With the length of a tough knotted staff,
Fit to drive the life flying like chaff,
  And leave a sheer carcase anon.

IX

That done, he sat, panted, and cursed
  The vile cross of this brute: nevermore
Would he house it to rear such a cur!
The dog dragged his legs, pained to stir,
  Eyed his master, dropped, barked at the door.

VI.1 Perched up] Perched high up *EI, TS*; high *del. proof de L*

X

Then his master raised head too, and sniffed:
    It struck him the dog had a sense
That honoured both dam and sire.
You have guessed how the tower was afire.
    The Shannon retriever dates thence.

XI

I mused: saw the pup ease his heart
    Of his instinct for chasing, and sink
Overwrought by excitement so new:
A scene that for Koby to view,
    Was the seizure of nerves in a link.

XII

And part sympathetic, and part
    Imitatively, raged my poor brute;
And I, not thinking of ill,
Doing eviller: nerves are still
    Our savage too quick at the root.

XIII

They spring us: I proved it, albeit
    I played executioner then
For discipline, justice, the like.
Yon stick I had handy to strike,
    Should have warned of the tyrant in men.

XIV

You read in your History books,
    How the Prince in his youth had a mind
For governing gently his land.
Ah, the use of that weapon at hand,
    When the temper is other than kind!

XV

At home all was well; Koby's ribs
   Not so sore as my thoughts: if, beguiled,
He forgives me, his criminal air
Throws a shade of Llewellyn's despair
   For the hound slain for saving his child.

A Stave of Roving Tim

(ADDRESSED TO CERTAIN FRIENDLY TRAMPS)

When this poem appeared in the February 5, 1888, issue of the *Reflector*, a weekly magazine, the following letter accompanied the title:

SIR,—The senior (see your Advertisement columns) who met that young Joseph Hofmann of politics, with the question as to the future of the youthful Tory, is impressed by the Reflector's repartee, in which he desires to find a very hopeful promise, that may presently dispel strange images of the prodigy growing onionly, and showing a seedy head when one appears. Meanwhile he sends you a lyric out of many addressed encouragingly to certain tramps, who are friends of his, for the purpose of driving a breath of the country through your pages, though he has no design of competing with the exquisite twitter of the triolets of the French piano which accompanied your birth, and bids fair to sound your funeral notes.

Yours, etc.
GEORGE MEREDITH

The advertisement referred to in the first sentence of this letter appeared on January 29, 1888: "The Gentleman who recently asked a younger man what the dickens he expected to come to if he started in life as a Tory, is referred to the precedent of Mr. Gladstone."

The "young Joseph Hofmann of politics" is probably an allusion to the famous Polish-born pianist (1876–1957) who had been touring Europe and America as a child prodigy.

The subtitle of the poem was added in the Edition de Luxe, and doubtless refers to the group of Sunday walkers who called themselves the Tramps, led by Meredith's great friend Leslie Stephen, uncle of James K. Stephen, editor of the *Reflector*. Meredith sometimes joined the Tramps in their ·rambles (see e.g., Cline, Letter 658 and note).

A STAVE OF ROVING TIM

Previously printed in the Reflector *1 (5 February 1888). MS:* Yale, *TS for "Scattered Poems."*

GM must have relished this poem, because eleven years later, on April 8 or 9, 1899, "he recited verses from his rollicking poem given to Jim Stephen for the *Reflector*" (*TLS-II*).

I

The wind is East, the wind is West,
   Blows in and out of haven;
The wind that blows is the wind that's best,
   And croak, my jolly raven!
If here awhile we jigged and laughed,
   The like we will do yonder;
For he's the man who masters a craft,
   And light as a lord can wander.
      So, foot the measure, Roving Tim,
         And croak, my jolly raven!   10
      The wind according to its whim
         Is in and out of haven.

II

You live in rows of snug abodes,
   With gold, maybe, for counting;
And mine's the beck of the rainy roads
   Against the sun amounting.
I take the day as it behaves,
   Nor shiver when 'tis airy;
But comes a breeze, all you are on waves,
   Sick chickens o' Mother Carey!
      So, now for next, cries Roving Tim,
         And croak, my jolly raven!   10
      The wind according to its whim
         Is in and out of haven.

III

Sweet lass, you screw a lovely leer,
   To make a man consider.
If you were up with the auctioneer,
   I'd be a handsome bidder.

But wedlock clips the rover's wing;
    She tricks him fly to spider;
And when we get to fights in the Ring,
    It's trumps when you play outsider.
        So, wrench and split, cries Roving Tim,
            And croak, my jolly raven!   10
        The wind according to its whim
            Is in and out of haven.

IV

Along my winding way I know
    A shady dell that's winking;
The very corner for Self and Co
    To do a world of thinking.
And shall I this? and shall I that?
    Till Nature answers, ne'ther!
Strike match and light your pipe in your hat,
    Rejoicing in sound shoe-leather!
        So lead along, cries Roving Tim,
            And croak, my jolly raven!   10
        The wind according to its whim
            Is in and out of haven.

V

A cunning hand'll hand you bread,
    With freedom for your capers.
I'm not so sure of a cunning head;
    It steers to pits or vapours.
But as for Life, we'll bear in sight
    The lesson Nature teaches;
Regard it in a sailoring light,
    And treat it like thirsty leeches.
        So, fly your jib, cries Roving Tim,
            And top your boom, old raven!   10
        The wind according to its whim
            Is in and out of haven.

VI

She'll take, to please her dame and dad,
    The shopman nicely shaven.
She'll learn to think o' the marching lad
    When perchers show they're craven.
You say the shopman piles a heap,
    While I perhaps am fasting;
And bless your wits, it haunts him in sleep,
    His tin-kettle chance of lasting!
        So hail the road, cries Roving Tim,
           And hail the rain, old raven!   10
        The wind according to its whim
           Is in and out of haven.

VII

He's half a wife, yon pecker bill;
    A book and likewise preacher.
With any soul, in a game of skill,
    He'll prove your over-reacher.
The reason is, his brains are bent
    On doing things right single.
You'd wish for them when pitching your tent
    At night in a whirly dingle!
        So, off we go, cries Roving Tim,
           And on we go, old raven!   10
        The wind according to its whim
           Is in and out of haven.

VIII

Lord, no, man's lot is not for bliss;
    To call it woe is blindness:
It's here a kick, and it's there a kiss,
    And here and there a kindness.
He starts a hare and calls her joy;
    He runs her down to sorrow:

>   The dogs within him bother the boy,
>   But 'tis a new day to-morrow.
>   So, I at helm, cries Roving Tim,
>   And you at bow, old raven!   10
>   The wind according to its whim
>   Is in and out of haven.

On Hearing the News from Venice

(THE DEATH OF ROBERT BROWNING)

Browning died in Venice on December 12, 1889, of a cold that was aggravated by a weak heart. William Stead of the *Pall Mall Gazette* must have asked GM immediately for a poem, because GM wrote him on December 13: "Browning's death takes me with a chokeing. I had hopes in his vitality. I cannot write of him at present—Love & reverence are in the way. There is the consolation that he died with the honours of his country upon him." Then he added a postscript, "—Yes, here is a Sonnet—perhaps worth nothing—But judge you. Really worth nothing, I think."

The sonnet was published on December 14 with the foreword: "We have much pleasure in publishing the following sonnet, which Mr. Meredith sent to us on hearing the news from Venice of the death of one whom he loved as a friend and reverenced as a teacher:—"

Browning and GM were not intimate friends, but had met many times and thought well of each other. As far back as 1862, after a particularly virulent review of GM's *Modern Love* volume, it had comforted him when Browning told him that he was "'astounded at the originality, delighted with the naturalness and beauty' of the poems" (LS, p. 112).

>   Now dumb is he who waked the world to speak,
>   And voiceless hangs the world beside his bier.
>   Our words are sobs, our cry of praise a tear:
>   We are the smitten mortal, we the weak.
>   We see a spirit on Earth's loftiest peak
>   Shine, and wing hence the way he makes more clear:
>   See a great Tree of Life that never sere
>   Dropped leaf for aught that age or storms might wreak.

ON HEARING THE NEWS FROM VENICE

Previously printed in the Pall Mall Gazette *49 (14 December 1889); and, with a facsimile of MS, in the* Pall Mall Budget *1108 (19 December 1889), title:* A Sonnet by Mr. George Meredith. *MSS:* BM 39, 927, *copy for the* Pall Mall Gazette, *title:* "The News from Venice"; *Yale, TS for* "Scattered Poems," *subtitle added not in GM's hand.*

Such ending is not Death: such living shows
What wide illumination brightness sheds   10
From one big heart, to conquer man's old foes:
The coward, and the tyrant, and the force
Of all those weedy monsters raising heads
When Song is murk from springs of turbid source.

The Riddle for Men

I

This Riddle rede or die,
Says History since our Flood,
To warn her sons of power:—
It can be truth, it can be lie;
Be parasite to twist awry;
The drouthy vampire for your blood;
The fountain of the silver flower;
A brand, a lure, a web, a crest;
Supple of wax or tempered steel;
The spur to honour, snake in nest: 10
'Tis as you will with it to deal;
To wear upon the breast,
Or trample under heel.

II

And read you not aright,
Says Nature, still in red
Shall History's tale be writ!
For solely thus you lead to light

THE RIDDLE FOR MEN

Previously printed in the Paternoster *2 (November 1890). MSS:* Huntington HM6748,
deleted title: "The Tragic Riddle"; Yale, stanza 1, corrected TS for " Scattered Poems."

I.2 History] Nature *del. TS*
I.3 To warn her] To all the *MS*; To all her *del.* Unto all *or* To all the *TS*
I.6 drouthy] sucking *TS*   for your] of the *TS*
I.7 silver] living *MS*; living *or* rosy *TS*
I.8 a lure, a web] a light; a lure *MS, TS*
I.10 spur to honour, snake] fiend at hand, the snake *or* spur to honour, snake *TS*
I.13 trample] tread it *MS, TS*

The trailing chapters she must write,
And pass my fiery test of dead
Or living through the furnace-pit:
Dislinked from who the softer hold
In grip of brute, and brute remain:
Of whom the woeful tale is told,   10
How for one short Sultanic reign,
    Their bodies lapse to mould,
    Their souls behowl the plain.

II.1–10 *MS*

    And read you not anew,
    Says Nature, nor have wish,
    Still red shall be that scrawl!
For nought is clearer to the view
Than this, when strong & weak are two:
That devilish makes devilish,
Angelical angelical.
And those who do the frailer hold
In bestial conquest beasts remain.
    Until [their *del.*] the dolorous tale is told,

II.12 lapse] passed *MS*

A READING OF LIFE
WITH OTHER POEMS
(1901)

A Reading of Life

About October 25, 1900, GM wrote Lady Ulrica Duncombe that this "long poem" was finished. (The poem consists of *The Vital Choice, With the Huntress, With the Persuader*, and *The Test of Manhood*.) On November 17 he wrote to her that periodicals would publish three of the four parts of the poem. "The part concerning Aphrodite [*With the Persuader*] is too much for magazines—and may be for you. Yet it is innocent as statuary." On December 1 he asked Lady Ulrica to point out any obscurities in the poem.

The Vital Choice

I

Or shall we run with Artemis
Or yield the breast to Aphrodite?
Both are mighty;
Both give bliss;

Previously printed in the Monthly Review *6 (April 1901); and in the* Critic *(New York) 39 (March 1901). Title in both:* A Reading of Life, I The Vital Choice. *MSS:* Yale. *MS 1, title:* [The Vital Choice *del.*] "The Test of Manhood"; *MS 2, fair copy.*
I.1 run] follow *MS 1;* speed *del. MS 2*
I.3 Both are] Each is *MS 1*
I.4 Both give] Each gives *MS 1*

Each can torture if derided;
Each claims worship undivided,
In her wake would have us wallow.

II

Youth must offer on bent knees
Homage unto one or other;
Earth, the mother,
This decrees;
And unto the pallid Scyther
Either points us shun we either
Shun or too devoutly follow.

With the Huntress

Through the water-eye of night,
Midway between eve and dawn,
See the chase, the rout, the flight
In deep forest; oread, faun,
Goat-foot, antlers laid on neck;
Ravenous all the line for speed.
See yon wavy sparkle beck
Sign of the Virgin Lady's lead.
Down her course a serpent star
Coils and shatters at her heels;   10
Peals the horn exulting, peals
Plaintive, is it near or far.

THE VITAL CHOICE
I.5 Each] Both *MS 1*   derided] *MSS, MR, erratum 1901 1st imp., 1901 2nd imp.,*
Mem. Ed., GMT; divided *misp. 1901 1st imp., de L*
I.6 Each claims] Both claim *MS 1*
I.7 *not in MS 1*
II.1 offer] render *MS 1*
II.2 Homage] Service[?] *del. MS 1*
II.5–6 *MS 1 del.:*

> Either to the deadly Scyther
> Dooms us, do we turn from either.

II.5 pallid] deadly *MS 1*
II.7 *not in MS 1*
WITH THE HUNTRESS
Previously printed in the Cornhill *83 (January 1901). MSS:* Yale. *Fair copy; TS.*

Huntress, arrowy to pursue,
In and out of woody glen,
Under cliffs that tear the blue,
Over torrent, over fen,
She and forest, where she skims
Feathery, darken and relume:
Those are her white-lightning limbs
Cleaving loads of leafy gloom.   20
Mountains hear her and call back,
Shrewd with night: a frosty wail
Distant: her the emerald vale
Folds, and wonders in her track.
Now her retinue is lean,
Many rearward; streams the chase
Eager forth of covert; seen
One hot tide the rapturous race.
Quiver-charged and crescent-crowned,
Up on a flash the lighted mound   30
Leaps she, bow to shoulder, shaft
Strung to barb with archer's craft,
Legs like plaited lyre-chords, feet
Songs to see, past pitch of sweet.
Fearful swiftness they outrun,
Shaggy wildness, grey or dun,
Challenge, charge of tusks elude:
Theirs the dance to tame the rude;
Beast, and beast in manhood tame,
Follow we their silver flame.   40
Pride of flesh from bondage free,
Reaping vigour of its waste,
Marks her servitors, and she
Sanctifies the unembraced.
Nought of perilous she recks;
Valour clothes her open breast;

22 Shrewd] Stirred *del. TS*   wail] dale *del. TS*
33 plaited lyre-chords] chords of the lyre, & *MS*
37 Challenge] Track a *del. MS*

Sweet beyond the thrill of sex;
Hallowed by the sex confessed.
Huntress arrowy to pursue,
Colder she than sunless dew,   50
She, that breath of upper air;
Ay, but never lyrist sang,
Draught of Bacchus never sprang
Blood the bliss of Gods to share,
High o'er sweep of eagle wings,
Like the run with her, when rings
Clear her rally, and her dart,
In the forest's cavern heart,
Tells of her victorious aim.
Then is pause and chatter, cheer,   60
Laughter at some satyr lame,
Looks upon the fallen deer,
Measuring his noble crest;
Here a favourite in her train,
Foremost mid her nymphs, caressed;
All applauded. Shall she reign
Worshipped? O to be with her there!
She, that breath of nimble air,
Lifts the breast to giant power.
Maid and man, and man and maid,   70
Who each other would devour
Elsewhere, by the chase betrayed,
There are comrades, led by her,
Maid-preserver, man-maker.

47 thrill] pitch *MS*
51 upper] mountain *del. MS*
55 sweep] pitch *MS*
68 nimble] mountain *del. MS*

With the Persuader

Who murmurs, hither, hither: who
Where nought is audible so fills the ear?
Where nought is visible can make appear
A veil with eyes that waver through,
Like twilight's pledge of blessed night to come,
Or day most golden? All unseen and dumb,
She breathes, she moves, inviting flees,
Is lost, and leaves the thrilled desire
To clasp and strike a slackened lyre,
Till over smiles of hyacinth seas,   10
Flame in a crystal vessel sails
Beneath a dome of jewelled spray,
For land that drops the rosy day
On nights of throbbing nightingales.

Landward did the wonder flit,
Or heart's desire of her, all earth in it.
We saw the heavens fling down their rose;
On rapturous waves we saw her glide;
The pearly sea-shell half enclose;
The shoal of sea-nymphs flush the tide;   20
And we, afire to kiss her feet, no more
Behold than tracks along a startled shore,
With brightened edges of dark leaves that feign
An ambush hoped, as heartless night remain.

More closely, warmly: hither, hither! she,
The very she called forth by ripened blood
For its next breath of being, murmurs; she,
Allurement; she, fulfilment; she,
The stream within us urged to flood;
Man's cry, earth's answer, heaven's consent; O she,   30

MSS: Huntington HM7462, *fair copy;* Yale, *TS.*

Maid, woman and divinity;
Our over-earthly, inner-earthly mate
Unmated; she, our hunger and our fruit
Untasted; she our written fate
Unread; Life's flowering, Life's root:
Unread, divined; unseen, beheld;
The evanescent, ever-present she,
Great Nature's stern necessity
In radiance clothed, to softness quelled;
With a sword's edge of sweetness keen to take   40
Our breath for bliss, our hearts for fulness break.

The murmur hushes down, the veil is rent.
Man's cry, earth's answer, heaven's consent,
Her form is given to pardoned sight,
And lets our mortal eyes receive
The sovereign loveliness of celestial white;
Adored by them who solitarily pace,
In dusk of the underworld's perpetual eve,
The paths among the meadow asphodel,
Remembering. Never there her face   50
Is planetary; reddens to shore sea-shell
Around such whiteness the enamoured air
Of noon that clothes her, never there.
Daughter of light, the joyful light,
She stands unveiled to nuptial sight,
Sweet in her disregard of aid
Divine to conquer or persuade.
A fountain jets from moss; a flower
Bends gently where her sunset tresses shower.
By guerdon of her brilliance may be seen   60
With eyelids unabashed the passion's Queen.

41 our] and *del. TS*
55 nuptial] pardoned *del. MS*
60 guerdon] mercy *del. MS*

Shorn of attendant Graces she can use
Her natural snares to make her will supreme.
A simple nymph it is, inclined to muse
Before the leader foot shall dip in stream:
One arm at curve along a rounded thigh;
Her firm new breasts each pointing its own way;
A knee half bent to shade its fellow shy,
Where innocence, not nature, signals nay.
The bud of fresh virginity awaits   70
The wooer, and all roseate will she burst:
She touches on the hour of happy mates;
Still is she unaware she wakens thirst.

And while commanding blissful sight believe
It holds her as a body strained to breast,
Down on the underworld's perpetual eve
She plunges the possessor dispossessed;
And bids believe that image, heaving warm,
Is lost to float like torch-smoke after flame;
The phantom any breeze blows out of form;   80
A thirst's delusion, a defeated aim.

The rapture shed the torture weaves;
The direst blow on human heart she deals:
The pain to know the seen deceives;
Nought true but what insufferably feels.
And stabs of her delicious note,
That is as heavenly light to hearing, heard
Through shelter leaves, the laughter from her throat,
We answer as the midnight's morning's bird.

62 Shorn of] Without *del. MS*
65 the leader] that tender *del.* that delicate[?] *del. MS*
66 One arm at curve along] An arm descending on *del. MS*
67 new] young *del. MS*
68 A] Her *del. MS*
69 signals] utters *MS*
71 will she burst] will burst *MS*
79 lost to float like] like the breathless *del.* is of the breathless *del. MS*
80 The] This *del. misp. TS*   phantom] vision *del. MS*

She laughs, she wakens gleeful cries;   90
In her delicious laughter part revealed;
Yet mother is she more of moans and sighs,
For longings unappeased and wounds unhealed.
Yet would she bless, it is her task to bless:
Yon folded couples, passing under shade,
Are her rich harvest; bidden caress, caress,
Consume the fruit in bloom; not disobeyed.
We dolorous complainers had a dream,
Wrought on the vacant air from inner fire,
We saw stand bare of her celestial beam   100
The glorious Goddess, and we dared desire.

Thereat are shown reproachful eyes, and lips
Of upward curl to meanings half obscure;
And glancing where a wood-nymph lightly skips
She nods: at once that creature wears her lure.
Blush of our being between birth and death:
Sob of our ripened blood for its next breath:
Her wily semblance nought of her denies;
Seems it the Goddess runs, the Goddess hies,
The generous Goddess yields. And she can arm   110
Her dwarfed and twisted with her secret charm;
Benevolent as Earth to feed her own.
Fully shall they be fed, if they beseech.
But scorn she has for them that walk alone;
Blanched men, starved women, whom no arts can pleach.
The men as chief of criminals she disdains,
And holds the reason in perceptive thought.

92 mother is she more   of] more is mother of our *del. MS*
93 For [our? *del.*] *MS*
94 would she] would she *del.* she would *MS*
95 Yon] Those *del. MS*
96 rich] sweet[?] *del. MS*
102 Thereat are shown] So says she with *del. MS*
104 skips] trips *del. MS*
108 *MS del.:* Herself she gives when she herself denies;
109 Seems it] It is *del. MS*
114 that] who *del. MS*

More pitiable, like rivers lacking rains,
Kissing cold stones, the women shrink for drought.
Those faceless discords, out of nature strayed,   120
Rank of the putrefaction ere decayed,
In impious singles bear the thorny wreaths:
Their lives are where harmonious Pleasure breathes
For couples crowned with flowers that burn in dew.
Comes there a tremor of night's forest horn
Across her garden from the insaner crew,
She darkens to malignity of scorn.
A shiver courses through her garden-grounds:
Grunt of the tusky boar, the baying hounds,
The hunter's shouts, are heard afar, and bring   130
Dead on her heart her crimsoned flower of Spring.
These, the irreverent of Life's design,
Division between natural and divine
Would cast; these vaunting barrenness for best,
In veins of gathered strength Life's tide arrest;
And these because the roses flood their cheeks,
Vow them in nature wise as when Love speaks.
With them is war; and well the Goddess knows
What undermines the race who mount the rose;
How the ripe moment, lodged in slumberous hours.   140
Enkindled by persuasion overpowers:
Why weak as are her frailer trailing weeds,
The strong when Beauty gleams o'er Nature's needs,
And timely guile unguarded finds them lie.

122 thorny] withered *del. MS*
124 For] From *del. MS*
125 tremor of night's] sound of midnight's *MS*
130 *MS del.:* The far notes of the [?] cruel bring
132 These, the] For these *del. MS*
134 these] & *del. MS*
135 veins] pride *del. MS*
136 flood] mount *del. MS*
137 Vow them] Would seem *del. MS*
138 and] for *del. MS*
139 undermines the race] fraility [*sic*] saps the strong *del. MS*
143 when] if *MS*

They who her sway withstand a sea defy,
At every point of juncture must be proof;
Nor look for mercy from the incessant surge
Her forces mixed of craft and passion urge
For the one whelming wave to spring aloof.
She, tenderness, is pitiless to them   150
Resisting in her godhead nature's truth.
No flower their face shall be, but writhen stem;
Their youth a frost, their age the dirge for youth.
These miserably disinclined,
The lamentably unembraced,
Insult the Pleasures Earth designed
To people and beflower the waste.
Wherefore the Pleasures pass them by:
For death they live, in life they die.

Her head the Goddess from them turns,   160
As from grey mounds of ashes in bronze urns.
She views her quivering couples unconsoled,
And of her beauty mirror they become,
Like orchard blossoms, apple, pear and plum,
Free of the cloud, beneath the flood of gold.
Crowned with wreaths that burn in dew,
Her couples whirl, sun-satiated,
Athirst for shade; they sigh, they wed,
They play the music made of two:
Oldest of earth, earth's youngest till earth's end: 170
Cunninger than the numbered strings,
For melodies, for harmonies,
For mastered discords, and the things
Not vocable, whose mysteries
Are inmost Love's, Life's reach of Life extend.

145 her sway withstand] withstand her sway *del. MS*
146 proof] mailed *del. MS*
147 incessant surge] wave aloof *del. MS*
162 She views] And eyes *del.* Regards *del. MS*
163 And of her beauty mirror] This mirror of her beauty *del. MS*
166 wreaths] her[?] wreaths *del. MS*
171 the numbered] unnumbered *del. MS*

Is it an anguish overflowing shame
And the tongue's pudency confides to her,
With eyes of embers, breath of incense myrrh,
The woman's marrow in some dear youth's name,
Then is the Goddess tenderness   180
Maternal, and she has a sister's tones
Benign to soothe intemperate distress,
Divide despair from hope, and sighs from moans.
Her gentleness imparts exhaling ease
To those of her milk-bearer votaries
As warm of bosom-earth as she; of the source
Direct; erratic but in heart's excess;
Being mortal and ill-matched for Love's great force;
Like green leaves caught with flames by his impress.
And pray they under skies less overcast,   190
That swiftly may her star of eve descend,
Her lustrous morning star fly not too fast,
To lengthen blissful night will she befriend.

Unfailing her reply to woman's voice
In supplication instant. Is it man's,
She hears, approves his words, her garden scans,
And him: the flowers are various, he has choice.
Perchance his wound is deep; she listens long;
Enjoys what music fills the plaintive song;
And marks how he, who would be hawk at poise   200
Above the bird, his plaintive song enjoys.

She reads him when his humbled manhood weeps
To her invoked: distraction is implored.
A smile, and he is up on godlike leaps
Above, with his bright Goddess owned the adored.
His tales of her declare she condescends;

181 a] her *misp. GMT*   tones] voice *del. MS*
191 star of eve] evening star *del. MS*
193 lengthen] crown their *del. MS*
196 hears, approves] listens, weighs *del. MS*
197 various] many *del. MS*
198 is deep] gives pain *del. MS*

Can share his fires, not always goads and rends:
Moreover, quits a throne, and must enclose
A queenlier gem than woman's wayside rose.
She bends, he quickens; she breathes low, he springs   210
Enraptured; low she laughs, his woes disperse;
Aloud she laughs and sweeps his varied strings.
'Tis taught him how for touch of mournful verse
Rarely the music made of two ascends,
And Beauty's Queen some other way is won.
Or it may solve the riddle, that she lends
Herself to all, and yields herself to none,
Save heavenliest: though claims by men are raised
In hot assurance under shade of doubt:
And numerous are the images bepraised   220
As Beauty's Queen, should passion head the rout.

Be sure the ruddy hue is Love's: to woo
Love's Fountain we must mount the ruddy hue.
That is her garden's precept, seen where shines
Her blood-flower, and its unsought neighbour pines.
Daughter of light, the joyful light,
She bids her couples face full East,
Reflecting radiance, even when from her feast
Their outstretched arms brown deserts disunite,
The lion-haunted thickets hold apart.   230
In love the ruddy hue declares great heart;
High confidence in her whose aid is lent
To lovers lifting the tuned instrument,
Not one of rippled strings and funeral tone.
And doth the man pursue a tightened zone,
Then be it as the Laurel God he runs,
Confirmed to win, with countenance the Sun's.

211 woes] pains *del. MS*
217 yields] gives *del. MS*
218 heavenliest] of her will *del. MS*
221 should passion head] if passion heads *MS*
222 hue] veil *del. MS*
223 must] should *MS*
229 brown] dark[?] *del. MS*

Should pity bless the tremulous voice of woe
He lifts for pity, limp his offspring show.
For him requiring woman's arts to please   240
Infantile tastes with babe reluctances,
No race of giants! In the woman's veins
Persuasion ripely runs, through hers the pains.
Her choice of him, should kind occasion nod,
Aspiring blends the Titan with the God;
Yet unto dwarf and mortal, she, submiss
In her high Lady's mandate, yields the kiss;
And is it needed that Love's daintier brute
Be snared as hunter, she will tempt pursuit.
She is great Nature's ever intimate   250
In breast, and doth as ready handmaid wait,
Until perverted by her senseless male,
She plays the winding snake, the shrinking snail,
The flying deer, all tricks of evil fame,
Elusive to allure, since he grew tame.

Hence has the Goddess, Nature's earliest Power,
And greatest and most present, with her dower
Of the transcendent beauty, gained repute
For meditated guile. She laughs to hear
A charge her garden's labyrinths scarce confute,   260
Her garden's histories tell of to all near.
Let it be said, But less upon her guile
Doth she rely for her immortal smile.
Still let the rumour spread, and terror screens
To push her conquests by the simplest means.

238 Should pity bless the tremulous] Calls he on pity under *del. MS*
239 He lifts for pity, limp] Should pity bless him, mild *del. MS*
243 through] though *MS, TS*
244–49 *not in MS; added in TS*
250 She is great] For she is *del. MS*
253 She plays] To play *del. MS*
254 evil fame] fright & shame *del. MS*
262 But less] 'Tis now *del. MS*
263 Doth she rely] That she relies *del. MS*
264 Still] But *del. MS*
265 To push her] For march of *del. MS*

While man abjures not lustihead, nor swerves
From earth's good labours, Beauty's Queen he serves.

Her spacious garden and her garden's grant
She offers in reward for handsome cheer:
Choice of the nymphs whose looks will slant   270
The secret down a dewy leer
Of corner eyelids into haze:
Many a fair Aphrosyne
Like flower-bell to honey-bee:
And here they flicker round the maze
Bewildering him in heart and head:
And here they wear the close demure,
With subtle peeps to reassure:
Others parade where love has bled,
And of its crimson weave their mesh: 280
Others to snap of fingers leap,
As bearing breast with love asleep.
These are her laughters in the flesh.
Or would she fit a warrior mood,
She lights her seeming unsubdued,
And indicates the fortress-key.
Or is it heart for heart that craves,
She flecks along a run of waves
The one to promise deeper sea.

Bands of her limpid primitives,   290
Or patterned in the curious braid,
Are the blest man's; and whatsoe'er he gives,
For what he gives is he repaid.

266 While man abjures not lustihead] As long as men are sons of Earth *del.* As long as
men have lustihead *del. MS*
267 labours, Beauty's Queen he] work, the Goddess they *or* work, the Goddess sought
will *del. MS*
279 Others parade] And here they walk *del. MS*
280 And of its] Of its bright *del. MS*
283 These] Such *del. MS*
284 Or would she] Then[?] *del. MS*
290 Bands] Groups *del. MS*
292 Are the blest man's] Are his *del. MS*

Good is it if by him 'tis held
He wins the fairest ever welled
From Nature's founts: she whispers it: Even I
Not fairer! and forbids him to deny,
Else little is he lover. Those he clasps,
Intent as tempest, worshipful as prayer,—
And be they doves or be they asps,—   300
Must seem to him the sovereignly fair;
Else counts he soon among life's wholly tamed.
Him whom from utter savage she reclaimed,
Half savage must he stay, would he be crowned
The lover. Else, past ripeness, deathward bound,
He reasons; and the totterer Earth detests,
Love shuns, grim Logic screws in grasp, is he.
Doth man divide divine Necessity
From Joy, between the Queen of Beauty's breasts
A sword is driven; for those most glorious twain   310
Present her; armed to bless and to constrain.
Of this he perishes; not she, the throned
On rocks that spout their springs to the sacred mounts.
A loftier Reason out of deeper founts
Earth's chosen Goddess bears: by none disowned
While red blood runs to swell the pulse, she boasts,
And Beauty, like her star, descends the sky;
Earth's answer, heaven's consent unto man's cry,
Uplifted by the innumerable hosts.

Quickened of Nature's eye and ear,   320
When the wild sap at high tide smites
Within us; or benignly clear
To vision; or as the iris lights
On fluctuant waters; she is ours
Till set of man: the dreamed, the seen;

308 Doth man] Would he *del. MS*
310 those] that *MS*
311 Present] Presents *MS*   armed] throned *del. MS*
316 While red blood runs to swell the pulse] While blood runs glad in veins of man
del. MS
317 the] from *del. MS*

Flushing the world with odorous flowers:
A soft compulsion on terrene
By heavenly: and the world is hers
While hunger after Beauty spurs.

So is it sung in any space   330
She fills, with laugh at shallow laws
Forbidding love's devised embrace,
The music Beauty from it draws.

The Test of Manhood

Like a flood river whirled at rocky banks,
An army issues out of wilderness,
With battle plucking round its ragged flanks;
Obstruction in the van; insane excess
Oft at the heart; yet hard the onward stress
Unto more spacious, where move ordered ranks,
And rise hushed temples built of shapely stone,
The work of hands not pledged to grind or slay.
They gave our earth a dress of flesh on bone;
A tongue to speak with answering heaven gave they.   10
Then was the gracious birth of man's new day;
Divided from the haunted night it shone.

That quiet dawn was Reverence; whereof sprang
Ethereal Beauty in full morningtide.
Another sun had risen to clasp his bride:
It was another earth unto him sang.

THE TEST OF MANHOOD

Previously printed in the Monthly Review *2* (*March 1901*); *and in the* Critic (*New York*)
38 (*March 1901*). *Title in both:* A Reading of Life, II The Test of Manhood. *MS:* Yale.
1 whirled at] between *del. MS*
8 pledged] bent *MR, Cr*

Came Reverence from the Huntress on her heights?
From the Persuader came it, in those vales
Whereunto she melodiously invites,
Her troops of eager servitors regales?   20
Not far those two great Powers of Nature speed
Disciple steps on earth when sole they lead;
Nor either points for us the way of flame.
From him predestined mightier it came;
His task to hold them both in breast, and yield
Their dues to each, and of their war be field.
The foes that in repulsion never ceased,
Must he, who once has been the goodly beast
Of one or other, at whose beck he ran,
Constrain to make him serviceable man;   30
Offending neither, nor the natural claim
Each pressed, denying, for his true man's name.

Ah, what a sweat of anguish in that strife
To hold them fast conjoined within him still;
Submissive to his will
Along the road of life!
And marvel not he wavered if at whiles
The forward step met frowns, the backward smiles.
For Pleasure witched him her sweet cup to drain;
Repentance offered ecstasy in pain.   40
Delicious licence called it Nature's cry;
Ascetic rigours crushed the fleshly sigh;
A tread on shingle timed his lame advance
Flung as the die of Bacchanalian Chance,
He of the troubled marching army leaned
On godhead visible, on godhead screened;
The radiant roseate, the curtained white;
Yet sharp his battle strained through day, through night.

28 has] had *MR, Cr*
32 pressed] urged *del. MS*
39 witched him her sweet cup] bade him now her goblet *del. MS*
43 A tread] As step *MR*; A step *Cr*
47 curtained] radiant *del. MS*

He drank of fictions, till celestial aid
Might seem accorded when he fawned and prayed;   50
Sagely the generous Giver circumspect,
To choose for grants the egregious, his elect;
And ever that imagined succour slew
The soul of brotherhood whence Reverence drew.

In fellowship religion has its founts:
The solitary his own God reveres:
Ascend no sacred Mounts
Our hungers or our fears.
As only for the numbers Nature's care
Is shown, and she the personal nothing heeds,   60
So to Divinity the spring of prayer
From brotherhood the one way upward leads.
Like the sustaining air
Are both for flowers and weeds.
But he who claims in spirit to be flower,
Will find them both an air that doth devour.

Whereby he smelt his treason, who implored
External gifts bestowed but on the sword;
Beheld himself, with less and less disguise,
Through those blood-cataracts which dimmed his eyes,   70
His army's foe, condemned to strive and fail;
See a black adversary's ghost prevail;
Never, though triumphs hailed him, hope to win
While still the conflict tore his breast within.

Out of that agony, misread for those
Imprisoned Powers warring unappeased,
The ghost of his black adversary rose,
To smother light, shut heaven, show earth diseased.

After 50 MS del.:
        And ever that [celestial *del.*] imagined succour slew
        The soul of brotherhood whence Reverence drew.   [*Cf. lines 53–54*]
58 hungers] *misp. MR, Cr*
70 Through] Through *del.* In *del. MS*
73 triumphs] trumpets *Cr, Mem. Ed.*

And long with him was wrestling ere emerged
A mind to read in him the reflex shade   80
Of its fierce torment; this way, that way urged;
By craven compromises hourly swayed.

Crouched as a nestling, still its wings untried,
The man's mind opened under weight of cloud.
To penetratc thc dark was it endowed;
Stood day before a vision shooting wide.
Whereat the spectral enemy lost form;
The traversed wilderness exposed its track.
He felt the far advance in looking back;
Thence trust in his foot forward through the storm.   90

Under the low-browed tempest's eye of ire,
That ere it lightened smote a coward heart,
Earth nerved her chastened son to hail athwart
All ventures perilous his shrouded Sire;
A stranger still, religiously divined;
Not yet with understanding read aright.
But when the mind, the cherishable mind,
The multitude's grave shepherd, took full flight,
Himself as mirror raised among his kind,
He saw, and first of brotherhood had sight: 100
Knew that his force to fly, his will to see,
His heart enlarged beyond its ribbed domain,
Had come of many a grip in mastery,
Which held conjoined the hostile rival twain,
And of his bosom made him lord, to keep
The starry roof of his unruffled frame
Awake to earth, to heaven, and plumb the deep
Below, above, aye with a wistful aim.

80 in him the] him as a *del. MS*
84 weight] press *del. MS*
88 exposed] revealed *del. MS*
91–96 *added in MS, not in MR, Cr*
102 its] his *MR, Cr*
104 conjoined] subdued *del. MS*
108 wistful] loftier *del. MS*

The mastering mind in him, by tempests blown,
By traitor inmates baited, upward burned;   110
Perforce of growth, the Master mind discerned,
The Great Unseen, nowise the Dark Unknown.
To whom unwittingly did he aspire
In wilderness, where bitter was his need:
To whom in blindness, as an earthy seed
For light and air, he struck through crimson mire.
But not ere he upheld a forehead lamp,
And viewed an army, once the seeming doomed,
All choral in its fruitful garden camp,
The spiritual the palpable illumed.   120

This gift of penetration and embrace,
His prize from tidal battles lost or won,
Reveals the scheme to animate his race:
How that it is a warfare but begun;
Unending; with no Power to interpose;
No prayer, save for strength to keep his ground,
Heard of the Highest; never battle's close,
The victory complete and victor crowned:
Nor solace in defeat, save from that sense
Of strength well spent, which is the strength renewed.   130
In manhood must he find his competence;
In his clear mind the spiritual food:
God being there while he his fight maintains;
Throughout his mind the Master Mind being there,
While he rejects the suicide despair;
Accepts the spur of explicable pains;
Obedient to Nature, not her slave:
Her lord, if to her rigid laws he bows;

116 struck] strove *del. MS*
117 ere] till *del. MS*
122 tidal] constant *del. MS, MR, Cr*   or] and *MR, Cr*
123 Reveals] Revealed *del. MS*
124 How] And *del. MS*   is] was *del. MS*
132 clear] own *del. MS*
135 suicide] comforting *del. MS*

Her dust, if with his conscience he plays knave,
And bids the Passions on the Pleasures browse:—   140
Whence Evil in a world unread before;
That mystery to simple springs resolved.
His God the Known, diviner to adore,
Shows Nature's savage riddles kindly solved.
Inconscient, insensitive, she reigns
In iron laws, though rapturous fair her face.
Back to the primal brute shall he retrace
His path, doth he permit to force her chains
A soft Persuader coursing through his veins,
An icy Huntress stringing to the chase: 150
What one the flesh disdains;
What one so gives it grace.

But is he rightly manful in her eyes,
A splendid bloodless knight to gain the skies,
A blood-hot son of Earth by all her signs,
Desireing and desireable he shines;
As peaches, that have caught the sun's uprise
And kissed warm gold till noonday, even as vines.
Earth fills him with her juices, without fear
That she will cast him drunken down the steeps.   160
All woman is she to this man most dear;
He sows for bread, and she in spirit reaps:
She conscient, she sensitive, in him;
With him enwound, his brave ambition hers:
By him humaner made; by his keen spurs
Pricked to race past the pride in giant limb,

144 Shows Nature's savage] Earth's sacrificial *del. MS*
150 stringing] prompting *del. MS*
151 flesh] flash *misp. 1901, de L;· corr. errata, de L 1911*
157 As] Like *del. MS*
159 Earth] She *del. MS*
162 *MS del.:* Now is it he who sows, & she who reaps.
166 the] her *MR, Cr*

Her crazy adoration of big thews,
Proud in her primal sons, when crags they hurled,
Were thunder spitting lightnings on the world
In daily deeds, and she their evening Muse.   170

This man, this hero, works not to destroy;
This godlike—as the rock in ocean stands;—
He of the myriad eyes, the myriad hands
Creative; in his edifice has joy.
How strength may serve for purity is shown
When he himself can scourge to make it clean.
Withal his pitch of pride would not disown
A sober world that walks the balanced mean
Between its tempters, rarely overthrown:
And such at times his army's march has been.   180

Near is he to great Nature in the thought
Each changing Season intimately saith,
That nought save apparition knows the death;
To the God-lighted mind of man 'tis nought.
She counts not loss a word of any weight;
It may befal his passions and his greeds
To lose their treasures, like the vein that bleeds,
But life gone breathless will she reinstate.

Close on the heart of Earth his bosom beats,
When he the mandate lodged in it obeys,   190
Alive to breast a future wrapped in haze,
Strike camp, and onward, like the wind's cloud-fleets.
Unresting she, unresting he, from change
To change, as rain of cloud, as fruit of rain;
She feels her blood-tree throbbing in her grain,
Yet skyward branched, with loftier mark and range.

168 Proud] Seen *del. MS*   primal] morning *del. MS*   crags] rocks *del. MS*
185–88 *not in MR, Cr*
191 Alive] Content *MR, Cr*   wrapped] clothed *MR, Cr*
193–96 *not in MR, Cr*
196 branched] bent *del. MS*

No miracle the sprout of wheat from clod,
She knows, nor growth of man in grisly brute;
But he, the flower at head and soil at root,
Is miracle, guides he the brute to God.   200
And that way seems he bound; that way the road,
With his dark-lantern mind, unled, alone,
Wearifully through forest-tracks unsown,
He travels, urged by some internal goad.

Dares he behold the thing he is, what thing
He would become is in his mind its child;
Astir, demanding birth to light and wing;
For battle prompt, by pleasure unbeguiled.
So moves he forth in faith, if he has made
His mind God's temple, dedicate to truth.   210
Earth's nourishing delights, no more gainsaid,
He tastes, as doth the bridegroom rich in youth.
Then knows he Love, that beckons and controls;
The star of sky upon his footway cast;
Then match in him who holds his tempters fast,
The body's love and mind's, whereof the soul's.
Then Earth her man for woman finds at last,
To speed the pair unto her goal of goals.

Or is't the widowed's dream of her new mate?
Seen has she virulent days of heat in flood;   220
The sly Persuader snaky in his blood;
With her the barren Huntress alternate;
His rough refractory off on kicking heels
To rear; the man dragged rearward, shamed, amazed;
And as a torrent stream where cattle grazed,
His tumbled world. What, then, the faith she feels?

197 sprout] shoot *del. MS, MR, Cr*   wheat] corn *del. MS*
200 guides he] who leads *del. MS*
206 would] may *del. MS*
207 Astir] And stirs *del. MS, MR, Cr*
218 her] their *del. MS*
220 days] times *MR, Cr*

May not his aspect, like her own so fair
Reflexively, the central force belie,
And he, the once wild ocean storming sky,
Be rebel at the core? What hope is there?   230

'Tis that in each recovery he preserves,
Between his upper and his nether wit,
Sense of his march ahead, more brightly lit;
He less the shaken thing of lusts and nerves;
With such a grasp upon his brute as tells
Of wisdom from that vile relapsing spun.
A Sun goes down in wasted fire, a Sun
Resplendent springs, to faith refreshed compels.

The Cageing of Ares

ILIAD, V. 385

[DEDICATED TO THE COUNCIL AT THE HAGUE, 1899]

The First Hague Conference, attended by representatives of twenty-six nations, sat from May 18 to July 29, 1899. Its purpose was to prevent an increase in armaments and to initiate an investigation into a future reduction of arms. It adopted several conventions in support of the pacific settlement of international disputes.

GM's mythological poem is based on this sentence from the *Iliad*: "So suffered Ares, when Otos and stalwart Ephialtes, sons of Aloeus, bound him in a strong prison-house; yea in a vessel of bronze lay he bound thirteen months" (trans. Lang, Leaf, and Myers [New York: Macmillan, 1930], p. 86).

THE TEST OF MANHOOD

227–30 *not in MR, Cr*

THE CAGEING OF ARES

Previously printed in the Daily Chronicle, *2 June 1899, title:* The Caging [*sic*] of Ares. *MS:* Yale, *fair copy, title:* "The Caging [sic] *of Ares." Subtitle added 1901.*

How big of breast our Mother Gaea laughed
At sight of her boy Giants on the leap
Each over other as they neighboured home,
Fronting the day's descent across green slopes,
And up fired mountain crags their shadows danced.
Close with them in their fun, she scarce could guess,
Though these two billowy urchins reeked of craft,
It signalled some adventurous master-trick
To set Olympians buzzing in debate,
Lest it might be their godhead undermined,   10
The Tyranny menaced. Ephialtes high
On shoulders of his brother Otos waved
For the bull-bellowings given to grand good news,
Compact, complexioned in his gleeful roar
While Otos aped the prisoner's wrists and knees,
With doleful sniffs between recurrent howls;
Till Gaea's lap receiving them, they stretched,
And both upon her bosom shaken to speech,
Burst the hot story out of throats of both,
Like rocky head-founts, baffling in their glut   20
The hurried spout. And as when drifting storm
Disburdened loses clasp of here and yon
A peak, a forest mound, a valley's gleam
Of grass and the river's crooks and snaky coils,
Signification marvellous she caught,
Through gurglings of triumphant jollity,
Which now engulphed and now gave eye; at last
Subsided, and the serious naked deed,
With mountain-cloud of laughter banked around,
Stood in her sight confirmed: she could believe   30
That these, her sprouts of promise, her most prized,

6 Close] One *MS, DC*
7 billowy] monstrous *MS*
13 grand] great *MS*
14 gleeful] joyful *del. MS*
19 Burst the hot] And burst the *del. MS*
22 yon] there *MS*
27 Which] That *del. MS*

These two made up of lion, bear and fox,
Her sportive, suckling mammoths, her young joy,
Still by the reckoning infants among men,
Had done the deed to strike the Titan host
In envy dumb, in envious heart elate:
These two combining strength and craft had snared,
Enmeshed, bound fast with thongs, discreetly caged
The blood-shedder, the terrible Lord of War;
Destroyer, ravager, superb in plumes;   40
The barren furrower of anointed fields;
The scarlet heel in towns, foul smoke to sky,
Her hated enemy, too long her scourge:
Great Ares. And they gagged his trumpet mouth
When they had seized on his implacable spear,
Hugged him to reedy helplessness despite
His godlike fury startled from amaze.
For he had eyed them nearing him in play,
The giant cubs, who gambolled and who snarled,
Unheeding his fell presence, by the mount   50
Ossa, beside a brushwood cavern; there
On Earth's original fisticuffs they called
For ease of sharp dispute: whereat the God,
Approving, deemed that sometime trained to arms,
Good servitors of Ares they would be,
And ply the pointed spear to dominate
Their rebel restless fellows, villain brood
Vowed to defy Immortals. So it chanced
Amusedly he watched them, and as one
The lusty twain were on him and they had him.   60
Breath to us, Powers of air, for laughter loud!
Cock of Olympus he, superb in plumes!
Bound like a wheaten sheaf by those two babes!
Because they knew our Mother Gaea loathed him,
Knew him the famine, pestilence and waste;
A desolating fire to blind the sight

37 craft] fraud *del. MS*
49 gambolled] sported *MS*

With splendour built of fruitful things in ashes;
The gory chariot-wheel on cries for justice;
Her deepest planted and her liveliest voice,
Heard from the babe as from the broken crone.   70
Behold him in his vessel of bronze encased,
And tumbled down the cave. But rather look—
Ah, that the woman tattler had not sought,
Of all the Gods to let her secret fly,
Hermes, after the thirteen songful months!
Prompting the Dexterous to work his arts,
And shatter earth's delirious holiday,
Then first, as where the fountain runs a stream,
Resolving to composure on its throbs.
But see her in the Seasons through that year;   80
That one glad year and the fair opening month.
Had never our Great Mother such sweet face!
War with her, gentle war with her, each day
Her sons and daughters urged; at eve were flung,
On the morrow stood to challenge; in their strength
Renewed, indomitable; whereof they won,
From hourly wrestlings up to shut of lids,
Her ready secret: the abounding life
Returned for valiant labour: she and they
Defeated and victorious turn by turn;   90
By loss enriched, by overthrow restored.
Exchange of powers of this conflict came;
Defacement none, nor ever squandered force.
Is battle nature's mandate, here it reigned,
As music unto the hand that smote the strings;
And she the rosier from their showery brows,
They fruitful from her ploughed and harrowed breast.

74 let her secret fly] make her secret known *del. MS*
75 the thirteen] thirteen *MS*
80 see] look on *del. MS*
81 fair] young *del. MS*
84 urged] waged *del. MS*
93 squandered] wasted *del. MS*
95 unto] for *del. MS*

Back to the primal rational of those
Who suck the teats of milky earth, and clasp
Stability in hatred of the insane, 100
Man stepped; with wits less fearful to pronounce
The mortal mind's concept of earth's divorced
Above; those beautiful, those masterful,
Those lawless. High they sit, and if descend,
Descend to reap, not sowing. Is it just?
Earth in her happy children asked that word,
Whereto within their breast was her reply.
Those beautiful, those masterful, those lawless,
Enjoy the life prolonged, outleap the years;
Yet they ('twas the Great Mother's voice inspired 110
The audacious thought), they, glorious over dust,
Outleap not her; disrooted from her soar,
To meet the certain fate of earth's divorced,
And clap lame wings across a wintry haze,
Up to the farthest bourne: immortal still,
Thenceforth innocuous; lovelier than when ruled
The Tyranny. This her voice within them told,
When softly the Great Mother chid her sons
Not of the giant brood, who did create
Those lawless Gods, first offspring of our brain 120
Set moving by an abject blood, that waked
To wanton under elements more benign,
And planted aliens on Olympian heights;—
Imagination's cradle poesy
Become a monstrous pressure upon men;—
Foes of good Gaea; until dispossessed
By light from her, born of the love of her,
Their lordship the illumined brain rejects
For earth's beneficent, the sons of Law,
Her other name. So spake she in their heart, 130
Among the wheat-blades proud of stalk; beneath

98 primal] simplé *del. MS*
110 Yet] But *MS*
117 them] us *MS, DC*

Young vine-leaves pushing timid fingers forth,
Confidently to cling. And when brown corn
Swayed armied ranks with softened cricket song,
With gold necks bent for any zephyr's kiss;
When vine-roots daily down a rubble soil
Drank fire of heaven athirst to swell the grape;
When swelled the grape, and in it held a ray,
Rich issue of the embrace of heaven and earth;
The very eye of passion drowsed by excess,   140
And yet a burning lion for the spring;
Then in that time of general cherishment,
Sweet breathing balm and flutes by cool woodside,
He the harsh rouser of ire being absent, caged,
Then did good Gaea's children gratefully
Lift hymns to Gods they judged, but praised for peace,
Delightful Peace, that answers Reason's call
Harmoniously and images her Law;
Reflects, and though short-lived as then, revives,
In memories made present on the brain   150
By natural yearnings, all the happy scenes;
The picture of an earth allied to heaven;
Between them the known smile behind black masks;
Rightly their various moods interpreted;
And frolic because toilful children borne
With larger comprehension of Earth's aim
At loftier, clearer, sweeter, by their aid.

138 When] And *del. MS*
144 ire being] fury *del. MS*
146 Lift] Raise *del. MS*
149 though] if *del. MS*
151 happy scenes] scenes of Peace *del. MS*

The Night-Walk

Awakes for me and leaps from shroud
All radiantly the moon's own night
Of folded showers in streamer cloud;
Our shadows down the highway white
Or deep in woodland woven-boughed,
With yon and yon a stem alight.

I see marauder runagates
Across us shoot their dusky wink;
I hear the parliament of chats
In haws beside the river's brink;   10
And drops the vole off alder-banks,
To push his arrow through the stream.
These busy people had our thanks
For tickling sight and sound, but theme
They were not more than breath we drew
Delighted with our world's embrace:
The moss-root smell where beeches grew,
And watered grass in breezy space;
The silken heights, of ghostly bloom
Among their folds, by distance draped.   20
'Twas Youth, rapacious to consume,
That cried to have its chaos shaped:
Absorbing, little noting, still
Enriched, and thinking it bestowed;
With wistful looks on each far hill
For something hidden, something owed.
Unto his mantled sister, Day
Had given the secret things we sought
And she was grave and saintly gay;
At times she fluttered, spoke her thought;   30

Previously printed in the Cornhill, *n.s. 7 (August 1899); and in the* Century *(New York)*
58 (August 1899). MSS: Yale. Fair copy corrected; TS corrected for the Cornhill.
25 With wistful looks] The while it looked *del. MS*

She flew on it, then folded wings,
In meditation passing lone,
To breathe around the secret things,
Which have no word, and yet are known;
Of thirst for them are known, as air
Is health in blood: we gained enough
By this to feel it honest fare;
Impalpable, not barren, stuff.

A pride of legs in motion kept
Our spirits to their task meanwhile,   40
And what was deepest dreaming slept:
The posts that named the swallowed mile;
Beside the straight canal the hut
Abandoned; near the river's source
Its infant chirp; the shortest cut;
The roadway missed; were our discourse;
At times dear poets, whom some view
Transcendent or subdued evoked
To speak the memorable, the true,
The luminous as a moon uncloaked;   50
For proof that there, among earth's dumb,
A soul had passed and said our best.
Or it might be we chimed on some
Historic favourite's astral crest,
With part to reverence in its gleam,
And part to rivalry the shout:
So royal, unuttered, is youth's dream
Of power within to strike without.
But most the silences were sweet,
Like mothers' breasts, to bid it feel   60
It lived in such divine conceit
As envies aught we stamp for real.

39 A pride] Young *del.* The joy *del. MS*
47 dear] our *del. MS*
51 earth's] the [?] *del. MS*
52 our] earth's *del. MS*
53 chimed] struck *del. MS*
57 *MS del.:* So prompt is Youth's unuttered dream   royal] rich *del. TS*

To either then an untold tale
Was Life, and author, hero, we.
The chapters holding peaks to scale,
Or depths to fathom, made our glee;
For we were armed of inner fires,
Unbled in us the ripe desires;
And passion rolled a quiet sea,
Whereon was Love the phantom sail. 70

The Hueless Love

GM sent this poem to Lady Ulrica Duncombe on August 29, 1900,
with the following remarks: "The enclosed little poem, recently written,
typed by a friend, is hueless, as befits the theme, and will not much interest
you. It refers to two that have gone. I send it because what verse comes
from me now is due to the lady who flatters me with her eyes on my former
pieces and is the one encouragement to fresh production." Lady Ulrica
evidently was puzzled by the fifth stanza, because on September 6 he wrote
her again: "Verse 5, is this: she had her moment of softness, and felt
surely that she need not be on her guard with him; could even, for the
instant, luxuriate in a vision of the richer human life it might be for them
if she were less respected—though it would be to love him less: and she
was aware, by the electrical current between them, that he likewise went
through his probation. They *nursed* no regrets, because each took up the
other's life as having prepared them for their mutual understanding. They
had a thought or two, but their love had in it the fire which does not admit
of retrospections. (And as to these, a woman who is made the victim of
them may know at once that the man is loving himself the most.) Indeed
the cry for times and circumstances to be altered proves the soul to be
absent in such a love. Is the case clearer?—In the days to come the owner
of the rational mind will read very accurately the person with whom she
is in very close intimacy, whether she speaks of it or keeps it fast, & it will
be the worse for him if she says nothing. This is when the tempered
emotions allow the rational mind to be active. The gift is one for cultiva-
tion."

THE NIGHT-WALK

65 peaks] heights *del. MS*
70 phantom] silver *del. MS*

THE HUELESS LOVE

Previously printed in the New Liberal Review *1 (April 1901); and in the* Bookman (*New
York*) *13 (May 1901). MS:* Yale, *TS.*

Unto that love must we through fire attain,
     Which those two held as breath of common air;
     The hands of whom were given in bond elsewhere;
Whom Honour was untroubled to restrain.

Midway the road of our life's term they met,
     And one another knew without surprise;
     Nor cared that beauty stood in mutual eyes;
Nor at their tardy meeting nursed regret.

To them it was revealed how they had found
     The kindred nature and the needed mind;   10
     The mate by long conspiracy designed;
The flower to plant in sanctuary ground.

Avowed in vigilant solicitude
     For either, what most lived within each breast
     They let be seen: yet every human test
Demanding righteousness approved them good.

She leaned on a strong arm, and little feared
     Abandonment to help if heaved or sank
     Her heart at intervals while Love looked blank,
Life rosier were she but less revered.   20

An arm that never shook did not obscure
     Her woman's intuition of the bliss—
     Their tempter's moment o'er the black abyss,
Across the narrow plank—he could abjure.

Then came a day that clipped for him the thread,
     And their first touch of lips, as he lay cold,
     Was all of earthly in their love untold,
Beyond all earthly known to them who wed.

18 heaved] rose *del. TS*

So has there come the gust at South-west flung
    By sudden volt on eves of freezing mist,   30
    When sister snowflake sister snowdrop kissed,
And one passed out, and one the bell-head hung

Song in the Songless

They have no song, the sedges dry,
    And still they sing.
It is within my breast they sing,
    As I pass by.
Within my breast they touch a string,
    They wake a sigh.
There is but sound of sedges dry;
    In me they sing.

Union in Disseverance

Sunset worn to its last vermilion he;
She that star overhead in slow descent:
That white star with the front of angel she;
He undone in his rays of glory spent

Halo, fair as the bow-shot at his rise,
He casts round her, and knows his hour of rest
Incomplete, were the light for which he dies,
Less like joy of the dove that wings to nest.

SONG IN THE SONGLESS

MS: Yale, *fair copy for printer.*

UNION IN DISSEVERANCE

MS: Yale, *fair copy for printer.*

2 overhead] seen[?] above *del. MS*
3 with the front] glowing soul *del. MS*   angel] heaven *del. MS*

Lustrous momently, near on earth she sinks;
Life's full throb over breathless and abased: 10
Yet stand they, though impalpable the links,
One, more one than the bridally embraced.

The Burden of Strength

If that thou hast the gift of strength, then know
Thy part is to uplift the trodden low;
Else in a giant's grasp until the end
A hopeless wrestler shall thy soul contend.

The Main Regret

WRITTEN FOR THE CHARING CROSS ALBUM

I

Seen, too clear and historic within us, our sins of omission
    Frown when the Autumn days strike us all ruthlessly bare.
They of our mortal diseases find never healing physician;
    Errors they of the soul, past the one hope to repair.

UNION IN DISSEVERANCE

11 impalpable] invisible *del. MS*

THE BURDEN OF STRENGTH

MS: Yale, *fair copy for printer.*

THE MAIN REGRET

Previously printed in The May Book, *compiled by Mrs. Aria in aid of Charing Cross Hospital* (London: Macmillan, 1901), *with facsimile of MS facing p. 38. MS:* Pierpont Morgan Library, *earlier than MS sent to* The May Book.

I.2 strike us all] strip us so *Morgan MS, MB;* strip men *canceled leaf in* A Reading of Life *(New York: Scribner, 1901. The N.Y. edition was set up before the cancellation of signature F); errata, de L 1911: "for 'strike' read 'strip.'"*
I.4 they of] charged on *Morgan MS, MB*   the one] all *Morgan MS, MB, canceled leaf N.Y. ed.*

II

Sunshine might we have been unto seed under soil, or have
    scattered
Seed to ascendant suns brighter than any that shone.
Even the limp-legged beggar a sick desperado has flattered
    Back to a half-sloughed life cheered by the mere human
    tone.

Alternation

Between the fountain and the rill
I passed, and saw the mighty will
To leap at sky; the careless run,
As earth would lead her little son.

Beneath them throbs an urgent well,
That here is play, and there is war.
I know not which had most to tell
Of whence we spring and what we are.

Hawarden

A eulogy on Gladstone, who died at his home, Hawarden Castle near
Chester, on May 19, 1898. The vast throngs that passed his bier in
Westminster Hall attest to the love and admiration felt by people of all
ranks for the "Grand Old Man."

When comes the lighted day for men to read
Life's meaning, with the work before their hands
Till this good gift of breath from debt is freed,
Earth will not hear her children's wailful bands

THE MAIN REGRET

II.1 under soil] *canceled leaf N.Y. ed., and cancel;* in the earth *Morgan MS, MB*
II.3 *Morgan MS:* Even the lowly of men some lowlier creature had flattered
II.4 a half-sloughed] acceptance of *Morgan MS, MB, canceled leaf N.Y. ed.*

HAWARDEN

Previously printed in the Daily Chronicle, *27 May 1898.*

Deplore the chieftain fall'n in sob and dirge;
Nor they look where is darkness, but on high.
The sun that dropped down our horizon's verge,
Illumes his labours through the travelled sky,
Now seen in sum, most glorious; and 'tis known
By what our warrior wrought we hold him fast.   10
A splendid image built of man has flown;
His deeds inspired of God outstep a Past.
Ours the great privilege to have had one
Among us who celestial tasks has done.

At the Close

This sonnet was written at the outbreak of the Boer War, October 11,
1899.

To Thee, dear God of Mercy, both appeal,
Who straightway sound the call to arms. Thou know'st;
And that black spot in each embattled host,
Spring of the blood-stream, later wilt reveal.
Now is it red artillery and white steel;
Till on a day will ring the victor's boast,
That 'tis Thy chosen towers uppermost,
Where Thy rejected grovels under heel.
So in all times of man's descent insane
To brute, did strength and craft combining strike,   10
Even as a God of Armies, his fell blow.
But at the close he entered Thy domain,
Dear God of Mercy, and if lion-like
He tore the fall'n, the Eternal was his Foe.

AT THE CLOSE

Previously printed in the Daily Chronicle, *16 November 1899.*

Forest History

I

Beneath the vans of doom did men pass in.
    Heroic who came out; for round them hung
    A wavering phantom's red volcano tongue,
With league-long lizard tail and fishy fin:

II

Old Earth's original Dragon; there retired
    To his last fastness; overthrown by few.
    Him a laborious thrust of roadway slew.
Then man to play devorant straight was fired.

III

More intimate became the forest fear
    While pillared darkness hatched malicious life
    At either elbow, wolf or gnome or knife
And wary slid the glance from ear to ear.

IV

In chillness, like a clouded lantern-ray,
    The forest's heart of fog on mossed morass,
    On purple pool and silky cotton-grass,
Revealed where lured the swallower byway.

V

Dead outlook, flattened back with hard rebound
    Off walls of distance, left each mounted height.
    It seemed a giant hag-fiend, churning spite
Of humble human being, held the ground.

Previously printed in Literature 3 *(9 July 1898)*.

VI

Through friendless wastes, through treacherous woodland, slow
    The feet sustained by track of feet pursued
    Pained steps, and found the common brotherhood
By sign of Heaven indifferent, Nature foe.

VII

Anon a mason's work amazed the sight,
    And long-frocked men, called Brothers, there abode.
    They pointed up, bowed head, and dug and sowed;
Whereof was shelter, loaf, and warm firelight.

VIII

What words they taught were nails to scratch the head.
    Benignant works explained the chanting brood.
    Their monastery lit black solitude,
As one might think a star that heavenward led.

IX

Uprose a fairer nest for weary feet,
    Like some gold flower nightly inward curled,
    Where gentle maidens fled a roaring world,
Or played with it, and had their white retreat.

X

Into big books of metal clasps they pored.
    They governed, even as men; they welcomed lays.
    The treasures women are whose aim is praise,
Was shown in them: the Garden half restored.

XI

A deluge billow scoured the land off seas,
    With widened jaws, and slaughter was its foam.
    For food, for clothing, ambush, refuge, home,
The lesser savage offered bogs and trees.

XII

Whence reverence round grey-haired story grew;
    And inmost spots of ancient horror shone
    As temples under beams of trials bygone;
For in them sang brave times with God in view.

XIII

Till now trim homesteads bordered spaces green,
    Like night's first little stars through clearing showers.
    Was rumoured how a castle's falcon towers
The wilderness commanded with fierce mien.

XIV

Therein a serious Baron stuck his lance;
    For minstrel songs a beauteous Dame would pout.
    Gay knights and sombre, felon or devout,
Pricked onward, bound for their unsung romance.

XV

It might be that two errant lords across
    The block of each came edged, and at sharp cry
    They charged forthwith, the better man to try.
One rode his way, one couched on quiet moss.

XVI

Perchance a lady sweet, whose lord lay slain,
    The robbers into gruesome durance drew.
    Swift should her hero come, like lightning's blue!
She prayed for him, as crackling drought for rain.

XVII

As we, that ere the worst her hero haps,
    Of Angels guided, nigh that loathly den:
    A toady cave beside an ague fen,
Where long forlorn the lone dog whines and yaps.

XIV.3 knights] nights *de L*

XVIII

By daylight now the forest fear could read
    Itself, and at new wonders chuckling went.
    Straight for the roebuck's neck the bowman spent
A dart that laughed at distance and at speed.

XIX

Right loud the bugle's hallali elate
    Rang forth of merry dingles round the tors;
    And deftest hand was he from foreign wars,
But soon he hailed the home-bred yeoman mate.

XX

Before the blackbird pecked the turf they woke;
    At dawn the deer's wet nostrils blew their last.
    To forest, haunt of runs and prime repast,
With paying blows, the yokel strained his yoke.

XXI

The city urchin mooned on forest air,
    On grassy sweeps and flying arrows, thick
    As swallows o'er smooth streams, and sighed him sick
For thinking that his dearer home was there.

XXII

Familiar, still unseized, the forest sprang
    An old-world echo, like no mortal thing.
    The hunter's horn might wind a jocund ring,
But held in ear it had a chilly clang.

XXIII

Some shadow lurked aloof of ancient time;
    Some warning haunted any sound prolonged,
    As though the leagues of woodland held them wronged
To hear an axe and see a township climb.

XXIV

The forest's erewhile emperor at eve
    Had voice when lowered heavens drummed for gales.
    At midnight a small people danced the dales,
So thin that they might dwindle through a sieve

XXV

Ringed mushrooms told of them, and in their throats,
    Old wives that gathered herbs and knew too much.
    The pensioned forester beside his crutch,
Struck showers from embers at those bodeful notes.

XXVI

Came then the one, all ear, all eye, all heart;
    Devourer, and insensibly devoured;
    In whom the city over forest flowered,
The forest wreathed the city's drama-mart.

XXVII

There found he in new form that Dragon old,
    From tangled solitudes expelled; and taught
    How blindly each its antidote besought;
For either's breath the needs of either told.

XXVIII

Now deep in woods, with song no sermon's drone,
    He showed what charm the human concourse works:
    Amid the press of men, what virtue lurks
Where bubble sacred wells of wildness lone.

XXIX

Our conquest these: if haply we retain
    The reverence that ne'er will overrun
    Due boundaries of realms from Nature won,
Nor let the poet's awe in rapture wane.

A Garden Idyl

With sagest craft Arachne worked
Her web, and at a corner lurked,
Awaiting what should plump her soon,
To case it in the death-cocoon.
Sagaciously her home she chose
For visits that would never close;
Inside my chalet-porch her feast
Plucked all the winds but chill North-east.

The finished structure, bar on bar,
Had snatched from light to form a star,   10
And struck on sight, when quick with dews,
Like music of the very Muse.
Great artists pass our single sense;
We hear in seeing, strung to tense;
Then haply marvel, groan mayhap,
To think such beauty means a trap.
But Nature's genius, even man's
At best, is practical in plans;
Subservient to the needy thought,
However rare the weapon wrought.   20
As long as Nature holds it good
To urge her creatures' quest for food
Will beauty stamp the just intent
Of weapons upon service bent.
For beauty is a flower of roots
Embedded lower than our boots;
Out of the primal strata springs,
And shows for crown of useful things

Previously printed in Scribner's *27 (February 1900). MS: Yale, fair copy, title: "A
Garden Idyll."*
14 We] You *MS*

Arachne's dream of prey to size
Aspired; so she could nigh despise   30
The puny specks the breezes round
Supplied, and let them shake unwound;
Assured of her fat fly to come;
Perhaps a blue, the spider's plum;
Who takes the fatal odds in fight,
And gives repast an appetite,
By plunging, whizzing, till his wings
Are webbed, and in the lists he swings,
A shrouded lump, for her to see
Her banquet in her victory.   40

This matron of the unnumbered threads,
One day of dandelions' heads
Distributing their gray perruques
Up every gust, I watched with looks
Discreet beside the chalet-door;
And gracefully a light wind bore,
Direct upon my webster's wall,
A monster in the form of ball;
The mildest captive ever snared,
That neither struggled nor despaired,   50
On half the net invading hung,
And plain as in her mother tongue,
While low the weaver cursed her lures,
Remarked, "You have me; I am yours."

Thrice magnified, in phantom shape,
Her dream of size she saw, agape.
Midway the vast round-raying beard
A desiccated midge appeared;
Whose body pricked the name of meal,
Whose hair had growth in earth's unreal;   60

30 she] we *misp. S*
41 This] The *del. MS*
45 the] my *del. MS*
46 a] the *del. MS*

Provocative of dread and wrath,
Contempt and horror, in one froth,
Inextricable, insensible,
His poison presence there would dwell,
Declaring him her dream fulfilled,
A catch to compliment the skilled;
And she reduced to beaky skin,
Disgraceful among kith and kin

Against her corner, humped and aged,
Arachne wrinkled, past enraged,   70
Beyond disgust or hope in guile.
Ridiculously volatile
He seemed to her last spark of mind;
And that in pallid ash declined
Beneath the blow by knowledge dealt,
Wherein throughout her frame she felt
That he, the light wind's libertine,
Without a scoff, without a grin,
And mannered like the courtly few,
Who merely danced when light winds blew, 80
Impervious to beak and claws,
Tradition's ruinous Whitebeard was;
Of whom, as actors in old scenes,
Had grannam weavers warned their weans,
With word, that less than feather-weight,
He smote the web like bolt of Fate.

This muted drama, hour by hour,
I watched amid a world in flower,
Ere yet Autumnal threads had laid
Their gray-blue o'er the grass's blade,   90
And still along the garden-run
The blindworm stretched him, drunk of sun.
Arachne crouched unmoved; perchance
Her visitor performed a dance;
She puckered thinner; he the same
As when on that light wind he came.

Next day was told what deeds of night
Were done; the web had vanished quite;
With it the strange opposing pair;
And listless waved on vacant air,   100
For her adieu to heart's content,
A solitary filament.

Foresight and Patience

In Huntington MS 1, both the title "In the Woods. Foresight and Patience." and the handwriting indicate that *Foresight and Patience* was written about twenty-five years before its first publication in the *National Review*, 1894. The poem was intended to be part of *In the Woods* (*Fortnightly*, 1 August 1870), a poem that GM subsequently dissevered, turning one part into *Whimper of Sympathy* (1887), others into *Woodland Peace* (1888) and *Dirge in Woods* (1888), and discarding a considerable portion. (For the discarded matter, see *In the Woods*, p. 774.) *Foresight and Patience* is associated with these poems. MS 1, written in GM's clearest hand, could easily have gone to an editor; in fact, it may well have, for it is fully endorsed, "George Meredith Box Hill Dorking," and was once tied together in the upper left-hand corner—his regular practice with a completed poem. One may reasonably conjecture that he wanted *In the Woods* to run in two instalments in the *Fortnightly* but that John Morley rejected this instalment—if for no other reason than its length. The manuscript runs to 448 lines and breaks off abruptly, suggesting the loss of two leaves in transmission. Conjectural date: 1868–70.

GM must have reread this manuscript in 1893, because on August 15, 1893, he wrote to a literary agent, William M. Colles, whom he employed briefly, "What would be given for a poem of about 400 lines, rather dull, full of morality and merit?" On August 17 he described the poem to Colles as "a glimpse at our marching world: with a star ahead and infernal machines around." On October 12 he asked Colles to look at the typed copy: "I have a fear that it is too didactic for present readers, though it says things that should be thought of." He sent the corrected copy to Colles in October. From a letter of December 1 it appears that Colles first submitted the poem to the *Century* magazine, where it was rejected. Huntington MS 2 would undoubtedly have been the manuscript for the typist.

FORESIGHT AND PATIENCE

See Supplementary Textual Notes.

Sprung of the father blood, the mother brain,
Are they who point our pathway and sustain.
They rarely meet; one soars, one walks retired.
When they do meet, it is our earth inspired.

To see Life's formless offspring and subdue
Desire of times unripe, we have these two,
Whose union is right reason: join they hands,
The world shall know itself and where it stands;
What cowering angel and what upright beast
Make man, behold, nor count the low the least,   10
Nor less the stars have round it than its flowers.
When these two meet, a point of time is ours.

As in a land of waterfalls, that flow
Smooth for the leap on their great voice below,
Some eddies near the brink borne swift along,
Will capture hearing with the liquid song,
So, while the headlong world's imperious force
Resounded under, heard I these discourse.

First words, where down my woodland walk she led,
To her blind sister Patience, Foresight said: 20

[FORESIGHT]
    —Your faith in me appals, to shake my own,
When still I find you in this mire alone.

[PATIENCE]
    —The few steps taken at a funeral pace
By men had slain me but for those you trace.

[FORESIGHT]
    —Look I once back, a broken pinion I:
Black as the rebel angels rained from sky!

[PATIENCE]

    —Needs must you drink of me while here you live,
    And make me rich in feeling I can give.

[FORESIGHT]

    —A brave To-be is dawn upon my brow:
    Yet must I read my sister for the How.   30
    My daisy better knows her God of beams
    Than doth an eagle that to mount him seems.
    She hath the secret never fieriest reach
    Of wing shall master till men hear her teach.

[PATIENCE]

    —Liker the clod flaked by the driving plough,
    My semblance when I have you not as now.
    The quiet creatures who escape mishap
    Bear likeness to pure growths of the green sap:
    A picture of the settled peace desired
    By cowards shunning strife or strivers tired.   40
    I listen at their breasts: is there no jar
    Of wrestlings and of stranglings, dead they are,
    And such a picture as the piercing mind
    Ranks beneath vegetation. Not resigned
    Are my true pupils while the world is brute.
    What edict of the stronger keeps me mute,
    Stronger impels the motion of my heart.
    I am not Resignation's counterpart.
    If that I teach, 'tis little the dry word,
    Content, but how to savour hope deferred.   50
    We come of earth, and rich of earth may be;
    Soon carrion if very earth are we!
    The coursing veins, the constant breath, the use
    Of sleep, declare that strife allows short truce;
    Unless we clasp decay, accept defeat,
    And pass despised; "a-cold for lack of heat,"
    Like other corpses, but without death's plea.

[FORESIGHT]
    —My sister calls for battle; is it she?

[PATIENCE]
    —Rather a world of pressing men in arms,
Then stagnant, where the sensual piper charms   60
Each drowsy malady and coiling vice
With dreams of ease whereof the soul pays price!
No home is here for peace while evil breeds,
While error governs, none; and must the seeds
You sow, you that for long have reaped disdain,
Lie barren at the doorway of the brain,
Let stout contention drive deep furrows, blood
Moisten, and make new channels of its flood!

[FORESIGHT]
    —My sober little maid, when we meet first,
Drinks of me ever with an eager thirst.   70
So can I not of her till circumstance
Drugs cravings. Here we see how men advance
A doubtful foot, but circle if much stirred,
Like dead weeds on whipped waters. Shout the word
Prompting their hungers, and they grandly march,
As to band-music under Victory's arch.
Thus was it, and thus is it; save that then
The beauty of frank animals had men.

[PATIENCE]
    —Observe them, and down rearward for a term,
Gaze to the primal twistings of the worm.   80
Thence look this way, across the fields that show
Men's early form of speech for Yes and No.
My sister a bruised infant's utterance had;
And issuing stronger, to mankind 'twas mad.
I knew my home where I had choice to feel
The toad beneath a harrow or a heel.

[FORESIGHT]
    —Speak of this Age.

[PATIENCE]
               —When you it shall discern
Bright as you are, to me the Age will turn.

[FORESIGHT]
    —For neither of us has it any care;
Its learning is through Science to despair.   90

[PATIENCE]
    —Despair lies down and grovels, grapples not
With evil, casts the burden of its lot.
This Age climbs earth.

[FORESIGHT]
            —To challenge heaven.

[PATIENCE]
                    —Not less
The lower deeps. It laughs at Happiness!
That know I, though the echoes of it wail,
For one step upward on the crags you scale.
Brave is the Age wherein the word will rust,
Which means our soul asleep or body's lust,
Until from warmth of many breasts, that beat
A temperate common music, sunlike heat   100
The happiness not predatory sheds!

[FORESIGHT]
    —But your fierce Yes and No of butting heads,
Now rages to outdo a horny Past.
Shades of a wild Destroyer on the vast
Are thrown by every novel light upraised.
The world's whole round smokes ominously, amazed
And trembling as its pregnant Ætna swells.

Combustibles on hot combustibles
Run piling, for one spark to roll in fire
The mountain-torrent of infernal ire   110
And leave the track of devils where men built.
Perceptive of a doom, the sinner's guilt
Confesses in a cry for help shrill loud,
If drops the chillness of a passing cloud,
To conscience, reason, human love; in vain:
None save they but the souls which them contain.
No extramural God, the God within
Alone gives aid to city charged with sin.
A world that for the spur of fool and knave,
Sweats in its laboratory, what shall save?   120
But men who ply their wits in such a school,
Must pray the mercy of the knave and fool.

[PATIENCE]
—Much have I studied hard Necessity!
To know her Wisdom's mother, and that we
May deem the harshness of her later cries
In labour a sure goad to prick the wise,
If men among the warnings which convulse,
Can gravely dread without the craven's pulse.
Long ere the rising of this Age of ours,
The knave and fool were stamped as monstrous Powers.   130
Of human lusts and lassitudes they spring,
And are as lasting as the parent thing.
Yet numbering locust hosts, bent they to drill,
They might o'ermatch and have mankind at will.
Behold such army gathering: ours the spur,
No scattered foe to face, but Lucifer.
Not fool or knave is now the enemy
O'ershadowing men, 'tis Folly, Knavery!
A sea; nor stays that sea the bastioned beach.
Now must the brother soul alive in each,   140
His traitorous individual devildom
Hold subject lest the grand destruction come.

Dimly men see it menacing apace
To overthrow, perchance uproot the race.
Within, without, they are a field of tares:
Fruitfuller for them when the contest squares,
And wherefore warrior service they must yield,
Shines visible as life on either field.
That is my comfort, following shock on shock,
Which sets faith quaking on their firmest rock.   150
Since with his weapons, all the arms of Night,
Frail men have challenged Lucifer to fight,
Have matched in hostile ranks, enrolled, erect,
The human and Satanic intellect,
Determined for their uses to control
What forces on the earth and under roll,
Their granite rock runs igneous; now they stand
Pledged to the heavens for safety of their land.
They cannot learn save grossly, gross that are:
Through fear they learn whose aid is good in war.   160

[FORESIGHT]
—My sister, as I read them in my glass,
Their field of tares they take for pasture grass.
How waken them that have not any bent
Save browsing—the concrete indifferent!
Friend Lucifer supplies them solid stuff:
They fear not for the race when full the trough.
They have much fear of giving up the ghost;
And these are of mankind the unnumbered host.

[PATIENCE]
—If I could see with you, and did not faint
In beating wing, the future I would paint.   170
Those massed indifferents will learn to quake:
Now meanwhile is another mass awake,
Once denser than the grunters of the sty.
If I could see with you! Could I but fly!

[FORESIGHT]
　　—The length of days that you with them have housed,
　　An outcast else, approves their cause espoused.

[PATIENCE]
　　—O true, they have a cause, and woe for us,
　　While still they have a cause too piteous!
　　Yet, happy for us when, their cause defined,
　　They walk no longer with a stumbler blind,   180
　　And quicken in the virtue of their cause,
　　To think me a poor mouther of old saws!
　　I wait the issue of a battling Age;
　　The toilers with your "troughsters" now engage;
　　Instructing them through their acutest sense,
　　How close the dangers of indifference!
　　Already have my people shown their worth,
　　More love they light, which folds the love of Earth.
　　That love to love of labour leads: thence love
　　Of humankind—earth's incense flung above.   190

[FORESIGHT]
　　—Admit some other features: Faithless, mean;
　　Encased in matter; vowed to Gods obscene;
　　Contemptuous of the impalpable, it swells
　　On Doubt; for pastime swallows miracles;
　　And if I bid it face what *I* observe,
　　Declares me hoodwinked by my optic nerve!

[PATIENCE]
　　—Oft has your prophet, for reward of toil,
　　Seen nests of seeming cockatrices coil:
　　Disowned them as the unholiest of Time,
　　Which were his offspring, born of flame on slime.   200
　　Nor him, their sire, have known the filial fry:
　　As little as Time's earliest knew the sky.
　　Perchance among them shoots a lustrous flame
　　At intervals, in proof of whom they came.

To strengthen our foundations is the task
Of this tough Age; not in your beams to bask,
Though, lighted by your beams, down mining caves
The rock it blasts, the hoarded foulness braves.
My sister sees no round beyond her mood;
To hawk this Age has dressed her head in hood. 210
Out of the course of ancient ruts and grooves,
It moves: O much for me to say it moves!
About his Æthiop Highlands Nile is Nile,
Though not the stream of the paternal smile:
And where his tide of nourishment he drives,
An Abyssinian wantonness revives.
Calm as his lotus-leaf to-day he swims;
He is the yellow crops, the rounded limbs,
The Past yet flowing, the fair time that fills;
Breath of all mouths and grist of many mills. 220
To-morrow, warning none with tempest-showers,
He is the vast Insensate who devours
His golden promise over leagues of seed,
Then sits in a smooth lake upon the deed.
The races which on barbarous force begin,
Inherit onward of their origin,
And cancelled blessings will the current length
Reveal till they know need of shaping strength.
'Tis not in men to recognize the need
Before they clash in hosts, in hosts they bleed. 230
Then may sharp suffering their nature grind;
Of rabble passions grow the chieftain Mind.
Yet mark where still broad Nile boasts thousands fed,
For tens up the safe mountains at his head.
Few would he feed, not far his course prolong,
Save for the troublous blood which makes him strong.

[FORESIGHT]
—That rings of truth! More do your people thrive;
Your Many are more merrily alive
Than erewhile when I gloried in the page
Of radiant singer and anointed sage. 240

Greece was my lamp: burnt out for lack of oil;
Rome, Python Rome, prey of its robber spoil!
All structures built upon a narrow space
Must fall, from having not your hosts for base.
O thrice must one be you, to see them shift
Along their desert flats, here dash, there drift;
With faith, that of privations and spilt blood,
Comes Reason armed to clear or bank the flood!
And thrice must one be you, to wait release
From duress in the swamp of their increase.   250
At which oppressive scene, beyond arrest,
A darkness not with stars of heaven dressed,
Philosophers behold; desponding view
Your Many nourished, starved my brilliant few;
Then flinging heels, as charioteers the reins,
Dive down the fumy Ætna of their brains.
Belated vessels on a rising sea,
They seem: they pass!

[PATIENCE]
                    —But not Philosophy!

[FORESIGHT]
        —Ay, be we faithful to ourselves: despise
Nought but the coward in us! That way lies   260
The wisdom making passage through our slough.
Am I not heard, my head to Earth shall bow;
Like her, shall wait to see, and seeing wait.
Philosophy is Life's one match for Fate.
That photosphere of our high fountain One,
Our spirit's Lord and Reason's fostering sun,
Philosophy, shall light us in the shade,
Warm in the frost, make Good our aim and aid.
Companioned by the sweetest, ay renewed,
Unconquerable, whose aim for aid is Good!   270
Advantage to the Many: that we name
God's voice; have there the surety in our aim.

This thought unto my sister do I owe,
And irony and satire off me throw.
They crack a childish whip, drive puny herds,
Where numbers crave their sustenance in words.
Now let the perils thicken: clearer seen,
Your Chieftain Mind mounts over them serene.
Who never yet of scattered lamps was born
To speed a world, a marching world to warn,   280
But sunward from the vivid Many springs,
Counts conquest but a step, and through disaster sings.

Fragments of the Iliad in
English Hexameter Verse

GM set particular store by these fragments. On March 26, 1890, he wrote to Sir Frederick Pollock, Professor of Jurisprudence at Oxford: "I wish to see you, to read you a few fragments from the *Iliad* in English hexameters—which I think are successful, as far as our tongue admits. In my opinion the whole *Iliad* is open to a rendering in fluent hexameter lines. And I am sure that all other measures are inefficient to give a single tone of the Homeric. That you will think, without granting the other. But come and take a taste." On April 7, Pollock not having visited him in the meantime, GM sent him the eight-line fragment, *Clash of the Achaians and the Trojans*, with the injunction to "remember, that Homer's terminations are not always good spondees. Our English supplies few. Latin is richer than either."

The following spring GM took more than usual pains about the printing of the fragments, writing Clement K. Shorter, editor of the *Illustrated London News*, on March 28, 1891, "Pray let me have the Revise, . . . for I am haunted by an omission of commas, vital to the meaning, also a spondee or two to be amended." He wrote again on April 1, 1891, saying that if the revise were already in the printer's hands, he wanted the accents he had marked on it omitted, for he had "falsified" one, and he indicated

FRAGMENTS OF THE ILIAD IN ENGLISH HEXAMETER VERSE

Previously printed in the Illustrated London News *98 (11 and 18 April 1891). MSS:* Yale. *Working draft; clippings from the* Illustrated London News *corrected for* A Reading of Life. *Cochran Library, Sweet Briar College,* Clash of the Achaians and Trojans, *transcribed by Cline, Letter 1262.*

corrections in the first two lines of *The Invective of Achilles*. But he did receive the revises and corrected them himself, begging Shorter, on April 3, to "put them into careful hands." On April 8, GM sent in one further improvement: in *The Horses of Achilles* "Ruler" should replace "Master" [line 19]; "It is much required to suit the sense."

GM's opinion of the best English measure for the translation of the *Iliad* had changed radically from the time of his favorable account in the *Fortnightly* (1 May 1869) of *Homer's Iliad in English Rhymed Verse* by Charles Merivale (London: Strahan, n.d. [1868?]). In this review GM declared that "the swell and rush, and the emphatic pause here and there—the seventh wave, as one may say," of Homer's verse cannot "be obtained from a sustained number of English hexameters pretending to dignity." "The hexameter sets our Muse on the slack-rope with a pole of very imperfect balance; she has neither the running nor the stamping foot for it." Merivale had primarily followed George Chapman in using the fourteener, but had varied the measure with the rhymed four-feet couplet or triplet of Scott's *Marmion*.

Prior to GM's condemnation of English hexameters as a medium for translating Homer, Tennyson, in a prose note to his "Specimen of a Translation of the Iliad in Blank Verse," had declared them impossible (*Cornhill*, December 1863). The controversy began with the publication in 1861 of Matthew Arnold's *On Translating Homer: Three Lectures Given at Oxford* and in 1862 of his *On Translating Homer: Last Words*.

The Invective of Achilles

i. 149

"Heigh me! brazen of front, thou glutton for plunder, how can one,
Servant here to thy mandates, heed thee among our Achaians,
Either the mission hie on or stoutly do fight with the foemen?
I, not hither I fared on account of the spear-armèd Trojans,
Pledged to the combat; they unto me have in nowise a harm done;
Never have they, of a truth, come lifting my horses or oxen;
Never in deep-soiled Phthia, the nurser of heroes, my harvests
Ravaged, they; for between us is numbered full many a darksome
Mountain, ay, therewith too the stretch of the windy sea-waters.
O hugely shameless! thee did we follow to hearten thee, justice   10

Before 1 MS: Then with looks under his lids unto him [spake *del.*] swift-footed Achilles.
2 Servant here to thy mandates, heed thee] Ready to heed thy hest here obey *MS*
3 *MS:* Either for ambush hie or to stoutly encounter the foemen? *or* Either the errand hie on or stoutly encounter the foemen?
6 horses or oxen] oxen or horses *or* horses or oxen *MS*
9 ay,] yea, [& *del.*] *MS*

Pluck from the Dardans for him, Menelaos, thee too, thou dog-
eyed!
Whereof little thy thought is, nought whatever thou reckest.
Worse, it is thou whose threat 'tis to ravish my prize from me,
portion
Won with much labour, the which my gift from the sons of
Achaia.
Never, in sooth, have I known my prize equal thine when Achaians
Gave some flourishing populous Trojan town up to pillage.
Nay, sure, mine were the hands did most in the storm of the
combat,
Yet when came peradventure share of the booty amongst us,
Bigger to thee went the prize, while I some small blessèd thing bore
Off to the ships, my share of reward for my toil in the bloodshed!   20
So now go I to Phthia, for better by much it beseems me
Homeward go with my beaked ships now, and I hold not in
prospect,
I being outraged, thou mayst gather here plunder and wealth-
store."

i. 225

"Bibber besotted, with scowl of a cur, having heart of a deer, thou!
Never to join to thy warriors armed for the press of the conflict,
Never for ambush forth with the princeliest sons of Achaia
Dared thy soul, for to thee that thing would have looked as a
death-stroke.

11 Menelaos, thee too] Menelaos, & thee, too *MS*; for thee *ILN*; for *del. corrected clipping ILN*
12 nought] nothing *or* nought *MS*
15 my] *my MS*
18 share of the] division of *MS*
19 while] & while *MS, ILN*; and *del. corrected clipping ILN*
20 my share] *my* share *MS*   my toil in the bloodshed] the toil of the fighting *MS*
21 much] far *MS*
22 not in prospect] it not likely *or* not in prospect *MS*
23 mayst] mayest *del.* may'st *MS*
[i.225]
1 deer] hind *MS*
2 to thy] to join thy *MS*   conflict] combat *MS*
3 sons of Achaia] of our Achaians *MS*
4 for to thee that thing would have looked as] such thing unto thee has the look of *or* for to thee that thing has *MS*

Sooth, more easy it seems, down the lengthened array of Achaians,
Snatch at the prize of the one whose voice has been lifted against
    thee.
Ravening king of the folk, for that thou has thy rule over abjects;
Else, son of Atreus, now were this outrage on me thy last one.
Nay, but I tell thee, and I do swear a big oath on it likewise:
Yea, by the sceptre here, and it surely bears branches and leaf-buds   10
Never again, since first it was lopped from its trunk on the
    mountains,
No more sprouting; for round it all clean has the sharp metal
    clipped off
Leaves and the bark; ay, verily now do the sons of Achaia,
Guardian hands of the counsels of Zeus, pronouncing the
    judgement,
Hold it aloft; so now unto thee shall the oath have its portent;
Loud will the cry for Achilles burst from the sons of Achaia
Throughout the army, and thou chafe powerless, though in an
    anguish,
How to give succour when vast crops down under man-slaying
    Hector
Tumble expiring; and thou deep in thee shalt tear at thy heart-
    strings,
Rage-wrung, thou, that in nought thou didst honour the flower of
    Achaians."   20

5 down] o'er *MS*
8 on] upon *del. MS*
9 Nay, but I tell thee] But I will tell thee *MS*   likewise] further *or* likewise *MS*
10 branches and leaf-buds] leaves & the branches *MS*
13 ay] yea *MS*
14 pronouncing the] when issuing *MS*
15 oath have its portent] sworn oath be weighty *or* have portent *MS*
16 Loud will the cry] Longing sure *MS*   burst from] will enter *MS*
17 in an anguish] troubled sorely *or* in an anguish *MS*
18 succour when vast crops] aid, when multitudes *or* succour when vast crops *MS*
19 deep in] within *or* then *MS*   heart-strings] bosom *MS*

Marshalling of the Achaians

ii. 455

Like as a terrible fire feeds fast on a forest enormous,
Up on a mountain height, and the blaze of it radiates round far,
So on the bright blest arms of the host in their march did the
    splendour
Gleam wide round through the circle of air right up to the sky-
    vault.
They, now, as when swarm thick in the air multitudinous winged
    flocks,
Be it of geese or of cranes or the long-necked troops of the wild-
    swans,
Off that Asian mead, by the flow of the waters of Kaïstros;
Hither and yon fly they, and rejoicing in pride of their pinions,
Clamour, shaped to their ranks, and the mead all about them
    resoundeth;
So those numerous tribes from their ships and their shelterings
    poured forth   10
On that plain of Scamander, and horrible rumbled beneath them
Earth to the quick-paced feet of the men and the tramp of the
    horse-hooves.
Stopped they then on the fair-flower'd field of Scamander,
    their thousands
Many as leaves and the blossoms born of the flowerful season.

2 on] o'er *MS*   mountain] mountain's *MS*
4 up] away *or* up *MS*
7 by] round *or* by *MS*   Kaïstros] Kaystros *MS*
8 pinions] wings there *del. MS*
9 shaped to] taking *del. MS*
11 On that plain of Scamander, and horrible rumbled] On the Scamandrian plain, *or*
On Scamander's plain, & terrific resounded *or* On that plain of Scamander, & terrible
rumbled *MS*
12 quick-paced] running *or* quick paced *MS*

Even as countless hot-pressed flies in their multitudes traverse,
Clouds of them, under some herdsman's wonning, where then are
    the milk-pails
Also, full of their milk, in the bountiful season of spring-time;
Even so thickly the long-haired sons of Achaia the plain held,
Prompt for the dash at the Trojan host, with the passion to crush
    them.
Those, likewise, as the goatherds, eyeing their vast flocks of goats,
    know   20
Easily one from the other when all get mixed o'er the pasture,
So did the chieftains rank them here there in their places for
    onslaught,
Hard on the push of the fray; and among them King Agamemnon,
He, for his eyes and his head, as when Zeus glows glad in his
    thunder,
He with the girdle of Ares, he with the breast of Poseidon.

Agamemnon in the Fight

xi. 148

These, then, he left, and away where ranks were now clashing the
    thickest,
Onward rushed, and with him rushed all of the bright-greaved
    Achaians.
Foot then footmen slew, that were flying from direful compulsion,
Horse at the horsemen (up from off under them mounted the dust-
    cloud,

ILIAD ii.455: MARSHALLING OF THE ACHAIANS

15 Even] Like *MS*   countless] the infinite *or* countless *MS*
16 Clouds of them] Clouding it *or* Clouds of them *MS*
19 dash at] rush on *MS*   crush] slay *MS*
21 all] these *MS*
24 in] of *del. MS*

ILIAD xi.148: AGAMEMNON IN THE FIGHT

1 now] then *MS*
3 footmen] the footmen *MS*
4 mounted] volumed *MS, ILN*

Up off the plain, raised up cloud-thick by the thundering horse-
    hooves)
Hewed with the sword's sharp edge; and so meanwhile Lord
    Agamemnon
Followed, chasing and slaughtering aye, on-urgeing the Argives.
Now, as when fire voracious catches the unclippèd woodland,
This way bears it and that the great whirl of the wind, and the
    scrubwood
Stretches uptorn, flung forward alength by the fire's fury rageing,					10
So beneath Atreides Agamemnon heads of the scattered
Trojans fell; and in numbers amany the horses, neck-stiffened,
Rattled their vacant cars down the roadway gaps of the war-field,
Missing the blameless charioteers, but, for these, they were
    outstretched
Flat upon earth, far dearer to vultures than to their home-mates.

Paris and Diomedes

xi. 378

		So he, with a clear shout of laughter,
Forth of his ambush leapt, and he vaunted him, uttering thiswise:
"Hit thou art! not in vain flew the shaft; how by rights it had
    pierced thee
Into the undermost gut, therewith to have rived thee of life-breath!
Following that had the Trojans plucked a new breath from their
    direst,
They all frighted of thee, as the goats bleat in flight from a lion."

ILIAD xi. 148: AGAMEMNON IN THE FIGHT

6 Lord] did Lord *MS*
7 Followed] Follow *MS*   aye] still *MS*
11 heads] the heads *MS*
15 home-mates] spouses *or* home-mates *MS*

ILIAD xi.378: PARIS AND DIOMEDES

1 shout] ring *MS*
2 pierced] hit *del. MS*
5 Following that] So likewise *MS*

Then unto him untroubled made answer stout Diomedes:
"Bow-puller, jiber, thy bow for thy glorying, spyer at virgins!
If that thou dared'st face me here out in the open with weapons,
Nothing then would avail thee thy bow and thy thick shot of
    arrows.   10
Now thou plumest thee vainly because of a graze of my footsole;
Reck I as were that stroke from a woman or some pettish infant.
Aye flies blunted the dart of the man that's emasculate, nought-
    worth!
Otherwise hits, forth flying from me, and but strikes it the slightest,
My keen shaft, and it numbers a man of the dead fallen
    straightway.
Torn, troth, then are the cheeks of the wife of that man fallen
    slaughtered,
Orphans his babes, full surely he reddens the earth with his blood-
    drops,
Rotting, round him the birds, more numerous they than the
    women."

7 stout] the *del.* stout *MS*
8 virgins] wenches *or* virgins *MS*
12 stroke] blow *MS*
13 noughtworth] worthless *del.* *MS*

Hypnos on Ida

xiv. 283

They then to fountain-abundant Ida, mother of wild beasts,
Came, and they first left ocean to fare over mainland at Lektos,
Where underneath of their feet waved loftiest growths of the
 woodland.
There hung Hypnos fast, ere the vision of Zeus was observant,
Mounted upon a tall pine-tree, tallest of pines that on Ida
Lustily spring off soil for the shoot up aloft into aether.
There did he sit well-cloaked by the wide-branched pine for
 concealment,
That loud bird, in his form like, that perched high up in the
 mountains,
Chalkis is named by the Gods, but of mortals known as Kymindis.

Clash in Arms of the Achaians
and Trojans

xiv. 394

Not the sea-wave so bellows abroad when it bursts upon shingle,
Whipped from the sea's deeps up by the terrible blast of the
 Northwind;
Nay, nor is ever the roar of the fierce fire's rush so arousing,
Down along mountain-glades, when it surges to kindle a woodland;

ILIAD xiv.283: HYPNOS ON IDA

MS, ILN *title:* Hypnos with Heré on Ida (with Heré *del. corrected clipping* ILN).
1 mother] the mother *MS*
2 ocean] sea there *MS*
4 vision of Zeus] eyes of great Zeus *or* vision of Zeus *MS*   was observant] had ob-
served him *MS*
6 spring] springs *MS*

ILIAD xiv.394: CLASH IN ARMS OF THE ACHAIANS AND TROJANS

MS title: "*Clash of the Achaians & the Trojans.*"
1 sea-wave so bellows] sea-wáve só béllows *Cochran*
3 fierce fire's rush] fire's fierce run *Cochran* rush] run *MS*

Nay, nor so tonant thunders the stress of the gale in the oak-trees'
Foliage-tresses high, when it rages to raveing its utmost;
As rose then stupendous the Trojans' cry and Achaians',
Dread upshouting as one when together they clashed in the conflict.

The Horses of Achilles

xvii. 426

So now the horses of Aiakides, off wide of the war-ground,
Wept, since first they were ware of their charioteer overthrown
    there,
Cast down low in the whirl of the dust under man-slaying Hector.
Sooth, meanwhile, then did Automedon, brave son of Diores,
Oft, on the one hand, urge them with flicks of the swift whip, and
    oft, too,
Coax entreatingly, hurriedly; whiles did he angrily threaten.
Vainly, for these would not to the ships, to the Hellespont spacious,
Backward turn, nor be whipped to the battle among the
    Achaians.
Nay, as a pillar remains immovable, fixed on the tombstone,
Haply, of some dead man or it may be a woman thereunder;   10
Even like hard stood they there attached to the glorious war-car,

---

ILIAD xiv.394: CLASH IN ARMS OF THE ACHAIANS AND TROJANS

5 in] on *Cochran*
8 Dread upshouting] Dreadfully shouting *Cochran*; Dreadfully shouting *or* Dread
upshouting *MS*

ILIAD xvii.426: THE HORSES OF ACHILLES

1 off wide of] at a stretch from *or* off wide of *MS*
3 low] there *MS*
4 brave] the brave *ILN*
6 Coax entreatingly, hurriedly; whiles did] Coaxed *del.* Coax them, entreating, hurried,
& while would *MS*
8 among] amongst *del. MS*
10 thereunder] beneath it *or* thereunder *MS*
11 like hard] so fast *or* so hard *MS*   glorious war-car] chariot splendid *MS*

Earthward bowed with their heads; and of them so lamenting
  incessant
Ran the hot teardrops downward on to the earth from their eyelids,
Mourning their charioteer; all their lustrous manes dusty-clotted,
Right side and left of the yoke-ring tossed, to the breadth of the
      yoke-bow.
      Now when the issue of Kronos beheld that sorrow, his head
        shook
Pitying them for their grief, these words then he spake in his
      bosom;
"Why, ye hapless, gave we to Peleus you, to a mortal
Master; ye that are ageless both, ye both of you deathless!
Was it that ye among men most wretched should come to have
      heart-grief?   20
'Tis most true, than the race of these men is there wretcheder
      nowhere
Aught over earth's range found that is gifted with breath and has
      movement."

The Mares of the Camargue

FROM THE 'MIRÈIO' OF MISTRAL

Frédéric Mistral's epic *Mirèio* (1859) won him honors. GM wrote
[May 31, 1861] to his friend, Bonaparte Wyse: "When you see M. Mistral,
pray tell him that it is my earnest wish to be introduced to him. *Mirèio*,
the more I look at it, strikes me as a consummate work in an age of very
small singing. It has in some parts the pastoral richness of Theocritus
and the rough vigour of Homer. I read your translation of the portion
describing the mares of the Camargue to Maxse, who was delighted."
    Several years later GM wrote at some length about *Mirèio* in an
unsigned review of "'Mirelle.' A pastoral epic of Provence. By F. Mistral.

THE HORSES OF ACHILLES

12 and of them so lamenting incessant] thus ever of them so lamenting *MS*
13 Ran] Coursed *MS*
14–22 *not in MS*

THE MARES OF THE CAMARGUE.   FROM THE "MIRÈIO" OF MISTRAL

Previously printed in an unsigned review, the Pall Mall Gazette 9 (*27 March 1869*).

Translated by H. Crichton (London: Macmillan and Co., 1869)" (*Pall Mall Gazette*, 27 March 1869). In this review GM translated the same stanzas that Wyse had previously translated to show how he thought Provençal verse should be rendered in English. On May 20, 1876, he wrote Wyse of his desire "to have drunk Chateauneuf du Pape with you, and to the health of Mistral. By the way, I am going to write a full review of him." There is no evidence that this review was written.

When GM decided to include *The Mares of the Camargue* in *A Reading of Life* he sent the printer a clipping of his review of 1869, deleting all of it except these five stanzas from Canto IV. See my article, "George Meredith on Mistral's *Mirèio*," *Yale University Library Gazette* 38 (October 1963): 67–74.

A hundred mares, all white! their manes
Like mace-reed of the marshy plains .
Thick-tufted, wavy, free o' the shears:
And when the fiery squadron rears
Bursting at speed, each mane appears
Even as the white scarf of a fay
Floating upon their necks along the heavens away.

O race of humankind, take shame!
For never yet a hand could tame,
Nor bitter spur that rips the flanks subdue   10
The mares of the Camargue. I have known,
By treason snared, some captives shown;
Expatriate from their native Rhone,
Led off, their saline pastures far from view:

And on a day, with prompt rebound,
They have flung their riders to the ground,
And at a single gallop, scouring free,
Wide nostril'd to the wind, twice ten
Of long marsh-leagues devour'd, and then,
Back to the Vacarés again,   20
After ten years of slavery just to breathe salt sea

12 captives] captive *PMG*

For of this savage race unbent,
The ocean is the element.
Of old escaped from Neptune's car, full sure,
　　Still with the white foam fleck'd are they,
　　And when the sea puffs black from grey,
　　And ships part cables, loudly neigh
The stallions of Camargue, all joyful in the roar;

　　And keen as a whip they lash and crack
　　Their tails that drag the dust, and back　　　　30
Scratch up the earth, and feel, entering their flesh, where he,
　　The God, drives deep his trident teeth,
　　Who in one horror, above, beneath,
　　Bids storm and watery deluge seethe,
And shatters to their depths the abysses of the sea.

Cant. iv.